THE
MIDDLE
AGES

Johannes Fried

Translated by Peter Lewis

THE BELKNAP PRESS OF
HARVARD UNIVERSITY PRESS

Cambridge, Massachusetts
London, England
2015

This book was originally published as *Das Mittelalter,* 3rd ed., copyright © Verlag C. H. Beck oHG, Munchen 2009.

Library of Congress Cataloging-in-Publication Data

Fried, Johannes.
   [Mittelalter. English]
   The Middle Ages / Johannes Fried ; translated by Peter Lewis.
       pages   cm.
   "This book was originally published as Das Mittelalter, 3rd ed., copyright (c) Verlag
C. H. Beck oHG, Munchen 2009."
   Includes bibliographical references and index.
   ISBN 978-0-674-05562-9 (alk. paper)
   1. Europe—History—476-1492. 2. Civilization, Medieval. I. Lewis, Peter (Translator)
II. Title.
   D117.F8513 2015
   909.07—dc23

2014014404

Contents

Illustrations follow Chapter 6, Chapter 11, and page 272.

Preface

The customary schema of historical eras—Antiquity, the Middle Ages, and the Modern Age—came into being at the end of the medieval period, but over the course of time its configuration has changed. It may have had its origins, as Johan Huizinga suggested, in the popular conception of a tripartite formula widely employed by heralds in the fifteenth century, which clearly demarcated the almost legendary period of Prehistory from their own present, and inserted between them a "middle era," *temps moien,* in other words a period that went back to the farthest limit of human historical recollection. Whether experienced as the present, as living memory, or as an ideal prehistory, the notion of a period lying between the contemporary age and the age of heroes and gods, of the patriarchs and matriarchs, occurs, albeit under various different designations, across a wide range of the world's civilizations. Yet mere identification of this kind of interim period did not in itself give rise to the concept of the "Middle Ages." In his *Historiarum ab inclinatione Romanorum imperii decades* (written between 1439 and 1453, and printed in 1483), the great humanist Flavio Biondo takes a more lucid and scholarly approach than any attempted hitherto (whether by heralds or in the popular imagination), presenting the historical period since the fall of the Roman Empire as a "middle age" extending from the conquest of Rome by barbarian Goths in 410 to the present; the humanist-educated Johannes Andreas (Giovanni Andrea Bussi), bishop of Aleria in Corsica, picked up on this concept in 1469, when he ascribed to the great scholar and cardinal Nicholas of Cusa a broad knowledge of the history and literature of three epochs: antiquity *(priscae [tempestates])*, the interim period *(media tempestas)*, and the present day *(nostra tempora)*. This formulation reached German humanists through the Latin world-chronicle of Hartmann Schedel (1493). However, at this stage, the idea of an era in its own right still did not exist. Such a concept was only devised by authors in later centuries, during the Baroque period and the Enlightenment. True, these commentators did not set hard-and-fast boundaries to this middle period—some dated it from Constantine the Great—or from A.D. 500 or 600—to the Reformation, while others saw it as having lasted variously to 700, or up to around 1100, or to the conquest of Constantinople by the Seljuk Turks in 1453, or even to other, quite different cutoff points. But even so, their endeavors only succeeded in presenting this "middle age" as some distant, self-contained era with no connection to the here and now, and in so doing gave the period its own identity. Specific hallmarks to corroborate this very rigid image of the period were soon invented. Henceforth, the Middle Ages changed from being barbarian and dark to being meaningful and enlightened, though this development brought its own particular dangers. Indeed, even up to the present day, various nationalisms and ideologies still appeal to a medieval period as defined by them to suit their own ends.

The present work therefore has as its subject matter a contentious phenomenon that has been shaped by contradictory and opposing traditions. It will thus eschew postulating any homogeneous picture of the Middle Ages or constructing any hermetically sealed whole. It will rather attempt to pursue certain lines of development through a millennium whose beginning and end have been solely determined by the customary practice of German university faculties of assigning responsibility for the period between around 500 to circa 1500 to those charged with teaching medieval studies; elsewhere, things are organized differently, with far-reaching implications for the tendentious concept of the "Middle Ages."[1] Consequently, whenever the term "Middle Ages" is used in the following account, it is not meant to denote any monolithic concept, of whatever kind, signaling

---

1. Johan Huizinga, *Zur Geschichte des Begriffs Mittelalter*, in *Geschichte und Kultur: Gesammelte Aufsätze*, ed. Kurt Köster (Stuttgart, 1954), 213–217; Peter von Moos, *Gefahren des Mittelalterbegriffs*, in *Modernes Mittelalter: Neue Begriffe einer populären Epoche*, ed. Joachim Heinzle, pp. 33–63 (Leipzig: Frankfurt a.M., 1994).

some irreducible identity, but meant simply to designate the given time span of 1,000 years or so.

In such an overview of a millennium, which aims to present humans of flesh and blood and not just trends and structures, it will naturally be impossible to treat the full range of all details exhaustively. Only the most stringent selection is possible, and this is of necessity subjective. The flow of the narrative will sometimes take a broad and straight course, while on other occasions it will split into tributaries, or flow around islands, but then its streambed will narrow once more, hastening the onward flow. Whatever it carries with it from here or there stands as an exemplar of many similar things, and hence should be regarded as symptomatic of cultural evolution beholden to the human spirit and as the social development of cultures of knowledge. The same applies to those particular historical instances that we have chosen to light upon as prime examples of the complexity of events within the realm of politics and power. Abstractions—"the monk," "the knight," "the townsman"—have been avoided. Rather, this account focuses on certain individuals—sometimes a pope, sometimes a king, or a scholar, a missionary, or an enterprising merchant. Their encounters with the unfamiliar, their grappling with new ideas, or religious movements, or scientific disciplines, their scope of action, and the expansion of their culture of knowledge are examined within the framework of political constellations of power and the proliferation of "international" relations, the growing complexity of societies, and functional differentiation.

Our focus, then, is firmly fixed upon cultural evolution, with both its continuities and discontinuities; and, just like any natural evolution, this does not develop teleologically. Only in retrospect does it appear to the historian to be linear, logical, and oriented toward progress. It is therefore a construct, necessarily subjective, no less so indeed than all the other spheres of reality in which we humans navigate, move, and act. It is a hypothesis, whose plausibility is conditioned by unprovable premises, our own subjective experiences, and familiar structural patterns. There can be no such thing as a generally binding history, any more than "my" reality could be "your" reality, even though both are indisputably forms of "reality." Likewise, the simultaneity of events also defies any authoritative account, since once such an account has been given, it is forever consigned to posterity, and is only capable of sequentially considering, combining, or describing things that in actual fact had a concurrent effect and were contingent upon one another and intermeshed in their impact. This is also consonant with our cognitive makeup as human beings, which prevents us from grasping simultaneity immediately, through our sensory perception, but which, rather, allows us to piece it together only in retrospect, on reflection, by adducing information from third parties and by deploying countless methodical preconditions and artifices. Flashbacks, forward shifts in time, and more minor interpolations by way of digression can only be an unsatisfactory literary expedient; for the same reason, it is impossible to avoid brief repetitions—these are quite intentional. Nonetheless, our intention is still to present an overview of a whole, namely that evolution mentioned above, a development that drew its dynamism from the confluence of political, social, religious, cultural (in the widest sense), economic, scientific, and natural forces, and whose guiding thread in the labyrinth of chance occurrences and exigencies, of plans and reactions, is constituted by the growth of the culture of reason in those supposedly "middle" centuries.

This book is intended to reach a readership that is interested in the past, yet is not blinded by any particular specialization. The choice of color illustrations has the dual purpose of illustrating the lines of development of religious mentalities, and of making clear how modes of visual perception changed over the centuries under discussion here; in doing so, it also has the effect of graphically underscoring the deliberate cultural evolution we have spoken of. The secondary literature on these thousand years of European history and culture fills entire libraries. No halfway manageable bibliography could hope to encompass this body of work; any such further reading list must of necessity remain incomplete. Accordingly, there is a great deal of scope for subjective emphasis. Any subject treated here confines itself to the bare necessities; there is no indication of all the sources that were consulted—rather, we are generally content merely to cite more recent pieces of secondary literature that digest the foregoing scholarship. With a few exceptions, only direct quotations are cited in the endnotes.

Many people assisted in the publication of this work. First, I am most grateful to Wolfgang Beck for his great patience and forbearance, and to Detlef Felken, without whose gentle but insistent prodding this book would never have seen the light of day. Wolfram Brandes, Jörg Busch, Heribert Müller and in no lesser measure Kerstin Schulmeyer-Ahl, Barbara Schlieben, Daniel Föller, and Peter Gorzolla were responsible for providing valuable advice, reading either individual sections of the manuscript or the complete draft at various stages of development, diligently offering constructive criticism and corrections on both detailed passages and the overall concept, and in promoting the project in a multitude of different ways. Alexander Goller compiled the index (for the German edition). My heartfelt thanks are due to all of them, but most of all to my wife for her enormous patience and unstinting help. It is to her that I dedicate this "Middle Ages."

I

Boethius and the Rise of Europe

Boethius, the most learned man of his time, met his death in the hangman's noose. He came from one of the most noble senatorial families of Rome and was a patrician, a consul, and a minister at the court of the Ostrogoth King Theodoric in Ravenna. Nevertheless, he fell victim to this same barbarian ruler; neither Theodoric himself nor his realm was to survive for long following the demise of his minister. Contemporary commentators believed that this tyrant had descended to the bowels of Mount Etna, into Hell itself, whence he would occasionally return as a wild horseman and a harbinger of doom. In truth, Theodoric simply passed away in 526. The precise reasons for the fall of his first minister have been lost in the mists of time. No proof of guilt for a crime was ever brought forth. It appears that this famous Roman was toppled purely by the mistrust of his king. This turned out to be a serious misjudgment, which the Goth ruler must instantly have regretted, albeit not soon enough to save himself.

And yet the life of Boethius was a triumph! The West owes this individual, Anicius Manlius Severinus Boethius, nothing less than its progression toward a culture of reason. Such a culture may be regarded as a blessing or a curse. Alongside many other gifts, Boethius left the Latin West, which was not familiar with Greek culture, a translation of one of the most seminal didactic texts in history, nothing less than a primer for the application of reason. This slim volume, really only a pamphlet, comprising the first three texts from Aristotle's *Organon,* provided an introduction to a mode of thinking that was subject to learnable rules and therefore susceptible to scrutiny and correction, was logically comprehensible, and obeyed the principle of causality. Coming at just the right moment, just as the tenth century was rediscovering and becoming enthralled with the concept of reason, these short tracts supplied a vital tool kit worth more than its weight in gold. They were a constant throughout the centuries that made up the Middle Ages, helping to shape scholars of the age from Scotland to Sicily, Portugal to Poland, and facilitating the growth of Western scholarship as a whole. It wasn't emperors and kings that made Europe great, but the categorical mode of thinking inspired by this translation, and the application of reason that ensued as a result.

Boethius added a number of writings to this body of work, notably a brief account of the "distinctions," his *Liber de divisione,* which dealt with the systematically arranged and logically "divided" order of the world and the sovereign principle guiding it. A similarly short treatise on arithmetic and a series of observations on music completed the literary legacy of the Roman; both of these likewise drew on ancient Greek sources and were instrumental in pointing the way forward for the future development of Western thought. It was Boethius who was responsible for introducing fundamental concepts such as "principle," "subject," or "substance" to European scholarly discourse. The decisive factor for the future was not that he had coined these terms himself, but that he employed them and taught others how to use them. He reminded people that knowledge is not some property that issues from the object of contemplation, but rather one that is inherent in the cognitive faculty of the thinking and perceiving subject. Boethius also, it seems, coined the term *quadrivium,* which in contrast to the *trivium* of grammar, rhetoric, and dialectics was an umbrella term for the four mathematical/arithmetical disciplines in the canon of the "liberal arts."

In his dungeon, however, so tradition relates, having been subjected to the cruelest torture, Boethius wrote his principal work, the *Consolation of Philosophy* in the last few months before his execution. This slim but profound volume bears witness to a final brilliant flash of ancient learning before its ultimate extinction. During the Middle Ages and the Modern Period it was transcribed hundreds of times, read and reread time and again, annotated, deliberated on, and made one of the first books to be set in printed type. It was also the impetus for Dante to portray himself meeting Boethius in the sunlit heaven of Paradise, together with the great heroes of Christian thought, such as Thomas Aquinas, Albertus Magnus, and the Venerable Bede, along with Solomon and other outstanding wise men (Paradise X, 124–129). And it has continued to resonate up to the present day, for example in the *Moabit Sonnets* written by the poet Albrecht Haushofer, a victim of the Nazi dictatorship. Nevertheless, this *Consolation* of Boethius dispensed with all specifically Christian content and remained strictly within the Neoplatonic tradition of which its author was a part.

The prisoner conducted an "internal dialogue." The embattled soul freed itself from all its bonds through conversations with Philosophia and Fortune—the personifications of wisdom and fate—and through meditations on God's foreknowledge, predestination, "intention," "reason," human emotions and free will, on "chance" and "necessity," and finally on the nature of true happiness the soul helped dispel all cares. Now all earthly prosperity and success and fame evaporated; true blessedness was only to be found in God and (in the approved Neoplatonist manner) in the liberating ascent to gaze upon God's countenance. "Hopes are not vainly put in God, nor prayers in vain offered. . . . If you would be honest, great is the necessity enjoined upon your goodness," the condemned man finally admonishes his readers with the words of Philosophy, "since all you do is done before the eyes of an all-seeing Judge." Here Boethius was broaching themes that were to underpin Christianity for many centuries to come, indeed over the whole of the following millennium. These themes were subject to constant adaptation and extrapolation, and have lost none of their relevance—note, for instance, his reference to free will—even in the twenty-first century.

The *Consolation* was a linguistic masterpiece. In both substance and form, it provided numerous literary models, musical and rhythmic patterns, and presented ancient metrical forms in all their beauty, which served as a template for the prosodic education of medieval poets:

Ó qui pérpetuá mundúm ratione gubérnas
Térrarum caelíque satór, qui témpus ab aévo
Iúre iubés stabilísque manens das cúncta movéri.

"O Thou, who by eternal Reason's law / The World dost rule! Great parent of the heavens / And of the Earth! By whose command supreme, / Time flows from birth of ages!" Thus begins one of the most famous, constantly translated and reworked "hymns" of the "Consolation." The work as a whole reminded the reader of the unity of scholarship and life and through its Neoplatonist approach made great play of the dispute between theology and philosophy. The yawning chasm that was time and again to force apart reason and faith over the course of the Middle Ages and the Modern Period first began to open up here. The Anglo-Saxon monk Alcuin was responsible for disseminating the work to the court of Charlemagne and to the kingdom of the Franks, where its effect soon began to be felt. As a monk from St. Gallen asserted in the tenth century, Boethius' teachings were "more philosophical than Catholic."[1] Still, the stimulus provided by his *Consolation* prompted the West to critique his specifically theological writings—*On the Trinity* and others—which had been known since the ninth century and by the twelfth century were instrumental in helping transform theology into a rational, reason-led discipline worthy of study at the leading universities. At the time, Peter Abelard, one of the greatest philosophers of his age, praised Boethius as the "greater Latin philosopher."[2]

Boethius, then, was the last Neoplatonist of note in late antiquity. The deaths of Boethius and his contemporary Cassiodorus spelled the end of an era. The abundance of schools of philosophy, educational institutions, and religions that the ancient world and Late Antiquity boasted, even in the Latin West of the Roman Empire, had all dissipated by now. Most of the academies had lost their patrons; even the School of Athens, where Plato had once been active, had just closed. The Byzantine restoration in Africa, Italy, and Spain extinguished the last few flickerings of life. Stoicism, Aristotelianism, New Pythagoreanism, mysticism, skepticism, mystery religions, and Mithraic and Dionysian cults (Manichaeism)—to name just the most significant belief systems—were all banned, or had fallen silent, died out, or become alien concepts. The few remaining writers adopted an overblown style in place of former clarity, while visual art ossified into the formalism of icon painting. The only thing left was Christianity, with its established church and its heresies. For all its growing hostility and opposition to Judaism, it could not deny its roots in the Jewish faith and in gentile adaptations of Judaic practice. But Judaism itself had also survived; forced in the Diaspora to come to terms with many and varied surroundings, it began to split into Sephardic and Ashkenazi traditions. Only in the East, in Byzantium and in the Arabic *koine* lingua franca that originated there, did the last isolated vestiges survive of the Ancient Greek body of knowledge comprising philosophy, medicine, cosmology or geography. And only there were Greek original texts or their Arabic translations passed on and preserved for posterity.

The church fathers of the Latin West—among whom Boethius, despite being a Christian, is not usually counted—made not the slightest attempt to style themselves as philosophers, despite the fact that many had been schooled in grammar and rhetoric or even—as in the case of Saints Augustine of Hippo or Jerome—had originally pursued careers as rhetoricians and lawyers. Taking issue with the Old and New Testament orthodoxy on the question of revelation, and in express opposition to the old modes of teaching, they developed their own form of literature, which consisted of apologias, exegetical and paraenetic works, and texts with a didactic or improving function, rather than scholarly research and experimentation. Their language, knowledge, thinking, and beliefs were to establish norms for the following centuries. Last, they preached a literary "simplicity" that shunned the traditional educational canon. Over a long period, great poets who continued to evoke the heathen pantheon were pilloried. After all, what did Christ have to do with Jupiter? Christian writers instead adopted a tone of lamentation or chiding. Later, the despised verses of, say, Virgil, Ovid, or Horace, had to be painstakingly sought out and copied from the dispersed remains of ancient libraries before they could begin, from the tenth century onward, to exert a renewed influence on the language of a blossoming renaissance among medieval writers and poets.

Accordingly, only a very sparse educational canon, a thin trickle of knowledge that carried little with it, flowed from Late Antiquity down to the Middle Ages. It comprised four, maybe five, books, no more. In any event, the earliest of these can only be deduced—an "instructional text for the study of the Arts, reworked in the Christian mode," written around 400; its influence can be surmised in the writings of Saints Augustine and Jerome and later in those of Cassiodorus and sundry excerpts from other writers.[3] With his treatise *De doctrina Christiana,* which was constantly read and reread from the Carolingian period onward, Saint Augustine had at least provided the basis for a theory of learning geared toward the Holy Gospel, while at the same time vindicating the "Liberal Arts"; but however important this tract was, it was by no means enough. In it, the bishop of Hippo Regius in North Africa directed his readers' attention to "things" and their "signs," in other words to semiotics and the questions of comprehension and expression. "Things are learned through signs" (I, 2.2.4). In time, medieval textual exegesis and interpretation of the world were to be imbued with the spirit of this work. Only from the twelfth and thirteenth centuries, however, do new, Aristotelian ways of interpreting knowledge begin to assert themselves. By contrast, in addition to the writings of Saint Augustine, the considerably shortened and simplified textbook written by Cassiodorus—which clearly drew on Augustine's works for inspiration, and which has come down to us via numerous manuscripts from the High Middle Ages—conveyed a Christian educational program and quite an extensive overview of the disciplines. In just a few succinct sentences, his *Institutions* outlined each and every one of the "Liberal Arts," which by this time—at variance with older textbooks—numbered just seven. Ultimately, the Middle Ages was also to have one further outline of the ancient canon of learning to draw upon: *De nuptiis Philologiae et Mercurii,* a work written in the fourth or fifth century by Martinus Capella, which he couched in verse form in the guise of a wedding present to celebrate the betrothal of Philology to Mercury. The Middle Ages took this allegorically framed foundation course in the arts to its heart, and following the rediscovery of the single surviving manuscript of the text in the ninth century, accorded it the status of one of its primary textbooks.

By the time Boethius fell victim to intrigue and mistrust, Europe was a conglomerate of formerly flourishing provinces that were now faced with decline. The ancient civilizations—Athens and Rome—had grown old and weak and collapsed. Just a century earlier (410), Alaric had overrun Rome—the first time this had happened for more than 700 years. The incident was both shocking and emblematic. The city was to suffer two further sackings by barbarian hordes during the course of the fifth century. Yet "what will remain standing if Rome falls?" as Saint Jerome asked presciently, in far-off Palestine, even prior to the first sacking, in 409 (Epistle 123). At that time, Augustine was moved to put pen to paper to write an apologia in defiance of the empire's collapse. This work—*The City of God*—became a comprehensive blueprint for the whole story of Christian salvation, and its effects are still felt today. In it, Augustine maintained that it was not, as the last pagans had claimed, the neglect of the old cult of the Roman gods that had brought about the city's downfall but rather the Romans' own failings. A thousand years later, fifteenth-century humanists would shun this insight, preferring instead to ascribe the empire's decline to the conquering Goths.

Wherever one looked, the land was ravaged by recurrent bouts of war, in the East and West alike. The great cities, including *Roma aeterna* (eternal Rome), and their public buildings crumbled into ruins. Over time, except for the stone that was reused to erect new churches, marble from the ancient palaces and temples and from the statues of the gods and heroes migrated into the lime kilns of a populace who were increasingly eking out a desperate existence. It was not some great rupture in cultural life that plagued people's lives, but rather bitter adversity, which eroded and destroyed all vestiges of civilization. Hunger and anxiety divested people of any aesthetic appreciation of beauty or of the "golden Rome" once hymned by the great poets. *Roma fuit*—Rome is at an end—sang Hildebert von Lavardin, one of the foremost poets of the eleventh century, when contemplating the ruins and rubble of the city on the banks of the Tiber. However, as he gazed at the buildings still standing and the works of art still in evidence, he saw himself looking on in awe and wonder as Rome rose again. Nothing, he claimed, was the equal of Rome: *Par tibi, Roma, nihil.* To be sure, at first large parts of the shrinking, decrepit Imperium Romanum were under the sway of barbarian rulers. And the city's last vestiges of vigor were swept away by the plague, which ravaged it in the sixth century, carrying off people and cities, life and culture alike.

It was only in the shadow of Rome that ancient groups and small confederations speaking a variety of Germanic dialects, who were not attuned to the cultural diversity of the Mediterranean world, finally coalesced into identifiable peoples such as the Goths, Franks, or Lombards. They began the arduous task of taking possession of Rome's treasures and institutions, assimilating its values and the relics of its spiritual legacy. With their arrival, a culture entirely devoted to the oral tradition met the highly literate ancient world, which could do nothing to counter this development, and in fact found itself increasingly dependent upon the barbarian culture. Research conducted in the twentieth century into preliterate nations has given us a new insight into what these barbarians brought with them. One key factor to emerge was that they displayed an additive rather than a subordinative way of thinking, approached things in an aggregative rather than analytical manner, essentially took cognizance of surroundings on the spur of the moment, and were incapable of abstraction. In other words, this way of thinking did not organize its environment systematically or according to categories, but instead preferred to cling tenaciously to familiar, traditional modes of thought and action.[4] These same observations may, with all due caution, also be applied to the so-called period of the barbarian invasions and the early Middle Ages. It entailed intensive learning processes— which, thanks to more challenging conditions regarding communications, were far more protracted than any comparable acquisition of cognitive skills nowadays—for societies such as these, which in any case were exposed to revolutionary changes, to advance to the high culture of Late Antiquity. Initially, as modern studies in developmental psychology have shown when comparing different civilizations, their traditional knowledge and their intellectual make-up must have been unsuited for the moment to progress toward a highly evolved form of culture and to the refined modes of living that prevailed in the Roman world.

And yet these outsiders brought with them the determination—manifested by all "barbarian" peoples who overrun advanced civilizations—to imitate those whom they conquered: a fact we know for sure thanks to the testimony of the Visigoth king Athaulf, which has been preserved for posterity. Like his brother-in-law and predecessor, the notorious Alaric, who sacked Rome in 410 and shortly thereafter died and was buried in the river Busento (near Cosenza), Athaulf severely harassed the Western Roman Empire. Yet having plundered Italy, he suddenly turned his back on it and embarked on an invasion of grain-rich Africa via Spain. Although this adventure eventually foundered, advancing no further than Gaul and northern Spain, Toulouse now became the center of a new Visigoth kingdom, which proceeded to put down firm roots there.

Having grown unaccustomed to agricultural labor over the long years of migration and warfare, Athaulf's warriors found themselves unable to cultivate the devastated fields of the lands they overran. The populace was hit by starvation and destitution. Sword in hand, the king sought help from the Roman emperor, a request he reluctantly agreed to, but which was never fulfilled. The Visigoths once more fell back on their own resources and came to an accommodation with the local populace. Athaulf forced the emperor's daughter Galla Placidia, who had fallen into his hands (and who would later be interred in the imperial city of Ravenna in a sarcophagus that is still admired today) to marry him. It is from his wedding speech that the famous passage comes down to us, in which Athaulf relates that he was eager to expunge the name of Rome and to transform the Roman Empire into a Visigoth Empire, before it suddenly dawned on him that the unchecked barbarity *(effrenata barbaries)* of his own kinsmen refused to be reined in by laws; realizing that no polity without laws could endure, he now sought to restore the empire, exalt the name of Rome once again, and secure his place in history as the instigator of Rome's renewal *(Romanae restitutionis auctor)*. Granted, this dictum has come down to us in Latin, not in Athaulf's native Gothic, and indeed the whole sentiment had a distinctly Roman ring to it.⁵ What he actually said, what he precisely meant by "Rome," and how he phrased his statement are all now lost in the mists of time.

Even so, the revival of Rome became the watchword for the ensuing centuries and indeed for the whole of the medieval millennium. The Renaissance of the fourteenth–fifteenth centuries merely completed what had already been set in train back in Late Antiquity; it was via the Visigoth kingdom that much of the priceless legacy of the ancient world was preserved in the first place. The calculation that Athaulf may have made was no less true of the other barbarian rulers. Time and again, the same sentiment was expressed, in countless different variations, and numerous steps taken to realize this ambition—in Rome itself by a succession of popes and ordinary citizens as well as by heretics and rabble-rousers and outside of the Eternal City by emperors and municipalities, intellectuals and poets. A broad current of plans, aspirations, and wishes for Roman revival bound the ancient world with all the centuries of the medieval period. Only the modern period has taken leave of this kind of restorative ideas.

Admittedly, at the time when Boethius was garroted the first priority was to salvage what could still be saved. One of those who took this task upon himself was Cassiodorus. Flavius Magnus Aurelius Cassiodorus, to give him his full name was, like Boethius, a Roman aristocrat, a scion of the illustrious Gens Aurelia, and was a consul and minister at the court of the great Goth king. He was bound up in some measure with the downfall of Boethius, but managed to escape being killed. Likewise, he also survived the end of the Ostrogoth kingdom by withdrawing at an opportune moment to a contemplative life in the country and founding his estate "Vivarium" in Calabria. This site, named after the stew ponds he kept for fish, was a kind of monastery, where Cassiodorus encouraged his fellow inmates to diligently copy Christian texts above all. This can be considered one of the greatest acts of preservation of the world's cultural legacy ever known, without which the world would be indescribably the poorer today. Moreover, Cassiodorus' own literary endeavors were of great significance. As the king's "secretary" he was responsible for drafting all official communications. He collected these writings, or *Variae,* in twelve separate volumes for posterity; as a result, we know a great deal about Theodoric, who was brought up in Constantinople. In addition, Cassiodorus wrote the schoolbook on the "Liberal Arts" already mentioned—the *Institutiones divinarum et saecularium litterarum*—a less significant world chronicle and a history of the Goths. This latter work is, strictly speaking, lost; however, parts of it are generally reckoned to have come down to us in the form of literal or analogous excerpts in the work *Getica* of the writer Jordanes, who was at least a generation younger. Another important work was Cassiodorus' history of the church *(Historia tripartita)*, which he likewise compiled from Greek-language sources from Late Antiquity, and which provided the Middle Ages with a sober corrective to the proliferation of legends that had by then grown up around the subject.

Almost nothing is known about the prehistory of the Goths. The idea that they originated in Scandinavia, as recounted in Jordanes (and presumably also in his source Cassiodorus) is now generally dismissed. Instead, it is thought that the Gothic people and kingdom only arose in the course of third century, under pressure from Asiatic steppe-dwellers pushing westward, from heterogenous elements (neither exclusively Germanic-speaking nor exclusively European) who inhabited the region around the northern Black Sea coast between the Lower Danube and the lower reaches of the Dniepr, and north of the Crimea; this development may even have occurred under Roman influence. The advance of the Huns forced the Goths, in their turn, to shift further west into Roman-controlled territory. Desperation made these peoples dangerous. In AD 378, under the leadership of their king, Athanarich, the Goths (whom their own bishop Ulfilas is reputed to have characterized as "loving war")[6] defeated a Roman army led by the emperor Valens himself at the Battle of Adrianople, killing the emperor in the process.

Yet wherever danger threatened, salvation was also to be found. Since the early fourth century, the Romans had been sending Christian missionaries to the Goths, and they expected from those whom they were sent to convert a readiness to radically rethink their worldview, an accommodation to alien worlds, values, and ways of perceiving and thinking. By contrast, the barbarians took this encounter with unfamiliar concepts as a challenge. Yet after some resistance on the part of these pagans, Arian Christianity did eventually gain a foothold among them, and with it an initial phase of Romanization. There is even talk of Gothic martyrs during this period. One of their own number, Bishop Ulfilas, a Goth who originally came from a Greek-Cappadocian family, translated the Holy Gospel into the Gothic vernacular—an enormous undertaking and a work of true genius. This also required that literacy take hold among a hitherto illiterate society. However, in the general climate of uncertainty and instability that obtained at the time, rapid successes could not be expected. Ulfilas' Bible translation, which drew heavily on the Greek, therefore also reflected the linguistic, semantic, and hermeneutic difficulties that the barbarians encountered in grappling with this foreign, book-based religion and its theology, and lays bare the comprehensive learning processes that an intercultural adjustment such as this demanded.

The Ostrogoth king regarded heaven as a kind of royal court. The concept of "mercy," though, presented the Goth mindset with an insuperable problem, and this central Christian virtue was (in accordance with its Latin root *miseri-cordia*) variously rendered as "poor heart," "joy," or "friendliness."[7] Pity thus had a struggle to inculcate itself into Gothic hearts and minds and in touching the Gothic soul. Yet come what may, that bold enterprise, the Ulfilas Bible, represents the oldest coherent text in a Germanic language. Unfortunately, though, it has only come down to us in fragmentary form in the precious "Codex argenteus" (the "Silver Codex," thus called because it was written with silver ink on purple-stained vellum)—which today is the most valuable holding in the library of the University of Uppsala, Sweden; a single leaf of the book is held at the library in Speyer, while Wolfenbüttel has a bilingual palimpsest fragment of Saint Paul's Epistle to the Romans. Other than that, only a few insignificant pieces of written evidence from this society—in transition to an advanced Mediterranean civilization—have survived by chance to the present day. Furthermore, up until now, aside from a few brief phrases, no "old-Frankish" or Lombardish text has even come to light, let alone any linguistic relics of the Vandal civilization. Everything that has been preserved from their era remained completely reliant upon intellectual elites who were conversant with Latin. Only among the Irish and the Anglo-Saxons, and thereafter via Charlemagne and during the reign of his son Louis the Pious did this situation change, and records of different vernaculars begin to be written down.

The long trek to the west saw the Gothic people split into two groups, the Visigoths and the Ostrogoths. When exactly and under what circumstances this occurred is uncertain; in an extent Gothic calendar (again, only surviving in fragmentary form), whose content appears to date it to the fourth century, only a single "Gothic people" *(gutpiuda)* is mentioned. The two groups began to diverge from one another more distinctly only around 400. In accordance with the political tenor of his age, but nevertheless inaccurately, in his *Getica* Jordanes presumed that the split had taken place in the third century. The learned minister of Theodoric the

Great, who we may assume was Jordanes' source for this as for so much else, was a gifted inventor of past histories. In short, we cannot rely on Cassiodorus' constructs in this matter. He also, as he put it, "rescued from the abyss of oblivion" (in other words, invented, we may fairly assume) the royal dynasty of the Ostrogoths—the so-called Amales—whom he traced back to a hero-figure named Gapt. His motivation in doing so was to create for his masters a noble prehistory in refined Roman society and thereby endow them with the respectability this entailed.

Our knowledge of the development of the Ostrogoths as a distinct ethnic grouping is only sketchy. It went hand in hand with their emancipation from Hunnish sovereignty after the death of Attila in 453 and their settling in Italy, where Theodoric, in an act of underhand brutality, usurped the rule of the barbarian king of Rome Odoacer by slaying him at a banquet to which he had invited him. Odoacer's wife was imprisoned and left to starve to death. Boethius' violent end (following a trial for treason conducted in accordance with Roman law) was not an isolated incident in the reign of terror of this Gothic king, who was much vaunted in legend. Like all despots, Theodoric made a "love of justice" his guiding principle.[8] But we may fairly assume that Boethius was the originator of the concept of "civilitas" in matters of law, settlement, and religion, with which Theodoric planned to regulate the cohabitation of his warrior people, who numbered just a few thousand, with the Roman people, who were prohibited from having any dealings with arms, but who were far more numerous.[9] In an attempt to foster a state of "general calm," Theodoric passed an edict that applied to "Romans and barbarians" alike, but which fell into disuse once Goth rule came to an end.[10] Many of his decrees harked back to Roman law, while others appeared very modern. Now Goths too were confronted with the death penalty—hitherto unknown to them—enacted, for instance, by burning at the stake for fomenting insurrection among the populace or the army or for desecrating a grave. Moreover, those who were bribed to bear false witness were put to death, if they came from the lower echelons of society *(humiliores),* whereas those who came from the upper class *(honestiores)* and committed this offence were divested of their fortune. Freeborn children who were sold out of desperation by their parents did not thereby relinquish their freedom, while no free man could be incarcerated without judicial approval.

Neither of the Gothic kingdoms that arose on the territory of the former Roman Empire formally seceded from the confederation of the empire, although the connections to the distant Eastern emperor in Constantinople grew ever weaker over time. When the Huns under Attila advanced as far as Gaul in 451, the Visigoths joined forces with the Roman commander Aetius to defend the territory at the Battle of the Catalaunian Fields. Meanwhile, a Burgundian contingent fought on the side of the Huns; their annihilation may have provided the subject matter for the Middle High German text the *Nibelungenlied,* assuming this work was based on any definite historical source. If Latin literary education can be said to have survived anywhere, then it was in the Visigoth kingdom. King Eurich (d. 484) promulgated common Roman law for his Visigoth subjects in the form of the "Codex Euricianus" and Roman law in the form of the "Lex Romana Visigotorum," while his successor Alaric II (d. 507) enacted the "Breviarium" with regard to the Roman inhabitants of his realm. Legal statute books were also created during the reigns of the Gothic kings. The law that was codified in them remained in force right up to the Middle Ages; it separated the "Romans" from the "Goths" and formed an integral part of the "Pays du droit écrit" (land of written law), a vital element in the development of medieval scholarship.[11]

Certainly, the Franks posed a major threat during this period. After triumphing in battle, their warlike king Chlodwig did indeed eradicate the Tolosan-Burgundian Empire and forced the Goths into the far south of Gaul, to Septimania (the westernmost part of the province of Gallia Narbonensis), and eventually to Spain (in 507). There, a new Visigoth Empire arose, with Toledo as its spiritual and temporal center for the next two hundred years. Originally Arian Christians, the Goths now converted under King Reccared (d. 601) to the Catholic faith. The Visigoth-Spanish synod of Toledo updated ancient canon law in a way that was later adopted by the church as a whole. In Bishop Isidor of Seville (d. 636), the country also produced the last of the church fathers. His encyclopedia *(Etymologiae),* which also set out to preserve the last remnants of elementary school learning, became one of the most widely disseminated books of the Middle Ages. At the same time, the other writings of the learned bishop testify to a broad knowledge of the ancient system of scholarship as nurtured by the "Visigoths," which in its later manifestations was integrated into the Carolingian educational reforms of the late eighth century. As was common practice in late antiquity, there were no formal legal ties to the Roman Church and the pope; rather, Gothic–Spanish Catholics retained their independence. Despite having legitimized the Catholic Church within his realm, in the master copy of his *Breviarium* Alaric II had already deliberately omitted the passage concerning this church's subservience to the papacy. Spain was only subsumed into the universal episcopate of the Bishop of Rome by the church reforms of the eleventh century.

Yet the form of royal investiture practiced here demonstrates that the Visigoth monarchy was intimately bound up with this independent church. Inner tensions and disputes brought about a rapid collapse of Goth rule under their last king, Roderic, when, in 711, "Arabs"—that is, Muslim Berbers—crossed the Straits of Gibraltar and invaded the Iberian Peninsula. Prior to this, the country had already been hit by plague and famine. In all likelihood, the Muslims were probably invited to intervene by one of the warring factions, but later accounts of this period of history, already colored by myth making, make it impossible to determine the facts.

In truth, neither the Ostrogoths under Theodoric nor the successors of the Visigoth ruler Athaulf were able to implement the program of renewal that must once have loomed large in their plans. Instead, this was only finally achieved, after several centuries had elapsed, by the Franks. Their great King Chlodwig, a contemporary of Theodoric, fashioned a realm with Paris at its center, which after numerous mutations still lives on in the form of modern France, and German history was also shaped by this development. With the exception of some minor territories, Chlodwig brought the whole of Gaul up to the Rhine under his control, conquered the Visigoths and Alemanni, and—at least according to legend—led his people, possibly after some initial hesitation, to adopt Catholicism, in contrast to other peoples who spoke Germanic languages, who all espoused Arianism. This move ensured him the support of the Roman church and was the catalyst to a fundamentally important change. Yet while the fact of Chlodwig's own conversion is in no doubt, the exact circumstances surrounding it are less than clear, being lost, unsurprisingly, in the fog of legend.

The "origins" of the Franks are likewise completely obscure. They themselves had absolutely no knowledge of their ethnogenesis, and it is wholly unknown when these people began to think of themselves as "Franks," in other words to form an emotional attachment to their own racial identity. It is thought that they, or at least certain groups among them, referred to themselves as the "Sicambri," a name that was attested even by Pliny the Elder. The earliest self-reference—as the "renowned people of the Franks" *(Gens Francorum inclita)* in the prologue of their oldest legal tome, the *Lex Salica*—only occurs in the later years of the reign of Chlodwig (d. 511), and is therefore too late to be very revealing. The Franks' first historian, the Gallo-Roman Gregory of Tours, who was writing toward the end of the sixth century, drew upon sources that have since been lost to affirm that they were immigrants from Pannonia (II,9); his view on this may also have been colored by the incursion of the Lombards into Italy. Around seventy-five years later, the Frankish chronicler known as Fredegar indulged in mythography on the subject. According to him, his people, who were descended from Priam and related to the Turks, escaped just like the ancestors of the Romans from the blazing ruins of Troy (III,2). This historian also knew the legend that claimed that King Merovech was conceived by a minotaur who had risen from the sea (III,9); it was from this semilegendary ancestor that the Salian Franks gained the name of "Merovingians." Over time, the Troy myth was elaborated still further, appearing again after more than 500 years in the *Grandes chroniques de France,* France's royal history par excellence, and ultimately taking on visual form in the tomb of the Emperor Maximilian I in the Hofkirche in Innsbruck.

This plethora of legends reflects the obscurity of their origin; however, their clear borrowing of elements of the ancient Europa myth and from Virgil illuminate the Franks' acculturation to the Roman world as well as Rome's accommodation to that of the barbarians. It is probable that the Franks coalesced as a people from several minor tribes that existed around the time when Tacitus was writing. The umbrella term "Franks," which grouped them as a single race, may well have been applied to them by the Romans in the third century; this was by no means uncommon at that time. The coinage derived from a Germanic word, and the Romans applied it indiscriminately to diverse groups such as the Salian Franks of Chlodwig and the Rhineland Franks around Cologne. It may even be the case that their kingdom arose at this same period, as a result of Roman development aid, especially the payment of subsidies to fund the creation of a group of loyal *foederati*. It may be that wealth and power served at that time to forge an alliance that would prove so characteristic of the further history of the West. The famous "Tabula Peutingeriana"—the sole surviving medieval copy (from the twelfth century) of a Roman map, named from its original owner, the Augsburg humanist Konrad Peutinger; the original is thought to come from the fourth or the fifth century—showed the territory of *Francia* occupying land only to the right of the Rhine, opposite the town of Xanten. Yet by the mid-fourth century we know that Salian Franks were already settled as *foederati* of the Roman Empire on the left bank of the river in the present-day province of Brabant, from where, around 500, they proceeded under Chlodwig's leadership to take control of almost all of Gaul. Certainly, this king was able to build on the successes of his father Childeric, who as the sovereign of his people and as a Roman confederate was able to attain a position of considerable influence and power.

The grave of this latter king, who died in 481 or 482, remained undisturbed until the seventeenth century; it was only in 1653 that it was discovered in the city of Tournai—possibly the first imperial capital of the Salian Franks—and opened, and the body identified through the golden seal ring with its mirror-image signature. The grave of Childeric is a tangible example of the acculturation of this barbarian people to the Roman world, and also points to the provenance of the treasure trove, which must have constituted the basis of the Merovingian rise to power. The finds were immediately publicized—fortunately for posterity, since they disappeared from the royal library in Paris and have never been seen again. Napoleon, the parvenu from the minor nobility and the first emperor of the French, gained the inspiration for the decoration of the coronation cloaks for himself and his empress Josephine from what were claimed to be the corresponding pieces fashioned for the very first rulers of the Franks/French. The painter Jacques-Louis David portrayed these imperial clothes several times on canvas. The precious grave goods of the Merovingian king were thought to have come from Byzantium or at least from craftsmen's workshops somewhere in the Levant.[12] This discovery points to the existence of formal relations between Childeric and the Eastern Roman emperor. Archeological excavations in the 1980s brought to light more culturally revealing and generally remarkable finds. The king of the Franks was buried under a massive long barrow in a wooden chamber amid gold-decorated and garnet-encrusted ceremonial weapons, a gold-reined horse, and a host of other lavish grave goods and—apparently—alongside a woman; at the foot of the burial mound, three more pits were discovered containing the bodies of a further twenty-one horses. Wherever the afterlife lay, this king was spirited away into it in the company of a whole retinue of horses. However, no evidence was found of any form of Mithraic bull cult, as supposedly indicated by Frankish legend. However, to sustain him on his journey, the dead king had been provided with a generous hoard of 200 silver *denarii* and more than 100 gold *solidi*; these led archaeologists to conclude that Childeric had entered into a *foederati* agreement with the

Romans. Indeed, this was the source of the Merovingian rise to power. Childeric's ceremonial golden clasp, richly decorated with crosses, might, along with other pieces of evidence, point to a hybrid religious culture, in which Christianity had begun to gain a foothold in the royal household, already perhaps paving the way in some fashion for Chlodwig's baptism.[13]

The Merovingians used the remnants of the Roman military and civil bureaucracy as the basis of their power; in conjunction with this, a key feature of their rule was the *Königsbann* ("exercise of royal jurisdiction"), which combined Roman and Frankish elements, and gave the monarch the right to issue commands and proscriptions, with penalties for any transgressions. Merovingian power was underpinned by the royal treasure, which consisted primarily of Roman subvention payments and was swollen by conquests. These barbarian kings were able to seize unowned domains and latifundia, as indeed all ownerless lands in the conquered territories devolved to their control—either to use for their own benefit or to pass on to their followers. Symbols of sovereignty such as the throne or displays of golden ceremonial weapons or clothing were a clear outward sign of royal dignity; precious gifts, lavish banquets, or the coercive use of terror were additional ways of asserting authority; in sum, personal attitudes with an institutional background. The church proved a useful handmaiden of this royal dynasty. It remained above all the last bastion of literacy; however, the gradual decline of literacy, together with an acute loss of sources—perishable papyrus continued to be used for manuscripts— mean that the era as a whole is largely sunk in obscurity.

Antiquity did not suddenly come to an end in the Merovingian Empire, any more than it did among the Visigoths; rather it underwent transformations—contracting, shifting (due, say, to emigration of the senatorial aristocracy) from north to south, and gradually petering out as the decades rolled by. Some customs and institutions were more resilient before they, too, disappeared, whereas others, such as the borders of those bishoprics in southern Gaul where the *civitas* mode of Roman provincial administration emerged in Late Antiquity, survived into the Modern Period. Although manufacturing declined in the cities at that time, it did not cease altogether. Even lawyers were still active in Frankish southern Gaul, despite the fact that the Merovingians, unlike their Visigoth counterparts, did not, as far as we can tell, systematically nurture Roman Law within their realm, but rather left this task to the discretion of local judges, while those lawyers played no part in framing Frankish legislation. The

Lex Salica, the most significant Frankish statute book, was compiled without their help; while jurisprudence, which had once been fostered by the great legal scholars of the second and third centuries—and remnants of which still survived among the Visigoths—did not exist in the Frankish kingdom. Long since defunct, this discipline had to wait until the Late Middle Ages to experience a revival. This development went hand in hand with a loss of mental acuity and of methodically controlled thinking, faculties that would only be reborn in the course of the Middle Ages.[14]

After Chlodwig's death, according to his wishes, his kingdom was split among his four sons, with this process of division leaving the Franks with a legacy that would ultimately spell the downfall of the late Carolingians in the ninth and tenth centuries. No other of the barbarian kingdoms would find itself exposed in the same way to the vicissitudes of royal fertility and succession. In this early period, none of the other realms divided kingly rule in this manner; with each struggle for succession that ensued, nothing was more effective at eroding royal power than these Frankish divisions. They did not result in the growth of stable Frankish subkingdoms, even in cases where certain traditions repeatedly led to the mutually agreed drawing up of frontiers. The leading polities to come to prominence during this period were Neustria, with the Île-de-France, in the center; Austrasia, with its heartland in the region around the Maas and the Rhine, and which was home to the Carolingians; and Burgundy, whose name recalled the Burgundian people who had perished in the upheavals of the Hunnish invasion, and which had its center at Lyons. Language may have played some part in these divisions, though by no means the major one.

The unstable Frankish subkingdoms could hardly be expected to instigate a process of renewal. Instead, they lived off the legacies of the Romans. At a cursory glance it might appear as though the Eastern Roman Empire, that is, early Byzantium, was the prime mover of such renewal. Emperor Justinian was on the throne there when Boethius was active, and he was pursuing a far-reaching policy of restoration. The emperor dispatched his armies to recapture the western provinces that already seemed to have been lost to barbarian rulers: the armies fought against the Vandals in North Africa, including Carthage, against the Visigoths and other separatist forces along the Spanish Mediterranean coast around the settlement of Cartagena, and first and foremost against the Ostrogoths in Italy and Rome, who put up a dogged resistance. Belisarius and Narses were the imperial commanders to whom Justinian successively entrusted these campaigns, the former a long-serving general, and the latter a eunuch. And indeed, in certain places and for varying lengths of time, they did succeed in restoring Eastern Roman rule. However, these wars placed too heavy a strain on Byzantium and its people. The centralization of power and the economy, which focused entirely on Constantinople, hampered the ongoing development of the reconquered provinces and weakened their performance and resilience; indeed, this phenomenon undoubtedly hastened the final decline and fall of the ancient empire.

In the empire of Justinian and his successors, all culture was concentrated on the capital Constantinople. The renowned Academy in Athens, where Plato had studied and Aristotle taught, was closed for being a hotbed of philosophical paganism. Yet from 529 onward Justinian was also responsible for framing the famous collection of Roman jurisprudence known as the *Corpus juris Justiniani,* including the *Codex,* the *Digesta,* and the *Novellae.* Both the closing of the Academy and the Code of Justinian were of lasting significance for the culture of learning that developed in the Middle Ages. Without the stimulus of the Academy and a diversity of schools, learning in the East was eventually to stagnate and produce no further scholarship of note, while in the West from the late eleventh century onward, the belated reception of the *Corpus juris,* which was tantamount to a complete rediscovery of the *Digesta,* sparked the development of Western university-based scholarship.

Byzantium was beset by external forces on all sides. Following the Hun invasions of the fifth century, the Central Asian steppes continued to dispatch waves of migration that threatened Constantinople and the Latin West; from the south, meanwhile, Arab groups fired by the new faith of Islam were pressing and encountering only token resistance against their advance northward and westward. The empire incurred major territorial losses, and only ever managed to regain small parts of its former holdings. A century after Justinian's death, apart from a few coastal strips, the most fertile regions of Italy had been lost forever, while the rich provinces of Syria and Africa—which even at the time of Augustine of Hippo were still an abundant source of grain and oil for the empire—had fallen for good to the Muslim invaders, as had extensive tracts of the Danubian lands to the Slavs, Avars, Pechenegs, and Bulgars. In Spain and Gaul, too, barbarian kings sat on the throne, unchallenged by Byzantium. This momentous upheaval still resonates to the present day.

In actual fact, then, the revived Roman sovereignty of Justinian did not last for even two decades, coming to an abrupt end when the Lombards of Pannonia under their great king Alboin invaded Italy in 568 and established an independent realm there with its capital at Pavia. Exhausted by the struggles against the Goths, the country was unable to mount any resistance to this new incursion. The Po Basin, Spoleto, and Benevento soon fell to the Lombards. Mainly thanks to their fleets, only the coastal regions around Genoa, Venetia, Naples, and Amalfi were able to hold out against these land-based conquerors, who were officially subjects of the Eastern emperor, but in fact were more or less independent agents. It was this period that saw the beginning of the rise of Venice. Only a narrow and unsecured corridor of land linked Ravenna, where the exarch resided as the representative of the emperor, and Rome, which put up stiff resistance against every attempt to conquer it and ultimately called upon the Franks for help in averting the ever-more-pressing danger posed by the Lombards. Also, the southernmost provinces of the "boot"—Puglia and Calabria—remained in Greek–Byzantine hands, as did Sicily, until it was finally overrun by the Arabs in the ninth century. Regional powers such as the exarch in Ravenna and the pope in Rome were responsible for organizing defenses. This was the first occasion on which the pope asserted himself as the political leader of the Eternal City. Meanwhile, as the years passed, the chances of any help arriving from Constantinople grew ever slimmer, with the Eastern emperors engaged in more pressing struggles of their own against the Arabs, Avars, and Bulgars.

Like the Vandals before them, the Lombards turned out to be a talented race of conquerors who knew how best to exploit the resources of the land they seized, and who were quick learners. Yet they were also riven by internal disputes, as the death of Alboin himself at the hands of a compatriot attests. Duchies were established in the major cities of Lombardy such as Milan and Turin. The king had his residence in Pavia, but found himself unable to assert strict rule. In particular, the dukes of Spoleto and Benevento jealously guarded their wide-ranging independence. Moreover, the invaders were too few in number to be able to displace the former populace of the empire. As a result, they had to reckon with the continued existence of an urban upper class, in evidence since late antiquity, as well as certain social and organizational structures, and last but not least with limited literacy and knowledge of the law. In any event, though, at no time does ancient scholarship ever appear to have died out entirely in the

Lombard kingdom, especially not in Romagna; the indigenous culture continued to thrive and blended with the Lombards' own strengths—thus forming a not insignificant strand of continuity from Late Antiquity to the Middle Ages. The Carolingian period was able to profit from this, and the intellectual ferment of the eleventh and twelfth centuries, as evidenced in the jurisprudence of the period or in the contemporaneous creation of the office of notary—a factor of huge significance for the development of European legal institutions—had one of its mainsprings in these lines of continuity.

The Ancient World thus shrank and eventually disappeared in the course of a long-drawn-out, uneven process of transformation. Spain, Gaul (which extended as far as the Rhine), and northern, central, and southern Italy, and possibly Sicily too, emerged as its independent and headstrong heirs. Revived Roman–Byzantine rule and its aftereffects clung on longest in Spain and the Visigoth kingdom, with Charlemagne still reaping the benefits, as well as in Lombardy and southern Italy, which was finally lost to the Normans only in the eleventh century. The exarchate continued to hold sway in Ravenna and Rome, until it was dissolved by the Lombards, the Franks, and the papacy in the latter half of the eighth century. This nonsimultaneous contraction of Western Latin Europe gave rise to specific tensions, whose implications were likewise felt into the Modern Period. Within its borders, there arose a culture of scholarship comprising competing interests and forces that spawned a tendency toward collecting and extrapolating from tradition and research, and indeed which required that such activities take place.

Yet like melting glaciers, the world that was in the process of vanishing left its traces behind everywhere, which for centuries—perhaps even up to modern times—have been evident as cultural lines of demarcations along the Rhine and the Danube and in southern England. It would appear that here, among a constantly present imperial populace, despite all the shifts of power and barbarian invasions, that a certain subliminal "orientation toward Rome" never completely died out. A dim awareness, perhaps no more than an inkling, survived, that the spiritual and cultural center still lay beyond the Alps, to which individuals still felt themselves attached. Beyond this demarcation line, according to ancient conceptions, there lived "barbarians." As a result of their material, social and cultural development up to that time, they had to content themselves with a considerably lower standard of civilization, involving only very few iron implements, no cities, no paved roads, limited communications, and a purely oral culture without the written word (the runes that barbarian peoples occasionally used were for a long time reserved for magic formulae and simple names), or learning, or any lasting historical tradition. Their small-scale social groups corresponded more or less to the requirements of a face-to-face society, while their religious cults are scarcely known. The practices that Pliny the Elder or Tacitus, the author of *Germania,* mentioned are no longer evident among the Franks in the fourth, fifth, or sixth centuries. Barely anything survived of their ancient cultures into the age of writing. Only in the tenth and eleventh centuries do more extensive runic inscriptions praising the deeds of hero figures find their way onto memorial stones—an early indication of a general acculturation to the advanced civilization of the Mediterranean region. The *Edda* was only written in the thirteenth century and contains just as many heathen as Christian allusions, and just as many scholarly as popular elements.[15] In terms of research methodology, it is unwise and unreliable to emulate the practice of the fairytale author Jacob Grimm and draw an arc from this work back a millennium or so to the so-called period of the barbarian invasions, which for the aforementioned reasons should more appropriately be called the "period when peoples originated," or even to the time of Tacitus, and draw conclusions from motifs appearing in the *Edda* about the conditions that existed then. In the north and south, east and west of the Western world that we are examining here, utterly diverse initial conditions pertained regarding the introduction or the revival of an advanced literary culture. The farther particular regions lay from the advanced civilization of the Mediterranean, the more distortions and obstacles become apparent, and the more delayed and weaker the act of assimilation. Only among the Irish was the situation different, and this would prove to be to the great benefit of Western scholarship, though the works of Boethius played no role in this civilization.

2

Gregory the Great and the New Power of the Franks

Pope gregory the Great (r. 590–604) must be counted among the most outstanding successors of Saint Peter. As a former Roman prefect and hence the city's highest-ranking civilian official, and subsequently permanent papal nuncio to the Byzantine court in Constantinople, Gregory, who came from the most distinguished Roman aristocratic family of the period, was the last pontiff to display the full panoply of ancient learning. After him, vulgarization and barbarity were the order of the day—comparable intellectual heights were only attained again several centuries later, without the immediate help of Antiquity. Repeatedly, Gregory's extensive theological works, comprising biblical exegeses, sermons, and letters, held the faithful in thrall. Yet the form of liturgical music that nowadays bears his name is from a later date, despite the fact that the very oldest books of liturgy do indeed date back to his time.

The later period of the Roman Empire—which was entirely given over to Christian observance—lived in expectation of the coming end of the world, in the belief in the Last Judgment, God's righteousness, and the everlasting nature of the soul. Natural disasters, such as the flooding of the Tiber in 589, which destroyed the ancient city of Rome, and the threatened invasions of the Lombards, made people fearful and seemed to vindicate their belief in the end time. This tenet of faith demanded that people exert their spiritual powers to the full, and required that they be steadfast in their faith in order that they might be prepared for the imminent upheaval. Gregory was well aware of this mind-set and geared his teachings to it. He exhorted Christians to keep in mind the power of the soul, to keep their eyes firmly fixed on the Eternal Life—albeit without in the process preaching escapism—and called for them to focus on the contemplative life and the practice of monastic spirituality. Consistently applying these principles to his private life, the wealthy Gregory vested all his family fortune in the church and urban monastic orders.

Gregory followed the doctrine, well-established since the time of Saint Jerome, of interpreting different layers of textual meaning in the Bible; according to this approach, the written word was not simply to be understood literally, but also in various metaphorical senses. In particular, the allegorical–typological and moral forms of exegesis were honed to perfection at this time. In these, Christ was seen as the bridegroom, while the church and the individual believer's soul were the bride. Later, the High Middle Ages was to interpret this kind of visual metaphor in legalistic terms. Gregory's *Commentaries on Job (Magna moralia)* explained the Book of Job typologically as a prefiguration of Christ and his Passion. This work is without doubt one of the great educational texts of the Middle Ages; it was widely disseminated and had an enduring influence. But perhaps even more significant was *The Book of the Pastoral Rule (Regula pastoralis)*. This was a seminal text for all future church leaders and bishops, and was read and absorbed over and over again; it even gained much currency as a book for the education of future rulers. Even in a thoroughly secularized society, this slim volume has lost nothing of its validity. Gregory, later to be canonized, outlined his own agenda in his introductory letter to the dedicatee of the treatise, Bishop John of Ravenna: "For, as the necessity of things requires, we must especially consider after what manner everyone should come to supreme rule; and, duly arriving at it, after what manner he should live; and, living well, after what manner he should teach; and, teaching aright, with how great consideration every day he should become aware of his own infirmity; lest either humility fly from the approach, or life be at variance with the arrival, or teaching be wanting to the life, or presumption unduly exalt the teaching." In other words, a person's life and teaching should be as one: "it is necessary that the good which is displayed in the life of the pastor should also be propagated by his speech." Gregory's correspondence, which has been preserved, and is organized chronologically, affords us a lively insight into his administration; as a result, it stands out like no other pope's reign from this early period.

Gregory's *Dialogues* are a remarkable work of lasting influence. Though doubt has been cast on whether these are actually the work of the pontiff himself—in any event, they don't match his customary style—they certainly come from his immediate circle. This work recounted the life of the great abbot Saint Benedict of Nursia, setting this paragon of the monastic life in the context of a host of other exemplary saints, especially monks and abbots; Benedict was renowned for performing twelve miracles and during the course of his lifetime progressed through seven stations, rising from the caves of Subiaco—the bowels of the Earth, as it were—up to the peak of Monte Cassino, and from there ascended still further above the earth, up a tower almost to the heavens, and gazed down upon the entire world, finally being reunited in death with his sister Scholastica. Twelve times and seven times, from below to above, from inside to outside, in the unity of benediction and knowledge—the symbolic richness of the language of the *Dialogues* reveals the true meaning of this saint's life. In addition, a kind of spiritual self-portrait of the author also shines forth from this text.

In all likelihood, the *Dialogues* owed their literary composition and execution to the papal interlocutors and notaries who wrote them down and edited them. Meanwhile, no real historical evidence of Saint Benedict can be found anywhere, and it is open to question whether he ever really existed at all. But that mattered little to the cult of the saint and the monasticism that drew heavily on this cult, which developed later—not in Rome and central Italy but to a far greater extent on the periphery, among the Anglo-Saxons and in Gaul. Likewise, the "Rule of Saint Benedict," which has come down to us, may well be apocryphal—that is, a post-Gregorian creation; in any event, Gregory did not know of it, and its early textual history (its provenance can only be traced back as far as the mid-seventh century) is lost in obscurity. It was only thanks to Charlemagne, and to an even greater degree his son Louis the Pious and his advisor Abbot Benedict of Aniane that it became the sole guiding principle of medieval monasticism. Only in the thirteenth century did the mendicant orders begin to diverge from it.

Exactly the same scruples that had bothered the early church fathers also oppressed Gregory—namely, whether and to what extent scholarship and religion, scholasticism and benediction were compatible with one another, and whether a Christian education, or indeed any form of religious learning, was even possible. On the contrary, weren't faith and scholarship (which had its roots in heathen society) mutually exclusive? This question troubled thinkers over all the ensuing centuries—and not just those from a Christian background, but Muslims and Jews in the Middle Ages, too. Across the board, the answers are contradictory and anything but definitive. Generally speaking, revelation defies all attempts by scholarship to explain it. The ramifications of this can be seen everywhere. Aberrant doctrines, scientifically based skepticism, even doubts about the truth of the Gospels and other religious tenets brought (and bring) animosity and persecution in their wake—even such atrocities as burnings at the stake, stonings, and bloody reigns of terror. The history of Christianity cannot be disengaged from this dark side. This problem was at the root of many of the clashes that arose in European intellectual history. Gregory the Great provided a radical answer, which can be said to have delivered the *coup de grâce* to school education in Late Antiquity, severely disrupting it for centuries to come. In regard to the attitude toward education of this church father, some scholars have even gone so far as to categorize it as blissful ignorance, a state of mind Gregory certainly preached, but which he was far from observing where his own learning was concerned (F. Schneider).

The intercultural transfer of knowledge was not confined to religion. The Christian church fundamentally changed social conditions and the exercise of authority among the barbarians, perhaps even more emphatically than in the Christianized Roman Empire. These barbarians learned how to rule and to integrate the new cult with new social institutions such as kingship, penal codes, and courts of law, which were designed to suit the newly created national groupings. It was precisely in this regard that barbarian societies had their first fruitful encounter with the rationalistic legal culture of Late Antiquity. This fundamentally altered the course of European history, entailing as it did a fundamental reorientation in social, ruling, church, and intellectual matters. In the process, secular rule and subjugation to Christ became etiologically intermingled. The church sanctified and spiritualized notions of authority and Roman concepts of law, while at the same time imparting to the barbarian peoples new, progressive values and social norms and unfamiliar interpretive models. When these peoples first came into contact with the advanced civilizations of the Mediterranean region, they had only just begun to coalesce into larger groupings and had scarcely transcended their former archaic tribal structures. As a consequence, they did not have affectively and normatively loaded distinctions like lay people, priests, and monks or women, widows, and virgins. These societies did not yet possess any sophisticated systems of norms with corresponding judicial and surveillance organs; there was still no consciousness of punishment. All of a sudden, they were confronted with the model of a Christian empire with its imperial and ecclesiastical law, and as a result—instead of the traditional individual agreements and negotiating processes between the parties concerning the maintenance, restoration, and regulation of peace—a quite alien ruling practice imposed itself upon their social order and their value system. From the outset, these were impregnated with ecclesiastical principles.

This gradual advance of Roman and ecclesiastical norms—such as the death penalty or corporal punishment—is especially noticeable in the realm of the penal code. Here in particular, the presumptuousness of the new learning was painfully apparent. Hitherto completely unknown crimes and statutory offences were introduced into law. Formerly, strategies were in operation in instances of conflict, which in the best cases led to an amicable settlement between the parties in question or in the worst-case scenarios to "self-help" in the form of a feud and endless blood vengeance. The institution of public punishment only obtained, if at all, in cases of treason.[1] Now, the so-called laws of the barbarians *(leges barbarorum),* which were introduced from the sixth century on, provided tariffs in order to try and stem the tide of incipient conflict, and which recommended compensation for various injuries—such and such an amount for a severed hand, for instance, or so much for a nose, or for the life of a high-ranking man, or a low-ranking one, or a woman of child-bearing age, or a maiden—indeed, a whole scale of gradations of compensation for all manner of wrongs. However, both warring parties still had to agree to abide by such settlement; matters weren't decided, say, by state-appointed judges.

Only very few misdemeanors were subject to public punishment. Not even murder came into this category, although, following biblical precedent, the worst kind of incest, namely marrying one's stepmother, did; such a practice could, in those days of early mortality and a far younger marrying age, be a highly attractive prospect. This transgression was punishable by death.[2] Disturbing the peace on a Sunday incurred God's wrath and was an offence that attracted a fine.[3] In addition, abortion was soon made a punishable offence; the following thoroughly dogmatic but also highly informative excerpt from the eighth-century Bavarian penal code (VIII, 21) explains the rationale—"the soul, once it has been made flesh but is unable to come into the world, and so never receives the sacrament of rebirth (that is, is not baptized), has to suffer eternal punishment, and is consigned to Hell by the practice of abortion." The effect of this kind of legal norm was clear, even though it emerged only gradually. Under the influence of Roman and ecclesiastical principles, a struggle ensued that would last for centuries, against blood vengeance and vigilante action and for the public persecution of wrongful deeds and their punishment by the state; the administration of Charlemagne and the introduction of a criminal penal code in the twelfth century represented another major step-change: thereafter, publicly administered justice carried all before it, and its strictures now permeate all our lives.

As acculturation proceeded apace, it raised new dangers. For example, the last strongholds of Roman–Byzantine rule in Italy found themselves under constant threat and attack by the Lombards. In particular, the two imperial cities Rome and Ravenna, had to fight hard to ward off attacks. Gregory the Great organized resistance and defense, and as a result, his role as a political leader was enhanced both in Rome and in the exarchate. And indeed, Rome did remain free. The Lombards, who were originally Arian Christians, were poised for an imminent conversion to Catholicism. Their queen, Theodelinde, from the Bavarian noble family of the Agilolfings, introduced them to the Catholic faith. In gratitude, Gregory sent a precious gem-encrusted cross to her, as a symbol of the impending Kingdom of God. This "Gregory crucifix" has been preserved to the present day. Yet the relief from the constant military pressure that the pope may have hoped would ensue from this conversion did not last long. To the contrary, it only served to encourage the Lombards to rearm all the more keenly for their attack on the *Urbs,* the mistress of the *Orbis.* After all, they too were Catholics now.

The peoples of northwestern Europe—the Irish (or Scots, as they were called on the mainland) and the Anglo-Saxons—had never been subjects of Rome: in the case of the Irish, because Roman fleets had never made it across the Irish Sea, and in the case of the Angles and the Saxons, because they only emigrated from an unconquered region (Denmark, northern Germany) to the British Isles during the late fourth and early fifth centuries when Roman rule there had already collapsed. Even so, both peoples did come under Rome's influence and were to emerge at an early stage as vectors of Latin culture. Christian missionaries came to the Emerald Isle, which was divided into a number of small warring kingdoms, by the fifth century at the latest. The missionary Saint Patrick, a Roman citizen from

Britain and a figure who is steeped in legend, is reputed to have been abducted to Ireland as a boy, and subsequently escaped, but returned to the Irish as a bishop, following a revelation, with the aim of baptizing them. This sketchy synopsis is all we know of his life. In a process that is often replicated in early history, the story of Patrick's life appears to have been conflated with that of the second missionary to come to Ireland: one Palladius from Gaul.

One decisive factor was that the Irish church came into being utterly beyond the sphere of Rome's influence. It was characterized by a special constitution with monasteries, abbots and suffragan bishops. These latter bishops did not have a diocese of their own, but instead only undertook consecrations and remained subordinate to their abbot. It was only in the twelfth century, after the British Isles had been absorbed into the Anglo-Norman empire under the successors of William the Conqueror, that the Irish submitted to the rule of the Roman pope and adopted the continental church constitution. However, the Catholic faith itself obliged the Irish, too, to take on board ancient learning. They became especially adept at grammar, and scholars from the island were soon becoming known for their excellent knowledge of Latin and Greek. Alongside this, a particular form of religious observance among the Irish came into being as the spiritual legacy of Saint Patrick: namely, voluntary exile, an aimless form of pilgrimage that, like the elaborately intertwined letters of ancient Celtic art, led people on wanderings that took them wherever God wished. This kind of *Peregrinatio religiosa* made the Irish the great carriers of the faith in the early Middle Ages. So it was that the abbot Saint Brendan embarked with a number of companions and after several stop-offs on fertile shores with abundant sheep, finally arrived at a small island that suddenly began to move and turned out to be a whale; it is at this point that God finally instructed him to turn back. This popular legend quickly spread far and wide, and saw Saint Brendan become the patron saint of seafarers, including the great navigators and explorers of the fifteenth and sixteenth centuries.

Like Saint Brendan, Saint Columba and his companions also left the British Isles, collected followers in France, and in collusion with the aristocracy of the western Vosges, founded the abbey of Luxeuil, which was soon to become famous. After being expelled from this region, they journeyed on to northern Italy and were instrumental in laying the foundations of the abbey at Bobbio. St. Gallen in Switzerland, too, recalls in the name of its founder Gallus one of Columba's companions. All these sites became centers of literary culture, rich library treasures, and further dissemination of the faith. From the seventh century onward, Bobbio especially proved to be a bastion of Irish-influenced learning on the continent. Yet even at the court of Charlemagne, Irish monks who had left their homeland on religious pilgrimages still kept arriving, spreading their great fund of knowledge and their religious message. The earliest advice on ethical rule and counsel to princes also came from Irish authors; they even saw fit to reprimand the great Frankish king.

The Angles and Saxons, who emigrated as heathens to the British Isles from the region of Angeln in southern Jutland, as well as from the lower reaches of the rivers Elbe and Weser and from Frisia, only came into contact with the new religion in their new homeland. The unique grave find at Sutton Hoo in Suffolk bears witness to the wealth of their heathen rulers. This ship burial was replete with gold artifacts, magnificent weapons, and precious silver dishes. It was Gregory the Great who was responsible for their conversion. This pontiff made a point of purchasing slaves from the islands at market, and freeing them and educating them as priests in order to send them back to their homeland as missionaries in the company of the Roman monk and prior Augustine. Augustine was to become the first Archbishop of Canterbury. Thereafter, the Anglo-Saxons preserved a close link with the Roman church, a tie that was only broken with the Reformation. Alongside Canterbury, York also came to prominence as an ecclesiastical center, with a history that stretched back to Roman times. Missionary work without education was unthinkable, and over time monasteries in the British Isles and the schools attached to them developed a unique reputation for scholarship. In York, Alcuin, the future teacher of Charlemagne, underwent schooling in the spirit of Pope Gregory and the Venerable Bede. Alcuin was to go on to be one of the great disseminators of Anglo-Saxon learning in France. Its reception laid the foundation for the intellectual unity of Western/Latin Europe, perhaps the most impressive result of the measures taken by this great pontiff. In particular, the "computus"—the method of time calculation that was of such central importance to Christianity because of the movable feast of Easter—reached the continent via the school of Bede and found a new home at the court of the Frankish king Charlemagne. After Bede, and through its widespread use in the Carolingian empire, the custom of numbering the years from the birth of Christ, which formerly had only been practiced in a few places, became the norm throughout Latin Christendom.

Not only the north contributed to the formation of Europe, however; the south, or more accurately the southeast also played its part. From the early seventh century onward, a new danger threatened from that quarter, like an impending storm. This storm blew up from Arabia. The Bedouin tribes that lived there, whose early history is lost in obscurity save for the odd inscription here and there, had hitherto known no common political leadership. Now, though, the Prophet Muhammad's proclamation of the Word of God served to unify them. The Prophet's entry onto the stage of world history is shrouded in mystery. The miracle of divine revelation surrounds the origins of the Qu'ran, while impenetrable uncertainty and—just as in Judaism and Christianity—a welter of contradictory oral traditions obscure the early history of Islam, including the *Hijra* and the activities of the Prophet. Written accounts of Islam begin late, in the ninth or tenth centuries. The first biography of Muhammad (the *sira* literature) only appeared around a century after his death, and the sole surviving version of this comes from a century later than that. Moreover, this document has only excited the interest of critical philology and academic history in Western scholarship. The Prophet's name means "the blessed One," Latin *Benedictus,* and it appears that, like the Christian–Latin Saint Benedict, Muhammad's life has dissipated into a comparatively late and somewhat idealized construct. In these circumstances, it is virtually impossible to attain any historical certainty; the Prophet's life is now the preserve of faith alone.

The new religion imbued the Arab world with unstoppable force. In the manner of Alexander the Great, from the early seventh century onward Arab caliphs and commanders conquered an empire that within a few centuries extended from the Arabian Peninsula and Mesopotamia east to the Indus River and west as far as Tangiers; soon, this area would increase to take in land up to the Ebro River of the northern Iberian peninsula and even beyond. From an early date, the center of this empire shifted from Arabia to Damascus, and then, from around 750, to the Euphrates and Baghdad. Christians and Jews lived physically unmolested under the sway of the Crescent Moon, which over the course of the Middle Ages became established as the prime symbol of Muslim rule. However, they were legally disadvantaged. Their monotheistic faiths were tolerated, since they were regarded as "peoples of the Book," but they were required to pay higher taxes *(jizya)*. The Jewish patriarch Abraham was also held by the Arabs to be a forefather, while Jesus of Nazareth, son of Mary, was regarded as a prophet ranking only just below Muhammad himself.

Byzantium, which had been weakened by wars against the Bulgars and the Sassanids, was unable to offer any effective resistance against this new onslaught. True, the emperor Heraclius (610–641) had won a series of important victories against the old enemies, the Persians, as well as the Avars, preventing an imminent collapse of the empire, and this enabled former imperial authority to be restored. Internal reforms brought, and Byzantium experienced a new period of cultural ascendancy, which exerted an indirect influence on the West. Yet the conquest of the Persians proved to be a pyrrhic victory, since it only served to hasten the Muslim advance. Byzantium could do little to ward off the attacks by the Caliph Umar. Syria and Egypt were irrevocably lost, and Jerusalem along with them. The remainder of Roman Africa soon followed. Only Antioch held out. Another factor that further weakened resistance was the sharp division among the Christian community between Orthodox Christians, who held the reins of power in Constantinople, and Monophysites, who were particularly prominent in Egypt. Not unreasonably, the Monophysites, who were persecuted for their beliefs, expected the attackers to grant them freedom of religion. Their doctrine only recognized the single divine nature of Jesus Christ, unlike the Orthodox Church, which identified a duality of natures, divine and human, in the one person of Christ.

Accordingly, the Byzantine Empire contracted, to embrace Asia Minor, Thrace, Macedonia, Greece, Sicily, and southern Italy, and despite a series of hard-fought and by no means unsuccessful defensive actions over the course of the Middle Ages, continued to shrink until it consisted of only the city of Constantinople. Finally, in 1453, it was overrun by the Ottoman sultan Mehmed II the Conqueror. Although Byzantium was decried in the West as arrogant, devious, and heretical, homage nevertheless continued to be paid to it because it served for centuries as a kind of defensive shield behind which the West could assemble and build up its forces; with the demise of Byzantium, Europe was thrown back on its own devices.

Even the sea could not halt the Muslims' expansionist tendencies. The first incursions of the forces of the Crescent Moon across the Strait of Gibraltar took place in 711; the name "Gibraltar" itself is Arabic in origin, deriving from *Jabl-i Tariq*, "the mountain of Tariq," which was named for the Berber Umayyad commander Tariq ibn Zayid, who led the initial assault on Iberia. Visigoth accession disputes had made the Muslim advance into Spain all the easier, and within two years they had conquered all the territory up to the Pyrenees. However, their armies did not even stop there. Toulouse was taken and southern Aquitaine overrun, and presently the whole of Gaul lay open before the Islamic forces. Soon after, namely from the early ninth century onward, Muslims from Tunis pushed through Sicily and encroached upon the southern Italian mainland as far as Apulia and Calabria. Sicily remained in Arab hands for a long time, to the end of the eleventh century, when the Normans finally expelled the Muslims and established their own kingdom on the island and the southern mainland, with the royal seat at Palermo.

Yet the Muslims were not the first people to disrupt the religious and economic unity of the Mediterranean region. Before them, the regime of the Byzantine emperor Justinian had, as mentioned above, despite all its success in restoration caused irreparable rifts and only succeeded in hastening the extraordinary development taking place in the east and west and the north and south. The centers of the Western world shifted northward from the Mediterranean, to the Île-de-France and the region around the Meuse and the Rhine (Neustria and Austrasia). Henceforth, the new intercultural vectors of communication throughout the entire Mediterranean region were the Jews. This development, which began in the ninth century and became especially widespread in the eleventh, emerges from the documents of the *Genizah* in ancient Cairo (Fustat), namely the records of the ritual repository for manuscripts containing invocations of God. The Jews of the diaspora constituted a "Mediterranean society" (Shmuel Goitein), indeed the only such society at this period, one might add. They were united by their broad outlook and their corresponding engagement in long-distance trade, from India via Aden to Sicily, Spain, and Narbonne. They acted as middlemen between the Far Eastern trade of the Arabian world and the Latin West. Jewish communities flourished in all the ports of Southern Europe. Efficient, large-capacity ships and a comparatively "modern" mercantile organization facilitated transport, trading, and commerce. These vessels carried goods and knowledge across the oceans, not to mention literary tropes, rhythms, songs, and poems. Each and every form of knowledge transfer was boosted by these developments.

A recovery in population figures following the ravages of plague became apparent throughout Europe. Even as early as the ninth century the heartland regions of France between the Loire and the Rhine were suffering from an increasing shortage of land for settlement. Villages grew in size, and farmsteads were first divided and then split into fourths, until they were incapable of sustaining anyone. Extensive forest clearances ensued, followed by a protracted process of internal colonization, the creation of new forms of governance, and new freedom for colonists. These developments saw settlements, ecclesiastical institutions, highways and streets, and modes of communication in general all multiply, and necessitated an intensification of trade and transport. This changing environment also represented a cognitive challenge to contemporaries, who had to engage simultaneously with new, Christian-generated patterns of interpreting the world, new intellectual methods inculcated by schools, and new living conditions.

In the Frankish empire, power shifted from the Merovingians to the Carolingians, whose rise can be traced from the seventh century onward. Over time, they were able to secure for themselves alone the post of the "mayor of the palace" *(Maior domus)*, the most important post in the Merovingian court, whose holders had arrogated considerable powers, which they claimed as their own. In this matter, the Carolingians relied upon the nobility of their Austrasian homeland, who for their part profited hugely from the rise of this dynasty, expanding their possessions and spheres of interest throughout the whole empire. The leading position within the ruling dynasty itself, however, was repeatedly contested and fought over.

Charles Martel, Charlemagne's grandfather, was ultimately able to claim sole power for himself in the face of fierce resistance from within his own family. He used his position to undertake warlike expansion of the mayor of the palace's authority as far as Aquitaine, the territory south of the Loire, as well as into Provence. Although the Merovingian monarchy remained nominally in power, it could no longer act independently. By contrast, Charles Martel was already being fêted as a king, without actually being one; Pope Gregory III endowed him with the title *subregulus*. Meanwhile, the trial of strength against the Saracens was still impending. The hosts of Allah had advanced as far as Toulouse and had begun to annex Aquitaine, or at least parts of it, into the Arab world. The decisive battle took place in 732 between Tours and Poitiers. Charles "the Unconquered" unleashed his full martial might against the enemy, killing their commander Abderrahman and vanquishing them with the aid of Christ. "Thus did he triumph as victor over his enemies," exulted the Carolingian chroniclers.[4] Never again were the Saracens to return to these regions, so distant from their Arabic–North African home territory, as conquerors. The "Europeans" *(Europenses)* had once and for all repelled the sons of Ishmael, as one Spanish writer noted.

And yet the significance of the Battle of Poitiers and some later engagements was deliberately exaggerated and overestimated by contemporary historians, with the aim of legitimating Charles Martel's authority. For Charles, the victory was just one battle among many others, but for the Arabs, Gaul lay too far away from their power base. All the same, the fame of the victory spread even as far as the Tiber. Pope Gregory III, who was coming under ever-increasing pressure from the Lombards, sent Martel the key to the grave of Saint Peter and his martyrdom's chains, a valuable religious relic and a significant gesture. He also asked the Frankish commander for help in 739, but Charles, who was in league with the Lombards, refused. It was only his son Pepin and his illustrious grandson Charlemagne who would eventually accede to such requests.

In Rome, a century after the papacy of Gregory the Great, the Apostolic Throne was occupied successively by Gregory II and Gregory III. They found themselves seriously at issue with their temporal master, the Byzantine emperor *(basileus)* in Constantinople, who had recently imposed a new tax on Italy and Sicily, and who refused the bishops of Rome the income from their Sicilian holdings when they dared to oppose this measure, ultimately requisitioning these funds for himself. The dispute started to loosen the ties between the Western and Eastern Roman Empires and hinted at a coming rift between the pope and the emperor.

However, of greater significance for the religious culture of the West was the rediscovery of the *Dialogues* of Gregory the Great, which found a new readership. But now, a century after their creation, these writings were taken quite literally. At the same time, especially on the periphery of the empire and not, at first, in Rome, Saint Benedict and his sister Saint Scholastica, were in the process of being resurrected. Clandestine efforts by Frankish monks and nuns to reveal a unique hoard of religious relics had, in miraculous fashion, led to the "discovery" of their grave and remains, which had been transferred to Fleury (near Orléans) and Le Mans. Finally, at the onset of the eighth century, the time was ripe to proceed to a monastery foundation at Monte Cassino itself. At the behest of Pope Gregory II and with the support of the Lombard duke Gisulf I of Benevento, a small group of Roman monks under the leadership of the Lombard Petronax from Brescia undertook this task. Thus began the meteoric rise of the cult of Saint Benedict of Nursia and of the Benedictine monastic order. Charles Martel's eldest legitimate son, Carloman was later to withdraw to Monte Cassino and take holy orders. The monastery there blossomed into one of the foremost religious centers of the West.

Far-reaching changes were looming in France, too. The wars conducted by the mayor of the palace were a huge financial drain on the country. In order to finance them, Charles Martel set about seizing church property, taking control of entire monasteries with their valuable land holdings. As a result, later generations were to consider this ruler as condemned to eternal damnation. This injustice nevertheless did bring some benefits: the new source of income undoubtedly strengthened the office of mayor of the palace, as well as the Carolingian monarchy. Further church reforms also became necessary. Charles carried these out, as his father Pepin of Herstal had done before him, with the aid of Anglo-Saxon monks, whose main sphere of activity would turn out to be the east of the realm. In particular, a monk named Winfrid, who had formerly been the abbot of the monastery at Nursling (near Winchester) enjoyed the confidence of Charles and his sons, at least initially. Winfrid, however, made certain of papal consent to his activities, hurrying to Rome to obtain the necessary legitimation. There, he took the name Boniface and was granted the *pallium* by Gregory III, the sash indicating the office of archbishop, which only the pope could bestow. He duly returned to the Franks as the "envoy of Saint Peter." Through his efforts, the Frankish Church, in accordance with Anglo-Saxon tradition, also forged closer and firmer ties with Rome than ever before.

Yet in Austrasia, Boniface—who ultimately became bishop of Mainz—was able to achieve very little. Only the abbey at Fulda, which he was responsible for founding, truly flourished; the establishment of bishoprics that he planned, however, came to nothing. Boniface was far more successful in Bavaria, where he not only enjoyed the backing of the mayors of the palace but also the support of Duke Odilo. Serious shortcomings were evident there, and demanded a comprehensive reform. For instance, there was one priest who was wont to baptize people "in the name of the Fatherland, the Daughter, and the Holy Ghost" *(in nomine patria et filia et spiritus sancti)*; and an Irishman by the name of Virgil, who misled the people with "perverse and false teachings," namely by maintaining "that another world with other people existed beneath the earth, with its own sun and moon" and who tried to turn the duke against Boniface.[5] It is possible that Virgil had some inkling of the spherical shape of the Earth. The remedy for such malpractices was to create fixed bishoprics, at Regensburg, Salzburg, Freising, and Passau, whose incumbents would henceforth be responsible for church discipline throughout the duchy.

Things also looked bad for the Franks; reforms were the order of the day there, too. The realm's first synod, the so-called *Concilium Germanicum* assembled at the behest of Carloman in 742. Its aim was to "renew the law of God and ecclesiastical order, which had fallen into decline." Its resolutions highlighted shortcomings and illustrated the urgent necessity for missionary work and reform. Henceforth, as laid down in the old canon law, which had since fallen into disuse, synods were to be held annually, in order to oversee church members and church discipline. Priests were required to obey their bishops and regularly give an account of their activities. False priests, and adulterous or lecherous deacons and clerics were to be removed from office and forced to do penance. Nuns who entertained lovers had their heads shorn, while priests who indulged in the same vice were savagely beaten, locked up for two years with only bread and water to eat, and sometimes punished even more harshly. God's servants were forbidden to carry weapons, engage in fights, or go to war. They were banned from taking part in the hugely popular activity of hunting with dogs, hawks, or falcons—a proscription that later needed to be repeated often. Spiritual and secular leaders were meant to act in concert to stamp out heathen practices.[6] And in general, the church was expected to shore up secular authority.

The populace had to reeducate itself. Albeit in secret, people still celebrated bloody sacrifices, indulged in fortune-telling and magic, placed their faith in amulets and soothsayers, sought salvation through spells, and believed in superstition (as the old cultic practices were now referred to). All of these beliefs were proscribed and persecuted. Familiar ways of life were now deemed unacceptable, and the magical interpretation of the world was robbed of its allure. The new religion called for an all-embracing enlightenment. In consequence, the reformers set in motion intercultural learning processes, and with them an evolution that continued for centuries and ultimately did not even shrink from questioning its own basic religious principles. Faith and learning once again found themselves at loggerheads and fanned the flames of an already fierce conflict which spared nothing—not the church, nor the monarchy, nor even the social order or humanity's conception of itself. The Austrasian aristocracy was therefore never able to make common cause with Boniface, the implacably zealous reformer. Finally, in 751, Boniface found his position seriously compromised by differences with the newly enthroned king Pepin the Short. In an attempt to relieve the pressure, the Anglo-Saxon archbishop embarked in 754 on a mission to Frisia; he had only just arrived there when he met a martyr's death. He was buried in Fulda Abbey; nowadays, in remembrance of Boniface, the German Bishops' Conference still meets there.

The rise of the Carolingians to a monarchy took place against a backdrop of bloody internecine struggles within the ruling family. Charles Martel, who for his entire life had aspired to autarchy, followed the Merovingian kings in the futile practice of dividing his kingdom up among his three sons Carloman, Pepin the Short, and Grifo. First of all, the youngest of them, Grifo, was imprisoned and taken out of the equation, and then Carloman found himself obliged to retire to Monte Cassino as a monk, and when he dared to return to the Frankish kingdom to challenge his brother, he was thrown into jail, where he died in mysterious circumstances in 753. Contemporary chroniclers pass over the question of how exactly the Merovingians were deposed in 751 or how Pepin won the assent of the Franks to his ascent to the throne. In any case, no exhaustive contemporary accounts of the Carolingian accession exist, let alone any from the losing side. History is written by the victors, and moreover is written in retrospect and heavily doctored into the bargain. It is doubtful whether the final act of transition from one dynasty to the next passed off peacefully; perhaps the interfamily conflicts were somehow bound up with it.

In a later historical account, Einhard, the biographer of Charlemagne, emphasized the unkingly poverty and the complete impotence of the last Merovingian. According to Einhard, he simply sat on the throne with long hair and a straggly beard, content with the empty title of king, and received envoys, merely giving them prepared responses. He also supposedly journeyed through his realm on an oxcart like a simple peasant and not on horseback and at the head of an army—as would befit a king, at this point Einhard feels it necessary to add. But what did the biographer of Charlemagne really know, writing as he was a century after the events he was describing? And what was he permitted to write?

Yet real skepticism must be reserved for the kind of legitimating accounts that appear in the semiofficial "Imperial Annals." According to them, Pepin asked Pope Zacharias who should be king—he who had real power or he who was king in name only? But such a question is clearly premised on the educational reforms that took place only in the late eighth century, which first made people acquainted with the Aristotelian doctrine of essentialism, namely the distinction between name and object, the *nomen* and the *res,* in this case the title of king and royal power. As such, this account is based on an anachronistic construction and was designed to retrospectively legitimate something that could not be legitimated. In an inversion of the normal sequence of reasoning, this kind of historical account therefore described the outcome rather than the cause of the Carolingians' success. Yet this description was to have far-reaching consequences for the relationship between the papacy and the restored monarchy in the High Middle Ages. For later jurists deduced from this account by the Carolingian annalists that the pope had the right to depose the Holy Roman emperor, a right that Gregory VII possibly first used, but which Innocent IV undoubtedly availed himself of in 1245, when he declared Emperor Frederick II deposed.

Of course, Pepin had no inkling of all this. His successes legitimized his rule as effectively as his newly won kingship. The whole of Gaul was unified, while Alemannia and Bavaria had once more been brought more firmly under Frankish control. The powers in Rome followed this radical development with great interest and recognized its legitimacy. When the Lombard king Aistulf conquered Ravenna, the seat of the imperial exarch, in 751, he demanded tribute from the Romans and the pope as his subjects, and subsequently made moves to bring Rome to heel. After he had already seized parts of the Roman duchy, Pope Stephen II journeyed in person across the Alps (753–754) to ask the Franks for help, and unlike his father before him, Pepin now heeded the pope's call. In retrospect, the pope's journey proved to be a first tentative step toward papal emancipation from Byzantine–imperial rule and toward full independence.

The new Frankish king received the successor of the Apostle Saint Peter in a carefully graduated ritual. Abbot Fulrad of St.-Denis and Duke Rothad met him at the border, and for the final hundred miles of his journey, to the Ponthion palatinate (in the Marne Valley), he was accompanied by Charles (Charlemagne), the king's eldest son. There, the king hastened to meet the pope in person and performed the service of *strator,* which involved leading the pope's horse for a short stretch by the bridle. This gesture was not only designed to show the heir of Saint Peter the respect due to him, but also, much more importantly, Pepin was at the same time demonstrating to his Frankish noblemen, who were inclined to turn down the pope's plea for help, the pre-eminent, unique rank and the humility-inspiring spiritual authority of the personage he was receiving.

The Frankish aristocracy was indeed very reluctant to be drawn into a war against the Lombards; in particular, Pepin's influential wife Bertrada turned him down. It was only at a reconvened imperial gathering in Quierzy that the king and the pope met with success; there, they forged a formal alliance. At once, Stephen—or rather not he as an individual so much as in some form of legal–mystical identification of the heir with the bequeather Saint Peter himself, holder of the keys to the gates of Heaven—anointed Pepin and his two sons Charlemagne and Carloman as kings in St. Denis. The belief in the heavenly acolyte of the Lord, the gatekeeper of Paradise, was deep-rooted among the Franks. At the same time, Stephen also bestowed upon all three Carolingians, the new king and his sons, a title—*Patricius Romanorum*—that it was not his to give, since only the emperor could grant such a title.[7] This gesture effectively obliged the Franks to protect Rome, but though its symbolic import was clear, its legal substance remained anything but. Pepin drew untold advantage from the pope's visit. For henceforth there was no question that his rule, which had been tainted with the stain of usurpation, enjoyed the blessing of Heaven and of the powerful vicar of the Prince of the Apostles. Indeed, the chroniclers lost no time in claiming that the pope had approved the deposing of the Merovingians and the raising of Pepin to the status of king, which had happened three years previously; to what extent this claim was true can no longer be verified.[8]

The anointed king duly crossed the Alps at the head of an army. With Saint Peter's help, the Franks successfully put the Lombards to flight and forced the defeated king Aistulf to hand back not only the papal lands—the *iusticia b. Petri*—but also all the regions belonging to the Roman *res publica* that he had seized (though these areas belonging to the empire were not outlined any more specifically).[9] Pepin had them formally restored them to the pope with a charter detailing his beneficence, but contented himself with a simple oath by the Lombards to remain peaceful before he returned home through the mountain passes. Meanwhile, Aistulf broke his word, threatened the pope, and prepared once more to conquer Rome. Fresh entreaties were dispatched to France, containing urgent pleas for help. These were couched in the form of an open letter by Saint Peter himself to the Frankish people and their rulers: "I, the Apostle Peter, . . . who adopted you as my sons . . . and who chose you Franks above all other peoples, . . . I hereby urge and exhort you . . . to protect my flock . . . defend Rome, and your brothers the Romans, from the heinous Lombards! . . . Come, come, in the name of the one living and true God, I beseech you, come and help before the spring of life from which you drink and in which you are reborn dries up, before the last spark of the sacred flame which illuminates you dies out, and before your spiritual mother, God's holy Church, . . . is desecrated."[10]

The sheer force of this address overcame the Franks: indeed, who could have resisted such a powerful plea? Once again, Pepin marched his army across the Alps, and once more Aistulf was defeated (756). This time, he was forced under Frankish supervision to give all his former conquests back to the pope, to hand over a third of his royal treasure, and to pay an annual tribute to the Franks. It seemed that only the kingdom of the Lombards would remain untouched, albeit now weakened. Pointedly, Fulrad of St. Denis had laid the keys to the gates of Ravenna and other sites before the pope, thereby signaling the handover of the former exarchate to the papacy.[11] Pepin evidently did not wish to see any restoration of Greek–Byzantine power in Italy, no revival of the exarchate, the Byzantine duchy of Rome, nor the return of the emperor there. He also forced Aistulf's successor Desiderius to "restore" the former imperial lands to the control of the pontiff.[12] Pepin had already signed a charter to this effect and handed it to Stephen at Quierzy. Now he duly "donated" the duchy of Rome to the pope—the exarchate, which comprised the region of Emilia and the duchy of the Pentapolis (the five cities of Ancona, Pesaro, Fano, Rimini, and Sinigaglia), together with a narrow land corridor between the two regions, along with a few specifically identified areas in the west of central Italy. This Carolingian ruler harbored no territorial ambitions in Italy. Pepin's son Charlemagne was later to follow his example in all matters except this latter one. Thus, despite its formal renewal, the donation of these regions remained a moot issue for the time being; neither Charlemagne's charter relating to this matter nor his father's has been preserved.

Even so, the substance of what had been sworn to in this act was not forgotten. Pepin's "donation" can truly be said to have laid the foundations of the Papal State right up to the nineteenth century. As enshrined in later treaties ("Pacta") signed by the Frankish kings and the Holy Roman emperor with successive popes—the oldest of these to be preserved was concluded with Louis the Pious in 817, the final renewal being granted by Henry II in 1020—all recovery plans, claims, and successes of the Holy See from the High Middle Ages can trace their origins to it. In these circumstances, any invented "Donation of Constantine" was superfluous; this infamous forgery, which was sometimes hallowed and sometimes condemned by the Late Middle Ages and the Reformation, and is still difficult even for modern scholarship to see through, therefore played not the slightest role for Pepin and his sons, despite a widespread view to the contrary; the document only appears in the ninth century, and in a completely different context.[13] But now it seemed that Gregory the Great's major preoccupation, to which he had devoted a central chapter in his *Life of Saint Benedict*—namely the lasting expulsion of the Lombards—had become reality thanks to the first Carolingian to occupy the Frankish throne. The alliance of the Franks with the papacy represented—at least from a European perspective—a major turning point in world history; it instigated a long and intensive cooperation between the Apostolic See with this ruling dynasty and later with the kings of France. Not least church ritual profited from this development. Monodic chant, as practiced in Rome, which emphasized the unity and clarity of the melody and lent each note its own weight, was now to become a feature of Frankish churches. Its popular name ("Gregorian chant"), already used in the Carolingian period, recalled Saint Gregory. Bishop Chrodegang of Metz sent his own choir members to the papal *Schola cantorum* to study this new form of singing. Gregorian chant spread from Metz throughout the whole of Charlemagne's empire.

The humiliation of the Lombards and the triumph of Saint Peter, however, did not really bring about peace. The situation changed when the election of a new pope sparked factional feuding in Rome. This prompted Desiderius to abandon the policy of acquiescence that he had originally adopted and to attempt to form an alliance with the Byzantine emperor *(basileus)* in Constantinople against the Franks and the pope. He enjoyed some early successes in his campaign; it seemed history was repeating itself. But this time, Pepin was detained in the Frankish kingdom. The new pope, Paul I, Stephen II's brother, was obliged to make peace with the Lombard king, who was even given access to Rome to pray. Then Pepin died, and his sons Charlemagne and Carloman divided the kingdom between them, viewing each other with suspicion. In Charlemagne's domain, a more friendly policy toward the Lombards prevailed. This king even married Desiderius' daughter—much to the displeasure of the pope, by this time Stephen III. The pontiff wrote to him that he ought not to be "besmirching" the nobility of his race by producing offspring "from the treacherous, evil-smelling Lombard people."[14] Yet Charlemagne only began to come round to this point of view when, following Carloman's death, Desiderius did indeed start to make preparations for war; now, he no longer had any need of a Lombard father-in-law. His divorce from his wife Desiderata was tantamount to a declaration of war and was, as it turned out, the prelude to a renewed round of fighting in Italy, in the kingdoms north of the Alps, and indeed throughout Europe that would go on for centuries.

Charlemagne and the First Renewal of the Roman Empire

T HE FIRST YEARS of Charlemagne's reign were overshadowed by conflicts with his brother, which were only prevented from culminating in
all-out war by the untimely death of Carloman. And yet the surviving
brother then proceeded to play the familiar, deadly power game that
Charlemagne's predecessors had played so skillfully in similar circumstances. Filled with dark forebodings as to what would happen to her and
her sons, Carloman's widow fled to the court of the Lombard king Desiderius at Pavia—all in vain, as it turned out, since she and her sons,
Charlemagne's nephews, disappeared without trace from history when
the Frankish king overran Pavia and the Lombard kingdom in 774.
Charlemagne ruled with an iron fist, not sparing even his closest relatives.
After many years of plots, tensions, and conflicts, he even sacrificed his
own son, who bore the portentous regal name of Pepin but had a hunch-
back that rendered him unsuitable for high office. His father banished
him to the monastery at Prüm when he disobeyed his wishes. At the same
time, Pepin's associates were summarily executed. As king, Charlemagne
was at war for fully thirty years; it was only when he became emperor that
he turned his attention toward maintaining peace.

Charlemagne inherited the bases of his power and of the administration of his realm from his father; these were overwhelmingly of a personal
nature, even including institutional bodies. Kingship in the Early and
Late Middle Ages manifested itself in ostentatiously displayed wealth (as
we have seen from Childeric's tomb)—in the glitter of gold and symbols

of authority such as the throne and the crown, as well as in symbolic gestures and rituals. A lavish, sophisticated banquet *(convivium)* was also an essential feature, and such official dinners have been laid on for centuries right down to the present day. Another was the aura of "terror" with which a ruler surrounded himself when he managed, say, to spear and kill a wild boar single-handed. In a similar vein were the liturgical "praises to the king" that were attested from the Carolingian period onward, which Mussolini imitated, and the gesture of "clemency" shown by a victorious ruler to those he had defeated or otherwise subjugated. Finally, an element whose significance—where the real power of the king was concerned—can scarcely be underestimated was the nature of his "friends and relatives." Through them, the queen and queen mother could gain in influence and political weight. It was through such signs, gestures, and personal constellations that a "language" with its own semantics developed, and like any other language, it underwent changes during the course of the Middle Ages. This idiom was rooted in a situational mode of thinking and rarely used abstracts; today we struggle to understand it. Aspects that are familiar to us, such as categories or a clear cause and effect or the operations of formal logic, were largely absent. After all, "terror" was more effective than argument and blood relations more important than logic. Only during the Late Middle Ages did this situation change. Even so, it is not true to say that formal institutions were completely missing in the Carolingian period, and particularly not under Charlemagne.

Institutional features were overwhelmingly to be found at the royal court, which, far from being merely an assemblage of buildings and facilities, also formed the personal, economic, and above all spiritual center of the empire, the institutional focal point of all royal rule. The court was organized around the king as head of the household; the queen, who played a leading role in the administration of the royal estate, also had her particular field of influence here. Like the ruler, the court moved throughout the royal lands, despite the fact that definite heartlands had grown up around the Île-de-France, the Meuse–Rhine region and the Rhine–Main region. In the later years of Charlemagne's reign, Aachen (Aix-la-Chapelle) began to take on the character of a permanent residence. Unlike their Merovingian predecessors, who primarily ruled from towns, the Carolingians preferred rural and hunting palatinates as their places of residence. Anyone who stayed at the court was subject to the domestic authority of the king. Charlemagne systematically reorganized the constitution of duchies, the institution of vassalage, and the feudal system. At the same time, these constitutional features represented the most prominent institutional export of the Frankish empire, insofar as they are found exclusively either within its borders or in places where Frankish forms of governance reached as a result of conquest. These places include Italy, Catalonia, and England (where they were introduced by William the Conqueror, duke of Normandy and himself a vassal of the French throne). The conquered regions also had to endure a significant influx of personnel from Franconia, Bavaria, and Alemannia, with whose help the king ruled his foreign territories.

Counts *(comites)* ruled clearly demarcated territories as the permanent representative of the king; their judicial authority derived from the royal writ, and they were responsible for upholding the peace, dispensing justice, and maintaining a standing army within each duchy. Vassalage encompassed the whole of the aristocracy, with whose help the king ruled; fiefdoms, however, were made hereditary only from the late ninth century onward. The possessions of certain lords, and especially of bishops and monasteries, enjoyed immunity; as such, they were under the direct control of the king in regard to their land holdings and their obligations of fealty. Charlemagne dispatched *Missi* (royal envoys), comprising one religious and one secular envoy, to oversee clearly defined domain of authority. In this respect, then, rational forms of rule made major advances in this period, even though not all elements were able to take hold or be sustained in the long term.

The Frankish empire was not a state as such. It did not appear to contemporaries as an entity, nor even as some notional, mystical "person" with its own "organs," and was not independent of the king. Nor did it have any clearly defined, unalienable areas of authority or any resultant guaranteed capacity to act, and was therefore not an independent legal entity. The empire was synonymous with royal power and royal authority, which had to prove itself afresh time and again. The empire was understood as the material possession of the king, the king's estate, and the realm in which the king could or should assert his kingly authority—it was effectively a group of individuals centered on the king and required the voluntary subjugation of the nobility on whom the king relied for support. The legal concepts of "heir" and "inheritance" transcended individual life spans. Things only began to change from the Late Middle Ages onward. Also, despite the fact that the words *office* and *ministry* did exist at this time, there was no concept of institutionalized bureaucracy. Rather, these terms had to do with personal (even, in its original sense, unfree) servitude. This was also true, especially so, of the king himself. He was, after all, the *Minister Dei,* a servant of God, not a minister of state.

Therefore, the Carolingian ruling elite was not completely devoid of institutions. The royal court, land ownership, vassalage and feudal tenure, the judicial system, duchies and the like, together with the plethora of churches, monasteries, and bishoprics combined to form a dense network of institutions. Yet, in the scholarship of the period, neither in its own right nor as part of the whole, did this network emerge as an autonomous entity. What was missing for this to happen was any kind of unifying concept, any handy metaphor or interpretative framework capable of embracing both the part and the whole and allowing them to be differentiated and the elements to be systematically correlated with one another. Without such a framework, no unity could be identified. Another aspect that was missing was any figure of abstraction separating the private and public realms. This shortcoming would prove to be an onerous burden that seriously hampered action. It was only counterbalanced over the course of the Middle Ages—step by step, and instance by instance, under the pressure of an increasingly formal, logical mode of thought and the discipline of jurisprudence that resulted from such a mind-set. Correspondingly, it was less orders and obedience that bound the nobility, on whom the Carolingians depended, to their king than it was consensus and reciprocity in the exchange of "goods and services." Of course, this could not exclude individual cases in which a nobleman might have cause to fear the king. But each downfall of a powerful aristocrat required a preceding rise of another who was prepared to help the king.

The royal treasure hoard and the manorial system intrinsic to the royal household formed the basic underpinnings of the empire's material wealth. The king was the largest landowner. Meanwhile, commercial production had overwhelmingly shifted to the proto-urban centers that grew up around the royal courts and the monasteries. Long-distance trade, markets, and hard currency did exist at this time but did not—as far as we can tell—play a significant economic role; their hour came when the population boom prompted shifts in the structure of society, including a far more widespread exchange of goods than hitherto. Even so, Charlemagne passed several edicts regulating weights and measures and monetary matters. The fundamental coinage reforms, whose consequences rippled down through the whole Middle Ages, were the direct result of this monarch's genius for planning. Charlemagne kept a close eye on the efficacy and organization of both the royal and the ecclesiastical landholdings. He demanded—and this was an entirely new element in the economic order—a written stocktaking to be made of farmsteads and their equipment as well as a regular report on their condition, and personally got involved in the management of his own country estates, right down to matters like chicken husbandry. Their administration came under the remit of the queen as lady of the household. In general, it is impossible to ascertain to what extent the reforms that the king or queen demanded were actually carried out. Yet it is clear from this example that rational, systematic organization was being deliberately put into practice here.

Basically, though not always in an identical fashion, the manorial landholdings were divided into the lord's lands, which the nobleman farmed himself with bondsmen, and into land consisting of "free" and "unfree" homesteads, disbursed respectively to freedmen and bondsmen, who were allowed to farm the land in return for regular levies and compulsory service. Free homesteads only had to pay levies, whereas unfree ones, although they had to pay less in taxes, were required to perform regular services for the lord ("corvée labor"), for example three days every week, or alternatively several weeks' labor tilling fields or harvesting per year. Admittedly, though, there was no question of any schematic uniformity. It appears that Charlemagne wished to see an administrative system based on "hide" (*hufe* or *mansus*) adopted universally. But in practice this only happened in those places where the king's authority was actually able to assert itself, particularly in the royal or monastic landholdings. If the need arose, the cadastral administration had the power to override the regional fragmentation of landholdings. Important inventions such as the horse collar, which allowed horses to be yoked, thereby facilitating a more efficient transport of goods, or the introduction of the heavy plow—which, since it could only be drawn by large teams of oxen, presupposed a greater degree of manorial or cooperative organization—soon began to appear on the scene. Complaints about inequalities saw the introduction of welfare measures to help the smaller and poorer free farmstead owners, yet these were only ever able to temporarily stem the long-term trend toward submission of these "farmers" under regional lords. Nevertheless, Charlemagne reigned over a dynamic, emerging society, not a late culture in decline; thus, limits to growth were never a problem that had to be contended with. Despite recurrent famines and epidemics, the population continued to increase, while farming was able to expand up to the thirteenth and fourteenth centuries through landowner-driven internal colonization, through the extension and reorganization of the manorial system, and through the improved legal status of large sectors of the independent peasantry. It was only in the fourteenth century that a farming crisis shook European society.

The church, too, was more firmly integrated into Charlemagne's ruling system, which stressed Christians' need for salvation as the Day of Judgment rushed ever closer. The king's most pressing concerns therefore focused on prayer, liturgical matters, canon law, and the constitution of the church. Correct, impeccable prayer was the order of the day. Otherwise, how was God to hear Man's supplications and dispense His grace? The king castigated the monks of Fulda and other communities when he heard their error-strewn Latin. He immediately demanded improvements, thus setting in train a fundamental and extensive education reform, which went far beyond mere liturgical needs. In particular, the writings of the church fathers, notably those of Saint Augustine, became required reading. Charlemagne led by personal example in this matter; the *City of God (Civitas Dei)* by the bishop of Hippo Regius was said to be his favorite book. But Augustine's *Confessions* were also known at this time. The impact of both works on European culture can scarcely be exaggerated. The *City of God* provided a template for how human society should be ordered, by stressing the importance of "peace" and "justice," as well as invoking the dualism of the "community of God" and the "community of the Devil" and reminding readers of the story of salvation and the end of days. The primary focus of the *Confessions,* on the other hand, was the individual, the innermost workings of human beings: "Thou, O Lord, turned me toward myself, taking me from behind my back, where I had put myself while unwilling to exercise self-scrutiny" (8.16).[1] This intense concentration upon the self and self-analysis, whether in the form of a confession of sins or an overview of a person's life—this liberation of the self through approaching a Higher Being—was a lesson that the West has never forgotten, even to the present day. Petrarch, who paved the way for the Renaissance and humanism, is said to have taken Augustine's *Confessions* from his pocket when he reached the summit of Mont Ventoux, a journey that afforded him a new view of the world and man.

Charlemagne's attempts at reform were aimed first and foremost at liturgical practice. The king requested a sacramentary (Roman missal) from

Pope Adrian in order to ensure liturgical unity with the Roman Church. Even Charlemagne's father had sought to forge closer ties with Rome when he instructed Bishop Chrodegang to teach Roman plainsong in Metz. Yet the manuscript that was sent to Charlemagne was by no means complete, and its content was not widely distributed; many additions were necessary, and numerous divergences from Roman practice remained. For instance, it was actually customary at that time in the Roman Church to sing the Creed without the *filioque*—in other words, without acknowledging that the Holy Ghost also proceeded from the Son of God, an omission for which the Greek Orthodox Church was later decried as heretical. In part, many regional and local differences still exist today in the liturgy and other observances.

The king integrated the church and its constitution into the fabric of his empire. This took place without any direct instruction or mandate on the part of the Apostolic See, though the Frankish king did make sure that he had the support of the papacy in his endeavors. Once again from Pope Hadrian I, Charlemagne requested a definitive collection of canon law (the so-called *Dionysio-Hadriana*), which henceforth was to form the basis of ecclesiastical law in the Frankish kingdom. The text of this document was repeatedly copied, but once again failed to achieve the uniformity that the Frankish king must have intended, with countless divergent norms remaining in force. The Frankish church was assigned to the Bishop of Rome, yet without being made completely and consistently subservient to him. This was only achieved in the church reforms of the eleventh century, though certain moves in this direction were made even during the Carolingian period. The most radical of such attempts was the forgery known as the *Pseudo-Isidorian Decretals,* which will presently be discussed at greater length.

Charlemagne was completely at one with the Apostolic See in his urge to introduce a consistent metropolitan constitution, that is, the organization of the church into separate provinces, each under the leadership of an archbishop whose remit extended over various bishoprics (dioceses). In Late Antiquity, such a constitution had only been implemented in a very rudimentary way at best, but now it became the general organizing principle of the whole church, a status it retains to modern times. Over time, it guaranteed strict control by the Roman pope as the head of the church over each archbishop and his suffragans, right down to the lowliest parishes. Diocesan and metropolitan synods were expected to meet, and visits to the parishes were to take place at regular intervals. These enabled the clergy and the people to be controlled, facilitating church jurisdiction. The Frankish imperial synods, however, never acted independently of the king, who was solely responsible for convening them.

The power to consecrate within a diocese lay exclusively with the respective bishop. Through this hierarchy of archbishops, bishops, and parishes, it really was possible to reach the entire populace. In addition, bishops were responsible for educating the clergy; they were charged with identifying the need for schools and establishing them. However, as yet there was no chapter, nor any council of clerics with settled livings at the central bishop's church. These institutions only arose, in the main, in the tenth century. When they did come into being, it fell to them to establish, lead, and maintain church schools, which were headed by either a *Magister scholarum* or a "chancellor." In the Late Middle Ages, certain cathedral schools that excelled through the quality of their teachers became the embryos from which universities grew. In particular, from the tenth century on, dialectics and the sciences flourished at the leading cathedral schools, which initially vied with exceptional monastery schools in these disciplines but soon outstripped them.

Yet Charlemagne would never have earned his sobriquet of "Magnus" if he had contented himself with merely reorganizing the existing power structure. Instead, he ventured beyond the former boundaries of the Frankish realm. A mixture of motives prompted this action: ensuring peace on the borders of the empire, conversion of the heathen Saxons, and an undisguised lust for power all played a part. Following his brother's death, the future emperor first unified Gaul, then conquered the Lombard kingdom, whose royal title he assumed for himself, then overran Saxony, which for centuries had posed the greatest threat to the Frankish borders. Using subterfuge, Charlemagne also deposed his cousin, the Bavarian duke Tassilo, while Frankish troops under Charlemagne's son Pepin, the king of Italy, vanquished the hitherto highly dangerous Avars once and for all. Finally, in 801, the March of Barcelona *(Marca Hispanica)* was also added to Charlemagne's conquests—comprising a chain of counties that stretched from Urgell in the High Pyrenees via Cedanya to Girona and Barcelona, the heartland of Catalonia with Barcelona as its most powerful center. There, for the first time, the Frankish feudal system was introduced, and the Roman liturgy supplanted the rites of the Visigoths and Mozarabs. This success was made possible by the fact that the Umayyad emir in Córdoba had broken away from the new Abbasid dynasty in Baghdad and lost the support of the central Muslim authority. As a result, the Caliph Harun al Rashid sought the support of Charlemagne, sending the Frankish ruler the keys to the Holy Sepulcher in Jerusalem as a gesture of friendship. Only the disintegration of Muslim authority thereafter allowed the gradual reconquest *(reconquista)* of the Iberian Peninsula, which began in earnest in the tenth century. Aside from the British Isles and the last remnants of Christianity in the overwhelmingly Muslim territory of Spain, the whole of Western–Latin Europe was now unified under the Frankish Empire. This generated long-term and momentous consequences in which the unified spiritual, religious, and cultural flavor of the whole of Western society was concerned.

Indeed, Charlemagne recognized at an early stage that military conquest needed to be consolidated and deepened by a spiritual dimension, and it is open to debate whether the great Frankish ruler gained greater renown for his feats of arms or for his efforts in ensuring that religious culture and its revival prospered in his empire. The king and later emperor instigated a dialog with the academic world. His court became a unique center of learning, setting a shining example for centuries to come. Moreover, the dialog between rulers and scholars that Charlemagne began was also sustained by his successors; in fact, his example ensured that it survived the decline of the Carolingian Empire. Already started in the reign of Pepin the Short (751–768), Charlemagne's court became the focus for a drive toward literacy par excellence, which the ruler personally made sustained and strenuous efforts to promote. The predominantly oral culture of the Frankish Empire required the revival of Latin studies on the part of the educated elite, who had no other lingua franca for scholarly or liturgical language at its disposal. And indeed, this elite developed a new virtuosity in the use of ecclesiastical and academic Latin. This, then, was another key factor that unified the West, and imprinted on its languages and modes of thought the seal of a decidedly Latin Europe.

Officially, the comprehensive educational program of antiquity was never abandoned; nonetheless, the efficiency of the "private" education system, which was not in "public" hands—not least because of Christian misgivings about its pagan orientation—had declined sharply in the dark centuries of the Early Middle Ages, when sources were few and far between. Certainly, the Merovingian kings must have had a comparatively good literary education; the entire system had not collapsed by any means.

And yet, there was no denying that knowledge and skills had dwindled and atrophied. Only under the Carolingian king Pepin and above all his illustrious son did a decisive move in the opposite direction begin. Here and there, ancient manuscripts with pertinent texts were still to be found, but it was a laborious task tracking them down, and then they required patient copying work to save them and once more disseminate the learning they contained. Despite the claims of the Renaissance and Enlightenment, Roman antiquity is only visible to us nowadays through the lens of this early medieval interest, and the efforts of these Carolingian conservators.

As a rule, the material from which these old volumes were made was the comparatively cheap but less durable papyrus. Following the slump of scribal activity and papyrus production, the consequences were catastrophic. Even by the Early Middle Ages, the stocks of papyrus were in decline; in the late eleventh century, only the papal chancellery still had quantities of this writing material. The rest of the Western world had to make a virtue of necessity and switch over to the more expensive but more durable vellum. Apart from a very few exceptions, virtually no papyrus roll with a scholarly text has survived down the ages. Fire, water, rot, and mice took a heavy toll on the vital transfer of knowledge. The results can be quantified in terms of sheer numbers: of the sometimes enormous ancient libraries containing as many as an estimated one million books, absolutely nothing survives. If the contemporaries of the Carolingians had not undertaken a systematic search for ancient texts and manuscripts with an eye to copying them, and if they hadn't used durable vellum in the process, most of the works of ancient, especially Latin, scholarship and literature would have been lost forever. No Cicero, no Quintilian, no Virgil, no Horace, no *Ars amatoria,* no *Gallic Wars* would have survived, let alone any of the ancient Christian authors. Charlemagne's thirst for knowledge effectively saved these texts, indeed the whole of the Latin educational program of the Liberal Arts and their handbooks of the Mechanical Arts, as well as the unique splendor of Roman literature. In the absence of this, the late medieval Renaissance is unthinkable.

The division of human capacities into the Liberal Arts and Mechanical Arts has its origins in the educational doctrines of the ancient Greeks and Romans. The term "Liberal Arts" denoted those disciplines that could be mastered without manual labor, and which one could pursue without having to make a living from them. In Antiquity, then, this conception was premised on the figure of the free, wealthy aristocrat, whose livelihood was maintained by an army of people more or less dependent upon him. But his social stratum no longer existed; his place was now primarily taken by monks and scribes, and very occasionally lay people. Every activity that required manual work, by contrast, was designated as "mechanical," including for example surgery and medicine, hunting skills, maritime navigation and any form of commercial enterprise.

These and other arts found a new home at Charlemagne's court and in his empire as a whole. The king loved the dulcet tones of the *fistula,* a kind of pan-pipes; this was soon augmented by the powerful sound of a (water) organ, an instrument long the preserve of the Roman and Byzantine imperial courts. And Charlemagne's royal library was reputed to have the best-stocked shelves of the Early Middle Ages. Many rarities could be consulted here, such as the surviving, richly illustrated manuscripts of the *Agrimensors,* which detailed the techniques of land surveying; their preservation down to the present day is thanks to the diligence of the royal collector. Charlemagne's court—and thereafter, every other medieval royal court, too, no doubt—became a center of education and learning, a headquarters of knowledge organization such as the world had not seen anywhere before. Its most recent heirs are modern government ministries of education and research.

Admittedly, the costs of such an undertaking were vast. Measured against the economic output and productivity (that is, its GDP, if one can talk in such terms) of society at that time, the Carolingian state's commitment to knowledge and education was certainly no less significant—in actual fact, far outstripped—governments' investment in these areas nowadays. Without it, our present culture of knowledge and our information-driven society simply would not exist. To make a single book in vellum required an entire flock of sheep; correspondingly, for large-format luxury tomes, huge numbers of animals were slaughtered. These technical circumstances naturally limited the breadth and the speed at which learning was disseminated, while also ensuring its survival in perpetuity. Nowadays, large documents, the contents of entire books or indeed libraries, can be sent round the world by e-mail in seconds or at most minutes, but back then it took many decades and even centuries for a work to have even a chance of extensive distribution, let alone the reality of becoming widely known. It took the vision of a new knowledge-based society—an infinitely patient undertaking—to pass down the collected scholarship of antiquity to future generations. Charlemagne, in his concern for the well-being of Christianity, harbored just such a vision, and his contemporaries and all their successors supplied the necessary patience and provided the financing that laid the foundations of our enduring culture of knowledge.

Only the most powerful patrons could bear such a heavy financial burden. Without the involvement of the monarchy, everything would have taken much longer, even assuming it had taken place at all. Without the pressure that Charlemagne personally brought to bear on the only institution that was then in a position to take this infinitely long view—namely the monasteries—the whole enterprise would have been infinitely more difficult. And so it was behind monastery walls that the incunabula of Western knowledge and skill took shape, forming the bedrock on which all later learning and technical skills imparted by cathedral schools, universities, and learned societies were based. In this undertaking, there was a curious separation of reading and writing, since the two activities were not learned in tandem as they are nowadays, with "reading" being regarded as a "free" art, while "writing" was seen as a "mechanical" one. The latter, then, was an aptitude of specialists, and not everyone who could read was a regular writer, too. In addition, "reading" meant reading aloud. Only over the course of the Middle Ages did this separation disappear, and anyone who learned how to read would generally learn how to write as well. This development represents one of the most enduring impulses toward literacy and the introduction of scientific method in Western civilization.

When Charlemagne had overrun the Lombard kingdom, he summoned scholars from all the peoples of the "Latin" West to the Frankish empire and his court, and gave them material security by endowing them with ecclesiastical offices and stipends. As well as learned Franks, they included Lombards, Visigoths, Bavarians, and soon Saxons too, alongside Irish and Anglo-Saxon scholars. Notable figures among them were Peter of Pisa, Paul the Deacon (Paulus Diaconus), Paulinus of Aquileia (Italy), the Anglo-Saxon Alcuin and his adversary, the Visigoth Theodulf of Orléans, the Irish scholar Clement Scotus II (also derided by Theodulf), and many others. There was no continuous central court school at which these scholars taught at the same time, nor any kind of academy or university. The teaching that took place at the court was on a more modest scale, directed at the children of courtiers. Whether and to what extent gifted children from the kingdom as a whole were assembled here is uncertain.

Charlemagne was content for these scholars to appear now and again at the court to give occasional lectures or classes. The decisive factor was that the court thus became the natural center for spiritual revival, and that corresponding initiatives rippled out from here to embrace the whole of the empire, and then flowed back to the court. Here, all the threads were drawn together that unified the empire as a spiritual entity.

The education that Charlemagne had in mind was an entirely purposeful one, being geared first and foremost to the worship of God. In order not to offend the Lord, religious services called for correct liturgical language, error-free Latin, proper liturgical plainsong, and reliable scholarship. Furthermore, the organization of the empire according to the principles of justice demanded intellectual techniques that were in accord with the growing complexity of demands. Templates of organization had to be available, criteria of organization developed, and knowledge to be adapted to practical requirements. As a king, Charlemagne may even be said to have been obsessed with the idea of organization. The landholdings, the coinage and weights and measures reforms, the network of duchies and their constitution, the consistent hierarchical organization of the church, the court, royal power, and even of time itself—in sum, Charlemagne wanted to ensure that everything was organized systematically, clearly, one might say positively schematically even, into a swift, reliable orientation in space, society, and time. The rationalism of this organizing principle knew no bounds.

Since there was no ready-made knowledge to hand, the Frankish empire and its court were characterized by a dynamic sense of activity. Restless curiosity impelled the scholars, with the king at their head, and their endeavors, despite Augustine's warning about it and its propensity for discrimination. This became clear in the matter of the *Computus,* the doctrine concerning the organization and calculation of time. What is time? Charlemagne wanted to know. Ever since humans began to think, this question had troubled them and spurred them to formulate new answers. Earthworks of the later Stone Age, which were designed to mark the solstices and the time for sowing and harvesting, along with numerous images, myths (such as Chronos, the god who devoured his own children), the astronomical theories of the ancient Egyptians, Babylonians, Greeks, and Romans, the six-day creation story in the Book of Genesis and the Talmud, the Christian church fathers, and modern relativity theories have all concerned themselves with the phenomenon of time, as has the metaphorical language of poets and writers. Nor were the Middle Ages unaffected by this development; ever since its beginnings in the Carolingian era, the question of time stimulated early forms of scientific enquiry in the West. Our current calendar and modern theories of time, as well as the whole time-based structure of our lives, have their roots in this development. The scholars at the court of Charlemagne and on its periphery also had recourse to pertinent treatises by the Anglo-Saxon monk Bede on this matter.

What was being undertaken here was more than the simple calculation of time, albeit a practical use had been clearly identified in scholarship on the calendar.[2] The astronomical work being conducted at the court of Charlemagne was designed to query the account of the fourth day of creation in the Bible and its description of the making of the firmament and of time, and was also an attempt to organize time so as to be able to order life. The scholars' endeavors highlighted three strata of time: a person's lifetime, which should on no account be wasted, calendrical time, which was to be heeded; and world time, that is, the lifespan of the earth, which would last until the Day of Judgment. The secret of creation was revealed in their calculations. So it was that an anonymous confident of Charlemagne (but in all likelihood Archbishop Arno of Salzburg) reminded him of the great solar–lunar cycle of 532 years, and significantly that its duration could be divided up thus: one hundred times five and six times five plus two. "The hundred times refers to the godhead, the six to its completeness, and the five to human beings. Thus shall the sum of all virtues be attained if all perfect things should be formed in the image of the godhead, while the godhead itself is wholly perfect. The remaining two denote joy in the love of God and in one's self." These scholars of the early Middle Ages intuited a sense of divine and human proportion. Awestruck, they contemplated the sublime order and beauty of the cosmos, its proportions, rhythms, and harmonies—which were all expressible in figures— and the spirit of God in his Creation. The lights of heaven, the stars, shone down on them like palpable signs of the virtues, demanding symbolic exegesis and admonishing people to use their time well. Time was a divine creation (one might well ask whether this act of creation took place before or after the advent of time) and was an act of salvation, given to mankind on probation after the Fall from Grace. Time was assessed and gauged in order to bring human life into harmony with the Supreme Being, and not so as to allow it to degenerate into some monetary value.

Chronologers of the Early Modern era such as J. J. Scaliger regarded these medieval calculators with disdain, and even went so far as to accuse the calendar makers of 1582 of half-heartedness. However, they misconstrued the absolute necessity of the first steps in this subject, and as a result disregarded earlier authors such as Wilhelm von Hirsau, Rainer von Paderborn, or Robert Grosseteste, who in the eleventh, twelfth, and thirteenth centuries respectively subjected the traditional calendar to close scrutiny, and through their experiments and calculations corrected it, for the most part accurately. Yet because their innovations were not immediately adopted, the modern period—in its ignorance and complacency—discriminated against those scholars and their entire era.

The most unfathomable questions being posed at the time—first and foremost "What is nothingness?" (that is, does it in fact constitute something, since God created the world from it?)—were not just idle speculation but were intended to stimulate enquiring minds that thought of themselves as scientifically oriented. Grappling with such questions helped lay the foundations for a more comprehensive analytical capacity than would otherwise have developed in the absence of such inquiries and the educational background needed to answer them—an intellectual facility that was flexible and deployable in many different contexts. This produced a wholly new systematically minded way of acting, and from this there developed a rational–operative *modus operandi,* which indeed manifested itself in the many new endeavors geared toward creating order.

"Knowledge before action" became the watchword of Charlemagne's court. In this, he followed the advice of religious counselors such as Alcuin, Theodulf of Orléans, or his cousin Adalhard of Corbie—an Anglo-Saxon, Visigoth, and Frank respectively—presenting himself as the first pupil of this new generation of tutors. Nowadays, it seems, the opposite approach is in vogue: act first, then ruminate on it later. The steady practicing of scientific language throughout these early centuries, and the way in which such discourse was effectively and extensively promoted by the monarchy and the church during this period may be counted as a key cornerstone for Europe's cultural and intellectual revival during the much-maligned Middle Ages, for knowledge and aptitude are intimately bound up with language. It was precisely in order to systematically promote language that the wise ruler gathered together scholars from Italy, Anglo-Saxon and Irish schoolmen, and Visigoths at his court. Through their efforts, the ancient canon of learning and the program of the Seven Liberal Arts were duly resurrected.

Language, thought, and research went hand in hand. In particular, grammar (that is, the revival of Latin), but also Aristotle's theory of categories and Ciceronian rhetoric came to the fore in this period. This laid the groundwork for a new virtuosity in oratory; however, speaking was always guided by thinking. The often misunderstood and misinterpreted phenomenon of linguistic *imitatio,* namely the use of a word in a different social and semantic context, simultaneously brought about both the transmission of knowledge and the generation of knowledge. Moreover, it did this in two ways: first by transferring learning from distant Antiquity into present and future early medieval society, and second through the ensuing introduction of scholarly Latin into the various vernaculars.

Thus, Aristotle became the mentor figure for Western logical thought. The oldest complete Aristotelian text to come down to us is the Latin pseudo-Aristotelian *Cathegoriae decem,* in a manuscript of 795. The person who commissioned this manuscript, Bishop Leidrad of Lyons, a Bavarian, maintained close contacts with Charlemagne's court; it may well be that the original was located there. Alongside this are the earliest medieval exegeses of this material, namely the two manuals that Alcuin wrote for the king and his court, one on dialectics and one on rhetoric. Although the latter derived from ancient Greek and Roman court cases, it outgrew its origins thanks to a change of context that could scarcely have been more radical. In the absence of a forum or a central courtroom, it became an established text in schools. But there was no presumption that the students reading it would necessarily become barristers or lawyers; rather, its sole purpose was to contribute to their broad intellectual education and to widen their linguistic horizons. Precisely because the social context of the ancient legal rhetoric no longer pertained, the text was received now as a universal, language-centered epistemology. Alcuin assigned both the discipline of rhetoric and that of dialectics to the broad category of logic.

Fittingly, the Anglo-Saxon scholar imparted his learning to the Frankish king in the form of a dialog. In his texts, he had the king play the role of the questioner, with the tutor providing the answers: *The king:* "What is the purpose of rhetoric?" *The tutor:* "To teach people how to speak properly." *Charlemagne:* "What matters does it treat?" *Alcuin:* "General ones—that is, those scholarly matters that may be grasped through the natural capacity of the intellect." *Charlemagne:* "How many circumstances *(circumstantiae)* need to be explained with regard to any given issue?" *Alcuin:* "Each matter has a total of seven circumstances: person, deed, time, place, mode, cause, and topic. These circumstances can be stylized as questions: Who was the perpetrator? What did he do? When? Where? How did he do it? Why did he do it? and How was he able to do it? In the Latin mnemonic, these questions run: *Quis? Quid? Ubi? Quibus auxiliis? Cur? Quomodo?, Quando?* In this manner, any issue could be circumscribed at least seven ways.

Furthermore, the *status causarum,* the main bone of contention between the disputing parties, which called for a special mode of questioning, was divided into matters that could be elucidated by "general reason" and those that posed special legal problems. The *status rationales,* namely the logical topoi, were in turn subdivided into four: conjecture, definition, quality, and legal procedure; while the *status legales,* the course of justice, was subdivided into two: according to the necessity of deliberating rationally between the norms in question, and according to the simple written proof. Through these kinds of distinctions, the logical realm of the *Causa* is brought into focus. Accordingly, every case and every phenomenon had to allow for seven circumstances, while every matter of dispute and every discussion of the facts of a case had to be analyzed from at least eight different graduated standpoints. This, then, is how analysis proceeded henceforth—becoming an ever more precise, sophisticated, and detailed art. To be sure, its origins lay in Antiquity, but now it became a completely refurbished basis for Western scholarship and perception of the world.

Differentiation, systematization, logical classification, and proper questioning—these were the keys to Western learning. The endpoint of all rhetoric was an ever more strictly differentiated and more narrowly subdivided and systematic questioning. This kind of rhetoric, conducted in this fashion, generated an insatiable curiosity, driving it inexorably onward and guiding it. In this way, the first steps were taken on the path to rational, reason-led science (moreover, this was a far more exclusive undertaking than it had ever been in ancient times). This teaching adopted intellectual techniques that could be deployed in many different fields, not least in the organization of rulership and commerce; and it was only a matter of time before this enlightenment began to produce disagreeable side-effects, for instance by shaking the foundations of faith or broaching contentious social issues.

In addition, there were the five predicables of dialectics: the genus of a thing; its species; *differentia* (between the genera or species); *proprium* (the characteristic feature of the genus or species); and *accidens* (chance attachments), as well as the ten categories or *praedicamenta* of Aristotle, which, without any word of conjunction, denoted either a substance or a quality, a relation, a where, a when, a posture, a condition, an action, or an affection and as such—so ran the ambitious claim of the ancient philosopher— enabled everything to be expressed. The Aristotelian doctrine of categories taught that the sensually experienced world could be subsumed under a system of categories and classifications, and distinguished the essential from chance circumstances. Teaching in schools adhered to this basic precept. Taking his cue from Aristotle, the great mentor Alcuin taught: "Whatever a person says must inevitably fall within these ten categories." This principle was drilled into every pupil in monastery and abbey schools, as well as the cathedral schools, which appeared somewhat later. Once again, it must be stressed that this was not some special training for lawyers that Charlemagne instigated. Rather, the king's aim was to establish a general school education founded on a categorical, analytical, and rational mode of thought that was capable of fathoming the mysteries of divine and human creation. As the king later said of the discipline of rhetoric, "The daily demands of our endeavors require that we practice it." The world was now being construed in terms of categories, in sentences that laid claim to truth and in questions that unlocked the truth.

Charlemagne and his teacher Alcuin continued their dialogs over a long period. The rhetoric that they revived, which following these instructions was taught in the same manner in all Western schools throughout the centuries of the medieval period, was much more than simply a debate about language and the art of "fine oratory." Once more, it is worth emphasizing that, in conjunction with the revived and steadily adopted discipline of dialectics, rhetoric provided a theoretical and practical epistemology, and gave rise to a mode of thinking that began to guide the way people acted, and without which the intellectual revival of the Latin West would have been unthinkable. Over time, both disciplines also taught people to pay heed to the "opposite side," in other words not merely to comprehend their own society and its world but to embrace what was alien, to approach it in an understanding way and to assimilate it intellectually. In this, these two disciplines constituted the essential character of European intellectualism.

The new learning encountered its first baptism of fire in truly urgent questions that reared their head at the time. Heresies such as Adoptionism, which was entering central Europe from Spain—and interpreted as a sign of the imminent end time—demanded tireless vigilance. Likewise, the image cult of the Greeks seemed to border on idolatry. It was vital that both these threats should be repelled, and Charlemagne set himself the task of doing so. Adoptionism—the doctrine which, invoking the teachings of Saint Paul, maintained that Christ had been God's adoptive son and so was potentially like any other human being—was opposed at the Synod of Frankfurt in 794. Meanwhile, the veneration (not "adoration," being rendered in Greek as *Proskynesis,* as opposed to *Latreia,* which could only be accorded to divine personages) and the cult surrounding images of Christ and the saints, especially the Virgin Mary, which according to Platonic teaching were integral to the essence of the subjects portrayed (the most famous example of this in the West being the legend of the conversion of Emperor Constantine the Great) were as much a part of everyday life in Byzantium as they were in papal Rome. Even today, Roman churches are still home to panel paintings from that period which were formerly the subject of great veneration, such as the Marian icon of the *Salus populi Romani* (Protectress of the Roman People) in the Basilica of Santa Maria Maggiore, or the icon of Christ in the *Sancta Sanctorum* of the Lateran Palace, quite apart from the iconostasis found in every Orthodox church. Many a simple-minded believer may well have identified the image with the subject depicted. The struggles against the Muslims, meanwhile, had made Byzantium aware of Islam's hostility to images of the human form; in addition, at the emperor's court itself, there were stirrings of Monophysitism, which diverged from Orthodoxy in recognizing only the divine nature of Christ. As a result, from time to time iconoclastic forces arose in the Eastern Roman Empire, and political conflicts broke out that also affected the West. In 787, the *basileus,* that is the Byzantine emperor, convened a council that rescinded the ban on religious images and permitted their veneration once more; a representative of the pope was invited to this meeting, the Second Council of Nicaea, but not one from the Frankish kingdom.

The Frankish king was wounded by this snub. Accordingly, he instructed his scholars to prepare a critique of the Proceedings of the Council, which had been leaked to him in a poor, error-ridden translation. The Visigoth Theodulf of Orléans, who had grown up in the iconoclastic environment of Muslim Spain, set about this work. His tract against the "shameless" adoration of images provided the first proof of the new-found dialectical skills in the Frankish realm, and testified to the diligent schooling that had gone on there. Theodulf drew a clear distinction between the created image *(imago)* as a genre *(genus)* and the venerated image, or idol, as a *species,* thus maintaining that every idol was an image, but that every image was not necessarily an idol. The vain Greeks, he claimed, had confused the issue, conflating the "possession" of images with their "adoration," and thereby mixing up the categories of condition and action. Yet the sole purpose of images was for instructing those who were unable to read, and they needed to be supplemented by a written explanation. However, no sooner was Theodulf's magisterial *"opus Caroli"* completed and approved by the king than news arrived from Rome that Pope Adrian I had had an indirect hand in drafting the Proceedings of the Council of Nicaea and had approved them; the Frankish king was loathe to oppose the theology of the pope. Thus, all this effort turned out to be in vain, and the proud work was consigned to the oblivion of the archives, an obscurity it retains to this day.

The pope's principal aim was for emancipation from Eastern Roman–Byzantine hegemony. Yet simply exchanging the distant power on the Bosporus for one closer to home, in the shape of the Frankish king—who by now also wore the Lombard crown—was by no means his intention. Moreover, as the *Patricius Romanorum* and the protector of the Romans, Charlemagne had an incontestable claim to their city; nor, it was clear, would he be content to play a merely supporting role. The most that Adrian I could hope to do, then, was to delay rather than thwart the monarch's plans to extend his control to Italy and Rome. The Frankish king had already rushed down to Rome on a previous occasion, when he was besieging Pavia in 774. On that occasion, he had pledged to renew the endowments bestowed by his father, but had never actually done so—a source of incessant complaint on the part of the pope. The rivalry between them inevitably led to tensions, which only became more acute when, from 798 onward, Charlemagne began to press for his imperial mandate to be reconfirmed. It seems that this concession was granted in agreement with the Byzantine empress Irene, who in her turn had to fend off an influential opposition to her own rule in Constantinople, and feared that Charlemagne might otherwise attack Dalmatia, part of her empire. A watchword in the Eastern Roman Empire at that time, at least if we are to believe Charlemagne's chronicler Einhard,[3] was "Have the Frank for your friend, but not for your neighbor." So in 798, envoys from the empress duly appeared at Charlemagne's court and "transferred" the "empire" to him *(imperium tradiderunt)*—at least, this is how the mission was construed at Charlemagne's court. It is impossible for us now to know precisely what the Byzantines were handing over.[4]

These diplomatic contacts coincided with dramatic developments in the city of Rome and around the papal court. Adrian I died, and his successor Leo III found that the previous incumbent's most important aides were all against him. Before long, complaints began to be voiced openly against him, and a bloody coup was attempted, which misfired. Escaping his persecutors by the skin of his teeth, Leo fled to Charlemagne, who immediately planned his fourth march on Rome. The charges against Leo—he was accused of pursuing an immoral life—were clearly not plucked out of the air. At the very least, they clearly required greater investigation, and the outcome created the conditions for Charlemagne to be crowned Holy Roman Emperor. The Frankish monarch spotted the unique chance that Leo's predicament offered and exploited it without hesitation. Whatever the foregoing negotiations with Empress Irene had concerned, Charlemagne was now free to attain the status of Holy Roman Emperor by his own efforts without any help from the Byzantine Greeks. For according to Roman law, the forthcoming proceedings against the pope required the involvement of an emperor, the *Imperator* and *Augustus.* Charlemagne did not allow the case to get as far as a formal trial of Leo, contenting himself (and even this was a delicate matter) with a pledge by the pope to mend his ways, which was made before the imperial investiture took place. And so the maxim "the pope is judged by no one"[5] (which owes its existence to a late medieval forgery) was borne out and gained legal force for all time. Thus purged, but not convicted, Leo III crowned Charlemagne emperor on Christmas Day 800; no one at the time could possibly have guessed the profound consequences this act would have for the history of Europe, nor how it would embroil the Holy Roman Empire and its leaders in a long-running conflict with Byzantium.

Indisputably, this pope was one of the most outstanding successors of Saint Peter. Despite his personal difficulties, he was skillful enough to rein in the most powerful of all the Carolingian kings. Although the new Byzantine emperor in Constantinople was also crowned by the patriarch, only accidental and no constitutive significance attached to the ceremony.

Leo, on the other hand, heightened the symbolic and hence also the political importance of the anointing and investiture ceremony that he conducted by combining it with the proclamation of the emperor by the people, in the process pushing this aspect into the background and assigning decisive significance to the coronation. The *Book of the Popes (Liber pontificalis)* handled the delicate affairs in that way. What might have been expected was a sequence of ritual actions according primacy to the constitutive acclamation of the people, and then following it with the corroborating coronation and the confirming *Laudes* of the clergy. But what actually happened was that the anointing and coronation appeared as the constitutive act, while the public acclamation and the *Laudes* were merged into a single act and were only accorded confirmatory status. The acclamation formula followed the Roman custom, but its precise wording has come down to us in two different versions. According the Frankish imperial annals, the Romans proclaimed: *Carolo augusto, a Deo coronato magno et pacifico Romanorum imperatori, vita et Victoria;* whereas the papal records insert, as usual, the superlative adjective *piisimo* before *augusto,* and leave out the word *Romanorum.*[6]

Charlemagne was well acquainted with the symbolic language of the liturgy and surely cannot have been pleased with this state of affairs, yet Leo's preferred staging of the coronation could not be undone. Nevertheless, the Frankish king later tried to revise the Roman form of coronation when he transferred the role of emperor to his son Louis, with the approval of his noblemen, and crowned Louis himself in the royal church of Saint Mary in Aix (Aachen Cathedral) without any involvement on the part of the priesthood. But all this was in vain, as it turned out, since three years later Louis the Pious had himself crowned emperor once again by the pope, who had traveled to the Frankish realm to conduct the ceremony. Thereafter, for the whole of the medieval period, anointment and coronation formed the constitutive act of coronation for all (Western) Roman emperors and were the exclusive right of the pope. Public acclamations were no longer mentioned. It was only the completely altered political landscape in the Habsburg Empire in the period (1558–1562) immediately following the reign of Charles V that enabled the exclusive papal right to coronation to be dispensed with. Even so, in Charlemagne's own coronation, actual power and the dignity due the imperial office—in other words, *res* and *nomen* in Aristotelian terminology, once more coincided. Empress Irene of Byzantium seemed inclined to acquiesce to Charlemagne's elevation, but she was deposed, and her successor Nikephorus I began arming himself in vain to wage war against the Franks before he and his own successor Michael were, after a decade or so (811–812), reluctantly obliged after all to accept the developments that had taken place in the West.

Since Late Antiquity, the ritual of the papal court had begun to conform to that of the imperial court in its symbolic acts and appurtenances. This development would dominate the history of the entire medieval period and, not least, come to define the papacy in a secular–political sense. The elaborate processional nature of the Stations of the Cross mass, which was celebrated in the most diverse churches of Rome, and which always began with a procession from the Lateran Basilica to the church in question, formed a direct link between the Roman pontiff and his *Urbs*. Under Leo III, this convergence found its most visible expression in some uniquely magnificent buildings. Two great halls were constructed and decorated with programmatic mosaics. Both of these buildings fell into ruin in the Late Middle Ages and were replaced by the present baroque Lateran Palace; nothing of them was preserved save for a few paltry, if still famous, remnants of an apse. Presumably, the relics of this construction as renovated in the Baroque period do not faithfully convey the symbolic imagery of the eighth century. Even so, accounts of these mosaics make it clear that they had more than just a representative function. The residence of the Bishop of Rome, the complex of buildings formerly known as the *Episcopium* or the *Patriarchum,* now appeared for the first time as the *Palatium Lateranense* (813); notably, they were designated a palace, like the residence of a king or emperor. This new terminology bespoke a new pretension on the part of the pope to autonomous rule and to independence from the Carolingian monarchy and empire. In the process, Leo III set a goal, which under his predecessor Adrian I had only ever been vaguely formulated, and which at most had only set its sights on emancipation from Byzantine control. Leo, though, harbored more ambitious and extensive plans, which were designed to stave off any imperial control either in Rome or in the territories granted to the See of Saint Peter by Carolingian endowments. This, then, saw the beginning of a development that, despite many setbacks and the most intense conflict, did eventually lead after several centuries to the complete independence and secular sovereignty of the Papal State.

As a king, Charlemagne had been all too keen to engage in wars, but as emperor his chief concern was to maintain peace. But to do this required keeping avarice, the root of all evil, in check. Charlemagne identified it as the key enemy of peace. But how might he set about countering a deadly sin? And what was "greed" anyway? Charlemagne's personal experience did not give him a satisfactory answer. For, so the contemporary wisdom maintained, destructive avarice was displayed by a person who "illegitimately covets possessions beyond all measure."[7] But what desire was "illegitimate" and what went "beyond all measure?" The traditional ethics of kingship found no answer to these questions, which had to do with the spiritual well-being of the individual, rather than with the exercise of power or the practice of authority, and focused not on power politics but more on the systematic interplay of antagonistic interests in society, time, and space. To resolve this matter and to have properly grasped the complexity of the situation would have required the application of sociological, economic, and political theories and corresponding mechanisms for implementing them. However, such methods were not available to Charlemagne's contemporaries, not even in embryonic form, rooted as they were in a totally different social order. Even the most heartfelt invocations of peace were unable to broaden the prevailing personal perspective into a systematic one.

Urgency was the order of the day; "the times were perilous" (2 Timothy 3:1). Wherever one looked, be it among the Byzantine Greeks, in Spain, or in Rome, there were insurrections, unrest, heresies, and other threats to religious life. Unmistakable signs indicated that the world was rushing toward destruction.[8] Dangers also loomed from outside. Especially in the north, strange enemies in the form of "pirates" were spreading terror; they were only defeated with great difficulty, and Charlemagne attempted to prevent them from threatening the frontiers of the empire through treaties. Insecurity also affected the south. Although the city of Barcelona was taken from the enemies of Christianity, Tortosa was unsuccessfully besieged on three occasions, and the danger that threatened from Spain was not overcome. The Muslims thirsted for revenge, and so attacked the islands of the Mediterranean and the coast of Gaul with their fleets. In Italy the citizens of Benevento rebelled against Charlemagne's rule. The Byzantine Greeks, long suspected of heresy, fought against Frankish authority in the southeast of the empire, Venice, and Dalmatia. The question of imperial authority in both East and West awaited resolution, and led time and again to tension and conflict with the *basileus,* especially since Nikephorus had ascended the throne previously occupied by Empress Irene.

The defense of the borders demanded constant combat readiness, costly watch duties, and an ongoing military presence. These expenses weighed heavily on all the imperial vassals, but particularly on the major churches and monasteries.

By now the Saxons had finally been defeated, though their ultimate absorption into the Frankish empire had yet to take place. Initially, the priority was to establish bishoprics and parish churches and found monasteries there. The Avars had also been conquered, but the expansion and consolidation of Frankish power and the spread of Christianity in Pannonia were still at an embryonic stage. Missionaries from Aquileia, Salzburg, Passau, and Regensburg vied with Greek Orthodox priests to incorporate this region within their separate diocesan structures; the only upshot of this was that they each hampered the other's efforts. The ecclesiastical administration of the entire country was in disarray; reports by royal messengers from all the administrative regions were alarming. Legislation had to be improved to protect the weak, and legal jurisdiction placed under effective control; the watchword of this period was justice. The situation required the utmost attention and demanded that no effort be spared for peace to be finally achieved.

From the day of his imperial coronation, then, the Frankish king found himself beset by a host of urgent tasks. After all, didn't the start of his reign coincide with the dawn of the new sixth millennium, which would bring the end of days and change everything? In any event, this is what some scholars who followed the prophecies of Saint Jerome believed. Cautiously, the emperor set to work. A series of measures aimed at securing peace were enacted, for the benefit of Christianity, the churches, and the peoples of his realm. Granted, the methods the ruler had at his disposal were in line with traditional knowledge, and they above all required renewal, expansion, and increased efficiency. But how might experience and knowledge be increased? There was a loathness to attempt new things. Other pressing questions were how to raise people's competence, and how to probe society's cultural memory and interpret the answers.

From the outset, only partial answers were offered, and these were strung together in an additive way rather than being structurally interlinked.[9] The spread and strengthening of the Christian faith and the improvement of the Mass, the *Cultus divinus,* were regarded as the first indispensable necessities. The Frankish king was a god-fearing Christian. Prelates were encouraged not to misuse their power, but to be an example to others in the way they lived and acted; Gregory the Great's *Regula pastoris* had already exhorted priests to do so. Anyone who proved unworthy of conducting Mass was to be dismissed. However, no exact guidelines were provided. Monks and nuns were expected to serve God by leading a sheltered and cloistered life. Law and justice were expected to prevail. The king's agents—bishops, abbots, dukes, and counts—were subjected to stricter controls. The people, meanwhile, were required to swear an oath of allegiance to the emperor. Widows and orphans were granted special protection. The poor were not to be oppressed, nor were vassal duties to be neglected. Poor freemen and hard-up vassals alike were offered the prospect of being absolved from military service. Incest and other sexual misconduct were to be prosecuted, while murderers (and especially those who killed their relatives) would have to face the full force of the law. When famine struck, people were still expected to pray to God for mercy, but now an additional relief measure came in the form of grain being sold at reduced cost to those in distress. Peace with God, among the powerful and within the populace at large, was the cardinal aim. Repeatedly, and in all areas of life, the emperor demanded that people should inquire after God's will and then act accordingly. Unity, friendship, peace, and love were both the means and the end; these virtues would underpin royal authority and lead the people toward salvation. But what was entirely lacking in Charlemagne's realm was any overarching institutional or structural planning.

Sources of danger to the state could be enumerated individually and in concrete terms only in ways the collective cultural memory permitted them to be identified. The principal focuses of public concern were the liturgical language of Latin, the Mass, and Christian care for the sick, and the respective remedies demanded were error-free texts, correct measurement of time, and medical knowledge; provision of these was to be monitored by the king's agents. But secular knowledge was also in demand. Criminals were subject to the same treatment meted out to rebels. It was forbidden to sport weapons—that is, a shield, spear, or coat of mail—in the home. Anyone who owned twelve *mansus* (or hides) of land was obliged to have a coat of mail, and if a person turned up to do his military service without one, he forfeited both the coat and the tenure of his fiefdom. Those who breached the peace had to appear in front of the king. Anyone who committed a murder despite having made a peace agreement would have the right hand cut off and be banished. Trade with the Slavs and the

Avars was conducted and controlled through certain frontier stations; the export of weapons was banned. Oaths of allegiance could only be sworn directly to the emperor and—for the ultimate benefit of the emperor—to a person's own master. People were sworn to uphold the law and justice and to protect the poor and destitute vassals, while ordinances were passed against priests or laymen who had gone astray or women who had absconded. In addition, measures were enacted against counterfeiting and to regulate marriages between freemen and female dependents on the state's finances. In short, the daily, all-too-familiar potential triggers of conflict, which time and again led to infringements and violations of the law culminating in feuding, were now to be strenuously opposed. A raft of individual measures were enacted to strengthen law and order and faith and religious observance, and to make the Realm of Peace on Earth a reality. However, peace imposed through royal authority necessarily entailed an intensification of the king's power. In order to stave off the apocalyptic end of days, therefore, a massive concentration of central authority was set in motion. But by this time, Charlemagne was approaching his dotage, and would no longer be able to achieve what he had planned. His main concern would now be to ensure the succession.

Yet the collective cultural memory of the Franks augured ill on this point. Every royal succession thus far—not just under the Merovingians, but also the Carolingians—had sparked conflict and been resolved through violence. Close relatives suddenly became deadly enemies who had to be eliminated at all costs through exile, forcible placement in a monastery, mutilation, murder, or civil war. These clashes between kings and pretenders to the throne never failed to drag the nobility and the common people into deadly warring. Charlemagne knew this from personal experience. To forestall it happening again, he took steps that had personal implications. To keep the peace and to limit the number of his heirs, following the death of his fourth (or fifth) wife Liutgard and since his coronation at Rome, he had only taken concubines whose sons were automatically excluded on the grounds of illegitimacy from the succession and the struggle over the realm that would inevitably ensue. Moreover, a timely ruling on the succession was intended to split the empire between the three · legitimate sons and thereby secure peace. This division *(Diviso regnorum)*, which took place in the year 806, flew in the face of all convention hitherto, and was never intended to apportion an equal share of the realm to each heir, as had happened in former times, on the last occasion in 768.

Rather, the eldest son was given the lion's share, perhaps precisely because no one expected him to produce heirs. But Charlemagne's two oldest sons, Charles the Younger and Pepin of Italy, both died before their father, leaving only one legitimate offspring, the youngest son, Louis the Pious, who was duly chosen to be Charlemagne's successor as emperor, and a grandson, Bernard (Pepin's son and a Carolingian also on his mother's side). Following the advice of his cousins Adalhard and Wala, Bernard's uncles, Charlemagne was concerned to ensure that Bernard would in turn be endowed with his father's legacy of the kingdom of Italy. In 812, a succession arrangement to this effect was devised, which Louis, unconventionally enough, was compelled to attest to in Aachen Cathedral when he was sworn in as emperor the following year. Quite how delicate this arrangement was is revealed not least by the *Consensus fidelium,* the consent of the nobility, which was specially demanded on this occasion, and which for the first time involved aristocrats close to the court in decision making about matters of power. This co-determination on the part of the nobility became a regular occurrence thereafter and represented a breakthrough on the way to a formal social contract.

The Crisis of the Carolingian Empire under Louis the Pious

Admittedly, Louis the Pious broke his oath just a few years after Charlemagne's death—the first royal perjury, which would open the floodgates for many subsequent ones. Thereafter, the empire and its ruling dynasty were granted not a moment's peace. Louis, who was given the sobriquet "the Pious" from the tenth century onward, was brought up to be the subservient king of Aquitaine. In other words, he was not raised in the Frankish tradition, or at least not exclusively, and certainly was not groomed for leadership of the whole empire. Indeed, he was not equal to the task. In his southern realm, for example, in accordance with Visigoth–Spanish custom, he had been imbued not exactly with animosity, but certainly with an attitude of reserve or even indifference toward the papacy. Accordingly, then, the young ruler, unlike his father, did not strive to find common ground with the Roman Church; upon becoming emperor, he did not undertake a single visit to Rome, or any pilgrimage to the grave of Saint Peter. Ostentatiously, he prohibited the *Renovatio imperii Romanorum* (Renewal of the Roman Empire) that Charlemagne had put in place and proclaimed in its place the *Renovatio regni Francorum* (Renewal of the

Frankish Empire). But first and foremost, barely after his father's death, he dismissed his leading advisors, in particular Abbot Adalhard of Corbie, who was a highly esteemed guest in Rome, but who now, like his younger brother the count palatinate Wala of Aix-la-Chapelle, was summarily banished from the kingdom. Moreover, Wala was forcibly tonsured and sent to a monastery. Nevertheless, the Carolingian Empire remained alive as a memory and a concept, serving as a constant warning to contemporary leaders, who were increasingly becoming overwhelmed by the conflicts in which they had become embroiled.

Abbot Benedict of Aniane, the son of a Visigoth count, became the chief advisor to the new autocrat of the Frankish kingdom; he had already played a prominent role at the Aquitanian court of the young ruler, and had clashed with Adalhard in the past. Benedict had an ambitious plan in mind, namely to standardize the monastic orders, and found a willing helper in his new emperor. While Louis's father had still tolerated divergent monastic practices, now the plan was for monasticism throughout the entire empire to fall in line with the Rule of Saint Benedict. At a series of imperial diets in 817–819, this monastery reform, along with one concerning canon law, was introduced and started to be implemented. The famous architectural drawing known as the Plan of St. Gall, which was drafted as part of these reforms, shows clearly how complex the organization of a monastic estate and its central working areas was, or was at least designed to be, with its own gold smithery and blacksmithing, maltings and brewery, as well as other workshops on site. The sharing of devotions between monasteries also aided the standardization program. In the wake of this collaboration, a new form of literature arose, the *Liber memoralis* or *Liber vitae,* in which the names of those for whom prayers were being offered, plus the names of beneficiaries of the convent or monastery in question, were noted down for reading out at the altar as part of the liturgy. Properly understood, these books represent a rich seam of knowledge for historians, because in addition to information on how such institutions commemorated people in prayer and the composition of names, they also passed on factual knowledge and, in the context of memorializing individuals, also stimulated the writing of historical accounts.

Louis's reforming zeal also brought changes to the social structure of the secular world and the aristocracy. This was especially evident in the spread of stricter rules governing exogamy in France, which were designed to bring about far-reaching changes in the marriage law. Hitherto, this legislation had adhered to proscriptions sanctioned by the Bible; conversely, though, this meant that marriage between two close relatives was allowed. In Louis's time, however, the schema of kinship encompassing seven generations present in Roman inheritance law, spread and was applied to ecclesiastical marriage law, thereby outlawing marriage between relatives to the seventh degree of removal. Even though the method of calculating these relations was not uniform—such broadly applicable definitions of what was incestuous could not be imposed either instantly nor even in the long term (thus occasioning repeated infractions and circumventions that were later to result in a welter of legal cases)—over the following centuries the whole model by which questions of relatedness and "family" were interpreted changed fundamentally, and still continues to have lingering effects in contemporary Europe. Henceforth, the concept of the agnatically organized group of relatives going back through generations began to take shape, the hitherto unrecognized construct behind the aristocratic family. Nevertheless, around 1100 even such exalted aristocratic families as the counts of Anjou in France or the Swabian Guelphs were unable, despite all their attempts to delve into their history, to trace their families back beyond the tenth century or to build up a proper picture of their genealogical tree. It was only after this point that genealogies started to become more reliable.

Meanwhile, Louis's reforming zeal petered out all too swiftly. The vexed question of the succession and especially the contradictory, inconsistent attitude of the emperor sounded its death knell. This turn of events sealed the fate of the Frankish empire. The most fortunate genealogical coincidences in the ruling house and the three generations of royal succession from Charles Martel via Pepin the Short to Charlemagne, which really did place the empire in a pre-eminent position, could in no way impair the principle of dividing up the realm. This remained in force, raising its head more imperiously than ever before and making a mockery of all the opposing aspirations that may have been harbored by supporters of the principle of indivisibility of the realm. Indeed, Louis himself had encouraged such hopes with the promulgation of an edict governing the succession *(Ordinatio imperii)* in 817; the aim of this ruling was to endow his eldest son Lothair with the office of emperor and the largely undivided empire, while compelling his younger sons to accept subkingdoms in Bavaria and Aquitaine. However, all this plan did was to sow the seeds of discord, since it divested the emperor's nephew, Bernard of Italy, of all power.

In an affirmation of the *Consensus fidelium,* Louis had personally taken an oath guaranteeing the integrity of Bernard's realm, but the ordnance of 817 effectively excluded Bernard from power and led to his death. Yet the plan ultimately fell victim to Louis's second marriage, which produced a fourth son, who was baptized with the portentous name of Charles. The emperor's aimlessness plunged the formerly happily unified Frankish empire into a rapid decline.

Judith, the second wife of Louis the Pious, was the daughter of a count in Bavaria and was in all likelihood related to the high-ranking "Robertians," if not a direct member of this dynasty, which now was coming to prominence. She was certainly not a Guelph, as has hitherto been assumed on the basis of the text known as the *Historia Welforum,* which was only written in the Late Middle Ages. Medieval historical writing was incapable of penetrating the obscurity of the tenth century, and many of its inaccurate conclusions also led modern research astray. The family history of the Guelphs in the twelfth century, from which modern scholarship took its cue, had misinterpreted the name of Judith's father "Welf" as his proper name; in all probability, this was only his nickname. As far as we can tell today, her father's actual name was *Ruadprecht* (that is, Robert). Judith's influence on Louis's government may well have been considerable, but it is hard to grasp at this remove. In any event, it seems that the "Robertians," who hailed from the southern Rhineland (Rheingau) and Bavaria, came with her to the West, establishing themselves in the Île-de-France region through such notable family representatives as Robert the Strong, count of Anjou, and Judith's nephew Hugh the Abbot. In the late tenth century, a descendent of this line, Hugh Capet, ascended the French throne as the first of the Capetians, a dynasty that only lost its grip on power during the Revolution and the upheavals of the nineteenth century, and which today (the royal Houses de Bourbon and d'Orléans) is the only surviving old European aristocratic family that can trace its male line unbroken back as far as the eighth century. Offshoots of this line, which later produced the Empress Adelaide, second wife of the Holy Roman Emperor Otto I, also managed to take power in Burgundy.

The violation of the succession order of 812–813 and the division of 806 that underpinned it, now hung like a sword of Damocles over Louis's entire regime. Furthermore, his *Ordinatio imperii,* though obsolete from an early date, still continued to influence affairs. Bernard of Italy's violent death reminded people of the effect of such plans, and acted as a constant reproach against Louis. The influential court clique around Louis the Pious was rightly characterized as "Foolishness covered by a cloak of pure stupidity." The former aide of Charlemagne, Adalhard of Corbie, and his biographer Paschasius Radbertus, from whom this quotation derives, could scarcely contain their anger at this situation. "Who," Adalhard enquired, "could have induced the People's Senate to countenance such madness?"[10] But disaster could not be averted when both of Charlemagne's cousins, namely Adalhard and his brother Wala, were readmitted to court after seven years' enforced exile. By this point too many serious and damagingly wrong decisions had already been taken, creating personal alliances and antagonisms that could no longer be dispelled. True, the emperor found himself obliged, many years after Bernard's death, to do public penance for his crime (822), an act which seriously undermined his "honor" and the "awe" that the office of king was supposed to inspire. Yet even so, Adalhard's promulgation of a courtly ordinance that was designed to hark back to the age of Charlemagne and impose discipline on the regime fell largely on deaf ears. The original of Adalhard's text is sadly no longer extant; some fifty years later, however, Archbishop Hincmar of Reims, who found himself in similarly dire straits, used it as a model for a warning tract of his own, entitled *De ordine palatii*; this treatise adopted much of Adalhard's text word for word and affords scholars a valuable insight into the way the Carolingians exercised power.

An endless succession of division plans now robbed the empire of all peace, since the king's sons and the various noble factions who were lined up behind each of them could not reach an accord, and because power gradually began to slip from the hands of the impotent emperor. Disputes multiplied, leading the factions that opposed one another after Louis's death in 840 to engage in the bloody Battle of Fontenoy (841) and culminating in the Verdun partition treaty of 843, which—aside from a brief interlude under Charles III—really did spell the end of all imperial unity and only guaranteed a very fleeting period of peace. Time and again, skirmishes and wars flared up, heightening the growing tension between the Carolingians and driving a wedge between the various parts of the empire.

Lending the altercations an added degree of volatility was the fact that they were closely bound up with one of the most burning issues of the Middle Ages—namely, the question of the world order, the relationship between the "priesthood" and "kingship," between *Sacerdotium* and *Regnum*. The polarity that existed between the universal nature of the church and the particularity of all forms of monarchical rule urgently needed to be resolved. But resolving this question was by no means straightforward. In the meantime, all that contemporaries could perceive was a disruption of the ordered relationship between secular and spiritual leadership, and the need for reform. Plans to settle this matter began to come together in 828, with the publication of Einhard's renowned *Life of Charlemagne,* which represented, in the guise of a biography, a kind of veiled admonishment to the emperor; other treatises later expanded on this. In particular Wala, who had succeeded his brother as the abbot of Corbie, was emphatic and consistent in his support of the aims of a reform program, calling for a proper relationship between the *Sacerdotium* and the *Regnum,* even if this should entail rebellion and the arrest of the emperor. Even during his time as a secular figure, this Carolingian count, who had been forced to take holy orders by Louis, had been instrumental in advising Charlemagne to institute reforms within his realm.

In 829, a synod was convened and assembled in Paris. It set as its principal aim a new, root-and-branch reassessment of the relationship between the two "powers." It took as its main guideline a missive from Pope Gelasius to the Emperor Anastasius from the year 494, which was set before the assembled bishops and abbots in Paris. This letter had almost certainly been discovered in the archives of those determined reformers who shortly afterward embarked upon the great undertaking of writing the *Pseudo-isidore.* Under the assumed name "Isidor Mercator," around this time or very shortly afterward, a counterfeiter of papal decretals and other canon law texts came to prominence, who had only recently been tracked down to the monastery of Corbie in Picardy, one of the foremost centers of scholarship at the time. This was the institution headed by Wala, and as far as we can tell, the most likely figure behind the deception was the abbot himself, aided by his closest confidant and assistant, Paschasius Radbertus.[11]

"There are two powers, august Emperor," Gelasius's letter ran, "by which this world is chiefly ruled, namely the sacred authority of the bishops *(sacrata auctoritas pontificum)* and the royal power. Of these, that of the bishops is the more weighty, since they have to render an account for even the kings of men in the divine judgment. You are also aware, dear son, that while you are permitted honorably to rule over humankind, yet in things divine you bow your head humbly before the leaders of the clergy."[12] This Doctrine of the Two Powers, as it has somewhat inaccurately been dubbed, was henceforth to shape all conceptions of worldly power in the Christian West. The dangers of the hereafter called for a new order in the here and now, geared toward the attainment of salvation. This order was, of necessity, under the control of the clergy. And who else but the king should be required to subjugate himself to its authority? All ethics of leadership were to be subservient to this regime. Incidentally, such concepts also developed within the traditions of Islam.

Wala, the cousin and the former leading secular advisor of Charlemagne during the final years of his reign, now proved his mettle as a rigorous church reformer. His outstanding significance emerges clearly through his identification with the polymath Pseudoisidore (although Paschasius Radbertus undoubtedly co-wrote this and lent it his intellectual weight). In addition, the biography of Wala, which was written by Radbertus for a small circle of initiates (the author gave it the misleading title *Epitaphium Arsenii*) and which retrospectively justified the extensive act of falsification, gives us an insight into plans, actions, and warnings. It is clear that his interests and concerns went far beyond matters pertaining to the running of an abbey and, as Wala was clearly accustomed to from his period advising Charlemagne, embraced issues relating to the church as a whole. With its fabrications, which drew on the church's entire historical tradition, the Pseudoisidore's primary aim was nothing less than defending the clergy as a whole, but especially the bishops and monasteries, from any encroachment by lay authorities, including the king, and from the despotism of the metropolitans. It did this by reinforcing the jurisdictional rights of the pope and of an envisaged instance of ecclesiastical authority interposed between the pontiff and the archbishops (the post of primate-patriarch, which, however, never came into being). The forgeries had hardly any effect in the ninth century, but the reforming powers of the eleventh and twelfth centuries, whose aim was to centralize the church around Rome and the pope, made some use of this work, which was highly relevant for their purposes.

During the reign of the Carolingians, then, the "realm," that is the sphere of monarchy and of personal secular authority, was still completely subsumed within the "church," that is, the mystical Body of Christ.[13] The logical distinction between "church" and "state" only began to assert itself gradually in the course of the eleventh and twelfth centuries. The interpretative frameworks of an as-yet undivided unity thus applied such concepts as "faith," "harmony," "peace," "order," and "status," along with "service" and other similar terms like "protection" and "help" exclusively to God. Secular thinking had yet to gain a foothold. The world was to become Christian, become the church, the Body of Christ. Radbertus never tired of praising Wala's urge to reform and unify the monarchy within the church, in order that this "monarchy should not fall to pieces," but above all praised Wala's concern "for the honor and reputation of the Christian Faith" and for the possessions of the church. Wala identified, in the correct placement of "clergy" and "monarchy," the basis for the survival of the Carolingian Frankish Empire. But in actual fact, the avarice of the lay authorities, on whom Charlemagne had attempted to crack down, and the resultant pressure on "the priests of Christ and the servants of the altar" had already driven many of them from their spiritual vocation; they were summarily divested of their property without any legal proceedings. Presently, the Pseudoisidore would make a point of stressing that monasteries had been affected by this despoliation, but above all bishoprics, which were allocated to new lords in contradiction to canon law. Wala's overriding concern was to protect the bishops; on their behalf, this reformer of church and empire pointed to the pope as the highest and final arbiter where they were concerned.

In 828, Wala, clear-sighted and apprehensive, complained to the emperor that everything was "corrupt and tainted." Yet still no one dared (as the *Epitaphium* dared, in retrospect) to speak the truth, despite the fact that "the sins of the empire had not yet reached their height," in other words were still on the increase and were threatening to bring down the state. In a comprehensive reform plan, Wala now outlined "of what estates the church of Christ consisted," and how these estates should behave toward one another. He emphasized that "the situation of the whole church" was governed by the two "estates," namely "the king, who in the exercise of his office should act modestly and not hanker after anything unfamiliar," and "the bishop and other servants of the church, who attend to what is particular to God." This, then, was a grave warning to the emperor—who, it seemed, had long since been preparing to destroy this order—but it was also entirely consonant with the aims of the Pseudoisidore.

Yet the problem ran deeper still. The Carolingian rulers, and especially Louis the Pious,[14] wielded an ecclesiastical authority that held sway over many aspects of the church, and laid claim to imperial power over the *Patrimonium Petri*.[15] It was vital to defend the church against both these encroachments and keep them in check. In doing so, the reformers took recourse in another fabrication, producing a document supposedly written by the very first Christian emperor of all, the so-called *Constitutum Constantini,* or Donation of Constantine, surely the most notorious forgery in world history. Over the course of the Middle Ages it was misconstrued, in a sense that encompassed the laws of endowment, property rights, and the power of disposition. Although it proved impossible to identify the counterfeiter by name, it is likely that this artifact originated in the monastery of St. Denis and its environs, perhaps even in collaboration with Pseudoisidore and Wala of Corbie. The document aligned the pope with the Roman emperor in the matter conferring insignia and civil rights, and endowed the pontiff, alongside his role as head of the universal church, with special patriarchal authority over the whole of the Latin West. This reformist tract, as the *Constitutum Constantini* may quite justifiably be construed, seriously delimited and called into question Frankish imperial authority over the church. With all the majesty of his spiritual power, the pope would either supplant it entirely or at least have the unrestricted freedom to vie with the Frankish king and emperor. Evidently, the "monism" that regarded the monarchy and the church as an indivisible entity and which—far from any "dualistic" thinking—was already prevalent under Charlemagne, was still calling the tune here. Even so, under the pressure of present circumstances, this monism had begun to lean more firmly toward the side of the church. Spiritual power appeared to be inextricably entwined with secular power, admittedly within the one church, but each with its separate realms of operation, whereby spiritual authority appeared as the polar opposite of all secular power.

In the contemporary Carolingian world, the reform endeavors represented by the *Constitutum Constantini* and the Pseudoisidore failed. Despite encountering enormous difficulties, Louis the Pious tenaciously defended his emperorship right up to his death in 840; he achieved no more notable successes during the latter years of his reign, though Wala did die in exile. Likewise, the abbot of St. Denis, Hilduin, was also later obliged to flee the Frankish West. Yet—and who could have predicted such an outcome?—the counterfeiters from Wala's inner circle in St. Denis, Corbie and elsewhere left behind for subsequent centuries a legacy that would continue to have an enduring impact on European history right up to the Reformation and even far beyond.

The two kingdoms of West and East Francia, ruled by Louis's sons and their successors from the Treaty of Verdun (843) on, were consolidated by the long reigns of their monarchs Charles (II) the Bald and Louis the German. At the same time, under the Treaty, Lothair had secured control of Middle Francia, a territory that stretched from Aachen down through Provence to Rome. However, his was the first dynasty to die out. In particular, Charles's western kingdom proved itself to be a final place of refuge for the blossoming of Carolingian culture. There was a far higher degree of literacy there than in Louis the German's eastern realm. Admittedly, it is only latterly, in the modern period, that the value of "symbolic capital" has come to be recognized. Knowledge is a phenomenon that proves its efficacy over the long term and only reveals its fruits gradually, over time. Yet initially the West was to see the full development of its potential hampered by several factors: the threat posed by external enemies, the Vikings; the plethora of powerful, quarrelsome aristocratic families; and the increasing frequency of succession disputes.

The pre-eminence of this Western realm also manifested itself in another factor, namely that its noblemen found themselves formally bound to their king through a treaty. The partition treaty of 843, for whose signing the three Carolingian brothers had assembled at Verdun in August, was followed in November by the Treaty of Coulaines. This latter agreement was a dual treaty, initially concluded among the retinue of Charles the Bald, and then ratified by the king himself. As had hitherto been the case, questions of the reciprocity of power and the exercise of power within the ruling elite were still not directly broached; rather, the treaty articulated the "affirmation of loyal noblemen" *(consensus fidelium)*, and with them the "people," of the sovereignty of the king, but also of the limits of his authority. The agreement was, in effect, a manifestation of the fact that the aristocracy and the monarch were in a relationship of mutual dependency. It is true that later, as the oral tradition of legislation gained ground once more, this treaty was never renewed. Nevertheless, the practice that it established retained its meaning and point, and in so doing helped regulate the real consequences of power sharing between monarchy and aristocracy. As such, it may be regarded as the first social contract in European history and as the founding charter not exactly of France but certainly of the polity that preceded it, as well as of its political practices and system of jurisprudence. In addition, it laid the foundation for the future independent development of the West Frankish–French kingdom, which culminated in the beginnings of the history of France.

Although an explicit doctrine of the social contract was only formulated by the sworn opponents of absolute monarchy in the sixteenth century, nevertheless the tradition of the social contract in France was enshrined and handed down by political practice. It runs through European history like a common thread, especially in those countries where the West Frankish–French tradition continued to resonate—and consequently it found expression not only in the English *Magna Carta Libertatum* of 1215, the *Joyeuse Entrée* of Brabant in 1356, and in the treaties concluded by the kings of Catalonia and Aragon with the *Cortes,* but also in countless coronation oaths. Even in those instances where no formal treaties were concluded, the concept of the social contract continued to exert its influence as an underlying template. The deep-seated roots of Western notions of constitutional rule, power sharing, codetermination, and democracy that would come to shape European history in the modern period all derive ultimately from this tradition.

4

Consolidation of the Kingdoms

Sᴄʜᴏᴏʟ ᴀɴᴅ its curriculum, which took the same form in all the educational landscapes that were shaped by the Latin language, laid the foundations for the intellectual unification of Europe. Everywhere one went, be it among the Anglo-Saxons or in France, and including Catalonia, Italy, or even at the seat of the papacy in Rome, schools always followed the same basic pattern. The only places where special forms of education arose were Spain and Ireland, as a result of their particular historical trajectory—in the former case, the conquest of *Al-Andalus* by the Arabs in the early eighth century, and in the latter an autonomous path of development separate from the Anglo-Saxon and Frankish centers. As a result, the illiterate populace became part of the culture this established, at the same time contributing to it their practical knowledge.

The principal monasteries and other ecclesiastical institutions were the main vectors not only of religious culture, but also of intellectual culture. In the process, in contrast to Late Antiquity, a noticeable shift took place, from the individual pursuit of knowledge that was widespread in the earlier time to the institutional pursuit, namely in monastery and other religious foundation schools as the most important places of learning. Faith and knowledge coalesced to form a whole, which only began to disintegrate once more in the Late Middle Ages. This unity was accompanied by a general awareness of sin, and this in turn called for an all-embracing, wide-ranging remembrance in prayer that would embrace both the spiritual and the secular élites, and whose traces, which are still visible today, would bring to the fore the spiritual and worldly contexts in which this culture could unfold. Schools outside monasteries and comparable religious endowments were seldom encountered during this period, only emerging gradually—in Italy initially—in the High and Late Middle Ages. An incomparable commitment on the part of these schools, together with the zeal of their pupils, who began to display growing pride in the academic achievements of their institutions, laid the groundwork for the extraordinary upsurge of the sciences in the formerly barbarian West.

The School at Tours, which blossomed under the leadership of Alcuin, enjoyed a brilliant reputation, while Orléans, where Alcuin's rival Theodulf was head of education, also stood out. In addition, St.-Denis and Corbie were already being spoken of as prominent seats of learning. Later, the teachers at Auxerre were to make a name for themselves. In the East, we may cite Fulda, St. Gallen or Reichenau, along with Freising and Regensburg. Moreover, several nunneries or convents, such as Chelles Abbey in the Carolingian period, or the Ottonian foundations at Gandersheim and Quedlinburg, also contributed to this educational boom. Under Charlemagne and Louis the Pious, even a comparatively good form of lay education occasionally took hold; however, during the war-ravaged decades of the internecine Carolingian feuding, this fell into almost total abeyance. War is not always the mother of invention.

The result was a far-reaching ecclesiastical appropriation of literacy and education; only in Italy does a certain degree of literacy appear to have remained continuously present since ancient times. Even so, a revival of literary activity became apparent, especially in the West, less so in the East, but scarcely at all in Italy, where instead a less elevated, more pragmatic form of writing became widespread. In any event, from the ninth century onward, an increasing number of works by contemporary authors have come down to us. Some of these writings have resonated far beyond the Middle Ages. Walahfrid Strabo of Reichenau, sometime teacher of Charles II, wrote commentaries on books of the Bible, which formed the basis of the standard commentary (the *Glossa Ordinaria*) that was in print right up to the Early Modern period. Drawing on his own life experiences, his Saxon friend Gottschalk of Orbais, who regarded his enforced monastic life as a form of imprisonment, devised a gloomy doctrine of predestination, which subjugated everything to the omnipotence of the Lord and allowed human free will little leeway. The bishops found this work less than edifying, and condemned him to lifelong incarceration in his monastery. And the works of Haimo of Auxerre appear to represent the first Christian attempt—and by no means a hostile or discriminatory one—to interpret the traditions of Judaism. Archbishop Hincmar of Reims came to prominence as a publicist and commentator, but primarily as a historiographer, without whose contributions the history of the ninth century could scarcely be written.

Hilduin of St.-Denis arranged for translations of the writings of Pseudo-Dionysius the Areopagite on the hierarchy of angels and men, which had just come to the West from Constantinople. He incorrectly identified their author as the patron saint of his abbey and, in common with his contemporaries, regarded him as the pupil of Saint Paul the Apostle. The results of this soon became apparent. The deeply scholarly Irish philosopher Johannes Scotus Eriugena, who was suspected of heresy, drew upon these writings for his doctrine of hierarchies and his theology of God's self-emanation, which were to have a lasting effect on scholasticism and younger mystics. In turn, these thinkers not only introduced various seminal theological works to the West, but even more momentous was the habit of thinking in hierarchies, which was set in motion by reading their works, and the whole hierarchical mode of thought that came into being after them. It set the tone for the rest of the medieval period. Indeed, only after the Late Middle Ages, and especially in the Renaissance (admittedly, the groundwork for this was laid by the whole arc of development of Western learning) can an increasing trend away from hierarchical thinking be observed. In accordance with this new tone, Lorenzo Valla recognized the work of Pseudo-Dionysius as a forgery, whose real author hailed from Late Antiquity and who had used the illustrious name to gain a following for his line of theology. This was one of the shining achievements of the scholarship of the Italian Renaissance.

Because of its wealth, the western part of the Frankish Kingdom was more frequently beset by external forces, primarily Vikings demanding tribute payment. In addition, due to the higher density there of a powerful nobility, as the century progressed, disputes over the succession multiplied. Even though both of these developments went unnoticed by people living at the time, they may be seen in retrospect as signs that the western regions of the old Carolingian Empire were undergoing a more progressive development then the eastern. Yet at the same time, both developments prevented the west from manifesting its superiority. In the east, it was undoubtedly the Abbot of Fulda and later archbishop of Mainz, Hrabanus Maurus, who exerted the most enduring influence as a teacher. He left behind numerous commentaries on the Bible and an extensive, repeatedly copied encyclopedia, which ultimately was even illustrated. The school attached to his abbey had an outstanding reputation.

This era also saw the beginnings of vernacular literature and poetry. Basically, all that is known from the eighth century are vocabularies and a few glosses, but thereafter the German-speaking peoples, such as the Franks, Bavarians, Alemanni, and even the Saxons, experienced a veritable flood not just of translations or concise prayer texts and magic formulae, but also of fully formed poems based on Bible stories using ancient verse forms. These include the Old Saxon Genesis (now only preserved in fragments); the "Heliand"—a New Testament verse story in the same language; the Gospel paraphrase of the Old High German "Tatian"; Otfrid of Weissenburg's gospel harmony in rhyming couplets; the apocalyptic poetry of the Bavarian "Muspilli"; the "calling of the people" *(de vocatione gentium)* in the Monsee-Wiener Fragments; the Murbach Hymnal, and many more, quite apart from the Psalms and versions of the Lord's Prayer. The fact that Germans still intone the Lord's Prayer or "Our Father" as the *"Vater unser"* with its clumsy inversion of noun and pronoun, can be ascribed to the word-for-word translations from the Latin made in the eighth and ninth centuries. Proudly and self-consciously, these poets and teachers transcribed the ancient material into their own, no longer merely barbarian, languages. 'Uuánana sculun Fráncon éinon thaz biuuánkon, / ni sie in frékiskon bigínnnen, sie gotes lób singen?' "Why should the Franks refrain from / singing the Lord's praises in the Frankish language?" (Otfrid). In these lines, one can almost sense the sheer elation felt by the cantor of Weissenburg as he was granted leave to recite his work in the presence of the king, the archbishop, and the bishop.

Nor did the Anglo-Saxons remain silent during this period. To the contrary, King Alfred (d. 899), who was justifiably known as the Great, had the *Cura pastoralis* and the "Dialogues" of Gregory the Great translated, as well as the works of Paulus Orosius and Boethius's *Consolation of Philosophy*. And older than all of these was *Beowulf,* the oldest of the few surviving heroic epics; this has been dated to around 700. It is not only a remarkable work for the poetry itself, but also for the fact that it should have been written down (in a character set akin to runes developed especially for rendering the vernacular)—and survived. There is nothing comparable to be found among the Roman peoples in the West or in Italy; all that has been preserved are a few scant fragments testifying to the existence of early vernacular tongues. The first poetry to emerge from this region was the "Sequence of Saint Eulalia" (dating from shortly after 880), dedicated to the patron saint of the bishopric of Barcelona. This difference once again highlights not only the difficulties experienced by the barbarians in steeping themselves in the high culture of the Mediterranean region, but also the enormous intellectual exertions that were called for in overcoming this hurdle.

To be sure, the ninth century was hallmarked in political terms by a new round of fragmentation, a process only partially reversed in the tenth century. As a result of the continuing existence of the Frankish–Carolingian partition law and of the divergent conditions of expansion that pertained in each of the subkingdoms, the unity of the Frankish kingdom could neither be maintained nor restored. Each heir demanded his share, and then some. In doing so, everyone's eyes were cast first and foremost on the entire former realm of Charlemagne. The collective memory of this entity framed his successors' individual aspirations. Anyone spotting a chance of expanding his kingdom at the expense of his brothers or nephews exploited the opportunity. The upshot was a succession of skirmishes and an endless round of wars. A particular victim of these circumstances was Lothar II, the second son of the emperor Lothar I, and the king whose realm of Lotharingia now bears the name of the French region of Lorraine. His realm was divided and soon fell entirely to the kingdom to the east, which thereby gained not just a considerable tract of land but primarily cultural and symbolic capital by dint of the great traditions of scholarship in such centers of learning as Cologne, Aachen (Aix-la-Chapelle), and Trier. When Charles II ("the Bald") fleetingly believed he was entitled to rule this realm, he had himself anointed king in Metz in support of his claim in 869. Though was not the first time this had happened, this anointing had a particular effect. For—as the presiding officiant, Archbishop Hincmar of Reims, was at pains to stress—it was conducted using the sacred oil preserved in Reims that had once, at the baptism of Chlodwig, induced a dove to fly down from Heaven; subsequently, all the kings of France kept faith with this "miraculous" oil at their investiture. But even Charles had to fight off attacks by his half-brother Louis II ("the German") and later attempted to pay back Louis's son, Louis the Younger, in kind. He threatened to advance with so strong an army that his horses would drink the Rhine dry so that he could cross without getting his feet wet. But he only got as far as Andernach, where a decisive battle saw Louis the Younger emerge victorious (876).

On only one occasion was the crumbling empire (leaving aside Provence, which now constituted a separate kingdom) reunified, when Charles III ("the Fat"), despite being terminally ill and raving mad, outlived a plethora of other Carolingian princes and kings. However, he only ruled this unified polity for three years (884–887) before being deposed by Arnulf of Carinthia, a Carolingian bastard; Charles died shortly thereafter (888). With his death, as the chronicler Regino of Prüm put it, in describing the year 888: "left in the lurch as it were by their legitimate heirs, all the kingdoms that had once been under his sway dissolved from their alliance and disintegrated into separate entities. They no longer awaited their natural sovereign ruler, but instead, each one of them decided to appoint its own monarch internally. Yet Fate condemned them all to ruin." A number of unstable small kingdoms thus came into being, before finally an East and West Frankish empire, Upper and Lower Burgundy, and Italy established themselves. Even in Aquitaine, the large region south of the Loire, separatist tendencies reared their head, albeit without any lasting effect, while a new dynasty also installed itself in Catalonia. As is well known, the collapse of the Frankish Empire continued right into the nineteenth century, when Luxembourg was declared neutral in the Treaty of London in 1869; together with Austria and the German Empire, it had been the last independent part of the old Carolingian Empire.

The loyalty of both noblemen and vassals was the only thing that enabled Charlemagne to rule at all effectively. However, their help came at a heavy cost in return favors. This kind of rule through consent either eroded the absolute power of the king or at least prevented it from developing further. As early as the ninth century, some aristocratic families attained truly prominent positions of power, which they were then able to greatly expand in the ensuing centuries. Thus it was that the Robertians came to the fore in the west of the empire, as did the Widonids (Guideschi) in the duchy of Spoleto in Italy, and the successors of Bernard of Septimania in Aquitania. In the eastern Frankish empire, meanwhile, three or four families came to prominence: the Conradins, who would in time supply the empire's first non-Carolingian monarch; the Liudolfings, who were to depose Konrad's family; the Babenbergs, who were related to the Liudolfings and who were also bitter adversaries of the Conradins; and finally the powerful Liutpoldings, whose power base was in the eastern marches of the Carolingian empire.

The Carolingian high nobility was characterized by vast landholdings, sometimes spanning the entire realm from the Atlantic to Pannonia, or from the River Eider in Schleswig-Holstein down to central Italy; hand-in-hand with this went power that also had the potential to spell danger for the monarchy. An extreme example of this is the testament of Eberhard, the son-in-law of Louis the Pious. In his capacity as margrave of Fiaul, he owned extensive estates in Swabia, Flanders, and along the River Meuse (Maas), was friends with a number of leading scholars of the age, and was himself a writer. In 888, his son Berengar ascended to the throne of Italy, and despite soon gaining—in Wido of Spoleto and his son Lambert—superior enemies who were crowned emperor, he was still able to maintain his position as king and emperor in the northeast of Italy right up until his death in 924. Even a man like Einhard, who owed his rise entirely to Charlemagne and Louis the Pious, owned property in every corner of the empire. The interests of these men and their families were correspondingly extensive. Yet the recurrent divisions of the empire forced them constantly to adopt new positions. Henceforth, regional focal points and concentrations of power developed. The Robertins, for example, established themselves on the Île-de-France, while they or close relatives also had footholds in Burgundy; the Conradins for their part established their power bases in the Rhine-Main region and the west of Alemannia, while the strongholds of the Babenbergs and of the Liudolfings (who later became the Ottonian dynasty) were in Franconia and East Saxony respectively.

Alongside the Carolingian empire's inherent predisposition to self-destruction and decay were the dangers that appeared from beyond its borders: in the south, the Saracens, mainly from Spain; and in the north the Normans (Vikings). From the late ninth century on, the empire's southeastern borders were menaced by the Hungarians. All these peoples were intent on plunder; the riches of unfortified monasteries and settlements were there for the taking. The necessary defensive measures and the experience of how best to deal with such attacks were highly variable and, taken as a whole, inadequate. Men were called to arms, a measure that likely helped from time to time against the Muslims. But the Vikings and the Hungarians came and went too quickly; by the time defensive forces had been mustered, the specter had disappeared. Thus many people sought salvation in prayer, fasting, and litanies, or in tribute payments to the invaders and hasty withdrawal, which only succeeded in provoking new campaigns of plundering.

From 888–889 pirates from Spain, mostly Saracens of Slavic descent who had once been kept as slaves, took up residence for almost a century in the town of Fraxinetum (La-Garde-Freinet near Fréjus). They demanded timber for shipbuilding, captured slaves of their own, and penetrated on their raiding expeditions to the Alpine passes, as far as the town of Vienne, the bishopric of Chur, and St. Gallen (939), where they seized control of the passes, threatening the pilgrimage routes to Rome. What a curious twist of fate for these people! Born in the area that lay both west and east of the River Oder, they were sold into slavery as children and dispatched to Spain, where they became eunuchs and were raised as Muslims. Some of the more fortunate ones carved out a career for themselves as advisers to the caliphs and emirs, while others—like the Mamelukes of Egypt in the thirteenth century or the Janissaries in Turkey—were engaged as soldiers and slave-hunters. Ultimately, by the eleventh century, they had formed their own élite, which in the east of Spain even seemed capable of taking power. In addition, several indigenous lords had already concluded pacts with them. King Hugo of Italy (d. 947), for instance, set the Muslims of Fraxinetum on his adversary, the emperor Berengar, who for his part called on the Hungarians for help. It was only in 975 that William the Liberator, count of Provence, finally intervened to put an end to the disruption in the Alpine region, after the Saracens had taken Abbot Maiolus of Cluny captive to try and extort a ransom. Events in the decades around the turn of the millennium saw Europe begin to coalesce in a very particular way.

The Frankish empire suffered the first Viking raids during the final years of Charlemagne's reign. The reasons for this incursion still remain unclear. In all likelihood, it was the result of a combination of factors—the prevailing social order, force of habit, struggles for prestige and power, maybe even a relative overpopulation or simply a lust for adventure driven by an urge to attain honor and glory, and most definitely the prospect of rich booty—as said, it may have been a mixture of all of these. The Vikings' long ships, which although they were seagoing were also extremely light and very fast for that period, and which sometimes used sails and sometimes oars for their propulsion, gave them an almost unbelievable mobility. The Vikings circumnavigated the entire continent, appearing to the north and west of the Frankish empire, sailing through the Straits of

Gibraltar, attacking the coastal areas of Italy, crossing the Baltic and rowing up and down the major rivers of Russia until they finally reached Constantinople, to which they (albeit unsuccessfully) laid siege in 860. Initially, the Mediterranean world was alien to them; after some of these northern people had sacked the small Italian coastal town of Luni, they celebrated having plundered the mighty city of Rome. But in no time they learned not only the art of effective plundering, but also of conquest and rule. In Byzantium, they formed the Varangian Guard, the personal body-guard to the Byzantine emperor; in Normandy and England they laid the foundations of modern rule; in Russia/Ukraine they established—or at least were heavily instrumental in the foundation of—an empire centered on Kiev, which bore their name: Kievan Rus' ("Rus'" denoting a group of Varangians). In Italy and Catalonia, they created powerful principalities and a kingdom, whose successors endured right up to the emergence of Italy as a unified state in the nineteenth century.

In particular, the British Isles were plagued by Viking incursions. Some of the earliest and heaviest raids were launched against these islands, severely weakening their cohesion and resistance. The old and extremely wealthy monastery on Lindisfarne (Holy Island, Northumberland), which was also the seat of a bishop, was the first place to be sacked, in 793. A century later, the "great army" was encamped on British soil; the cautious King Alfred was only able to gain temporary respite from their depredations. Thereafter, the Danelaw came into being—a long-term colonization by the "Danes," which left a lasting imprint on the country between the ninth and eleventh centuries, and whose effects are seen most clearly today in East Anglia. Over time, the eyes of the Vikings turned ever farther north. Before long—this age witnessed an optimal period of global warming between two "small Ice Ages"—they ventured out into the Atlantic. The Vikings settled Iceland in the tenth century, which as early as around 1000 adopted Christianity. This period also saw Erik the Red journey as far as Greenland, where an initially thriving colony was founded that lasted until the early fifteenth century and enjoyed regular connections with Norway, until overgrazing, maladministration, and a new worsening of climatic conditions spelled an end to the experiment. Erik's son Thorwald ventured even farther west, taking women and livestock with him (with the clear intention of founding a colony) and, having discovered land, duly settled in "Vinland," as he christened it. In the meantime, this brief account in the Nordic sagas has been confirmed by clear archaeological evidence: in the north of Newfoundland, at the site of L'Anse aux Meadows, the remains of a longhouse were discovered that bear the hallmarks of Scandinavian workmanship. But because this is the sole surviving such artifact, experts have concluded that the site has all the signs of a colony that was quite deliberately abandoned again. It appears that the few Norsemen who ventured here finally ceded the land to the original inhabitants of the region, be it the Inuit or the Beothuk.

Even to the mighty Frankish empire, the creation of Charlemagne, these "Norsemen" represented a challenge to which the state seemed ill-equipped to respond. There, the plunderers were regarded as "pirates," albeit ones dispatched by kings, and so were seen as the fighting force of a particular civilization. But of what civilization exactly? And how was it organized? In order to take appropriate action, a proper assessment of the danger was called for; this in turn demanded apposite interpretative models and an accurate picture of the environment from which this threat emanated. In other words, what was needed was a coherent plan that would serve as a guide for action. Yet despite all the educational reform that had taken place in the Frankish empire, no assessment was forthcoming that might have allowed the state to react effectively to the Viking incursions. Only King Alfred of England took the trouble to find out about the Vikings' cultural milieu, and responded by ordering the construction of a fleet of larger and taller ships. For instance, into the Saxon translation of the theological writings of Orosius, the king had inserted the account of a Norwegian seal-hunter named Ohtere, who visited Alfred in 890 and told him about the great herds of seals and walrus he had seen when he rounded the North Cape, a natural spectacle that no longer exists. Not even the slightest hint of such curiosity and investigation is evident in contemporaneous Frankish sources.

So this striking ignorance of the Scandinavian environment and society, and the resulting difficulties in assessing the dangers coming from that region, engendered a widespread sense of helplessness among contemporaries in organizing defensive measures. This tendency was particularly noticeable among the Franks—in their reports, and in the wholly inadequate defensive precautions they undertook. Accordingly, there was no let-up in the succession of attacks. The promise of booty attracted new, ever larger and ever bolder raiding parties to venture farther inland. The Franks hardly ever emerged victorious; the situation only changed when the Normans tried to conquer the country. The monarchy failed utterly to mount a defense; regional lords such as the count of Flanders, the Robertins and other noblemen bore the brunt of the effort to repel the invaders. Robert IV the Strong was killed during the successful defense of Paris in 866. His death brought the family renown: Robert's sons Odo and Robert were subsequently crowned king in the West Frankish empire—in actual fact, the first Capetians to ascend the throne, though it was Robert's grandson Hugh Capet who founded the dynasty that bears his name. In 882, the Vikings staged a serious incursion that overran Aix-la-Chapelle (where they turned Charlemagne's palace chapel into a stable); they then moved on to Trier and Mainz, where evidence of their burning of the towns can still be unearthed today. It was during this period of decay and Viking invasion that Abbot Regino of Prüm, who had been forced to leave his monastery and move to Trier, wrote his handbook *(De ecclesiasticis disciplinis)* on ecclesiastical discipline for use in the visitation of dioceses; this was an attempt at a systematic organization of the body of canon law, which had expanded greatly over time. It represented nothing less than a marvel of scholarship during a time of political chaos.

The situation only changed from the early tenth century on, when the ethnogenetic processes that were gradually taking place among the Normans had reached an initial stage of completion, that is, when the Danes and Swedes had become distinct peoples, ruled by relatively firmly established kings, and had finally embraced Christianity. The attacks on England now took on the character of royal campaigns of conquest. Canute the Great ruled as king over Danes and Anglo-Saxons. But even as early as the second half of the eleventh century, a man like Harald Hardrada came to prominence, who as a Varangian Guard had earned a fortune in Byzantine service. He used this money to raise an army and seized the crown of Norway, whereupon he set off westward with the intention of conquering England. However, his ambition was thwarted when he was defeated and slain at the Battle of Stamford Bridge. This took place in 1066, the same year when, just a few weeks later, another Norman ruler, William the Conqueror, duke of Normandy, invaded from the south and, enjoying better fortune, succeeded in conquering England. The nations that make up modern Europe were slowly emerging in this period.

Italy, though, appeared to follow a separate path of development. The south was part of the Byzantine empire, while Muslims from Africa had overrun the island of Sicily in the ninth century. In the north, as a successor to rule by the Carolingian emperors, an independent kingdom came into being that was fought over by various rulers, many of whom were short-lived. However, the most tenacious of these proved to be Wido and Lambert of Spoleto, albeit constantly threatened by Berengar of Friaul. Later King Hugh of Vienne and his son Lothar seemed poised to be the most successful northern Italian rulers, but both died prematurely, and their last adversary, the Saxon Otto, inherited the realm after he, having just lost his wife, married Lothar's widow Adelheid. With this development, all embryonic attempts to forge an independent empire in Italy were thwarted for centuries, a process also hampered by the deep divisions among the Italian nobility. The dream was only revived during the *Risorgimento* in the mid-nineteenth century.

Hugh maintained close contacts with Byzantium. His envoy was called Liudprand, and later became bishop of Cremona. His experiences in Constantinople left him with a negative impression of the "Greeks"; he found imperial court protocol and Byzantine diplomacy highly suspect. Admittedly, he was also angry with his master King Hugo at that time, who had in his view denied him the appropriate reward—namely, a bishop's see—for the dangers to which he had exposed himself by traveling to the Bosporus to take up his post. But the negative typecasting evident in Liudprand's attitude took root and remained in place for a long time. The Greeks were henceforth seen in the West as having succumbed to godless sybaritism, and so were regarded as "decadent," and "degenerate," as well as being thought arrogant, devious, and heretical. Once again, ignorance set the tone in the contact between two cultures and in the perception of foreigners; knowledge of Greece or the Greeks was not widespread in the West. Superficially the West imitated Byzantine courtly ceremonial, which derived from Hellenistic royal ritual, without really understanding it in its entirety. Moreover, "Westerners" had not the slightest feel for the fine art of diplomacy, which enabled the Byzantine emperor *(basileus)* to deal with Christians, Muslims, and heretics alike. Now that Classical Antiquity was well and truly a thing of the past, the "Romans," as the Byzantines called themselves, had become wholly alien to Latin westerners; the ensuing discrimination caused a schism in Christianity and separated Byzantium from Europe. In Italy, which by dint of its southern regions and the trading position of Venice remained closer to the Bosporus than the rest of the Western world, the implications of this alienation were recognized earlier than elsewhere.

The Mediterranean world of Italy was quite different from the remainder of the Christian West. Here (as in parts of Languedoc, as well) the ancient city culture had survived in a rudimentary form. This manifested itself not least in the country's economic life, which had retained since antiquity, albeit in reduced form, a particular form of commercial organization, characterized by division of labor and monetary transactions. Yet it was also evident in a certain kind of continuous literary education, and in written legislation and jurisprudence. This was perhaps not institutionalized in schools, but rather passed down through legal practitioners; the Lombard monarchy seems to have set special store by judges and advocates who were active in its courts having a formal vocational education. These circles were responsible for reviving the discipline of jurisprudence, which began to blossom once more beginning in the late eleventh century. Yet at the same time historiography languished; the only outstanding Italian historian of this period was Paulus Diaconus (Paul the Deacon) who was active in Monte Cassino in the eighth century. And literary figures only began to emerge in the tenth century. Notable among these was Ratherius of Verona, a restless spirit who for various reasons was torn between his homeland in Lorraine and Italy. Having immersed himself in Saint Augustine of Hippo's *Confessions,* Ratherius became a scrupulous observer of his own inner life. Another early Italian author was Atto of Vercelli, a clever, perceptive observer of his age and a critical pioneer of urgent church reform, who penned incisive critiques of the practices of simony and priests entering into marriage. Finally, there was Liudprand himself, who in his historical writings displayed, behind a mask of irony, a keen interest in ecclesiastical reform; ultimately, he owed his appointment as bishop of Cremona to the patronage of the Holy Roman Emperor Otto I.

Furthermore, very special circumstances prevailed in Rome at this time. During the early years of Carolingian rule, the papacy had enjoyed something of a heyday. The most successful popes of this period were Gregory IV and Leo IV, and to a lesser degree Nicholas I, Adrian II, and—despite his assassination—John VIII. In particular, Nicholas (r. 858–867) asserted the prerogatives of the Roman church and of the Apostolic See as the universal ecclesiastical authority over emperors and kings, prelates and princes more effectively than virtually any other pontiff of the Carolingian era. The *Decretum Gratiani,* the fundamental compendium of canon law in the High Middle Ages, used his letters as the second-most-frequent source, after the writings of Gregory the Great. Nicholas demanded that "the decretals of the Roman bishops are to be accepted even if they are not included in the *Codex canonum.*"[1] He even turned his attention to "the

Christians of Asia and Libya" (that is, Africa). This pontiff legitimized Cyril and Methodius, the Slavonic apostles from Byzantium, appointing the latter to be an archbishop, and also promoted missions among the Moravians and Bulgarians. Belatedly, he also intervened in the destiny of the Frankish Empire, when in the divorce proceedings instituted by Lothar II, he ordered that the king should remain married to his first wife, even though the union had been childless. In doing so, he effectively excluded the son who was born of the king's affair with another woman of all inheritance rights and so provoked the end of the realm of Lotharingia and the new round of wars of division that ensued. At least where these core regions of Europe were concerned, Nicholas's ruling meant that monogamy was definitively established as an imperative. The pope's judgment even held sway in Constantinople. As two archbishops who were dismissed from their posts by him complained, "This pope regards himself as an apostle among the Apostles and has appointed himself emperor of the whole world." Indeed, Nicholas's pontificate acted as a prelude to the great church reforms of the eleventh century. The Roman librarian Anastasius reminded this successor of Saint Peter: "Your role is to act as God's representative here on Earth."[2]

Meanwhile, the more important a position was, the more bitter the struggles became to occupy it. In the absence of any protective intervention by kings or emperors, the office of pontiff became caught up in the machinations of the desperate power struggles being played out by Italy's urban nobility. Adrian II was married, and his wife and children were still alive when he was elected pope, but they were summarily murdered. John VIII himself met a violent end. The end of the ninth century, though, saw the hitherto most serious instance of such degeneracy when the enemies of the deceased Pope Formosus were so hell-bent on humiliating him that they exhumed his corpse, sat it on the papal throne and clothed it with the pontifical robes, in order to then tear them from his body in a symbolic act of deposition. They then proceeded to mutilate his corpse and hurl his remains into the Tiber. Even though its judgments were later revoked, this so-called Cadaver Synod of 897 saw the medieval papacy sink to an absolute low point. Reform was now the order of the day—but how and by whom?

But in almost miraculous fashion, the first stirrings of reform began to make themselves known at this time. Rome, golden Rome, the Eternal City, was to be reborn. The pope who made this restoration his main aim was Sergius III (d. 911), a sworn enemy of Formosus. Sergius drew support from the secular rulers of the city, the "senators" Theophylact and his son-in-law Alberic. Even this title they gave themselves was a deliberate part of their agenda, as they ruled Rome with a firm hand and openly embraced the reform efforts. Yet hopes of true change proved premature and false, as both men died without producing a son. All the more remarkable, then, was the achievement of Theophylact's daughter Marozia, who even ruled the city at times under the title of *patricia*. Before, during, or after her first marriage—it is now impossible to determine—she is reputed (though this may be a exaggerating caricature by the proponents of canon law) to have summoned Archbishop John of Ravenna to Rome as her lover and pope, installing him as John X. Ultimately tiring of him, though, she had him strangled in prison and conceived a son, the later Pope John XI, with his successor Sergius. Marozia disappeared from the political stage in the same year that Otto I succeeded to the throne. Her son from her first marriage to the margrave of Spoleto was called Alberic II, who went by the grandiose title (reflecting his ambition and his agenda at the same time) *princeps ac senator omnium Romanorum* (prince and senator of all Romans), and his son in turn was christened Octavian (Ottaviano). This boy with the portentous name was destined, in the absence of any further heirs, to unite the spiritual and secular offices of the city in his hands. Accordingly, at the tender age of eighteen, he was installed as the successor of Saint Peter. In memory of the lover, or maybe the bastard, of his mother—or was it just that the name Octavian was unseemly for any pope?—the young man henceforth called himself John XII. This was the first instance of a pontiff taking a regnal name; many others were to follow. Just as Pope Adrian I had done in his era when calling on Charlemagne for assistance Pope John asked the Saxon ruler Otto for help when the Italian king Berengar of Ivrea made moves to seize Rome. This move saved the papacy, but spelled the end for the pope himself, as John was soon relieved of his post.

The rise of the Saxon Liudolfings (or Ottonians) to the monarchy had been a gradual process. One prerequisite was the demise of the Carolingians in East Francia, as was the collapse of the most powerful Carolingian aristocratic family, the Conradins, along with Conrad I, the first non-Carolingian to ascend the throne in the East Frankish empire (only in the west had others preceded him in this). Conrad's death without an heir in 918 had thrown the question of succession wide open. The way in which it was resolved remains a mystery; all that has come down to us is the questionable account of the victors, steeped as it is in myth, and later merged into the legend of Henry the Fowler. Only this much is certain: the different branches of the Conradins were at loggerheads with one another, while several of their representatives were too young to assume the crown. The Saxon Henry seized the chance that thus presented itself by appointing himself king. Quite how this came about was not recorded; in order to fill the gap left in popular memory, posterity came up with the legend of Henry being offered the crown as he sat trapping birds.

Henry's family, the Liudolfings, had for a long time been fostering close ties to the Carolingian royal house. Large landholdings in the foothills of the Harz Mountains and an aggressive campaign against the Slavs between the Elbe and the Oder furnished them with the vast wealth that they needed to make a bid for the royal crown. The means the Liudolfings employed to achieve this were brutal. They launched attack after attack; those victims who survived—provided they were young enough—were sold into slavery to the Moors in Spain, or to Byzantium, or farther afield into the Islamic caliphates of the Middle East. Even some decades later, the chronicler Thietmar, who as bishop of Merseburg himself had jurisdiction over such Slavonic peoples, was lamenting the sad fate of these people, whose families were torn apart and scattered to the four winds. But he could do nothing to alter the situation, still less did he reflect upon the benefit that their subjugation had brought his bishopric, too. One may speculate on whether these Slavs converted to Christianity of their own free will.

Henry was able to assert his position as king, winning over the Alemanni and the Bavarians to his cause, while Lotharingia also capitulated to him. Yet he only resorted to the use of force infrequently and reluctantly, preferring to seal unions through friendship accords. These treaties formed the basis of a general common assent to his reign. In 921, he also concluded an agreement with the Carolingian king of West Francia, Charles the Simple, in Bonn, on the borders of Lotharingia, which not only recognized the existence of Henry's, kingdom, but also formally acknowledged the emancipation of East Francia from the sovereignty of the Carolingian king. Yet despite the presence of a Saxon on one throne, the realm still remained Frankish. Meanwhile, the Saxon–Frankish court did not exactly present a resplendent picture; above all, it lacked any literary figures. The royal chancellery didn't even leave behind records in any great numbers, inasmuch as we can even grace with the name chancellery an institution that never generated more than sporadic writing activity.

The real baptism of fire for Henry's kingdom was provided by the Magyars. In their alien appearance seeming more like devils than men, these Asiatic mounted nomads spread fear and terror with their "godless" fighting methods and their pagan modes of living. When they attacked and burned Augsburg in 955, they drove forward their foremost ranks (comprised of captive foreign peoples) with whiplashes to storm the city's ramparts. Driven by inner-Asiatic mass migrations, the Hungarians or Magyars had themselves initially been forced to emigrate westward into the steppe lands of southern Russia. However, they found no peace there; trapped between the fronts of new threats from Asia—on the one hand attacks by the Pechenegs, a horse-based people like themselves, and on the other by Byzantine military expeditions—they reacted violently. They incurred heavy losses as a result. Their enemies exploited the opportunity when the Magyars' armies were away fighting to attack their yurt camps, cutting down women and children or abducting them. Year after year, the Hungarian hordes shifted inexorably west; in search of gold, silver, and women, they invaded Italy and Henry's kingdom almost in annual rotation. They then advanced into Burgundy and Spain, sacking, burning, and destroying monasteries and villages as they went.

Henry found himself obliged to reorganize his army and to introduce new tactics and stricter discipline. This enabled him to successfully repulse the Hungarian threat. The construction of large fortified towns helped protect the surrounding countryside. The chroniclers hailed Henry's victory at the River Unstrut in 933, which brought the country peace for the following two decades, as a major triumph. It is possible that the king first carried the Holy Lance at this engagement as a kind of military colors. He had acquired this relic shortly before (possibly in order to stake a claim to control of Italy); in any event, it became the outstanding symbol of royal authority of the Ottonian and Salian monarchies.

Yet Henry was also concerned about the spiritual life of his people. Accordingly, he and his wife Mathilde founded a number of convents in Saxony. The town of Quedlinburg in particular, benefited from the patronage of both; this is also where both of them were buried, though their graves were deconsecrated and destroyed in the twentieth century when the collegiate church and castle were made into an SS shrine during the Nazi period. The surviving convent treasure hoard was hidden during the Second World War and misappropriated in 1945 by an American officer, but was ultimately repatriated under dramatic circumstances, and can now be viewed once more in its home town. It tells us a great deal about the wealth the country acquired as a result of Henry ascending the throne. One of the foremost historians of his age, Thietmar von Merseburg, was educated at the Quedlinburg convent school; he died in 1018.

The "army reform" that Henry I set in motion may indeed hint at deep-seated social shifts and upheavals. New kinds of fighting men, the so-called *agrarii milites,* were the result—though it is not clear precisely what they were. But at least this development proves that a paucity of sources, which characterizes the tenth century overall, by no means points to a state of historical stasis. This century, which has hitherto been thought of as "obscure" because of this lack of historical sources, in fact witnessed further fundamental changes, though these seem to have entirely escaped the attention of the small number of contemporary historians. Archeologists have found traces of a groundbreaking technical innovation whose importance can scarcely be overestimated, a truly brilliant invention whose creators are completely unknown, as indeed is the context of their work.[3] The earliest evidence of a horizontal, treadle-operated loom—which would come to supplant the vertically mounted warp-weighted loom, on which all weaving had been done hitherto—has been discovered at Haithabu (Hedeby), near Schleswig, the now-deserted major harbor site on the River Schlei, which was a busy port in early medieval times. It is thought that the earlier vertical looms were used exclusively by women, who often congregated in "women's work houses" *(genicia).* The goods they produced were relatively small. The new type of loom, however, increased the efficiency of production by virtue of the fact that it could be extended, allowing, for instance, two weavers to work in rotation; this meant that longer, wider, and finer pieces of cloth could now be turned out in less time than ever before. A whole new industry thus opened up, with many new separate processes and spin-off trades, and a new long-distance trade commodity came onto the market, offering the chance to many people to earn a living and amass wealth. The first social consequences of this innovation soon became apparent: the treadle-operated loom now turned men into weavers, at least in towns.

No less significant was the spread of the watermill with a vertical waterwheel. Vitruvius, the Roman writer on architecture, had described such mills; however, in the arid Mediterranean region, animal-powered mills with horizontal wheels were far more common. But in the Frankish empire, the former type predominated and became widespread. Lords exploited this technology in order to establish so-called seigneurial mills, much to the chagrin of their tenant farmers, who were obliged to pay a toll to have their grain milled there in return for payment. In water power, the motive force generated by means of a camshaft and a cogwheel found a widely available source of energy. Nor was it just used for pounding and milling the grain for making bread—rather, it gave rise to technologies that found application in many different ways. Mills could now be employed for pumping or hammering, or for fulling cloth—in short for any mechanical operation that could conceivably be driven by water power. This in turn helped foster an entrepreneurial spirit, which spawned countless new branches of industry organized on the principle of the division of labor. These kinds of innovations first came into evidence in the context of the manorial system, which in turn succumbed to this historical change and unleashed new social forces. They helped bring about a huge leap in the efficiency of labor, making it less onerous, and in so doing promoted a desire for things to be "longer, wider, faster." In other words, a ceaseless yearning for "more" was thereafter to characterize European commerce and provide an ever-increasing population with livelihoods. Such growth called for denser communications networks, and these were duly created. No matter where such innovations first appeared, they swiftly became widespread throughout the West and precipitated economic, social, and political advances across the whole length and breadth of Europe.

The mining industry also gained momentum in this period. In around 960, deposits of precious metals were discovered in the Rammelberg on the northwestern fringes of the Harz Mountains near the town of Goslar, which proved to be rich seams of copper and silver. Deep mining became possible as pumps (running on water power) were used to drain underground water. Energy requirements for smelting ores steadily increased, and were mainly supplied by burning charcoal. The first depredations of the environment by this industry became evident around 1000, by which time the Harz Mountains had been largely clear-felled and had to be painstakingly reforested. This in turn gave rise to the first systematic attempts at silviculture (forest management). As the whole range of mining technology was modernized, the resulting profits were considerable. Nor did this simply accrue to the benefit of the monarchy; again, a series of new trades and spin-off enterprises came into being, which owed their existence to mining, smelting, and metalworking. The royal palatinate region of Goslar profited hugely from this undertaking. These innovations, plus the needs of a growing population, also saw great improvements to the transport network. Roads were built and bridges constructed, while the number of marketplaces, coinage offices, and customs houses multiplied. Money gained in importance. People's spatial mobility also increased, even over long distances.

Not least, the Ottonian empire also profited from these developments. It soon had at its disposal a fortune the scale of which may be guessed at even today from the priceless manuscripts and goldwork that have been preserved, for instance in Trier, and which were without equal in the West. Such artifacts served to project the kind of power that was commensurate with this kind of wealth. When Henry was on his deathbed, he refused to divide his realm. Even while his father was still living, his son Otto was anointed king in 930, almost certainly in Mainz, even though in his own time just such a ceremony had hampered Henry's ascent to the throne. But now, the religious underpinning of his kingship served to distinguish Otto from his three brothers, while also raising him out of the ranks of the lords who were known as the "pillars of the realm." This act represented a decisive rejection of the tradition of partition that had operated hitherto; certainly, the new arrangement was not accepted without demur, but once resistance had been overcome, it did manage to assert itself. Conceivably this is why Otto, when he succeeded his father in 936, may possibly have had himself anointed a second time—this time in Aachen and for Lorraine, so to speak—before he ascended the throne of Charlemagne. Equally, though, the uncertain report of this event may just as well relate to his son Otto II and his anointment in 961. Whatever the truth of the matter, the character of the "empire" had changed fundamentally, insofar as it no longer just denoted the sphere of the king, but at the same time the allodial participation of these lords, without having to seek the consent of the Ottonian monarchy, in the former royal domain of the Carolingians.

The coronation itself reflected this new inclusiveness. During the ceremony, the young king was required to engage in the following litany of questions and responses: "Do you promise to guard the faith that the Catholic fathers have handed down to you and honor it with righteous deeds?"—"I do!"—"Do you promise to be the guardian and keeper of the Holy Church and its servants?"—"I do!"—"Do you promise to rule and protect the realm that God has granted you according to the just practices of your forefathers?"—"I do, and furthermore pledge to be true in all my dealings, so far as I am able with God's help and the support of all the

Faithful." Thereafter the bishop turned to the congregation and said: "Do you promise to submit to this prince and leader, and strengthen and consolidate his kingdom through steadfast loyalty and obey his commands?" Whereupon the clergy and the people thrice made the following vow: "So be it! So be it! Amen!" This, then, amounted to a reciprocal pledge of good faith, a exchange of gifts fortified by religion. The "people" were represented by the princes and the nobility, while the "clergy" were the bishops and abbots. Liturgically, and solemnly sworn in the sight of God, they concluded a kind of ruling compact with their lord prior to his investiture. The future ruler was thereby reminded of his responsibility before God, in other words, before the norms and the knowledge of the priesthood, not yet before ordinary men, while the people vowed to be obedient and to give "succour" to their king and "consolidate" his kingdom. "Justice" was the overarching norm, which required that each party in this compact keep their word.

Only a limited number of people were involved to a greater or lesser extent in the king's rule, and they were all known to one another. Covering a period of sixty years, the monk and chronicler of the early Ottonian period, Widukind of Corvey, who came from the upper echelons of the aristocracy, cited by name only 130 such active contemporaries from both the spiritual and secular realms of the Ottonian empire, including just a handful of queens. Ordinary people were seldom mentioned; only occasionally, when plague or famine hit the populace or when they tried to escape oppression or exploitation, did historians even touch upon their concerns. Just a few gestures and rituals sufficed to reveal and manifest the rank and status of the lords. For instance, dukes were not only required to subjugate themselves to the king during the coronation, they also "served" the newly crowned monarch by waiting upon him at the coronation banquet. This initial ritual act of fulfilling their pledge of obedience helped set it firmly in place. The semantics of this kind of ritual, which only became established in the Ottonian empire, were easy to decipher. In a semiliterate society, this kind of literal enactment took the place of any "theoretical" demonstration of loyalty. Even so, a distinction must be made between ritual, ritualistic acts, and ceremonial. Only full ritual could implement the will of God and reaffirm the divine order of things. Everything else was merely the work of man.

Nevertheless, disputes still arose. Time and again, Otto had to overcome deep hostility not only from his brothers Thangmar and Heinrich, who became rallying points for other malcontents, but also from his own son Liudolf, who after his father's second marriage not unreasonably feared for his position as the rightful heir. As the king weathered all these challenges, his authority was strengthened. However, it is inappropriate to talk in terms of him engaging in "politics"—this intellectual concept of human activity deriving from, and for the benefit of, the common weal is an anachronism for the tenth century. Such notions, at least where the West is concerned, may be said to have arisen only in the thirteenth century, as a consequence of the late reception of the works of Aristotle. The Ottonian period was still some centuries removed from that development. Accordingly, its lords did not think in "political" categories, indeed the habit of thinking in categories at all was still only in its infancy then; instead, they would explain their motivations by means of signs, gestures, and rituals. There were no conceptions of "domestic" or "foreign policy," or of "politics" and "the state"; nobody would have understood them as templates for interpreting the world or for acting in a particular way, nor could anyone have associated a particular attitude with them or have advocated such a mind-set. The organization of human coexistence followed quite different schemata. Proximity to the king, noble provenance and property, forestry rights and seigneurial rights, tributes, and duties were the criteria by which those in the top strata of society measured one another; rank and status duly devolved from these. The deadly sin of cupidity was a firm guiding principle informing their actions, albeit tempered by norms of behavior laid down by the church and the threat of being found guilty in the eyes of the Lord and condemned to eternal torment—strictures intended to keep the power of greed within some bounds.

God, too, revealed His will in signs, and they were everywhere to be seen for those who knew how to read them: they manifested themselves in the sun, moon, and the stars in the sky, in the natural world and among people, and even in animals. God and Man, the Devil and sinners, the cosmos and the world of human endeavor all conversed with one another in this language of signs. Heaven and Earth, and the Here and Hereafter, permeated one another. The aristocratic lust for power, the oppression of the poor, and unconfessed sins could all invoke natural disasters—drought and hunger and plagues—bring enemies into the country and ensure their triumph, and cause people to perish bereft of any salvation. God's punishing justice terrified and admonished humans by means of eclipses of the sun and "bloody rains," or through packs of ravening wolves, or the birth of double-headed calves. These signs were there for everyone to see, and everyone came to feel their effects. Skillful interpreters could always be relied upon to proclaim their import with hindsight. Pious souls were struck by fear and implored God with supplications, litanies, and processions to show them mercy and grace; they founded monasteries as places of prayer and attempted to ward off impending doom through charitable donations and constant devotion to prayerful contemplation. People's readiness to invest in orders of strictly observant monks who gave over all their time to prayer was forever being whipped up, and many monasteries were established and richly appointed and defended in times of hardship. So it was that even the rich and powerful did not cease to call for earthly justice. Such a demand had the power to engender scruples or even a growing fear in the face of God's punishing omnipotence.

At this time, the tireless promotion of religion, the cult of the saints, and worship appeared to be an absolute necessity of life within the community. Ecclesiastical ritual, prayer, and liturgy were accorded the greatest significance. These observances could be deployed to invoke divine mercy, which gave life and maintained God's order, and to ask the saints for their continuing help in leading a blessed life in the earthly world, and not just for eternal bliss and salvation from the terrors of the Day of Judgment. The king bowed to the divine laws and proclaimed his submission through regular participation in ritual observances. If anything could have been regarded as "politics," it would have been the fact that the king and his court played a full part in the Mass, prayers, and the benedictions of the church. It was a ruler's duty to celebrate Mass.

A hitherto unknown sense of religiosity began to permeate the office of monarch. By means of anointment and coronation, regality was ritually tied into the church. This all took place more consistently and more extensively than in the Carolingian period. The Ottonian and Salian kings now appeared as the *Christus Domini,* the "Anointed One of the Lord," almost as the "vicar of Christ" *(Vicarius Christi).* In return, he was expected to strengthen religion in his realm and combat heathen practices. "O Lord, You who are the glory of the just and who show mercy to sinners, who sent his only son to bring salvation to man with His blood, You who abolish all conflict and are the champion of all those who believe in You, and in whose will the might of all kingdoms is founded," so runs the service of coronation of the "Romano-German Pontifical," a manuscript of liturgical practice compiled during the reign of Otto the Great, most likely in Mainz; "we humbly beseech You: bless [Otto] Your servant on this royal throne, who trusts in Your mercy, and graciously grant him your succor, so that he may, under Your protection, prevail over his enemies. Bestow on him Your blessings and let him conquer all his foes. Crown him with the crown of righteousness and piety, so that he may believe in You with all his heart and mind, serve You, protect and exalt Your Holy Church, and rule justly over the people whom You have entrusted to his care, and may no one through evil counsel ever mislead him to commit injustices. Kindle, O Lord, in his heart a love of Your grace through this anointing oil, with which you anointed priests, kings, and prophets, that he might love justice and lead his people on the path of justice and, after completing the life span that you have granted him in regal grandeur, may he earn the right to enter into eternal bliss."

And indeed, the Ottonian kings were notable for their prolific foundation of churches. Many bishoprics were created and monasteries established by them; in return, they were constantly remembered in prayer. But in general the powerful were expected to act as patrons of religious institutions. The Ottonians fulfilled such obligations in exemplary fashion; many monasteries, other ecclesiastical endowments, and bishoprics owe their existence to their beneficence. Furthermore, while they were not responsible for inventing it, they did reorganize the court chapel—the institution which brought under one roof the court clergy, the liturgical functions within the royal house, and the royal physical collection of holy relics. Above all, Otto's youngest brother Brun, the archbishop of Cologne and duke of Lotharingia, played a leading role in this regard. At a church synod which met at Ingelheim in the royal palatinate in 948, the mission to northern Europe and among the Slavs was initiated. Around the same time, the bishoprics of Havelberg and Brandenburg were founded. Protracted negotiations finally led, two decades later, to the founding of the archbishopric of Magdeburg, whose cathedral is still home to the tomb of Otto, its founding monarch.

Charlemagne had advocated a policy of strict separation from the Slavs. Henry the Fowler and Otto I, on the other hand, after an initial phase of conflict and enslavement, promoted their integration into their own realms. This fostered the meeting of two distinct cultures on a social, regnal, religious, and material plane and also facilitated learning processes and intercultural transfer of knowledge. Certainly delimitations and hostilities were in part the result of this encounter, but on the other hand, there was no fundamental ostracism. Moreover, numerous marriages among the nobility were made across all ethnic and linguistic divides. This all made the mission task easier, to incorporate the new converts into Western culture.

Conditions in Italy were especially unstable during this period. A cry for help came to Otto from the young, beautiful Adelheid, the widow of Lothar II. She found herself under threat from Berengar of Ivrea, who was attempting to seize the throne of Italy. Otto heeded her pleas and in 951 assumed the Italian crown himself, freeing Adelheid from her state of siege and taking her back to Saxony as his wife. When she became pregnant and bore a son, the question of succession reared its head once more. Otto's son from his first marriage, Liudolf, had already been chosen as his successor, but now found his status threatened, since he was motherless and faced with a stepmother installed in his father's house. Seeking help from his brother-in-law, Conrad the Red of the Salian dynasty, they jointly staged a rebellion that proved extremely dangerous for Otto I. Meanwhile, the Hungarians exploited the opportunity to launch another invasion of the Ottonian empire (954). Some contemporaries accused the rebels of having deliberately invited the Hungarians' incursion; there were certainly some opponents of Ottonian rule who were prepared to make common cause with the Hungarians. No sooner had Otto finally seen off the rebels and the Hungarian incursion than he was faced with an uprising by the Slavs, and barely had he managed to suppress this than news was brought to him of further invasions by the Hungarians into Bavaria and Swabia (955). With a powerful army, the Magyars laid siege to Augsburg, whose defense was led by the city's bishop Ulrich. Otto promptly marched south and met his enemies in battle at the River Lech. The exact location of the engagement is disputed, as are Otto's tactics and the precise course the fighting took. But what is beyond doubt was the decisive outcome of the Battle of Lechfeld, as it is known, which once and for all put a stop to Hungarian incursions into the Ottonian empire.

Berengar of Ivrea, however, tried to capitalize on these conflicts. Yet when he made moves to seize control of Rome, the same kind of situation that had occurred in the eighth century arose once more. Admittedly, this time, the last of the Carolingian line were experiencing its death throes in West Francia, battling in vain against the entrenched position of power of the Capetians under Hugh the Great on the Île-de-France. This meant that no help could now be expected from that quarter; the Carolingian kingdom by this time was just too weak. The only conceivable person to whom the pope could turn for help now was Otto I, conqueror of the Hungarians. Accordingly, John XII summoned him to Rome; for a second time, then, the Saxon monarch marched across the Alps and on February 2, 962, had himself crowned Holy Roman Emperor by the pope. The following year, however, Otto deposed John XII for being unworthy of his office. Henceforth, Italy and Rome were to play a central role in the unfolding of Ottonian power. It was here that the "Germans"—the *Tedeschi*—first emerged as a community, virtually as a distinct people, and were given a name that derived from their language (loosely translated, *Tedeschi* means "speakers of the vernacular"); scholars soon came to associate this designation with the "Teutons," the name of those ancient barbarians who in around 100 BC had put mighty Rome under enormous pressure.

Immediately, the term was revived from the concept of the *Furor Teutonicus* and transferred to the contemporary "Germans." The Roman monk Benedict of San Andrea lamented: "Woe unto you, oh Rome, you who have been oppressed and humiliated by so many peoples. Now the Saxon king has taken you. He has brought your people to heel with the sword and sapped you of your strength. They have carried off your gold and silver in their bags." None of Benedict's elegy was untrue, but it was one-sided. The emperor did extract material profit from the region; once again, he found himself in a position to reward services with gold. But at the same time, he did try to bring peace to this deeply divided land. For many years, he remained stationed in the south of Italy with his forces. Even so, he never managed to secure any enduring success in Rome. The Lombards and the Romans did not see the Saxon as one of their own, and occupiers were never looked upon favorably, even in those days.

In regard to its consequences, the revival of the empire can be seriously overestimated. From this point on the Ottonians pursued imperial goals that marked all the later history of their empire. The caliph of Córdoba, who in the early tenth century had split from the central caliphate of Baghdad, entertained diplomatic relations with the Ottonian court, though for various reasons these links never really flourished. Yet the Ottonians' main rivalry for imperial grandeur and rank, plus control over Italian provinces, was with Byzantium. This competition was not without its consequences, even if it was impossible for contemporaries to identify these from the outset. The enormous costs in manpower and matériel that the Ottonian expansion into Italy entailed overstretched the financial resources of the Saxon kingdom. For every campaign fought in Italy, vassals had to be compensated with gold or fiefdoms; over time, this expenditure drained the economic potential of the Ottonian kings; the modest gains made in the south did little to make up for the massive outlay. Indeed, as we shall see, in the long run this expansion only served to dissipate the king's power—authority that would have otherwise been an essential ingredient in bringing internal cohesion to an empire that comprised many different peoples and countries.

Otto I's extended absence in the south was the cause of much resentment in Saxony and other parts of the empire north of the Alps. His closest confederates were offended by it, and the most loyal of his allies—the margrave Herman Billung and Archbishop Adalbert of Magdeburg—now seemed prepared to plot rebellion. Otto hurried back, but died after convening a final imperial diet in Quedlinburg (973). His heart was buried in Memleben, while his body was interred in Magdeburg. Otto the Great's son and grandson had to pay the costs of his reign with their young lives. Otto II died at the age of twenty-eight in Italy, while his son Otto III didn't even make it to twenty-two. Whole armies of knights went with them to the grave. Warned by the fate of these two young Ottonians, it was left to their successors, Henry II and Conrad II, to learn how to keep well clear of Italy in person—without thereby relinquishing the royal and imperial crown of the country—and largely leave the exercise of authority on the ground there to indigenous forces. And so it remained until the Holy Roman Emperor Henry V and above all Frederick Barbarossa revived the disastrous policy of intervention in Italy.

As Charlemagne had done before them, the Saxon emperors now turned their gaze toward Constantinople, the yardstick of all imperial authority. Otto I entered into long-running negotiations with Byzantium, with southern Italy and Venice, the two westernmost outposts of the *basileus's* domain, as the key points of discussion; the Saxon king was bidding for a princess of imperial birth as a match for his successor. However, no daughter of the Eastern emperor—traditionally known as the *porphyrogenita*, meaning "born in the purple chamber," that is, of imperial provenance—was available, only his niece Theophanu. The imperial princess Anna, the only potential bride of the highest rank then of marriageable age, was already betrothed to the incumbent to the Rus' throne in Kiev, which was closer to Constantinople and was more urgently in need of a peace alliance. And indeed, this marriage did bring Kievan Rus' great benefits, with the recently enacted baptism of Russia into the faith being strengthened and the link with Orthodox Christianity firmly established, a connection that endures to the present day. The Ottonian empire also gained lasting benefits from the dynastic marriage with the emperor's niece. The Western empire's own self-awareness and the image it projected were to all intents and purposes set by this alliance. In particular, the empresses took an active part in these innovations. They appeared together with the ruler in images and were regarded as full participants in the realm, as the *Consors imperii,* the imperial consort.

In his youthful arrogance, the husband of Theophanu, Otto II, challenged Byzantium. Presumptuously, he styled himself the "Emperor of the Romans," something his father had always avoided; it was a sensitive matter that deeply offended the Byzantines' identity. For, in their eyes, only they were the true Romans. The one true emperor of the Romans was the *basileus.* Otto's urge to act knew no bounds. He wanted to extend his realm in southern Italy as a bulwark against Muslim expansion, true to the oath he swore at his investiture to become the conqueror of the heathens, who had begun to gain a foothold from the ninth century and whom the Byzantines had not been very effective in repelling. The *basileus* viewed his endeavors with suspicion. Right at the southernmost tip of the boot of Italy, at Cotrone on the Gulf of Taranto, their forces duly clashed. The battle ended in a terrible defeat for the Latin emperor, who barely escaped with his own life. After six months he was carried off by the plague, leaving behind a three-year old son as his heir. Unhappy the land, though, that has a child as its king.

Nevertheless, Otto II's reign was brilliant in its cultural achievements. Could it have been that the presence of the Greek princess from Byzantium among the Saxon-German barbarians acted as a spur to artistic endeavor? Certainly, her bridal treasure chest brought them face to face with the art of the East, which spawned a string of imitations. The very marriage certificate of Theophanu was a case in point—painted in imperial purple, and with calligraphy probably done by the foremost artist of the era, the Master of the "Registrum Gregorii." Book illumination flourished in its wake; schools of painting with significance far beyond regional boundaries arose in the Reichenau, Trier, Echternach, and Fulda. Works from Reichenau in turn became known in Italy, where imitators soon sprang up. In general, the culture of books experienced a great revival at this time. As patrons and clients, monarchs naturally played an active part in this development. Book production was a matter for the ruling classes. Liturgical volumes under the Ottonians might be decorated with images glorifying rulers, as they had once done under the Carolingians. And the donation of richly illuminated books became established as a piece of royal protocol. Images came to be regarded as the visible presence of a monarch who was absent in reality, but who might thereby be included within the prayer congregation of the recipients. Goldsmiths and silversmiths found their work in demand once more. Poetry also underwent a revival, though only in Latin and not in the vernacular. In this context, we may mention Hrotsvith von Gandersheim, or the Latin epic *Waltharius*. Another realm of cultural life to reappear was the sciences. In particular, a dispute in the presence of the emperor between Gerbert d'Aurillac and Ohtrich von Magdeburg about the classification of science became widely renowned; the whole of the court attended and witnessed— the defeat of the Saxon schoolmaster.

And yet all this could not disguise the fact that the high-water mark of Ottonian power had already passed. Major military defeats and bitter setbacks heralded the change. Had the Saxons overreached themselves? Or underestimated the dangers of getting involved in Italy, or at least failed to appreciate the magnitude of the task they faced? The armies there were carried off by plagues. The rival Lombards and Romans were not about to be reconciled by a foreign lord from the north; their partisan wrangling ground down imperial authority. Otto II was the first to feel the destructive effects of all this. His premature death could have served as a warning, but was not heeded as such. Theophanu buried her husband in Rome— the only German emperor who would ever be interred in Saint Peter's Basilica. His three-year-old son Otto inherited a difficult legacy. His own uncle, Henry the Wrangler, was threatening to depose him. But his mother's skill as regent saved the crown for him; Theophanu, the only Latin *Coimperatrix* there ever was, was a remarkable woman. Under the male title of *Theophanius imperator augustus* she held the reins of power until Otto came of age. In doing so, she made a number of enemies.

It was during the period of Theophanu's regency and the uncertain situation of her empire that a decisive sea change occurred in the west of the old Frankish empire. Consolidation of the kingdom there had been a long time coming. The last of the Carolingian line steadily lost more and more influence and dynamism. Charles the Simple had already had to look on helplessly as the northwest of his kingdom, around the mouth of the Seine and Rouen, was settled by Norman invaders. A treaty signed on the border between his realm and the Norman-controlled lands, at St.-Claire-sur-Epte in 911, legitimized this development in a new way, which had only occasionally been practiced to date; the invaders took the land they had seized from the king as a fiefdom. At the point where Rollo, the future Norman duke, was expected to bow down like a dutiful vassal and kiss his lord's feet, the historian Dudo of St.-Quentin (admittedly a full century after the event took place) reported that, instead, the duke pulled the king's foot up so violently that his lord toppled backward off his throne—a gesture of humility, pride, and presumption all at the same time.

This anecdote may well be a myth, but it does afford us an insight into the mind-set of the forebears of William the Conqueror, the victor of the Battle of Hastings in 1066. The Norman dukes proved to be extremely capable conquerors. They enforced peace not only in their own domains, but also permanently saved the future kingdom of France from further Viking invasions. Vassal status meant legitimacy to them, not submission, and meant recognition of authority as legal title—authority they had usurped and won by violent conquest. This mode of legitimation would enjoy a long history. Wherever Normans from Normandy carved out new rights of sovereignty, they always reverted to this same model. Even when the individual principalities of southern Italy were due to be unified under a single crown in 1130–1139 the future king accepted his new realm of Sicily from the pope as a fiefdom.

In the remainder of West Francia, too, the regional power of the nobility intensified. Anyone who failed in the tenth century to lay the foundations of future ducal authority would find it impossible to achieve thereafter. But this only served to put the Carolingian monarchy under even greater pressure. Its end, when it came, was heralded in quite a low-key fashion. For a long time, the duke of "Francia," Hugo the Great, had wielded more power than his feudal lord the king, and had authority over more duchies and bishoprics, whose bishops he—and not the king—was entitled to appoint. Charlemagne's successors remained loyal to the end to the old Frankish tradition of dividing up their possessions and the domain under their sway among all their legitimate sons, until eventually there was nothing left to divide, and besides the sheer honor of the title, precious little to bequeath. A final division was planned in the year 953, but lapsed due to wider developments. For it was at that point that Hugh Capet, the most powerful of the new echelon of dukes, finally swept the Carolingians from the throne, or to be more precise, when he refused to allow the last Carolingians to ascend the throne. Instead, he now took it for himself, and with it the royal dynasty, which continues to this day in the male line. Furthermore, according to more recent tradition and the gradually evolving religious self-image of the dynasty, Hugh's son Robert the Pious was reputed to have been the first person to heal scrofula—a power that was henceforth said to be granted only to the anointed monarch.

Through the fertility of its kings and as French monarchs did not, unlike the Ottonians, put their young lives on the line with reckless adventures in malaria-ridden Italy, France was spared internal conflict over succession to the throne. This was an extraordinary stroke of luck for the French crown. Moreover, the might of this new kingdom was no longer based, first and foremost, on the old Frankish tradition and royal feudal rule over the nobility; instead, it relied to a far greater extent on the inherited property (which now became crown lands) and the allodial rights of the Capetians. Both of these multiplied over the coming centuries in precisely the same way as the power of the nobles had hitherto. And because, for the time being at least, the French kings were not intent on pursuing any more far-reaching aims, there was no danger that property that had been acquired might be misappropriated by some confederate or other. After the toppling of the Carolingians, Count Borell of Barcelona, Urgell, Girona, and Osona was the only vassal to refuse to swear allegiance to the usurper (988). Thus began the legal emancipation of Catalonia from the Frankish empire, which over time led to full independence. Henceforth, the history of France unfolded under completely different structural conditions than those affecting Germany, despite the fact that both polities had the same origin in the Carolingian Frankish empire.

Another factor was a symptomatic distinction between political mentalities in the east and the west, which also began to become apparent from this period onward. The French lay princes, powerful as they were, maintained contacts to the papacy independent of the king, whereas in the Ottonian empire the king intervened as a rule, with the result that no negotiations independent of the monarch could take place between the aristocracy and the Apostolic See; it was only during the Investiture Controversy that German noblemen who opposed the king circumvented this convention and appealed directly to Rome. Accordingly, different trends in communication with long-term implications became visible in west and east; they made any approaches on the part of the German nobility to the Apostolic See a truly explosive issue, while those by the French aristocracy were largely uncontroversial.

This agrarian-oriented aristocratic society was predisposed to think in martial terms, was competitive in its basic make-up, and was correspondingly rife with conflict. Every nobleman viewed his fellows with deep suspicion. "Be on your guard, Leo!" was the watchword that the loyal Ottonian paladin in Italy, Bishop Leo of Vercelli, constantly called to mind; he was always deeply mistrustful of his own lord and master, whether this was Otto II or Henry II. No advocate was worthy of unqualified trust, no intercessor ever acted unselfishly, and no growth or extension of authority ever happened without envy, discord, or violence rearing their heads. How might just rule take root in such conditions? Even so, this society was Christian, or at least claimed to be so. How, then, to maintain God's grace and not squander it?

In a climate of continuing violence and growing sin, there was a constant need for a renewed hope and certainty of salvation. The sword-wielding nobility thus set great store by the intercession of monks. The ongoing process of civilization required that readiness to resort to violence and raw expression of emotions be held in check. And, last but not least, the excessive costs of waging war, which in the long term simply consumed too much cultural capital, militated strongly in favor of a strategy of peace and reconstruction. Christian doctrines of education therefore got a hearing once more, and pointed the way forward. Peace, humility, and piety were messages that, after the experience of excessive violence and suffering, fell on fertile ground. In this, monastic orders acted on behalf of all of society.

The momentum of Saint Benedict's reforms had long since ebbed away; however, new monastic reforms came in their place that were now about much more than simply observing the rules. A much stricter sense of discipline was called for, and appropriate modes of living were demanded. Teamed with these requirements was a demand for freedom from secular power—which in the past had proved so dangerous to churches and monasteries—whether this was in the form of the king, a duke, or a count; the monasteries should be protected and free to hold Masses, prayers, and observances for the dead. The abbey at Cluny (northwest of Mâcon), which was founded in 910 at the instigation of Duke William III of Aquitaine, realized these objectives in a unique and exemplary way. The abbey was subject to no secular authority, and the designation of successors as abbot and the free choice of candidates for this post were in the gift of the members of the institution. The abbey was under papal protection but not subordinate to papal authority and was exempted from the episcopalian power of the local diocese: these were the favorable conditions under which Cluniac freedom unfolded over the tenth and eleventh centuries, and which no authority would ever violate, be it king or emperor, bishop, or priest. The abbot took his staff of office from the high altar and used it to "invest" himself—or rather, Saint Peter, the divine patron of the abbey, used it to invest the abbot. A succession of important and extremely successful abbots took it upon themselves to disseminate the Cluniac way of life. Above all in the west and in Burgundy, monastery after monastery was bequeathed to them, with most of them becoming priories subservient to the great abbot of Cluny; this confederation encompassed no fewer than 1000 separate communities in its heyday. However, decline set in during the twelfth century, as new reforming orders, chief among the Cistercians, began to spread. In the following century, during the reign of Louis IX, Cluny Abbey finally fell under the jurisdiction of the king. Reduced to the status of a commandery, it was finally abolished by the Revolution in 1790, and nowadays welcomes tourists as a small village with an impressive set of abbey ruins.

The Cluniac reform movement radiated out as far as Rome and Monte Cassino, to Anglo-Saxon England, and even to Spain—but at first, with a few exceptions, scarcely at all on the territory of the Ottonian empire. There, other reforming monasteries and abbots were active independent of and in parallel to the Cluniac movement, especially in Lorraine and radiating out, such as Gérard de Brogne (near Namur) or John of Gorze (south of Metz). This reformist movement, too, spread its influence over large swathes of Western Europe, particularly Italy, France, and Burgundy, whereas the monasteries on the right bank of the Rhine were hesitant in recognizing their need for reform, or even in some cases rejected it outright. Only in the period of church reform, from about 1070 on, did the Cluniac reforming idea cross the Rhine, or perhaps came from the south through the Alps. By this stage, the reform could sometimes have a political, antimonarchical edge to it. The new centers east of the Rhine were Hirsau and Siegburg.

The medieval prayer service, whose roots reached far back into ancient Christianity, and which in a new guise became institutionalized during the reigns of the first Carolingian kings and emperors, touched upon extensive connections between faith, education, society, politics, art, and science, as well as communication, and while all of these areas were inextricably linked to contemporary modes and locations of action, they were also at the same time of a general nature and so generated paradigms that enabled contemporaries to weigh up the social factors involved. This was even true of the earliest known example, namely the "death confraternity" of Attigny, which comprised forty-four ecclesiastical officeholders, bishops, and abbots under the leadership of Chrodegang of Metz; at a synod in Attignu in 762, they had in the event of the death of any one of their number reciprocally committed to hold liturgical prayer services, in the presence of all their assembled clergy and lay members, for the deceased individual. Such prayer associations reflect a form of social integration and supraregional community formation that transcends purely ecclesiastical forms and that was by no means confined to religious life, but rather made its presence felt in extraecclesiastical and political affairs. One example that can be observed in its long-term effect was the prayer confraternity of Dortmund, which was concluded in 1005 between King Henry II and a number of bishops and noblemen, whose charitable obligations were demonstrably fulfilled over a period of at least 150 years. In this way, communities dedicated to peace and common interests come to the fore that were highly significant for their age. The Cluniac death association, which appears to have been highly efficient, represented the highpoint of this entire development. The names of the deceased were written down on scraps of parchment, together with the remembrances that were to be offered up, and circulated to all the communities in the confederation, who in turn added their own notes detailing what observances they had made. Long narrow scrolls *(rotuli)* of sewn-together notes enumerating acts of piety were created, and these made the rounds among the monasteries within the Cluniac sphere of influence, spreading the comforting message far and wide: namely, that for each and every one of the dead under the aegis of Cluny Abbey hundreds of requiem masses would be said, with attendant feedings of the poor. Only rarely did these scrolls cross the linguistic boundary to the east—a striking indication of the communitarian and yet also exclusive effect of the prayer confraternity.

Certainly, it was primarily a select few individuals who were explicitly remembered by name—kings, bishops, noblemen, abbots, and monks; with very few exceptions (one being the Battle of Lechfeld in 955), no events were commemorated, nor any abstract concepts, organizations, or institutions. The religious and secular hierarchy thus remained intact even in death, and there are no extant commemorations of members of the lower orders. "Stretch out to me the hands of prayer and solace" was the plea, for example, that Pope Urban II, famous for dispatching the First Crusade to Jerusalem and who had formerly been a monk at Cluny, sent to his erstwhile abbot Hugh. Prayer and politics went hand in hand. Accordingly, for historians who learned to pay heed to these commemorations and interpret their testimonies, extended groups of related noblemen began to become visible. Indeed, it is through commemorative testimonials that we have come to identify the early Robertins/Capetians, the Conradins, and other groups of relatives, along with aristocratic factions such as the "friends" of the Ottonians or extended peace confederations. These preserved all the signs of personal-historical and social connections of historic significance, which if such testimonials had been ignored, would have remained hidden, and virtually invisible to posterity. The prayer texts and liturgical formulas that have come down to us reveal the religious and spiritual horizons of people at that time and the gravity with which they surveyed them.

Extant documents indicate massive material outlay that was necessary for the commemorative observances. Monastic foundations, the building of churches, the cult of saints, painting and goldsmithing, music and liturgy, welfare for the poor, and other factors were all deployed in the service of such memorials, and were promoted by them. Yet all this had to be paid for, a fact that lends this phenomenon of commemoration a cultural relevance whose importance can scarcely be overstated. The business of memorializing was therefore fed back into the entire society and its economy, causing the monastic "enterprises" sometimes to flourish and sometimes to overreach themselves, and occasionally even to collapse; it conditioned their development and in the process unleashed a social and economic dynamism of enormous significance. The dead, for the good of whose souls the Cluniac monasteries undertook distributions of food to the poor, placed monastic finances under a huge strain. It has been estimated that in the late twelfth century there were usually more than 18,000 such meals organized annually, while on occasion they even exceeded 30,000. These figures may appear insignificant to a contemporary world accustomed to dealing with populations in the millions, but for the economic capacity of hostelries in the High Middle Ages, which also had to cater to their own large number of monks and lay members, it represented a challenge impossible to meet on a continuing basis. In effect, the dead wasted away the living and bankrupted the richest and most powerful monasteries in history.[4] The duties in service of commemoration were just too massive. The internal management of monasteries was clearly incapable in the long term of squaring the charitable and the economic activities of these institutions. Nevertheless, the commemoration of the dead and cultural memorializing awakened and directed dynamic forces that could not help but eventually transform the world.

Consequently, the business of memorializing may be regarded as a phenomenon in which everything at the time in society and culture was reflected and ruptured: profane life as well as religion, "political" matters and the economy, science, art, and technology every bit as much as the social order and interpretative schemata, modes of communication and perception, society's capacity for innovation and its dynamism. For instance, although old Europe's hierarchy-conscious doctrine of the "estates," that is the tripartite division of "religious men," "warriors," and "artisans," which had begun to assert itself in Western European society from the tenth century, was not created by the act of memorializing, it still played a significant role in shaping this doctrine. The freedom of action of monarchs, the organization of monastic life and the church in the Early and High Middle Ages by the nobility, and aristocratic assertion of authority could all now be seen in a context that would appear to be more in accord with contemporary social and cultural activity than the earlier constructs of historical scholarship, which were overwhelmingly predicated on larger conceptions of power politics and political authority. Not least, the enduring influence of the business of commemoration made itself felt on the development of historiography in the Early and High Middle Ages and hence directly on the cultural memory of groups of that era.

Yet this extensive business of commemoration was anchored in the education and socialization of each and every individual monk. Customarily, from the Carolingian period on, a monk was entrusted to a monastery (including Cluny) when he was still just a little boy, a *Puer oblatus* of an impressionable age, around six years old. From the outset, he was burdened with the expectations of his parents and relatives, aspirations that in turn had been dinned into their flesh and blood from earliest childhood: namely, that the boy should fulfill his intercessionary duties on behalf of all of them, and thereby assure them of God's mercy in both the Here and Now and the Hereafter. It was in this kind of education and socialization, of aspiration and obligation expected to weather all the extensive innovations and catastrophic failures of the age, that the psychological correlate to the social reality of the monastic life resided.

5

The End of Days Draws
Menacingly Close

THE WORLD WAS superannuated, well over 5,000 years old; it was
rushing toward its demise, an event that many people thought would occur exactly 6,000 years after its creation. This deadline had been conveyed
to Jews and Christians alike by Talmudic scholars. Admittedly, it was
seen as presumptuous to calculate the precise time when the world would
end; knowledge of when this would take place was the preserve of the Lord,
and not even the angels were party to the secret. Even so, some scholars were
unable to contain their curiosity and continually tried to start their calculations afresh on this score. After all, living in anticipation of Christ's Second Coming and the Day of Judgment, which would coincide with the
End of Days, had been a central principle of Christianity since its inception, and was a familiar feature of Medieval and Early Modern faith. This
concept derived its power over the souls of believers from the terrors that
the Last Judgment would hold, which were ever more luridly portrayed as
time passed. As suggested by the prophesies of the Gospels, the Book of
Revelation, and other sacred texts, as well as the church fathers, the turn
of the millennium awakened both in Byzantium and in the Latin West
corresponding expectations that the Day of Judgment would soon come
to pass. "Satan's millennium" was now upon the world, pronounced one
Western scholar;[1] the Antichrist had been unchained, an event that the
renowned *Bamberg Apocalypse* actually captured in a manuscript illumination. A century characterized by prevailing thoughts about the End
Time was thus ushered in, to be followed by a succession of new phases

and waves of adventism anticipating Judgment Day—sometimes such notions were widespread and at other times were only harbored by a few members of sects. This process would continue on to Luther, and thereafter right up to the twentieth century.

We, who fancy that the world will endure forever, may well scoff at this simple faith, or seek to refute it. Yet it was a faith that could move mountains and that was responsible for unleashing an abundance of cultural endeavors, as well as giving rise to scientific practice and writings, literature, art, and architecture. It was also the motivating force behind popes, bishops, emperors, and kings, and finally bodied forth in the Age of Science and the Enlightenment. Religiosity and piety were hallmarked by their patient anticipation of the Day of Judgment. Yet such adventism was not a debilitating force; rather, as the prophesies exhorted, it called for the utmost exertion of all efforts and the greatest engagement, encouraged people to do pious deeds, militated in favor of reform, and culminated in innovation.

Furthermore, books of expiation, which began to arrive on the continent from Ireland in the ninth and tenth centuries and thereafter enjoyed a highly successful "career," recommended that a person—quite apart from atoning for the deadly sins—should also undertake in their lifetime a number of "tariff atonements," each calibrated to the particular transgression, in order to be able to stand one day before the Supreme Judge with as light a burden of sins as possible. Just like Saint Augustine's *Confessions,* these books involved a series of questions (in the format "Have you done this or that?") and in so doing required the person confessing their sins to look to himself. Now, however, something more was being demanded, not just self-contemplation and expiation; rather, the soul should now prepare itself to receive its "bridegroom." Not least the Pax Dei movement, which had its origins in the late tenth century in southern France and during the eleventh century spread to embrace the whole of France, with the exception of Normandy, may well, as certain pieces of evidence would seem to indicate, have been stimulated by apocalyptic expectations. For one of the earliest preserved decrees of the Pax Dei movement sets forth as a guiding tenet the principle that "no one shall see God without Peace."[2] By means of conjurations, a state of peace was invoked, which placed named persons, objects, and animals at specific times—say from Thursday evening to Saturday morning—under the protection of those who had sworn the oath, and prosecuted and punished anyone breaching the peace. This movement also seems to have had an influence on the commune movement in northern Italy, which likewise used the expedient of conjuration to maintain peace within cities, and over time to assert municipal authority over the local lords and bishops. Indeed, the commune may well have been the specific form taken by the Pax Dei movement in the towns of northern Italy. Pressing concerns about the question of the End Time also occupied the thoughts of the highest ecclesiastical circles, demanding answers to old, vexatious questions and setting new forces in motion. The perceived proximity of the Day of Judgment reminded the church reformers of the eleventh century, chief among them Pope Gregory VII, of the urgency of this reform.

Not least because of the impending end of the world, contemporaries living during the decades around the turn of the millennium undertook missionary work on the frontiers of the known world: for their task, as outlined by Saint Augustine, was to proclaim to even the most remote islands the good news of the resurrection of Jesus Christ prior to their preordained destruction. This missionary task demanded knowledge of the entire inhabited world and the expansion of Latin Christianity across its surface, wherever human beings were to be found. The carrying of the message "to the whole world" set in train a globalization of desire and knowledge, still in the context of a complete absence of a global economy. It was deemed especially important to win the immediately neighboring peoples, the still-heathen Slavs—who it was assumed lived on the fringes of the Christian community—over to the true faith. People's knowledge of the Earth was really still very sketchy at this period. Notions of geography fed solely on direct experiences, which seldom went beyond the immediate environs of people's home region. Only the aristocracy in the service of the king knew more about the world. Despite the fact that scholars of the period had access to the learning of antiquity to a limited degree, this fund of knowledge was in no way applicable to the actual business of wielding power or to the Christian mission to embrace the whole world. Accordingly, the world had to be discovered anew, as it were, in order to carry out the global mission, and the West set about preparing itself for this task.

The Earth was conceived of as a ball, but the inhabited Christian world was only a tiny island surrounded by ocean. Traditional maps from antiquity, such as the sketch map from Macrobius's commentary on Cicero's *Somnium Scipionis (Scipio's Dream)* presented it in this way, showing an inhabited northern region separated from the Antipodes by a vast ocean at the equator. Imaginative works of this kind depicted the whole of the earthly cosmos and, as such, were primarily of interest to scribes and other scholars. In other words, such schematic representations were of no practical "political" use for anyone seeking to secure control over territory or people particular regions. Under these circumstances, strategic or logistical planning, or any insight into regional conditions preceding action, was impossible. Cartographic knowledge remained the preserve of scholars, and it did not transfer into practical knowledge. Instead, pragmatic knowledge was gleaned on the job, over the days and weeks that it took to cross the region in question. Maps with information on distances in accordance with a definable scale first appeared at the end of the fifteenth century. Space at this early stage was still conceived of as woods and fields, rivers and mountains, and scattered islands of settlement; space also embraced the people who inhabited this landscape and tilled it, and the tributes that were collected there. Covetousness to possess a region and success in wresting control of it had to take place on the spot. Control was visible, present, and threatening, but also dependent upon the constraints of knowledge at that time.

Data supplied by historians barely points beyond their immediate environment. The Saxon writer Widukind, for instance, did not know equally well all areas of the region where his people had settled, although he purported to write their history. Nor, despite several differences on points of detail, do the descriptions of the chronicler and bishop Thietmar von Merseburg go much farther. If anything, the horizons of the anonymous, though well-informed nun from Quedlinburg, who also wrote annals of the Saxon people, were even more narrow. Under these circumstances, where cognizance of the extent of royal authority was concerned, the "empire" appeared to be a regionally highly diffuse entity, so despite its hard-and-fast borders it was not a homogeneous territory—not a realm where the writ of royal control ran uniformly, but rather a region where claims of manifold complexity had to be continually refreshed. As a general rule, knowledge of foreign and even of neighboring peoples was no better. Thus equipped with correspondingly limited experiences and conceptions, the missionaries embarked on their journey. This demanded the same courage as that displayed centuries later by astronauts when they began exploring the universe.

The world of the Slavs, so far as we know it, was formed in the context of this mission. Their early history has been lost in the mists of time due to a lack of source material, which archeological and linguistic evidence can offset to only a limited degree. They lived as peaceful farmers, and their collective organization was on a relatively simple level. They were organized into small tribal alliances, most likely concentrated around cult centers. Overall, they had still not coalesced under a strong, empire-forming power, which would have been in a position to coordinate resistance to Frankish or Saxon incursion and against the threat of Viking raids. It was only during the course of the ninth and tenth centuries that a powerful principality was first established in Moravia, and thereafter a Czech duchy in Bohemia and Upper Silesia, and then finally, around the rivers Oder and Warthe, the first Polish kingdom, which endured until the early eleventh century.

There is, however, one solitary report dating back to the seventh century, which tells of a merchant from the Frankish kingdom by the name of Samo, who after an uprising against the Avars is said to have founded a kingdom among the Slavs, which also held its own against the Franks, but which collapsed after his death. No more detailed information is available. Historical data only become thicker on the ground from the High Carolingian period onward. At that time, missions were undertaken to the Carantanians (a Slavic principality around modern Carinthia in Austria and Slovenia) and to the Moravians, who were busy establishing a highly successful kingdom of their own. Two missionaries from Byzantium, Cyril and Methodius, were active among the latter group. The Bavarian and East Frankish bishops looked upon this action with disapproval, for with the support of Pope Nicholas I, these Greek faith emissaries were threatening to revive the ecclesiastical province of Sirmium, which had existed in Late Antiquity but had since disappeared, or even to incorporate the Moravian Church into the Orthodox Patriarchate of Constantinople, at a time when Salzburg, Passau, and Regensburg were entertaining hopes of expanding their own dioceses. The Greek missionaries not only spread the Glagolitic, early "Cyrillic" script, which takes its name from Saint Cyril (who ended up buried in the church of San Clemente in Rome), but also employed the vernacular liturgy to great success. At that time, such an act was considered heretical, and provoked a great deal of anger among the Latins.

This undertaking received a setback in the form of a Hungarian invasion, to which the Moravian kingdom and the Bavarian conscript army both fell victim (907). This also sounded the death knell of the rule of the Bavarian princes in Prague. By that time, this was already the largest city in the Western Slavic lands, boasting, as the Moorish traveler from Spain

Ibrâhim ibn Yaqûb noted with astonishment, stone buildings. It dominated trade, particularly the slave trade, to Kraków and Kiev, and further
on to Samarkand, Constantinople, and Arabia. Wealth accumulated in
this city, and it was a seat of power. Prague became the seat of the
Premyslids—the family of Saint Wenceslaus, who was murdered in a
power struggle with his brother and martyred—and this dynasty established a strong duchy there. It fostered close connections with both Saxony (hence the dedication of the cathedral in Prague to Saint Vitus) and
the Bavarian ducal city of Regensburg, from where an important road ran
on to Italy. From the reign of Otto I onward, Regensburg had been integrated as a duchy into the Ottonian Empire.

Christianity flowed from both the north and the south into Bohemia.
However, it only gradually managed to make headway there. Finally, in
972–973, the diocese of Prague was founded and—possibly in order to
neutralize the competition from Saxony and Bavaria—incorporated into
the ecclesiastical province of Mainz. This province thereby took control
of a broad diocese that encompassed the Prague Basin, Silesia, and all of
the eastern lands to a point far beyond Krakow, as well as some areas in
northern Hungary. Adalbert von Weißenburg, the future first archbishop
of Magdeburg, traveled on a mission via Prague and Krakow to bring
Latin Christianity to Russia, but returned disappointed. Back in Prague,
he confirmed Wojciech, who himself took the name Adalbert and became
the city's second bishop. This future saint harbored ambitious plans, which
were undoubtedly ultimately aimed at detaching Prague from the Mainz
ecclesiastical province and raising it to the status of an independent Slavic-
Hungarian archdiocese. Since their defeat at the Battle of Lechfeld (955)
the once-dangerous Magyars had been eager to find a home within the
Christian community, either with Byzantium or with the Latin West.
Adalbert spread his message among them, while missionaries also came
from Bavaria. Gisela, the daughter of Duke Heinrich of Bavaria, married
the Hungarian prince Vajk, who took the name Stephen when he was
christened and became the first king of Hungary. Adalbert may well have
undertaken the baptism himself. Yet once again a power struggle in Bohemia, this time between Duke Boleslav and Adalbert's family, compromised the success of this union and thwarted more ambitious plans. The
bishop withdrew first to Rome, and ended up leading a mission to Prussia, where he was martyred (997). Hungary and Poland also became eccle-
siastically independent, while it was only under the Holy Roman Emperor

Charles IV (r. 1355–1378) that Prague was elevated to the status of a metropolitan archdiocese with its own ecclesiastical province.

Admittedly, for a long time national prejudices clouded any impartial view of the millennium and the rise to prominence of the peoples to the east of the Ottonian Empire. The weighty legacy of the more recent past in the nineteenth and twentieth centuries had cast heavy shadows on the historical images, which were taken as ciphers of national identity. Only gradually are they beginning to become clearer and opening up new transnational perspectives. As they do so, they are shifting the development far more firmly into a religious and ecclesiastical context than was hitherto the case. This is exemplified particularly by the "baptism" of Poland and the difficulties encountered by Christianity in establishing itself in the region between the rivers Elbe and Oder.

As already noted, the Liudolfings had already subjugated this region and begun to impose ecclesiastical order there. Then Otto I, in the face of considerable resistance by Mainz and Halberstadt, founded the archdiocese of Magdeburg, incorporating the suffragan bishoprics of Merseburg, Meissen, and Zeitz (Naumburg), as well as the slighter older sees of Brandenburg and Havelberg. However, a major revolt of the Slavs after Otto II's death in 983, directed against their decades-long subjugation, provoked a reversion to paganism by the Western Slavic Lutitians, thus putting a stop to the complete Christianization of this region for at least another century and a half; for the time being, the bishoprics of Brandenburg and Havelberg were lost once more to the resurgent pagans. Certainly, one result of paganism having free rein was a considerable degradation of "cultural capital"; archeological finds make clear that development was retarded during this period, and without the stimulus of the church, culture stagnated.

History took quite a different course in the lands east of the Oder. There in 1000, with the assistance of Pope Sylvester II and the Polish count Boleslav Chrobry, Emperor Otto II, who was fully aware of the End Time, founded the archdiocese of Gnesen (Gniezno) on the frontiers of the known world. Contrary to the plans of the count, Adalbert's younger half-brother Gaudentius was dispatched from Prague to become its first archbishop. As far as we can tell, it was at this time, in the context of eschatological expectations and the founding of the archdiocese that Poland first received "its" name, which, following the example of the Prophet Isaiah was then transferred, so to speak in its christening, to Boleslav Chrobry's land and people. Certainly, there is no evidence of an older West Slavic tribe of "Polans," as posited by some modern etymological researchers as the source of the country's name. The young emperor was also instrumental in the founding of the archdiocese of Gran/Ezstergom (1001). He sought the friendship of princes to the east of his empire's borders, and in an imperial gesture reminiscent of Rome, and learned from the example of Byzantium, he ensured their elevation and recognition as kings. The intention of this was not, however, secular integration of their realms into the Ottonian empire, as many commentators have assumed from looking at some of the miniature illuminations of rulers in liturgical manuscripts; thus, the provinces of *Gallia* or *Sclavinia,* which in these imaginative depictions are shown paying homage to Otto III, do not represent either France or Poland, but—as the parallel verses and other texts indicate unequivocally—the Ottonian empire's province of Lotharingia and the Slavic region west of the Oder, which had also long been integrated into the empire. The first rulers to transgress against Polish sovereignty and wage war against Boleslav Chrobry and his son Miesco II were Henry II (r. 1014–1024) and Conrad II (r. 1027–1039). This was a major blow to Poland, which could only be made good in the second half of the eleventh century, and then without a monarch at the helm.

Strangely, Venice also attracted the attention of the young emperor Otto III. In secret, given that the lagoon belonged to Byzantium, he visited the doge, though the exact reason for his trip was never stated. It may be that plans were afoot regarding Dalmatia, the burgeoning maritime republic's outland and one of its spheres of interest. Venice, over which Charlemagne had renounced control in his peace settlement with Basileus Michael in 812, came to occupy a peculiar intermediary role between East and West and in so doing became important and influential in its own right. The wealth of this still young state was initially founded on the production of salt and a monopoly on the trade in this commodity; also, timber from the Alps, which was in widespread demand for shipbuilding throughout the Mediterranean region, as far afield as Constantinople, was traded through Venice (unless it was used in its own shipyards). Alongside these commodities were "luxury goods" like slaves and eunuchs. The first contacts between Venice and the major trading centers north of the Alps were forged during this period. Since the Byzantine fleet declined over the coming centuries, while the threat increased, the Venetian fleet took on an increasing significance for the Eastern Roman Empire, as the valuable customs and trading privileges that were dispensed in the tenth and eleventh centuries make clear. Also Western emperors from the Carolingian period onward signed special trade agreements with the lagoon city, regulating reciprocal relations.

Venice, however, was an exception. Prior to the twelfth century, cities in the West played only a subordinate role, despite the fact that industrial production was beginning to shift once more into (proto-) urban centers at this time. There was no shortage of merchants, but their heyday was yet to arrive. These early medieval traders were hard-bitten men, as revealed by a snapshot of life that has happened to survive from Tiel in the Lower Rhine area. Carousing, perjury, and adultery were supposedly the order of the day there—though these remarks tell us more about the incomprehension of the chronicler that these merchants could ever form a guild than it does about their actual mode of existence. Yet long-distance seaborne trade and piracy often went hand in hand. At this time, the merchants themselves would undertake the journeys, on land and sea alike; they would be armed and equipped for all eventualities. These men took extended trade voyages in their stride. Local peddling is also well attested in this period. Scruples about mercantile rectitude were only very tentative. "Do you want to sell your wares as cheaply as you bought them?—Of course not! Otherwise, how can I profit from my endeavors? So I sell them at a higher price to make a profit, which I use to feed my wife and children." Thus did the schoolmaster Ælfric of Eynsham instruct his pupils about the rationale of the merchant around the turn of the millennium.[3] But this situation would change before long.

So Venice, Hungary, and Poland were all the beneficiaries of important support by Otto III. Broadly speaking, this was the counterpart of the efforts of Byzantine diplomacy; Otto, the progeny of Saxon and Byzantine imperial dynasties always kept Constantinople constantly in mind as the model and yardstick for his actions, anyway. In lively competition with the Eastern Roman Empire and always mindful of his role as the successor of his idol Charlemagne, he planned the regeneration of the Roman Empire. The Palatine Hill in Rome, seat of the ancient emperors and the place from which all other "palaces" took their name, would once again become the residence of an emperor. And indeed, despite the fact that he was to reign for only short six years, this Byzantine Saxon would spend more days in Rome than any other medieval emperor before or since. Seals of imperial office showing him enthroned face-on were created for him, taking as their model images of ancient Roman emperors, and henceforth not only every subsequent Holy Roman Emperor but foreign rulers too would adopt this mode of representation. Otto looked for and opened the grave of Charlemagne and planned to canonize the first Frankish emperor, whom the Saxons revered as the man who had brought them Christianity. However, the premature death of the young emperor at the tender age of twenty-one—which was interpreted as divine punishment for the sacrilege of disinterring the former ruler—stymied Charlemagne's elevation to sainthood at that time. During his time in Rome, this youngest of Ottonian rulers had for the first time chosen non-Romans from within his inner circle as popes, initially his cousin Bruno of Carinthia, who took the papal name of Gregory V, and then his former tutor Gerbert d'Aurillac, who ascended the apostolic throne as Sylvester II. Did Otto II perhaps see himself as the new Constantine the Great?

Contrary to all worries about the End Time—indeed seen in a proper light, precisely because of such concerns—the tenth century, which is beset by a paucity of historical sources, may be said to have witnessed the dawn of the Age of Reason. For faced with the threat of an imminent end of days, people thirsted after reason. This faculty required a differentiating ability to judge when interpreting all the manifold signs that made themselves apparent everywhere, but which were unclear in their actual meaning—signs that the Lord himself had prophesied (Matthew 24:4 ff.): wars and rumors of wars, nation rising against nation, and kingdom against kingdom, pestilence, famine and earthquakes, false prophets, abounding iniquity and godless injustice and love waxing cold, and the darkening of the sun and moon, and "bloody rain" and the stars falling from heaven and so forth. This all demanded great powers of discrimination, as laid down in the study of dialectics. This discipline helped usher in the rise of the sciences from belief in the Apocalypse.

In actual fact, then, it was the tenth century, which has gone down in history as belonging to the "Dark Ages," which like no other era before or since in European history grappled with logic and dialectics. It is no exaggeration to say that this age fell under the sway of reason *(ratio)*. The seeds that Charlemagne had sown were now beginning to germinate. Admittedly, contemporaries first had to discover and resolve the necessary concepts for themselves. The first part of Aristotle's *Organon* became their indispensable point of orientation. It was at this time, from the first half of the tenth century onward, that the original doctrines of categories and syntax as enunciated in the Latin translations of Boethius began to be disseminated;

these writings were read ever more frequently now and were eagerly absorbed. There are no manuscripts extant from the period in question that
are not covered with Latin (not vernacular) glosses. Glosses in the margin
and between the lines, glosses to aid comprehension and to clarify terms,
glosses that range from an initial engagement with the subject matter to a
sovereign extrapolation from the material at hand. Some people even ventured to make translations once more. For example, the monk and schoolmaster Notker Teutonicus of St. Gall translated Aristotle's *Categories* into
Old High German, a bold undertaking, since the crude Teutonic language
had not hitherto shown itself to be particularly suited to conveying philosophical thought, dialectics, or knowledge. A long hard road lay ahead for
this tongue, as indeed it did for all the various vernacular languages that
now began to develop; but at least this was a start. The whole medieval period took infinite pains with the business of translation, and in conjunction
with this, with the attainment of great virtuosity in foreign languages and
the formation of its own mode of Latinity, which was characterized by great
intellectual achievement and linguistic elegance.

However, the application of reason was no headlong, rushed affair; its
progress was all the more tenacious for that. Thorough practice of the art
of logic and dialectics, of logical division and differentiation was called
for, along with a proper grasp of the distinction between "accident" and
"proprium" in Aristotelian thought. The glosses testify to how deeply scholars delved into the bases of an abstract, systematizing mode of thought.
One particular incident that caused a stir at the time and that was characteristic of the entire era was the public disputation that took place in 982
at the imperial court between the Magdeburg cathedral scholar Ohtrich
and his opposite number from Reims, Gerbert d'Aurillac, which concerned
the classification of the various branches of learning. Yet no one was there
to delight in some intellectual sparring contest for its own sake; rather, the
new knowledge and sense of order was firmly grounded in its sense of social relevance. Since every transfer of knowledge went hand in hand with
a new generation of knowledge, these properties served to broaden the horizons of the burgeoning languages of intellectual discourse, spawning ne-
ologisms and engendering whole new sets of differentiating terminology,
and bringing about advances in perception and an increase in the sum total of cognitive capacity. The end result was an internalization of a methodically schooled mode of thought, which precisely for that reason was
amenable to criticism. This increasingly became the dominant way of

thinking guiding the actions first of all of the intellectual elites and there-after society at large; in fact, as we shall presently see, it gave rise to a to-tally new way of acting.[4] One leading representative of this new trend was the prior Abbo of Fleury (ca. 945–1004), who was a strict member of the Cluniac order and a church reformer, as well as being a dialectically schooled scholar and an advisor to the French kings Hugh Capet and Robert II.

This new ferment in intellectual affairs was closely bound up with the centers of power and life. New perspectives on and approaches to the complexity of the world and the cosmos opened up, and to the phenom-ena and circumstances of human existence and society. Now things that had never even been imagined came within peoples' purview, while famil-iar things were seen in a new light, placed in a new relation to one an-other, and reaffirmed afresh. Nor did knowledge remain on the level of linguistic mediation; rather it was geared toward the practical. This can be shown through the example of music; around this time, in 1025, the ca-thedral scholar Guido of Arezzo greatly facilitated the training of singers by inventing a system of musical notation that used four staff lines and the C and F keys; this innovation, as Guido proudly predicted it would, shortened singers' period of training from ten years to just one. The ques-tion as to its practical application soon became a standard introduction to every treatise published in the High Middle Ages. In communicative in-teraction, theoretical knowledge now availed itself of social and political practice. This dialectical access served to reestablish the natural order of things and thereby changed them fundamentally. The social consequences of this educational revolution made themselves immediately apparent.

The word "freedom," for example, took on a whole new flavor. "I only know of free and unfree people," Charlemagne had once said. Yet the ac-tual development of society had long since eroded this simplistic, unsubtle dichotomy. Demands for freedom could not be ignored. Many serfs now simply renounced their former unfree status by fleeing; Otto III had al-ready issued an edict outlawing this kind of autonomous emancipation, but it had little effect. Social stratification was as impossible to hold in check as scientific progress. Daily life called for a correspondingly nu-anced "language," for apposite concepts and sentence constructions, for the capacity to abstract and express oneself in different ways, and for new templates by which to classify and interpret phenomena. The culture of learning was intrinsically bound up with social reality, hastening its pace of change and at the same time being contingent upon it. "Anyone who ignores me," reflected one man of letters in the eleventh century, referring to dialectical instruction, "is incapable of differentiating between things."[5] We may take this to mean that such a person was not equal to the pressing demands of the age, which kept on growing in complexity. This brief statement succinctly encapsulates the interdependence of language, thought, planning, and action.

The notion of "more" or "less" freedom, of relative degrees of freedom, duly arose; the upshot was a multiplicity of freedoms, all requiring accommodation within a hierarchy. For instance, in his *Colloquy,* Ælfric of Eynsham had a plowman lament: "Alas, what hardship and drudgery [*labor*]. I am not free." This passage in this Anglo-Saxon writer's work is likely the first mention of the tribulations of being a bondsman. Plus, this lament also highlights the value of "work"; as this value increased, it began to tug at the shackles of serfdom, demanding that it justify its existence and turning it into a social problem. Hitherto, human action and suffering were deemed to be somehow beholden to God's providence and will. But the phenomenon of labor not only accentuated the question of greater or lesser degrees of freedom and its constituent "elements," not only made this or that person appear "freer" than others; more than this, it also demanded that the *proprium* of freedom be defined, a fundamental question that could not be suppressed any longer. The boldest scholars of the age—early on, say, Johannes Scotus Eriugena, who was suspected of heresy—discovered the answer in the free will of man, which unlike in the Augustine tradition, was now not simply free to do evil. But the longer the question of free will was discussed, the less tenable it became to deny the "worker" *(laborator)* and other bondsmen this capacity. For even those who were under the control of human masters had to answer for their actions before God.

Accordingly, over time the whole idea of being unfree purely by dint of one's lowly station by birth came under intense pressure for legitimation. To be sure, a long time was to elapse before any general distinction between legal and social vassalage was attempted. For the present, by way of counterbalancing their doctrine of free will, theologians and philosophers, along with ecclesiastical and secular legislators and authorities, simultaneously provided rulers with legitimation strategies to justify the very real existing state of vassalage in which their bondsmen lived. It was only certain revolutionary movements of the Late Middle Ages that began radically to question the whole concept and raise demands for judicial and political freedom. Only then did the famous questioning refrain arise: "When Adam dug and Eve span, / Who was then the gentleman?"[6]

No less far-reaching in terms of political life and the history of the nobility were the exogamy precepts of ecclesiastical marriage law, which had been consolidated since the reign of Louis the Pious and which the power of conviction of religious scholars now imposed upon aristocratic society. At least this was the case in central and western Europe, whereas the marginal zones adhered to the older, "archaic" practices for far longer—retaining for instance several diverse forms of polygamy. In his *Decretum,* which was soon widely disseminated, the learned bishop and great canonist Burchard of Worms assembled the questionable norms and reconciled them with the familiar terms of consanguinity, thus making the whole question more generally manageable. Those on trial and their judges were henceforth to turn to Burchard's text for guidance. Around the turn of the millennium in Germany, for example, a series of trials of people deemed to be too closely related to get married greatly unsettled the upper echelons of the nobility and the monarchy alike. Frequently, the main point at issue was the legitimacy of heirs, and hence the survival of the whole social stratum of the aristocracy. Indeed, insofar as this class represents a social interpretative schema, it may be said to have arisen precisely at this historical juncture, conditioned by social change, from the spirit of ecclesiastical law. For sure, the exogamy precepts were framed so broadly as to be impracticable and had over time to be toned down considerably. Nevertheless, the advance in systematic legal knowledge and in the widespread diffusion of norms, passed down for the most part in historical order, is clearly in evidence here. Burchard did not hesitate in applying these accomplishments to the business of ordering his own estate; his *"Lex familiae wormatiensis ecclesiae,* a collection of customary laws for the workers of the Worms episcopal estate, represents one of the first such undertakings of this kind.

A comparison of the famous Strasbourg Oaths of 842 with the newly conceived legal theories sheds light on the radical sea change from symbolic to categorial thinking that was now underway. Formerly a person would swear brotherhood with another: "Thus do I pledge to protect my brother as one is duty bound by law so to do" ("so haldih thesan minan bruodher, soso man mit rehtu sinan bruodher scal"). If a person at that time had posed the question, "What is allegiance?" he would have been given the answer, "Allegiance is the way in which a vassal is beholden to his master." But in the interim, people had learned to distinguish *proprium* and *accidens* from one another, to divide things up logically, to determine the *differentiae,* and to grasp the categorical essence of an object. The discipline of dialectics took on a stirring dynamism of its own and transcended all barriers. The mysteries of religious belief were just as much a challenge to it as the requirements of social life. It found a home predominantly in schools in the West, particularly in the Île de France. The renown of scholars such as Fulbert of Chartres (d. 1028) spread far and wide; his teaching was reputedly like hearing an angel sing, at least according to the fulsome account of a cleric from Regensburg who had had the benefit of his tuition. Fulbert's many pupils disseminated his ideas throughout Gallia and beyond.

Fealty was also subjected to this same procedure of categorical thinking. This, the medium binding together masters and vassals, indeed the whole feudal system, now no longer consisted of simple loyalty, but was now fanned out into individual factors that combined to make up the concept, and the consequences that flowed from these factors. Fulbert, then, differentiated between fealty and oaths of allegiance, categorizing and naming their defining and distinguishing criteria, when Duke William V of Aquitaine sought his advice on this subject in 1020: "He who swears fealty to his lord ought always to hold these six things in mind; what is harmless, safe, honorable, useful, easy, practicable" ("incolumen, tutum, honestum, utile, facile, possibile"); these aspects encompassed, as Fulbert went on to explain, the honor and possessions, and the actions and accomplishments of the vassal on behalf of his master, and were subject to an obligation of reciprocity on the master's part. Personal vassalage and feudality began to form a veritable legal system that clarified the complex relations between lords and their bondsmen, as well as differentiating and shaping relational modes of existence in a normative fashion. In the twelfth and thirteenth centuries, Fulbert's letter to William was incorporated first into the *Decretum Gratiani* and from there into the *Libri Feudorum,* the two authoritative collections of ecclesiastical and feudal law, which remained in force until well into the Modern Period, and which also formed an essential part of university study until the nineteenth century.[7]

Fulbert's concern was not just to dissect the concept of fealty and the oath into separate categories; he was also the first to detach the *regnum* from its purely subjective attachment to the king, a position it had occupied throughout the entire period of Carolingian and Ottonian rule, and through objectifying it and dividing it up into its constituent parts *(par-*

tes) to establish it as an independent factor: "Just as a house cannot exist without foundations, walls, and a roof, so there can be no kingdom without a country, a people, and a king. If a country, a people, or a king are lacking, so there can be no kingdom anymore."[8] The bishop of Chartres formulated this thought in order to characterize contemporary Jews as a people without a kingdom. Yet leaving aside its anti-Semitic context, the logical form of dualistic thinking that this sentence represents had a great future ahead of it. Even nowadays, the terms "body politic," "national territory," and "state power" define the "state." Fulbert's method of division was destined to theoretically underpin the conflict between *regnum* (the secular state) and *sacerdotium* (the clergy) which broke out shortly thereafter, insofar as the *regnum* itself, and not just a person such as the king, could now be regarded as a legal agency.

Schools proliferated teaching the same ideas as those espoused at Chartres. As a result, aside from a few final instances such as Fleury, this diminished the importance of the monastery schools in France, though for the time being these retained their significance within the Ottonian–Salian realm. This gave rise to a evenly dense educational landscape there, which prevented a concentration on just a few "elite schools" as future universities. By contrast, from the eleventh century on, the cathedral schools of narrowly defined "Francia" (alongside Chartres, Reims, Laon, Paris, and various others) rose to prominence, acting as a magnet for the whole of the "Latin" West. Before long, fierce competition arose between the pupils of the different schools; accounts have come down to us from the eleventh century of a rivalry of this kind between the cathedral schools of Würzburg and Worms, and a failed bid to have the cathedral school at Mainz perform the role of adjudicator.

One of the prime areas in which reason began to assert itself was in matters of faith and church administration. School education paved the way for the (re)birth of learned heresy. This had reared its head at Orléans in the early eleventh century; even the confessor of the French queen found himself in the ranks of the heretics. To demonstrate her fury at being thus deceived, the lady in question is said to have put out his eyes with her hairpin on the way to church. Such extreme displays of emotion do not appear in any of the records of the Late Middle Ages. Heterodoxy also increased, and the concerns of the church grew. Yet these were the very spirits of learning and dialectical training that it had invoked itself, and of which it was unable to rid itself henceforth.

Kings and their realms felt this change in intellectual and religious culture directly. For instance, Abbo of Fleury fell out with King Robert after questioning the monarch's marriage to his queen on the grounds of too close a blood relationship; this dispute created major discord within the royal household. Nor did Abbo's zealotry stop at the walls of monasteries; while attempting to restore discipline at one such institution in Gascony, he was murdered by rebellious monks. King Henry II was praised for his humility and his openness to reprimands by the clergy, but his successor Conrad II, who controlled the church with an iron fist, found himself subjected to growing censure from this quarter. However, he did manage to intervene and restore peace to the cities of Lombardy, chief among them Milan, when he issued an edict promising the *valvassori,* the subvassals of the great captains, that their fiefdoms could be passed down to their heirs; this directive would later form the introduction of the *Libri feudorum.*

Conrad's son and successor Henry III showed himself amenable from an early stage to reformist monasticism and ecclesiastical reforms. He was keen not to see the clergy become the preserve of priests' sons. Likewise, he was determined not to tolerate simony, the "purchase" of religious offices; despite this, though, he as king still continued the age-old practice of dispensing bishoprics and imperial monasteries and of investing his chosen candidates with a crozier and a ring. When he felt guilt as a result of his military campaigns in Bohemia and Hungary, the king and his army would do public penance, with Henry appearing barefoot and in a penitent's hair shirt. He completed the cathedral at Speyer as his dynasty's chapel of remembrance. Up to the demise of the old empire, the memorials of the Salian kings were maintained here.

The radical change in thinking had a particularly enduring influence on the co-operation between monasteries, the church, and the monarchy. Clerics and monks formed the intellectual elite of the empire. Indeed, monks would often confront the king and emperor to remind them of the church's independence. Not least, the spirit of reformist monasticism reminded the church of its vocation. The Cluniac demands for freedom did not echo emptily behind monastery walls, but resonated throughout France, and even as far as Italy and Rome; nor did they confine themselves to monastic matters. The Cluniac order's priors and ecclesiastical supporters were active in the world, expounding and spreading the idea of ecclesiastical freedom, the *Libertas ecclesiae,* namely the freedom of the church from the influence of the power of the laity. This demand combined with advances in dialectics, lending the discipline a conviction that immediately won over the educated clergy to the cause, along with the preachers and the spiritual advisors of secular rulers.

The prelude was promising. The monk and recently elected archbishop Halinard of Lyons, who had previously been abbot of the Cluniac-inspired monastery of St.-Benigne in Dijon, refused to swear an oath of fealty to the king (1046). Halinard appealed to the proscription against taking oaths in the Rule of Saint Benedict: "If I were to abandon the commandments of the Eternal King and the monastic rule that I pledged to hold to, then how could I be trusted to observe any oath of fealty that I might swear to the emperor? . . . In the Gospels, the Lord tells us; 'Thou shalt swear no oaths'; moreover the Rule of Saint Benedict commands us 'to take no oaths' . . . it would be better for me never to be appointed a bishop than to transgress against God's order." Whereupon Bishop Sigebaud of Speyer replied: "Who is this man who dares to voice insubordination in the palace of the emperor, something none of us ever dared to do. He must swear an oath to the king or be thrown out."[9] At this stage, then, it was just a single messenger of freedom offering resistance to the king; the majority of the bishops did not follow his lead. Even so, Henry vacillated; he sensed danger for royal authority, but still wanted to avoid conflict and accepted Halinard's refusal without demur. This was the first success of the church reform movement against the monarchy; many other such victories, and more significant ones at that, were to follow.

For example, during the act of paying homage *(homagium)* the consecrated hands of the priest were no longer to rest in the bloody hands of the king. The consequences of this ruling for the king were profound. Despite being anointed into his role, henceforth he counted as a lay person; the monarchy thus became secular, and any hint of sanctity that still clung to it was entirely in the gift of the priesthood. Another of these reformers who caused a stir at the time went by the name of Wazo, who was bishop of Liège and died in 1048; Wazo brusquely pointed out to the king the fundamental difference between the investiture of kings and bishops: "We owe obedience to the highest pontiff," he once told Henry II, "but only fealty to you. We must cede accountability to you in worldly matters, but the pontiff has supreme authority over all things relating to service to God." On another occasion, he is reputed to have stated that kings are anointed to kill, whereas bishops were anointed to awaken people to a new life in God: "Just as life stands so much higher than death, so our anointment is far superior to yours."[10] Such words were calculated to cause uproar. This "far superior" became, as it were, the leitmotif of the ensuing disputes between the priesthood and the monarchy. This confrontation ushered in the irrevocable secularization of the latter institution. The separation of church and state, and European dualism. And subject to this confrontation was the was the newly conceived order of the world with all its consequences; this was in no way understood as purely spiritual, but instead soon saw itself normatively interpreted and set down in ever clearer and more ambitious legal formulations. Political notions of freedom owe their latitude to this dualism.

The reformists' ideas spread slowly; they had still not caught on in Rome, which was still, in the first half of the eleventh century, beset by terrible conditions. The city's noble families were feuding with one another, as they had done since time immemorial, over control of the highest office in the *Urbs*. The two clans in dispute at this time were the Tusculani and the Crescentii (whom Otto III had also clashed with); both families had already had several candidates on the papal throne. Each side had recently elevated one of their own to the papacy; the youngest successor of Saint Peter, the representative of the Tusculani, Benedict IX, was just twelve years old when he was made pope. Then a total of three pontiffs found themselves disputing the legacy of the Apostle. The situation was clearly untenable and, as in the reign of Charlemagne, necessitated the intervention of the monarchy. This was the turbulent prelude to fundamental reforms. Who other than the king could have set the church's house in order? As the future would show, this in fact was the last occasion on which this would happen, but even so it was the cause of bitter recriminations over the encroachment of royal power into church affairs:

Romana superstitio . . . indiget iuditio // Romanum adulterium . . . destruet imperium // Papa sedet super papam . . . contra legem sacram . . . Propter aurum et argentum . . . hoc malum est inventum.[11] Inelegant verses such as this spurred Henry III into action. The church was regarded as the bride of her highest bishop; and several bishops at the same time appeared to be adulterous, in a kind of bigamy or even worse. Also the accusation that gold and silver ruled the papacy was never to go away from this point on. Henry II went to Rome and called a synod, which met in 1046 in Sutri. There, three popes were deposed by the members of the synod and the emperor, and a fourth raised to the papal throne in their stead. He then in turn crowned Henry emperor. It appeared, then, as though the empire had ascended the highest peak of power.

But it was precisely among the reformers that criticism began to be voiced about the king and emperor's intervention to save the papacy, in spite of the fact that it was they who had gained the greatest advantage from his presiding judgment. The pope, they demanded, was subject to nobody's jurisdiction. Although this phrase, as noted previously, derives from a forgery in late antiquity, by the time of Charlemagne at the latest it had nevertheless gained general acceptance. The most important consequence of this event was indeed the introduction of church reform to Rome; the papacy had finally been wrested from the grasp of the local nobility and the traditional Roman clans; not only this, but the rights of the emperor had also been pushed back. Once again, as under Otto III, when the secular Holy Roman Emperor attempted to purge the Roman church of the aristocratic feuding of the Eternal City, non-Romans were elevated to the throne of Saint Peter. On this occasion too, this move was not without its risks! The first of these men to be enthroned in the Lateran church, Clement II, formerly Bishop Suidger of Bamberg, was poisoned in 1047; his remains are interred back in Bamberg and still bear witness to the unnatural cause of his death; his successor, who reigned for just a few years as Victor II, was Bishop Gebhard of Eichstätt; finally, after the Romans had lobbied in vain for Halinard of Lyons, the cousin of the emperor, Brun of Toul from Alsace, ascended the throne of Saint Peter. He called himself Leo IX, and with his accession to power the papacy put itself at the very head of the reform movement. The monarchy, however, saw itself driven ever further into secularity.

A batch of newly created cardinals, whom Henry III had put forward and Leo IX had then instituted, brought Lotharingian reformers to Rome. It was as a result of this that such men as Frederick of Lotharingia ended up in Rome, or Humbert, who later became the cardinal-bishop of Silvia Candia and acted as one of the foremost advisors of Leo IX. Italy as a whole stood on the verge of far-reaching changes. Dangers were mounting above all in the south of the peninsula. There, Normans had invaded, the descendants of former Vikings, seized certain areas as sovereign territory and, having been recognized by Emperor Henry III, now sought the same recognition from the pope. However, Leo was disinclined to accede to their wishes. To the contrary, experienced as he was in military command, he assembled an army—of bandits and robbers, as people would subsequently complain—and attacked the invaders. This was the first campaign in history to be fought under papal leadership and the sacred banner of Saint Peter—an initial step in the development of the concept of the Crusade. This enterprise, though, was to end in a debacle.

Yet it all began so harmlessly and happily. On their return from the Holy Land in 1016, forty Norman pilgrims from Normandy, brave old campaigners one and all, supposedly put in at Salerno. To the Lombard prince Guaimar III who ruled Sicily at the time, they appeared as his salvation from dire straits, for his capital was being besieged by Saracens, and with the help of the Normans he was able to break their siege. After they had gone home, Guaimar later sent emissaries to Normandy to recruit more knights for the defense of Sicily. In the event, he would have been well advised not to have done so. Some 250 fighters, eager to escape the strict rule of their own duke, are said to have heeded Guaimar's call; as they passed through Rome, they were given the pope's blessing. In the south, they were first sent into action against Byzantine forces, which still laid claim to Calabria; despite defeat at the hands of the Greeks, the Normans still managed to gain a foothold in Aversa. Presently, an ever-growing number of their compatriots took refuge in southern Italy from the tyranny of their ruler. Foremost among these banished Normans were the ten sons of Tancred of Hauteville, led by William Iron Arm; these warriors distinguished themselves in battles against the Saracens. They are believed to have brought around 300–500 Norman knights with them. They soon came to hold their Lombard commander in disdain and started to fight for their own benefit. By the time Iron Arm died (1045), he was count of Apulia; his brother Drogo inherited his lands and title. Another of the Hauteville brothers was Robert Guiscard, whom the German writer Heinrich von Kleist (1777–1811) planned to immortalize in a tragedy (which was never finished). Guiscard succeeded in taking control of Calabria following victories over both the Byzantines and the Saracens. Pope Leo duly appeared at the head of his force, but suffered a crushing defeat—immediately ascribed by contemporaries to the godlessness of his bandit army—at the Battle of Civitate in 1051. Leo was taken prisoner, and was fortunate in that the Normans paid him due respect as Saint Peter's successor; they were primarily concerned to gain legitimacy and recognition for the lands and booty they had taken.

After his defeat, Leo IX threw himself into the business of church reform, even more single-mindedly than before. As they began to take effect, these reforms caused quite a stir. "The Holy Roman church is to be revered and loved, not because Rome was built on sand by Romulus and Remus but because it was built on the Rock of Christ by saints Peter and Paul." Thus wrote Cardinal Humbert of Silvia Candia, in his compendium of all available information on the office of primate of the Roman church and its incumbent.[12] Over time, a lively industry in producing polemical pamphlets arose, and nowhere were the advances in literacy more apparent than in the ensuing flood of scurrilous tracts that swamped the German kingdom not least of all; political differences between the king and some of his lords further exacerbated this overheated debate. In Rome, too, commentators were sharpening their pens ready to weigh into the controversy. Humbert himself played a prominent role. His *Three Books against the Simonists* were a clear and comprehensive summary of the demands of those who opposed this practice, which derived its name from Simon Magus in the Gospels, who offered to buy from Simon Peter the apostle's gift of miraculous healing. Humbert's tracts helped formulate a clear and irrevocable line against this sin, of which the cardinal identified three distinct forms. The first of these was the purchase of holy offices with money; the second a verbal form of simony through false promises; and the third through gifts or actions such as presents or services.

Alongside simony, "Nicolaitism" also came in for severe criticism. This was the name of a heretical sect cited in the Book of Revelation (2:6, 15; also in the Acts of the Apostles 6:5), but it was only during the church reforms of the eleventh century that this became identified with married priests or those living in a state of concubinage. This controversy marked the beginning of the struggle over priestly celibacy. Nowhere in the dogma of the early church fathers had this been mentioned as a requirements for priests; only now did it become a peculiarity of Catholic ecclesiastical law, marking a clear deviation from the practice of Orthodox Christianity and so driving an even deeper wedge between the Eastern and Western churches. Later, in the thirteenth century, this issue would prove to be the stumbling block to a unification of the two churches. Yet now, as it was implemented, it served the objectives of church reform. Altar service demanded purity and sexual immaculacy. The priest was supposed to be married only to his church, and not to be a "bigamist." Women who cohabited with priests were seen as the epitome of whores, and the children of priests as bastards. Certainly, material reasons also militated in favor of priests being unmarried. Bachelorhood preserved the church's wealth from being whittled away through inheritances to priests' offspring. Even so, in pressing through this reform, the church created a weighty burden for itself in the future. As immediately became evident, realization of the ideal of celibacy was illusory. Indeed, by the fifteenth century, the end of the Middle Ages, no question was to occupy the papal court so much as recognizing the legitimacy of priests' sons (primarily so that they might be ordained as priests themselves). One of the most famous such cases concerned the great humanist thinker Erasmus of Rotterdam.[13]

Yet the Eastern church, which was accused of a lack of orthodoxy, also found itself facing tough challenges. The old bone of contention of the missing *filioque* in the Creed and the dispute concerning whether leavened or unleavened bread should be used in the Communion (the so-called Azym Question) provided ample scope for mutual suspicion. But in actual fact the matter that brought the Eastern and Western patriarchs to loggerheads over was the priority in the hierarchy. Should Rome or Constantinople occupy the highest position? In order to supply an answer to this thorny question, the document called the "Constitutum Constantini" (Donation of Constantine) was unearthed from the archives in Rome—probably by Humbert—and adduced as evidence against the case of the *basileus* and the Orthodox patriarchs. This caused a schism between West and East, with the two primates, Michael Kerullarios and Leo IX, excommunicating each other (1054). These execrations did not come out of the blue for Christians; they had been building for a long time, and were symptoms of a long-lasting alienation rather than a sudden outbreak of hostilities, a direct consequence of the papal universal episcopacy, as Western reformers saw it when they made realization of this ideal their key objective, just as Byzantium utterly rejected it.

During this period of momentous upheaval and change—upon which schools, urban culture, and a growing professionalization of intellectual elites all left their mark—the monarchy and the papacy came across as fossilized relics. It was vital that they now fall in line with these developments and evolve. This happened only partially, though, with the educated ecclesiastical powers that be embracing change at an earlier stage and more wholeheartedly than the largely illiterate secular powers, who remained dependent on clerics for their doctrines and exegeses. In particular, the Salian monarchy made heavy weather of this change. This dynasty was affected especially profoundly, inasmuch as Otto III and to an even greater extent Henry II, the last representatives of the Liudolfing line, relied heavily on the great imperial churches, monasteries, and bishoprics. These two kings had assigned to these ecclesiastical institutions all manner of dispositions, such as counties, forests, and various other sovereign territories, which they transferred to the incumbent of the respective church office at the same time as they invested them with their spiritual authority through the gift of the crozier and ring. In return, those elected to these offices gave their oath of fealty or allegiance and undertook to perform the corresponding services. Power of dispensation over the offices of abbot and bishop were thus a matter of vital concern for the monarchy.

But it was precisely the assigning of ecclesiastical offices by the king that the church reformers had been railing against from the mid-eleventh century on. They feared for the freedom of the church if it was too closely allied to the king and called for a total separation, not merely for the church to renounce the endowment of any lands belonging to the king. Granted, the king was anointed and consecrated, too; since Ottonian times, the monarch had been regarded as "God's Anointed One." Yet this anointment did not culminate in altar service or any other spiritual function whatsoever. Thus, as the reformers saw it, the king remained nothing but a simple lay person, however much he might argue to the contrary. There was clearly need for fundamental clarification in this matter, and indeed this was not long in arriving.

The "two powers doctrine" of Saint Gelasius was invoked once more. Priests and worldly authority should be separated, with the priesthood taking precedence; this had always been the traditional position, and this was the line taken by the reformers as they reappraised the old values. Apposite metaphors and images were readily to hand; the Old and New Testaments offered them—albeit modified—in abundance. Thus, there was talk of the "proper entry through the gate," of the two swords, and of the pope as the head of the body of Christ. One of Pope Gregory VII's favorite maxims was that Christ had not said that he was the "Custom" but the "Truth." Attempts to more closely define the content of the "Truth" then ensued by means of new norms and values and through the binding power of the successor of Saint Peter to impose interpretations. In return, as if in a dialectical process, the formation of a monarchical papacy led to the demarcation of a worldly sphere with its own legitimacy. In the process, the methods of early scholasticism proved to be an aid to the growing specialization of the language of the ecclesiastical and worldly realms.

Nor did this fundamental reappraisal of the nature of the church spare the very center of the institution, the papal palace. Quite the opposite, in fact: this place in particular was in dire need of purging reforms; the means by which popes were chosen especially required an overhaul. The pillars of the living God, it was claimed, looked battered and in danger of collapsing, while the net of the supreme fisherman was at risk of sinking amid a shipwreck. So, in order to refresh the spiritual order, and to guard against the "depravity of evil, hostile men" and facilitate a "clean, sound, and corruption-free election," Pope Nicholas II issued an Election Decretal (1059), which really did represent a radical break with tradition.[14] Hitherto, the choice of a new pope had fallen to the clergy and the people of Rome, which in practice meant the urban aristocracy of the city. Henceforth, the cardinal bishops were to meet and discuss candidates for the papacy before summoning the other cardinals and finally the clergy and the laity of Rome to give their assent. In addition, the right of the king and future emperor, at the time the nine-year-old Henry IV, to be involved in the election was also, albeit very imprecisely, taken into consideration—the very last time this would happen. For the time being, election of the cardinal deacons was not mentioned; over the ensuing decades, though, they were also included. The precise number of votes needed to elect a pope was not yet stipulated—as a result of disagreement among the cardinals, not outside intervention—a factor that set in train a full century of papal schisms and seriously threatened the unity of the Latin church, until the Peace of Venice was concluded between Pope Alexander II and Frederick Barbarossa in 1177. But the principle of having the cardinals exclusively elect the pope has remained in force, right up to the present day; never again after 1177 would an emperor have any involvement in the choice of a pontiff.

The first people to benefit from this reform were the cardinals themselves. In a process that was only hastened by the schisms, the cardinal deacons attained widespread parity with the two other ranks of cardinal. The designation "cardinal" came from the original function of these priests; they were "incardinated" into (that is, placed under the jurisdiction of) one of the churches within the precincts of Rome. The seven bishops of the suburbicarian sees (Ostia, Palestrina, Sabina, Porto and Rufina, Albano, Velletri, and Frascati) were required to officiate as representatives of the pope at the weekly liturgical service at the cathedral church of Rome, Saint John Lateran. Meanwhile, every day each of the priests of the parish or titular churches in the city, twenty-eight in total, would officiate at one of the weekly or hebdomadal services held in one of the four patriarchal churches (Saint Peter's, San Paolo dentra le mura, San Lorenzo fuori le mura, and Santa Maria Maggiore). The final group was the cardinal deacons, who were in charge of the ministration stations in the then eighteen or nineteen suburbs of the city. Thus, when all the positions were filled (which was seldom the case) there were just over fifty cardinals in all.

The church reforms transformed the cardinals' college into the "Papal Senate," the collective executive committee of the Roman and hence the Universal church, which gained ever greater influence over all decisions of the Apostolic See. The distribution of privileges, as evidenced by the list of cardinals' signatures at the bottom of all papal documents (a practice that began at this time), legal decisions, the formulation of decretals, and papal policies—henceforth, everything was agreed upon beforehand with the cardinals. The cardinals also constituted the Papal Court (Consistory), which from the twelfth century on was deluged with an increasing number of cases from all over Europe—not just regarding ecclesiastical matters. Parallel with this, the Roman–canonical trial became the authoritative form of hearing for all ecclesiastical cases and furthermore for secular law as well.

By the time the new Electoral Decretal was promulgated, one man had already attained a position of overriding influence within the papal patriarchy, and became a decisive figure in shaping the future of the church: Archdeacon Hildebrand. In his dealings with Pope Nicholas, Hildebrand had, so the rumor went, "fed him like an ass in the stable," while one of his compatriots in Rome, Cardinal Petrus Damiani, called him a "holy Satan." He was no scholar, not even a dialectician, but was a staunch ambassador of the Roman church, who was well versed in the traditional prerogatives of his church and in these spiritually turbulent times knew how to say the right thing and translate it into action. Moreover, he was a sworn enemy of all simony and married priests, of whom there were many at this time, yet he was also a man who deeply divided opinions. In 1073, the cardinals elected him Pope Gregory VII. He turned out to be one of the great revolutionaries of world history, but he achieved his aims not through force of arms but rather through taking hold of old, rediscovered doctrines and putting them into practice, with a clear sense of his own objectives and an unbending will for reform.

6

"The True Emperor Is the Pope"

CHRIST WAS the body and the pope the head of the universal church. Mysticism was made real, with all that that implied; it was as old as the church and yet still managed to appear revolutionary each time it was realized afresh. Now, in the late eleventh century, thanks to Gregory VII's efforts, the universal church assumed the form that it would basically retain for the whole of the ensuing millennium. The church's agenda emerges clearly from the twenty-seven guiding principles enunciated in Gregory VII's *Dictatus Papae* of 1075—a mysterious document, since it was addressed to no one yet was subsumed into the records of papal correspondence without any further explanation. These guidelines stressed the monarchical exclusivity of the pope and, as a consequence, the subservience and unquestioning obedience of the entire church, namely all prelates and lay people including the king. The *Dictatus* stipulates "that the Roman church was founded by God alone (1); that the only person legally entitled to be known as the universal pontiff is the pope in Rome (2); that he is solely empowered to dismiss bishops and reinstate them (3); that he can depose the absent (5); that for him alone is it lawful to make new laws, according to the needs of the time (7); that he alone may use the imperial insignia (8); that all princes shall only kiss the feet of the pope (9); that he has the power to depose emperors (12); that no synod may be deemed a general one [namely, a *concilium*] without his say-so (16); that no chapter and no book shall be considered canonical without his authority (17); that a sentence passed by him cannot be retracted by anyone, but that he alone can rescind the judgments passed by others (18); that he may be judged by no one (19); that the Roman church is never in error and, as Holy Scripture attests, never shall be so to all eternity (22); that the Roman pope, as soon he has been canonically ordained, shall undoubtedly be made a saint through the good offices of Saint Peter (23); that anyone who is in disagreement with the Roman church shall not be considered righteous [Catholic] (26); and that has the power to absolve subjects from their oath of fealty to unjust men (27)." All these guiding principles have precursors and a long history, and yet the brusque manner in which Gregory formulated them and the consistency with which he subjugated all the institutions of the church to them and imposed his new order indicate that his pontificate was a turning point in the history of the papacy and of the Catholic church. "The Roman church opens and closes the Gates of Heaven to whomsoever it chooses according to its unique privilege," is another principle stated elsewhere, but fully in keeping with Gregory's edicts.[1] Rarely have so few words summed up in its entirety the change from one era to another and, moreover, one of the greatest revolutions in European history.

To be sure, these principles reflected legal norms, but nevertheless did not themselves gain widespread acceptance as such; Gregory did not issue any papal decretals. Even so, the papal universal episcopate was henceforth constituted rationally and in an increasingly legalistic fashion. The sources from which Gregory may have gleaned his knowledge of canon law—possibly from a compendium known to scholars in this field as the *Collection in Seventy-Four Titles*—is uncertain and ultimately immaterial. He thought more in spiritual than in juristic terms, despite the fact that he provided the initial impetus to the systematic collections of canon law that now began to be laid down. He was primarily concerned about the "perilous times" through which the world was passing as it came to its end. For instance, Gregory, who was fond of quoting Scripture,[2] believed that the last of the signs that Jesus Christ himself revealed would herald the coming of the Antichrist and the Day of Judgment—"the love of many will grow cold"—had already come to fruition. His actions were protection against the End Times. The church had to be prepared for this. "We who are charged above all others with the care of the Lord's flock, must . . . keep watch; for it seems to us far preferable to confirm God's justice through new measures than to let men's souls go to perdition along with laws that have fallen into disrepute."[3]

The church therefore had to be prepared, while its head, the universal pope, "the servant of the servants of God," had to be responsible for this state of readiness by effecting a correct order of things in the temporal world; accordingly, everything had to be made subservient to this head. Gregory's predecessor Alexander II had already identified portents of the impending advent of the Antichrist in the great increase in simony and a massive upsurge in those professing "Nicolaitism." "Who knows how little time we have remaining before God comes down to Earth to judge the world," warned Petrus Damiani. Concerns about spiritual purity were also much in evidence at this time, as expressed in the strict demand for celibacy (now firmly enforced) for the entire clergy and especially among priests. The methods that Gregory VII employed brought about a new centralization within the church. The concept of the papal monarchy, which had been a dictum of the church for centuries, now became a reality. In its external manifestation, it took its cue extensively from the secular role of emperor.

However, Gregory was far from throwing down any gauntlet to the Holy Roman Empire; rather the church, the body of Christ, was seen as overarching all earthly powers, be they of a priestly or a lay class. Now, in imitation of the "royal court," the former *Patriarchum* was now transformed into the Roman Curia *(Curia Romana)*, and in the process became an agency with the authority of central leadership and was furnished with armies of professional notaries and other functionaries. Whenever a new incumbent ascended the Petrine Throne, the start of the chosen candidate's term of office was marked by a coronation with a "crown," the papal cap *(regnum)*, and a tiara, which over the succeeding two centuries was reshaped into a triple crown. Gradually, papal ceremony was divested of its early mediaeval features. The processional nature of the papal service marking the Stations of the Cross, which had lent ritual observance a particular character and bound each bishop directly with his city, was increasingly scaled down and soon abandoned entirely. For, the reasoning went, the bishop of Rome was the pontiff of the whole world anyway.

Innovations were implemented beyond the bounds of the cities, too. As representatives of the pope, legates with wide-ranging powers were dispatched to oversee the episcopate and the regional synods. At the same time, this system of legates effectively meant that the papacy and papal power became ubiquitous; the legates were soon joined by a judicial apparatus comprising judges delegated by the Apostolic See. Both of these institutions offered an effective means of establishing firm papal leadership of the church and realizing the papal universal episcopate.[4] In addition, consistent with this goal and under pain of punishment, Gregory VII required that all metropolitans and bishops should come to Rome on a regular basis to attend the Lenten Synods and the Synods of Legates; anyone who was absent without an acceptable excuse risked suspension, deposition, and excommunication. This demand, which went far beyond any existing conventions, provoked anger and opposition. "This dangerous man [that is, Gregory] wants to order bishops about as though they were his bailiffs," wrote Archbishop Liemar of Bremen to Bishop Hezilo of Hildesheim after Liemar was suspended in 1075. Liemar went on: "And if they do not do everything that he wishes, then they have to come to Rome or be suspended without trial."[5] And yet, as happened so often, animosities within the German episcopate prevented it from adopting a united front against Gregory. Liemar, too, was forced to climb down. In France, however, there was a better understanding of Gregory's aims, and the clergy there largely shared and applauded them.

No less significant for the future of the papacy were the development that occurred in Rome itself during this period. The *Patrimonium Petri* and the other possessions of the Apostolic See now became—undoubtedly in imitation of the Holy Roman Empire—the *Regalia b. Petri,* and (possibly harking back to the Donation of Constantine) were made the inalienable sovereign property of the Apostolic See. For the ninth-century *Constitutum Constantini,* which had only been rediscovered during the course of a dispute with Constantinople, was now subject to a new interpretation conditioned by a fundamental change in the history of ideas, a reinterpretation which—in the so-called Leo-Humbert version—even made itself apparent in the text of the document, since it transformed the allocation of patriarchate rights by the Pseudo-Constantine, which had been relevant in terms of canon law, into an actual conferring of authority on the papacy by the emperor. It was this emendation that first turned the original text into the notorious Donation of Constantine. Awareness of this—regardless of whether it was based on an intimate knowledge of the text or not—now quickly spread far and wide. This fabricated document still antagonized church reformers in the sixteenth century (when it had only just been exposed as a forgery). Admittedly, Gregory VII appears not to have drawn on this document as a basis for his reform plans, or to try and legitimize them.[6] Direct consequences from the Donation were first drawn under the rule of Pope Urban II, who in 1098 laid claim to all the islands of the Earth, thereby establishing an idiosyncratic theory of islands, which was still operative in 1493 when Pope Alexander VI divided the world up between Portugal and Spain (Treaty of Tordesillas).[7] In general terms, indeed, it is true to say that the papacy had no need of the forgery to legitimize itself. Rather, it appealed to the tradition of the Roman church and to Christ's words to Saint Peter: "And I also say unto Thee that Thou art Peter and upon this rock I will build my church." (Matthew 16:18). These words now increasingly came to be interpreted in a legalistic way.

Sooner or later, the demand for "freedom of the church," the inflexibility of Gregory VII, and the traditional hegemony of kings and princes over the church would clash and set in motion the most serious of conflicts. Henry IV's disputes with his Saxon adversaries and the sheer inexperience of this monarch, who was then just twenty-five years old, only served to accelerate this process. Conflict with the pope flared up in 1075, when Henry intervened to occupy vacant dioceses within the domain of the *Patrimonium Petri* and also attempted to impose his chosen candidate upon the see of Saint Ambrose in Milan. The ill-advised monarch misread the situation and overestimated the extent of his power. He imagined he might rule Italy from Germany, assert his wishes in the teeth of opposition in Milan from the *Pataria*—the first known popular religious movement of the Middle Ages, which was predisposed toward radical reform—unilaterally appoint an archbishop of his own in that city against the express wishes of the pope, and finally even be strong enough to depose the pope himself (1076). From far-off Worms, the king fancied he might be in a position to threaten the pope and browbeat him into abdicating from the Apostolic Throne: "I Henry, king by the grace of God, do say unto thee, together with all our bishops: Step down, step down!" Gregory VII's instant response was to make a solemn supplication to the assembled cardinals at the Lenten Synod in Rome, which pronounced Henry's excommunication, and to ban him, by virtue of the power invested in him by Saint Peter to appoint or dismiss monarchs, from exercising any further royal authority. In other words, Gregory's pronouncement amounted to a dismissal, or at very least a suspension of the king. The effect of this was immense. Latin Christendom, indeed the whole world, was shaken to the core.

The beginnings of propaganda were evident in the ensuing exchange of manifestos and proclamations, which soon found widespread distribu-

tion. Indeed, with and through church reform a radical structural transformation of the public sphere made itself apparent, and in the period that
followed it only deepened to a point where it could no longer be effaced.
This development was due not least to the new urban society that had grown
up, and pointed, as it were, to a profound societal shift toward modernization and to the establishment of corresponding intellectual elites through
Europe, who began communicating with one another. They sharpened
their pens and started to engage in a lively exchange of opinions and re-
buttals, objective analyses and polemics, which were disseminated around
the world. As a forum for their views, these scholars used sermons, open
letters and pamphlets; the art of rhetoric and the art of dictation (*Ars dictandi* and *Ars arengandi*) taught in schools proved a fertile seedbed, while
historiography, which at first was taught only in monasteries but later
flourished in towns, was the grateful beneficiary of such training. The
populace were overwhelmed with a veritable flood of polemics and treatises; in consequence, public opinion came into being as a distinct phenomenon, and immediately found itself exposed to manipulation from all
sides. Henceforth, everything that had to do with the monarchy or the
papacy, and everything that united or divided secular and ecclesiastical
authority, or prompted them to cooperate or conflict, became the subject
of intense interest among these elites and those who acted on their instructions. The long series of papal schisms that took place in the eleventh
and twelfth centuries served to further entrench these developments, and
in the thirteenth and fourteenth centuries, Italy resounded to the orotund
manifestos of both imperial and papal propaganda.

As it turned out, Henry IV had acted precipitately. His following
quickly dwindled, especially once his old adversaries, the kings of Saxony,
Bavaria, and Swabia became restive once more and this time, legitimized
in their campaign by Henry's excommunication, managed to garner even
greater support.[8] This must have opened the king's eyes. True, the following events have all been distorted, sometimes to the point of becoming
unrecognizable, by being passed through the prism of historical accounts
that are for the most part one-sidedly against the king, and that have also
often been written at considerable distance in time from the actual event
and under false premises. But if we cannot trust the antimonarchical pro-
pagandistic version of events that was generated in the eleventh century,
and spread by historians from the sixteenth century on, and which basically still shapes our view of the incident today—or still less that version

that became one of the founding myths of the "second" German Empire, namely the Protestant–Prussian war cry "We're not going to go to Canossa!"—we have no choice but to heed those contemporary witnesses who followed events from close at hand.

Henry realized his mistake as early as the summer of 1076. Taking the advice of his godfather, the senior abbot Hugo von Cluny, his mother, and his closest relative in Italy, the margravine Matilda of Canossa, feelers were put out to try and find a way of healing the rift. Gregory too was concerned to restore peace, though admittedly not at the price of sacrificing the "freedom of the church." His true enemy was not in fact the German king but rather the world that lay beyond the reach of the church—false Christians, the sworn adversaries of the Apostolic Prince and his teachings, and the enemies of justice. A face-to-face meeting with the king was agreed, and at the same time papal mediation was arranged to settle the clash between Henry and his opponents within his own realm. Henry's domestic enemies fully expected the pope to sweep in and issue a resounding condemnation of Henry, and they made preparations for choosing a new Holy Roman Emperor.

In actual fact, Gregory gave the "Germans" clear advance notice of his arrival. The letter he wrote stands as a key piece of evidence testifying to the self-awareness of this powerful pope. Even the manner in which he addressed them and the formulaic salutations he offered were unusual and never repeated in any of the missives he subsequently sent to the Germans: "To all those," his words run, "in the whole kingdom of Germany who are defending and keeping the faith and teaching of Christ and of Saint Peter, the prince of the apostles, greeting and the blessing of the blessed apostles Peter and Paul, also the absolution of all their sins." The blessings and the letter alike were addressed equally to the priesthood and the laity. No other papal missive began in this way, namely with the word "I" *(Ego)* which was customarily reserved for oaths or used in the parables of Christ. "I such as I am, a priest and servant of the prince of the apostles . . . am coming to you!" *Venio ad vos!*—this was a "messianic formulation" if ever there was one. "I am coming to you, ready to suffer death for the honor of God and the salvation of your souls, even as Christ laid down his life for us. For your part, my brothers whom I love and long for, strive by all means to ensure that I may with God's help come to you and profit you in all things. May he bless you by whose grace it was said to me at the body of Saint Peter on the day of my ordination: "Whatsoever you bless shall be blessed, and whatsoever you loose upon earth shall be loosed in heaven." Here, Gregory was proclaiming an epiphany, in imitation of Christ he was prophesying a ritual theophany.[9]

Understandably, the king stayed clear of the initial meeting arranged on German soil between the pope and the princes, which was held in Augsburg, right in his enemies' center of power, and instead without their knowledge hurried after the pope as he headed back to Italy. They met at Canossa, a fortress and monastery complex belonging to Matilda, in 1077. Henry sent his godfather Hugo of Cluny ahead as a courier to lay the preparatory groundwork for this meeting. After three days of symbolic penance, Henry's excommunication was lifted, and the pope and king concluded a treaty in which Henry agreed to stop supporting the Lombard enemies of the pope, including Archbishop Tedald of Milan, whom Henry himself had appointed. In return, Gregory pledged to do the same vis-à-vis the king's enemies. At the end of their meeting, Henry wanted to accompany the pope back across the Alps for a joint meeting with the German princes, but the opponents of both men thwarted this final success by taking prisoner the papal legates and electing Rudolf of Rheinfelden as a rival king, acts that undermined the peace treaty that had just been signed.

It was only after this incident that the conflict came to a head, despite the fact that at first the king and the pope did not get involved. The ripples caused by the dispute soon touched the whole of Europe, though France and England were less affected by them than the Salian empire, and Spain first came fully under the aegis of the Roman church during Gregory's papacy. Civil war raged in large parts of Germany and Italy. The Benedictine monks of Hirsau left their monastery and went out to preach to the public against Henry IV, "in contravention of the divine order of things, and undermining both the empire and the church," as their enemies claimed.[10] It took until 1080 for Gregory VII to excommunicate Henry for a second time, but the sanction had lost much of its sting through being repeated. Meanwhile, just a few years later, after leading a campaign against Rome and capturing the city, Henry appointed his own antipope, Clement III, who crowned him Holy Roman Emperor in 1084. Though Henry garnered little support in the long term, he did force Gregory to flee to Salerno, where he died in 1085, stubborn to the last. His last words were reputed to have been "I loved justice and hated iniquity, and that is why I am dying in exile." These are an adaptation of Psalm 45, and everyone who knew their prayers could readily supply the unspoken end of the original verse in the psalm; "therefore God, thy God, hath anointed thee with the oil of gladness." Gregory, banished as he saw it for upholding the freedom of the church, was filled not with bitterness but a sense of joyous hope, and saw himself as an instrument of the Lord.

Looking back, the historian Bishop Otto von Freising, who compiled a chronicle of the world shortly before 1150, recognized in the conflict that raged during the time of Gregory VII and his own grandfather Henry IV—a conflict that he regarded as over for the time being but still as a portent of the impending End Time—a "struggle concerning the Investiture." Thereafter, German historians in particular exalted this designation into the epoch-making concept of the Investiture Controversy. However, this view of the matter only touches upon one aspect of what was at stake, and even then not the most important, for the entire edifice of the Latin church—the papacy, canon law, and ecclesiology—was reformed by the clash. It seems more apposite to talk about an Era of Church Reform, or a Rediscovery of the Church, and of a return to the universality that defined its very essence, and the resultant consequences. Indeed, it would be no exaggeration to speak of a Church Revolution.

In fact this radical upheaval in the church's conception of its self threatened the fundamental being of the Salian empire. The first proscriptions against investiture can be dated to 1075, and in 1078 they were enshrined in the general canon law. They must have had an especially debilitating effect on a kingdom that relied upon its control over the great imperial churches. It could not countenance releasing these into a state of independence. In France and England, by contrast, bishoprics and monasteries were by no means furnished with such extensive sovereign rights as they had been in Germany since the Late Ottonian period. Nevertheless, a widespread conflict flared up, whose inevitable outcome was one that demarcated the "freedom of the church" from the sovereignty of secular rule, established those separate rights as inalienable (even when such rights were delegated to churches), and gave rise to new patterns of order.

It was necessary to discover theoretical solutions that would fracture traditional ways of thinking. This could not be done simply by dividing the property of the church into its spiritual possessions *(Spiritualia)* and its worldly holdings *(Temporalia)*. Not even the further distinction between on the one hand *Temporalia* in votive offerings by the faithful (which as such were to be counted as *Spiritualia*) and on the other allocations of funds by monarchs to churches would suffice. Thirty years of conceptual wrangling were to elapse before the inalienability of those things that the king assigned to the church was established, namely the rights devolving exclusively to the king *(Regalia)*. Indeed, this may be seen as having carved out for the very first time the concept of the empire as a legal entity in own right—a decisive step in the conception of the political organization as an independent legal person. The Concordat of Worms in 1122 was able to take its point of reference from here; yet not all legal scholars subscribed to the theory of *Regalia*, nor did every contemporary understand it.

Cardinal Petrus Damiani had developed a political "doctrine of the two swords" from the account of the Last Supper in the Saint Luke's Gospel (22:35–8), according to which any ruler was to be deemed fortunate, who could unite the "sword of kingship" with the "sword of priesthood" in such as way that the latter would temper the former, while conversely the king's sword would sharpen that of the priest.[11] It was not stated who had originally conferred the two swords, especially the sword of kingship. Yet the church had immediately, in a hierocratic sense, claimed both swords, the *gladium spiritualis* and the *gladium materialis,* for itself, in order to be able to confer the latter on secular rulers (including the pope investing the emperor with one). In this sense, as one anonymous canonist expressly put it in the early twelfth century, it appeared that the pope was the true emperor. In this context, the Donation of Constantine could serve as a way of corroborating the ecclesiastical-papal power of disposition over the worldly sword. Henry IV and his religious aides appealed in vain to Gelasius's doctrine of the Two Powers, which conceived of each of the two swords, and hence each of the two distinct powers having been placed directly in men's hands by God. The monastic doctrine gained precedence and, strengthened by papal decretals, was adopted into general canon law. This was the cause of endless controversies concerning the supposedly divine immediacy of worldly power.

Doctrines such as these forced the monarchy ever deeper into secularism, while at the same time the church became thoroughly clericalized. In the last decade of the eleventh century, Manegold, the prior of the foundation at Lautenbach in the Vosges—a formerly much-vaunted, dialectically schooled peripatetic teacher, who had admittedly foresworn dialectics—devised a theory of royal authority that was more radically secular than any that had gone before it, so much so that the institution was positively consigned wholly to the worldly realm. Manegold demanded that incumbents of the royal office display wisdom, justice, and piety. Kings were elected, he claimed, in order to punish reprobates and protect the virtuous. If a king should abrogate his duty, then his subjects should consider themselves absolved of all obligation to be obedient, since the king had broken the very compact he had been elected to uphold *(Pactum, pro quo constitutus est)*. Nor, in order to illustrate his contention that such "tyrants" could be deposed, did this high-profile publicist for church reform shrink from comparing kings with the lowliest of servants, who stood on the lowest rung of the social ladder, and who would be dismissed and deprived of his earnings if he should ever willfully leave his flock to their own devices—in other words, Manegold dared to equate kings with swineherds. It was quite right, he went on, that Henry should have been stripped of his office—Henry the nun-violator, the arsonist, the sodomite, he called him.[12] There was no hint in this diatribe of the notion of the king as "God's Anointed One," the *Christus per Gratiam,* as a few isolated voices in the church still described the monarch. The elected king now simply appeared as the servant of his electors, and resistance against him was perfectly admissible, if he should break the electoral compact.

All these disputes had far-reaching consequences. The demand for freedom was not confined to the church, but spilled over into society at large, and became a fundamental postulate of European history. It coincided with a thirst for freedom in the cities, in the bourgeoisie, and among the intellectual clergy. In this process, the two powers of the "church" and the "state" monitored one another, held each other in check, and in the long term prevented either of them from attaining a monopolistic position from which it could control everything. Independent of all questions of faith, this led to a general dismantling of hierarchies in everyday life and in the political sphere, legitimized the opposition to "tyrants" and, with its tentative conceptions of the electoral compact and the social contract, genuinely helped pave the way for thinking in terms of the "state."

The growing encroachment of legal process and legal language upon ecclesiastical affairs set in at the same time as the church began to reform, and it was scarcely a surprise that the following centuries witnessed an exponential increase in ever more systematically organized collections of canon law, and that the discipline of jurisprudence that developed at the same time also embraced ecclesiastical doctrine. Gregory himself was not able to use any of these collections. The first of them was compiled by

Bishop Anselm II of Lucca (d. 1086), a close confidant of this pope, but almost certainly only sometime after 1083. This was followed by the compilation of Cardinal Deusdedit, and then the outstanding figure of Bishop Ivo of Chartres with his *Decretum* and *Panormia*. Pseudo-Isidore, too, was discovered for the church; henceforth, no prelate would be able to get by without consulting professional authorities of canon law. Especially in France, where the rather humble dioceses—in terms of property law— bore no comparison with the principalities of the German prelates, theological or legal studies became an indispensable prerequisite for any ecclesiastical career, right up to the office of bishop, while the German dioceses and princely abbeys largely remained aristocratic churches whose prelates were raised to the status of lords of the manor.

The pope as the true emperor brought the world no peace. He fought for the freedom of the church, for a new claim to precedence over the worldly powers. But did he really free the church from its bondage? Doubts were raised, and criticism began to be voiced even within the ranks of the clergy, centering first on the contradiction between a rich, powerful, and worldly-wise clergy and the apostolic early church, and second on the feudal lifestyle of many prelates. In Milan, opposition arose first among the lower classes. Yet this grassroots movement, known as the *Pataria,* failed and was ultimately absorbed into a reform movement controlled by the papacy, and so never slipped into heresy, though its most radical activists did trample underfoot the sacraments of unworthy priests, namely those who were indulging in sins of the flesh. The clashes between the pope and the king only exacerbated such expressions of discontent and lent them a political edge. Notions of the revival of the apostolic church, and of voluntary actual and not just symbolic poverty (as had hitherto been the case) were voiced. These notions immediately found themselves at variance with the elevation of the church in general to a position of huge wealth and power. And so, before long, criticism the imperial papacy was indeed taken up as a rallying cry by truly heretical movements. These critics identified the cause and beginning of the church's decline in the Donation of Constantine. Yet preachers of repentance also made their voices heard at this time.

Religious unrest and the desire for a radical break with established practices became widespread. Notions of imitating the life of Christ found concrete expression in the urge to pursue a *vita apostolica* in a state of apostolic poverty. Such modes of existence became popular particularly in France in the final decades of the eleventh century. They can be interpreted as indications that it was no longer just the aristocracy but the entire populace that was gripped by this religious movement that was taking place outside the walls of the monasteries. On occasion, its protagonists would teeter on the edge of heresy or descend fully into it. A series of itinerant preachers offered literal interpretations of the Bible, living strictly in accordance with its commandments and encouraging the people to do likewise. One of these was Robert of Arbrissel, who roamed the countryside and preached repentance—dressed in rags and accompanied by a throng of men and women, including some noblemen. Finally, in 1098, he founded the abbey of Fontevrault near Poitiers, a religious institution for both men and women, which included houses for lepers and repentant whores; Robert entrusted the running of the abbey to two women and went on to found further monasteries, which he also had run by women. The poverty movement thus ultimately became a religious women's movement. Another preacher was Peter the Hermit, who rode around on a mule, with a shock of unkempt hair, brandished a document he claimed had divine authorship, and recruited believers for the First Crusade; ultimately, he was to lead his poor followers to destruction by the Turks as they attempted to reach Jerusalem (the so-called People's Crusade of 1096). Indeed, many of the early crusaders may well have been inspired to go on this venture not by a papal sermon but by listening to the messages of ragged preachers such as these. Another, somewhat later, preacher of this kind was Tanchelm of Antwerp, who inspired by the Holy Ghost and (it was said) married to the Virgin Mary, gained a mass following that was by no means confined to his home town; from 1112 on, he led a band of simple followers throughout Flanders, Zealand, and Brabant. Eschatological considerations may well have played a more frequent part in these movements than the sources would have us believe. Some people mocked these itinerant preachers, while for others the joke soon turned sour. Barely two decades after Tanchelm, heretics turned up in Cologne apparently preaching Cathar doctrines to the masses. But the ideal of the contemplative life of renunciation was also taken up by orthodox reformers. Many hermitages were founded, the most famous of them by Saint Bruno the Carthusian, a priest from Cologne, who had formerly been a pupil of the cathedral school in Reims before renouncing the world and establishing the Great Charterhouse (Grande Chartreuse) in Grenoble, whence the Carthusian order originated—the strictest monastic order of all, renowned for its ascetic lifestyle and its vow of silence.[13]

Faith now became caught up in the mill of early scholastic dialectics. The doctrines of Berengar played a key role in this movement; this cathedral scholar from Tours interpreted the Eucharist in a symbolic way, thus imparting a mystical flavor to Christ for believers, and in so doing he stirred up the first controversy concerning the Eucharistic Presence in European history. For Lanfranc—the abbot of Bec in Normandy and soon to be Archbishop of Canterbury—and others took issue with Berengar's thesis. These authorities took the view that the believer had no need of rational disputation in this matter, and that in matters touching upon the mysteries of faith, the faithful should take their cue from the religious authorities, not from any dialectical arguments. This directive was not meant as an outright rejection of dialectics, but it definitely was designed to consign it to a subservient role within theological discourse as a whole. Lanfranc and his allies taught that the Eucharistic bread and wine underwent a very real and substantial transformation into the Body and Blood of Christ, which the believer ate and the priest drank. Thus it was that the doctrine of the sacraments came within the purview of scholars. Could it really be that the host, the Body of Christ, was chewed, digested, and excreted? Dialectics were of no use in this question; there was clearly an urgent need for dogmatic clarification. However, the doctrine of transubstantiation, which was now formulated, only succeeded in digging an even deeper trench dividing the faithful. Once more, doubters made their voices heard; Peter of Bruys, for example, a preacher who had been suspected of the Cathar heresy and who gained a large following in Italy and the south of France, interpreted the Eucharist purely as a feast of remembrance and repudiated any idea of transubstantiation. Furthermore, he refused to recognize the church hierarchy and rejected the idea of the communion of the living and the dead. In many regards, these decades in the history of church reform appear to anticipate the confessional conflicts of the sixteenth century, which were sparked by the self-same controversy. In the event, Peter of Bruys met the common fate of heretics at that time, being burned at the stake in Saint Gilles in Provence in 1125. His ideas were subsequently taken up by Henry of Lausanne, until he was captured by Bernard of Clairvaux and thrown into jail, where he died.

The curtain opened onto an initial prelude of endlessly protracted debates that have continued up to the present day, and which turn on the two fundamental philosophical positions adopted regarding the nature of the general terms *(universalia)* employed by dialecticians and theoreticians.

Did these terms possess some kind of real actuality *(realia)* or did they represent nothing more than conceptual abstractions *(nomina)*? A scholar named Roscelin maintained that the latter was the case, but because he dared to apply this to the dogma of the Holy Trinity, which for him represented three separate deities, he found himself condemned, while all his writings were destroyed. We can only gain some inkling of his teachings through the polemic of his opponents. Roscelin appears to have regarded the universalia simply as "names," as a mere "sound" *(flatus vocis),* and to have seen no species as having any actuality, in other words, he did not recognize "man" as such, preferring to recognize the reality only of individual humans and things, and not of any genera. Because Roscelin was condemned to silence, his teachings did not find any resonance; his brilliant pupil, Peter Abelard, did not follow his doctrine unreservedly. It was only in the late phase of scholasticism in the later Middle Ages that the controversy about realism versus nominalism flared up again, more animatedly than ever before. Incidentally, the question of the reality of genera and species, say in the fields of biogenetics, linguistics, and semiotics, has nowadays been decided in favor of Roscelin.

This first "nominalist" found an implacable adversary in Anselm of Canterbury. Anselm's chief concerns were faith and God, not dialectics, which he only used as a means of seeking the Lord's countenance: "Now then, Lord my God, teach my heart where and how to seek and find you." *Credo, ut intelligam,* "I believe in order to understand." This faith, which seeks understanding—*fides quaerens intellectum,* as in the original title of Anselm's *Proslogion*—was geared toward the contemplation and experience of God, not to physics.[14] Anselm's search eventually led him to formulate his ontological proof of the existence of God. According to the theologian, God is the greatest, most perfect entity ("that than which nothing greater can be conceived"); however, in order to attain perfection a being must possess real existence, and not just "the quality of being imagined"; therefore, God must exist. This argument convinced many people at the time, but on the other hand even some contemporaries refuted Anselm's "proof," and his *Defence (Liber apologeticus)* did nothing to change their views. More successful was Anselm's doctrine of "free will," which unequivocally pronounced this faculty capable of doing right and good, and not just evil, as had been the case in Saint Augustine's writings. This outstanding theologian and philosopher operated solely within the worlds of grammatical and logical book-learning and in enquiring after the nature of the human soul; his thinking, as already noted, had no bearing on the natural world. And yet it was during his lifetime that astrology first made its entry into Western intellectual history, becoming one of the most important impulses toward the growth of a mathematically determined discipline of natural sciences. Astrology excited both approbation and rejection. Manegold of Lautenbach, for example, considering the inevitability of the "end of times," disparaged "this measuring of celestial spaces and passing of judgment on the conjunction of planets."[15] But it was precisely the expectation of the End of Days that prompted people to seek refuge in astrology and hence in a mathematical study of the heavens (astronomy) that culminated in the growth of the physical sciences.

Nor was it just souls that were suffering hardship at this time; the world too was in disarray. Eastern Rome, the mighty Byzantium, was by now in dire straits. The Seljuk Turks had inflicted a catastrophic defeat on the Byzantines at the Battle of Manzikert (1071) on the shores of Lake Van. Anatolia was now lost without any hope of being regained, while Nicaea, the old imperial residence of Constantine, was now in Seljuk hands. Antioch on the Syrian coast had also fallen. The Norman knight Bohemond of Apulia, the adventurer son of Robert Guiscard, took advantage of this weakness. In 1087, he set off intending to conquer Constantinople. He got as far as Salonika before his crusade disintegrated. Near Dyrrachium on the Adriatic coast of Albania, his fleet was defeated by a Byzantine force with the decisive assistance of Venetian galleys. This gave the ruler on the Golden Horn a modicum of breathing space, but the fear of invasion still remained. The *basileus* sent out calls for help to Count Robert of Flanders, who had recently visited Constantinople on his way back from pilgrimage to Jerusalem. Around 150 years before, urgent pleas for help from the then-*basileus* had also been sent to Pope Gregory VII; the records are vague on this matter, but Gregory may have sought military assistance in the form of mercenaries for the campaign against the Seljuks; and, more recently, pleas for help had also reached the Curia during Urban II's papal reign, the second pope after Gregory. But what the West mustered in the way of help and dispatched to Byzantium was by no means welcome. The *basileus* John Comnenus made the best of the situation, concluding fealty agreements with Crusaders as they swept through Constantinople, treaties which admittedly were later broken by the Latin Empire.

Urban II did heed the pleas for assistance, and answered them with a decisively new line of attack. He convened a synod at Clermont-Ferrand in the Auvergne in 1095, and those attending witnessed a curious piece of stage management that was designed to announce to the whole world the objectives of the pope and his followers. Urban gave a sermon whose thrust was a call for Christians to desist from fighting amongst themselves: "Set sail for the Holy Sepulchre, seize from the accursed heathen the land that God gave to the People of Israel as their own and bring it to heel!" His call was received with tumultuous applause: "It is the will of God! It is the will of God!"[16] What Urban had done was to announce the dispatch of an armed pilgrimage to Jerusalem *(peregrinatio),* a Crusade, as it would later be called. It seemed as though the West was attempting to export abroad the wars that were raging within its borders. And scarcely had the pope concluded his speech, scarcely had he appointed the bishop of Le Puy as the legate to the Crusade, than messengers arrived with the news that the count of Toulouse, Raimond de St. Gilles, was already hastening hence with a mighty army in order to lead God's Army *(exercitum Dei).*[17] It was plain for all to see: the *Sacerdotium* and the *Regnum* had found their way to a God-ordained union under the leadership of this pope. "The whole world" was in uproar. Bohemond too, the belligerent Norman and the scourge of kings, appeared among the crusading knights; his fame as a warrior already resounded around the world, and, as the inscription on his grave in Canosa di Puglia maintains, he could be called neither a man nor a god.

All the claims of modern historians that the Middle Ages had no conception of planning in any targeted way are patent nonsense when one considers this piece of political theater in Clermont-Ferrand. But as is invariably the case when the major powers gird their loins for battle, the small players are the victims. Thousands of ordinary people, seduced by the pope's sermon promising redemption of sins, heeded the call to arms, but were hopelessly ill-equipped. Without the slightest idea of what they were about to face, they rushed headlong to their deaths; moreover, in their delusional state, while they were still on home territory they carried out atrocities against the people that their preachers taught them were "Christ murderers," namely the Jew. In Troyes, the largest Jewish community in France with its widely renowned synagogue (1095), in Mainz (1096); indeed, on their journey east, wherever the mob of cross-bearing crusaders descended, they slaughtered the Jews. In Mainz, admittedly in desperate peril and perhaps in some kind of messianic expectation, the Jewish community, who had managed to take refuge in the bishop's palace there, committed mass suicide. And in parallel with the crusade to Jerusalem, a second front also opened up against the Muslims, with a crusade directed at Tarragona in Catalonia, which was supposed to bring the same salutary benefits to the participants as the Jerusalem adventure.

What is a Crusade, exactly? Such an enterprise required the leadership of the pope, who alone was entitled to call for one, not leadership in person, but through a legate; it was here, at Clermont, that the essentially unarmed papacy was first able to summon up an army, which it was later to send into the field against objectives other than Jerusalem. Other factors that came into play were the institution of the plenary indulgence, which absolved a person of all temporal punishment for sins, and the guaranteed protection by the pope of any individual who had taken the Cross, along with his wife and children and his property. The cross in question was a cloth one sewn onto the right shoulder of the crusader's tunic so that it should be clearly visible. Following the First Lateran Council in 1123, these benefits were further augmented by special crusaders' privileges, which initially simply assured them of papal protection, but from the Second Crusade onward (1146–1149) also explicitly granted them favorable terms regarding taxation, loans, and interest rates. Of course, this war had to be a truly just one, holy in some measure, if its full salutary effect was to be realized. Accordingly, crusades were officially declared holy wars, since they were after all directed against the "enemies" of the Christian faith and conducted at the behest of the pope. It was these aspects, the defense against a common enemy and the leadership of a king or pope that defined a just war in the eyes of contemporaries.

The hordes who set off in 1096 for Jerusalem were by no means only knights. Countless poor people also joined the Crusade, under the leadership of Peter of Amiens, who instead of a military banner waved his "letter from heaven" above his head. Their main motivation was the hope of attaining salvation and a better life for themselves. Among the knightly class, admittedly, the urge for salvation was not the only driving force, even if this did undoubtedly provide a powerful stimulus. Rather, a social–historical perspective tends to focus our attention on the reinforcement of the wider brotherly and hereditary community, or *frérèche*, which was a social prerequisite, at least in France, for the recruitment there of the vast majority of knights for the First Crusade, and which excited a person's willingness to participate in a dangerous military adventure. This institution points to momentous upheavals in French aristocratic society, indeed the European nobility in general. In a family with several brothers, only the eldest inherited the entire estate, while the younger ones remained at home and were prohibited from marrying, and were obliged either to join the clergy or leave the family home as squires or professional soldiers or perhaps hire themselves out as stewards to princes. Many of these "juniors" undoubtedly also ended up settling in the burgeoning cities and, if they were adept enough, carving out a place for themselves in the urban elite. In the French royal dynasty, this development toward primogeniture was firmly in place by the tenth and early eleventh centuries.

For these younger sons of the aristocracy, the campaign against Jerusalem presented a unique opportunity; granted, it required considerable investment and had some incalculable economic risks inherent in it. A horse, weapons, and armor represented a major outlay. Many crusaders pawned or even sold everything they owned in order to finance the trip to the Holy Land. At best, this was just enough to set them on their way. Underway, they would have to forage from the territories they passed through. This won the Crusaders no friends, either in Hungary or Constantinople, where the armies quite literally descended upon the produce markets like a plague, plundering them and eating every last item. At least Pisa declared itself willing to deploy its fleet to aid the enterprise; the city's Archbishop Dagobert actually joined the army marching east and following the success of the campaign was installed as the first Latin patriarch of Jerusalem. On the other hand, Venice and Genoa were unwilling to commit their maritime forces at first; but when Pisa's involvement paid off, its rival cities were quick to follow suit—Genoa first and, a little later, Venice. These maritime communities subsequently set up their own fixed quarters in the ports of the lands they conquered.

The ambition, competition, lust for power, and envy that dogged any individual crusader in his homeland were not, of course, effaced by the religious objective of the enterprise. Quite the contrary, in fact—as soon as they were able, every one of the great lords that had affixed the cross to his shoulder sought to establish his own principality in the Holy Land. The investment costs in so doing would pay handsome returns. The Crusader states included Odessa (1097), where Balduin de Bouillon established himself, and Antioch, where Bohemond set up his domain once the city had finally been taken and held (1098). The forces of the "Franks" (that is, the French), as the Crusaders were known in the Holy Land, fragmented and no longer remained under a unified command. Nevertheless,

almost miraculously, Jerusalem was indeed captured, in 1099, and after
some delay the Latin Kingdom was established in the Holy Land. The
Crusaders had had to overcome unimaginable hardships and fears, and
their success in taking Jerusalem was preceded by remorseless, bloody
combat on both sides. Their relief is evident in the sheer joy of their victory songs: *Ierusalem laetare, / Quae flebas tam amare, / Dum servam tene-
bare, / Ierusalem, exsulta.* Be joyful, Jerusalem, rejoice! And then comes a
stanza celebrating their triumph: *Rivi fluuunt cruoris / Ierusalem in mo-
ris / Dum perit gens erroris, Ierusalem, exsulta.*[18] Rivers of blood—even at
this early stage in the history of the Crusades. The success of the "Franks"
was made possible by the disunity of the Muslim forces, just as later, when
these forces were once again unified, Jerusalem was retaken and the Crusader kingdoms, whose history cannot be discussed here, proved unsustainable in the long term.

The world was out of joint. The papacy was split, the successor to the
throne of Saint Peter was preaching war, the abbot of Cluny was embroiled
in the dispute between the king and the pope, the mysteries of faith were
being openly questioned, there were monks preaching on the streets, and
fanatical mobs roaming the countryside slaughtering Jews. Everywhere,
civil war seemed to be raging, while Byzantium teetered on the verge of
collapse, and many believed that the advent of the Antichrist was nigh—
where was peace in all this, and the power of prayer and salvation? The
conflict ground down the forces of religion. Clearly, there was an urgent
need for a new way of thinking. Once again, monks were at the forefront
of a call for the revival of Christian values. One such reformer was Robert, abbot of Molesme (near Langres). He and six of his fellow brothers
left their monastery and, in imitation of Saint Benedict, went into retreat
to Cîteaux near Châlon in 1098, in order to pursue a more strictly ascetic
way of living. Although the abbot found this existence too solitary and
presently returned to Molesme, his companions remained at Cîteaux, and
the monastery that they founded in a wilderness of thickets and thorns,
began to flourish. Their example inspired others. They aspired to be the
"new soldiers of Christ," *novi milites Christi;* "poor together with the poor
Christ." The secret of their success was their absolutely literal adherence to
the Rule of Saint Benedict *(puritas regulae),* prayers at the canonical hours
from matins through to compline, life within a community, hard manual
labor, and the renunciation of all wealth. All this was combined with a
rejection of the traditional practice of commemoration of the deceased,

yet alongside their "desire for God," the brothers of this order laid particular stress on learning. A unique mystical spirituality spread throughout this order in the form of a cult of courtly love for Jesus, in which the Savior appeared as a kind of mother figure.

Contemporary lords in need of salvation, foremost among them Duke Odo of Burgundy, granted land to these "Cistercians," often wasteland, which the monks had to first till in order to make it arable. Before long, the young theologically educated elite was beating a path to the Cistercians' door. By 1113, in similar surroundings, the order's second institution, La Ferté, was founded, and so it continued. Soon, one monastery after another was being established, particularly thanks to the efforts of the most eloquent and renowned Cistercian of the age, Bernard, abbot of Clairvaux; every one of them was tucked away in remote solitude, in land that had not been heavily settled, and often in the middle of marshland that needed to be cultivated. Cistercian monasteries were located in as diverse places as Burgundy, France, Italy, Germany, England, Ireland, Spain, Portugal, Hungary, Poland, and Scandinavia. Outlying holdings were administered by special estate centers known as "granges"; the monasteries also engaged in commercial activities. Poverty soon became a thing of the past. The Englishman Stephen Harding, the second abbot of Cîteaux, organized the growing community, which found a sense of cohesion through the "charter" that he wrote for the institution, which he entitled the *Carta caritas* (Charter of love). This charter thus laid the foundation of the first monastic "order" to truly warrant the name. Each of its monasteries was linked to a mother abbey, which was obliged to conduct a yearly visitation of all its satellites, but which still remained independent and under the control of its own abbot. All the abbots would assemble annually for a "general chapter" at the mother abbey of the whole order, and the decisions made by this meeting were binding on all. Asceticism even governed the method of construction of each individual monastery. The opulent architectural magnificence of the Cluniac churches and monasteries was rejected in favor of a building program characterized by simple severity. Every monastery complex followed the same plan, with the church and the dormitory immediately abutting and with direct access to the oratory and other communal spaces, and with the cloister in the center. The only decoration consisted of the ubiquitous flowing well set within the cloisters. Before long, lay brothers (also called "converse monks") were also admitted, who were primarily employed on manual tasks.

This model spawned many imitators, but also disputatious competitors. A welter of new religious orders and communities appeared on the scene, many of which engaged in polemical exchanges. Norbert of Xanten, a prosperous secular priest who turned to a life of asceticism and solitude after being struck by a thunderbolt, also became an itinerant preacher of repentance. After proclaiming that the advent of the Antichrist might happen even in his lifetime, he was suspected of heresy. However, as a friend of Bernard of Clairvaux, in 1120 Norbert was permitted by Pope Calixtus II to withdraw to the remote location of Prémontré (near Laon) and, like the Cistercians, to follow the example of Jesus and the Apostles and live as a "true pauper in Christ" *(verus pauper Christi)* by combining the contemplative monastic life with pastoral care ("naked, to follow the naked Christ on the Cross"). As yet, though, this monastic program had none of the radicalism that Francis of Assisi was later to exhibit in calling for a life of poverty.

Members of Norbert's new institution, which consisted of canons regular, not monks, and which was known as the Premonstratensian Order, took the same vow of poverty, chastity, and obedience as monks, but lived according to the Rule of Saint Augustine rather than that of Saint Benedict. As such, then, they remained attached to the world outside the cloisters, concerned themselves with both church and imperial affairs, and worked as assiduously for the salvation of others souls as for their own. At many sites—for example, in Prémontré itself, joint monasteries and nunneries were built for men and women. Some of their enemies accused the Premonstratensians of sanctimony; their case in particular highlights the intense rivalry that existed between monastic orders and religious movements. Nevertheless, Norbert's foundation flourished. In 1122, the nobleman Gottfried von Cappenberg donated his castle to the preacher to found a monastery there; its provost, Otto, became the godfather of the Holy Roman emperor Frederick I (Barbarossa). By the late thirteenth century, there were well over a thousand such Premonstratensian foundations throughout Europe. Norbert himself was appointed archbishop of Magdeburg in 1126 at the urging of King Lothair III.

Without going into the full history of them here, mention should be made of other reform movements that also came into being during this period, notably in Bavaria, such as the canons regular of Saint Augustine. However, what all these new foundations had in common was their refusal to admit *pueri oblati* (children dedicated at an early age to the monastic life) or to perform elaborate requiem masses or other commemorative du-ties, both of which factors had played such a significant role in older mon-asteries. Rather, they subjected themselves and their mode of existence to strict rules of conduct and promoted the *vita communalis*. Around this same time, Cluny was undergoing a period of crisis, which manifested it-self in the fall of its abbot, Pontius, in 1119: the institution that had paved the way for a new order of things now found itself being overtaken by that new order. The church in general was in a state of flux. The schism even spread as far as the college of cardinals, which divided into representatives of Gregorian reform and the more modern trends, which were character-ized not least by Early Scholasticism. Accordingly, following the papal election of 1130, the church found itself once more with two rival popes, Anacletus II and Innocent II, and monarchs had to decide in favor of one or the other. The main question now was whether the papacy and its king-like position would be able to survive these upheavals.

Boethius is consoled by the Lady Philosophy *(Philosophia)* during his imprisonment. Illustration from an early eleventh-century manuscript. The Art Archive at Art Resource, NY.

Sixth-century gilded bronze forehead plate portraying Lombard king Agilulf (r. 590–616). At center, the ruler is shown seated on his throne, bare-headed, with long hair and beard and wearing his royal cloak. He is flanked by heavily armed warriors, while from the sides winged spirits carrying plaques with the legend "Victoria" and dukes bearing gifts approach the throne. This artifact was found near Lucca, Italy, and is thought to have been presented as an honorary gift. Nicolo Orsi Battaglini / Art Resource, NY.

Merovingian jewels, sixth to seventh century. The Merovingians ruled the Franks until replaced by Pepin, the son of Charles Martel, in 751. Chroniclers claimed the pope approved deposing the Merovingians, but no authoritative account of the Carolingian accession exists. Gianni Dagli Orti/The Art Archive at Art Resource, NY.

This small rock-crystal crucifix in a gold and pearl setting was given by Pope Gregory the Great to Queen Theodelinde of the Bavarian Agilolfing dynasty in thanks for her conversion of the Lombards, formerly followers of Arian Christianity, to the Roman Catholic faith. As was customary in Late Antiquity, the crucified Christ is shown wearing a short sleeveless tunic *(colobium)*. Treasury of Monza Cathedral, Italy / De Agostini Picture Library / M. Carrieri / The Bridgeman Art Library.

A gilded table centerpiece in the form of a hen with seven chicks (ca. 600). The Bavarian Lombard queen Theodelinde is thought to have donated this piece to the cathedral at Monza, Italy. Aside from its religious symbolism, this stunning example of the goldsmith's art demonstrates the advanced state of craftsmanship in Late Antiquity. Treasury of Monza Cathedral, Italy / Giraudon / The Bridgeman Art Library.

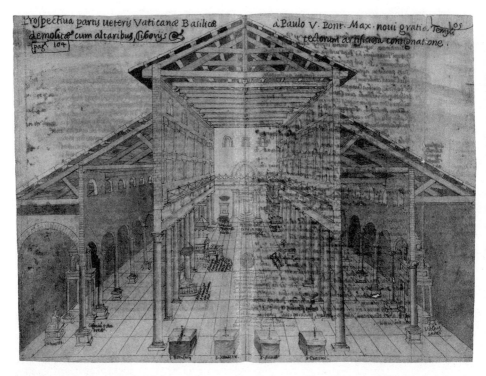

Cutaway view perspective of the ancient Basilica of Saint Peter by Giacomo Grimaldi, seventeenth-century drawing. Biblioteca Apostolica Vaticana, Vatican City / Mondadori Portfolio / The Bridgeman Art Library.

A silver denarius coin depicting Charlemagne in the idealized guise of a Roman emperor, clad in an imperial toga and garlanded with a laurel wreath. It bears the inscription KAROLUS IMP AUG (Emperor Charles Augustus). Münzkabinett, Staatliche Museen, Berlin / Karin Maerz / Art Resource, NY.

The Palatine Chapel at Aachen Cathedral in Germany, which houses the marble throne believed to have been used by Charlemagne. Alfredo Dagli Orti / The Art Archive at Art Resource, NY.

PECCAIORVM CARNIS RESURRECIIONEM UITAMAEIERNAM AMEN

INCIPITFIDESCATHO LICAM

QUICUQUEUULT UNAESTDIUINIIASAE SIMILITEROMNIPOTENS
SALUUSESSEANTEOMNIA QUALISGLORIACOAET PATER OMNIPOTENSFIL
OPUSESTUTTENEATCATHO NAMAIESTAS LIUSOMNIPOTENSETSPSSO
LICAMFIDEM QUALISPATERIALISFILIUS ETTAMENNONTRESOMNI
QUAMNISIQUISQUEINTE TALISETSPIRITUSSCS POTENTESSEDUNUSOMPS
GRAMINUIOLATAMQUE INCREATUSPATERINCRE ITADSPATERDSFILIUS
SERUAUERITABSQUIDU ATUSFILIUS INCREATUS DSETSPIRITUSSCS
BLOINAETERNUMPERIBIT ETSPIRITUSSCS ETTAMENNONTRESDII
FIDESAUTEMCATHOLICA INMENSUSPATERINMEN SEDUNUSESTDS

An early church council, as depicted in the Utrecht Psalter. The Psalter is a Carolingian-era copy (ca. 830) of an original document from Late Antiquity. Shown is an animated assembly of priests in whose midst scribes sit documenting the proceedings, while three figures holding an unrolled scroll engage in lively debate. On the two lecterns, manuscripts with authoritative texts lie open, ready to be consulted if necessary. Bibliothèque Nationale, Paris, France / The Bridgeman Art Library.

Siege of a city, from the Utrecht Psalter. Despite its stylized portrayal, this illustration conveys something of the turmoil of a battle during the Early Middle Ages. Bibliothèque Nationale, Paris, France / The Bridgeman Art Library.

The Susanna Crystal, crafted at the behest of King Lothar II (d. 869), depicting the slaughter of the two lustful elders who had watched Susanna bathing. The expressiveness of the image demonstrates the high level of artistry in crystal cutting in the Carolingian period. © The Trustees of the British Museum / Art Resource, NY.

The Gokstad ship is an outstanding example of a Viking longboat from the late ninth century. It had room for thirty-two oarsmen. Werner Forman / Art Resource, NY.

A tenth-century Viking helmet from Gjermundbu, Norway. Universitetets Oldsaksamling, University of Oslo, Norway / Photo © AISA / The Bridgeman Art Library.

The Golden Madonna of Essen, ca. 980, one of the oldest preserved free-standing sculptures in the world. It is made from a wooden core covered with sheets of gold leaf. Foto Marburg / Art Resource, NY.

The Abbey of Saint Philibert near Tournus, France (the surviving building dates from the twelfth century) was originally built as a fortified compound for protection against Viking raids, as can still be seen from its configuration. Gianni Dagli Orti / The Art Archive at Art Resource, NY.

Detail from the Christ Column in Hildesheim. Commissioned by Bishop Bernward (ca. 960–1022), the column shows twenty-eight scenes from the life of Christ. Modeled on Trajan's Column in Rome, it symbolizes the conscious attempt made during the reign of Otto III to revive the Roman Empire. Erich Lessing / Art Resource, NY.

The Antichrist slaying Elijah and Enoch, eleventh century. Given people's high expectation of the End of Days around the turn of the first millennium, the Apocalypse and Last Judgment were frequently addressed topics. ART167537.

The so-called Gero Crucifix was created in the late tenth century. It represents a decisive stage of medieval piety: this was the first time that the dead Christ was shown nailed to the Cross, and it became the model for many similar life-sized Romanesque works. Dendrochronological dating has shown that the piece comes from the time of Saint Heribert (970–1021), not his predecessor as archbishop of Cologne, Gero (ca. 900–976). Foto Marburg / Art Resource, NY.

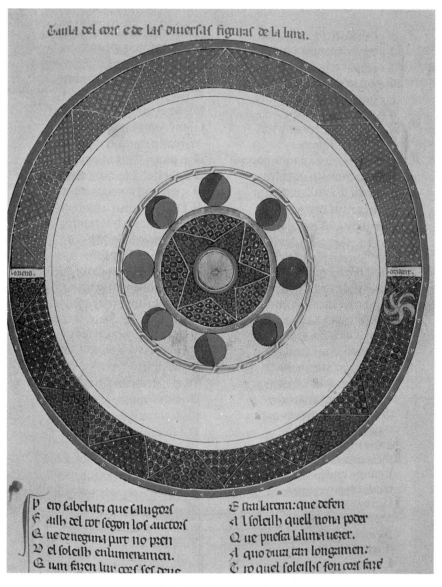

Table of the Movements of the Moon in Relation to the Sun, on vellum, Master Ermengaut (d. 1322). Biblioteca Monasterio del Escorial, Madrid, Spain / Giraudon / The Bridgeman Art Library.

Equestrian statue in Padua, Italy, depicting the mercenary leader *(condottiero)* Erasmo da Narni (d. 1443). Nicknamed "Gattamelata" ("Honeyed Cat"), the former butcher's apprentice rose to become ruler of the city. Four years after his death, this statue was carved by Donatello. It was the first equestrian statue since Antiquity and was commissioned as a striking public display of authority. Alfredo Dagli Orti / The Art Archive at Art Resource, NY.

7

The Long Century of Papal Schisms

THE EFFECT of the papal schisms, which from 1061 onward continued to rock the church for a whole century and more, until 1177–1180, extended much farther than merely reorganizing the college of cardinals or the influence it exerted on the politics of the Roman curia. This century witnessed not only the rebirth of the church; the whole of society also entered a state of flux, as Europe quite literally went out into the streets, not just to become itinerant preachers, on pilgrimage or on Crusade, but also as a result of people fleeing their native countries, clearing land for development, colonization, or engaging in long-distance trade. The West burst out of the boundaries it had hitherto occupied. Intellectual culture in its entirety was in a state of upheaval; church reform itself was simply one indication of this trend. The reform movement, which demanded a more clear-cut division than ever before between spiritual and secular power, really did spread to encompass the whole of Europe, except for the Orthodox East, and in the process lent this continent its particular spiritual stamp. Last but not least, kings and other instances of authority found themselves caught in the undertow of this momentous change.

This all becomes clear precisely through examining the schisms themselves. If it had been the case hitherto that the Carolingian or Ottonian-Salian rulers had had the last word where contentious papal elections were concerned, now the papacy's recently constituted and newly articulated claim to universality required that all interested parties, first and foremost the whole of Latin Christendom, that is, the universal church, should be canvassed in the same way, and that each of those who were elected pope should thereby solicit recognition especially by kings and princes, and in exceptional cases also by individual priests. Yet many kings and princes were also well versed in turning crises of the church to their own advantage. For the universal monarchical papacy demanded the consensus of all, not simply the judgment of one individual king. Meanwhile, kingdoms and principalities found themselves in the grip of no less a significant meta-morphosis than the universal church.

The population continued to grow steadily, since, despite repeated bouts of famine and feuding, it was never threatened by epidemics. The living conditions to which every person was thus subjected constantly increased in complexity, without contemporaries particularly noticing it; once again, these conditions called for a greater efficiency in economic output; the foundations of economic activity, which had been laid in the Carolingian period, were now no longer up to the task. Communication networks grew ever denser, while the demands to supply the entire popu-lace with food and clothing kept increasing, calling for an ever more spe-cialized division of labor and more streamlined organizational forms for production, communication, transport, warehousing, and bringing com-modities to market. Spatial and intellectual mobility were sought-after, along with entrepreneurial spirit, inventiveness, and innovative thinking. This growing diversity of needs and interests demanded new templates of social order and a commensurate capacity for abstraction, as indeed was already being practiced in educational establishments at the time. Not least, a finance system now became an indispensable requirement, and in turn spawned the need for an effective money market with credit and in-terest facilities. Admittedly, this last requirement contradicted the moral principles of religion and so was denigrated as usury. Power relationships had to react to this, and in promoting this development some found them-selves faced with hitherto unimagined challenges. Trading, like knowl-edge, demanded differentiation; the division of labor and professionalism increased, and the world became ever more minutely "analyzed." Clearly, a new knowledge-based society was on the rise.

Estates were confronted with a long drawn-out process of radical change. From the final years of the tenth century onward, we find signs of a society in flux: bondsmen deserted their masters and sought their for-tune in far-off lands. "I was young, I was an orphan, I had no one who would feed me. And so I left my homeland, went abroad and earned a living there by the sweat of my own brow." This was mobility out of necessity. This particular case was debated by Bishop Burchard of Worms in his canon law *(Decretum)* of 1023. He quite literally made a society in upheaval the theme of his work. Before long, new settlement communities were springing up everywhere. Forest clearances, drainage of swamps and other low-lying regions, new agricultural technologies such as the heavy wheeled plow, which allowed a plowman to turn over heavy, clay-based soils, new forms of organization and husbandry and increasing division of labor all helped bring about an increase in production and furnished the growing populace with sufficient provisions. The farmer, who from the tenth to eleventh century onward was regarded as occupying his own social class, played a key role in this economic upturn, while at the same time relinquishing much of his former freedom by becoming downgraded to the rank of mediate vassal and forced to acknowledge his fealty to a feudal lord or lord of the manor. The former differentiations in rank between free and unfree tenant farmers now disappeared. Subsequently, "free" became largely synonymous with "aristocratic." Things only looked more favorable in the areas of new clearance and expansion. There, people's rights as colonists reduced the tributes they had to pay while also granting certain privileges and enduing liberties. Repercussions for the old empire were not long in making themselves apparent; there, too, ties to former estates were also loosened, and the collective organization of villages began to assert itself ever more forcefully. More clearly than ever before, the countryside began to separate from the city. In this way, many bondsmen fled to the towns and "emancipated" themselves.

A Return to Urban Culture

Indeed, urban culture made a comeback during this period. But what now emerged—even in places where Roman *civitates* still survived—bore little resemblance anymore to ancient conditions. Formerly, cities had been hallmarked by spaciousness and special public cultural facilities such as for a, public baths *(thermae)* or theaters. The new urban culture, by contrast, was characterized by confined space and legislation, by walls and towers and guarded gates that were locked at night, by churches and ecclesiastical communities, by confederations and the formation of communes, by trade and commerce, and not least by Jewish communities. Even by Late Antiquity, the loose building style (albeit in stone) of the

Roman period had given way to a tendency to set buildings cheek-by-jowl. Insofar as it was possible, ancient remains were put to new use. Yet even in cities that had been imperial residences, such as Rome, Ravenna, Milan, Arles, or Trier, only very few ancient buildings—mostly in the possession of the church—withstood the ravages of time. A more homely vernacular style of building developed in places with no Roman legacy. In towns such as Lübeck or Hamburg, say, most construction was in wood—tightly packed log houses, which could be several storeys high. These buildings had little light, being set on narrow alleyways and with tiny windows which in winter were covered with parchment; these were mostly unfortified and were at best roofed with simple boards. Accordingly, the cityscape as a whole took on a primitive aspect in the twelfth century. It was only from the thirteenth century on that solid stone-built or half-timbered houses began to proliferate here.

Italy, however, enjoyed a head start that was for a long time unassailable. It was there that the medieval city had its origins. The ancient townscapes on the Rhine or the Danube, on the coasts of the Mediterranean, or on the great rivers like the Rhône already existed at this time, but from the late eleventh century on, they spread to regions like Flanders, on the territory of modern Belgium and the Netherlands, or—from the twelfth and thirteenth centuries—to the areas controlled by the Hanseatic League in northern and eastern Europe, which became urbanized only at that time. Milan, Pisa, and Barcelona may be taken as representative of the first wave or urbanization in the first two regions mentioned, while Bergen in Norway or Novgorod on the River Duna are emblematic of the latter phase. In addition, urban centers began to develop along the long-distance trade routes to the East and the North, for instance those leading to Kievan-Rus or to Constantinople, or even on the Ox Trail (Haervejen) leading to the Jutland peninsula. These towns included Prague and Krakow; likewise, Leipzig also grew up on a long-distance route from the Rhine–Main region to Poland. The Muslim cities of Al-Andalus (Spain), however, underwent their own particular development. In typological terms, a distinction can be drawn in the growth of cities between ones that expanded and ones that were newly founded, and in functional terms between palatinate, royal residence, and episcopal cities, as well as between market, commercial, and mountain cities. Other typologies can also be devised. A bishop had to reside in a city *(civitas)*; alongside the cathedral church, ecclesiastical foundations and monasteries were essential elements. Canon law thus caused settlements to grow more dense. One early newly established city was Freiburg im Breisgau, whose founding charter dates from 1120. The local lord of the manor, Conrad I, duke of Zähringen, granted the city its rights, while the "constituent" citizenry of the town emerged from a sworn alliance of the founding merchants. Over the subsequent course of the Middle Ages, cities were often established as commercial undertakings, many of which were in clear competition with already existing conurbations.

The municipality movement can be identified from the tenth–eleventh century onward. It spread northward from Italy, taking in Burgundy, France, and Flanders, before expanding eastward. The first places in Germany where its effects become evident are Worms, whose citizens were granted an initial privilege in 1074 by Henry IV in gratitude for their loyalty to the king in his dispute with the bishop who was the overlord of their city, and Cologne, whose inhabitants rose up in that same year in defiance of an order from their lord, the archbishop, and who since that time had succeeded in asserting their rights ever more effectively against him, despite the fact that they had not gained imperial immediacy (the privileged status of being subject to the direct authority of the emperor).

A town charter absolved the citizenry both from the feudal organization of the manorial system, which they had been able to join during the early Middle Ages, and from the common law. It bonded the inhabitants of a town into a defensive and peace-keeping union and into a judicial community; indeed, we may go so far as to say that it forged them into a political alliance. Moreover, viewed from a sociological perspective, clear differences can be identified between the past and the situation that now pertained. The Roman city had been inhabited by Roman citizens, while the medieval city was not only inhabited by the confederates and their dependents, but regularly also by Jews; in these circumstances, in Germany at least, the dominant force in the cities were often the *ministeriales*—the knightly and in many cases still unfree, but occasionally also wealthy, bondsmen of the lord of the town. Cities invariably had the right to convene markets and in most cases the right to fortify themselves. In Germany, from around the turn of the millennium on, a transference of an older right to hold markets to newly established cities can be identified, with the result that extended families of those entitled to hold markets arose. In the same way, older municipal rights were also later conferred upon newer cities, thereby bringing various families endowed with municipal rights to prominence. The later Middle Ages saw the establishment of patriciates and guilds, while a characteristic religious, intellectual, and political culture came into being in the cities, in spite of the fact that the municipalities, especially those in Italy, had in many cases fragmented into various quarreling and warring factions.

It is true that no medieval town ordinance enshrined *expressis verbis* the familiar principle of law (in Germany) that "city air makes you free" *(Stadtluft macht frei),* which was actually an invention of the nineteenth century. But this principle was always present in spirit if not in letter: "Anyone who moves to the town and resides there without being challenged [by a master] for a year and a day may never thereafter be reclaimed by anyone as their serf"—thus ran a clause in the municipal charter of Hildesheim from 1249, regardless of the fact that the inhabitants of that city continued to recognize the local bishop as their lord. Nonetheless, blatant legal and social differences existed within the urban populace as well, but these generally manifested themselves in matters of trade control, labor commitment, wage dependency, and economic hardship, but hardly ever in terms of legal status, as had been the case in the early Middle Ages. Cities acted as a magnet for population growth; they continued to grow as a result of people fleeing the countryside, and this made for a regular influx of new inhabitants. Markets and commerce in the cities gave people the opportunity to make a lucrative living and to participate in the economic boom.

This period thus saw the rise of the merchant class. The status of the merchant experienced a meteoric rise that has never been matched in world history. Traders grew rich and became powerful; as citizens of medieval towns they secured positions of authority, even that of legislator, inasmuch as they were instrumental in codifying common law. Indeed, merchants became the quintessential archetype of the politically powerful bourgeoisie and the epitome of the culture of reason. "Capital" and power came together under their leadership. This was a thoroughly European development, and represented the decisive historical breakthrough to the hegemony of precisely this "capital," driven by entrepreneurial spirit, calculation, and the weighing up of risks. The first general proscription of usury, issued by the Second Lateran Council in 1139, was evidence of the greatly increased demand for capital by the expanding "economy" of that time, especially in the towns; for the earning of any form of interest was considered "usury." The ban affected Christians, but made no mention of

Jews. The process in question had undoubtedly begun some years prior to this, although there are no records charting its origin; now, however, the practice was brought out into the open. At the same time, by means of trade contacts, the transfer of knowledge and leagues of towns, this new bourgeois class expanded intellectually beyond the narrow confines of city walls, paving the way for the future growth of nation-states and the expounding of new social theories.

Economic growth and power were based on long-distance trade, commerce, and manufacture, though in many cases, particular cities rose to prominence as a result of a favorable location on a river, at a ford, or on a coastline (or through being sited on valuable mineral deposits). As early as 1009, a merchant who is thought to have come from Flanders and who dealt in cloth, made his will in Barcelona.[1] Prominent mining settlements grew up at Goslar, Dinant, Freiberg in Saxony, and Kuttenberg in Bohemia. Specialized centers of production came into being wherever, say, cloth or linen-weaving enterprises congregated, manufactures that had since the tenth–eleventh centuries on increasingly moved from the countryside into the cities. English, Flemish, or Italian towns (for example, Florence) made wool and other textile manufacture into a major industry, while linen production and processing and fustian weaving was concentrated in the cities of southern Germany, and particularly Swabia. And the Low Countries continued to employ multifaceted manufacturing processes that took the organizational structure of the publishing industry.

A favorable transport location brought economic advantages, which were systematically exploited. Accordingly, many a city such as Cologne managed to secure for itself "staple rights" (which required vessels to unload at their ports and display goods for sale); these cities owed much of their subsequent wealth to this measure. Staple rights were originally a logistical necessity, since the Rhine was navigable for oceangoing ships as far as Cologne, but in order to be carried farther upstream, the goods had to be transferred to smaller barges; however, after the introduction of large "cog" merchant ships with such a deep draft that they weren't able to get up the Rhine even as far as Cologne, stapling simply transformed into a particularly expensive customs duty. River and sea ports alike profited from the expansion of long-distance trade. Over time, an infrastructure of bridges and roads followed. One of the most well-known of such projects was the first stone bridge over the Danube at Regensburg, which was under construction for eleven years and was opened in 1146. Many contemporaries considered it a wonder of the world, and it set in train such an extensive diversion and rerouting of traffic that not just the city itself, but also countless local landed noblemen around the city profited greatly as a result of the tolls they levied. Sometime later, it became necessary to provide merchants traveling overland with an armed escort in order to protect them from being robbed; in particular, major market cities such as Frankfurt or Nuremberg provided this escort service for traders coming to do business within their walls.

A number of groundbreaking innovations emerged in the eleventh and twelfth centuries especially in the realm of long-distance trade. Several commentators have even gone so far as to speak in terms of a "mercantile revolution."[2] Business organization based on the division of labor, staged capital investment, and corresponding profit-sharing became widespread. Merchants no longer always undertook journeys in person, instead devolving this to a partner, generally the shipowner. A distinction was thus drawn between the *socius stans* (the stationary partner who put up most of the capital and remained at home) and the *socius tractans* (the active partner who put to sea). The beginnings of the idea of insurance can also be seen in the "maritime commandery," namely simultaneous involvement in several enterprises with only a small capital investment in each, an arrangement that entailed a new distribution of risks. Every loss was borne by several people and therefore did not result in one person's ruin. For the time being, financial activities were concentrated on the trading fairs, particularly in the Champagne region, and always in urban centers. Large-scale financial transactions, that is, money exchange, indeed the whole concept of the "bank," only arose first during the thirteenth century. The first major accumulation of capital can be identified at the end of the twelfth century at the latest, with an early form of European high finance appearing shortly thereafter. Like the Champagne fairs, this may well have been deployed to facilitate trading links between Italy, France, England, and Germany. Venice was one of the first places to emerge as a financial center. In 1198, *ministeriales* of the archbishop of Cologne who were involved in financial transactions intervened actively in imperial politics, when they bankrolled the election of the Guelf Otto IV as Holy Roman Emperor against the candidacy of the Ghibelline Philip of Swabia (including all the necessary bribes) and in so doing provoked a serious succession conflict. Frankish kings, too, were obliged to rely increasingly on credit. Money was about to become the prime mover in world affairs.

The rationalistic basis of trade was apparent both in its public organization and in the rise of the institution of civil law. The municipalities of Lombardy and Tuscany played a leading role in this development. It was within the safety of the walls of the cities in these regions, above all—and much less in the remote religious foundations and monasteries—that the clerical intellectuals of the High and Late Middle Ages were active, and there too schools flourished, and from the twelfth century onward universities as well. The privileges of the municipality, whose benefits the citizens enjoyed, such as autonomy, independent town charters, political order, and self-determination, now combined with the world of scholarship. In Italy the urban traditions of Antiquity and the Early Middle Ages also came into play; additional factors here were the remoteness of monarchical authority and the successful exclusion of the feudal powers of counts and bishops alike (the latter were sometimes the representatives of cities prior to the advent of municipalities). The *Inhabitatio* compelled the feudal aristocracy to live in the town at least temporarily (say, for a few months a year).

These cities were hallmarked by certain characteristic features. Rarely was there any unity within them. Individual families and larger groupings were often in open rivalry. This makes it all the more remarkable, therefore, that a sense of political pragmatism became the norm in these towns, transcending all wrangling, and fostering a respectable culture of disputation (even though the tale of Romeo and Juliet seems to run counter to this). A series of innovations ensured a generally stable constitution. These included the annually elected body of municipal consuls; the group of officials known as the Podestà, which from the twelfth century on was charged with governing the city and which with its full staff of magistrates and notaries was brought in from outside the city; the popular assembly; representative seats; churches and communal palaces; from the twelfth century on in the Italian municipalities notaries and educated jurists; a tendency to record things in writing, increasingly among lay people also; the instrument of the notary's office; written proof in place of mere testimonial evidence; and in general a growing level of literacy and legal scholarship. All these new factors lent the Italian cities an intellectual and political air of epoch-making modernity and great efficiency. In short, these cities laid down the model for the municipal movement to spread north and west of the Alps.

It was precisely within cities that freedom became an urgent, indispensable requirement, in order that there should be no restrictions placed on the entrepreneurial spirit and to keep economic risk at an acceptable level. From the outset, peace, freedom, and justice formed the central demands of the entire municipal movement. Venice, for instance, made justice into a state cult. The inhabitants of cities and municipalities called on city founders and lords to grant them corresponding freedoms. Individual privileges attest to the fact that such freedoms were forthcoming from the eleventh century on, while more comprehensive privileges endowed upon cities ensued in the following century. These were granted to municipalities as a whole, with individual citizens enjoying them collectively as a community. A whole series of freedoms were encompassed within these privileges. Leaving aside safety and security, which had already been guaranteed by city rulers, citizens now had freedom of trade and exemption from paying excise duty, individual rights, unrestricted right of succession, freedom of expression, freedom before the law, the right to elect bailiffs and juries, the freedom to settle anywhere they wished (at least for anyone who was not beholden to a master as a bondsman), and numerous other privileges. The city itself was the supreme authority, governed by consuls, *podestà* or other *signori,* or by councils and mayors. Taken together, this represented a founding of corporative and personal freedom, which ultimately would have repercussions beyond the jurisdiction of the city. "Anyone who is not a citizen cannot call himself a human being," *(Et si non est civis non est homo)* preached the Florentine Dominican priest Remigius in the early fourteenth century, alluding to Aristotle and his fellow Dominican Thomas Aquinas.[3] The majority of all the freedoms that since the eighteenth century have come to be regarded as basic human rights were first formulated during the Middle Ages in the context of municipal privileges.[4] Their enduring effect can scarcely be overestimated; in the long term, they were responsible for the legal, economic, political, and intellectual emancipation of the bourgeoisie from the conditions of feudal rule. By the fourteenth century at the latest, the relationship between municipalities and sovereign rulers was codified in formal contracts.

Alongside these technical innovations came legal ones, a vital requirement in such realms as entrepreneurship, the publishing and contracting industries, the credit economy, providers and acquirers of capital, or inheritance law; the objectives were increased profit and more efficient business operations. The rediscovery of Roman Law, and in particular the Justinian Pandects, was a decisive factor here. This did nothing less than create civil law anew. A whole new profession, namely that of lawyers, came into being, precisely in the "modern" Italian municipalities. Yet emperors and kings too, foremost among them Holy Roman emperor Henry V and Frederick Barbarossa, also sought counsel from legal advisers. Soon, every municipality in Lombardy had several "judges" *(judices)* on its books, each of whom had been required to undergo special training—and from the thirteenth century on had to have completed a course of university education; in addition, there were also notaries on the cities' payrolls. Education and study now proved to be urgent and essential prerequisites. The fact that city dwellers now lived cheek by jowl—along with the growing complexity of life, and the various forms of profit sharing in mercantile activities and other forms of business—created a need for legal regulation and, sooner or later, for jurisprudence. The further development of the legal system can be sketched out in the following broad terms; it progressed from oral tradition to codified law, from enshrined practice and private privilege to a written and continually updated public statute book and to mercantile law and formal articles of association. Over time, all European countries were to fall in line with this development.

From an early stage, some cities came to especial prominence. For example, the cities where kings established their residences may be mentioned, chief among them Paris, but also London, Rouen, Bordeaux, and Barcelona; or the main ports of the Mediterranean such as Marseilles, Genoa, or its rival Pisa. In the north, Lübeck developed into a notable city from the second half of the twelfth century on. In the south, meanwhile, the rise of Venice was now unstoppable; its intense rivalry with Genoa only served to spur it on rather than hamper it. The old Roman imperial residence of Milan benefited from its favorable transport location near the Po Basin and on the main road leading over the Alps; this position enabled the city to control long-distance trade across the Alps and into northwestern Lombardy. Kings from the north had left the city in peace since the eleventh century. It was in Milan that the law on feudal tenure was codified in the following century; this was then added to the *Corpus Iuris Civilis* by the universities and taught in the context of this body of law. In the twelfth century, the maritime municipality of Pisa likewise became renowned for its legislative achievements, such as the *Constitutum maris* and the *Constitutum de legibus,* the two oldest comprehensive codifications in all of medieval Europe; as well as treating municipal law, they also covered maritime and commercial law.

Even prior to the mid-twelfth century, Bologna had become a magnet for thousands of students from all over the continent who were drawn by its university (alongside Paris the oldest in Europe); as in Paris, their encounters there led to an revolution in knowledge as intellectual elites now met one another in person at Europe's universities and exchanged views thus giving rise to a hitherto unknown "market of ideas." This sea change engendered a flow of information and an international transfer of knowledge that went far beyond the universities. For it was university graduates who presently found themselves in demand as preachers and confessors, or who in other circumstances acted as political agitators. So it was that the lay elites and the broad church community as a whole came to participate in intellectual innovations; and it was through this urban culture that Europe coalesced intellectually.

The city was at once both a legal entity and a way of life; both of these produced new mental horizons among the various ranks of the bourgeoisie and the citizenry. These ranks were characterized by a close co-existence, but one that never resembled the face-to-face society that existed in the countryside. Among the bourgeoisie a characteristic sense of equality held sway; yet new prospects of social advancement served to generate considerable social pressure and a corresponding dynamic for change, even though it is also true that the class demarcations within urban society only hardened in the course of the Late Middle Ages.[5] Glaring contrasts between rich and poor, work and idleness, hunger and satiety, conspicuous wealth and destitution, plus the immediate juxtaposition of success and economic ruin or of education and illiteracy or laity and clergy all combined to reawaken tensions and conflicts. No larger city was without its complement of monasteries and ecclesiastical foundations; above all, the mendicant orders came to the fore from the thirteenth century on as confessors and preachers within the cities. Welfare for the poor had to be organized, a task in which religious institutions usually played a prominent part, but lay organizations were also involved. In addition, brotherhoods and guilds played a major role. The cityscape behind the walls, beginning in the north, was characterized by both soaring buildings and lowly, poor hovels; stone buildings and half-timbered constructions only came to dominate the picture over time. Public amenities were quite different than those in the countryside, with the contrast between rich and poor heightened by the co-existence of narrow streets and prestigious squares. In the Late Middle Ages, ordinances concerning styles of building and clothing were to curb the worst excesses in these areas. But this contrast affected all walks of life, from money-related activities to people's mode of thinking. Envy and greed, and indeed all the other deadly sins, gained a new relevance among city dwellers; usury and the debtor's prison were two sides of the same coin.

The sheer density of the urban population brought new problems with it. Population figures of up to 50,000 or 100,000—which were not to be seen again for several centuries—required new patterns of order, a more refined understanding of burden-sharing (say, for the wall construction or street cleaning) and novel administration methods. In Germany there were some small towns with not even a thousand inhabitants that were granted a municipal charter. As always, in large and small towns alike, the authorities were always in evidence. Their principal task was keeping the peace. Accordingly, the legislative process came to play a role in the towns considerably earlier than in, say, the provinces; criminal law especially came into its own during this period, which fell in line with a growing and ubiquitous process of criminalization that had been in evidence since the twelfth century and that represented a significant departure from the formerly presiding principle of "composition" (where the guilty party paid a sum of money in compensation to the victim's family). Taxes were continually levied and collected; urban courts were now immediately at hand to dispense justice and as such were comparatively efficient. The police carried out their duties competently, and every significant city was familiar with the figure of the executioner (one of whose tasks was to control prostitution). The town was a citadel and a fortress for the local ruler, but also protected its own citizens, who were required to perform military duties for the defense of the locality in times of war. Ordinances on the construction of walls and appropriate taxes regulated this burden on finances. Later—especially in Italy—mercenaries were also recruited; with the requisite skills, their commanders could sometimes exploit the opportunity to assert their own enduring authority over a town and establish their own territory. All this helped the urban regions under discussion to emerge as centers of enhanced social dynamism, institutional modernization, and ever-denser communications networks.

The new wealth and its corollary, the new power of the cities, was evident everywhere. The twelfth century witnessed the construction of many notable castles, palaces, and royal residences, such as the royal palace on the Île de la Cité in Paris or Dankwarderode Castle in Braunschweig, the stronghold of Duke Henry the Lion. In addition, this was the age when the building of Europe's great cathedrals got underway, which still remain the pride of every episcopal city. They were the tangible manifestation of a competitive mind-set, which was by no means restricted to the bishops but which gripped the different municipalities and their citizens. The cathedrals were visible signs of their wealth, ambition, and actual power. The Early Middle Ages left behind very few major buildings, despite the fact that archaeology has shown that a great deal of construction was undertaken in the tenth and eleventh centuries. Charlemagne's royal church of Saint Mary at Aachen (Aachen Cathedral), which when consecrated was the largest new building north of the Alps, is one of the rare exceptions from the Carolingian period to this general rule. But the churches of the centuries that followed are still standing, defying the ravages of weather and man. In Germany, Speyer Cathedral was an early precursor of the new wave of ecclesiastical construction; the beginning of its construction goes back to the early eleventh century. In France, the outstanding examples of the medieval cathedral are Chartres and Notre-Dame in Paris, along with the Abbey church of Saint-Denis, the first Gothic structure (ca. mid-twelfth century); the remains of the third Cluny Abbey (1088) should also be mentioned in this context. Italian cities are still home to numerous grand ecclesiastical and secular buildings dating from the twelfth century, England and Spain likewise.

Stabilization of the Kingdoms

In this world of profound change, kings and princes had to adopt a completely new stance. The long century of papal schisms compelled them, when the college of cardinals was split over its choice of candidate, to choose between the true successor to the throne of Saint Peter and the antipope who pretended to this august position. This situation was as dangerous for kingdoms and independent principalities as it was for the church, which saw itself at risk of permanent division. Every wrong decision brought their ruling lords, who were constantly involved in open or latent conflict with their peers, setbacks in their struggle for earthly power, in any event diminishing their authority within their own realm and in extreme cases even threatening them with the loss of their crown, civil war, and death. On the other hand, a correct call on the part of their rivals would immeasurably strengthen their position. This situation exacerbated the already intense pressure for change, since not a single one of these rulers was in a position to act without the assent of his entire realm. Furthermore, it presented these kingdoms with political, legal, and social ramifications, both internally and externally, which sometimes combined to strengthen and consolidate them, but on other occasions weakened them.

The consequences of this were twofold. The first of these concerned the integration or disintegration of alliances of rulers depending upon whether they had made the right or wrong choice for the true or false pope, while the second brought with it the necessity—not only for kings and princes but also for the churches within their realms—of making their decisions with circumspect restraint and with consideration for their opponents, indeed even sometimes in consultation with them. Ostensibly, the schisms culminated in a European-wide series of declarations of reception, amounting to formal legal documents, which initially consisted of a kind of confirmation of the candidate chosen and necessarily entailing the obedience of the person making the declaration. Thus a diplomatic network came into existence, forming the prelude to the "concert of great powers," which soon constituted a full complement of nations and which has been center stage in European diplomacy for centuries, right up to the present day.

Canon law inevitably came into conflict with this new reality. The claim of the papacy to have the exclusive and legally binding right to determine the norms of the papal election for the whole of Christianity could under no circumstances sanction this kind of "reception," nor was there any way in which canon law could codify it. But the outcome of this was that it had an even more enduring effect on the "receiving" groups. For political necessity led to the development of a quasi-normative order, which sought to regulate precisely that which was extraordinary (that is, schisms). To do so not only meant closer scrutiny and a reassessment of the relationship between the worldly powers and the papacy's claim to universal authority. Far more significantly, rulers, for their part, now needed to swing their "national churches" (which were just emerging at this time and being defined as such) behind them in support and win them over; and above all rulers had to take other rulers into consideration, lest by recognizing the wrong pope they hand sworn enemies, or potential enemies and rivals, an insuperable advantage and do irremediable damage to their own position.

This situation—underpinned by the newly emerging disciplines of jurisprudence and canon law—resulted in a new legal fixing and legitimizing (as well as a theoretical analysis) of rulers' power, to a stronger spatial awareness of this power, and so to a hitherto unachieved legal integration and consolidation of ruling alliances. In short, its effect was to concentrate and intensify public power. But first and foremost, beyond all these processes of integration, it compelled kings and princes to engage in a calculated interaction, to a kind of concert of the powers, in which each participant had to play an instrument tuned to his fellow musicians if he wanted to survive. Thus, this century of papal schisms saw the emergence of the multifaceted world of kingdoms and principalities, which shaped the following centuries, and that extensive, tension-laden, and conflict-rich interdependence, which was to characterize the history of Europe from that time forward. This development was accompanied by sometimes favorable, sometimes disparaging prejudices about this or that "nation," which over time became highly potent, action-guiding, and enduring. These kinds of repercussions stabilized the western monarchies, above all, especially France, while the Holy Roman Emperor during this period (the eleventh and twelfth centuries and thereafter) was repeatedly found on the wrong side. But these repercussions also had a strengthening effect, especially on the papacy. Supported by the university disciplines of jurisprudence and theology, which flourished from the twelfth century on, the papacy now hastened unstoppably toward the era of its greatest power, as it became the unchecked, absolute representative of God's power on Earth.

The Investiture ban, which ushered in these changes, shook most European kingdoms and principalities to the core, yet nowhere did it have such a cataclysmic effect as in the Holy Roman Empire. The rulers of most European realms managed to turn the repeated schisms of the Roman Church to their advantage in quite a different way from the Roman-German kings, since most European rulers were not faced with the strong opposition from their princes that these Roman-German rulers met. Moreover, in most European domains even the leading churches and great monasteries did not as a rule have at their disposal any authority beyond the boundaries of their (in any event modest) land holdings; therefore most rulers could forgo the former investiture rights without incurring any great loss of power. Nowhere in Europe, not even in the areas of Italy under the Holy Roman Empire, were bishops and abbots also secular princes, as they were in Germany; in France, in any case, the renunciation of investiture rights affected the king and royal vassals in equal measure, yet kings there still retained the so-called *regalia* rights, namely the right to temporary use of church revenues when a living fell vacant, so long as these revenues belonged to the Crown's domain. So it was that both there and in England, concordats ending the dispute were able to be concluded far earlier than those eventually reached with the German king. In the wake of the contention surrounding the papal schisms of 1130 and 1159, the many individual churches in England and France ultimately came together under the leadership of the king to form their respective national churches, the *Ecclesia Anglicana* and the *Ecclesia Gallicana*. These churches attained a sense of closeness and cohesion that the "princely churches" of Germany never managed to achieve at any time.

Around this time, the English chronicler John of Worcester, a perceptive contemporary observer, painted a disturbing picture of his age. He couched it in the guise of a dream of his sovereign, King Henry I, who had a nightmare that peasants were attacking him with hatchets, rakes, and flails; alarmed, he woke with a start, calmed down, and fell back to sleep. Then knights appeared in full armor, with swords and shields, toying menacingly with their weapons and crowding round the king. Once again, he woke from his dream in terror, and then fell asleep again for a third time. Now abbots and bishops appeared, raising their crosiers above their heads as if to strike him. Henry awoke in a cold sweat, proclaiming: "Such things can frighten a king!"[6] In this narrative, the chronicler was sketching the image of a society in disarray, in a state of flux and upheaval with new aims, wishes, and desires. People's horizons were widening, and no one knew where things were heading or how everything would end. And that was indeed enough to terrify even a king.

However, the European horizon was widening not least as a direct result of the papal schisms, as those who were elected to the Petrine throne dispatched envoys to all corners of the continent to solicit support. No royal court, let alone any individual, had such a comprehensive and accurate knowledge of Europe at that time as the Roman Curia. Its register of interest payments, of which a written record had been kept since the late twelfth century, noted every country, every diocese, and every church and community that was liable to pay interest. Yet corresponding maps—an abstraction of spatial and geographical knowledge—only came into being in the Early Modern period. Even so, Latin ecumenical Christianity now began to coalesce in a way that had been inconceivable since Antiquity. This new union of many diverse peoples and realms—which had not been produced by the schism but was nevertheless decisively shaped by it—aimed to be all-encompassing.

Developments on the Iberian peninsula, hitherto somewhat marginal and overlooked, now drew the world's attention. This all took place under the auspices of the *Reconquista;* only now, in concert with the church reforms and under entirely different conditions from other European kingdoms, did the country begin to seek closer ties to the Roman Church and the papacy. After the swift collapse of the West Gothic Kingdom in 711, only small pockets of territory had remained in Christian hands. Nevertheless, they did manage to survive and gradually, beginning in the ninth but especially from the early eleventh century on, began to harbor thoughts of expansion. This was made possible by the decline of the recently flourishing caliphate of Córdoba, which was now torn by civil war, and its consequent fragmentation into various minor realms. The same basic truth always emerged: division weakens and destroys and allows one's opponents to prevail. To be sure, the beginnings of the new Christian kingdoms in Spain were very modest. Yet a series of effective and militarily successful leaders managed to consolidate these kingdoms internally and to expand them externally. Henceforth, the main problem was *Repoblación,* "repopulating" the territories that had been taken from the Moors but were depopulated by the ravages of war. New settlers were recruited especially from France, but the Muslim population was not completely expelled at this point but rather, like the Jews, granted protection and made subject to high taxation, thus creating a lucrative source of income for the new Christian conquerors. It is not beyond the realms of possibility that many a Hernán Cortes, many a *conquistador* who ravaged the Americas in the sixteenth century gained his inspiration from the centuries-long and much-vaunted *Reconquista* of Spain.

Indeed, Spain began to become a focal point for Christians. During the reign of Louis the Pious in the Frankish kingdom, in the far northwest of the Iberian peninsula, in the Asturias region centered on Oviedo, a miraculous discovery was made by King Alfonso II (d. 842)—doubtless in order to counter the rise of ever more virulent Adoptianistic doctrines in the country—namely, the supposed tomb of the Apostle Saint James the Elder. Over the ensuing centuries, this tomb was to prove an invaluable piece of symbolic capital, an investment that paid handsome dividends. But even above and beyond that, Saint James (Santiago de Compostela) became the patron saint of the struggle against Islam. Belief in him awakened and intensified people's willingness to fight. People imagined him as a heavenly warrior mounted on a white charger and riding bravely into battle against the Moors carrying a white flag emblazoned with a red cross, and spurring on the downhearted Christian forces to a famous victory. The apostle thus earned himself the nickname of *Matamoros,* the "Moor-slayer." Later, the Castilians would ride into battle against the Saracens with the war-cry *"Santiago;"* on their lips. Moreover, even at this early stage, there were embryonic signs of the *Reconquista* idea, which found their apotheosis in the myth of Covadonga, a cave in the Pyrenees, outside which rebellious Western Goths under the leadership of Pelagius of Asturias had, supposedly even in 722, sworn to devote their lives to "the salvation of Spain and to reforming the army of the Goths . . . and to put our trust in God's mercy for the restoration *(recuperatio)* of the church, the People, and the Realm" (as recounted in the early tenth-century *Chronicle of Alphonso III).* This legend of Covadonga, where the "Goths" were thought to have scored their first victory over the Moors, founded the kingdom of Asturias, and inaugurated the reconquest that would end in the capture of the caliphate of Toledo. Over the years, this myth became ever more vividly delineated.

In the eleventh century, skillful propaganda made the discovery of the apostle's tomb into an event that concerned the whole Western world. Pilgrims began to venture there from all over Europe. The Way of Saint James pilgrimage route now reunited long-marginalized Spain with the rest of Latin Christendom; and Santiago de Compostela became, along-side Rome and Jerusalem, one of the three principal pilgrimage sites of the Catholic world. Even today, it still stands as a stronghold of faith in a rising tide of faithlessness. The evolving cult of Saint James was, not least of all, an effective means of recruiting Christian settlers to come and occupy the areas vacated by the defeated Moors. The Cluniac monks who were invited to settle in Spain took it upon themselves to provide pastoral care to the new arrivals. At the same time, not unlike modern tourism, mass pilgrimage and the calculation of the remission of sins took on enormous economic significance for all those churches and monasteries that lay along the pilgrims' route, assuring many of these institutions—such as the diocese of Antun in Burgundy or the monastery of St.-Gilles in Provence—a sizable income that enabled them to commission new church buildings, each one large, grander, and more opulent than the last. Money seemed to follow pilgrims.

Over the centuries, the kingdoms of Léon and Castile evolved from the old polity of Asturias. Its neighbor was the realm of the Basques—Navarre—with its royal seat at Pamplona. A third political center to appear was

Aragón, including the region of Catalonia under the earldom of Barcelona, which legally belonged to France. Catalonia owed its establishment
to the Carolingian king Louis the Stammerer, who in 878 granted Wifred,
the count of Urgell and Cerdanya, the territories of Barcelona and Girona as
well, and gave his brother Miro the Roussillon district. This was the last occasion on which the West Frankish/French kingdom was able to intervene
in the capacity of a feudal lord in this region; after that, Catalonia became
independent, while through their own efforts its rulers projected its power
far and wide. From 1162 on, they also wore the crown of Aragón, and their
dynasty only died out in 1410, 500 years after its inception.

The *Reconquista* reached its most decisive and intensive phase in the
latter years of the eleventh century. In this period, around 1060–1090, the
saga of El Cid (which was only set down for literary posterity in 1235)
became the anthem of the whole *Reconquista*. This rebellious soldier, one
Rodrigo Díaz de Vivar, who was exiled from Castile, spent some time
aiding Christian rulers against the Moors, yet on other occasions fought
in alliance with them against Christian opponents, but eventually won
control over the kingdom of Valencia. He was known to the Moors as *El
Cid* and to Christians as *El Campeador,* but after his death, Christian
forces could not hold Valencia for long, and it was another 150 years before
the city was retaken by them, under Catalan leadership. Just as the First
Crusade was setting off for the Holy Land, another Crusade-like expedition was assembling to try and conquer Tarragona. According to legend,
this city fell on the same day as Jerusalem in 1099.

The kingdoms of Léon and Castile were allied briefly in the eleventh
century before being finally unified under Ferdinand III in 1230. By the
late eleventh century, they could look back on a period of relentless
expansion—despite early disputes over the succession, serious aristocratic
rebellions, and occasional setbacks in the struggle against the Moors.[7]
True, in the years around the turn of the century al-Mansur and his son
Abd al-Malik al Muzaffar, the rulers of Córdoba, had made serious in-
roads against the Christians, even taking Santiago de Compostela, the
spiritual and religious center of the *Reconquista* and hotbed of Christian
confidence in ultimate victory, and razing it to the ground. Yet internal
wranglings weakened al-Andalus, and a series of new Christian victories
soon erased all memory of their recent defeats. This phase came to a peak
in 1085 with the capture of Moorish Toledo. The following decades saw
this city become the seat of a highly productive and far-reaching intellec-

tual culture that synthesized Arab, Jewish, Mozarabic, and Latin learning; the Catholic bishop appointed to the city became, with papal privilege, the primate of the Spanish Catholic Church.

The influence that Muslim culture exerted on the whole of the Latin world was to fundamentally change this Western civilization. From the eleventh century onward, astronomy and astrology began to spread throughout Europe, alongside medical knowledge. Scholars from all arts of the continent began to flock to Spain to study the natural sciences, and it was there too that long-forgotten ancient Greek authors and their Arab exegetes (notably Avicenna and Averroës) first became known to Westerners. For it was in al-Andalus, and on the former Arab-controlled island of Sicily, that translators were active whose work enabled the Latin West to engage once more with this long-untapped treasure trove of knowledge, thereby enriching the whole intellectual culture of the West and its way of life. At least two of these scholars working in Spain should be identified by name: Gerard of Cremona (d. 1187) and Dominicus Gundissalinus (d. sometime after 1181).[8] The Lombard Gerard translated more than eighty works on philosophy, astronomy, mathematics, geometry, and medicine from the Arabic; in particular, he was responsible for making Ptolemy's *Almagest,* the most important work of Antiquity on astronomy, available to Latin world once more. Dominicus, for his part, devoted his efforts to translating the philosopher Avicenna (whose works have an almost Enlightenment feel to them); he also wrote tracts of his own on psychology and the taxonomy of philosophy. His writings influenced many other scholars, including Thomas Aquinas. At the same time, the defensive battles fought by the Moors against advancing Christian forces were hard and brutal. For example, even today the remains of the caliph's palace at Ronda still bear witness to the bitterness of the conflict, with its 200-meter high staircase leading down to the river, a staircase hewn from the solid rock inside the cliffs by the forced labor of prisoners of war and other captives.

Meanwhile, Navarre remained more or less confined to the Basque lands, since its hemmed-in location precluded it from expanding through conquest. Its neighbor Aragón, which had split from Navarre, could count itself more fortunate in this regard. It began its expansion from two valleys in the Pyrenees and the small episcopal seat of Jaca; soon, the town of Huesca had been taken, and presently Aragón succeeded where even Charlemagne had once failed, in capturing the city of Zaragoza. From the reign of King Peter I of Aragón (r. 1094–1104) and Pope Urban II (r. 1088–1099), the rulers of Aragón, far removed from any schisms, were granted papal protection (1095). The most successful of these kings, Alfonso I (known as "the Warrior"), left no heirs; in 1131 he wrote his will bequeathing everything to the knightly orders and the Holy Sepulcher, though his wishes were not ultimately carried out. Instead, the Aragonese raised Ramiro, the man they called their *dominus naturalis,* to the throne. Ramiro, however, was a monk. He was taken from his monastery, installed on the throne, and—necessity knows no law—given as a wife a widow who already had children. That same year, she bore Ramiro a daughter, Petronilla, who was married off at the age of one year to Count Ramon Berenguer IV of Barcelona, so that the monk might renounce his royal role and return to his devotions.

As it turned out, a better choice of husband could scarcely have been conceived; the Catalan count can fairly be regarded as one of the great ruling figures of the twelfth century. The marriage between him and Petronilla marked the birth of a new major power: the throne of Aragón. Presently, alongside Aragón and Barcelona, it also included Roussillon and the city of Montpellier as well as numerous smaller counties and other domains. A branch of the royal house of Aragón-Barcelona even gained control of the county of Provence, which had formerly been part of the Kingdom of Arles. Thus it was that in around 1200 the English chronicler Roger of Hoveden was able to report that the territories controlled by King Alfonso II of Aragón (r. 1164–1196) extended as far as Nice.[9] The whole of Languedoc seemed to align itself with the Aragonese throne; at that time even the count of Toulouse was closer to the Spanish king than to his French lord. Yet the first Aragonese king to acknowledge the feudal supremacy of the papacy and to be crowned by the pope in Rome (Innocent III, in 1204) was Peter II, the grandson of Raimund Berenguer IV and Petronilla.

Aragón's expansion into Provence was abruptly reversed by the Crusade against the Albigensians. Despite being a protégé of the pope, Peter found himself forced into the role of a protector of the Cathar "heretics," alongside his brother-in-law and vassal, Count Raymond VI of Toulouse. The Crusader army, which recruited knights from all over Europe was skillfully led by Simon de Montfort the Elder. Presently, the decisive battle of the campaign against the Albigensians loomed and was fought at Muret outside Toulouse in 1213. Peter, supposedly exhausted by a night of lovemaking before the battle, was killed at this engagement; he has gone down in Catalan history as Peter "the Catholic." Henceforth, the Aragonese kings turned increasingly toward the south, while the Capetian monarchy of France consolidated its control over the lands bordering the Mediterranean coastline.

Our attention now shifts from the south to the far north, to Scandinavia in fact, and the homeland of the Vikings, who had once been the scourge of the West, even as far as Asturias. Certainly the Viking "islands" including Denmark—as Scandinavia had been thought of since Antiquity and was still conceived of at this time—lay far removed from the centers where historians wrote their chronicles, but it was no longer beyond the reach of the Christian world. The first missionaries had set out in the ninth century (829–831) to convert the Svear (Swedes) living around Lake Mälaren and old Uppsala; the mission was led by the monk Ansgar, formerly of Corbie and Corvey abbeys; indeed, Abbot Wala of Corvey recommended him for this mission. However, Ansgar and his fellow missionaries only had limited success. Around the turn of the millennium, the first Christian ruler of the Svear and Götar is thought to have been Olaf Skötkonung, but aside from some sketchy details about the advent of Christianity and violent battles, very little is known about how this king came to power or how this new religion managed to assert itself in the north, which traditionally worshipped a whole pantheon of gods. Likewise, we have no information on how Olaf's reign or Christianity developed over the ensuing period. Historical data for this region only becomes thicker on the ground from the thirteenth century on. Yet all that we do know points to a long-lasting state of unrest in this northern realm and to revolutionary upheavals throughout Scandinavia as a whole. It would appear that church reform acted rather as a stabilizing factor for the monarchy, the sole entity that enabled the church to achieve any success here in the first place.

The picture is somewhat clearer where Denmark is concerned, a region that seems to have been unified from the first half of the tenth century onward under the rule of Gorm the Old and his son Harald Bluetooth. The first place where the term *dena mearc* is mentioned is in the sections relating to Scandinavia in the late ninth-century translation of Orosius's *Historiae adversus Paganos* often attributed to Alfred the Great. In the country itself, the great rune stones erected in commemoration of the country's unifiers Gorm and Harald at the church in Jelling are the first to call the country thus created by the name *tanmark*. As early as c. 700 Willibrord had undertaken missions to Denmark—albeit without any tangible result; and during the reign of Louis the Pious, King Harald

Klak was baptized in Ingelheim, which likewise failed to spark mass conversion. Then Ansgar established churches in Ripen and Schleswig, whose immediate history thereafter is unknown. However, these foundations resurface, along with Aarhus, in the reign of Otto the Great as the first dioceses of Denmark, under the aegis of the metropolitan region of Hamburg–Bremen. By this stage, then, Christianity had gained a firm foothold in the country, and both institutions, the monarchy and the church, mutually reinforced each other. Even so, or perhaps precisely because of this, King Canute IV died a martyr's death in 1086 (and was later canonized). His predecessor Sven Estridsen found in Adam of Bremen a chronicler who had much to report but who also passed down much anecdotal material, the historical accuracy of which cannot always be verified. Nevertheless, gradually the darkness lifted over this land without writing (aside from various runes carved in rocks). Around 1100, Eric I was able to found the archbishopric of Lund, to which the whole of Scandinavia was made subservient, and hence to disengage the Danish church from its fealty to the Hamburg ecclesiastical province, much to the displeasure of the metropolitan there, who had recently harbored dreams of a great northern patriarchate. Following wars of succession in the early twelfth century, the situation stabilized. Waldemar the Great (1153–1182), whose reign was distinguished by the forging of closer relation to the apostolic see, was also the first Danish king to pursue a policy of expansion in the western Baltic, which brought him into conflict with the Saxon ruler Henry the Lion. His son Waldemar II (1202–1241) intervened in the upheaval of the German succession dispute by bringing the imperial territory of Holstein and Lübeck under his control, but was forced to relinquish his new conquests after defeat at the Battle of Bornhöved in 1227, despite the fact that the emperor, Frederick II, had already renounced his claim. Furthermore, the period around 1200 saw the emergence of the first Danish chronicler, Saxo Grammaticus, who recounted a rich treasure-trove of ancient sagas.

The North Sea realm of Canute the Great, which in the early eleventh century extended as far as England and Norway, proved to be unsustainable. Olaf Trgyggvason and Saint Olaf had already united the latter country and introduced Christianity there by the time that Canute defeated the younger Olaf. In trying to win back Norway, Olaf was killed in battle in 1030 and has been honored ever since as a martyr and patron saint of the country. After Canute's death, the Norwegian monarchy managed to reestablish itself, even though there were sometimes several kings on the throne simultaneously. Before he ascended the throne, one of these, Harald Hardrada, was in the service of the Byzantine emperor in Constantinople. It was only in 1152–1153 that Norway was granted a single archbishopric, the metropolitanate of Drontheim. Norway's history becomes far less opaque after that date.

Far-reaching changes also occurred in the age of church reform and papal schisms in the British Isles, the territory that had suffered most from Viking raids. Here, too, conditions stabilized over time. The last Anglo-Saxon kings had barely been able to defend their lands against the Danes. Svein Fork-beard, Harald Bluetooth's son and father of Canute the Great had subjugated England and in 1011 raised his banner over Canterbury. He imposed a tribute, known as Danegeld, on his new conquest and two years later deposed King Ethelred the Unready. Svein was widely acknowledged as the country's new ruler, and became the first "Norman" on the English throne. When the captured Bishop Aelfheah refused to pay his ransom, he was first mocked and taunted by his Danish captors before being slain with axes "out of pity." Ethelred's son Edward, though, went into exile at the court of the Duke of Normandy. In England, meanwhile, Svein was succeeded by his son Canute the Great (1016) who held a tight rein over the country and soon wrested for himself the crowns of Denmark and Norway (1019). When he died, his three kingdoms were plunged into disarray, a story that lack of space precludes us from describing here.

This situation enabled Edward the Confessor to return from Normandy and ascend the throne. However, his reign was beset by constant wrangling with his earls. One of them, Harold Godwinson, became king on Edward's death in 1066, but immediately found himself faced with a dangerous rival in the shape of William, duke of Normandy, to whom Edward the Confessor had promised the English throne in return for granting him sanctuary. William made preparations for war and invasion, which duly ensued. Battle was joined at Hastings; Harold Godwinson, who had just won a hard-fought battle against Harald Hardrada at Stamford Bridge in Yorkshire, rushed down to engage William on the south coast, but was defeated, losing his life in the process. The Bayeux Tapestry depicts the entire history of the event. The tapestry may be regarded as an authentic source that is comparatively close in time to the actual incident and to the ruling dynasty; it was probably woven in Canterbury for William's half-brother Odo, the Bishop of Bayeux, and represents a unique pictorial document of the history of this period. Ships, weapons, armor, fighting tactics, pillaging, and other features are all show here in great detail, and shining down on all the action is Halley's Comet, the arrival of which had marked 1066 as a year of both terror and good fortune.

William the Conqueror was immediately proclaimed king of England, which he ruled until his death in 1087. He successfully established a "realm of two peoples" straddling the English Channel. Yet this could not be achieved without effecting major changes in the traditional order of the island. The Anglo-Saxon ruling elite was completely disempowered and was replaced by Norman barons. As a vassal of the French king, which William was by law, he imported continental feudal law and other institutions of his duchy to England, not least French as the language of authority and the courtroom. This "Law French" endured for a long time; only after 1362—a result of the Hundred Years' War—did it become permissible to plead one's case in English; not until the eighteenth century did the ancient judicial language vanish completely. The new king brought over a succession of reforming abbots from Bec Abbey and assigned to them the principal archbishopric in the country, Canterbury. The first of these was Lanfranc, who was succeeded by Anselm, and over the following six decades, all the English dioceses were entrusted solely to faithful followers from either Normandy or France.

William was succeeded on the English throne by his sons. Under William Rufus (d. 1100), the question of the investiture dispute first raised its head, which was then resolved and regulated during the reign of his brother and successor Henry I Beauclerc under pressure from Archbishop Anselm, who forced the king to comply with the papal ruling that only the pope, and not a secular ruler, could invest a new bishop. Henry's soubriquet apparently derived from his education in the liberal arts. It was reported that he once angrily lashed out at his father, the illiterate Conqueror, telling him that *Rex illiteratus quasi asinus coronatus* ("An uneducated king is nothing better than an ass with a crown"). Overall, he was a worthy successor to his father and brother; yet even he was visited by disaster when his only son[10] was drowned when the "White Ship" foundered and sank in the Channel in 1120. The consequences of this tragic loss reverberated over centuries, as England immediately found herself in the throes of a succession dispute ("the Anarchy"), and the ensuing coronation of another French royal vassal (Stephen of Blois) opened up a vista of dynastic disputes that were to culminate, centuries later, in the Hundred Years' War. Certainly, Stephen was initially able to consolidate his control of the island, but he too died without leaving a legitimate heir. As a result, his adversary Henry Plantagenet, duke of Anjou, the son of Geoffrey of Anjou and the Empress Matilda, widow of Holy Roman Emperor Henry V, was able to seize control of the English throne. Around this time, the Celtic–Welsh legend of King Arthur crossed the Channel and soon gained a presiding influence over the epic poetry tradition of the continent. Power and culture were often closely linked, but did not always follow the same premises. Now, in real life, the vanquished was to prevail over the conqueror.

Out of a combination of the Anglo-Saxon legacy and Norman and French innovations, the Normans and Angevins managed to fashion comparatively modern polities on both sides of the Channel, characterized not only by strong ducal or royal rule but also by a highly efficient financial and fiscal administration and a centralized judicial system. These institutions remained effective even when—as was the case most of the time—the kings were absent, spending long periods in one or other part of the realm. Following the reign of William the Conqueror, the monarchy had had to find ways of institutionally compensating for long, regular absences on the part of the ruler. Indeed, these absences were the catalyst to creating precisely those institutions that were designed to represent the notional presence of the personage of the "king," even when he was physically remote. In doing so, they were the very first bodies to generate a figure of abstract statehood, in the legal personage of the Crown.

In this context, special attention should be drawn to William the Conqueror's *Domesday Book* and the *Exchequer*. Both of these represent singular undertakings for the period. The *Domesday Book* is first mentioned by name in the 1179 work by Richard FitzNigel (Richard of Ely) entitled *Dialogue Concerning the Exchequer,* where the author also notes that the information it contains is every bit as inalterable as the sentences passed on Judgment Day. Shire by shire and borough by borough—insofar as William had gained control of them—this overview of England was conducted in 1086, and methodically (albeit not comprehensively or without some errors) notes the following information for each of these areas: the number of inhabitants, the extent and value of the holdings of the king and of those belonging to his vassals and barons, the number of estates ("hides"), plow teams (of eight oxen apiece), and other pieces of infrastructure or topography (for example, mills or forests), in addition to the taxation revenue accruing from all of these lands, respectively during the reign of Edward the Confessor, in 1006, and "now." This data was compiled on the basis of systematic questioning of landowners. The *Domesday Book* was a survey of the country that not only displayed a high degree of rational organization but that also, for all its shortcomings, pointed the way forward for all future state bureaucracies. The book was preserved in the royal treasury, and is now held at the Public Record Office in London.

Richard FitzNigel's much-admired *Dialogue Concerning the Exchequer*—whose Latin name *Dialogus de scaccario* derives from the word for abacus *(scaccarius),* the device used to make calculations—was only written almost a century after the *Domesday Book,* although the institution that is its subject, the Exchequer, dates back to the reign of Henry I. The work was about the collection and administration of taxes and described the techniques and principles that were employed in this area, including—and this is significant in a period that saw the first general proscriptions against usury—the distinction between "public" and "nonpublic usury," together with hints on covert interest-paying lending activities. The author set great store by the writing down of accounts; indeed, from this period on, all the crown's financial records are extant in a continuous sequence from the "pipe rolls," which were drawn up annually from 1130 on, right up to the present day. In his preamble, Richard straightaway offered the insight, remarkable for this period, that "money *(pecunia)* is indispensable not only in war but also in times of peace." And he was at pains to warn his readers: "Those who lack such worldly means will fall prey to his enemies, but those who have this wherewithal shall prevail over their foes." This may well be the first occasion in the West on which a writer had, so succinctly and appositely, made the connection between money and politics. A new age was dawning, a change of era. Granted, Richard of Ely can have had no inkling of how right he actually was. His final great achievement was to raise the ransom money needed to release his king, Richard I (the Lionheart) from his captivity in Germany during his return from the Third Crusade. This incident set in train a whole new chain of events, largely played out in the Norman kingdom of Sicily, that not only caused England to shed more blood but that also brought about the end of the Hohenstaufen dynasty. For all this, though, the Exchequer still serves as the treasury of the British crown.

Southern Italy was indeed the scene of major upheavals during this period. There, too, the restlessness of the Normans metamorphosed into a ruthless pursuit of power. Though this process cannot be seen as a result of the papal schisms, nevertheless it was fundamentally hastened and shaped by them. Following their victory over Leo IX in 1051, the sons of Tancred of Hauteville did not rest on their laurels, but instead set about conquering further territory, county by county and duchy by duchy. The Lombard princes of Dalerno, Capua, and Benevento, who had formerly asked the Normans for help, now found themselves deposed and stripped of power by them. Richard of Aversa, who had begun as a vassal of the Hautevilles but who then managed to seize Capua, legitimized his rule by becoming the very first of the Normans to swear an oath of fealty to Pope Nicholas II (1059). By 1060, the Normans had secured control of virtually the whole of southern Italy, a campaign in which Robert Guiscard, despite family feuding, obtained the support of his younger brother Roger. Twelve years later, Palermo and almost all of Sicily was in the hands of Roger, who quickly established his rule over the island. Meanwhile, in Rome, Archdeacon Hildebrand was pulling the political strings; the following year (1073) he duly ascended the papal throne as Gregory VII. He immediately turned to the new Catholic rulers of southern Italy for their help. Though they were parvenus, from the start of the period of church reform, they proved themselves to be effective partners in shaping the political and intellectual culture of Europe.

Likewise, Urban II and Pascal II, who were also threatened with schisms, found it expedient to be well-disposed toward the Normans. Once Count Roger I had completed his conquest of Sicily, he was granted a legation privilege by Pope Urban, which named him as the legitimate papal legate on the island and accorded him special rights. His son, also named Roger, inherited the mainland territories of the Hautevilles and during the schism that began in 1130 was not only able to assert his control there against the will of the pope, but in return for a pledge of allegiance was also succeeded in having Sicily raised to the status of a kingdom, first by the antipope Analect II, and then (in 1139) by the legitimate successor to the Petrine throne, Innocent II. Roger II was one of the outstanding rulers of his age. The pursuit of shrewd policies within its multilingual realm of many diverse cultures—which contained a mix of Catholic Latins, Orthodox Greeks, Muslim Arabs, and Jews—involved an efficient economic policy that used similar methods and—in exchange—the same skilled labor as the English Exchequer, and finally an ambitious foreign policy that relied on a powerful fleet and that projected its reach as far as Africa; the new kingdom was soon able to emerge as one of major powers in the Mediterranean. Roger II's court in Palermo became a center of learning; outstanding scholars from all countries and regions gathered there. It was here that Plato's *Meno* was first translated into Latin, and the geographer al-Idrisi drafted a world map for the Sicilian king, which was the first such map in centuries to be based on the findings of Ptolemy. Byzantine mosaic makers decorated the chapel of the king's palace in Palermo, as well as adorning the newly built cathedral churches in Cefalù and later in Monreale with unique decorative motifs and programmatic images of the king. Here too, with the assizes at Ariano, there arose one of the most modern legislatures of the age, which was based on learned Roman Law, mixed with Byzantine and Norman traditions; this court covered both general "public" law and the specialties of canon law, feudal law, marriage law, and criminal law. Even so, despite the vow of fealty, the kingdom of Sicily's relations with the popes remained tense, with this new power in the south of the peninsula representing a latent threat to the papacy.

France, too, after the demise of the Carolingians, witnessed the steady rise of a royal dynasty—the Capetians. This nation is perhaps fortunate to have known, to this day, only this single dynasty, with its agnatic branches of the Valois, Orléans, and Bourbons, whereas all other European monarchies without exception were characterized, and shaken, by numerous changes of ruling houses and succession disputes. Philippe I (d. 1108), who made his peace with the pope in 1107, and Louis VI (d. 1137) were the first monarchs of this dynasty to extend the Crown's domain—in Berry and Vexin respectively—and above all to consolidate royal power internally. Unlike the kingdom of the Salians, this regime was able to retain lapsed fiefdoms, since no one else emerged to claim them, and the king was no longer obliged to recompense anyone for such costly military service as the Italian campaigns. The Crown lands were now administered by bailiffs who could be hired and fired, and not by vassals with a hereditary claim to their tenures. New acquisitions were placed in the temporary care of younger side branches of the royal house; as such, these acquisitions were withdrawn from control of the central monarchy only for a while instead of disappearing completely, a common fate elsewhere given the vicissitudes to which ruling dynasties were prone. The central royal court grew in importance. Paris truly became the capital city, with all the central institutions of royal authority, in particular the treasury and judicial system, congregating and all the various threads of power converging here. In all likelihood, the university also flourished and expanded due to the proximity of the king in the capital on the Seine. As for the church in France, it could not bring power-political pressure to bear on the king through military resistance; rather its best hope was to exert moral influence on him, by insisting upon canon-law norms such as marriage law.

A very particular form of patriotism made itself apparent among the French from an early date. The author of the *Chanson de Roland* (from the first half of the twelfth century) had already spoken of *la douce France*. When France found herself threatened by attacks from Henry I of England and then by the Holy Roman Emperor Charles V (1124), the otherwise feuding royal vassals rallied round their king and assisted him in defending the country—the first sign of a newly awakened awareness of community, which in the following centuries would grow ever stronger, uniquely in Europe. This merged with a new sense of the sacredness of the monarchy, which in the ensuing century and a half was to endow the "Most Christian Majesty" of the French monarch with its own special aura. At that time, in 1124, the "Oriflamme," the battle ensign of the Capetian dynasty, was raised from the high altar of the Abbey church of Saint Denis, and before long was reinterpreted as the banner of the sacred Charlemagne and also came to symbolize the reception of the kingdom as a fiefdom from Saint Dionysius (Saint Denis). Right up to the fifteenth century, it represented a preeminent insignia of the French monarchy; only after the Battle of Agincourt in 1415, the last great battle of the Hundred Years' War, did its significance wane.

The abbey of Saint Denis became the royal sepulcher, the supreme memorial shrine to the French kings, the site where the sacred anointing oil was kept, which, as Hinkmar of Reims had reported in the ninth century, had supposedly been brought down from heaven by a dove in order to baptize Chlodwig. From the twelfth century on at the latest, all French kings were anointed at their investiture with this heavenly oil. Even as late as 1824, the last occasion on which a Bourbon monarch—the ultraroyalist Charles X—received unction, a drop of this wondrous oil was applied which was said to have been rediscovered, miraculously, on a shard of glass from a holy oil ampoule deliberately smashed during the Revolution. And so the "Oriflamme," Saint Charlemagne, and the heavenly oil, together with the hands of the king, which were believed to cure people of scrofula, combined to make up a curious sacred ensemble. This was augmented in the thirteenth century by the exclusive privilege accorded to the king to be anointed on the head, although this practice had been reserved for priests alone ever since the reign of Pope Innocent III, and also to have the prerogative during the coronation to take communion by receiving both the Body and the Blood of Christ, despite the fact that otherwise only the clergy drank from the chalice was from the twelfth century on. Finally, there was the question of the sanctity of the royal personage himself, as represented by the canonization of King Louis IX. The French monarchy thus created, like no other royal household in Europe, a veritable *"religion royale,"* and embellished this concept ideologically and liturgically in a completely inimitable way.

In this same period, no such undertones of patriotic allegiance to homeland were observable in the Holy Roman Empire, and the sacredness of its rulers, formerly the "Lord's Anointed Ones" had long since been called into doubt. To be sure, in this realm too there were lavish and heavily symbolic emblems of royal authority, foremost among them the Imperial Cross and the Holy Lance. Yet unlike when Otto I went into battle against the Magyars, no one rallied round the Holy Lance anymore when the king raised it in a desperate situation. Saxony, Franconia, and Bavaria retained their own sense of ethnic identity, which only served to separate them from one another rather than imparting any unifying concept of "Germanness." Apart from their own legal system and territory, those peoples had no central institutions—no "clan assemblies" or "clan duchy," for example, even though there was only, say, one Bavarian or Saxon duke. Rather, these places were characterized by the rivalry of a set of petty principalities, which also caused the empire as a whole considerable problems. Only the king could guarantee the unity of the overarching ruling assembly. Yet if, this body's power of integration waned, as had been the case since the reign of Henry IV, the only things remaining were the ever-weaker feudal bonds and authority over the imperial churches, which had been jeopardized by the Investiture Controversy.

Henry V (d. 1125) turned to Italy once more, in the expectation of receiving the rich inheritance of Matilda of Tuscany and doubtless also in the hope of using it to reassert the realm's authority north of the Alps as well. He took an uncompromising line toward Pope Paschal II, to try and force him to climb down on the investiture question, but this only succeeded in strengthening the opposition of the nobility and the clergy to his rule back in Germany, while bringing him no advantages in his disputes in Italy or with the other crowned heads of Europe. People were growing increasingly weary of endless discord. For a moment, it even seemed as though Paschal—prompted by the ideal of poverty—might give way and completely renounce his claim, on behalf of the churches, to the *"regalia,"* as they were then defined, insofar as the right of the empire had been transferred to the imperial churches (1111). However, even if this intention had been meant seriously, it foundered anyway on the clamorous opposition of the German bishops, who had no desire to relinquish their worldly power and developing principalities. For a while, Henry supported an antipope (1119). Consequently, it took another three years before the Concordat of Worms (1122) seemed finally to have brought a formal end to this dispute. This agreement guaranteed the free election of the clergy and conceded to the king the right to invest priests with the *regalia*; in Germany before the bishops had consecrated the priest, but in Italy and Burgundy within six months after the consecration. Thus began the inexorable rise of the German high churches to become worldly principalities under the control of ecclesiastical princes (which famously led the German historian Samuel Pufendorf to describe the Holy Roman Empire in 1667 as "an irregular body like some misshapen monster"); though this entity endured for centuries, in actual fact it was increasingly hamstrung.

Henry V duly waited to come into possession of the bequest of Margravine Matilda of Tuscany (d. 1115) beyond the Alps. Indeed, the Salian king did manage to persuade his aunt to sign over possession of her holdings to him. Or so it seemed; but the lady in question, a last descendant of the Conradin dynasty, had in fact repeatedly promised the apostolic see that it would inherit her territories. The ensuing wrangling developed into a row of major proportions, which every new papal schism only aggravated. Scarcely had the Investiture Controversy drawn to a close than new causes for conflict reared their heads. And so things were to remain for the next few centuries. No sooner was the matter of Matilda's possessions resolved than the question of the *Unio regni cum imperio*—namely, the union of the Hohenstaufen kingdom of Sicily with the Holy Roman Empire— came to the fore, which threatened the very existence of the papacy. And scarcely had this question been settled by the demise of the Hohenstaufen dynasty than the papal demand that Rome should henceforth vet all German kings as suitable future candidates for the emperorship shattered the peace once more. Finally, with this matter seemingly dealt with by the so-called Golden Bull of 1356, the Western Schism (1378–1417) promptly sowed uncertainty and unrest, and in turn, when this appeared to have finally been resolved, the Reformation was already looming on the horizon, which split Germany along confessional lines and generated decades of civil war. The German lands, indeed, never witnessed a genuine peace between the *Sacerdotium* and the *Imperium*. Given this situation, it is easy to understand the broad political consensus in Germany that greeted Bismarck's defiant utterance (during the *Kulturkampf* in 1872): "We will not go to Canossa—neither in body nor in spirit!" This was emblematic of a nation whose whole character had been forged by the clash between secular and ecclesiastical forces.

Impact of the Crusades

Nor did the tensions in the West leave the "Franks" in the Orient unscathed. The sense of unity that seemed momentarily to have been achieved by Pope Urban II was destroyed by the ensuing schisms. The kings for their part were at odds with one another; none of them would have been able to mount a Crusade without help from the others. In these circumstances, any lasting help for the Crusader states in the Holy Land was out of the question. The "Latins" who had settled there after the conquest of Jerusalem in the First Crusade, steadily accommodated themselves to the conditions prevailing there. Short-lived gains were made in Syria and Palestine. But before long, difficulties began to mount; the trickle of people arriving from Europe by no means met the needs of the Crusader states. Furthermore, the routes leading from the ports to Jerusalem and Christianity's other holy sites were still extremely unsafe, with the soldiers of the Latin Kingdom unable to defend themselves against ambushes. This desperate situated gave rise to the creation of the orders of knighthood. The most successful and momentous of these was the order founded by Hugues de Payens, a French nobleman who with a handful of followers took on responsibility in 1118 for defending the groups of pilgrims traveling on routes across the Holy Land. These knights lived like monks, and indeed had sworn a vow before the patriarch of Jerusalem to remain poor, chaste, and obedient, at the same time pledging their lives to the struggle against the heathens and all enemies of the Cross. This small community got its name from the site that they were assigned on the Temple Mount in Jerusalem, immediately next to the Al-Aqsa Mosque; the buildings of the Knights Templar are still preserved in this location today.

In its combination of monasticism and chivalry, such an undertaking was highly scandalous. But Bernard of Clairvaux, a relative of Hugues de Payens, pronounced this new mode of living legitimate—which ran counter to every knightly or monastic ethos that had gone before—in a programmatic treatise entitles *De laude nove militie* (In praise of the new knightly order). They did not fight for glory, Bernard claimed in his work, but for Christ; he maintained that they permitted themselves no superfluous word, no pointless action, and no immoderate laughter, that they shunned the hunting and falconry that were otherwise the great pastimes of men of their rank; and that they listened to no heroic lays or bawdy songs, but rather shaved their heads and lived a frugal life. "They arm themselves with faith within and steel without . . . they attend to battle rather than display, to victory rather than glory . . . they fling themselves against their foes and treat their adversaries like sheep, ever fearless alike, however few in number they may be, of barbarous savagery and the numberless horde." He went on: "What can be said, but that this is the Lord's work and a miracle in our eyes?" And indeed, it was a miracle; the creation of the Knights Templar answered an almost insatiable yearning. This unconventional community offered the potential to combine noble rank with noble poverty and service to God with a chivalrous mode of existence. The pope, convinced by Bernard's propaganda, recognized the new order, the first military order, and granted it privileges. It enjoyed immense success. Especially in France and in England (less so in Germany), the sons of the highest aristocracy and of knights flocked to join the order. The Templars spread throughout Europe, and were granted land and income; in Paris, they were given the fortress called the Temple, where Louis XVI and his wife Marie Antoinette were held in 1791 prior to their execution two years later. The Templars' corresponding home in Berlin was the Tempelhof, later the site of the main airfield used to defy the Soviet blockade of the city in the Berlin Airlift of 1948–1949.

The Templars then served as a model for the creation of a second order, the Knights Hospitallers (Knights of Saint John), and finally, at the end of the twelfth century, the Teutonic Knights. Likewise, Spain and Portugal had their own knightly orders, known as the Order of Santiago, the Order of Calatrava, and later the Order of Christ, which took over the legacy of the Templars in Portugal in the fourteenth century. How urgently necessary the military orders were everywhere is illustrated by the phenomenon of the mercenary, which developed and spread parallel to them—these soldiers were ruthless and effective but soon found themselves reviled and opposed. Like the knightly orders, bands of mercenaries found their recruits among the younger sons of noblemen and in impoverished knights.

However, there was widespread discord among the Crusaders, and little cooperation was forthcoming. In 1144, Edessa was lost once more. Pope Eugenius III pressed for a Second Crusade (1147–1149). The saintly Bernard of Clairvaux, the "oracle of God" as one contemporary called him, lobbied strongly in favor of this military campaign: "O ye sinners, [now] is the opportunity for your salvation, for God will grant you remission of your sins and eternal glory. I pronounce this race of men fortunate who have been granted so much time for the remission of their sins, and who have seen this year of great rejoicing dawn. But now, O brave knight, now, O warrior hero, here is a battle you may fight with impunity, where it is glory to conquer and gain to die." Bernard went on to exhort anyone who was a prudent merchant to join the Crusade, for the investment would be minimal and yet the beatitude of the kingdom of heaven the reward. Many people heeded his call. The image of the merchant was compelling; it seemed to many to epitomize the whole idea of profit.[11] The fundamental change in society and its workings could not have been put more succinctly.

After receiving certain diplomatic assurances, Louis VII of France was immediately ready to embark on the Crusade. But the German king Conrad III hesitated before Bernard won him over with his preaching, appealing to him not in his own voice but in that of Christ: "O man, what more can I do for you than I have long since done?" And so this man, this king, stirred into action by the letter and by public opinion, duly hoisted the cross onto his shoulders. Two heavily armed armies immediately set off for the East—in the vanguard the Germans, and just a few weeks behind them the French, both taking the same road, through Hungary to Constantinople, and then across Asia Minor and on to inevitable ruin. Only a very few of them ever made it as far as Jerusalem. After its experience during the First Crusade, Byzantium was anything but overjoyed at the new influx of knights from the West, and failed to supply these new adventurers with either competent guides or sufficient provisions. Indeed, how could it do otherwise when faced with two huge armies who marched along the same road and plundered the same markets as they went? Things got even worse in Asia Minor; the terrain was harsh and food scarce. But armies cannot fight on empty stomachs. Only at the last moment did the *basileus* intervene with his fleet to save at least the kings. Conrad fell ill and returned to Europe, where his adoptive daughter Bertha-Irene was ruling as empress and looked after him. According to a tried-and-tested formula, Bernard of Clairvaux subsequently explained this catastrophe by claiming that too many evildoers and criminals had attached themselves to the well-intentioned enterprise and harmed it; this was exactly the same explanation given for the defeat of Leo IX against the Normans a century before. Even so, the monk's lust for war remained undimmed; Bernard went on zealously preaching in favor of the Crusades. Small groups of fighters continued to journey to the Holy Land, keen to fight but inexperienced, and consequently found themselves more feared than welcomed by the "Franks," who had since learned the lie of the land in Palestine.

Human tragedy followed hard on the heels of the débâcle of this Crusade, and its ramifications were to ripple down through world history. Louis VII of France, who was more of a scholar than a knight, had gone on campaign with his lady, Eleanor of Aquitaine. In the event, this proved a fateful decision. His spirited young wife was besotted with military heroes and is reputed to have immediately embarked on an affair with her uncle, the valiant Raymond of Antioch. This indiscretion plunged the royal couple into dreadful quarreling, and—following their return—a divorce, despite the attempted mediation of Pope Eugenius. But how shocked Louis must have been to see, shortly afterward, his banished former wife on the arm of Henry of Anjou, his most powerful vassal lord, whose marriage to Eleanor now secured him a rich dowry, namely the country of Poitou, and the duchy of Aquitaine with its capital, Bordeaux. And it was precisely this same Henry who, as a result of inheritance and military conquest, presently ascended the throne of England as King Henry II. A realm extending from Scotland to the Pyrenees was thus created; moreover, its borders lay just outside Paris—a mortal danger for the king of France. His realm was to feel the consequences until long after the end of the Hundred Years' War. To counter this threat, France had to summon up and intensify its powers, by enhancing the authority of the king. Yet for centuries, Bordeaux remained the residence of the English kings. Henry II also conquered Ireland, which thereby became part of the Roman Catholic Church's domain.

For German history, too, the Second Crusade likewise presented a small episode with major consequences. At one encampment on the campaign, the wealthy margrave of Tuscany, Welf VI, who had extensive territories in Bavaria and Swabia, pitched his tent aside from the main camp; there, he was attacked by Muslim warriors and surrounded, and would have been lost had his nephew Frederick of Swabia not rushed to the rescue.

Welf showed his gratitude to his savior for ever thereafter, the first time in 1152, when he intervened decisively to ensure that this Frederick (whose red beard earned him the soubriquet "Barbarossa") prevailed over Conrad III's own six-year-old son Frederick when the monarch appointed his successor as king of Germany. Later, in 1175, after Welf VI's only legitimate heir had died of malaria, he assigned all his prosperous estates to Barbarossa, rather than to the person who was next in the line of inheritance, Henry the Lion. Both of these decisions were to have a profound impact on both German and wider European history.

Yet it was not only the German monarchs and their princes who were affected by these events; relations with Byzantium were henceforth colored with a latent mistrust and an unquenchable animosity toward the young Hohenstaufen king. Conrad III had concluded a peace treaty with Manuel I Comnenus, which made provisions for a campaign against their common enemy, the Normans in southern Italy. This agreement was strengthened by the marriage in 1145 of the *basileus* to Conrad's adopted daughter Bertha, who upon becoming empress in Constantinople assumed the symbolic name Irene (meaning "peace"). But beyond this, the peace treaty never came into force as intended, not least due to the Crusade, when the Western king—who moreover in diplomatic relations with Byzantium always styled himself as the emperor—stood menacingly outside the gates of Constantinople with a mighty army and demanded access through to Asia Minor. After his humiliation at the hands of the Seljuk Turks, Conrad renewed the peace treaty from his sickbed in Constantinople; but even then he refused to commit forces to fighting Roger II of Sicily, despite the fact that the Norman ruler was at that moment threatening Constantinople. The death of the Hohenstaufen ruler a few years later (1152) caused the whole agreement to lapse. Tensions immediately increased between the Eastern and Western emperors. Frederick Barbarossa, who had effectively usurped his young cousin Frederick, Conrad's second son and the brother of the Empress Irene, had quite different objectives from his uncle, and before long Manuel counted himself among his sworn enemies. One aspect of Conrad's rule that Barbarossa did keenly adopt, however, was the *Augustus* formulation in the king's title, hitherto reserved for an emperor, but which Conrad had first used to style himself. It basically proclaimed that the "German" king was tantamount to an emperor, and so in terms of royal ambition put him on a par with the *basileus*. Not least, it also represented a clear barb directed at the pope, since the title had formerly been conferred only after coronation by the bishop of Rome. And so, unwittingly, the Second Crusade only served to sow the seeds of calamity in both East and West.

So what was the effect of all these events on the culture of the East? It was certainly not restricted to a considerable expansion in Western trade with Constantinople, in the export and import of commodities from this region. New learning also flowed from there: in production and distribution techniques and communications and languages, alongside a new appreciation of foreign countries and societies. Church reform with its attendant developments had also ushered in an intellectual revolution, which introduced the Latin West to learning on a hitherto unimagined scale; the Crusades only deepened and widened this process. Constantinople and the East as a whole, so to speak, suddenly came much closer, opening the Latins' eyes to worlds beyond their once narrow, familiar horizons. This was especially true where the Holy Land was concerned. No sooner had Jerusalem been taken than advance parties—real expeditions—were dispatched to scout out the region as far south as the Red Sea. The sheer fact that this happened is not perhaps so surprising—after all, who doesn't scout out territory they have just conquered? What is remarkable is that extensive reports of these expeditions were compiled and put down in writing, in order to serve as information and instruction for future generations. Knowledge thus became durable, and Western intellectual society was reformed on a new basis, with its rationalism being challenged and heightened through this direct encounter with Byzantium and the East. People's curiosity was piqued; they wanted to fathom this new realm, amass "experience" *(experimentum),* and draw conclusions that were not just hypothetical. Certainly, some commentators offered deeply inconsequential observations on lands and peoples, on date palms and Bedouin tribes, during this period, for instance that the Dead Sea really was "bitter," or that the waters of the Red Sea weren't red at all, because they'd seen it with their own eyes. But it's not this kind of harmless investigation, or travelers' initial sense of wonder and tasting the sweet fruit of new experience that's astonishing—but rather what holds our attention is their whole attitude, the desire to know and fathom things, the thirst for empirical evidence that followed the initial wonderment and that manifested itself in action.

Indeed, Christian Latins saw and learned things in the Holy Land and on the way there that were completely alien and unfamiliar to them and that contradicted the negative stereotypes that they brought with them concerning the "Saracens"—for example, the admirable humility of Muslims when praying to Allah, their foreheads smeared with dust as they prostrated themselves. As had happened in the far West as a result of the successes of the *Reconquista,* in the East the Christians entered a new phase in their encounter and engagement with the monotheistic religion of Islam, and so embarked on a gradual process of relativizing—not using that stereotype as a benchmark, though, but their own faith. The first stirrings of criticism of the Crusades began to make themselves felt in the West too as early as the twelfth century. There appeared the very first, still tentative germs of tolerance, which called for broad toleration of the Other while not quite yet embracing the concept of full acceptance of the Other in all its Otherness. New impulses for missionary work were the result, but also a sense of loosening of ties to the mother church, which was increasingly beset by heresies.

Certainly, missionary work had already been going on for some while in Spain and was far more effective there. Cluny Abbey had extensive possessions in the country, partly inhabited by Muslims. The Cluniac abbot Petrus Venerabilis, though, was not content merely to carry out enforced conversions. He wanted to learn in detail about the faith of those who were to be converted and took a systematic approach to the matter. The result was the publication of the first translation of the Qur'an into Latin, as well as a Life of Mohammed. In the interim, some extraordinarily good knowledge about Islam was circulating in the West, though this was soon to become clouded with all manner of myths and defamatory observations. Extant knowledge and new insights from the Holy Land complemented one another and engendered a new sense of reflectiveness regarding foreigners and their customs and religion.

New Branches of Learning

In addition, Byzantium challenged Western scholars with a hitherto unknown intensity. No diplomatic mission from the West arrived there without provoking the old theological controversy with the Greek Orthodox Church over the provenance of the Holy Spirit not just from the Father, but also from the Son—the centuries-old *filioque* question—as well as other articles of faith. This intercultural dispute required each party to broaden its own intellectual horizons, to perfect its methods of enquiry, and for European scholars to acquaint themselves with Ancient Greek texts frequently used by the Byzantines and Arabs but that had not been available to consult before in the West. It was virtually impossible to know in advance what one should be searching for in this quest; yet what emerged was an extraordinary treasure trove of learning. The key discovery was Aristotle, the master whose works plunged the traditional Neoplatonic-tinged worldview into chaos and then reassembled things in a new order.

One example will suffice to show how this came about and how it subsequently developed. The *Categories* of Aristotle required that a person should repeatedly adopt a skeptical or analytical stance on the difficult question of whether substances can be relative: *Dubitare autem de singulis non erit inutile* ("To entertain doubts on particular points will not be unprofitable"). Scholars from Worms, who around the mid-eleventh century are thought to have conducted a year-long dispute with cathedral scholars from Würzburg on this topic, seized upon this sentence—divorced from its context and in all likelihood without properly understanding it—to try and galvanize the scholars of the Mainz Cathedral seminary, well-versed as they were in the discipline of rhetoric, to pronounce on who had won the debate, exhorting them to "scrutinize while doubting:" *dubitando inquirere.*[12] The scholar Peter Abélard (d. 1142) took a quite different approach; pointing to Aristotle, he raised doubt to the status of a cognitive principle in itself: "For it is from doubt that we arrive at questioning; and in a state of questioning we apprehend the truth."[13] Once this basic premise was accepted, apparent contradictions in the works of the Christian Fathers could be plausibly clarified.

Abélard exempted nothing from this doubting and questioning, neither the Trinity, nor the anti-Semitic prejudices of Christians, nor his own biography. Above and beyond the immediate goal of an argument, a fundamental methodological principle had been established that proceeded to take firm root in the Western scholastic tradition and the civilization that was conditioned by it, namely methodical doubt and the systematic pursuit of the "way of inquiry," the *via inquisitionis,* as it was to become known in the thirteenth century.[14] Yet at the same time, this clearly meant taking an ax to the root of simple blind faith. As Abélard provocatively formulated it in his *Dialectica*: "Dialectic, to which all judgment of truth and falsehood is subject, holds the leadership of all philosophy and the governance of all teaching." According to him, the dialectical method is the "Discipline of disciplines; it teaches us how to teach, and how to learn; reason itself comes to the fore in it and reveals its nature and its purpose. Dialectic knows knowledge."[15] This kind of apotheosis of reason forms the bedrock of Abélard's theology and epistemology. God has ordered the world along rational lines, but He has allowed man, as the pinnacle of His creation, to be party to this faculty of reason; in this way, man can apply his rationality to recognize God as the "nature of all things," as the "soul of the world," and as the "highest good." Cicero, Plato, King Solomon, and Saint Paul—the great wise men of the pagan, Jewish, and Christian traditions—are all adduced in Abélard's theology as evidence of the philosophical insight that there is only one God.

It was precisely around this time, between 1120 and 1130 or very shortly thereafter, that the previously unknown second, and more extensive, part of Aristotle's *Organon* first became known in a Latin version in the West (it had hitherto only been available in Greek), which contained the *Prior Analytics,* the *Posterior Analytics,* the *Topics,* and the *Sophistical Refutations (De sophisticis elenchis),* and covered the syllogistic method, demonstration and definition, and logical fallacies. It may have come to light thorough the more frequent and intensive contacts with Constantinople arising from the Crusades. One Jacob of Venice, who was active in Constantinople at the time, is cited as the translator (presumably not of all these writings). The earliest traces of this "logica nova" can be traced back to the schools of the Île-de-France, to Paris and Chartres; from there knowledge of this philosophical approach quickly became widespread. The new learning fell on fertile ground cultivated by Abélard. You could hear his theses on the Trinity being discussed on every street corner, complained his opponent Bernard of Clairvaux,[16] who attempted in vain to blunt the effect of the Breton scholar's theology by having a synodal judgment issued against him. The physical expansion of the cities was paying intellectual dividends. And now the long march of the Middle Ages (and with it Western thought as a whole) through the work of Aristotle received a new impetus, as presently—and continuing on into the twelfth and thirteenth centuries—the complete works of the Ancient Greek philosopher, his physics and psychology, his political reflections along with the Arab commentaries on them (insofar as they were available) all flowed into the scholarly culture of the West. Four cultures were now combined within this Western civilization: alongside the Latin were also the Jewish, Greek, and Arabic traditions.

Abélard was not just a logician, he was also a theologian and not least a moral philosopher. In this area, too, he broke new ground with his examination of the role of intention in ethics. Thus, Abélard claimed, it was not what a perpetrator actually did, but was his intentions were; in other words, it was the "proprium" of his guilt that counted in moral terms. According to the degree of reason he possesses, a person avails himself autonomously of his free will *(liberum arbitrium)*; sin therefore resides in the premeditation of an evil deed, not in the act itself. Even the Jews who crucified Jesus and believed that they were acting in good faith had not, according to Abélard, committed a sin. It followed that they were not deicides. Free will directed by one's own intelligence now became the basis for people to shape their lives, through an independent, but thoroughly correctable, exercise of will.[17] And because this "free will" could not be denied to anyone, be they a farm laborer or housemaid, this idea represented a decisive step toward establishing the concept of human freedom as a whole, which came to form an unmistakable characteristic of Western culture, even though in Abélard's time this step was still a very long way off. One of Abélard's most mature works, "his *Dialogue between a Philosopher, a Jew, and a Christian,* was at variance with the old tradition of Christian anti-Semitic treatises, inasmuch as it did not admit any authoritative decision against the Jews or pass such a judgment itself, but ultimately allowed the two religions, when questioned by the figure of the philosopher, to complement one another and unite. It appears to be a cruel irony of history that, at around the same time, in the mid-twelfth century, the first unequivocal accusations are attested—namely by Thomas of Monmouth in England—of "blood libels" against the Jews, a charge that was repeated time and again in the Late Middle Ages. According to this initial accusation, the Jews had sacrificed a boy by the name of William of Norwich at Easter/Passover.[18] Envy, xenophobia, and fear combined into a deadly mixture.

Meanwhile, Abélard spoke with great reverence about the Jews, their philosophers, and their scholarship. Indeed, it was around this time, in the twelfth century, that rabbis in communities in Provence and Languedoc—and also in Catalonia, with its center at Girona, a location the much-traveled Benjamin of Tudela (ca. 1160/1170) would presently describe—began to unfold the first beginnings of the Kabbala. This "theosophical" form of mysticism, which was directed against Aristotelian trends, would over time enrich not only the intellectual history of Judaism but of the whole of

Europe as well. It was sometimes received with praise, and at other times with reservations or even outright rejection, but time and again European intellectuals found themselves challenged to take a stance on this phenomenon. Granted, the Kabbala (leaving aside modern schools) only reached its high-water mark in the decades around 1300, and continued to flourish in the Late Middle Ages and Early Modern Period. Its doctrine of the emanation of the godhead across the intellectual, numerically comprehensible stages of being into the "lower" world continued to make its influence felt in the Renaissance, but also much earlier than this on Christian thinkers. Furthermore, literature and poetry received new impetus from the Jewish culture that was being transmitted to Aquitania and France from Spain and Catalonia. Not least, the courtly love poetry of the southern French troubadours and trouvères was heavily influenced by Jewish models.[19] *Meu Sidi Ibrahim / ya tu omne dolge / vent'a mib / de nohte.*

While it is not the case that Abélard had already directly addressed the question of the Kabbala, the learned man certainly did sense—like no other before him save perhaps Haimo of Auxerre in his commentary on the Letters of Saint Paul[20]—the importance of Jewish philosophy and learning; Christianity would be much the poorer if it stayed aloof from it. Moreover, he unflinchingly applied the yardstick of his own ethics to his own biography—entitling it *Scito te ipsum* ("Know thyself"). Accordingly, it turned into a *Historia calamitatum,* a brutally honest history of his personal failures. He pointed to the fact that scholarship called for a singular lifestyle, which because it was totally new and unfamiliar at that time struck many people as scandalous. He claimed that he, Abélard, had rejected the knight's girdle in favor of teaching "for fame and money." Nobody had ever dared say this so directly and forthrightly before, and he was duly punished for his audacity. However, the business of vying with one another to attract a steady stream of (paying) students and fees from people attending lectures was a chief concern of all scholars at this time. The urge to win renown by getting their name known at the courts of princes, kings, and popes, as well as rivalry with their colleagues, motivated each and every one of them, even to the extent of (occasionally) taking up arms against each other. But Abélard the scholar and clergyman was also a man, and so he followed his urges and took a lover, Héloïse—a fateful step for both parties. But the philosopher and ethicist in him unhesitatingly owned up to his desires and deeds and calmly accepted the disastrous consequences of his self-determined actions.

The renewed influence of Boethius on the disciplines of philosophy and theology—which by now had firmly established themselves as university subjects—can scarcely be overstated. The outstanding scholars of the twelfth century, such as Gilbert de la Porrée, Thierry of Chartres, William of Conches, or Alanus of Lille, now read the *Consolations of Philosophy* in a new light, as well as all the writings on logic and theology by this renowned thinker from Late Antiquity. In particular, the theological works, which had been paid scant regard hitherto, now came into their own as pieces of remarkable scholarship. The theologian Peter Lombard of Novara, who ended up teaching in Paris, was especially fond of citing Boethius. Lombard's *Four Books of Sentences* became the primary theological handbook of High and Late Scholasticism. His teaching on the Trinity was officially approved by the Fourth Lateran Council in 1215. All subsequent scholastic philosophers—Robert Grosseteste, Thomas Aquinas, and William of Ockham—studied and were influenced by Lombard's works. His four books dealt systematically with the Trinity and Unity of God, the Creation and formation of things corporal and spiritual, Salvation through Christ, and the doctrine of the Sacraments. In his *Divine Comedy* (*Paradiso* Canto X, 106–108), Dante imagines himself meeting the author in Paradise: *Quel Pietro . . . che offerse a Santa Chiesa il suo tesoro.*[21] Before long, every doctor of theology had written commentaries on the *Sentences*; however, opposition to the ideas they contained did not begin with Luther.

This new climate of learning provided the seedbed for many major works of scholarship. Historian Otto of Freising, for instance, and John of Salisbury, the author of the *Policraticus,* both studied under de la Porrée in Paris. Disappointment or even anger about the failures of kings—say the Plantagenets in England or the Hohenstaufen dynasty in Germany—prompted John of Salisbury to put pen to paper, as he revived the genre of admonitions of rulers. He drew a clear distinction between the good princes and the tyrant. Against the latter, the English philosopher sanctioned people's legitimate right to resist. The era of the Monarchomachs, the sixteenth century, would rediscover John's writings, but even before this it made its effect felt. With Bishop Otto of Freising, however, the writing of history attained one of its rare high points. His works offer a unique combination of direct contemporary experience and imaginative reconstruction of the past. Basing his text on the eternal struggle between the realms of God and the Devil (the *civitas Dei* and the *civitas diaboli*) that Saint Augustine had revealed, and deeply troubled by the "change-ability of all things" *(mutabilitas rerum)* that he perceived when he con-templated the "Investiture Controversy"—a term first coined by him, incidentally—Otto produced a model of interpretative writing that truly did embrace the history of the world. It combined the notion that had been abroad since Carolingian times of a *Translatio imperii* with a concept that he, Otto, had devised himself, namely the *Translatio studii.* In other words, Otto put forward the thesis that over the centuries a dual transpo-sition had taken place—on the one hand of the concept of empire and on the other of scholarship—from the Far East to the Far West, in which latter location the two phenomena were now epitomized respectively by the Holy Roman Empire in Germany and higher learning in France. As such, therefore, the history of the world had almost reached its conclu-sion; the final chapter, which still had to be written, was the advent of the antichrist, whose reign Otto had already incorporated into the account of the history of human salvation that he gave in his World Chronicle.

Meanwhile, it was not just theology and philosophy, or historiography and admonitions to rulers, that saw themselves raised to the status of sci-ences in the mid-twelfth century; natural philosophy too attracted many students to the colleges of the Île-de-France at this time. The basis for this branch of learning was study of the *Timaeus,* the only Platonic dialog known to the Latin West for over 800 years, which had been translated by Calcidius in the fourth century. A reading of this text, accompanied from an early stage by the long-rekindled interest in astrology, prompted many scholars to come up with new interpretations of the six days of the Divine Creation. Intellectual curiosity in the natural world paved the way for a coming reception of Aristotle, who had become known to the West dur-ing the period of the Crusades through increased contact with Byzantium and Arab scholarship.

Of course the impulse for venturing to the East in the first place had been faith, and the quest to "liberate" the Holy Sepulcher. Yet ironically, the effect of this faith-driven venture in the West was, if not exactly to provide the basis for faith's ultimate destruction, then at least to accelerate it. The first of these works of Aristotle to reach the West and revolutionize European intellectual history was the *Physics.* It came to Europe by two routes from around 1170 onward. One of the translations was made di-rectly by Venetians working in Constantinople and was transmitted via the Hohenstaufen court, while the other arrived through the Norman court at Palermo. Both routes point to the growing position of influence that scholars and higher institutions of learning were beginning to occupy in monarchs' coteries of advisers. The *Physics* prompted a shift in the West toward an interpretation of nature that diverged from the traditional belief in the six days of Creation. Especially as a result of the early inclusion of Avicenna's commentary on the *Physics* and the interlacing with the discipline of astrology (another import from the Arab world), scholarly debate on Aristotle's text actually became such a serious threat to theology that lectures on the work were banned in Paris by the pope. However, this intervention came too late to save the West from the Scientific Revolution, which began to spread as early as the thirteenth century, with the first traces of materialism, and has prevailed thereafter over all forms of Creationism.

In these times of great upheaval, charges of heresy against intellectuals were not uncommon. Gilbert de la Porrée (d. 1154), who according to John of Salisbury was the most learned man of his age, had to endure such an ordeal. Later, in the backlash against Aristotle's *Physics,* heresy trials increased. In particular, the much-fêted Abélard had repeatedly given cause for offense. His stress on doubt and his unsparing directness shocked and unsettled his contemporaries, and also generated enmity. Accordingly, he was accused of heresy—a charge that carried with it the death penalty. The Crusade preacher Bernard of Clairvaux was prominent among Abélard's critics. He was guilty of presumptuousness, the cleric reproached him, as well as violating the mysteries of faith and flouting all boundaries. "Peter Abélard is out to destroy the reputation of the Christian faith, for he takes the view that the entire nature of God is within the grasp of human reason."[22] Abélard was repeatedly put on trial, and eventually condemned (1141). Only the intervention of Peter the Venerable, the abbot of Cluny, helped save the renowned philosopher. Yet some adherents of his doctrines were also to be found in the college of cardinals in Rome. This heavily persecuted individual, whose only crimes were to have fallen in love with a woman and displayed consistent reasoning—and to have openly admitted to both—this thinker who was cast adrift by his peers, but who pioneered the whole concept of free will and paved the way for the expression of human freedom and must count as one of the greatest minds of the Western world, finally found peace at the end of his life in the abbey of Cluny.

Despite the reservations of Saint Bernard—and unlike in Byzantium—scholasticism and the subordination of theology to Aristotelian dialectic could not be suppressed, nor could the light of reason be extinguished or excluded from the precincts of schools or from people's thoughts; it permeated through every crack and shone into every corner of intellectual culture. Peter Lombard, whose "Sentences" became the universal theological primer of the Late Middle Ages, was a pupil of Abélard. Furthermore, it was not just theology and philosophy that got caught in the slipstream of dialectics. The application of the scientific method to the law had an even more enduring and profound effect upon society. For it subjected the law to the strictures of Aristotelian reason, which required proofs, and like some newly arisen Sun of Justice dispelled the darkness of trial by ordeal and "oath-helpers," which legal custom had hitherto required. This new rationalization followed the rediscovery of Justinian's *Digests*. It is thought that this unique legacy from Classical Roman jurisprudence had survived the intervening barbarian centuries in just two manuscripts. It was rediscovered toward the end of the eleventh century, presumably quite by chance, somewhere in Tuscany, or Pisa, or at another location within the domain of Matilda of Canossa. Scholars read it and, realizing its import, copied it. This text truly fired the interest of academic jurists in the West, who unlike their ancient Roman counterparts, did not stop at applying it to civil law, but rather applied its method to fundamentally reshape canon law, as well as feudal and criminal law, and above all to open up an entirely unknown field of operation to jurisprudence, namely common public law.

Bologna rapidly became the center of such studies. Its school of law flourished in around 1120–1130 through the efforts of the renowned "four doctors"; Martin Gosia, Bulgarus, Hugo de Porta Ravennate, and Jacobus de Boragine, the first academics who are definitely known to have taught Roman civil law; alongside Paris, Bologna became the oldest university in Europe. Yet the "glossators," so called because of the principal literary form they employed—glosses, or commentaries in the margin or between the lines of the old texts—held sway in the lecture theaters for only around 150 years, before being supplanted by the "conciliators," named for their extensive writings. Around 1230, one Accursius, a Bologna jurist *(Legum doctor)* organized the *glossa ordinaria* into the *Corpus Juris Civilis,* which subsequently became one of the first texts to find its way into print (in five folios), and until the seventeenth century dominated legal proceedings as the standard commentary on the law. The higher institutions of learning arose in parallel and in interdependency with these interests. Arranged by "nations," they established themselves as constitutive associations, or *uni-*

versitates. In Paris, the dominant group were the *Magistri,* mainly consisting of teachers of the Seven Liberal Arts, while in Bologna it was the law students, who were generally older than the scholars in Paris and who in addition had already completed a course of study in the *Artes.* Strictly speaking, the fêted law professors, the famous *Doctores legum* did not form part of this group in Bologna. Henceforth, these two universities provided a secure home for scholarship, though it was by no means the only one. *Lectio, quaestio,* and *disputatio* were the favored methods of teaching—that is, reading aloud the text to be glossed; followed by a formalized session of questioning; and finally a dialectical dissection of the text and answers; the material under study was systematically abstracted by means of the tractate, the commentary, and finally the summation.

Soon, other universities came into being, Oxford in England, for instance. From the early twelfth century on, droves of students gravitated to Paris, Bologna, or Oxford as well as to the more recently created universities in France, Italy, or Spain, such as Salerno or Montpellier to study medicine, or to Salamanca, whose higher institution of learning had been founded long since, but which only blossomed gradually. These institutions were established and granted special privileges from the thirteenth century on by kings and popes, and in addition to teaching the curriculum of the Seven Liberal Arts also boasted at least one of the three "higher" faculties of theology, jurisprudence, or medicine, and in accordance with said privileges granted their graduates the right to teach at any comparable institution *(licentia ubique docendi).* For the present, Germany, Hungary, and the Slavic lands were the only places to establish no universities, and so rather than attracting students to the banks of the Rhine, Danube, or Vltava, instead sent their young men abroad to study. Royal and princely courts could not afford to stand aloof from these new branches of scholarship. Academic training became indispensable to them, creating new elites and opening up new career possibilities.

The Roman Curia found itself infiltrated by the new learning from an early stage and had no choice but to foster it if it wished to exert influence on an increasingly scientifically constituted world. The Curia had only just emerged from the schism of 1130, which had broken out because of a lack of unity within the college of cardinals. It seems that the majority of the cardinals, who had cast their votes in favor of the antipope Analect II, represented the traditional clergy who were less inclined to think dialectically, whereas Innocent II could count on the overwhelming support of those cardinals who had been schooled in the new methods; indeed, some of them had even attended Abélard's lectures. Before long, historiography was flourishing once more at the papal court; the Chancery developed not just as a key institution within the Vatican, but also provided an example to numerous princely and royal courts on how to draft and archive official documents.[23] The Apostolic Camera—the papal treasury—which was also headed by a cardinal, likewise assumed far greater significance from the second half of the twelfth century. All sources of papal revenue were now scrupulously recorded once more, the most famous of these inventories being the *Liber censuum* of 1192, which was drawn up by Cardinal Cencius, who was later elected Pope Honorius III; moreover such records, organized by diocese, represent the most comprehensive geographical survey of Europe during the era in question. And last but not least, the liturgical observances of the papal court entered a new Golden Age from around this time, which was to endure until the end of the medieval period. Immantation (that is, the ritual enrobing of a new pope with the cloak of imperial purple), taking possession of the Lateran Palace, and the enthroning or crowning of the chosen papal candidate were staged particularly lavishly as rites of passage; nor was the rich processional ritual ignored, although the extravagance that the Early Middle Ages expended on this feature diminished considerably over time.

Canonistics, the science of ecclesiastical law, soon became a familiar part of the curriculum at the emerging universities; it developed, in parallel and in close interplay with civil law and its methodology, into a real discipline of jurisprudence. Its principal textbook was the *Concordia Discordantium Canonum* as the *Decretum Gratiani* was properly known. Initially, this existed in two editions, the older of which had possibly been compiled before 1130 while the more recent edition, which ultimately came to be the only definitive one, was fundamentally expanded only around 1150. The work was divided into two parts, the distinctions and the *Causae,* and was remarkable for its systematic presentation of the legal material. The *Causae* were themselves elucidated through *Quaestiones* and lucidly exemplified the application of the scientific method. For instance, Case number 24 concerned itself with heresy: "A bishop, who fell prey to a heresy, dismissed some priests from their posts and excommunicated them. Accused of heresy after his death, he was found guilty, together with his acolytes and their entire families. The first question to be asked is: whether a heretic can divest others of their positions and excommunicate them; secondly, whether a person can be posthumously excommunicated; and thirdly, whether a whole family can be condemned for the sins of an individual." As an addendum to this "inquisitorial" dissection of this "case" the appropriate canons that deal with such instances are cited verbatim, commented upon in the introductory heading to each one; in his way, a decision is reached on the particular case. The heading of the first canon cited for the first case, for example, reads: "anyone who commits a heresy that has already been condemned is complicit in their own damnation," and it continues in the same vein. Like the civil law, the *Decretum Gratiani* was also glossed; this enabled scholars to make cross-references to other canons and in general to create a dense network of legal norms, which penetrated the entire material under discussion and provided a wealth of information to the user. The *Glossa ordinaria* on Gratian's *Decretum* by Johannes Teutonicus was included in 1215, and again in the definitive revision of the text by Bartholomaeus Brixiensis thirty years later. Presently, the welter of decretals being issued by popes also called out for a comprehensive collection, which after various unsuccessful attempts was finally completed by Raymond of Peñafort's *Liber Extra* of 1234, which was likewise straightaway given its own *Glossa ordinaria* by Bernard de Botone. Right up to the Council of Trent (1545–1563) and until the proclamation of a new *Corpus Iuris Canonici* in 1917 Gratian's *Decretum* and the *Liber Extra* were regarded respectively as the authoritative statute book and handbook of canonistics. The only revisions they experienced in this time were the addition of the *Liber Sextus* in the early fourteenth century, a collection of new papal decretals up to the reign of Boniface VIII, and the *extravagants* (constitutions) published by John XXII.

As we have already noted, the introduction of legal process into the church began in the twelfth century; hand in hand with this development came a specific mode of thought, which soon took hold of the whole of the West. Pope Alexander III began the process by scouring France for clerics with a theological or canonical schooling in order to appoint them to the Roman Curia as cardinals. The pope himself was the highest lawgiver and judge of the Catholic Church. It was not long, then, before canonists, including lawyers who had received a university training, began to ascend the throne of the apostolic princes. One of them, Innocent IV—the pontiff who deposed Emperor Frederick II (1245)—published an extensive commentary on the decretals when he was pope. And although secular princes did not attend seats of higher learning, monarchical and political actions also followed the same trend. Jurists became indispensable. Legal records of the "Consuetudines" and "Coutumes" were drafted from the twelfth century on in Pisa, as well as in France and Barcelona. The German realm/Holy Roman Empire participated in this development in a very particular way. There, Roman Law was seen as synonymous with "imperial law." From the reigns of Henry IV and Henry V onward, German kings had sought the advice of lawyers. Moreover, the theologians enjoyed a similar success to the rise of the jurists. Now, it was generally no longer the case that being of noble rank alone was enough to secure a person a high position in the church; in addition, theological training was also normally expected of princes' spiritual advisers and confessors. In particular, the Italian municipalities had an inexhaustible need of university-trained officials—preachers and lawyers, not to mention armies of academically schooled notaries; gradually, physicians were added to this list, too. Only in Germany, where the aristocratic church endured in part right up the end of the Old Empire, were the conditions completely different.

Law as an academic discipline did not just mean jurisprudence; rather, this discipline gave students a broader grasp of complex relationships concerning society and rulers' dispensing of justice. Indeed, it expounded a theory of society that was intrinsically bound up with a theory of rule. Like dialectics, in the absence of which it could never have come into being in the first place, the discipline of law taught students how to abstract, and it put a correspondingly technical language at their disposal, which enabled them to analyze and express precisely those relationships. New methods, ways of thinking, and metaphors were devised in order to express the juxtaposition and relationship between *Regnum* and *Sacerdotium,* customary law and new statutes, dominion and communality, and hierarchy and self-determined action; in short, to present politics with a clarity never before attained. The inception of this new approach to the law was, it appeared, essential for people to henceforth get their bearings in the church and the world, and within a society controlled by secular authorities and economic interests. Methodical and factual distinctions on the basis of the logical technique of division came to form an ever denser normative orientation grid. One result of this was the emergence of a hitherto unknown mode of public discourse conducted in a technical language that was unintelligible to outsiders.

It was only now, in the late twelfth century, that the "office" began to be thought of as an autonomous entity distinct from the person holding it;

prior to this, there had only been "servants" of God or the king, and their "servitude." Yet John of Salisbury was already familiar with the concept of a *res politica,* a "body politic" *(est autem res publica corpus quoddam)* that was positively animated by equity *(aequitas)* and reason *(ratio),* whose "principate" (that is, position of supreme power) was occupied by the priesthood, and whose head was the prince, and its heart the senate, while its eyes, ears, and tongue were the judges and provincial governors, its hands the officials and knights, its stomach and lower organs the quaestors and manciples, and finally whose feet were the peasants.[24] Soon, namely over the course of the thirteenth century, the doctrine of the *persona ficta,* the "fictitious person" was discovered, a concept of the legal personality embodying, say, a suprapersonal group, or a whole community, or even the "empire." There had been no inkling of such a concept in the ninth century. Henceforth, by referring to John of Salisbury's definition, the "official" was perfectly capable of serving as the "organ" and "limb" of this fictitious legal person, which would have been a completely alien notion in the Early Middle Ages. In addition, jurisprudence was further complemented by a discipline that only arose in the course of the twelfth century and that also established itself as a university subject, namely the *ars dictandi.* This was particularly significant for the profession of notary. The effects of the application of the scientific method to intellectual and political culture made themselves felt in political life from early on, yet so surreptitious was this process that contemporary chroniclers failed to register it. In fact, this transformative process only become apparent from the sequence of scientific texts and commentaries that begin to appear. In concert with the rise of these academic disciplines, new legitimation strategies also emerged for political strategies in disputes arising both between crowned heads and between kings and the ecclesiastical authorities.

Royal Strategies

So it was that kings and their realms took center stage once more. The concept of "la douce France" was joined by that of the "Honor of the Holy Roman Empire," as propagated by Frederick Barbarossa. But what a difference there was! In the West, the power of the king was definitely intensified under the influence of the new sciences; the abstraction processes that we have touched upon progressed more rapidly. In the East, by contrast, all attempts to set the same process in motion were hindered by structural conditions and the politics of the ruling elite. No clear dividing line could be drawn between the law of the empire and the personal honor of the emperor. The personage of the king and the suprapersonal empire were only distinguished from one another in a very rudimentary way; as yet, the differences were by no means sharply defined. And it was precisely in the reign of Frederick I that this problem became apparent. He had obtained the assent of his princes that he should come to the throne, despite the fact that an underage son of his predecessor Conrad was still alive and had a prior claim. Presumably, as always, in this instance Barbarossa had simply overridden the contrary wishes of his uncle. If that was indeed the case, then Barbarossa's elevation to the throne already betrayed the same lack of scruples that would later become evident in other matters, not least in his policies toward the pope, or in the downfall of the man who had been his most important confederate in the early years of his reign, Henry the Lion. In any event, Barbarossa's reign was not a happy one, as the future would show: for it placed greater stress on coercion than on diplomacy, on aggressive expansion rather than peaceful integration, and on an antiquated notion of "imperialism" rather than on a recognition of equality among kings. Accordingly, this approach fanned the latent tensions with the papacy into open conflict, persecution, and war. And so this Hohenstaufen monarch embarked on a mode of politics that, once his son and grandson followed the same prescribed line, was destined to drive the empire to the brink of destruction, and that set the seal on the fragmentation of the German lands into petty states.

Initially, though, things ran smoothly. Pope Eugene III required assistance against the Commune of Rome, which (as with many popes before and after) was doing its utmost to make his reign over the city difficult or even impossible. The commune regarded itself as a "senate" and hoped to revive Rome's ancient greatness, even offering that the senate would invest the Hohenstaufen monarch the emperor's crown, but at the same time sought help against Roger II of Sicily. In the event, Pope Eugene III concluded a treaty with Frederick I, which pledged to preserve and restore each side's rights, but which was also explicitly directed against Byzantium; Adrian IV, Eugene's successor after the brief reign of Anastasius IV, renewed this compact. When he was still a cardinal and papal legate, Nicholas Breakspear, the future Adrian IV, had successfully brought about the reform of the Scandinavian Church and had founded the independent archepiscopal see of Trondheim (1152–1153); but it was precisely this success that the new king Frederick I was soon to curtail. Barbarossa marched to Rome at the head of a strong army, had himself crowned emperor, and fulfilled his pledge to the popes by crushing the antipapal communal faction in Rome led by Arnold of Brescia (1155). But the glitter of ancient Roman imperial glory dazzled the Swabian king. And the revival of academic law only served to fire the ideologues of the Holy Roman Empire. The king from Alemannia saw himself as being in a direct line of succession from the great Roman emperors and lawgivers. Barbarossa's aim was nothing less than to reassert the universality of the empire; *Honor imperii*—whether this was construed as status, honor, wealth, jurisdiction, prestige, or preeminence—and a new sense of Roman imperial hegemony came together in Frederick's ambitious goal. Using a consciously archaic formulation, the Hohenstaufen monarch dubbed his Roman Empire the "Holy Roman Empire," and later had himself portrayed as a laurel-wreathed Caesar on the battlements of Rome, and lauded as the *mundi dominus* (master of the world) and the *princeps principium* (prince of princes). Adrian IV, the first (and thus far only) Englishman to occupy the papal throne, deeply mistrusted Barbarossa; not only was he devious and unscrupulous in his dealings, he had also recently razed the city of Tortona to the ground and was threatening to do the same to Milan. Worst of all, Frederick appeared to be planning to strip the pope of his honorary right to invest emperors and to restore imperial power on a scale that had long since ceased to be.

All too soon, the pope saw his worst fears realized. Adrian IV was outraged that Frederick, in spite of the fact that the Roman Church had invested him as emperor and was prepared to endow him with even greater *beneficia,* had done nothing to secure the release of Archbishop Eskil of Lund, who had been arrested in Germany while returning from Rome; he duly wrote to Barbarossa to express his anger. At that time, Frederick's principal aide was Rainald von Dassel, the son of a count, who had just been appointed the king's chancellor and was presently to be installed as the bishop of Cologne, though he was never consecrated and was at best a power broker. One anecdote—which was supposedly told about Rainald by his fellow students in Hildesheim, and neatly encapsulates the man's character—recounted how he had once dozed off during the day and muttered to himself, *"Ego sum ruina mundi"* ("I am the scourge of the world"). Whether this story was a fabrication or not, this spiritual shepherd brought his master and the Holy Roman Emperor no blessings. Acting as translator of Adrian's letter, which had reached the emperor at a diet at Besançon in 1157, Rainald rendered the formulaic expression *beneficia* as "fief" rather than "benefaction," thereby turning the empire into a fiefdom of the pope, which incensed the illiterate lay members present, men like Otto von Wittelsbach. Enraged, he drew his sword and made to attack the papal legate at the diet, Roland Bandinelli of Siena (whom the college of cardinals later elected as Alexander III, Adrian IV's successor). It was only with great difficulty that Frederick was able to restrain his furious vassal. It is entirely plausible, though, that Rainald and Frederick had agreed beforehand that the former should deliberately mistranslate the letter precisely in order to stir up the German nobility (who did not know Latin) against the pope—a nefarious piece of skullduggery that was, however, entirely indicative of Barbarossa's unscrupulous *modus operandi*. For the papal legate and the Curia, though, it merely confirmed their long-held suspicions. Once again, then, the old adage proved to be true: uneducated rulers are particularly dangerous.

Pope Adrian subsequently reached an agreement with Roger II's successor, William I of Sicily, meaning that henceforth he was no longer reliant on Barbarossa's help. The pope's success rendered the claims of the emperor and Italian king to southern Italy null and void; as it turned out, these had to be renounced forever; only the *Risorgimento* in the nineteenth century created a new situation. Hereafter, then, Sicily found itself on the side of the enemies of the Hohenstaufens. However, the next year, Barbarossa reappeared in Italy with a mighty army and launched straight into a war against the municipalities, with Milan at their head. He secured the support of the four renowned doctors of law at Bologna (see above), and with them all of the faculties of law at the early universities. At a diet in Roncaglia (near Piacenza) in 1158 these scholars, together with other "judges" from the communes, defined the *regalia* with a clear bias in favor of the emperor. The privileges he was granted included financially advantageous rights such as tolls, treasure troves and the like, all manner of jurisdiction including the right of dominion over duchies or counties, all royal palatinates along with the right to establish such entities wherever he saw fit, and finally a poll tax that was to be paid by everybody.[25] First and foremost, the intervention of these scholars was to have a profound effect on the communal society of northern Italy; they gave scant attention in their deliberations to the German princes or cities. Barbarossa appeared to be trying to revive ancient imperial authority in Italy through force of arms. After a long siege, Milan was forced to surrender in humiliating circumstances; its defensive walls were demolished and its populace dispersed (1162).

Frederick's policy of aggression might at first have seemed sensible in the not unjustified expectation of huge financial gains. But in the long run, this policy dragged the forces of the kingdom into the internal struggles of Lombardy and the central Italian municipalities, where they were exhausted. Barbarossa's success was thus short-lived. After just a few years, the citizens regained and redoubled their former power, and no medieval emperor was ever able to conquer them again. Likewise, the doctrine of the *regalia* was ultimately reduced to a series of financially advantageous rights and integrated, albeit without the slightest power of disposition attaching to it, into the *Libri Feudorum,* books of feudal customs produced in Milan in 1158. Through these, it remained in force right up to the nineteenth century. Posterity judged the Bolognese jurists who had colluded with Barbarossa harshly; they were decried as the *miseri Bononenienses* (miserable wretches of Bologna) by one of their younger, but equally renowned colleagues, Placentinus, who, when he came under pressure from the emperor, is thought to have fled to Montpellier, where an important rival university to Bologna was flourishing. This rebuke not only reflected the mood of the citizens of Milan or Piacenza, but more importantly also expressed the deep unease felt toward the Germans and their incursion into Lombardy and Italy, which now began to spread apace.

But however remarkable the legislation drafted at Roncaglia, it availed the Holy Roman Empire nothing. The most significant law to emerge from this imperial diet could only remain in force in a roundabout way and without alluding to its provenance: namely, the stipulation that all jurisdiction lay with the emperor and that each "judge" "received" his "authority" from the emperor. Late medieval lawyers such as Baldus or Bartholus cited this principle without naming its source; and it was via a report by the renowned Nicolò de' Tudeschi (known as Panormitanus), a jurist of the Basle Council, that Jean Bodin came to know of it and included it in his *Six livres de la république* (1576). It can be found there in the key chapter (I,8) on the sovereignty of the highest state authority *(puissance absoluë).*[26] But by then this supreme authority had long since passed from the hands of the emperor, but instead resided in the "sovereign" authority exercised by the nation-state; this, too, formed part of the legacy of the High and Late Middle Ages.

The consequences of Frederick's unsubtle policies now became apparent all too swiftly. The emperor had failed to weaken the communal element; on the contrary, all he had done was strengthen the citizenry's will to resist. And presently every autocratic ruler who in worldly matters recognized no authority higher than himself had requisitioned the newly formulated principle of jurisdiction. However successfully this principle was applied elsewhere, there is no denying that it profoundly damaged its originator. Various communes led by Verona formed an alliance against Barbarossa (1164), and within a short time this had expanded into the Lombard League (1167). Even the *basileus,* Manuel Komnenos, and William I of Sicily supported this body from afar, while Venice, which belonged to the League of Verona, did not join the Lombard League. Soon, this League found itself in alliance with the pope—forming a many-headed, unbeatable opponent of imperial restoration. Not even the constant presence of a Holy Roman Emperor in Italy—the last to do so was Barbarossa's grandson Frederick II—could prevent the empire's power there from being steadily eroded.

Adrian IV died in 1159; he was succeeded in a schismatic papal election by Cardinal Roland, who came to the throne as Alexander III. His rival, the antipope Victor IV, only managed to attract three votes, yet still insisted upon the legitimacy of his election. Ill-advised and in the deluded hope of thereby securing himself an advantage in the struggle for Italy, which was a complete misreading of the situation, Barbarossa opted for Victor. And when this antipope died a few years later, the emperor immediately had a successor, Paschal III, installed, so prolonging the dreadful schism. Despite unbearable pressure from Barbarossa, which drove him into exile in France, the scholastically trained Alexander III proved himself more than a match for Frederick I. Successive Italian campaigns on the part of the emperor failed to bring this pope to heel. Even nature itself conspired against Barbarossa's plans. In 1167, just when the German army seemed poised to take Rome, they were carried off by the plague. This fate could have been predicted; even a cursory glance back into the Ottonian past would have served as a warning. Many Swabian noble lines were wiped out by this pestilence, and often their inheritance fell to Barbarossa, who thus actually profited from this catastrophe. Indeed, for a very brief spell it even increased the power of this ruler; but in the long term it brought the crown and the royal house no benefit at all.

In summary Frederick I pursued outmoded policies; he failed in historical terms. Nor was it simply a concatenation of unfortunate circumstances that denied him success, but rather the countless ill-conceived decisions and poorly executed plans enacted by him and his closest advisers. And with all the fear that they instilled, Frederick's policies severely damaged the reputation of the Germans within Latin Christendom. Moreover, however successful the fiscal and economic policies pursued by Barbarossa might have been (in these, he was advised by experienced merchants)—even his "imperial land policy," the creation of linked complexes of imperial estates such as the Vogtland region around Plauen, the Wetterau district, or the "empire" between Aachen and Duisburg, all of which were administered by *ministeriales*—none enjoyed any lasting success. The disastrous policies of the emperor undermined everything that might have served to strengthen the crown, the empire, and transpersonal associations, and their consequences destroyed everything.

By contrast, France proved to be a great source of support for the beleaguered pope, despite the many differences between them. At the same time, the special role played by the higher seats of learning in France made itself felt. In the Schism, they were at the forefront of opposition to Barbarossa; their graduates wielded considerable influence at the Parisian court, as well as on the French Church, the Ecclesia Gallicana, and the Roman Curia. "Who appointed the Germans as the judges of nations? Who endowed these rough and short-tempered people with such great authority?" So ran the bitter complaint of an Englishman in France, and one of the leading intellectual spokesmen of the pro-Alexander faction, John of Salisbury, about Barbarossa's posturing as a world ruler.[27] The international nature of the universities, the cross-border migration of teachers and students, and the supraregional, Europe-wide community of scholars that was developing all combined to produce an increasingly sensitized body of public opinion. Barbarossa paid this opposition little heed—much to his own detriment. Only the ensuing military débâcle, the victory of the Milanese over the imperial army under the personal leadership of Barbarossa at the Battle of Legnano in 1176, forced him to make peace with Pope Alexander III. The emperor, as the chief military strategist was solely responsible for the defeat, thanks to his negligence in planning, but even so he sought to shift the blame, no doubt at the urging of the Philipp of Heinsberg, the archbishop of Cologne, onto Henry the Lion, whom Philipp considered too powerful, and thus Henry's downfall was engineered and staged. His duchy was broken up in 1180, with the lion's share—along with the province of Westphalia, which had itself been raised to the status of a duchy in the interim—falling to the archbishop of Cologne. But presently he too was to become the emperor's bitterest enemy.

Frederick's peace accord with the pope was celebrated in Venice (1177). The emperor recognized Alexander as the sole legitimate successor to the Petrine throne and vouchsafed all the rights and possessions "which the pope holds, save authority over the empire," while the pope in turn made a similar concession to the emperor, once again "with the exception of authority over the Roman Church."[28] Contentious questions of disputed territories were, it seems, excluded from the agreement so as not to jeopardize the accord. Over the ensuing two decades, these were to remain unresolved, though matters largely panned out in favor of the emperor over this period. However, the ritual of the meeting between the pope and the emperor, and the way in which later events laid a deforming stratum over this ritual in the cultural memory of Venice, conspired to generate a myth around this settlement, the effects of which the papacy was to still feel during the Reformation in the sixteenth century. The peace treaty also embraced Byzantium and the kingdom of Sicily, with which Frederick concluded a fifteen-year armistice. He then set about preparing a new peace accord, which was sealed by the marriage in 1186 of Barbarossa's eldest son Henry to Princess Constance of Sicily, Roger II's daughter, who was no longer in the first flush of youth. What no one at the time could have anticipated was that this marriage would, a few decades later, plunge the papacy into a serious crisis.

The humiliated emperor now found himself facing new dangers in the West of his realm. There, Southern Burgundy, the much-disputed kingdom of Arles—in which the kings of Aragón, France, and England, the counts of Toulouse, the municipalities of Genoa and Pisa and even the *basileus* all pursued their own self-serving interests—threatened to slip from Frederick's grasp. He devised a new method of keeping control of it; hurrying from his base in Italy to Arles, he promptly had himself crowned king of the region in 1178 (which had not had its own king for 150 years). This event was staged, as one contemporary English observer put it "in order to at least embellish the nefarious goings-on with a proof of title of the highest rank," or to quote Frederick himself, "to glorify the grandeur of the imperial Majesty." In any event, it was a gesture of laying claim rather than of real power; for all that, though, it was not without immediate success.[29] Frederick had to thank developments in the East for a sudden relief from his problems in the West. There, the *basileus* Manuel I Komnenos had suffered a crushing defeat at the hands of the Sejuk *sultan* Kiliç Arslan II at Myriokephalon in 1176. As soon became apparent, this defeat fatally weakened Byzantium; the Eastern Roman Empire found itself unable to recover from the consequences of this catastrophe. The West felt the effects of this momentous event shortly thereafter; it had lost its most formidable defensive shield to the East.

The Peace of Venice smoothed the way to the Third Lateran Council (1179), at which Alexander assembled all the prelates of the Latin Church. The most important resolution concerned regulation of the papal election, which finally—in order to prevent future schisms arising from the disunity of the cardinals ("when the enemy sows tares among the wheat"; Matthew 13:25)—established the principles of a two-thirds majority of voters and the immediate transference of power to the new pontiff through the election. In addition, a series of internal church reforms were also implemented, such as a ban on simony, the establishment of episcopal schools (poor students were exempted from paying fees), and a ban on jousting. Some measures that had fallen into abeyance were also revived, such as setting a canonical age for various forms of consecration—a bishop, say, had to be at least thirty and be of legitimate birth—and a proscription against Christians practicing usury. Particular stress was laid on the fight against heresy; the council issued a sweeping condemnation of all renegades, from the Cathars to assorted mercenary bands from Brabant, Aragón, and beyond, threatening them all with the most severe excommunication. Anyone taking up arms against these groups was accorded the same privileges as a Crusader.

The allies of the pope, the cities of Lombardy, were only partially included in the peace accord between Alexander and Frederick I. The emperor was only prepared to commit himself to a six-year armistice where they were concerned. Only after this had elapsed was a treaty signed in Constance, which assured the municipalities a large measure of autonomy and guaranteed the emperor certain financially beneficial rights; this latter clause was broadly similar to the award of *regalia*, divested of any power of disposition, that had been enshrined in the 1158 *Libri Feudorum*. However, this success was modest when compared with the huge military and political cost at which it had been secured, and the damage that had been caused. Indeed, it is questionable whether the end result can even be construed as a success.

While France tenaciously consolidated its monarchical power precisely as a result of the Schism, Henry II of England had to bear the consequences of his hesitant attitude. The archbishop of Canterbury, Thomas Becket, who had originally been the king's lord chancellor and a loyal supporter, switched allegiance when he became archbishop and became a staunch defender of church freedom and an avowed ally of Pope Alexander III. As a result, he was forced to go into exile. However, he returned to England too soon, and was murdered in the precincts of his cathedral. The infamous Murder in the Cathedral, for which the king was popularly held responsible, weakened the Crown's position toward the apostolic see. Thomas was immediately made a martyr to the cause, and Henry II was obliged to do penance at his tomb; this incident served to open up the hitherto more or less insular England to the papacy. In its aftermath, a deluge of papal decretals flooded the island, and the final years of the reign of Henry II (d. 1189) were blighted by conflict with his three sons, who were all in various ways manipulated by the king of France. Barbarossa's mistaken policy of dividing the church thus precipitated the ruin of other realms too.

Philip II of France, though, was a wily operator; he knew how to foment the discord between Henry II's three sons and how to play them off against one another. The Plantagenet king on England's throne was, after all, the vassal of his French counterpart in the territories where his family originated (Anjou, Normandy, Aquitaine) and which England still controlled on the French mainland. Though this potentially posed a threat to Philip, it could also be used to his advantage. Under Louis VII (d. 1180), for various reasons matters had remained on an even keel between the two nations. But Philip (d. 1223) took a tougher line than his father; the popular nickname "Augustus" which was given to him in the early years of his reign, expressed his expansionist approach. The English royal house was to feel this painfully at first hand. Internecine feuding had destroyed many a realm prior to this. Furthermore, Henry's sons, it seemed, were characterized by a distinct lack of ability, each less gifted than his elder brother. Only the eldest son, named Henry for his father, appeared to have much promise; he gave his father much cause for concern, but died young. Richard, the second son, was regarded as an exemplary knight, a son after his mother's heart (Eleanor of Poitou, a vivacious woman in her youth). Finally John, to whom posterity has given the nickname "Lackland," was hot-tempered—as a young prince, he had once smashed a chessboard over his Latin tutor's head in a blind rage—spurned all counsel, and lost the most valuable continental possessions of the Plantagenets.

The Third Crusade, which was called in 1189, at least provided some respite to the beleaguered Angevin Empire, since both kings—Philip and Richard I (the Lionheart), who had only just succeeded his father—both found themselves compelled to take part out of mutual suspicion. But while hostilities between the two nations flared up again with full force once Richard had returned from almost two years' captivity, Philip could never prevail militarily over the Lionheart. Only Richard's death in 1199 changed the situation.

In the Near East, while the West was preoccupied with the papal Schism and the conflict between the pope and the emperor, the period witnessed the revival of Islam's former might and a new regrouping and strengthening of its forces. By 1187, Sultan Salah al-Din, the *milte Saladin,* had recaptured Jerusalem and large parts of the Holy Land. Alarmed, the West took up arms and prepared to launch the Third Crusade. The Holy Roman Emperor Frederick Barbarossa and two kings, Philip II of France and Richard the Lionheart, set off for Palestine; Leopold V of Austria also joined the campaign to "liberate" the Holy Sepulcher. No previous undertaking of this kind had ever been better organized. The logistical problems encountered by the Second Crusade were taken into account, with no army taking the same route as another, and yet the whole enterprise still ended in a series of catastrophes. Certainly, the Germans planned the campaign thoroughly; only well armed and properly equipped knights were permitted to join the emperor's retinue. Barbarossa concluded a special treaty with the *basileus* to regulate his army's passage through the lands belonging to Byzantium. Yet the emperor drowned while trying to cross the River Saleph (Göksu) in Anatolia in 1190; his death spelled an ignominious end to the grandiose operation. Several of the accompanying knights swiftly buried the funds they had brought with them; the German army largely dissolved, with only a few princes continuing on their journey. They ended up fighting alongside the English and French kings. Others, though, went straight back to their homeland. It is a mystery why Frederick Barbarossa, of all German rulers, should have become the focus of a legend, according to which he will return from a deep, centuries-long slumber to bring peace to his country. The myth first appeared in a fifteenth-century prophesy and gained further impetus from a poem by the nineteenth-century author Friedrich Rückert, which claimed that "he lies hidden in a subterranean castle . . . but will one day return" (the underground cavern in question was thought to lie beneath the Kyffhäuser hill in the Harz Mountains). Certainly, the real Frederick Barbarossa never brought his land good fortune and peace—nor did the enduring nationalistic legend of him as a supposed savior and redeemer, which only stoked up fantasies of superpower status for Germany; the most ironic invocation of his name was Hitler's Operation Barbarossa (the invasion of the Soviet Union in 1941), which ended in the unmitigated disaster of Stalingrad.[30]

The success of this hugely costly Crusade was only modest; Jerusalem was not retaken; only the important port of Acre (Akko) was recaptured and thereafter became the last stronghold of the "Franks" in the Holy Land. Leopold of Austria claimed to have played a decisive role in storming this city and was incensed when the glory and booty that he believed were due to him were refused by the English king Richard I. Leopold duly withdrew, embittered and with his pride deeply wounded. He got his revenge, however, when the Lionheart was shipwrecked on his return voyage from the Holy Land and was forced to take an overland route through Austria. Although he had taken the precaution of disguising himself, he was recognized and taken prisoner; Leopold handed him over to the new Holy Roman Emperor, Barbarossa's son Henry VI. After the sinking of the "White Ship," this was the second shipwreck to hit the English royal household, and it too ushered in devastating historical consequences for the whole of Europe. For Henry only agreed to release the king in exchange for an excessive ransom, and this sum—150,000 silver marks—which was obtained illegally, having been extorted by violating the principle of free passage for all Crusaders, was then used to fund his own invasion of Sicily. Henry VI laid claim to the island as Queen Constance's rightful heir after her husband William II had died childless—but also through recourse to long-outdated imperial rights. When he invaded, the Sicilian king Tancred was struggling to assert his authority over hostile local barons. The new Hohenstaufen monarch summarily rode roughshod over the rights of the pope, Celestine III.

Yet this illegally funded campaign did not bring the emperor, his realm, or his household any lasting good fortune. After barely three years of harsh and unpopular rule over Sicily, Henry VI died of malaria, without ever having received papal assent to his conquest of the island. The demise of two Holy Roman Emperors within a decade effectively extinguished the glory of the Hohenstaufen dynasty and brought about the collapse of their empire, as it turned out, in a crisis that was impossible to overcome in the long run. In vain, Henry VI urged the imperial princes and the pope to agree to his plan to transform the Holy Roman Empire from an elected monarchy into an hereditary Hohenstaufen empire.[31] He felt that the prosperity or ruination of his kingdom and empire was still too dependent upon the assertiveness of individual monarchs. But the idea of a Hohenstaufen global monarchy was a chimera. Circumstances proved quite different: while the crowned heads of Europe submitted to the ecclesiastical leadership of the papacy, they only recognized the regional sovereignty of secular rulers. France's and England's rulers thus appeared on a par with the emperor even though they themselves lacked this title. Moreover, the papacy was itself intent upon warding off the threat of universal imperial hegemony.

Intellectual Culture

As kings and bishops found themselves embroiled in these disputes, the most significant up-and-coming social force of the twelfth century—the cities and their citizenry—seemed to have played no major part in developments, leaving aside Barbarossa's campaigns in Italy. Nevertheless, kings required money, and this was only amassed in the cities. Correspondingly, the power and the influence of the urban bourgeoisie were on the rise everywhere. Even as early as the twelfth century, the Italian municipalities had given evidence of the fact that this group, despite internal divisions, was also highly potent in military terms. Its influence was even growing in Germany. At this stage, only the largest European cities—Paris, London, Barcelona, Milan, Genoa, Venice, or Rome—had more than 50,000 inhabitants; in addition, Cologne may have been just as populous, but other than that German cities had far fewer people. Immigration was growing fast, though. The bourgeoisie was by no means homogeneous.

The middle classes were largely led by the merchant class, who were increasingly proving their worth both as entrepreneurs and in financial transactions, as well as by a patrician class that drew its members from the ranks of the lower aristocracy. The cities of Lombardy were characterized by a rivalry between the resident aristocracy and representatives of the people, which manifested itself not in formal political parties pursuing a set agenda but rather in general trends. Fierce competition, even to the point of long-running feuds, hallmarked dealings within the cities, but, overall, competition tended to stimulate the entrepreneurial spirit rather than hamper it. Furthermore, this urban society of the twelfth and thirteenth centuries was permeated with heresies. In German cities such as Cologne or Frankfurt, episcopal or royal ministers played an important role. Wealth, and a rank that was not inherited enabled a person to have a stake in power in the cities. As a result, new legitimation strategies characterized the upper echelons of urban society. New patterns of behavior, new values, and new ethics took hold—the ethics of money, and of usury and its avoidance or retrospective penance. People's prime interest was in trade and commerce, in the market and in the unimpeded flow of goods and commodities. In the twelfth and thirteenth centuries, the famous Champagne Fairs, which were held according to a strict rota throughout the year in the four towns of Lagny, Provins, Troyes, and Bar-sur-Aube, constituted, a central European location for the exchange of goods, because the counts of Champagne were in a position to guarantee the necessary safety of traders. Their importance declined as soon as the monarchy took over the powers once vested in the counts. In Flanders and Brabant, the towns enjoyed and secured by coercion a similar sense of security and likewise used it to consolidate their autonomy and their economic power, aided by their proximity to the sea. In particular, cloth production both here and in Tuscany gave the region a high-value export commodity that was traded widely, as far away as Spain and the Near East. Recently, cloth making had been made less onerous by technical innovations. For example, the spinning wheel became widespread, most likely imported from the East—from China (in the case of silk) and from India (for cotton). Initially, its use was banned for fear of ruining the quality of the thread; it was only in the fifteenth century, after technical improvements, was it adopted throughout Europe.

The seats of power, of kings and princes, began to migrate once more from rural palatinates and country residences into the cities (as in ancient times and during the Merovingian period). Leaving aside hunting and pleasure palaces, this picture was to remain the same throughout the Middle Ages. Paris, Bordeaux, Rouen, London, Barcelona or Dankwarderode in Brunswick, Meißen, Vienna, and Heidelberg—the list of palatinate or royal residential cities could be extended *ad infinitum*. Only the German realm and empire had to make do without a capital city; its empire was too large, too heterogeneous, and too poorly integrated; and the policies enacted by the Hohenstaufen dynasty permitted no change in this situation. And yet the similarly diffuse empire of the Angevins

(Plantagenets) drove them to embrace a corresponding mobility. In the episcopal cities—which only in the West also played host to royal and princely residences—literacy and education flourished, as did innovation: for instance, these cities saw the rise of the Gothic idiom of architecture. Saint Denis and the cathedral of Notre Dame in Paris are considered its finest examples; by contrast, Germany continued for a long time to build in the old Romanesque style. Elsewhere, cathedrals arose over many decades, or even centuries. Famously, Cologne Cathedral, like many other cathedrals begun in the same era (for example, Sagrada Familia in Barcelona) was only completed in the nineteenth century, no doubt an expression of political romanticism and of burgeoning nationalism.

Courtly culture was another vitally important phenomenon that flourished within this urban milieu of residences, successful trade, and intellectual elites. It was in Paris that Abélard, the renowned tutor, and Héloïse, his beautiful student, lived and loved one another, and where they were forcibly separated. Their ensuing correspondence, whose authenticity has sometimes been doubted, is once again regarded as genuine. All the same—however flawed, stylized, or retrospectively composed it may be—this exchange of letters represented a beginning, epitomized a new departure and sea change that could only have been possible in an urban environment. A new world of feelings was being articulated here, a hitherto unknown display of free will: infamous and yet multifaceted, reprehensible and yet enthralling. The unconditional earthly love and the endangering of one's spiritual salvation through the urges of the flesh are the overt themes here, but other elements that also shine through are the beginnings of human self-realization and the shaping of an individual's own life.

The story itself can be quickly recounted: Abélard was appointed as tutor to Héloïse, the young, enchanting niece of a Parisian canon, and, as can sometimes happen, the professor fell in love with his student. She became pregnant; beside himself with rage, the canon had Abélard waylaid and castrated. This was only the start of his woes, however. Héloïse, meanwhile, did not press Abélard to marry her, quite the contrary in fact: she realized that a crèche and the constant sound of children's prattle was no place for a scholar like Abélard. Accordingly, she turned down his offer of marriage for his sake, while never renouncing her love for him: "Lord God, bear witness when I say that if Augustus, Emperor of the whole world, were to think fit to honor me with marriage and conferred all the Earth on me to possess forever, I would rather be called your whore—and wear the name with pride—than his Empress. For a man's worth does not reside in his wealth or power; these depend on fortune, whereas worth depends on his merits. And a woman should realize that if she marries a rich man more readily than a poor one, and desires her husband more for his possessions than for himself, she is offering herself for sale. Certainly any woman who comes to marry through desires of this kind deserves wages, not gratitude, for clearly her mind is on the man's property, not him as a person, and she would be ready to prostitute herself to a richer man if she could."[32] Héloïse, though, was deeply in love.

Abélard could not have formulated his ethics of free will any more drastically than this, nor spelled out its enormous power—mighty enough to shatter society—any more forcefully. For the heart has an innate propensity to sin: "and it yearns for past pleasures with an undimmed ardor." Admittedly, such an unbridled passion could not go uncorrected; Héloïse duly became abbess of a nunnery, a home for fallen women known as the Oratory of the Paraclete, which the castrated Abélard had founded. Nevertheless, the words "rather your whore . . . than his Empress" were out there for all to see, and Abélard's fall from grace was now famous; the revolution had happened, and with a body of well-reasoned argument behind it, it could no longer be banished from European history. However hard Andreas Capellanus, chaplain to King Louis VII's daughter Marie de Champagne, may have tried, in his widely distributed *Tractatus amoris et de amoris remedio* (ca. 1180?), to repress physical love with canonistic and theological arguments, it remained an untamable force that only obeyed its own rules. For anyone who thought of containing it was implicitly recognizing its immensity. The stories in Boccaccio's *Decameron* treat precisely this theme in many and varied ways. Of course, Immanuel Kant—more a thinker than a lover, and one of those Enlightenment scholars who sweepingly denounced the Middle Ages for its supposed lack of reason—had no conception of such momentous upheavals. Yet even he stopped short of claiming that love in the Middle Ages was nothing more than a formulaic posture—a charge he leveled against the period in many other regards.

This, then, was the age of courtly love poetry. This genre was undoubtedly influenced by verse from the Arab world, which came to Europe through Moorish Spain (Al Andalus). William IX of Aquitaine, Eleanor's uncle, is widely regarded as the first troubadour. Those of his poems that have survived have lost none of their original freshness; another famous love poet was Marcarbru, his slightly younger contemporary: *Dirai vos d'Amor con signa:/De sai guarda, de lai guiga,/sai baiza, de la rechigna* ("I shall sing to you about Love, and how it sends its signals: from here it peeps, from there it winks, here it kisses, and there it grimaces"). It is often said that "high" and "low" forms of courtly love were at odds with one another, but was this really the case? A quite different picture emerges from many of the actual poems: *Robins m'aime, Robins m'a/Robins m'a deman-dée/Si m'ara/Robins m'acata cotele/D'escarlote bonne et belle/Souskanie et chainturele,/Aleuriva!/Robins m'aime, Robins m'a/Robins m'a demandée/Si m'ara* ("Robin loves me, Robin loves me alone, Robin burns for me, and so he will be mine. Robin gave me a fine and beautiful skirt of scarlet, a camisole and a girdle. Aleuriva! Robins loves me"). Arthurian epic poetry flourished at the Angevin court of Eleanor and her children in Rouen, but also at the French court in Paris and those of the principal royal vassals such as the counts of Champagne in Troyes. The epic poet Chrétien de Troyes or the poetess and daughter of the French king Marie de France, countess of Champagne and Eleanor's daughter, performed their works there. After a delay of a generation, this art form also reached the German lands along the Rhine.

However, knighthood was not just an ideal, it was first and foremost a harsh and miserable reality; knights found themselves under pressure from a combination of dwindling income (from agricultural holdings) and a lifestyle of bounden duty, together with a correspondingly demanding code of honor and status and rising costs. Their expenses included horse, armor, travel to jousts far and wide (the Lateran Council's ban on jousting went largely unobserved)—and their only recompense for this was the honor of one day dying in battle for their master. Younger sons found it especially difficult maintaining their status and rank; often, the family had nothing left to give them. As a result, many people renounced their knighthood, entered a knightly order, took up holy orders, or sought their fortune in the cities. Some even took refuge in favorable marriages to the daughters of wealthy farmers, a quick and effective means of augmenting their working capital. The knight who spent the morning toiling behind a plow and rode to take part in a joust in the evening became something of a cliché. In economic terms, they began to find themselves outranked by the urban bourgeoisie and the emerging class of the minor aristocracy. And yet princes found themselves unable to entirely do without this band of warriors. Accordingly, one of the main purposes behind the idealization of knighthood was to compensate for and legitimize its distinct drawbacks.

The beginnings of mercenary service, in other words the origins of the professional soldier who earns his sole living from war or the threat of war, can also be traced back to this same period, namely the second half of the twelfth century. The monetary economy thus now also made its influence felt on the concept of armed force and its practice. The earliest names for bands of mercenaries—say, the now-obscure term "Brabanzons" or "Aragonese"—reveal the regions where the urgent need of the local nobility first gave rise to this way of earning a living. Contemporaries who found themselves inadvertently caught up in conflict—kings, above all—despised the new mercenaries just as much as they needed them. They decried them as rash adventurers, hiring and firing them at will, and washing their hands of their atrocities: these godless soldiers of fortune became a convenient scapegoat to blame for the outbreak of war. At a summit meeting held in Vaucouleurs in 1171, which sealed a decades-long friendship between the Hohenstaufen and Capetian dynasties, Frederick Barbarossa and Louis VII of France agreed to ban the use of mercenaries. But this did little to stem the tide; their sons and grandsons deployed mercenaries in their skirmishes and battles against their royal adversaries. War made a mockery of all attempts at proscription. And so there arose a whole new professional specialty of men, who could be hired or purchased, and upon whom the constant scramble for money by secular powers and popes alike soon contrived to place an astronomical premium; at the same time, this situation presented the salaried commander or *condottiero* with previously unimagined opportunities. The most famous municipal regimes *(signorie)* of the Late Middle Ages, such as that of the Sforza in Milan or the Malatestas in Rimini, were founded on mercenary service performed by their forbears.

There was no getting round the fact that money now ruled the world. A satirical work from the twelfth century was in no doubt on this score: *Nummus vincit, nummus regnat, nummus cunctis imperat,* ran a poem by Walter of Châtillon, which mimicked a section of the *Laudes* by replacing "Christ" in the refrain with "Money;" "Money is the victor, money is the king, money reigns supreme over all." Corruption was rife in the Roman Curia: a famous eleventh-century satire the *Treatise of Garcia of Toledo* had lampooned bribery there by referring to payment for the relics of the fictitious cardinal-saints "Albinus" and "Rufinus" ("silver" and "gold" respectively). To be sure, different taxation jurisdictions created different systems of government, prompted princes and landowners to explore new economic interests, and generated a demand for new specialists. Rulers now made a point of promoting trade and commerce, and founded cities as economic enterprises in deliberate competition with existing ones belonging to rival neighbors. The counts of Champagne were renowned for their wealth because they had promoted the holding of markets within their domain.

Indeed, the beginnings of European high finance are found in this same period. The new capitalism transcended the frontiers of all empires, made kings and princes, and even men of the church intent upon chasing profits dependent upon money, and presently began to make effective interventions into politics. Early high-water marks of this trend were, for instance, Barbarossa's entry into the Third Crusade, which generated enormous financial transactions, and the German succession dispute from 1198 on, following the death of the emperor Henry VI. The dual election of that year was made possible only by financing it with massive sums in bribery, which Cologne merchants and money brokers—foremost among them the archepiscopal *ministerialis* and chief customs official Gerhart Unmâze—transferred from England to the Holy Roman Empire. "We are in desperate need of money," complained the Sicilian king and emperor Frederick II in the next century, and this was to become the abiding watchword of all the centuries that followed.[33]

8

The Vicar of God

JUST AS THE founder of the universe established two great lights in the firmament of heaven, the greater light to rule the day, and the lesser light to rule the night, so too He set two great dignities in the firmament of the universal church . . . , the greater one to rule the day, that is, souls, and the lesser to rule the night, that is, bodies. These dignities are the papal authority and the royal power. Now just as the moon derives its light from the sun and is indeed lesser than it in quantity and quality, in position and in power, so too the royal power derives the splendor of its dignity from the pontifical authority, and the more closely it cleaves to the sphere of that authority the less is the light with which it is adorned; the farther it is removed, the more it increases in splendor." Far away—like the full moon from the sun—according to Innocent III, that was how remote secular authority should be from the ecclesiastical. His entire policy was geared toward realizing this goal: namely, keeping the Holy Roman Emperor at arm's length from the seat of papal power. Only in such circumstances could royal power truly shine. If it were to come too close to the church, it would dim like the new moon. In creating this analogy, Innocent was conjuring up an image that had a long history, and that Gregory VII had used to symbolize the notion that royal grandeur was subject to the leadership of the church. Subsequently Boniface VIII was also to have recourse to the same image, extracting every last drop of symbolic value from it in comparing hieratic and secular authority in his assertion: "The moon has no light except insofar as it obtain it from the sun; in the same way no earthly power has anything which it does not receive from the ecclesiastical authority."[1] Moreover, the commentary on Innocent II's decretals helpfully worked out the precise difference in magnitude between the two powers: "Since the Earth is seven times larger than the moon, while the Sun is in turn eight times larger than the Earth, so it follows that papal dignity is fifty-seven times greater than that of a king."

There is no question that the thirteenth century saw an illustrious series of outstanding rulers ascend the royal thrones of Europe: in the Holy Roman Empire and Sicily, Emperor Frederick II (r. 1212–1250); in France, Philip II Augustus and Louis IX (Saint Louis r. 1226–70) and at the end of the century Philip IV the Fair (1285–1314); in Aragón, James I the Conqueror (r. 1213–1271) and Peter III the Great (r. 1276–1285); in Castle Ferdinand III (r. 1217–1252), who was also later canonized, and his son Alfonso X the Wise (r. 1254–1284). And yet the thirteenth century remained for all that a century of popes, beginning with Innocent III (r. 1198–1216) and ending with Boniface VIII (r. 1294–1303), and which in the interim also witnessed an extraordinary succession of pontiffs: Gregory IX (r. 1227–1241), Innocent IV (r. 1243–1254), and Celestine V (Pietro Angelerio, r. 1294).

By now, the doctrine of *plenitudo potestatis* in both ecclesiastical and secular affairs had been fully formulated and clearly laid down in legal terms, along with that of the "representative of God." The latter had evolved quite logically from the whole notion of the pontiff being the successor and heir of Saint Peter, aided by theology and especially the discipline of jurisprudence. Ramifications for canon law and for church dogma then emerged with the same consistency. Pope Gregory VII was the first to apply phrases to himself that played on the papal role as the imitator of Christ. Allied to this were both the incontrovertible impact of the decretals and the ever-increasing practical role of the popes in framing legislation. Marriage law, inheritance law, and representation were constantly refined by the law faculties of Bologna, Paris, and elsewhere. Even as early as the twelfth century, the Curia had become the central ecclesiastical court. Lay people, too, could bring actions here, and frequently did so. Innocent III regulated the competence of this court. Henceforth, it was open to any lay persons to appeal directly to the pope if found themselves in distress and felt that they had been failed by the secular justice system and so submit themselves to the judgment of the Roman Curia. This "emergency justice" could, at least in theory, be far-reaching; it was especially effective during imperial interregna, or in cases where a judge was lacking in competence, or where there was a denial of justice, or where the case was intractably ambiguous or difficult to solve, also when a crime had been reported direct to the ecclesiastical judges.[2] The pope now appeared to fill the role of an international court of last instance, since priests, princes, and kings really did begin to appeal to the pontiff, thereby breathing life into the theoretical doctrine of the pope as the vicar of Christ.

Granted, genuinely poor people, small-scale farmers, the dispossessed and the oppressed stood very little chance of bringing their case before the Curia or the Rota, as the special papal court of law soon came to be known. People contemplating bringing an action there had to dig deep into their pockets, nor could they hope for a swift resolution. This was the same for lay people as for clerics. On top of the court costs—expenditure for witnesses, advocates, notaries, judges, and general administrative expenses—there was also the outlay for travel and accommodation and all manner of bribes, which might be required for a person to even find out how to proceed in the first place, or what to do in particular cases, or to discover who was to be paid what fees. In addition, anyone who lost a case had to pay the successful plaintiff's costs. Furthermore, over the ensuing centuries, a tightening-up of the court process, the introduction of honor codices for advocates and judges, and an endless succession of new ordinances were all aimed at stemming the tide of cases and limiting the explosion in costs, or at least ensuring that they could be calculated in advance. The idea was that only lawsuits where a large amount of money was at stake were to be dealt with by the papal court. However, nothing seemed to quench the litigiousness of the people in dispute with one another, and so throughout the Middle Ages the papal legal system remained an area in need of constant regulation and a matter of central concern to the Curia.[3]

The doctrine of the vicar of Christ was worked out in full by the lawyer-pope Innocent IV. Jesus Christ—so this pontiff, or rather his propagandist proclaimed—handed over the reins of both the spiritual and worldly empire to Saint Peter and his successors, and constituted at the apostolic see the papal and royal "monarchate" (*monarchatus*: the word is far from familiar even in medieval Latin).[4] The pope is, so Innocent IV's own teaching maintained, the representative of Christ on Earth; he has dominion over all people, whether Christians or heathens; he is the vicar of the Creator-God *(vicarius Creatoris)* and as such all creatures that are graced with the gift of reason should be subservient to him.[5] This development reached its high-water mark and conclusion in the Papal Bull *Unam sanctam,* promulgated by Boniface VIII in 1302, which stated that outside the Roman Church, a person could attain no salvation or remission of sins. The church, though, has only the one head: "Christ and the vicar of Christ, Saint Peter and his legitimate successors." When the Greeks announced that they were not beholden to Peter and his succession, they ceased to be part of Christ's flock. In other words, both "swords" (in Gelasius's "Two Swords" doctrine) were wielded by Saint Peter and the church. Anyone who denied this was guilty of misinterpreting the Bible. It was in the gift of the spiritual power to appoint the secular and to sit in judgment over it if it turned out not to be "good" and went astray. But if the pope himself should ever err *(deviat),* only God was in a position to judge him. "We hereby proclaim and pronounce that each and every human being must for the sake of his own salvation be subservient to the Roman pontiff."[6] Later, doubt was to set in on this score; its outcome is well known. It was not long before dissidents like John Wycliffe and Jan Hus were preaching their sermons, or before the appearance of the Lollards. Soon, the whole fabric of the church would also be rocked by the dogmatic clashes between the papalists and the conciliarists, and the Western Schism loomed on the horizon.

Innocent III, one of the most outstanding of Saint Peter's successors, occupied the papal throne right at the beginning of the new century. His pontificate took the medieval papacy to its highest point, indeed to one of the pinnacles in the entire history of the papacy. Before becoming pope, Innocent had studied in Rome, Paris, and Bologna; he was undoubtedly a theologian, therefore possibly with canonistic training. From the very start of his papacy, Innocent was faced with a welter of the most difficult questions. Yet at the same time, some unique opportunities opened up for him, too. After all, he was embarking on his reign just as a bitter succession dispute was raging in Germany between Otto IV, a son of Henry the Lion, and Philip of Swabia, the youngest son of Frederick Barbarossa, creating turmoil throughout Central Europe (1198), and soon the king of England was in urgent need of his assistance as well. The succession dispute in Germany triggered the first collapse of Hohenstaufen power, reaping the harvest of the crisis sown by the last two monarchs from that dynasty.

The worst fighting took place north of the Alps, where civil war raged; crops were burned in the fields, and famine was rife wherever one turned.

Failed harvests only heightened the state of terror. At the time, Henry VI's widow Constance headed the government of Sicily as regent; yet despite the fact that her four-year old son Frederick (the future Holy Roman Emperor Frederick II) had already been elected king of the Germans, she apparently did not wish to see him succeed as Holy Roman Emperor and renounced all his claims. However, Constance died the following year (1199), leaving her royal offspring in the hands of warring regents and the care of the pope, who was the supreme feudal lord of Sicily. The misery of the Holy Roman Empire continued until Frederick II, duly installed as emperor, was able to reassert the authority of the Hohenstaufens. And yet, in spite of all the desperate hardship, this period saw poetry and literature attain a unique high point in Germany, with the courtly love lyrics of Walther von der Vogelweide, and Wolfram von Eschenbach's epic poem *Parzival*. These two troubadours were said to have met at the so-called minstrels' contest *(Sängerkrieg)* held at the court of one of the most notorious "turncoats" in the succession struggle, Landgrave Hermann of Thuringia. Walther may even be called the poet laureate of the succession dispute: *So wê dir, tiutsche zunge, / wie stêt din ordenzunge! . . . untriuwe ist in der sâze / gewalt vert ûf der strâze, / fride unde recht sint sêre wunt* ("Alas for the German-speaking territories and the parlous state they find themselves in . . . treachery lurks everywhere, violence stalks the highway / law and order are gravely stricken") from his political poem the "Reichston"). It was sheer crisis that spawned such verse. Certainly, no comparable political poet emerged in France or England at this time.

Innocent had not provoked the succession dispute, but he knew precisely how to exploit it, with inimitable virtuosity, to the advantage of the Roman Church and the papacy. Indeed, he even deliberately made sure the dispute lasted longer than seemed absolutely necessary for the church. In doing so, he struck a great blow for the emancipation of the church from the clutches of the empire. His most pressing concern was for the possessions belonging to the Roman Church. With a clear grasp of political realities, he recognized the unique opportunity that the succession dispute presented for the church to regain the lands that had apparently been snatched from it by a series of emperors from Germany. The Peace of Venice of 1177 had at the time purposefully excluded any clear ruling on the territorial borders between the papacy and the empire in Italy, such as delineating the possessions of Matilda of Tuscany or the *Regalia b. Petri* (that is, the papal lands). It seems that Henry VI offered major territorial concessions in this treaty, but Pope Celestine refused to enter into any trade-off at this juncture. Now there was a chance to make good this missed opportunity.

In setting out his "recuperations," Innocent did not appeal to the Donation of Constantine, but rather to the Ludovicianum of 817, namely Louis the Pious's bequest of lands to the Roman Church, and presumably also to the draft treaty concessions by Henry VI that were never implemented, and that were now presented as his last will and testament. Claims were now made to far more extensive tracts of land than had ever been the case during the period of Hohenstaufen rule: the Marche, Spoleto, and Ravenna, Umbria and Tuscany, as well as the whole of central Italy. Step by step, all these areas were absorbed into the Patrimonium Petri. Innocent III was able to assert control over the Maritima, Campania, and Tuscia regions; the remaining areas were secured in perpetuity after Frederick II's death by means of a treaty with Rudolf of Habsburg (1279). This was the genesis of the "Papal State," a process that was consolidated over the following centuries, not least thanks to the steady advance of nepotism, until Italian unification was finally achieved in 1870, when only the narrow confines of the Vatican State remained as the worldly sovereign territory of the pope. But one side effect of this development was to implant for half a millennium in the very heart of the church the deeply disruptive struggle over the precedence of *Regnum* and *Sacerdotium*. For it was not uncommon at various periods in the church's history to find a concern for the welfare of the Papal State predominating over a concern for the Universal Church. Yet the German princes and kings were deeply divided among themselves from 1198 on and simply had to accept what was happening in Italy.

North of the Alps, too, the succession struggle—which did not cease with the murder of Philip of Swabia in 1208 but dragged on until 1214 or even 1218 (the respective dates on which Otto IV was deposed and died)—resulted in an extensive selling off of monarchical lands, royal rights, and privileges. It was at this juncture that the German principalities came into being. Indeed, the princes and the pope had many interests in common. The fall of Henry the Lion two decades previously proved to be a harbinger of momentous change within Germany. The Guelf ruler had not simply sought a territorial balancing but rather an intensification of his authority to the extent of mediating the church and the aristocracy. He had failed in this plan, and ultimately found himself opposed by everyone, including the emperor. Now, however, in the succession dispute the monarchy had finally to foot the bill; moreover, this was a costly affair both for the ruler and by extension the whole empire. Every king had had to secure the support of vassals with remuneration, and frequent shifts of allegiance were the order of the day. This progressive weakening of the material means of the kingdom and of the whole authority of the king could not subsequently be counteracted.

Innocent intervened directly in the succession dispute. With the bull *Venerabilem* he addressed basic principles of electing a king, which ultimately came to be associated with the Electors' College, which came into being in the thirteenth century. First and foremost, however, in this bull the church's chief legislator proclaimed the papal right to vet the person who was to be crowned emperor; over the following decades, this demand was worked up by canon law experts and subsequent popes into a positive right of veto over the future emperor and culminated, in the reign of Ludwig the Bavarian (1314–1347) in an inevitable confrontation between pope and emperor. In the end, in 1201, Innocent declared in favor of the Guelf candidate Otto of Brunswick, since Philip of Swabia had been excommunicated, and he, Innocent, had already come to fear the young Hohenstaufen ruler in his capacity as duke of Tuscany. Many Germans, including Walther von der Vogelweide, held the pope responsible for causing the succession dispute: "Ahî wie kristenliche nû der bâbest lachet, swenne er sinen Walhen seit, ich hanz alsô gemachet! . . . er giht 'ich han zwên Allamân undr eine krône braht, daz siz riche silen stoeren unde wasten'" ("So, what a beatific Christian smile the pope now gives when he tells his Italian subjects 'Look what a good job I did!' . . . and goes on to explain, 'I have forced two Germans to dispute one crown, so that they will end up destroying and ravaging the Empire'").

Innocent duly crowned Henry the Lion's son Holy Roman Emperor, as Otto IV, in 1209, but immediately excommunicated him when he attempted to conquer Sicily with an eye to adding this territory to his possessions. Otto—who was brought up to live in the urbane society of the English court in France, far from any German or Holy Roman monarchy, who was made Count of Poitou by his uncle Richard the Lionheart, and who in all likelihood spoke better French than he did German—doubtless had his great-grandfather Lothair III in mind when he launched his invasion of Sicily: Lothair had been the last of the Roman–German rulers who (albeit with the help of Pope Innocent II) had forced the Normans of

Southern Italy to recognize his sovereignty, in 1137. But by now circumstances had changed fundamentally. Sicily was now unequivocally regarded as a papal fiefdom. Like his predecessors, Pope Innocent III would tolerate absolutely no claim on the part of the Italian king to the formerly Lombard principalities; deceived in his choice of emperor and finding himself in dire straits, he took the last resort that was open to him. He pressed Frederick II of Sicily, who had only just come of age, to assume the German crown, and in so doing helped breathe new life into the very thing that he had wanted at all costs to avoid, namely the unification of the Sicilian kingdom with the Holy Roman Empire.

And so, guided by good fortune the *chind von Pülle,* the "boy from Apulia" embarked on his adventurous journey to the north, where he accepted his father's inheritance at his coronation in Aachen (Aix-la-Chapelle) in 1214; at the same time he surprisingly pledged to lead a new Crusade. Certainly, he helped his cause by ensuring that the flood of privileges that had hitherto washed over the German princes, did not abate. The new Hohenstaufen ruler—the first king ever to do so—even ceded imperial territory, in the shape of the province of Holstein and the city of Lübeck to the Danish king Waldemar II. Meanwhile, his adversary Otto IV went into battle alongside his uncle John Lackland against Philip II of France at Bouvines in Flanders (1214). Otto's defeat there cost him his authority, his prestige, and to all practical intents and purposes, his crown. He died in 1218, without ever having regained it, at his castle of Harzburg near Goslar, which he had recently renovated. Frederick, though, proceeded to show his true colors; he circumvented the agreement with the pope, the terms of which stipulated that he was to bequeath control of Sicily to his son Henry in order to focus his own rule solely on the empire. Instead, he got the German princes to elect Henry to be their king, while he himself bent all his efforts toward returning to Italy to be crowned emperor and resuming control of his hereditary realm in Sicily (1220). This decision would provoke endless struggles and bring about the downfall of his dynasty.

Other matters turned out just as badly for the papacy. Christian forces suffered bitter setbacks in the Holy Land; as the Third Crusade had amply demonstrated, rule there could not be sustained for much longer just through occasional military expeditions. Accordingly, fresh calls were repeatedly issued for a new Crusade. Were all the previous efforts in "God's own land" to have been in vain; were none of the campaigns to be blessed with success? This outcome seemed inconceivable. Furthermore, the church was threatened by internal heresies, too; pastoral care was largely nonexistent. And the English–French conflict began to assume dangerous proportions. The pope was beset by all these problems; presently, Innocent made plans for a new synod to try and solve these difficulties at one stroke.

The pope's chief concern had long been the Holy Land. Straight after his election, Innocent called for a Crusade. But in spite of intensive attempts at recruiting, the number of knights who rallied to the cause did not meet expectations. In the interim, too many of them had absolved themselves from their vows to go on Crusade by making payments in lieu, though this money was not redeployed to secure the services of mercenaries instead. Yet what the Holy Land urgently needed was troops, not money. In addition, the Crusade taxes that the pope levied on the faithful provoked widespread anger. Walther von der Vogelweide was once more to hand to voice opposition: "Sagt an hêr Stoc, hât iuch der bâbest her gesendet, daz ir in rîchet und uns Tiutschen ermet unde pfendet? . . . hêr Stoc, ir sît ûf schaden her gesant, daz ir ûz tiuschen liuten suochet tœrinnen und narren" ("Tell me, Mr. Offertory Box, has the pope sent you here so that you can make him rich while impoverishing us Germans and draining our resources? . . . Mr. Offertory Box, you've been sent here to do us harm, and to search out silly women and fools among us Germans"). But even this fierce critic of the pope was only decrying taxation, not denouncing the notion of the Crusade as such. Indeed, Walther joined others in praising this venture: "Kristen juden und heiden / jehent daz diz ir erbe sî / got müez ez ze rehte scheiden / dur die sîne namen drî / Al diu welt diu strîtet her / wir sîn an der rehten ger, / reht ist daz er uns gewer" ("Christians, Jews and heathens claim this as their heritage. God must settle the matter justly, for His three names. The whole world is coming to do battle here—our cause is just. It is right that He is granting it to us"). But who would God choose to support? Endless conflict seemed inevitable.

In the event, the army that assembled in Venice could not even fill the transport ships that the municipality had promised to put at the disposal of the Crusade nor raise the agreed sum owing for this facility. The doge, Enrico Dandolo, exploited this situation to get the Crusaders to do his bidding, directing them first to sack the Dalmatian port of Zara (modern Zadar), which was claimed by Venice but at that time belonged to the king of Hungary, and had himself pledged to join the Crusade. The city was taken and handed over to Venice (1202). The Crusader army then set sail under the banner of Saint Mark for Constantinople instead of the

Holy Land and, under the leadership of the Doge, captured this city too, which had not been overrun for the last 900 years. Byzantium was sacked, and for the next almost 60 years became the capital of the so-called Latin Empire, in which Venice played the leading role. This spelled the end of the Byzantine Empire; rocked by murderous succession disputes, and sacked and ravaged by barbarous destruction, it lapsed ignominiously into foreign rule in 1204. Two insignificant successor states, the Empire of Nicaea and the Empire of Trebizond, could not disguise this sad end. Even after Constantinople, with Genoese help, became Greek once more after less than sixty years and the Lion of Saint Mark was banished from the Golden Horn (1261), there was no rebirth of the Byzantine empire. The rump that remained, comprising the capital city with a small hinterland in Asia Minor and Thrace, was weak and ineffectual and prone to a constant shrinkage through losses to the Seljuk Turks. It survived for almost another two centuries before Mehmet the Conqueror finally raised the Crescent banner of Islam over the Hagia Sophia (1453).

The assaults on Zara and Constantinople could never have been regarded as "just wars," though the size of the booty they plundered may have caused those responsible to forget this. Both sackings were carried out in defiance of the express wishes of the pope, though it is true that the attack on Constantinople was sanctioned by a papal legate. Innocent III could do nothing to avert these disasters; only the prospect of an ecumenical union with the Greek Orthodox Church could console him. Subsequently, the West was to pay dearly for this incident. The assault by Crusaders on a king who professed the same faith and his Christian subjects was a source of huge resentment. New legitimation strategies had to be devised. After all, had not God permitted Satan to rage against his servant Job? And didn't this fury ultimately emasculate Satan and redound to the greater glory of the saint in the end? As the chronicler Arnold in far-off Lübeck reflected, having studied the reports of those who had participated in the evil act: "Much of what happens in the church seems to occur more with God's acquiescence than through His actual deeds; looked at in this way, then, God's permission must also be construed as His will being done. . . . Everything that God wills shall come to pass, even against the will of the Devil."[7] Venice as the tool of Satan? Such reflections clearly sat very uneasily with this moralist.

As for Venice itself, it glossed over, even positively expunged, its scandalous triumph from its collective cultural memory. Its chroniclers made only brief mention of the consequences of the Fourth Crusade, without making any great play of them or praising them. Instead, they chose to commemorate a victory of 1177 that was genuinely supposed to have been gained for the good of the Roman Church and the pope, what is more a victory over a Holy Roman Emperor, that is, Frederick Barbarossa, off Punta Salvore (the southernmost point of Istria). In actual fact, though, this naval engagement never took place. No matter, all triumphal posturing, all the collective memory of the municipality, and all the ritual of victory focused on this fiction, whose fabrication nobody saw through until the Reformation. Over time, it came to be accepted as fact in the Doges' Palace, the Lateran, and by large sectors of the populace of both Italy and Germany. Moreover, in spite of the fact that large amounts of booty from the 1204 raid on Constantinople duly turned up at the Rialto, and was widely dispersed around Saint Mark's Basilica, the Doges' Palace, and the city in general, it was never acknowledged as having come from the perverted Crusade of 1204. Rather, the maritime commune chose to base its mastery over the sea, its *trionfi,* and its symbol of authority, the winged lion, supposedly endowed by the pope, on historical fictions. Admittedly, all this only happened after Frederick II's excommunication, deposition, and death, possibly even after the last legitimate member of the Hohenstaufen line, Conradin, had been publicly executed in the marketplace in Naples (1268); in other words, once this dynasty of persecutors of the church, as the Hohenstaufens were regarded by the Roman popes, had been safely extinguished. The recollection that had been implanted in the collective memory of large sectors of Christendom found, as we have already noted, widespread credence and centuries later gave rise to a disturbing image—the foot of the victorious Pope Alexander, whose triumphs had been won through the support of the doge, on the neck of the Holy Roman Emperor, lying prostrate on the ground. This was to become one of the most potent antipapal propaganda images of the entire Reformation.

All these events heralded a new structural transformation of the public sphere, whose foundations lay in an ever denser, Europe-wide communications network, which was maintained by pilgrims, merchants, transient people, and men of letters. This network created the phenomenon of public opinion, which continued to gain in importance and which neither the people nor the social elites nor the rulers could escape. Venice in particular came to feel the pressure of this public sphere, as it threatened to confer on its rival cities, foremost among them Genoa, military and commercial advantages that had to be forestalled at all costs. Indeed, for the whole of the thirteenth century and beyond, Venice and Genoa found themselves locked in a surreptitious yet endless war. Marco Polo, for example, later fell victim to this great enmity after his return from China, when he fell into the hands of the Genoese and was thrown in jail there, where he began to dictate his account of his travels, *Il Milione*.

Meanwhile, notwithstanding the debacle of 1204, Europe began to make preparations for a Fifth Crusade, a campaign that also ended in catastrophe (1219). Prior to this expedition, there had also been the Children's Crusade of 1212—a procession of unarmed young men and women from France and Germany, who followed a shepherd boy claiming to possess a "letter from heaven" and who believed that they might miraculously be able to cross the Mediterranean on foot and liberate the Holy Land. Their expedition came to an end (for those of them that had not already died of starvation) when they fell into the clutches of slave traders in Genoa and Marseilles. However, the young king Frederick, the *chind von Pülle*, came across this procession of lost souls at Cremona, as he made his way across the Alps to his investiture. Might the terrible fate of this venture have been behind his own decision to take the Cross? As ever, the strategists of the Fifth Crusade realized what a danger Egypt posed to the Christians in Palestine, and so attacked the ruling Fatimid caliphate in its very heartland. It is related how Francis of Assisi sought an audience with the sultan to try and convert him, and how—if we are to believe the story—the Muslim leader listened to this quaint Franciscan friar with all the amused indulgence of a great ruler toward a fool. Yet the Crusaders had reckoned without the terrain of Egypt and the Nile; after some initial successes, their army found itself encircled in the town of Damietta by water and enemy forces and were forced to surrender. Even the knights among them, unless they were able to purchase their freedom, succumbed to a lingering death or slavery. It was against this background that Pope Honorius III and his successor Gregory IX urgently exhorted Frederick II to fulfill the promise that he had made in Aachen.

In the interim, matters had come to a head between England and France. John Lackland could not match the political and military skill of his French counterpart, Philip II. For a variety of reasons, including the suspicion that he may have been personally responsible for murdering his nephew Duke Arthur of Brittany (a legitimate claimant to the English throne), John was repeatedly summoned to appear at the court of his feudal lord, namely the king of France, but refused to comply. Accordingly, in several legal proceedings, he was stripped of all his fiefdoms. War ensued in the wake of these court cases, fought on the English side by expensive mercenary forces, and from which in any case Philip emerged as victor (1204). He immediately began to make plans for the invasion of Britain, which were then temporarily put on hold. The dispute with King John gradually expanded into an affair that drew in the whole of Western Europe, in which dynastic marriages and candidatures, shifting alliances and small-scale military campaigns generated an atmosphere of continuing unrest, whose direct end result, in the south, was the crusade against the Cathars. Above all, it was the kings of Castile and Aragón, alongside numerous regional dynasties of noblemen, who found themselves drawn into this dispute. John was able to assert his authority in the south, in Guienne and Gascony, and the decisive Battle of Muret near Toulouse in 1213 had major and long-lasting ramifications for Aragón and France and the local lords of those kingdoms.

In addition, John had also made an enemy of the pope, in refusing to recognize Stephen Langton, the man whom Innocent had consecrated as archbishop of Canterbury in 1207. This caused the fighting between France and England, between the emperor and the pope, and between the Guelfs and the party of the Hohenstaufens in Germany to coalesce into a single great Europe-wide conflict. Langton subsequently led the opposition against King John, and Philip Augustus revived his plans to invade the island. In desperation, John sought the help of Innocent III, though he had been excommunicated and under a papal interdict since 1209. He offered the pope the kingdom of England and Ireland to hold in fee against an annual payment of 1000 silver marks. The imminent invasion was called off. Yet the truly decisive event, which resolved all the entanglements in Europe and ensured the final triumph of Philip II was the Battle of Bouvines (near Tournai) in 1214, which despite assistance from his imperial nephew ended in a catastrophic defeat for John. Philip's victory set the seal on the irrevocable loss of most of the Angevin possessions on the Continent, the dynasty's original homeland; the only area they retained control of was Guyenne, with Bordeaux at its center. This battle also settled the succession dispute in Germany in favor of Frederick II, who had traveled to Vaucouleurs to meet the French dauphin, the future Louis VIII, before the engagement to renew the old French–Hohenstaufen alliance against Otto IV and King John. However, in a prophetic gesture, the victor of Bouvines sent the imperial eagle standard captured on the battlefield to Frederick II with its wings broken.

It was around this time that the English barons began to conspire against the king. Under Langton's leadership they wrested from the defeated John Lackland—who, in order to recruit new levies of mercenaries, had once more raised taxes and pledged to go on Crusade—the concessions of the Magna Carta (1215). In its sixty-three articles, this seminal document set forth a list of personal and political freedoms that were henceforth to be enjoyed not only by the barons and knights of England, but also by all freeborn men and by cities, in particular London. It also guaranteed the right to inheritance and chattels, imposed strict limits on the king's authority, who was obliged hereafter to seek the counsel and judgment (*consilium* and *iudicium*) of the barons before taking action. Magna Carta represented a comprehensive manifestation of the demands for freedom that were abroad throughout Europe at this time. In addition, extraordinary taxes were only to be levied with the approval of the "general council of the kingdom"—a precursor of the English Parliament—on which bishops, abbots, counts, and barons were to be invited to sit. Chapter 39 of the document stated: "No free man shall be seized, or imprisoned, or dispossessed, or outlawed, or exiled or injured in any way . . . except by the lawful judgment of his peers, or by the law of the land." All judges and other officials were required to have a thorough knowledge of the law and observe its requirements—this marked the beginning of special legal education in England. Alongside the king there now came into being a body called the *communa totius terre* (which the king was prohibited from circumventing in all state affairs)—a committee of twenty-five barons to oversee the king's actions and, if necessary, impose sanctions on him or even initiate full resistance to his rule within the bounds of the law. In short, Magna Carta severely curtailed the king's power, while at the same time clearly delineating the limits of his authority within these confines, and defining royal authority as a concept independent of the personage of the king. Even if the king was absent in person, he was always present in the form of his legal counsel; in other words, the notion of the "Crown" as the embodiment of royal authority came into effect even at this early stage.

As England's feudal lord (and in order to protect the monarch who had just pledged his service as a Crusader), Innocent III instantly invoked his power of binding and loosing to declare Magna Carta invalid, stating:

"The charter with all its undertakings and guarantees we declare to be null and void of all validity forever."[8] Yet while this cassation remained without consequences for the development of the English constitution, elements of Magna Carta itself, repeatedly renewed and modified, still represent valid aspects of constitutional law even today. The resistance of the barons was not going to be broken by any papal intervention. They deposed John and asked the French dauphin Louis to assume the English throne. And Louis did indeed land on the island at the head of an army. But at this point the papal commitment to protection came into force; Innocent issued threats and dispatched a legate, Cardinal Guala, to England, whose intervention managed to rescue the crown for John and, when he died in 1216, for his son Henry III (r. 1216–1272), who was still a minor at the time. One of Henry's first legislative acts when coming to power, with the approval of the papal legate—was to renew Magna Carta. Louis was not in a position to conquer England; however, Innocent did not live to witness his success there, dying three months before his royal vassal John.

None of these machinations harmed France. Innocent himself declared that France's elevation was tantamount to an advance for the Apostolic See also, since France was a country that had been blessed by God, a country that was steadfast in its respect for the Apostolic See and would never in his estimation lapse from the one true faith. And so the pope never called into question the outcome of France's trials of the English king and its defeat of him in battle, despite the fact that he, Innocent, had come down in favor of John Lackland as early as 1204. This lavish praise of France came in the opening of his *Novit,* one of the outstanding decretals issued by this great legislator of the Roman Church; it was presently incorporated into the *Liber Extra* and, addressed to the French episcopate, summarized the pontiff's basic right of intervention in worldly affairs.[9] In this missive, Innocent declared that he had no intention of passing judgment on a fiefdom, but rather his target was the sin of breach of the peace. After all, the pope maintained, Philip II himself had called for precisely this sanction in his similar dispute with Richard the Lionheart. However, the peace that was now being disrupted had been solemnly confirmed by oath at the time, and since a question of a religious oath *(iuramenti religio)* was at stake, this legitimized the pope's jurisdiction. Even so, Innocent accepted the development that had occurred as a result of the legal actions taken against the vassal of the French throne, especially as King John of

England was also in dispute with the pope at the time. Nor did Innocent later question the results of the Battle of Bouvines, since it had also succeeded in breaking the power of an anathematized emperor.

All in all, Bouvines bestowed upon France one of the most magnificent victories—perhaps even the greatest of all successes—ever achieved by a French king. The new acquisitions it brought, including Normandy, one of the richest and best-run territories of the age, were incorporated into the Crown's domain and used to furnish newer branches of the ruling dynasty with lands to administer. So, the county of Anjou was acquired by a side branch of the Capets who then soon inherited the county of Provence as well and a little later, in 1264 (and with the pope's help), the kingdom of Sardinia in addition, plus the Hungarian crown, after the illustrious Arpad dynasty finally died out (1301). Since the beginning of the era of church reform, the Roman Curia and France had grown ever closer. There were no French ambitions of hegemony over Rome to compromise and hinder the fundamental solidarity binding together the pope and the French king.

Certain key elements of ecclesiastical and papal doctrine, in fact, were even formulated in France and tested though argumentation there. Numerous cardinals and popes of the twelfth and thirteenth centuries studied there; many of them were themselves French. Seen in this light, the rise of France was an early triumph of the universities. As the Holy Roman Emperor increasingly proved himself an enemy of the Roman Church, so the influence of France on the church grew.

This whole development was of direct benefit to the French monarchy. It profited from the papal decretals, even when they were not addressed to the king. Thus, to cite just one prime example, the lord of Montpellier, Guillem VIII, separated from his first wife, who had borne him only one child, a girl named Maria, in order to take a second spouse, who had already given him the male heir he longed for. When this union was declared illegitimate, Guillem attempted to legitimize his bastard son by pointing to a similar procedure undertaken by King Philip Augustus. Innocent II intervened to prevent this from happening, in the decretal *Per venerabilem* (1202).[10] This turned out to be a directive in favor of the French monarchy, even though Guillem did not hold a royal fee. France's king, the first to be thus honored and archetypal for all sovereigns thereafter, was attested as having no superior in worldly matters: *quum rex ipse superiorem in temporalibus minime recognoscat* (since under no circumstances does the king himself recognize a superior in temporal matters) as the original phrase put it—a formulation that was repeated time and time again subsequently, either verbatim, or in paraphrase, by canonists, jurists, and publicists. This edict was immediately deployed as the theoretical foundation for future state "sovereignty." As it turned out, Maria, Guillem's sole legitimate daughter, unloved though she was by her father, ended up allying Montepellier with the crown of Aragón. She became the wife of Peter II of Aragón, and the mother of James the Conqueror. Not least, the pope's struggle against heresy effectively allied the interests of the Curia with the benefit of the French crown. This was in stark contrast to the situation in Lombardy, where the pope's ongoing battle with the emperor actually sometimes worked to the advantage of the heretics.

Ever since the reforms of the eleventh century, the church's monopoly over salvation had seen itself increasingly threatened by heresies. The Cathars, the Waldensians, and other heretical movements, which were not always clearly distinguished from one another by contemporaries, spread rapidly during the twelfth century and not just in France (where they thrived especially in Languedoc, in the domain of the rural nobility). Merchants and artisans who traveled around a great deal spread the heretical message across the continent. Large areas of Europe were gripped by the new religiosity. Favorable conditions prevailed not only in municipalities like Milan or Bologna, but also in towns like Assisi. Reasons for the success of the heresies can be identified in the evolution of the church and of society: for instance in the fraught situation of the lower aristocracy, who, once they lost the power of disposition over the lesser churches, saw themselves deprived of a large portion of their income. But an explanation can also be found in the specific tensions arising within urban communities, where the old controlling powers found themselves confronted with the bourgeoisie's sudden and ostentatious wealth. Similar indications also emerge, say, from the descriptions of the early life of Saint Francis. These indicate sharp contrasts between the poor and the rich—all the more stark when they were cheek by jowl—the decline of individual churches despite the wealth of the church as an institution, plutocratic modes of existence and the growing moral scruples that such inequalities aroused, physical and spiritual crises, and last but not least the demand for equity and the "curing" of social ills, alongside a yearning for the certainty of salvation. The excess that the church was also guilty of indulging came into conflict with the precepts of poverty and love for one's fellow man inherent in the Christian message—precepts that the powerful and wealthy church was in danger of overlooking. Its increasing involvement in worldliness and temporal matters stood in striking contrast to the demand that spiritual concerns *(spiritualia)* should always take precedence over worldly concerns *(temporalia)*. Many people feared for the salvation of their souls.

The early history of the Cathars, especially concerning their origins, is completely uncertain. Various commentators mention influences from the East, from the Bogomils. The Cathars's doctrines have been largely reconstructed from the counterarguments of their opponents; only a single more extensive authentic Cathar text has so far come to light— the *Liber de duobus principiis* (Book of two principles)—alongside a series of smaller texts. As far as we can make out, those professing this faith referred to themselves as "the good people," or "the pure ones," while their spiritual elite, men and women alike, were called the "perfects" *(Perfecti)*. They despised the church hierarchy, but in their heyday themselves had their own churchlike organization. While devoid of any uniform dogmatic focus, their theology followed a consistent dualism of the Two Principles, that is the two powers of God and Satan, with the latter being seen as the true demiurge (that is, the creature responsible for creating the material world). Light encountered darkness, with spirit and soul as the good principle confronting the physical universe as the evil principle. The soul fell prey to the evil realm of the material, where Satan held sway, since it was incarcerated within the body, though ultimately it would be freed from this and reunited with the spirit that had remained in the heavenly realm. Man was seen as a fallen angel, banished from heaven into the satanic world of physicality and darkness, where he did penance so that his soul might be redeemed and take its place in heaven once more. Redemption, then, was less an act of grace and more one born of personal effort. This interpretation dispensed with the idea of Christ the Savior and Redeemer. Had he really become a man, and died, and risen again? The Cathars questioned this. His descent into Hell (between the Crucifixion and the Resurrection) was rejected. Likewise, the Cathars would hear nothing of the Resurrection of the Flesh. They refused the sacraments; the only ritual that was permitted was a "spiritual baptism," the *consolamentum* or *baptismum spiritus sancti*, conducted by the "perfects," since they were the ones who had come closest to the spirit. The Cathars lived very frugally, from their lands or the sweat of their brows, and journeyed around, encouraging one another in their faith and winning new converts. They were expected to undertake regular bouts of fasting and to observe strict dietary rules: no meat, no milk, and no eggs. Other injunctions included sexual abstinence and continual mutual confessions. Such forbearance, in a world where priests were often seen to violate their vow of celibacy, would surely have made quite an impact. Their practice of mutual help and charity also drew many poor and destitute people to their ranks. Yet poverty was not an absolute requirement for either the "perfects" or the common faithful. However, the radical rejection of physicality and embrace of the spirit, along with the solidarity among the Cathar faithful, convinced many to join.

The history of the Waldensians, the "Poor of Lyons," the second great medieval religious movement to create major problems for the Roman Church, began with their "founder," the wealthy yet illiterate merchant Waldes of Lyons, who only took the Christian name "Petrus" in the fourteenth century. Deeply moved by the parable of the rich man and the pauper Lazarus, he gave away all his possessions to the poor; at the same time, he taught people to embrace a life of voluntary poverty and model themselves on Christ and His apostles. He had the Bible translated into the French vernacular, and then, heeding the word of the apostle to "go into all the world and preach the gospel to every creature" (Mark ch. 16, v.15), immediately became an itinerant lay preacher, without episcopal sanction. Straightaway, he found himself accused of "usurping the office of the apostles" and "usurping the office of Saint Peter." At the Third Lateran Council of 1179, Waldes sought recognition by Pope Alexander; but while the pope welcomed the vow of voluntary poverty, he forbade Waldes from preaching. When he refused to comply, in 1184 he was placed on the list of heretics, despite having made an avowal of adherence to the one true faith. It was from this point on that Waldensians began to criticize the church; they also began to differentiate themselves dogmatically, by rejecting the church's doctrine of the sacraments and accepting the principle of lay baptisms. In place of university teaching, their own program of study equipped Waldensian preachers with a comparatively good education. In ca. 1260–1266, an ecclesiastical chronicler known as The Passau Anonymous, an opponent of the Waldensians, highlighted another matter in which they diverged from the Roman Church: "The second cause of their heresy is that men and women, great and small, day and night, do not cease to learn and teach; the workman who labors all day teaches or learns at night. . . . Whoever excuses himself, saying that he is not able to learn, they say to him; 'Learn but one word each day, and after a year you will know three hundred, and you will progress.'"[11] The great and lasting success of this lay teaching program, which used the vernacular Bible and Gospel texts, once again points up the neglect of people's spiritual needs by a church that was increasingly preoccupied with struggles over power and possessions. Moreover, despite being subjected to intense persecution, Waldensian communities are the sole medieval heresy to have survived right up to the present day.

The church now found itself under the severest pressure. Its response was characterized by a keen self-awareness and drastic practical measures. Beginning with a synod convened at Reims by Pope Eugene III in 1148, it began to deploy the weapon of mass excommunication against the new heresies. People were forbidden to offer protection or lodging to the leaders of the sects in Provence. In the decades that followed, a whole series of new normative ordinances and persecution strategies were implemented. Before long, the threats became even more dire. Fifteen years later, Alexander III ordered that heretics were to be arrested and stripped of all their possessions. This had little effect. "So far has the stinking slurry of heresy spread already that anyone who adheres to it believes that they are obeying God's commandments," complained Raymond V of Toulouse to the general chapter of the Cistercians in 1177, with no notion that his own noble house would be wiped out within two generations after siding with the Cathars.[12] Pope Lucius III's decretal on heretics in 1184 threatened to turn them over to the secular authorities for summary justice, the destruction of their property, banishment into exile, and even burning at the stake. This latter punishment, which had been used previously, was first enacted against heretics by Peter II of Aragón in a law of 1197–1198.[13] What an irony of history it was, then, that precisely this good Catholic, who enjoyed the protection of the pope, should have ultimately met his end not exactly at the stake, but in the Battle of Muret (1213) while fighting alongside the heretics. For, as his son later commented on the death of his father, "it was always the custom our family to either triumph in battle or be killed."[14] Heresy plunged the order of the world into chaos, invoking as it did a thoroughgoing spiritual, social, and institutional renewal without providing any indication of what shape or organizational form a society thus changed would take. In consequence, Emperor Frederick II proceeded against heresy as though it were a crime against the Crown, a threat to the world order and salvation, and as a rebellion against God.

Above all, though, heresy threw down a challenge to the head of the church, the pope. Innocent III resorted to the most fearsome weapon in his armory by calling for a Crusade against the Cathars. Furthermore, any secular authority which chose to ignore the warnings and resisted persecuting heretics—either, depending upon one's viewpoint, "refusing to purge their land of the filth of heresy," or simply trying to protect their own territory from being ravaged by the fury of war—was threatened with excommunication and interdict and, after a grace period of one year, usurpation of their leadership by staunch Catholics. Scarcely had Innocent issued his proclamation than Crusaders fell upon Languedoc and the county of Toulouse and the surrounding areas (1208). Leading this force was Simon de Montfort, a minor northern French baron and a capable military commander, who had formerly refused to participate in the attack on Zara because he was appalled at the injustice of the Venetians but now found himself in a position to fulfill his Crusader vows in the service of the church; his brutal campaign of plunder saw him rise to become a major landowner in southern France. The fighting spared neither princes nor peasants, neither heretics nor loyal Catholics. It is salutary for us to remember that similar acts of terror were carried out then in the name of Christ as are nowadays committed in the name of the Prophet. When the city of Béziers was besieged in 1209, its inhabitants, Catholics and heretics alike, took refuge in the cathedral, which had been built on an unassailable rocky outcrop high above the plain. It was only vulnerable to fire; and so the papal legate, Abbot Arnold of Citeaux, ordered that it be burned to the ground, with all those inside, irrespective of their loyalties. Before the building was put to the torch, he is alleged to have calmly announced: *"Tuez les tous, Dieu reconnaitra les siens"* ("Kill them all, God will recognize his own.") Nine thousand people are reputed to have died in this atrocity. The legate duly gave thanks to the Lord: "Oh miraculous revenge of God!"[15]

Even so, military force was not enough; the heresy outlasted the Crusade. In the long term, even Simon de Montfort and his son Amaury, who succeeded him, could not sustain their authority there; neither the region nor the king wanted them to have a power base there. Yet what this holy war did achieve was, after the final elimination of the counts of Toulouse (in 1229 and 1243), to open up the south to the French crown. The king now established his writ there, submitting the Midi to his governance and taxation, and imposing *sénéchaux* and *prévôts* on it. But the persecution did not end with the Crusade. Efficient measures against the Cathars were called for. Inexpressible suffering was now visited upon the inhabitants of the cities of Carcassonne, Toulouse, and Albi. One anecdote speaks volumes: one time, a noblewoman near Toulouse, who was on her deathbed, called for the *consolamentum*; hearing of her plight, the local Catholic bishop rushed to her side and spoke consolingly to her about the contemptibility of all earthly things, so that she took him for a Cathar and confessed her faith to him. The bishop duly had her burned at the stake.[16] Truth demanded sacrifices, but what was the truth? This incident demonstrates the two levels on which the fight against heresy was now carried forward: the indoctrinating sermon and the most subtle, perfect, lasting, and implacable persecution the church had ever known; henceforth, the latter would—albeit in many different forms—come to characterize European regimes right up to the present day. One need only think of the network of spies deployed by the Inquisition or of various state intelligence services, torture chambers, and gulags. Here, then, was the ultimate origin of what R. I. Moore has termed the "persecuting society."[17]

The efficiency of the Inquisition (literal meaning: "questioning, investigation") lay in the fact that it brought together may different competencies. In contrast to the principle of accusation, according to which an individual plaintiff could set a trial in motion, an inquisition proceeding in the canon, and later the secular, judicial system was instigated by the authorities, meaning that from the outset there was a presumption of guilt on the part of the accused. During the trial, witness statements alone were taken as proof of guilt, and denunciations were the order of the day; no testimony or adducing of any other material evidence was allowed. From the papacy of Innocent II onward, this official principle of suspicion was initially only practiced against clerics, and it has continued to evolve into the phenomenon of the public prosecutor (district attorney) in modern states. Then, from around 1230 on, a corresponding procedure began to be used against heretics, becoming a fully evolved system by the middle of the century.

However, the heretic-inquisitor was not merely a public prosecutor, but rather a persecutor, accuser, and judge all rolled into one; people who dared oppose him exposed themselves to the suspicion of promoting heresy and so would find themselves caught up in the machinery of the Inquisition (which were active throughout Europe with the exception of England and

Scandinavia). An abbreviated, summary hearing, which was justified through the supposed imminence of the danger posed by heresy, and swiftly fabricated proofs condemned the accused, and enforced the sentence (which fell to the secular authorities to execute). From 1252, torture came to be employed in the interrogation process, either in order to force a confession—the "queen of all proofs"—out of the suspect or to compel witnesses to make a damning statement. If those accused expressed remorse and confessed their guilt, their punishment was to be thrown in jail, but in cases of obstinacy or recidivism, the penalty was to be burned at the stake. Acquittal was possible, but in these prevailing circumstances only rarely happened. The church authorities quickly learned how to invest even secular affairs with the semblance of heresy. For example, Joan of Arc was condemned to be burned at the stake after a heresy trial; the Spanish Inquisition used the same approach to persecute the *marranos,* Jews who had been forcibly converted to Christianity but who secretly continued to observe Judaism. The witchcraft trials of the Late Middle Ages and the Early Modern Period were based on the same procedure. The notorious work *Malleus Maleficarum* (Hammer of the witches) by the two inquisitors Jakob Spengler and Heinrich Institoris gives a detailed description of the inquisition process.

Yet the Inquisition and torture could do nothing to heal the wounds that had been inflicted upon people's expectation of salvation. Nor could the heresies, which continued to escalate, heal them in the long run either. Rather, pastoral care and preaching were required to address the social and psychological challenges of the age, and there was a pressing need for a new religiosity and new modes of living such as those that had once been preached and pioneered by the Poor of Lyons, but this time incorporated into the church and in full accordance with the episcopal magisterium. Admittedly, the religious poverty movement, especially in its most radical form, always teetered on the fine line between high church acceptability and heresy. How might the latter be prevented?

The help that was so urgently hoped for came from new orders, especially mendicant ones, which now came to prominence at the beginning of the thirteenth century and which were astonishingly successful. The first signs of this development became apparent in 1206 in the ecclesiastical province of Narbonne. In that year, certain canons-regular in the group around Dominicus, a canon-regular of Saint Augustine from the small Castilian town of Osma, were granted permission by Pope Innocent "in imitation of the poverty of the poor Christ," as the program of all Christian poverty movements had framed their mission from the late eleventh century onward, to "dissuade the heretics from the errors of their ways" by preaching and by setting a good example.[18] A precursor of these mendicants was the Waldensian proselyte Durandus of Huesca; he, too, had been granted leave by the pope to preach sermons against his former coreligionists, an enterprise in which he scored some notable successes. Just nine years later, at the Fourth Lateran Council, Innocent conferred on Dominicus and his fellow Augustinians the task of supporting the bishop of every diocese by assuming responsibility for preaching and education; the pope also formally regulated the organization of their General Chapter.

In total contrast to all former monastic or canonical reform movements, these preaching brethren, the *Ordo Fratrum Praedicatorum,* quite deliberately established their communities in the great centers of societal change, namely the cities—which especially in northern and central Italy were also hotbeds of heresy—and in the environs of the universities. In regard to their mode of living, their clothing, their fasting, and their vow of poverty, they followed a stricter form of the Rule of Saint Augustine, and were canon-regulars as opposed to monks. Like the Cistercians before him, Dominicus won many converts among students. In 1217, the General Chapter under his leadership declared pastoral care and learning to be indispensable elements of his community; in a departure from all previous practice, study became an integral part of the order's rule. At that time, the order sent its brethren to all corners of the world, but particularly to the University of Paris; Saint Jacques became their center there, precisely the same convent which, some 500 years later, served as the meeting place of the most radical wing of the French Revolutionists (that is, the Jacobins). Bologna was another early stronghold of the Dominican order; indeed, it was there that its founder was buried following his death in 1221. The Dominicans were henceforth to prove their mettle in the fight against heresy; before long, they were conducting their own university-like courses of study for order members, for example in Paris and Cologne. The outstanding scholars of the period, such as Albertus Magnus and Thomas Aquinas in addition to many others, joined their ranks. Other prominent Dominicans were the mystics Heinrich Seuse, Johannes Tauler, and (somewhat earlier) Meister Eckhart, who was also a leading logician and linguistic innovator. Pope Gregory IX assigned the duty of carrying out inquisitions to the order. Its members were decried as *Domini canes,* the "Lord's hunting dogs," and depicted as black-and-white patterned hounds on many a polemical tract. One of the authors of the *Malleus,* Heinrich Institoris, was also a Dominican. The fact that the order assumed responsibility for the Inquisition, however, did not prevent even its greatest scholars, such as Thomas Aquinas or Meister Eckhart, from being investigated by the Inquisition or from writing sentences that were condemned by it.

All the reform measures were summarized and thoroughly regulated by the Fourth Lateran Council in 1215. Certain fundamental questions of the Middle Ages, which transcended the particular period, emerged at that time in Rome and were concentrated there like light rays in a magnifying glass. Antiheretical, jurisdictional, institutional, and pastoral measures all intermingled. The pope directed the assembly with a sure hand. When the archbishop of Bremen raised objections, he was sharply rebuked. The council's proceedings began, remarkably enough, with a communal confession of faith. Momentous resolutions followed, beginning with a decretal against heresy, which brought together all measures used hitherto against heretics. The council then proceeded to condemn the "arrogance" of the Greeks—after all, the Latins were still in control of Constantinople at this time—and to threaten them with excommunication if they refused to submit to the Roman Church. Theological studies, moreover, also needed greater depth. Preachers were to be installed throughout the church, who would be entrusted with education that was to be established alongside the cathedral schools, with the "poor" being able to study the liberal arts and theology free of charge.

Accusations of heresy were also leveled around this time at the mysterious Calabrian abbot and soothsayer of the Apocalypse, Joachim of Fiore, whose teachings had spread far and wide. He was banned from preaching, although no formal condemnation followed. Joachim (d. 1202) was one of the most extraordinary yet at the same time highly effective religious thinkers of this age. The small, insignificant abbey that he ran lay far distant from any other religious centers, in the mountainous wilds of Calabria. Raised for a life of service at the Sicilian royal court, Joachim first became a Cistercian. In 1184, at his own request, he was relieved of his duties as abbot by Pope Lucius III and granted leave to devote all of his time to writing his "Revelations." When the General Chapter threatened to punish him for his views, he withdrew to the abbey of Fiore, which he had founded. His exegetical works, which rely heavily on the allegorical mode of expression, are difficult to comprehend, but their unique musings on the nature of history had a powerful effect on his contemporaries. Joachim taught that there was a tripartite division of the history of man's salvation: first, an "Age of the Father" (up to the time of Jesus), an "Age of the Son," and a third "Age of the Holy Ghost," which was, he claimed, represented by monasticism and which was to commence with the year 1264 (the date he said had been revealed to him). This final era would be heralded by the appearance of the first antichrist, who would be vanquished by an outstanding representative of the church. Speculation was understandably rife as to who these two figures might be.

Many further resolutions of the Council concerned church reform and pastoral care. In caring for the sick, it was stipulated that the priest should be summoned first, and then the doctor, who in those days was also an astrologer, and so was helpless and clueless in cases of serious illness. The faithful were expected to go to confession at least once a year and always to attend the Easter Communion; these were possibly the two most effective injunctions of the Council. For the individual acknowledgment of sin that lay at the root of a person's confession before his or her confessor demanded self-examination, and a close scrutiny of one's ego, and as such allowed people to intensively educate their conscience. Up to this point, confession had merely punished a person's actions, whereas now the intention behind the deed came to the fore, stressing free will and the question of personal guilt. This shift of emphasis was soon universally accepted. The history of the psyche and human attitudes, and hence the entire history of the West was profoundly affected by this change. In the light of this nexus of guilt and confession, and the consequent forgiveness of sins, the emotions of fear and despair, yet also confidence in faith, charity, and social institutions, experienced a widespread revival; likewise, the practice of selling indulgences now entered its decisive phase. Immanuel Kant's formulation of the Categorical Imperative ("act as though the maxim of your action were to become a universal law") can be seen as a late flowering of the principles laid down by the Fourth Lateran Council.

The Council adopted several resolutions relating to court procedure and marriage law. One issue that the assembled prelates returned to repeatedly was secular interference in ecclesiastical matters. Clerics were not allowed to be taxed. Specific ordinances were passed against usury, especially against the "interest-related usury of the Jews." Jews and Moors were ordered to wear distinctive apparel in order that Christians might easily recognize them and so that "carnal intermingling" could be prevented. Jews were forbidden from appearing in public during Eastertide, and as "blasphemers against Christ" they were disbarred from occupying any official position. Finally, after advancing exhaustive justifications for it and passing wide-ranging resolutions concerning its funding (including a law on the refund of interest by Jewish creditors), a new Crusade was proclaimed and an arms embargo imposed on Muslims.

Interest, usury, and money did not, of course, banish poverty from the world. Quite the contrary, rather than provide any relief, they only exacerbated it, inasmuch as they extensively undermined familiar ways of living. The spread of a monetary economy brought with it new modes of existence, which were responsible for much suffering and sorrow but also gave rise to a new economic upturn and prosperity. The Lateran Council's injunctions that people should search their conscience and confess their sins had little effect on this. Economic prosperity, founded on easy credit and usury, was widespread, yet this same period saw the rise of the under classes in the cities and tied laborers in the countryside. The Dominicans followed "the poor Christ in poverty," but they did not preach any radical poverty. In addition, it was impossible to complete a course of study "without income or property," as the regulations required; a student's books alone cost a fortune. As a result, it was left to Saint Francis of Assisi to realize the strictest and most radical form of voluntary poverty. Francis—a lay preacher and the son of a rich family of merchants who maintained a decidedly aristocratic-knightly lifestyle and possibly hailed from a Cathar background—exalted the emulation of the poor Christ to an almost accusatory religious ideal of radical voluntary poverty that was guaranteed to cause offense among the authorities. He embarked on his path of spiritual renewal—quite literally naked. Yet for all his radicalism, he submitted himself and his community to the church hierarchy in all matters and traveled to Rome to have the first rules for his community confirmed by Pope Innocent III. The spinning of legends around the figure of Saint Francis began even during his lifetime, with the result that the real life and the mythical account of this saint can scarcely be disentangled anymore. The legend portrayed Francis as emulating Christ impressively, including receiving the stigmata. The saint, who became known as *Il Poverello,* exuded a charisma akin to that of Christ, which was preserved and heightened when he stepped down from leading his order, thereby willingly subjugating himself in his own lifetime to one of his fellow monks, first the jurist

Petrus Catanii, one of his earliest companions, and then Elias of Cotrone. When the order was still emerging, he prescribed that it should shun all possessions and that its members should wear the simplest of habits, a brown tunic tied with a cord, and that even these should be loaned to them. Furthermore, Franciscans were to carry with them "no bag, and no staff," nor should they ever handle money or build any great churches. The saint finally impressed these rules on his associates in his "Testament"; however, no sooner had he died than Pope Gregory IX declared that this document was not binding.

The Minorites, or *Ordo Fratrum Minorum,* were an itinerant Franciscan order who preached about sin, atonement, and the Day of Judgment. Because they were lay brothers, they were precluded from addressing any questions of dogma or theology. Invariably, two or three would be dispatched in advance to smooth the way for the reception of the rest of the order in the region in question. For example, Giovanni da Pian del Carpine and his companion Barnabas arrived one time in the southern German city of Würzburg, asking for *brot durch got* ("bread from the Lord"); from there they moved on to Mainz, Worms, Speyer, Strasbourg, and Cologne. "Each time, they would appear and preach a single sermon, so paving the way for their fellow monks." Thus did the chronicler and Minorite Jordan of Giano recall (sometime after 1262) the first footholds of his order in Germany, a place greatly feared at the time for its barbarity; later, he and two other brothers traveled to Salzburg, while others set off to Regensburg.[19] In this way, Germany was gradually divided up into several Minorite provinces; the same method was subsequently used by the order to spread throughout the entire domain of the Latin Church.

The embryonic Franciscan order had to endure many a test of its endurance, which carried on up to the Poverty Dispute of the early fourteenth century. The radical message of poverty preached by Saint Francis—which was not without its criticism of the official church and ran the risk of drifting into heresy—could clearly not be allowed to endure; instead, it was diverted into institutional channels and so divested of much of its acerbity. Soon, Franciscans began to apply Joachim of Fiore's doctrine to their patron saint Francis, who was distinguished through his stigmata as a "second Christ"; correspondingly, Emperor Frederick II was interpreted as the first Antichrist. After his death, this movement slid ever further toward heresy. Despite the fact that Francis had solicited papal assent for his new way of living right from the outset, the Christomimetic self-image of the saint and the claim to be revitalizing the church were at variance with Christ's representative on Earth, namely the pope. Evidently, the relationship needed clarifying. The *Poverello* soon found an influential protector in the form of the cardinal-bishop Ugolino of Ostia, who ascended the papal throne in 1227, and who after the death of Francis (1226) exerted a lasting and guiding influence over the early history of the order. The master-general of the order, Elias, who had been appointed by Francis, was dismissed and excommunicated, turning up a short while later at the court of the likewise excommunicated Frederick II. The Spiritual Franciscans *(Fratelli)*, who were heavily under the influence of Joachim's teachings and had strong millennarian tendencies, broke away; here was another potential source of heresy. These tensions, which were no doubt conditioned by the necessary transformation of a charismatic poverty movement into a well-organized monastic order, were mirrored in the intractable confusion arising from the transmission of the original rules of the Franciscan order and in the various accounts, repeatedly rejected, of the early life of the saint, the oldest of which were banned and replaced by an official version in 1266—the only one recognized as valid—from the pen of the master-general Bonaventura, the *pater seraficus*. Nevertheless, the Franciscans became established throughout Europe; they were particularly sought after as confessors. They were also much favored to lead missions to the heathens, and entrusted with sundry other sensitive special tasks or legations that were fraught with danger. Thus, to cite just one example, when the Mongol hordes invaded Europe in 1238–1242, the Franciscan provincial (minister) responsible for Germany, Giovanni da Pian del Carpine, journeyed as the papal legate of Innocent IV to the court of the great khan Ögedei in Mongolia. This was, as the future would show, the dawn of a new era, as the Age of Exploration began and globalization took great strides forward. A new knowledge of the Earth and its countries and peoples was required before it could become a global marketplace.

The men were not alone; alongside them, religious orders for women also evolved. These first emerged around 1100, but now became more clearly defined. They point to the social emancipation of women, who hitherto had always been neglected in comparison with men; for this very reason, such orders were viewed with suspicion. From the early twelfth century onward, satellite convents had grown up near Cistercian monasteries, following the same strict regime as their male counterparts. Yet it was 1228 before they were formally incorporated into the order; admittedly, this meant that they lost their independence insofar as each convent was now placed under the control of a "father abbot." The Premonstratensians also had a female branch to their order. The women's religious movement expanded noticeably in the early thirteenth century. The reasons for this may well be akin to those governing the rise of the mendicant orders, especially the Franciscans.

In addition, numerous communities also arose at this time who wished to live according to the precepts of the Gospel, prayer, and atonement, but who followed no set regime. Deriving mostly from the ranks of city-dwellers, they lived in secure houses within the precincts of the city or its environs, mainly supported by donations and income from modest land holdings. In Brabant, these "pious women," whose most famous mother superior was Maria of Oignies (d. 1216), were the Beguines; they lived a chaste life devoted to prayer, asceticism, meditation, and deep contemplation of the sufferings of Christ; they also practiced religious ecstasy. Could these women be said to have usurped the traditional roles of the sexes? The absence of any rule for their order certainly cast the Beguines in a suspect light. The Fourth Lateran Council's proscription of new religious communities may well have been aimed at them; however, in the principal preacher of the Fifth Crusade, Jacques de Vitry, they found an influential and eloquent advocate.

The beginnings of women's mysticism are closely associated with the Beguines. Maria received visions of the stigmata and sufferings of Christ.[20] Meanwhile, not all the practices observed by these early nuns were in accord with established ecclesiastical customs, and the suspicion of heresy was never far from the surface. Christine de Saint Trond (d. 1224), for instance, reputedly a cowherd who knew Latin, was wont to enter a state of ecstasy in which she would whirl herself to unconsciousness like a dervish. This trancelike state carried her quite literally to new heights, as she would clamber up into the rafters of churches and climb towers and trees, flirting with death. She also tried to replicate the torments of sinners in Hell by putting herself in ovens, plunging into boiling water, having herself lashed to mill wheels and hanged on gallows, and lying in open graves. She claimed that while she was still alive, she had a near-death experience where she had stood before God's throne. Likewise, Margaret of Ypres (1216–1237) flagellated herself into an exaggerated perception of her own sinfulness, a state of self-loathing even, with briars and scourges, before immersing herself in prayer; ultimately, she came to see herself as the

Bride of Christ. No less a person than Thomas of Cantimpré, a high-minded author, portrayed the lives of both women. Other women took a different approach: Mechthild von Magdeburg described the mystical union of the soul with Christ with all the visual immediacy of the "Song of Songs" (in her book *The Flowing Light of Divinity*). Mechthild began as a Beguine, but later joined the Dominicans in Magdeburg, and in her later life entered the Cistercian nunnery at Helfta, where she met the mystic Saint Gertrude the Great. Meanwhile, the French mystic Marguerite Porete, whose widely read *The Mirror of Simple Souls* describes the simple soul united with God in love, and who was repeatedly condemned as a heretic, was finally found guilty of being a "recidivist heretic" and burned at the stake in 1310. In his *Book of the Twelve Beguines,* Jan van Ruysbroek (d. 1381) celebrated the intense love of Jesus and oneness with God. Despite intense hostility toward it, the Beguine order spread east, west, and south over the course of the thirteenth century. Before long, every central European city played host to several Beguine houses; in Cologne, by the fifteenth century, there were reputed to be 105 such establishments. And yet the order has survived to the present day only in Flanders and the Lower Rhine region.

At the same time, yet another women's religious movement came into being in Italy; like the Beguines, it ultimately developed into a formal order. It was the creation of Clare of Assisi, who contemporaneously with Francis and under his guidance, led a group of like-minded nuns. Ugolino of Ostia also took this movement under his wing, and furnished them with a rule. The order of Saint Clare developed as rapidly as the Franciscans. Toward the end of her life, Clare herself formulated a new rule, which later, with papal approval, became binding for her order—the first monastic rule to be formulated by a woman (1253). However, it is also possible that Elisabeth of Hungary was influenced by Clara; this princess, who died at the early age of twenty-four, unconditionally embraced the idea of voluntary poverty and, when she was widowed aged twenty, devoted the rest of her life to asceticism, prayer, and charitable care of the sick at the hospital in Marburg that she founded. All the women mentioned here are now venerated by the church as saints.

Nevertheless, even the women's movement itself sought male leadership. For "women are naturally subordinate to men, since nature has ordained that man is blessed with greater faculties of reason"; and "man is the Alpha and Omega of woman, just as God is the Alpha and Omega of all Creation." Thus ran the teachings of all theologians, represented here by Saint Thomas Aquinas.[21] To be sure, Thomas construed this subordination as operating in a domestic context *(oeconomica vel civilis)*, not as absolute servitude *(servilis)*, and as the necessary corollary of a world that had been arranged hierarchically ever since the Creation. Even so, such sentences and postulates strike us nowadays as discriminatory, and would indeed be precisely that if applied to the social order of the early twenty-first century. But at that time, namely the thirteenth century, and throughout the Middle Ages, they were entirely of a piece with a thoroughgoing conception of the world and of humanity as sanctioned by every type of authority—be it Biblical, ecclesiastical, moral, legal, or philosophical—as hallowed by social tradition, and as recognized by the religious women's movement. Anachronistic criteria and judgments have the added disadvantage of obscuring the great novelty that this scholastic doctrine represented, namely that every person, women included, was created in the image of God the Father, God the Son, and God the Holy Ghost, and that the story of Creation and the tale of Adam's Rib were susceptible of rational and "scientific" interpretation and corresponding criticism. Indeed, the application of reason was deemed to lift Man out of a state of "immaturity"; the path, though, was not clear but strewn with thorns and difficult to travel. For the rest, women of this period by no means shied away from acting independently, either in their capacity as urban entrepreneurs, or as princesses, abbesses, or indeed Beguines, saints, and heresiarchs.

9

The Triumph of Jurisprudence

The King Is Emperor within His Realm

The ringing of alarm bells ushered in the new century. Religious movements registered it like a seismograph. Kingdoms and cities throughout the length and breadth of Europe were seized by unrest and upheaval. Dispute over the succession was raging in Germany; the Angevin Empire was disintegrating; and crusading had deviated from its original purpose, with its fury directed against Byzantium rather than the enemies of the Faith—Constantinople was conquered by the Latins and the Byzantine Empire collapsed. It was never to recover from this blow. Furthermore, never again was a king or prince to rule in isolation from others: Philip of Swabia had married a Byzantine princess; the Latin emperor of Constantinople hailed from Flanders and was a vassal of the French throne; in Languedoc, the kings of Aragón, France, and England vied with one another for power and influence, alongside indigenous princes such as the counts of Toulouse and Provence; and for a brief spell a daughter of the Castilian king ruled over France with an iron fist. Shifting marital allegiances and fulfilled or frustrated candidatures for this or that legacy kept the whole carousel of power in motion. Lords married repeatedly, as did their ladies, making the whole situation so complicated as to make it impossible to explain concisely here. Suffice it to say that with each marriage, the regional and supraregional power relationships became interlaced afresh; a chaotic system over which nobody was able to gain a comprehensive overview and which somehow regulated itself.

Vassals of the French throne and English barons formed alliances against their respective kings, so placing the network of relationships under extreme stress. The English king found himself obliged, *in extremis,* to subjugate himself to the pope and to urgently seek his assistance. The fierce rivalry between the Italian maritime municipalities sucked the major powers into disputes between these cities. As the feudal lord of Sicily and England, and Portugal too—but also from the point of view of its own secular interest—the papacy became heavily, even decisively, involved in these wranglings. In external affairs, anyone with ambitions to be successful had, to keep a weather eye on the whole of Europe and, in internal matters, to deploy the most up-to-date ways and means that the age had to offer in organizing and consolidating his own grip on power. This involved not only an adept handling of jurisprudence and the sciences, of scholars and mercenaries alike, and of both the capital markets and theological and ecclesiastical doctrines, but also matching the efforts of foreign powers in garnering reliable support from the mendicant orders and the papacy.

Intellectual life was also in a state of flux at this time. Nothing was as it had once appeared. Old yardsticks and value judgments lost their force and dissipated. The major seats of learning, in particular, became the site of ongoing intellectual ferment, which, feeding on novelty, posed questions, and spread uncertainty and a sense of a new beginning. In particular, the scientific and metaphysical writings of Aristotle excited curiosity and engendered controversy. Other treatises also fostered speculative thought. For example, the dialectician Amalric of Bena (d. 1206) formulated pantheistic ideas that he had developed from Johannes Scotus Eriugena's *Periphyseon,* while David of Dinant, who occasionally served as chaplain to Pope Innocent III and who could speak Greek and so had translated several of Aristotle's works, which scarcely anyone in the West had been able to read up to then, disseminated dubious philosophical aphorisms. "The World is God," he wrote, "and the spiritual and the material are one and the same." That had a truly dangerous ring to it, since it departed radically from the tame form of theology taught in the universities. A synod held in Paris in 1210 considered Amalric's pantheism and David's speculations, mixing them up somewhat, and posthumously condemned both *Magistri.* Amalric's followers were subjected to a formal heretics' trial and sent to be burned at the stake (even in the process consigning Eriugena's work to the flames), while the reading of David's *Quaternuli,* the notes accompanying his lectures, was banned under pain of severe punishment. It became clear just how unsettled the ecclesiastical authorities were five years later, when a total ban was imposed on the reading and teaching of all the problematic texts of Aristotle, which were enshrined in the statutes of the universities. However, this changed nothing. As early as 1230, Averroës's commentaries on Aristotle were translated, and before long the Arab philosopher came to be regarded as "the commentator" *par excellence,* and Paris became the scene of furious debates concerning Aristotelianism and Averroism. Materialistic ideas also began to creep in from various sources, along with recent advances in the scientifically—that is, theologically, canonically, and legislatively—supported ruling doctrine. Admittedly, this doctrine also had its dark side: after some preliminary thoughts in the previous century on this matter, the ensuing period saw the formulation, especially by canon law experts, of the theory of the "shadow" king—the *rex inutilis*—which was then invoked to legitimize the toppling of many a monarch.[1] In sum, the centers of scholarship— namely the universities of Paris, Bologna, Montpellier, or Oxford, soon to be joined by Salamanca—attained a position of great influence not only over intellectuals but also over the Western powers, notably their internal order and their foreign policy agenda and on the legitimization of both these areas.

Formulation of new theories began with the exegesis of the papal bull *Per venerabilem* of 1202. The concept it broached of a "king who acknowledges no higher authority in worldly affairs" *(rex superiorem in temporalibus non recognescens)* created an exact equivalent, in canon-law doctrine, of the judicial *Lex regia,* according to which the Roman people had once irrevocably ceded their legislative authority to the *princeps.* However, there was no longer any such supreme emperor; he had long since been supplanted by a multitude of kings, each of whom recognized no higher authority in worldly matters. Scholars drew the logical conclusion from this, and it was just a small step to the theory they devised of the king who is emperor within his own realm *(rex est imperator in regno suo),* a doctrine that evolved around 1200 or shortly thereafter in canon-law circles, and that was then belatedly taken up by legislators, assuming all the greater force in the process. Its basic implication was that a king in his domain was on a par with an emperor in his *imperium,* who was completely free to do as he pleased in his capacity as ruler, legislator, and judge and that he was subject to no higher authority, not even that of an emperor.[2]

Saint Gregory the Great (590–604) was the last pontiff for several centuries to master the full range of classical learning. His *Book of the Pastoral Rule* was a seminal text for all future Church leaders and bishops. Gianni Dagli Orti / The Art Archive at Art Resource, NY.

Frankish king Charlemagne (742–824), surrounded by his principal officers, receiving Flaccus Alcuin, Anglo-Latin poet, educator, and cleric, in 781. Cianni Dagli Orti / The Art Archive at Art Resource, NY.

The Great Satan from the Gates of Hell, mosaic floor of the cathedral of Otranto, Italy. The cathedral was built under Roger, Norman Duke of Apulia, and consecrated in 1088. The mosaic floor of 1166 is a compendium of early medieval knowledge and lore. Erich Lessing / Art Resource, NY.

The Coronation of Otto III. This key ruler planned to revive the Roman Empire.
Bayerische Staatsbibliothek, Munich, Germany / Lutz Braun / Art Resource, NY.

Gilded bronze statue of Pope Boniface VIII, who frequently had himself depicted in this kind of opulent guise, to the great displeasure of many contemporaries. Scala / Art Resource, NY.

Transporation of spices to the west and unloading spices in the east, miniature from the *Book of the Wonders of the World* by Marco Polo and Rustichello, France, fifteenth century. © DeA Picture Library / Art Resource, NY.

This detail from *Saint Luke Drawing the Virgin's Portrait* by Rogier van der Weyden shows an idealized medieval city. Groeningemuseum, Bruges, Belgium / © Lukas—Art in Flanders VZW / The Bridgeman Art Library.

Detail from *Martyrdom of the Franciscans* by Ambrogio Lorenzetti
(c. 1336–1340). On this fresco, painted for the Church of San Francesco
in his hometown of Siena, the painter portrayed the martyrdom of three
Sienese Franciscan missionaries in China. This detail represents the earliest
"realistic" depiction of Asiatic peoples in Western art, marking a shift from
the archetypes to figures drawn from real life. Scala / Art Resource, NY.

The elderly emperor Charles IV visiting his nephew King Charles V of France in Paris. According to medieval custom, the color of the horses ridden by monarchs indicated who had sovereignty over the territory in question. Thus, the fact that it is the French king riding the gray horse emphasizes that Charles V held sway in France. By contrast, the emperor is mounted on a chestnut horse draped with a caparison in French royal livery (the fleur-de-lys). The two rulers greet one another bare-headed and with a handshake; the young man behind the emperor (and wearing a hat) is his son Wenceslas. © Bibliothèque Nationale de France, Dist. RMN-Grand Palais / Art Resource, NY.

Hans Memling's *Last Judgment*. Memling created for the Renaissance city of Florence a work imbued with the contemporary anticipation of the Day of Judgment, thought to be drawing close. Scala / Art Resource, NY.

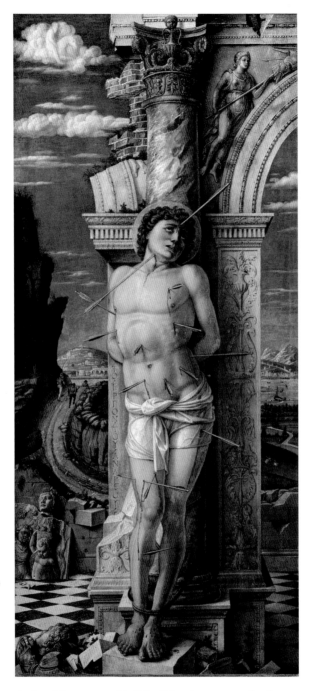

Andrea Mantegna set his Saint Sebastian among a landscape of ancient ruins. To add to the ancient atmosphere of the piece, and at the same time display his own learning, on a pillar below the right arm of the martyr the artist painted in Greek the words "the work of Andrea." Erich Lessing / Art Resource, NY.

Masaccio's fresco of the Trinity in the Church of Santa Maria Novella in Florence (1429) is the first painting to apply the laws of single-point perspective formulated at that time by Brunelleschi. Through the bold strategy of setting the standpoint of the viewer below the scene, the painter made the devout onlooker feel as though he were standing directly underneath the Crucifixion and drew his eye into the side chapel. Erich Lessing / Art Resource, NY.

The famous *Pietà* by the Venetian artist Giovanni Bellini (c. 1470). Over the course of the
fourteenth century, painterly imagery changed fundamentally, moving from the cold abstraction of icons to an emotional narrative content. The Latin inscription below the painting
underlines this development: "When these swelling eyes evoke groans, this work of Giovanni
Bellini could shed tears." Images like Bellini's *Pietà*, if regarded as a form of meditation, can
be seen as a parallel development to the growth of the "Devotio Moderna" north of the Alps.
Scala / Art Resource, NY.

The Angel Pietà of Antonello da Messina (c. 1475) can be seen as a rival piece to the Brera Pietà of Giovanni Bellini. Pain and suffering are etched on the faces of Christ and the mourning angel standing behind Him, eliciting an empathetic response from the viewer. Moreover, images of this kind were not solely commissioned in an ecclesiastical context; rather, collectors became increasingly interested in such works, as the palazzi of Venice became the haunt of art connoisseurs. Bellini would go on to paint several "ripostes" to Antonello's Pietà. Scala / Art Resource, NY.

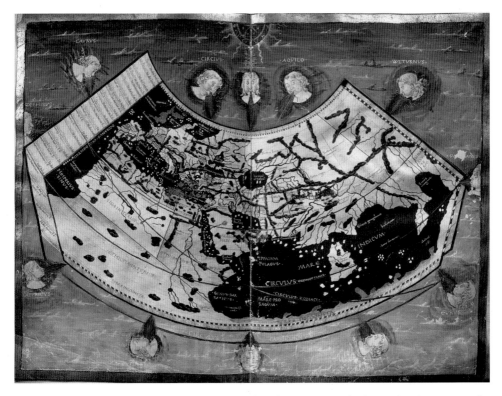

A map from a late fifteenth-century manuscript of Ptolemy's *Geography* depicts his description of the Oecumene (the inhabited world). The *Geography* (or *Cosmographia*), originally written in the second century AD, and familiar to Arab scholars, only became known in the Latin West around 1400. This manuscript—the Naples Codex—is believed to be the work of the renowned cartographer Nicolaus Germanus, who incorporated the latest findings of European scholarship into his maps. Thought to date from sometime before 1470, it represents geographers' conception of the world before the Portuguese voyages of exploration to Africa and before the "discovery" of America. Scala / Art Resource, NY.

Painting by an unknown artist of the execution of Savonarola on the Piazza della Signoria in Florence in 1498. The revolution that Savonarola instigated and his ensuing death marked a decisive turning point in the history of Florence. Scala / Art Resource, NY.

The three scenes on this painted panel (c. 1500) show the investiture in 1469 by Emperor Frederick III and the papal legate Bishop Michael of Pedena of Johann Siebenhirter as the first Grand Master of the Austrian chivalric Order of St George. This military order was founded to fight the Ottoman Turks, but had little success, its existence threatened from the outset by a lack of funds. It has, however, survived to the present day, albeit in a much altered form. Erich Lessing / Art Resource, NY.

The Calumny of Apelles by Sandro Botticelli. Every detail of this dramatic late work by Botticelli, which was based on a description of a painting by the Ancient Greek artist Apelles, is replete with symbolic meaning. Its female figures also represent a striking departure from the ideals of feminine beauty that Botticelli created in his early works. The naked, helpless and pleading Apelles is shown being dragged by his hair before a judge-king by the figure of Calumny; she is attended by two beautiful companions, Conspiracy and Fraud, who adorn her hair with rose petals and white ribbons. Meanwhile, Envy denounces the painter to the king, whose long asses' ears are whispered into by Ignorance and Suspicion. At far left, the figure of Truth stands, likewise naked and helpless, and implores Heaven for help, while Regret, dressed in ragged widow's weeds, glances in vain toward Truth. Alfredo Dagli Orti / The Art Archive at Art Resource, NY.

Botticelli's *The Story of Virginia*, which illustrates a tale by Livy. Appius Claudius, a judicial official of ancient Rome, lusted after Virginia, a beautiful Roman woman. When she rebuffed his advances, and despite pleas for clemency by her father, Appius Claudius sentenced her to be his slave. To preserve his daughter's honor, her father stabbed her to death. Few medieval works convey the same kind of outrage and disillusion at the misuse of power by the ruling classes evident in this painting; Botticelli used the classical incident as a veiled social criticism of abuses carried out under Medici rule in Florence. Scala / Art Resource, NY.

Martin Waldseemüller's world map of 1507 was the first not only to acknowledge the existence of the New World, but also to show it as a separate continent and to give it the name "America." Staatsbibliothek zu Berlin, Stiftung Preussischer Kulturbesitz, Berlin, Germany / Ruth Schacht, Map Division / Art Resource, NY.

This doctrine can be seen as one of the classical principles, one of the fundamental maxims that form the basis of the concept of state sovereignty, which (perhaps only just) still holds sway today. Around the middle of the thirteenth century, the jurist Jean de Blanot applied it explicitly to France. Alfonso X (the Wise), king of Castile, the great legislator under whose reign the statutory code known as the *Siete Partidas* was compiled, attested to his fellow monarchs: *Vicarios de Dios son los reyes cada uno en su reyno, puestos sobre las gentes para mantenerlas en justicia e en verdad cuanto a lo temporal, bien assi como el emperador en su imperio.* Before long, every prince, every baron, and every municipal leadership was subscribing by analogy to this principle. This surreptitious development marked the beginning of the dissolution of hierarchical modes of thought. For no pontiff drew the conclusion from it that these emperor-like monarchs derived their power from the successor of Saint Peter.

One final step related to the doctrine of the institution, which at this time was being given shape by the academic discipline of jurisprudence. The *universitas* was now counted as a "fictitious person," *persona ficta*, and so the ruling authority now also came to be regarded as a juridical person. Granted, this was customarily identified with the personage of the ruler himself. Regents or judges could therefore, following Roman Law (C. 9.8.5), be seen as *membra corporis regis (imperatoris)*, as members or organs of the body of the king, as it were, as thought the king had two bodies, a transient one and a superhuman, immortal, and eternal one. A whole new future conception of the state appeared to be taking shape. The trend in this direction made itself apparent in all the major kingdoms of this period. Politics and science, the profane and the sacred, and the institution and doctrines all combined forces to bring this about.

Frederick II

The aims of Frederick II, the Holy Roman Emperor at this time, were never expressly formulated; instead, they can only be deduced, albeit at the risk of circular reasoning, from hints and from actions that he undertook. Frederick seldom revealed what made him tick quite as candidly as he did toward the end of his life, in 1249, when corresponding with John III Doukas Vatatzes, but conversing with the emperor of Nicaea he did not need to pull any punches: "How fortunate Asia is, and how happy the rulers of the East, who do not fear armed insurrection by their vassals or intriguing by their bishops!" The *basileus* was no friend of the Roman Church.[3] The Hohenstaufen emperor regarded those rulers as fortunate who had no inkling of "the abuse of pestilential freedom"—an allusion to the power of the Lombard municipalities—and who did not live in fear of any pope.

Many of his contemporaries saw in Frederick II the "marvel of the world" *(stupor mundi)* and its "miraculous transformer." Such desperate hopes augured ill. Frederick was orphaned when still a young boy; many people then tried to bring the royal child, resident in Palermo, under their influence. Throughout his life he remained mistrustful of others, even his closest circle of associates. Even so, he must have enjoyed an outstanding education. The scope of his intellect went far beyond most of his contemporaries. The sciences and arts captured his imagination as much as the noble pursuit of falconry, which he not only practiced with a passion, but which he also wrote about and taught with a true enthusiast's love and meticulous attention to detail. Time and again, he was portrayed as a winning, even an enchanting, personality. Even the Franciscan Salimbene of Parma, a longstanding antagonist of the emperor, admitted that "I loved him once, too."

Early on, when still a boy, he gave evidence that he was imbued with the singularity of his royal–imperial majesty. He was resolved, however, to bring freedom, the pope, and the communes all to heel under his rule; in this, he was taking on the most powerful forces of the age. It seems that he aspired to bring the whole of Italy under imperial control, from Sicily in the south to Spoleto and territories even farther north, and was particularly intent on subjugating the municipalities. Yet the time was not yet ripe for such an enterprise. The most opportune moment for the first objective had already passed, while that for the second had not yet arrived; both aims were out of time—the struggle against the freedom of the cities and their inhabitants and the unification of Italy. The pope and the townspeople mounted a strong defense. Furthermore, the two realms of the Hohenstaufen ruler were undergoing diametrically opposed developments. While in Sicily Frederick was able to expand the relatively modern system of rule, which had been in force since the Norman era, royal power increasingly ebbed away in the rest of the empire, especially north of the Alps. To some extent, indeed, this was sacrificed to Frederick's ambitions in Italy. The Lombard municipalities revived their League (1226). The emperor won a series of battles against one or other of the League's members, and Imperial loyalist Ghibellines opened the gates of cities under their control to Frederick's forces; he also defeated the League at the Battle of Cortenuova in 1236, after which the communes appeared more amenable to negotiation; and Innocent IV, believing that he was no longer safe in Rome, decamped to Lyons. But despite all these successes, which remained long in the memories of succeeding generations, for a variety of reasons Frederick's triumphs were transitory and achieved little of any lasting value beyond some more or less profitable sources of income from his conquests. The whole campaign came to a close with Frederick's death in 1250.

As a young man, Frederick had been sent to Germany by Innocent III as an alternative king to oppose Otto IV. At that time, the old Hohenstaufen vassals flocked to the colors of this "son of Apulia." Unopposed, the eighteen-year-old was able to undertake an extraordinary and speedy triumphal procession from Constance to Aachen, where he was crowned king in the shrine housing the mortal remains of Charlemagne; on this same occasion, he also gave his ill-fated vow to go on Crusade. In the succession dispute, the young monarch sought to win back imperial rights that had been lost, but for the most part was forced to concede the territories that had been wrested from the competing kings. He was unable to rescind anything. The privileges granted to the princes in 1220 and 1231–1232 turned out to be highly significant for the history of Germany. These concessions embraced all the rights which the princes—who for the first time were designated as "sovereign rulers" *(Domini terrae)*—had been granted over the preceding decades. To be sure, their "sovereign rule" did not extend over any large integral tracts of land, but rather over a multitude of fragmented domains and land easements. The first person to finally abolish the political fragmentation of the German lands was Napoleon; earlier, in 1667, the political philosopher and jurist Samuel von Pufendorf had called the Holy Roman Empire "a body that conforms to no rule and resembles a monster."[4]

In one of history's ironies, the first privilege conceded by Frederick, which particularly concerned the ecclesiastical princes, was granted in order to facilitate the election of Frederick's eldest son Henry (VII) to the German throne; in the event, Henry was unable to assert any form of independent rule but instead was to become, in his capacity as German vassal king, something of a burden to the emperor—a squandered opportunity. The second privilege was, with the emperor's assent, wrested precisely from this monarch and renewed by Frederick with only minor dilutions as the price for ensuring the princes' continuing support for his policies in Italy, which were increasingly directed against the pope. Finally, mention should also be made here of the great Imperial Peace of Mainz of 1235; although this actually failed in its intended aim of guaranteeing the empire lasting peace, justice, and stability, it did, nevertheless, lay down a series of regulations and institutions that were repeatedly renewed and that were therefore important for the future. The most noteworthy of these were the clauses relating to the curtailment of the right of feuding, to judicial procedure and the imperial court, and above all to the prosecution of injustice and crime not being triggered solely by a complaint by the injured party (as had previously been the case) but instead being initiated by the authorities. The influences of Norman–Sicilian law are evident in this framing of legislation, even though everything was enacted much more completely in that realm. The Imperial Peace of Mainz was hampered in its immediate efficacy by the actual weakness of the king's authority for all practical purposes.[5] The contrast between the royal policies of Henry VII and the imperial policy of his father led to complaints from the princes and to Henry's being effectively stripped of his office; after seven years' imprisonment in Calabria, he ended up taking his own life in 1242 (he may also have been suffering from leprosy); his miserable demise was a baleful omen for the future.

Frederick II's taking of the cross was the catalyst for a series of deadly conflicts with the papacy. The successors of St. Peter manipulated the delaying of the Sixth Crusade, ultimately occasioned by Frederick and much of his army being laid low by an epidemic, to their own, decidedly secular, ends. In particular Gregory IX pressed Frederick more insistently than had been the case with any crusading king before him to fulfill his vow, refusing to countenance any excuses or to accept payment in lieu and release the emperor from his obligation. The pope expected the emperor to lead the Crusade to Jerusalem in person; when he failed to do so, Gregory excommunicated him in 1227. When the excommunicated, Arabic-speaking king finally did go on Crusade to the Holy Land, he immediately entered into friendly talks with Sultan al-Kamil and negotiated a treaty which granted the Christians exclusive control over the sacred sites of pilgrimage in Jerusalem for ten years. This signal success was roundly condemned by the papal loyalists. They had hoped for a bloodbath rather than diplomacy. Moreover, no sooner had the emperor set off for the East than the pope ordered foreign troops, his "key forces," to invade Sicily, with a view to conquering the island. This action made it abundantly clear that the dispute between emperor and pope was about far more than merely a Crusade, that a struggle for temporal control over Italy had ignited, and that the pope was bent on stripping the Hohenstaufen ruler of all his power in the peninsula. Despite many other differences between them, this effectively made Gregory an ally of the Lombardy municipalities, who for their part had reconfirmed their League. Although the pope and the emperor did reunite once more in a peace agreement of 1230, this only lasted for a few years, ultimately ending, to the sound of apocalyptic-sounding imprecations from Rome, with Frederick's second excommunication in 1239 and the final demise of the house of Hohenstaufen.

Frederick was not an emperor who ruled for the benefit of the German monarchy. On the contrary, he consciously drove it to destruction. The experiences of Henry VII, the son he left behind in Germany, who tried in vain to assert his authority there alongside and over the princes, should have acted as a warning to him. However, he disregarded them and even disavowed the young ruler in favor of his fruitless struggle for Italy. He abandoned Germany entirely to the princes, the "sovereign rulers," and during his reign they gained an unbreakable grip on power. As a result, despite his having aided them, they became increasingly disinclined to serve the emperor. The father effectively emasculated his own son, whom he had once helped gain the German throne by mobilizing his best diplomatic efforts, by taking him into custody in 1235, allowing him to languish in prison, and installing the heir to the throne of Jerusalem, Conrad IV, as the German king instead. Anyone who plays games with kings ends up disempowering the monarchy as a whole; in effect, then, Frederick II himself was responsible for provoking the imminent demise of his own dynasty.

By contrast, Frederick put in place one of the most modern regimes of the age in his hereditary kingdom of Sicily. It was characterized by an efficient bureaucracy, a judicial system ultimately directed by the king but managed by the legal profession, a centralized system of finance (the *doana*), and a standard currency. Other institutions that brought the realm great stability were a succession of appeal stages culminating in a royal supreme court, a cadre of jurists who had undergone university training (especially in Naples), an economic system that no longer depended on serfs but on wage-earning temporary laborers, and checks and balances on the privileges of the nobility, the clergy, and the cities. This all culminated in an outstanding legal code unrivaled by anything else in the contemporary world—namely, the Constitutions of Melfi (1231).

The norms and institutional arrangements that were codified in this document were devised as an urgent method of healing the wounds that the war with the pope had inflicted upon the authority of the king and on the country in general. In more than two hundred separate laws, which were augmented by numerous new pieces of legislation in the years that followed, the Constitutions regulated the administration, criminal law and legal procedure, and feudal and civil law as well; they remained in force in the kingdom of Naples right up to the beginning of the nineteenth century. It is likely that the emperor had the help of learned jurists of the Bologna school in drafting this statute book; after all, it was with the intention of fostering the study of jurisprudence that, as early as 1224, he had founded the *Studium*, the university in Naples, and granted it special privileges; henceforth, this institution was to become independent from Bologna, a city that found itself in conflict with the emperor.

The new constitutions followed on from the assizes held by Roger II and William II, quoted Roman Law *in extenso*, and aside from the legal matters also united monarchical ideology with Hohenstaufen imperial ideology. Its prologue represented a challenging manifestation of Frederick's conception of kingship. The legislator went back to basics: he began with the creation of the world, following more the twelfth-century scientific exegesis of this event rather than the account in the Book of Genesis, then proceeded to discuss the origins of man, mentioned the Fall from Grace, which was explained as a transgression of the law that had placed the whole of Creation in jeopardy. But in order to ensure its salvation, God populated the Earth. Even so, the consequences of the transgression rippled on; people, who had been created by God as "open and without sin," now "became involved in strife." In other words, the Fall from Grace continued. And so, out of dire necessity, God's providence saw to it that princes were elected to lead the people, in order to curtail the wantonness of men's transgressions. "They were to set themselves up as judges who had the power of life and death, so to speak as executors of the divine judgment which determined what destiny and what rank and position was to be allotted to each and every person." This formulation thus ascribed to kings the role of intermediaries. The legislator appeared as the "father and son of justice," as an individual who both created laws and followed them, and as a mediator between God, the "Father" of all justice, and the world, where justice was meted out. Henceforth, the princes kept watch to ensure that the Holy Church, the mother of the Christian religion, was not besmirched by those "who vilified the faith" (that is, heretics), defending it with the temporal sword and so bestowing peace and justice upon the peoples of the Earth. Accordingly he, Frederick, "whom alone the power of God, in all its rectitude and responding to the hopes of men, had exalted to the pinnacle of the Holy Roman Emperorship and to dominion over sundry other realms" claimed to have offered up "a sacrificial calf of his lips [that is, praise] to God through his nurture of justice and his framing of laws, and promulgated this statute book "in order to use the talents that have been entrusted to us in the service of revering the living God in the figure of Jesus Christ."[6]

This was secularized theology. Completely in accordance with theological tradition, the legislator was following God's commandment to save his Creation. Frederick's reign thus appeared as a form of salvation, with the emperor as the high priest of justice, and as an intermediary between God and the world of men: without making any mention of Christ's deeds, his legal code formulated a kind of worldly doctrine of redemption. A concern for justice would heal the Fall from Grace. And although the church was mentioned, it was not assigned any explicit, recognizable task in this process; indeed, it appeared to contribute little to the transmission of salvation. It was a matter of irrelevance whether or by what method the church might dispense the means of grace; the spiritual sword remained sheathed and invisible. This church, whose faith was protected by the princes, represented nothing other than the totality of people for whose salvation the Creator-God held the kings to account and whose religion was called justice. Within a few years, the emperor would also take action against the strongholds of heresy—which he identified as the Lombard municipalities. A form of state cult was being preached here, couched in theological language, a process that ultimately amounted to secularization; this concept had a great future ahead of it. At no point in the Constitutions was there the slightest mention of the pope, the vicar of Christ, whose vassal ruler in Sicily was Frederick, and with whom he had only recently concluded a peace treaty. It appeared, then, that kings had a direct connection with God, no matter what laws they ruled by. Frederick's statute book would later become a key primer for the education of princes.

The Hohenstaufen ruler's personality lent his court a unique splendor. He attracted scholars and poets from far and wide, and was renowned throughout the Arab world. Some commentators have even suggested that the beginnings of the *dolce stil nuovo* (the dominant literary movement of thirteenth-century Italy, exemplified by Dante) are evident in Frederick's court. It was certainly a cultural and scientific center without parallel. Politics and scholarship went hand in hand here, indeed they were inseparable.[7] The chancellery, which for a long time was headed by the "judge of the great curia" *(judex magnae curiae)* Pietro della Vigna, and which had a division archiving Greek and Arabic documents, sent rhetorically impressive manifestos out into the wider world, which continued to resonate even several centuries later. For instance, Johann von Neumarkt, Charles IV's chancellor, used them as a model at the dawn of the Renaissance. Frederick's scientific endeavors were assisted by Michael Scotus, Theodor of Antioch, and Jews from Spain and Languedoc. Indeed, the emperor may be seen as the person who introduced Jewish learning into the Latin world; in no other court of the period do we find it held in such high esteem as in Sicily. The earliest knowledge of the works of Maimonides is attested there, and Judah ben Solomon ha-Kohen resided for a long period at the Sicilian court as the emperor's guest. His principal work, the *Midrash ha-Hokhmah,* the oldest Hebrew encyclopedia, which he originally wrote in Arabic while in Spain, was completed during his sojourn in Sicily, and was closely associated with the academic culture of this polyglot court. This culture brought together Latins, Greeks, Jews, and Muslims. However, such openness aroused suspicions elsewhere, with Frederick being regarded as a dangerous epicurean and heretic by his enemies.

The lurid calumnies of the propaganda campaign against the emperor appeared to be confirmed. When Pope Gregory excommunicated Frederick II, he used the occasion to warn the other kings of Christendom against having any contact with the Sicilian emperor (1239), using words that he borrowed directly from the Revelation of Saint John the Divine: "A great beast rises up out of the sea full of the names of blasphemy" (cf. Book of Revelation 13:1). In response, Frederick flung back the following accusation at the vicar of God: "The bishop of Rome seated in the chair of perverse doctrine, that Pharisee anointed with the oil of pestilence above the rest of his consorts, who for his abominable pride is cast down from Heaven, endeavors with his power to destroy and to undo all. . . . But we say, he is that monstrous beast of whom we read: 'And there went out another horse that was red, and power was given to him that sat thereon to take peace from the Earth, and that they should kill one another.'" (Book of Revelation 6:4). Long after the emperor's death, the Franciscan monk Salimbene offered the damning verdict that Frederick had always sought conflict with the church that had nurtured, protected, and raised him; furthermore, maintained Salimbene, the emperor was devious and sophisticated, avaricious, profligate, malicious, and irascible. But even Salimbene had to concede that Frederick had his good sides, and "if only he had been a good Catholic, if only he had loved God, the church, and his own soul, then none would have been his equal among emperors, or indeed in the world as a whole."[8]

However, the Hohenstaufen ruler had long since ceased to be regarded as a good Catholic. The full ferocity of the rage and fear felt toward this persecutor of the true Faith was discharged in a seemingly endless tirade issuing from a source close to the papal legate in Rome, Cardinal Rainier of Viterbo, who denounced Frederick as "This Prince of tyranny . . . this overthrower of the church's faith and worship, iconoclast of the Faith, master of cruelty, confuser of the age, shatterer of the Earth and hammer of the entire world." These harsh words prepared the ground for the deposition of Frederick II. This act was duly carried out by Innocent IV, a leading jurist in his own right, at the First Council of Lyons in 1245. Furthermore, the pope did not restrict himself to words. The deposition decree was accompanied by a call to the Germans (which was indeed heeded) to elect a new king. Heinrich Raspe, a brother-in-law of Saint Elisabeth of Hungary, and Landgrave of Thuringia, put himself forward for this shabby charade. In vain, Frederick appealed to a sense of solidarity among the crowned heads of Europe. But this truly important figure had underestimated the capacity for resistance of the bourgeoisie, which was divided amongst itself, and had failed to pay sufficient heed to three key factors: the alliance between this group and the papacy; the moral and intellectual weight of the church, which had learned how to exploit the new learning even more effectively than the emperor; and the latent opposition of European kings and princes to a dominant empire that stretched from Palermo in the South to Lübeck in the North. So it was that none of them raised their voice and intervened on behalf of the emperor. The reward for their inaction was the corrosion and finally the complete collapse of Hohenstaufen power and with it the monarchy in Germany. Frederick's death in 1250 hastened both.

And yet the Germans yearned for redemption. They found it in the last will and testament of the dead emperor, and abandoned themselves to certain curious and enduring illusions. For example, a turn of phrase in this document, which is very close to a formulation In Roman Law, spoke of the deceased, the testator, appearing to live on in his heirs, was seized upon and transformed into the sibyl-like incantation "He lives not; yet he lives" (from Dante's *Purgatorio*). False Fredericks began to appear, attracted a following, and awakened millenarian-sounding hopes for the reform and cleansing of the church, for peace on earth, justice, and the unification of the empire. The beginnings of the legend of the "sleeping emperor" can be traced to Frederick II's will; it was only in the Late Middle Ages that this myth was transferred to Frederick's earlier namesake and grandfather, Frederick I. Henceforth, the story grew up that Barbarossa lay sleeping under the Kyffhäuser hill in the Harz Mountains—or elsewhere—until the time of his reawakening arrived, when he would return to complete his work.[9] Even the Prussian king William I, or "White Beard" as some German contemporaries dubbed him in a flush of romanticism, was seen as linking hands with Barbarossa over the centuries in order to complete the task of national unification. But what actually ensued in Germany after Frederick II's death was an "emperor-less, terrible time," the interregnum, when a series of kings who lacked any royal authority was followed by a period of no kings at all, while among the members of curias, canon law experts, and theologians, the long-running debate about the status of the imperial role—was the emperor a vassal of the pope?—gained new momentum, foreshadowing the many conflicts that would arise over the coming decades.

The impending disaster came to a head within a few short years. Frederick's son Conrad IV invaded Italy after his father's death in an attempt to hold the empire together militarily, but far from consolidating his realm and ensuring himself a long reign, he died shortly thereafter from malaria in 1254. For a decade thereafter, his brother—Frederick's talented son Manfred, who sought to emulate his father as a patron of the sciences and arts—sat on the Sicilian throne, before he lost both his crown and his life to Charles of Anjou (whom Pope Urban IV had proclaimed as vassal ruler of Sicily two years before and who through marriage already held the title of count of Provence) at the Battle of Benevento in 1266. Conrad's only son Conradin did not fare much better; setting out from Bavaria to conquer the Sicilian realm that was bequeathed to him, he was defeated in battle, fell into Charles's hands, and was publicly executed in Naples in 1268, at the tender age of sixteen. His last words were reputedly: "O Mother, what grief I am preparing for you!" Conradin was the last legitimate male member of the Hohenstaufen line, a dynasty that had attempted to realize anachronistic ideals of kingship, and that finally found itself isolated, after (with very few exceptions) its subjects, vassals, and neighboring princes had abandoned it; at least, though, James I of Aragón had, in defiance of the express wish of the pope, allied his son and heir Peter through marriage to the house of Manfred of Sicily (1262), giving cause for both later hopes and subsequent wars. Two older cousins of Conradin, the sons of the deposed Henry VII, died unmarried and without any claim or hope for a crown.

Following Raspe's death, a group of German princes elected Count William of Holland as king in 1247; but when he fell in battle against the Frisians in 1256, the princes were split, with some opting for Richard of Cornwall, the brother of the English king, and others for Alfonso X of Castile, a distant cousin of the Hohenstaufens, who had never set foot on German soil. This period (1254–1257) saw an alliance to help maintain the peace, strengthened by several princes such as the three Rhineland archbishops and the count palatine, between German cities from Basel and Strasbourg in the south through Frankfurt and as far north as Mühlhausen in Thuringia and Münster in Westphalia and west to Cologne and Aachen. This was the first city league in Germany; thereafter, such alliances were concluded on a more regular basis. Not least, they now had the power to confront feudal lords and others who disrupted the peace, and even to threaten the king. The urban bourgeoisie thus began to free itself from feudal rule and to play an active role in politics. This came about primarily in order to safeguard economic interests; yet the major cities like Frankfurt and Cologne were also pursuing political objectives. Symptomatic developments in royal cities, say, were the withdrawal of the imperial reeve and the appointment instead of a royal sheriff (ca. 1220), freedom from the obligation to marry (1232), and the transformation of the college of lay assessors into a city council (first attested 1266). Only the tax revenues from Frankfurt am Main, largely levied on the Jews of the city, remained the preserve of the king. Admittedly, as an electoral city, Frankfurt was always close to the monarchy.

The Mongol Invasion of 1238–1242:
A New Impulse toward Globalization

All of a sudden, a new enemy appeared on Europe's horizon—one that was utterly alien and terrifying, and which swept all before it. Yet while most rulers took note of this threat, with the exception of the Hungarian king, none of them made any attempt to find out about these horsemen from the East who were spreading terror. They overran everything that dared to stand in their way. The first empire to fall victim to them was Kievan Rus (1240), and soon after the Polish-Silesian army was annihilated in battle at the pilgrimage site of Legnica (1241). That same year, Hungary was depopulated, and its king, Béla IV, took refuge on an island in the Adriatic. A sense of apocalyptic fear became widespread. Sinister rumors spread, claiming that the mythical peoples of Gog and Magog, whose coming signaled the end of the world, had sallied forth to usher in the end of days; other people pinned their hopes on the mysterious Christian ruler Prester John (whose kingdom was said to lie in Africa) arriving with his armed hordes to defend Christianity against Muslim incursion. And yet, however strange, threatening, and catastrophic everything appeared to be, and however paralyzed the West was by horror and fear, the Mongol invasion—for this was the event in question here—brought about, despite heavy losses in places, especially in Hungary, a key moment of transformation in world history.

Except for the single engagement at Legnica, the West did not respond with force, which it was ill-equipped to do anyway, but rather with a rational and systematic application of reason and with the intellectual adeptness that it had acquired. It also reacted with a sense of curiosity and thirst for knowledge, underpinned by the entrepreneurial spirit of merchants and the dauntless zeal of Christian missionaries. It was not the temporal powers that took the initiative in this but the pope. Innocent IV sent the Franciscan Giovanni da Pian del Carpine as an envoy to find out what the Mongol's objectives were, to spy out their military strategies and tactics with an eye to devising more effective countermeasures, and above all to investigate the possibilities of dispatching missionaries to them (1245–1247). Carpine's report was a unique attestation of his skill in ethnographic observation; and, in the modes of perception and powers of discrimination and deduction it employed, it bore eloquent practical witness to how well the style of thinking practiced in the West for the past three and a half centuries had proved itself. A few years later, William of Rubruck set off on a mission, yet reaching his ultimate goal, the court of the Great Khan, required a commission as a royal envoy. King Louis IX of France (Saint Louis) duly granted him one while he was resident in the Holy Land (1253–1255). William's depiction of the Mongols surpassed any ethnographic work that had been written hitherto. All aspects of their lives were described in exhaustive detail: their government and society, their ways of life, their uses and customs, their traditions, and the diversity of peoples and religions represented at the court of the Great Khan. No such clear-sighted description of a foreign people was to appear again until the nineteenth century.

Traditional learning combined with new scientific knowledge in this period. The geographers of antiquity were well aware that the Earth was round and a single entity, and explored it, amassing their findings. These were taken up by early Christianity: the good news of the imminent kingdom of God quite literally drove messengers of the Faith to visit "all four corners of the Earth"; even the earliest missionaries such as Saint Paul tirelessly criss-crossed the Roman Empire in their efforts to spread the Word. Later missionaries followed in his footsteps, traveling throughout Europe and half of Asia, admittedly without any knowledge of one another and without exchanging information about their experiences. This factor set them apart them ancient scholars. For example, Saint Boniface knew nothing of the Christians of India or the Christian Uigurs of central Asia. And when Saint Adalbert of Prague embarked on an audacious mission to bring Christianity to the neighboring Prussians, which at the time was considered a journey to the very frontiers of the known world, no one had any inkling how many peoples there were still to be "discovered" farther to the east. Irish missionaries ventured far and wide on missionary quests without committing the knowledge they gleaned in the process to paper; accordingly, no written records of their voyages have come down to us. And when Columbus made preparations for his voyage across the Atlantic to find a passage to the Far East, he was impelled by thoughts of spreading the Christian Gospel and concern about the impending end of the world. In the Early Middle Ages, then, it was only the Jews who, thanks to their extensive trading contacts, would have been in a position to impart to Europe knowledge about India, Persia, or Arabia; however, Christians at this stage still shunned taking any advice from them.

The Crusades then sensitized Europeans in a new way about interactions with alien cultures, yet it was only the Mongol invasion that opened their eyes to the immense dimensions of the world, which dwarfed their own communion in a quite incredible and frankly alarming way, far exceeding all previous conceptions of its scale. "Even I who am here in the country do hear things averred of it that I can scarcely believe," wrote Andrew of Perugia in 1326 from Cambaluc (modern Beijing). So it was that the invasion of this foreign people, who were completely unknown even to ancient scholars, and the eruption of the Incomprehensible into the academic culture of the West, clearly called for missionary efforts to be redoubled, and for Europeans to urgently reassess their worldview. This event truly did herald a turning point in the process of globalization. In its aftermath, Europeans began systematically to explore the entire Earth, to investigate its peoples and their ways of life, and to plumb its manifold riches. No sooner had the first men to venture to the Far East, Carpine and Rubruck, submitted their reports than contemporary scholars began to correct the knowledge that had been passed down from ancient sources and to exploit the new information that supplanted it to commercial ends. In the process, the concepts of universalism and particularism were wrested from their original, exclusively theological, context. The integration of the new knowledge into the general worldview and into the corridors of power stimulated discussions not only in the realms of canon law and "politics," but also in economic and military circles as well; over time, an expertise began to evolve, which took possession of the Earth in both intellectual and material terms, and which provoked a wholly secular sense of curiosity. When Giovanni da Pian del Carpine set off on his journey to meet the Mongols, nobody from the Latin West was in a position to offer him assistance; but when Rubruk set out just ten years later, he was already able to glean helpful initial information from Venetian merchants who over the preceding years had established trade links with the Mongols. A new picture of the world came into being and instantly found expression in a totally new form of world map. Extreme communication problems also arose; a pressing need became apparent to integrate alien cultures, unknown languages in which no available interpreter was fluent, and what were at first sight quite abhorrent customs and practices into the emerging and recently systematized horizons of experience. Merchants made immediate use of the new knowledge. Thanks to the account he wrote of his travels *(Il Milione)*, Marco Polo is only the most well-known of these. Latin trading settlements were founded in Tabriz, Samarkand, Hormuz, and China, while the Catholic archdiocese of Cambaluc was established in 1307.

Even in the few decades separating the Mongol invasion from the foundation of this first oriental bishopric, people found themselves confronted with intellectual challenges and with the social consequences of globalization, which only became more acute over time, as awareness grew of alien cultures and social and power structures, and of foreign religions, ambitions, and modes of thought. Through the repercussions it had on traditional societies, as for instance the history of the Italian mercantile cities tells us, the inception of commercial contacts with the Far East sharpened competition and created a hitherto unknown poverty among the urban lower classes—this unpalatable fact could not be concealed, and indeed soon became glaringly obvious in the social conflicts that began to erupt everywhere. The opening up of the world called for a new intellectual flexibility and spatial mobility, an entrepreneurial spirit that did not shy away from taking risks that were almost impossible to calculate, and demanded a knowledge of foreign markets and trading conditions, the mastering of several languages, as well as of technical innovations and expansion strategies. In short, a comprehensive facility for learning, re-thinking, aptitude, and knowledge was the order of the day. It is an abiding hallmark of Late Medieval Europe that it was both able and willing to meet this challenge.

Western Judaism did not remain immune from these developments either. The year 1240 in the Christian calendar equated in the Jewish calendar to the 5000th year since the creation of the world—an apocalyptic moment. Many Jews prepared themselves for the coming of the Messiah, even arming themselves in anticipation of the struggle to renew the kingdom of God on Earth. This may also have been a response to the Mongol invasion, the first news of which began to reach the West precisely around that time, from 1238 onward.

Anti-Jewish Pogroms

But instead of the expected advent of the Messiah, a new round of pogroms now devastated the Jewish communities of Europe. In Marburg they were accused—as they had been before in Lauda and elsewhere in Germany—of ritual murder; papal decretals against this slur could do nothing to prevent such allegations, either now or in the decades that followed. In Frankfurt am Main, a full-scale "slaughter of the Jews" ensued, which claimed the lives of the entire community (1241); even the cemetery there was desecrated, with the gravestones being dug up and reused in the construction of the cathedral. The accusations of ritual murder were soon to peak in the story of a youth named Werner of Oberwesel, whose body was found in undergrowth near the Rhineland village where he lived. Local Jews were immediately accused of his "murder," and the boy was venerated as a martyr. People began to make pilgrimages to the site, and a chapel was erected at Bacharach, a little jewel of late-Gothic architecture, but like the sainted boy himself tarnished with the worst excesses of anti-Semitic persecution, a symbol par excellence of the "persecuting society." Finally, in 1963, Werner was removed from the calendar of Christian saints. In 1298 in the Tauber Valley in southern Germany, an impoverished nobleman by the name of Rintfleisch incited the local residents to carry out a pogrom to avenge an alleged incident where Jews had desecrated the consecrated host (sacramental bread). And so it continued; in eastern Franconia, a person styling himself "King Armleder," another down-at-the-heels nobleman led a mob that terrorized Jews in the region for forty years.

Dreadful atrocities were carried out against the Jews in other countries, too. In Paris, King Louis IX arranged a formal disputation and at the behest of Pope Gregory IX ordered the burning of the Talmud (1242), an act that was then repeated throughout France and beyond its borders; countless manuscripts, reputedly more than 10,000, fell victim to this religious vandalism. Innocent IV, Clement IV, and other popes renewed the burning order right up to the Early Modern period. In 1248, Parisian scholars delivered an expert opinion, signed by forty-one professors (one of the last on the list being the great medieval theologian Albert of Cologne),[10] maintaining that the Talmud contained numerous errors and calumnies against Christianity, and recounting the fear that this sacred text evoked among Christians. Around this time Rabbi Meir ben Baruch from Rothenburg, one of the great teachers of medieval Judaism in Germany, composed an elegy *(kinah)* on this destruction of the holy books—undoubtedly including the Torah—which is still recited nowadays every year on Tisha B'Av, the day in the Jewish calendar commemorating the destruction of the First and Second Temples in Jerusalem: "O you who burn in fire, ask how your mourners fare . . . I marvel at the light of the day, which dawns for everyone, but it also brings both you and me darkness . . . After the days of your suffering, may God console you and break the bondage of the cities of Yehurun and lift up your arms." Threat and persecution lent the Kabbalah during this period a unique flavor. This strain of Jewish mysticism reached its first high point with Moses ben Nahman (known as Nahmanides) from Girona in Spain. In 1265, he was invited to take part in a disputation with Christians in the presence of King James I of Aragón, where he was accused by Dominicans of insulting the Christian faith. Persecuted as a result by Pope Clement IV, Nahmanides left Spain shortly afterward in order—like all pious Jews—to spent his final days in the Holy Land (ca. 1270). After hostility toward the Jews grew in Germany in the reign of Rudolf of Habsburg, Meir of Rothenburg along with many of his co-religionists also took the decision to emigrate to Palestine (1286). However, the group of refugees was arrested in Lombardy. Meir was imprisoned in Ensisheim in Alsace until his death; his grave can be seen today in the city of Worms.

The systematic exclusion of Jews from urban society was now conducted ever more radically. Not least, Late Medieval Christian devotion, which increasingly chose to stress the sufferings of Christ rather than the image of God as king, only served to exacerbate this particular trend. The cult of the consecrated host also provided repeated cause for acts of persecution. Even though the Jews were not "heathens" *(gentiles* or *pagani)* they were still seen as "nonbelievers" *(infideles)* and as "blasphemers against Christ,"[11] who poured scorn on the Cross and the crucified Jesus. Cohabitation with them was banned by ecclesiastical and secular legislators alike. Just like the Moors, they were required to wear clothing that distinguished them clearly from Christians, in order to prevent there being any unconscious "sexual congress" between them. This was how the Lateran Council of 1215 demanded and justified a statute (ca. 68) calling for the Jews to be visibly separated from the rest of society. And yet it was only the fifteenth century that saw a greatly increased emigration of Jews from Germany to lands to the east.

Thinking in Terms of "Politics"

The situation in Europe following the demise of the Hohenstaufen dynasty, though, was by no means characterized solely by wars and power struggles or by repercussions from developments taking place in Central Asia and the Near East. The cultural landscape had changed fundamentally, too. A symptom of this change was the so-called Mendicants Dispute" in Paris, a disagreement between the mendicant orders and the secular clerics over who had the right to teach at the university there. Yet this was also an argument primarily about content, which revisited the thorny question of how to interpret the psychological and scientific works of Aristotle, Once again, a newly discovered text by the ancient Greek philosopher was the cause of a radical sea change in thought. In 1264, precisely the same year when Charles of Anjou was granted control of Sicily by the pope, William of Moerbecke translated Aristotle's *Politics*. Though his translation is more clumsy than elegant, this was still an epoch-making step.

The academic world was best equipped to receive this text. Dominicans in particular had embraced the subject matter of the "Mirror for Princes," that is, instructions to rulers on how to govern correctly. This theme could point to a long tradition, which had been revived in the twelfth century first and foremost by John of Salisbury's *Policraticus*. Moreover, Louis IX of France, with the assistance of the Dominican monastery in Paris, had only recently commissioned a comprehensive work that was designed to provide instruction on the status of princes, the royal court and the ruling family, and on administration and governance in general. Its most significant compiler was the "encyclopedist" Vincent of Beauvais; the royal household took a keen interest in the progress of this work.[12] This *Opus universale* gathered together and edited a broad sweep of material from Cicero, Seneca, and Macrobius on a diversity of topics ranging from the Bible, Saint Augustine, and Gregory the Great to Bernard of Clairvaux, and even farther afield to Aristotle and the Arab authors Alfarabi and Avicenna; in doing so, it offered an historical perspective on the subject in hand. It was intended to teach kings to act in a just way and to organize their kingdoms according to the yardsticks of a Christian-inspired practical philosophy.

This work maintained that it was precisely princes who needed to be in possession of the highest and best learning, not just in order to educate himself and his people, but also in order to lead his council effectively, to dispense justice, to oversee his country's bureaucracy, and provide wise stewardship of its economy and firm leadership in times of war. A prince's education should be in tune with the entire scholastic program of study, embracing grammar, rhetoric, and logic, as well as theology and civil law. Yet he should also learn humility, and lead a life of self-denial, cleanliness, and chastity; if he were to display all these attributes, this would indeed be a "gift from God." Just as a world without light would only result in confusion and a lack of any security, so human existence without such "understanding" would always be in a perilous position, being nothing but a picture of the misery of Hell, and would have no order, merely terror. From childhood on, a ruler should always be mindful of aging, death, and the Day of Judgment. At this point, the mendicant monks who compiled this work revealed something of an "antifeudalist bias." For, they claimed that the terms "knight," "servant," or "freed man" were concepts "born of ambition and injustice." The prince and the pauper were the same inasmuch as they were both limbs of the body—namely the church—of which Christ was the head. Anyone who stole from the poor was "truly ignoble" *(rusticissimus)*. And it was precisely the barons and princes who were oppressing and exploiting the people; bread was being snatched from the mouths of the poor. In summary, the ethics of the mendicant orders, should be permitted to infiltrate the ruling order. They reminded princes that they obtained "their power from the people's assent," that they required "consensus" from the same source, and that the purpose of all government was "the common good."

This work has only come down to us in fragmentary form—the so-called Paris Mirror of Princes' Compendium—and, furthermore, does not present a unified picture in its doctrine; the final editing contradicted in part the teachings of Vincent of Beauvais, who had died while the work was still in progress. Even so, it was of enormous significance and set in train a development that soon rendered its own teachings obsolete. Admittedly, the overarching catch-all concept of "politics" had still not been formulated to encapsulate the *res politica* or *politia*. This was only introduced via the critical reception of the work of this name by Aristotle, which was translated in the same year that Vincent of Beauvais died (1264). Certainly, the West already had a dim inkling of this text, given that many of Aristotle's ideas had been transmitted to the medieval world through the intermediary of the classical tradition. But now, suddenly, the adjective *politicus* or the noun *politia* took on real substance, and before long *politici* emerged as specialists in this academic discipline, and the concept of "politics" truly began to take shape, and the first "political theories" began to be formulated in the Western world.

Immediately, new interminable debates and controversies broke out among philosophers, jurists, and theologians over the best form of government, and for the first time a genuinely "political" mode of thought evolved, together with a new theoretical form of argumentation. Over time, a quite special style of thinking duly developed, with its own particular categories and patterns of disputation. These taught people to identify connections that nobody had ever noticed hitherto. Soon, the first commentaries were published, the most outstanding examples being by Thomas Aquinas and others. Paraeneses to princes, which hitherto had been the most characteristic and important form of treatise on the theory of kingship, now no longer took center stage. Instead, attention was now focused upon the systematic study of the origin, development, and organization of different modes of rule; other prominent topics of discussion included the practical aspects of ruling, administration, waging wars, the ways and means of realizing the common good, and the economy—the latter of which Aristotle identified as being a key consideration for each and every ruling system, be it democracy (polity), aristocracy, or monarchy. The upshot of this was an endless advance toward professionalism. Henceforth, it would prove impossible to prevent scholarship from becoming an integral part of "politics." Royal counsel, jurisdiction, financial administration, chancelleries, even provincial governance and the cities—in short, anything and everything that had to do with the written word could no longer do without qualified personnel. From now on, rulers and administrators had at their disposal concepts of order that enabled them to direct human activity in a way that had up till then been inaccessible.

The "mirror to princes" body of literature was given a new impulse, with works of this type becoming more technical and professional. One of the most mature works of this genre was begun for King Hugo II of Cyprus by none other than Thomas Aquinas; it was completed by his pupil Ptolemy of Lucca. It is right at the very beginning of this treatise that we find Aquinas's famous definition of the natural human propensity to be a social and political creature (which he derived from Aristotle), as well as the long-undisputed justification of monarchy as the best form of government. Yet the most widespread publication at this time, which was translated into numerous vernaculars, and even into Hebrew, was the work *De Regimine Principum* by Giles of Rome (Aegidius Romanus). With Aristotle's *Politics* in the arsenal of disputation, not only did the strategies for legitimizing rule and the language of pamphlets and paraeneses change fundamentally; rather, a systematic permeation of "political" correlation now became possible, allied with practical recommendations for the education of princes. The world of the princes responded swiftly;

henceforth, it would be imperative that all forms of rule be more thoroughly legitimized and more efficiently organized than ever before.

Europe after the End of Hohenstaufen Rule: Sicily

The papal fiefdom of Sicily appeared to be the hub of all the complex developments in European politics. Not only the pope but also the kings of England, France, and Aragón cast their eyes toward this island. Despite Pope Urban IV's objections, in 1262 James I of Aragón had organized a marriage between his son and heir Peter and a daughter of King Manfred of Sicily, before the pope's own choice as ruler, the Capetian Charles of Anjou, took control there. The youngest son of this union, who was only born after the French seized power, was christened with the portentous name of Frederick. Southern Italy pinned great hopes on this infant and his father, for Charles did not win over the hearts and minds of his subjects. Indeed, a rebellion known as the Sicilian Vespers presently broke out on the island, supported by the Palaiologan emperor in Constantinople. Peter of Aragón immediately landed there and was welcomed as king by a jubilant population. The pope, now Martin IV, responded by excommunicating Peter, exercising the papal power to loose and bind to divest him of all his realms, and calling for a crusade against Aragón (1283). Armed with the pope's sanction to wage war, French troops under Charles of Valois, the younger son of Philip III, who had been selected by Martin to be the next king of Aragón, then launched an invasion of Sicily. Yet the methods that had recently brought about the fall of the Hohenstaufen dynasty, failed in the case of the crown of Aragón. Although the nobility there seized the opportunity to form a conspiratorial "union" against Peter, so forcing the king to restore many of their privileges, their failure to lend their support to the French ended up preserving the indigenous ruling house from the fate of the Hohenstaufens. When he was on his deathbed, Peter III waived all claims to Sicily (1285), but his successor Alfonso III was intent on retaining control. His younger brother James II finally gave up the island kingdom in 1295 after a reconciliation with Pope Boniface VIII, and in recompense was granted the Kingdom of Sardinia (including Corsica) as a hereditary realm (1297). However, in the meantime, possibly in consultation with James, his younger brother—the youth with the Hohenstaufen name of Frederick—had taken possession of the island, which duly paid homage to him. Ruling as Frederick III, he remained in firm control of Sicily until his death in 1337; no excommunication or war was ever able to unseat him. This brought about the long-term division of the kingdom into the island realm of "Trinacria" (which also laid claim to the entire former Norman-Hohenstaufen empire) and the mainland rump kingdom of Naples in the hands of the counts of Anjou (which claimed Sicily). It was only with the accession of Alfonso V of Aragón (d. 1458) that the old Norman-Hohenstaufen empire was finally reunified once more—after long-running conflict from 1421 onward—to form the "Kingdom of the Two Sicilies."

Meanwhile, the Angevin rulers of Naples found themselves recompensed in 1301 for the bitter loss of Sicily, when Andreas III of Hungary, the last in the line of the native royal house of Arpad, died without leaving an heir and King Charles Robert of Naples, by virtue of his paternal grandmother, laid claim to the Magyar succession. After initial resistance, he was finally able to assert his claim with papal support (1308). Close relations with Philip the Fair of France helped consolidate his hold on power. During the reign of the last Arpad rulers, the kingdom of Hungary had risen to become a respectable power located strategically between the West and Constantinople. Its kings had established themselves in Croatia and Dalmatia after successful campaigns against the Venetians, while its clergy was alive to the latest cultural trends in Italy. The Golden Bull issued by Andreas II of Hungary, the father of Saint Elisabeth, in 1222, may serve as an indicator of the general developments taking place in Europe, and was of supraregional importance. The king was striving after the Byzantine crown and overall was pursuing costly and inconsistent policies. This proclamation was wrested from him by the Hungarian nobility and granted them—much like the English "Magna Carta"—the right to resist the crown. But now, in 1301, the male line of the glorious house of Arpad, the dynasty that had given Hungary Saint Stephen, had died out, and for three-quarters of a century the country was ruled by the Neapolitan side branch of the house of Anjou, until it too died out with the death of Louis the Great in 1382. In this case of succession, the Holy Roman Emperor Charles IV and the French king Charles V, together with the aristocracy of Bohemia and Poland, came to a mutual agreement about who should next ascend the Hungarian throne. And so it was that the crown of Hungary fell to Mary, who then ruled as co-regent when she married Sigismund of Luxembourg.

The royal and princely landscape of Europe was characterized by the lives and marriages of the various crowned heads, the acceptability of heirs, endless wars but also compacts concerning sovereignty between the monarch and groups of noblemen, or between the "Cortes" and the "common people." In cases of dispute, the papacy would step forward as the supreme court of law, and rule on the legality of the matter in hand. However, after the demise of the Hohenstaufen dynasty, it could only assert its authority when it intervened on the side of the victor. Worldly powers were now once more in the ascendancy over the spiritual, as the pope himself, Boniface VIII, would soon learn at first hand. Nevertheless, the vicar of Christ remained the only instance in Latin Christendom with the power to lend a veneer of legitimacy to naked power. This development was not only epitomized by the kingdom of Aragón, but also made itself apparent in England.

England

The death of King John Lackland did not bring the civil war in England to an end. The nine-year-old Henry III, for whom initially the experienced though aged William Marshal acted as regent (later replaced by a regency council), swore fealty to the papal legate Guala Bicchieri. In order to placate the rebellious barons, the Magna Carta was renewed (albeit with some revisions) with the agreement of the legate in 1216 and 1217. But like his predecessor Innocent, Pope Honorius III imposed ecclesiastical penalties on the king's opponents and on the person directing their insurrection, the French dauphin Louis. This papal intervention undoubtedly saved the English crown for the infant king, and isolated the Capetian pretender, who ultimately suffered a military defeat too, forcing him to renounce his ambitions of gaining the English crown and turn his back on the island. Immediately, the struggle for control of the Plantagenet territories on the continent, both those already lost and those that still remained, flared up anew; this scramble for land, though, only succeeded in consuming human lives and enormous amounts of money, and despite the early death of Louis VIII (1226) and several other favorable opportunities, did not result in a decisive English victory. On the contrary, in the Peace of Paris of 1259, Henry was forced to acknowledge all his father's losses and content himself with control over the region of Gascony alone, but even then only as a fiefdom of the French crown. Yet throughout this period, the Plantagenet king remained a loyal vassal of the Roman Church and the pope and was constantly prepared to plunge headlong into military adventures or heavy financial commitments in his service.

The irreversible loss of Normandy and Anjou meant that Bordeaux became the continental residence of the English king, while London (with Westminster, where the king was the driving force behind construction of a magnificent new Gothic palace), as the seat of the most important state institutions such as the royal chancellery, the exchequer and the high court (which sat, as it still does today, in nearby Holborn), rose unchallenged to become the capital of the island kingdom, and provided the Crown with a permanent home. More and more of the barons, too, had to relinquish their formerly wealthy holdings in France and settle in England. Certainly, this situation only exacerbated the recent confrontation with the king. The heavy financial support required by Henry III's foreign policy on the continent stirred up resistance; in addition, for a long time the king had clearly preferred southern French advisors and bureaucrats (on a divide and rule principle deliberately choosing men who were at odds with one another) over his own barons. And if all this were not bad enough, Henry made a point of bringing in bishops from Italy. All of these measures alienated the country's nobility. Furthermore, countless new marital alliances changed the political landscape throughout Europe. No kingdom could stand aloof from another any longer; instead, each nation found itself entwined in several networks of relationships, and its rulers and leading nobility were involved in far-reaching interests and diverse extended family connections and inheritance claims. So it was that the progress of the conflict between the Hohenstaufen dynasty and the pope also drew Henry III's attention to Germany, Provence, and Sicily. Innocent IV offered Henry's brother Richard of Cornwall the Sicilian crown, but he declined it; however, after the deaths of Conrad IV and the rival king William of Holland, Richard was elected "king of the Romans" (that is, German king) by a group of princes in 1257. In the meantime, Henry made preparations for his own younger son Edmund, who was only eight years old to ascend the Sicilian throne with papal assent, but this plan failed as well, not least due to the resistance of the English barons, despite the fact that a treaty including this provision had already been concluded with Alexander IV (1255–1256).

Endless problems awaited Henry back in his own homeland. Archbishop Stephen Langton of Canterbury issued a clear warning to a royal advisor who wanted to have Magna Carta declared invalid because it had been signed under duress; "If you loved the king, then you would not thus thwart the peace of his realm!"[13] The freedoms of the barons and the citizens and the peace of the kingdom converged. This made England's need for the Magna Carta all the more pressing, embodying as it did a root-and-branch reorganization of the country's power and authority structure. The lords began to pose an increasing danger to the king. The *Commun de Engleterre,* or to give it its Latin title the *Concilium totius regni Angliae,* the Council of All England, was convened in Oxford in opposition to the monarch. Its first success was to force Henry to concede the "Provisions of Oxford" in 1258, which were expanded the following year into the "Provisions of Westminster"; the latter granted the lower aristocracy too the right to occupy the most important posts in the country's administration. The French advisors were expelled, and English barons and knights henceforth gained a decisive influence over the kingdom's policies and finances; this was why Henry found himself obliged to sign the Peace of Paris. The oaths taken in the bureaucratic language of Law-French by the members of the *Commun* reveal exactly what was going on here: members swore "that each of us, whether individually or collectively, shall provide mutual support to one another . . . and against all others . . . saving faith to the king and the Crown" *(salve la fei e rei e de la corune)*; the highest royal officials also took this same oath, along with the judiciary, the exchequer, and the chastelains.[14] The "Crown" now took its place alongside the personage of the monarch as the suprapersonal ruler of the kingdom.

It was in the midst of this period of violent conflict that Henry de Bracton, a legal counsel of the king, wrote his work *De legibus e consuetudinibus Angliae* (On the laws and customs of England), one of the great theoretical legal works of the entire Middle Ages. While paying due regard to canonistics and legistics, this learned man still succeeded in drafting the English "Common Law," which as a form of case law defied all codification—indeed, it is not too far-fetched to claim that in bringing this phenomenon into being in the first place, Bracton lent considerable impetus to the creation of the modern state! According to him, "Those connected with justice and peace belong to no one save the Crown alone and the royal dignity, nor can they be separated from the Crown, since they constitute the Crown *(faciant ipsam coronam).* For to do justice, give judgment and preserve peace is the Crown, without which it can neither subsist nor endure. Neither these rights nor the exercise of them can be transferred to person or tenements, or be possessed by a private person unless it was given to him from above as a delegated jurisdiction." The treatise stated further: "As the vicar and servant of God, the king may do nothing on Earth except that which is he is permitted to do by law . . . and which following the counsel of his magistrates has been deemed to be lawful and just."[15] Here, then, the authority of the monarch was being clearly separated and demarcated from the person of the king, and thereby strengthened. England's sovereign was therefore not actually the king, but the God-like exercise of justice. Even so, according to Bracton, it was still in the king's unique gift to interpret the law.

Although the Provisions were repealed following fighting, almost on the scale of a civil war, and military success by Crown Prince Edward, Bracton's treatise survived; in retrospect, then, the Provisions symbolized the general trend following the struggle for power in England. Adopting the designation for the circle of royal advisors, the gathering of secular and church dignitaries soon took the name of *parliamentum* (the first attested use of which is in 1237); from 1258 onward this body was to meet three times a year, and indeed quickly began to function as the definitive counterpart to the king. The first figure to come to prominence in its service was the young Simon de Montfort, the son of the notorious anti-Cathar crusader of the same name, and Henry III's brother-in-law. In opposition to the king, in 1264 and 1265, de Montfort convened parliaments to which the knightly class and the cities sent delegates, alongside the barons and the leading clergy—a first breakthrough in the long history of parliamentary representation, which began here. The year 1264, in fact, was remarkable, witnessing the first "parliament," the appointment by the pope of Charles of Anjou as king of Sicily, and the translation of Aristotle's *Politics*. Subsequently, both the English parliament and Aristotle's *Politics* would fundamentally change public life throughout Europe, though contemporaries had no inkling of their huge importance.

In 1265, Simon de Montfort was killed in battle against Prince Edward. But in a shrewd move, and despite his military victory, in 1267 King Henry III renewed Magna Carta once more as well as confirming his assent to all the main points enshrined in the Principles of Westminster; he was likely persuaded to do so by Louis IX's arbitration and the desire to maintain peace. In doing so, he laid the groundwork for an enduring pacification of his realm. This agreed, rather than coerced, compliance was probably Henry's greatest achievement. Certainly, his son and successor

Edward I was able to build on it. A text called *Modus tenendi parliamentarum* (Method of holding parliaments), published soon after 1330, gave an (admittedly idealized) insight into parliamentary procedure; this work makes clear how firmly entrenched in the kingdom's life this representative assembly had become by this stage. Individual freedoms and peace, the cooperative involvement of the country in governance in place of a parliament merely confined to the barons, legal theory, justice, the court system and common law, and finally the Crown as the epitome and manifestation of the transpersonal state all went hand in hand. The kingdom of England, which not long before had seemed on the verge of collapse, now showed the Western world one—though by no means the only—way toward realization of the modern state.

Spain

The kingdoms of Spain followed a similar trend, though the individual paths they pursued in each case was very different. Barely one hundred and fifty years after the conquest of Toledo by the Moors, the Battle of Las Navas de Tolosa (1212) successfully halted the last truly threatening incursion into al-Andalus of the Almohads from North Africa. This key engagement was contested on the Spanish side by Alfonso VIII of Castile with an army that included a few Crusaders from France, plus the forces of kings Sancho VII of Navarre and Peter II of Aragón. The city of Toledo welcomed the Christian victors with great jubilation: "Blessed are you who come in the name of the Lord!" In 1143, Galicia under King Alfonso I had seceded from Spain to form the independent Kingdom of Portugal, which stood under papal protection; Galician forces were not present at Las Navas. The Castilian conquests continued under Ferdinand III, who allied his kingdom permanently with León in 1230. Córdoba, which had been the seat of the emirs and caliphs since 711, was taken in 1236, to be joined (albeit less stably) by Murcia in 1243. Five years later, Seville fell to the Christians, whereupon its magnificent Grand Mosque was reconsecrated as a cathedral; 400,000 Muslims are said to have fled at this time from the city and its environs, to be replaced by just 20,000 Christians. Despite the occasional insurrection by *Mudéjares,* as Muslims living under Christian rule were known, the fall of Seville signaled the interim cessation of the *Reconquista* in Castile. Ferdinand III (d. 1252)—the king who had scored these great successes, and who had allegedly swooped "like an eagle on its prey" (in reference to Córdoba), who founded both the cathedral at Burgos and the University of Salamanca, has been venerated as a saint since 1671.

The refugees, though, who fled to North Africa, even in some cases as far as Egypt, bemoaned the loss of the territories, where their forefathers had lived and worked for the past 500 years. "Where is my homeland?" lamented one of the great poets and intellectuals of Moorish Spain, the Sufi scholar Ibn Sa'id al Maghribi. "When I recall it, tears rolled endlessly down my cheeks. It was madness to leave you, you magnificent al-Andalus. When I call to mind my happy life in Seville, the rest of my life seems to me nothing but a tribulation." Anyone who was present at these expulsions must have understood the poet's pain. Those Muslims who remained saw themselves gradually pushed back to the emirate of Granada, whose borders held firm for the time being. Even nowadays, countless places in Andalusia still bear the byname of "de la Frontera." But even this tiny Moorish enclave, the remains of al-Andalus and the mighty caliphate of Córdoba, still experienced a remarkable cultural efflorescence during this period. Granada was graced with many gardens, fountains, and public baths, while scholars emerged with whom Latin rulers, notably the Holy Roman Emperor Frederick II, were keen to undertake academic exchanges.

Ferdinand's son Alfonso X, who thanks to his outstanding academic interests earned himself the soubriquet of "the Wise," was one of the greatest ruler figures of the thirteenth century, "one of the most important and powerful men on Earth," as his father-in-law, the Catalan conqueror-king James, who was not always well-disposed toward him, once conceded.[16] The son of a daughter of Philip of Swabia, Pisa and Marseilles elected Alfonso as emperor after the death of William of Holland, followed by certain German princes in 1257, who proclaimed him "King of the Romans." The Castilian ruler acknowledged his election, but at no time—despite clear intentions to do so—made a move to actually assume power in Germany, Italy, or Burgundy; subsequently, he tried in vain to have his position as emperor recognized by the Roman Curia. All that happened was that Italian notaries appeared at his court in Castile, which appeared to corroborate his imperial standing. This undertaking only came to an end when Rudolf of Habsburg's election in 1273 extinguished the Spaniard's imperial ambitions once and for all. In his own country Alfonso successfully expanded his kingdom to the south and the east, as far as Jerez de la Frontera and—after a dangerous uprising by the *Mudéjares*—to gain a permanent hold with Catalan help over Murcia (1266).

Spanish historians nevertheless declared that he had failed in his political ambitions. One prime reason for this judgment was the unrest within his own country, namely rebellions by his son and the Castilian grandees, which put great strain on Alfonso's regime toward the end of his life. For, in the wake of his elder son Ferdinand's untimely death, a conflict over the succession between his younger son Sancho IV (who eventually did end up as successor) and his grandsons cost Alfonso the Wise his throne in 1282; he died two years later in enforced exile. Younger contemporaries subsequently saw in his fate a divine punishment for godless pride and for the worst type of "blasphemy." They had been scandalized by the disruptive atmosphere of academic inquiry and the restless intellectual curiosity of the king, especially his interest in the banned disciplines of astronomy and astrology and the *quadrivium,* studies that he embraced with a true scholar's passion. The king also had Arabic texts translated into the vernacular. At his behest, Ptolemy's tables of planets—tables showing the position of the sun, moon, and the planets Mercury, Venus, Mars, Jupiter, and Saturn relative to the fixed stars of the firmament—were recalculated with hitherto unknown accuracy by a team under the guidance of the Jewish scholars Yehuda ben Moshe and Isaac ben Sid. These so-called Alfonsine Tables came to form the foundation of all astronomical studies right up to the time of Copernicus, and also, especially, of astrology, the most important ancillary field of study to medicine in those days; even Tycho Brahe and Johannes Kepler still knew of them. The tables' calculations were based on a year lasting 365 days, 5 hours, 49 minutes, and 16 seconds. And yet "while Alfonso studied the heavens and watched the stars, he lost the Earth," as the historians mockingly asserted; nothing less than a godless presumption, a mortal sin that consigned him straight to Hell, was ascribed to him. For this scholar-king was commonly supposed to have claimed: "When God gave the Earth form and set to work on His Creation, if He had been able to seek advice from him, Alfonso, then He would have done a better *(melhor)* job." This damning judgment against the Castilian king resurfaced once more during the furor over Galileo's support for the theory of a heliocentric universe. In the light of this, the belated canonization of his father was at the same time an antiacademic sideswipe at his son.[17]

Even so, consigned to exile just as his younger contemporary Dante would be from Florence twenty years later, Alfonso still undoubtedly merited his soubriquet for his laudable patronage of the sciences and his fostering of the Spanish language, as well as for his achievements as a legislator. As with the *Chroniques de France,* the innovation of keeping chronicles would prove to be a great impetus to the advancement of the vernacular language in Spain. One of Alfonso's most famous legacies is his *Games Book,* in which he explained, developed, and annotated the rules of chess, dice, and other board games; this same work also represented an early example of game theory instructing people in how to successfully exploit chances that presented themselves. Alfonso the Wise is credited with having introduced the concept of "checkmate" into chess; in formulating this term, he may well have been reflecting on the real political situation in Castile at the time, and conceived it as emblematic of a political theory of cooperation between between the monarch and his grandees, and its breakdown.

In particular, Alfonso's concern for law and justice, which had its apotheosis in the grandiose *Siete Partidas*—a mixture of statute book, legal encyclopedia, and commentary—deserves special mention here. This seven-volume work was designed to create a single basis for the law throughout the kingdom, and hence dissolve the various regional *Fueros.* This principle was announced in 1265 (or possibly even earlier), though its effect remained only limited, before it was ratified in 1348 and from 1501 onward became the foundation of the country's legal code. The king, who presented himself in the *Siete Partidas* as both legislator and commentator, had entrusted the drafting of the work to jurists, who were adept in processing a wide range of source material, namely Roman civil law including the *Libri Feudorum* and the commentaries of the glossators, the *Liber Extra* with the *Glossa Ordinaria,* works by Aristotle and Thomas Aquinas, and sundry other writings. The almost 2,600 "laws" that resulted presented the material (and this in itself was a sign of a progressive intellectualization of legal matter) in a systematic fashion, rather than in the historical order in which they had been introduced, as in previous statute books. They provided an introduction to legal theory and the theory of legal sources, addressed the responsibilities of the secular authority, discussed the principles of justice and the common good, which it was the ruler's duty to put into practice, considered the areas of the law relating to the family, private matters, and inheritance, and finally concluded with an examination of criminal law. Any legislator, it was asserted, should be literate so as to be able to distinguish justice from injustice and to have the capacity to amend his laws whenever he should deem it necessary. His concern for the common good over personal advantage was what distinguished him from the tyrant. Furthermore, it was stated that daughters could not be married off in their absence or without their express agreement with the arrangement, and, if they so wished, that they should be permitted to retain their possessions and not surrender them to the husband. The position of the Jews and the "Moors" in Spain was discussed repeatedly, and in a discriminatory way. So, although their life and limb and their property were all under the protection of the king, as were synagogues and mosques, and Jews enjoyed the right to observe the Sabbath unmolested, Jews and Muslims were forbidden under pain of death from proselytizing among Christians or from sexual congress with Christian women. Moreover, as the Fourth Lateran Council had prescribed, their headgear and their clothing should be such as to clearly distinguish them from Christians.

Yet what would the wise king have achieved without the conqueror? The last great political success scored by the Castilian king, significantly in alliance with Aragón, was the conquest of the Moorish kingdom of Murcia. The "crown of Aragón," which had been under the protection of the pope since the era of the reforming papacy, rose to become a major regional power in the Mediterranean, with its royal capital in Barcelona. It united the two historically divided (in both social and legal terms) realms of the actual kingdom of Aragón and the county of Barcelona, which in the course of the *Reconquista* had expanded through the annexation of "New Catalonia" (Tarragona); in addition, extensive lands south and north of the Pyrenees were beholden to the king-count in varying degrees of dependence. The king must have been intent upon integrating these diverse legal titles into an empire and legitimizing it. Peter II had certainly intended something of this nature when he reached a new agreement to render his realm *(regnum meum)* liable to paying interest to the Roman Church and the pope but without assigning it to feudal tenure, and was duly crowned by Innocent. But in the meantime, the pope refused his assistance in creating a closed transmontane kingdom centered on the Pyrenees. The consequences of this would have been incalculable. The various provinces of this Spanish crown—leaving aside Aragón and Tarragona but definitely including the county of Barcelona—had since the Carolingian period legally continued to belong to the *regnum Francorum* (the Frankish empire) and hence to France; and the pope had not the slightest intention of curtailing the rights of the French king. As far as we can tell, though, neither Peter II nor his successors ever made interest payments to Rome again.[18]

After Peter II's defeat against the Crusaders at the Battle of Muret (1213), a second candidate for the Aragónese throne appeared, while various aristocratic factions threatened the king's authority. Once again, it was the papacy—first Innocent III and then Honorius III—under whose protection Peter's son also stood, that saved a throne for a child ruler, namely the five-year-old James I. At that time, before the king had reached the age of majority, Aragón began to turn away, albeit slowly, from its policy of expansion in Languedoc and look instead to the south, and a resumption of the *Reconquista* against the "Moors." Like many other rulers who were prepared for high office through long years of minority, James tended to be a mistrustful and impulsive man. He is said to have ordered the tongue of a confessor who betrayed his confidence to be torn out; he calmly accepted the act of penance that was imposed on him for this cruel act. He hunted down dissenters who did not surrender promptly, and put them to death. His nickname of the Conqueror was well earned; no sooner had he brought his country's nobility back into line with the threat of harsh reprisals than he proceeded to overrun one kingdom after another. He began, as his father had already planned and as was only appropriate for a ruler of Barcelona looking out over the sea with an eye to long-distance trade, by conquering the island of Majorca (1229; Ibiza was added in 1235), and then the rest of the Balearic Islands, which thereafter belonged to "Spain," and then Valencia (1238), the former domain of the warrior El Cid, whose praises were just then being sung in the "Cantar del mio Cid," a rousing battle-song probably composed in the early thirteenth century. With the help of Alfonso X of Castile, James then took Murcia (1264), which according to their agreement was to be ruled by the latter, but which in the event was settled primarily by Catalans. The suffering of those displaced in such campaigns is always the same; here, too, then, Moorish refugees nostalgically memorialized their lost homeland: "The fall of Valencia wounded Muslims deeply; this catastrophe was a bitter blow to them. . . . The city was nothing less than a Paradise / Of Beauty 'beneath which the rivers of Paradise flowed.' / The balm of the day would be followed by the fragrant scent of the evenings, / and the trees and bushes were imbued with a mild breath of wind . . . but now even the day here is shrouded in darkness."[19]

Henceforth, the Catalans were to distinguish themselves as one of Europe's foremost seafaring nations. The king took further measures to found the administration of his kingdom on the principles of learned Roman and canon law. James I once noted in passing in his *Book of Deeds* (see below) that it was essential for legal trustees, decretalists, and experts from the *Fueros* to be constantly present in his household, for cases involving all three of these different types of law were always cropping up; if a different arrangement were in place, it would be to the detriment of his court, "for neither we nor any lay person can possibly be familiar with all the legal texts in this world."[20] As a shrewd politician, James was careful not to overestimate his abilities and instead surrounded himself with the most competent advisors. Among the king's counselors was Ramón de Peñafort, the most important canon lawyer of the age, and the compiler of the most authoritative collection of decretals to emerge from this era, the *Liber Extra*. Ramón was also the author of a seminal work on penitential discipline *(Summa casuum)* as well as the standard commentary on it. The results of consulting such experts soon became apparent: jurisdiction became more technical and financial administration more efficient, while the power of the Cortés was held in check.

In Aragón too, which was militarily successful and culturally vigorous through the agglomeration of Latin, Arab, and Jewish knowledge and skills, the culture of reason had long since become firmly embedded in political practice. The constitution of the kingdom of Aragón can fairly lay claim to being a model for the rest of Europe: for the position of *justicia mayor* (constitutional judge) was the first such post in world history, a person appointed to arbitrate between the Crown and the country's representatives, a body which in the "Cortes" comprised three castes, the *Ricos hombres* (the high aristocracy), the *Infanzones* (middle and petty nobility), and delegates from the cities. Here, too, then, a trend toward institutionalization was evident, which accelerated the process of state formation. James also brought a definitive end to the disputes with France, when in the Treaty of Corbeil (1258), he and Louis IX agreed upon the national boundaries that, basically speaking, still form the frontier between the two countries. Furthermore, wars were not the only thing to result from the confrontation with Islam: lively commercial and cultural contacts between Spain and the Maghreb can be identified at this period. As a way of promoting both Christian missionary work and learning, the eminent Catalan scholar Ramon Lull, the tutor of James II and professor of theology at Paris and Montpellier, called for the introduction of systematic course of language study in Hebrew, Aramaic, and "Chaldean" (the latter doubtless a reference to the Mongols) at the universities of Paris, Bologna, Oxford, and Salamanca. An important center for cartography was presently established on Majorca, which produced the most modern and accurate maps of the world yet seen; this was also where the famous *Catalan World Atlas* was created (1387). All these enterprises were accompanied by improved language teaching and the founding of schools for translators.

At the end of his life, James compiled an autobiographical *Book of Deeds*, which it appears he committed to paper in several attempts; though highly selective and riddled with errors, this exhaustive account nevertheless offers valuable and unique insights into the psyche of the ruler and the scenes he portrays from his personal life and his role as monarch. Written in Catalan, this *Llibre dels fets* is the very first undertaking of its kind. It reveals how the king was able to assert his authority even when beset by rival groups of noblemen, and how he managed to galvanize the two very differently disposed courts in Catalonia and Aragón into taking common action. In one passage, for instance, we learn of how a dispute over ownership of a falcon drove two aristocratic families into a fatal feud; in another, the tale is told of a king who while gambling was killed by being struck on the head with a gaming piece. Elsewhere, we hear of two men, a bishop and his brother, who defying the king's express wishes and the recently concluded armistice, conducted a private war against the Moors, an incident where James was obliged to deploy deadly force in order to exercise his will; another story recounts how, in order that he might produce a son and heir, a royal prince who was just twelve years old and "had not yet come of age" married for fear of falling victim to illness or deliberate poisoning before the succession could be secured.

Looking back on his life, the author of the *Llibre* gives joyful thanks for his long, healthy, and blessed life: "My Lord Saint James wrote that faith without good works is dead (James 2:17–20, 26), and our Lord Jesus Christ wanted to fulfill this word in our deeds—a warning to his successor Peter III, to all sons who are due to come to the throne, and indeed to all people on Earth to follow his, James's, example and make sure "that they do the same as us, and place their faith in God Almighty." James even looked upon his own birth as being a portentous moment. To be sure, his father did not love his mother, and only at the insistent urging of a paladin did he spend a night with her, with Maria, the heiress of Montpellier, who had to assert her claims in Rome in an audience with Pope Innocent III; and when her son was born, the queen was overjoyed and dedicated twelve great candles, each for one of the apostles, and gave her son the name of the apostle whose candle flame burned the longest, namely James. Maria herself, though—the "saintly Queen," as the autobiographer calls her—died while she was in Rome and was buried in Saint Peter's; and subsequently, several miracles were reputed to have occurred at her tomb.

After James the Conqueror's death in 1276, in accordance with his wishes, the kingdom was divided up among his sons. His eldest son Peter succeeded his father on the throne of Aragón and as ruler of Valencia, while his brother James II inherited the kingdom of Majorca, along with the county of Roussillon and the dominion of Montpellier, which despite being constituent parts of the kingdom of France were still added to his realm, and took up residence in Perpignan. Peter never recognized this division, and forced his brother to hold his island kingdom in fee. Nor was Aragón's urge to expand in any way curtailed by these developments, as attested by Peter III's invasion of Sicily in 1284. Though this adventure momentarily threatened the collapse of the Crown, in the event the Aragonese monarchy emerged strengthened from the conflict in Sicily. Peter IV (r. 1336–1387) not only succeeded in revoking, or at least severely curtailing, the privileges accorded to the nobility in the Union of Aragon, but he also managed to seize part of the realm of Sardinia, entrusted to him as a fiefdom by the pope, from the Genoese, and—following a sensational trial and a brief military campaign—to snatch back the special realm of Majorca and reincorporate it long-term into the kingdom of Aragón. The last king of Majorca, James III, a great-grandson of the Conqueror, fled to France, sold Montpellier to Philip VI of France to finance his campaign to take back Majorca, but died in the attempt to do so (1343–1344) without leaving an heir. So it was that "Northern Catalonia" also devolved to Peter's control, and only fell to the French crown in the Treaty of the Pyrenees of 1659.

France

During this period, France consolidated her position both internally and externally and became, after a fashion, the foremost power in Europe. Outstanding rulers such as Louis IX (Saint Louis) or Philip the Fair guided the country's destiny at this time. When Louis IX came to the throne in 1226 at the age of twelve, his mother Blanche of Castile acted as regent, performing this task extremely energetically and effectively. The barons were subdued, the counties of Provence (1247) and Toulouse (1249) were finally secured for the royal house, and military ventures by the English king successfully repelled. Louis IX's coronation witnessed a convergence of all the various aspects of the *religion royale,* as devised and developed over the preceding century, and which would endure right up the end of the French monarchy: the coronation oath committed the young ruler not only to protect the church, and uphold the law and the peace of the country, but in all likelihood also to persecute heretics, a prescription expressly included in the protocol for French coronations from 1270 onward. The eve of the coronation witnessed the induction of the royal youth as a knight, a ceremony that henceforth also became a feature of the French coronation ritual. Throughout his life Louis, whose personal piety, awareness of sin, and propensity to do penance were never in doubt, took the duties that attached to the coronation ritual—which went back to the Carolingian period—extremely seriously. Indeed, his entire ruling ethos was sustained by them.

In a letter of advice to his son Philip III, probably written toward the end of his life, Louis encapsulated the fundamental guiding principles of his own reign. This text drew heavily on the lessons imparted by the "Mirrors to Princes" body of literature, which was widespread around the University of Paris, and which had received new impetus from the reception of Aristotle's *Politics.* In his letter, Louis wrote as follows: "My dear son, I advise you to appease wars and contentions, whether they be yours or those of your subjects, just as quickly as you can, for it is a thing most pleasing to our Lord." "If you have anything belonging to another, either of yourself or through your predecessors, if the matter is certain, give it up without delay, however great it may be, either in land or money or otherwise. If the matter is doubtful, have it inquired into by wise men, promptly and diligently. And if the affair is so obscure that you cannot fathom the truth, make such a settlement, by the counsel of upright men, that your soul may be wholly freed from the affair." This latter statement was an appeal to the dauphin to examine his conscience and search his soul, a warning comparable to, or even more stringent than, the Fourth Lateran Council's injunction to make regular confessions. Indeed, Louis always acted in accordance with his conscience in all his actions: supervising the courts, undertaking investigations, persecuting heretics, relieving the Jews of the profits they made from charging interest, and preparing to personally take part in two Crusades. Louis made the ultimate aim of all his advice to his son abundantly clear: "My dear son, ensure that the people of your realm love you, for in truth, I would rather that a Scotsman came from Scotland and ruled our subjects well and loyally than for you to govern them badly."[21] But for all this reverence, the rights of the king over the church were still jealously guarded; and in the conflict between the pope and the Holy Roman Emperor Frederick II, this "Most Christian King" *(Rex Christianissimus; Roi Très Chrétien)* attempted to fill the role of moderator and mediator. Only after the death of Frederick and Innocent IV (1250 and 1254 respectively) did the Capetians move against the last Hohenstaufen rulers in Italy, King Manfred of Sicily and his nephew Conradin.

The repercussions of Louis IX's character for the French kingdom were felt in both internal and external affairs. The lessons that the king had imbibed from his schooling by the Dominicans of Paris ran deep. The justice system, for instance, was reformed, with trial by combat being outlawed, while the collection of taxes was made more efficient and more equitable. In cases of repeated complaints against certain *prévôts* and *baillis,* the king had investigations conducted throughout the realm and appointed standing inquisitors to supervise the officials. The results of these enquiries were collated and evaluated in Paris. In general, despite the regions enjoying a large measure of autonomy—as reflected in their own laws, the *Coutumes*—the overall organization of the kingdom was focused centrally upon the king and his court. Centralization was intended to neutralize any exploitative middlemen in the power hierarchy. In England and France alike, tax sovereignty and the formation of a supreme court with no right of appeal proved to be the essential elements in the formation of the modern state from the High Middle Ages onward. Yet France became increasingly attractive to foreigners. This was not just due to the fact that the French king acted as a mediator in the conflict between the English barons and their king; from the demise of the Hohenstaufen dynasty, the Francophone princes on the western borders of the Holy Roman Empire also began to look to Paris ever more frequently. It was there, at the court of Louis IX and his successors, that they had their sons educated, while they themselves concluded treaties of fealty and other agreements with the French king.

Furthermore, there evolved in France a unique doctrine of legitimation, namely the construction of the *Reditus regni Francorum ad stirpem
Karoli* (the return of the realm to the House of Charlemagne). This doctrine had gradually taken shape from the reign of Philip II Augustus onward: a contemporary troubadour, Bertrand de Born, praised Charlemagne as *Charle, que fo dels mielhs de sos parens* (Charlemagne, the best
of his [that is, Philip's] ancestors). Innocent III's decretal *Novit ille* of 1204
already acknowledged Philip's illustrious lineage, adumbrating the new
doctrine that would become firmly established under Louis VIII and his
son. Presently, in 1244, the widely read encyclopedist Vincent of Beauvais
coined his pithy *Reditus* phrase, which from Philip III onward conditioned French kings' image of themselves. In 1274, during this monarch's
reign, the *Grandes Chroniques de France*—which related the history of
France through a chronography of its kings and which became a quasi-
official primer for all French rulers thereafter—looking back at Philip II
Augustus was inscribed thus: *"Le royaume est retourné à la lignée de Chal-
lemaine le Grant."*[22] Thereafter, the Christian–monarchical ideal was used
to legitimize the reign of the Capetians; according to God's will, prophesied early on, this found its confirmation and corroboration in precisely
that sense of "return."[23] In it, the greatness, the sublimity, and the sovereignty of France was manifested anew. Henceforth, the name of the great
Frankish ruler became the preferred one with which to christen young
Capetian princes, beginning with Charles of Anjou, the brother of Louis
IX and the future king of Sicily, as well as Philip III's second son Charles
of Valois, who tried and failed to seize the Aragonese crown. Later Cape-
tians with this name were Charles of Valois's nephew, the youngest son of
Philip IV the Fair, who ascended the French throne as Charles IV. The
Grandes Chroniques became, so to speak, the Bible of the *religion royale*.

The regained sacredness of the Most Christian King reached its apotheosis in the person of Louis IX. At the age of just twenty-five, he collected holy relics with a zeal unmatched by any other monarch of the period; the next ruler to show such devotion was Emperor Charles IV. In
1239 Louis purchased Christ's "Crown of Thorns," the most valuable sacred relic that Constantinople had to offer, from its ruler Baldwin II, who
was heavily in debt to the Venetians and Templars for funding his Latin
Empire; when it arrived in France, the king went barefoot to collect it,
carried it away in his own hands, and so created a new royal cult of relics.
To house it, Louis founded the free-standing, two-story Sainte-Chapelle

within the precincts of his palace on the Île de la Cité—still an architectural jewel of the French capital—with the lower chapel dedicated to Our Lady and the upper—illuminated with the glow of gold and the light from the stained-glass windows—as a chapel for private prayer by the king. The king's own canons performed liturgical services in both places. Soon afterward, the king added to the crown a splinter of the True Cross and other holy relics he had obtained from Baldwin: sacred blood, pieces of the vinegar-soaked sponge passed to Christ by centurions as he suffered on the Cross, fragments of the Holy Lance, the purple cloak the soldiers used to mock Christ, and the reed that was pressed into Jesus' hand instead of a scepter, as "King of the Jews."[24] This collection not only assembled all the things that Christ may have possessed; these relics also envisioned the instruments of Christ's suffering, which he would in due course present at His Second Coming on Judgment Day. The sight of these holy relics was a spur to examine one's conscience, something Louis spent his whole life doing, and to repentance and asceticism; the king would flagellate himself in front of them in emulation of Christ's Passion.

There was a popular belief that a number of other treasures from the Holy Land were also housed in the chapel: these included the swaddling bands of the Christ child, links of the chain with which He was bound at his capture, the board His head rested upon after the Deposition, a stone from His tomb, a drop of Mary's breast milk, the skullcap of John the Baptist, and the heads of Saint Blasius, Saint Clement, and Saint Simeon. In any event, Louis spent vast sums amassing his treasure trove of relics (1241), and reputedly stored the whole lot in Sainte-Chapelle, where he venerated them and put them on show for the public, so turning Paris, as it were, into a second Jerusalem.[25] One might have thought that Christ himself had blessed France with the presence of these gifts. When Innocent IV dedicated the chapel for the king in 1244, he sent him the following message: "The Lord himself has set His Crown of Thorns on your head, and miraculously entrusted Your Majesty with its safe keeping."

In actual fact, Louis ended up treading a path to the real Jerusalem, both to the one in the afterlife and to the one in the here and now. In the same year that work on his chapel began, he took it upon himself to take the Cross and pledge to go on Crusade.[26] And two months after Sainte-Chapelle was consecrated, in 1248, he set off, to Aigues-Mortes, Cyprus, and Egypt, with the aim of launching a campaign from there to liberate the Holy Sepulcher. But, just like his chapel of relics, a harbor had first to be built from which the king could embark on his journey east; nominally, at least, the port of Marseilles still belonged to the Hohenstaufen Empire. The king's actions attest to a high degree of coordination. Prior to the start of the crusade, there is evidence that large sums of money were transferred; after all, transportation, knights, and 5,000 archers all had to be paid for. Genoese bankers in particular were entrusted with this task, and Louis also appointed sailors from this city to captain his fleet. A tithe that the king personally imposed upon the churches and cities to finance this venture raised far in excess of a million *livres tournois*—an enormous sum. Even so, the outgoings still outstripped income. Some considerable time later, in the fourteenth century, the Royal Treasury estimated the entire cost of this Crusade at 1.3 million *livres tournois,* or more than five times the annual income of the French crown. The fortress of the Templars in Paris served as the king's treasury during the campaign—the very same building that was to play such a sinister role in the French Revolution, as the final place of incarceration of Louis XVI and Marie Antoinette before their execution.

The Muslim caliphate to which Jerusalem was also subject had its capital at the court of the Ayyubids in Cairo. Logically, therefore, Louis directed his initial assault against Egypt. Damietta was taken without a fight. Optimistically, Louis immediately founded an archiepiscopate there. But in the meantime an epidemic, almost certainly dysentery, instantly annulled all his military successes, and the king and his entire army were forced to surrender to the sultan. Louis now found himself imprisoned, while his pregnant queen, whom he had left in Damietta, went into labor and bore a son. This proved to be a stroke of good fortune for him, for Margaret of Provence was such a redoubtable woman that she was able to hold the army together, even as it threatened to disintegrate, mounted a successful defense of the town, and in so doing secured a bargaining chip for the Christian forces, which (in addition to a large ransom) was soon paid over to obtain the release of the king and his army. Four days before this occurred, the Mamelukes, an elite military caste comprised of captured slaves, had staged a coup in Cairo, toppling the Ayyubids and seizing control.

Despite the initial catastrophe of the Seventh Crusade, these events now ensured Louis a certain freedom of action. He sailed from Egypt to Palestine, where he remained until 1254. By now, though, the crusade had definitely failed, and the French army broke up. But Louis was able to exploit the conflict between the Ayyubids in Aleppo and the Mamelukes in Cairo to intervene constructively in the Holy Land, improving or rebuilding the Crusader fortresses there, and signing pacts with the local princes. Again, this created a grace period for the region for a generation, before the final Christian stronghold, the port of Acre (Akko) fell in 1291. During Louis' absence, the regency in France was led by the king's mother, the canniest of women, until her death in 1252, and thereafter by his brother. In vain, Louis had hope to recruit the Mongols as allies against the Muslims; even while he was still making his way home, he dispatched from Cyprus William of Rubruck as an envoy to the court of Möngke Khan in Karakorum; the Franciscan missionary duly returned from there in 1255 to bring news to Louis, who by that time was back in Paris once more; William's accounts were useful yet sobering. Shortly after, the Mongols captured Baghdad (1258), though their further advance into Egypt was thwarted by defeat at the hands of the Mamelukes (at the Battle of Ain Jalut, 1260), whereupon both the Mongol Ilkhans of Persia and the Khan of the Golden Horde both converted to Islam.

Despite the failure of his crusade, Louis then set about preparing for a second campaign against the Muslims. Again, Africa was his objective; this time, however, the king got no further than Tunis, succumbing most likely to dysentery there in 1270; though he died peacefully, his demise acted as a warning to future monarchs. Henceforth, no French king would ever embark on a crusade again. Although Louis was soon canonized for his endeavors, all the other Christian kings and princes of Europe were too preoccupied with their internal affairs to be won over for overseas adventures. After the fall of Acre, successive popes kept pressing for a new crusade, commissioning both from the knightly orders and other experts a whole series of reports on the viability of such an enterprise. Some of these are completely fanciful, while others take a far more realistic approach; the most interesting read like actuarial risk assessments, which display a positively mercantile and sanguine calculation of likely success. The distinctly uncertain chances of victory would not, most experts concluded, justify the enormous costs involved in mounting such a campaign, and given the lack of peace and unity among the various Christian forces, no ruler could afford to get involved. Evidently, under the influence of economic and political realism, a long but slow learning process had set in and begun to prevail over simple religious convictions.

The final balance sheet of the Crusades presents a shocking picture rather than one of success. On the profit side, these campaigns were the first occasions on which Europeans had ventured beyond their narrow home horizons on any grand scale, and there can be little doubt that the Crusades helped overcome certain mental barriers, as well as furnishing the mercantile world and early European high finance with huge profits; finally, around 1100, when Urban II preached a doctrine of "armed pilgrimage," the fight against the Muslims also helped relieve the constant pressure of internecine feuding in the Western world by effectively "exporting" war, at least for a time. And yet, on the debit side, the immediate successes were strictly limited; indeed, after the initial successful conquest of Jerusalem, all that came to pass was an unstoppable melting away of all the former gains, consuming vast amounts of human, financial, and symbolic capital. Furthermore, the "exported" war returned all too swiftly from the Holy Land to its original source, providing fuel for a new round of conflict in Europe, quite apart from the anti-Jewish pogroms and associated injustices—at their most extreme the accusations of ritual murder—that had been sparked by the Crusades. Many of the recurring bouts of upheaval and long-running conflicts in European history were set in train by these ventures: Louis VII of France's worsening marriage crisis while on Crusade; Duke Welf VI's preference for Frederick Barbarossa as king; the papal excommunication of his grandson of the same name (Frederick II); the incarceration of Richard the Lionheart; the sidelining of Byzantium, which had long provided protection for the West against dangers from the East; the catastrophe of the Children's Crusade; the misuse of the preaching of the Cross against political opponents; Louis IX's humiliating ransoming; and the destruction of the errant Knights Templar after the fall of Acre—to name just a few examples—indicate clearly to what extent the history of Europe in the High Middle Ages was permeated by the Crusades.

One significant effect of this expansion into the Near East was the peculiar blending of a religious urge for salvation with economic advantage. Contradicting Max Weber's assertion, this combination turns out, therefore, not to be a late invention specifically of Protestantism or Puritanism at all. From the very outset, the Crusaders were supported by the merchant class; faith, ideology, and commerce all went hand in hand, and God sanctified every military success. Without the aid of the merchant fleet from the city of Pisa, Jerusalem would not have been conquered in 1098. Before long, all the seafaring municipalities had set up their own quarters in the ports of the Holy Land. The West had no intention of doing without the spices, silks, and other luxury goods of the Orient. But in the interim, after the opening up of the Silk Route by the Mongols, the maritime municipalities of the West had no need of crusading any more. Venetian, Pisan, Florentine, Genoese, Marseillaise, and Catalan merchants had long since learned, without imposing a military presence or invoking an ideology, how to transcend all religious boundaries and establish trade contacts with Mongols and Muslims. And, in the West and East alike, the Jews emerged as the middlemen of this mercantile system. Commercial enterprise expanded, as trade treaties and diplomacy supplanted crusades and conflict. Piracy also brought rich rewards, though over time the profits and losses for both sides may well have canceled one another out. The same year that Acre fell, 1291, also saw the Vivaldi brothers set sail from Genoa to circumnavigate Africa. We do not know how far they got, since they disappeared without a trace. But success or otherwise was not what counted here, rather the intention; and this urge to explore survived the failure of other such expeditions too. In short, waging war in the Holy Land became too expensive. Only in the twentieth century did Europeans once again, for a while, occupy Syria and Palestine.

Germany

Many European kingdoms consolidated in this period and constituted themselves as national confederations. The only place, conversely, to disintegrate was Central Europe during the interregnum and the ensuing internecine warring of the princes. The German kingdom grew steadily weaker as a result of the absence of the king and emperor, who was intent on pursuing his aims in Italy. Moreover, the country's eastern neighbors were disunited as well. The Piast dynasty in Poland did not act in any concerted manner, despite the fact that their constitution was based on the principle of agnatic seniority. On occasions, there were as many as six separate duchies in existence in Poland at the same time, whose rulers were regularly engaged in feuds with one another. Masovia in the northeast, Greater Poland around Poznan and Gniezno, and Lesser Poland with Krakow at its center formed the center of gravity. Although the duchy of Silesia was governed by a Piast, it went its own way from an early stage, a move that saw it grow increasingly close to Bohemia. A new reunification of Poland was only achieved at the start of the fourteenth century, by Vladislaus I and his son Casimir III the Great. In addition, following a request for assistance by Duke Conrad of Masovia in 1234, the

Teutonic Order established itself in the Chelmno region and in Prussia, a development that eventually led to serious conflicts with the Polish and Lithuanian counts there. Propaganda, legal advice, court actions, and open warfare were the consequences. Though Emperor Frederick II had confirmed the Teutonic Knights' possessions in Prussia—lands that he would later acquire—in his Golden Bull of Rimini in 1226, at the time this was a writ for territories outside his realm, and his actual authority as emperor and was therefore of doubtful legitimacy. This bull was unable to forestall future difficulties. The Teutonic Order's desire to achieve independence was unequivocally at the cost of the local Polish lords.

The failure of the Hohenstaufen dynasty was most impressively in evidence in Germany itself. Indeed, how could imperial authority be expected to survive the decades-long interregnum that followed the death of Frederick II? None of the rulers with the title of king was able to fulfill the role of emperor any longer; the extent of the power now enjoyed by the vicar of Christ had entirely eclipsed it. Unlike the situation in England under the Plantagenets, whose king was regularly absent from the country for long periods, the Holy Roman Empire had not evolved any enduring institutions that existed independently of the king and that embodied royal authority. Nor was there any central taxation system for collecting and administering taxes and other levies on a continuing basis, nor a supreme court that could administer justice even without the king being present, and that excluded any right of appeal. The imperial supreme court that Frederick II had planned to institute at the Imperial Peace of Mainz of 1235 only existed on paper (a material, incidentally, that was just then beginning to arrive in Europe from the Arab world through Spain and Italy, and was fast replacing vellum). It was only right at the end of the medieval period that an Imperial Chamber Court was finally put in place; however, even this was unable to assert is authority over the regional lords, who had been furnished with courts of last resort of their own—the *Privilegia de non appellando* or *Privilegia de non evocando*—and yet, through the sheer volume of work it had to cope with, it still shelved many cases. This "empire" was present in the personage of the king, and at the same time embodied entitlement, ritual, usage, tradition, and memory and possessed hallowed customs and practices, and theoretically rights, lands, and seigneuries too, but no institutions that could have administered these independently of the king, in other words no exchequer or lord chief justice. In sum, there was no concept of the "Crown" coexisting alongside the monarch.

Likewise, Rudolf of Habsburg (r. 1273–1291), whose reign ushered in a new phase in the history of the German kingdom and the Holy Roman Empire, was only able to ascend the throne with papal approval and in exchange for burdensome concessions—a heavy legacy for future rulers. Prior to his election, Rudolf had only been a count, not a powerful duke like all previous lords who had been made king. But the pope, Gregory X, made it clear that he did not want a "Hohenstaufen," that is, any blood relative of the royal house that had been excommunicated, to be elected as the next emperor; moreover, Ottokar of Bohemia, who was some people's favored candidate, was too powerful for the majority of electors, and in any event was excluded by dint of not being German. But scarcely had the Habsburg count been elected king than bad news reached the pope's ears. Feuding had broken out throughout the empire. It was said that serious unrest *(turbatio)* was hampering any chance of peace there and preventing the church from realizing its aims—the planned Crusade, for example. But the "territories" did not want an emperor who would actually punish the omnipresent wickedness, while the German princes had no desire for one who would really govern them. The East was rife with heresies; plus, there was widespread fear of another Tartar invasion.

Bitter complaints about the situation, such as the following one—which unsurprisingly came from a bishop, Bruno of Olomouc (Olmütz)—came to a head in lengthy diatribes directed at the mendicant orders (Beguines) and in cliché-ridden attacks on "the Jews, who keep Christian women as wet-nurses, who frequently practice usury, and who sorely press a person who is obliged to pay interest by charging more in a single year than the initial loan. They occupy official positions, gaining control over excise affairs and currency, but since they are unbelievers they disregard the Christian faith in performing their duties. They misappropriate chalices and sacred vestments, take stolen manuscripts in payment and put them under lock and key, and while any Christian found hoarding such sacred books is obliged to hand them back, the Jews are not required to restore them to their original owners."[27] These complaints concerned the "Jewish ordinances," which Duke Frederick II of Austria (in 1244) and King Ottokar II of Bohemia (in 1254 and 1255) had passed in favor of the Jews in their territories, and against which a provincial synod held in Salzburg had recently tried, and largely failed, to mount opposition.[28] A new church council had already been convened, Bishop Bruno maintained, in order to redress these grievances. "Usury" in those days meant money-lending with interest; all forms of interest were held by theologians and canon-law experts at the time to be extortion.[29] But the bishop chose to turn a blind eye to the fact that the worst "usurers"—who charged interest rates far in excess of 50 percent and in some extreme instances even 200 percent and more—were actually Christians, and to ignore that the accusations made against the Jews were colored, possibly even motivated in the first place, by a desire on the part of these Christian moneylenders to dispense with unwelcome competition and, even worse, that this endeavor did not stop short of organizing pogroms.

Nevertheless, in some regards Rudolf could look back at the end of his life on a largely successful period in office. First and foremost, he had managed to massively increase the dynastic power of his family, without which no king could hope to rule. He secured control over Austria and emerged as the victor in the so-called brothers' war against Ottokar II of Bohemia from the Premyslid dynasty. The Bohemian ruler did not want to hand back the imperial territories that he had won during the interregnum and so was placed under the imperial ban; finally, he was defeated in the Battle on the Marchfeld, and assassinated immediately after (1278). With the approval of the electors, Rudolf duly enfeoffed his son Albrecht (1282–1283) with the principalities thus gained—alongside Austria, the provinces of Styria, and Upper and Lower Carniola—an act that instantly raised Albrecht's status in the hierarchy of imperial princes. Thereafter, Habsburgs were to remain on the throne of Austria until 1918. Rudolf's marriage politics were also of great legal significance; he married or rather was obliged to marry four of his six daughters to the princes who were foremost in supporting his election: two of them on the coronation day itself, and two some years later. A series of public truces were enacted to pacify the empire. Individual bailiffs were charged with the responsibility for regaining the imperial rights that they had lost during the interregnum. Even so, Rudolf only really enjoyed success in this regard in the south of his realm; the north was to remain resistant to his authority. Moreover, one major goal was not achieved: the evolution of the Holy Roman Empire into a homogeneous state. It remained an unwieldy entity, whose monstrosity only grew rather than diminished with the passing centuries.

And this monster of a polity devoured its own rulers. For almost thirty years from 1246 onward, until the election of Rudolf of Habsburg, there were always two rival kings laying claim to the empire. And when Rudolf himself died in 1291, the electors voted against his son Albrecht, initially opting, it would appear, for Conrad of Teck, who was slain on the day of his election, and immediately replaced by Adolf of Nassau. Only when he was deposed in 1298 did they settle on Rudolf (this was the occasion when the Prince-Electors' College of seven "Electors" first came to prominence),[30] but he was murdered in 1308. He was followed by the first emperor of the House of Luxembourg, Henry VII, upon whose death in 1314 two rivals laid claim to the crown, the Habsburg Frederick the Handsome and the Louis of Bavaria of the House of Wittelsbach; the latter prevailed, but in 1346 a group of electors made Charles IV king of the Romans in opposition to him. After an entire century of division and declining power under thirteen kings from nine different dynasties, Charles's election finally brought stability to the Holy Roman Empire.

Rudolf's death also provided the impetus to the formation of the Swiss Confederation. In 1291, out of justifiable fear of outside intervention, the three alpine cantons of Uri (which following the recent opening of the Saint Gotthard Pass had emerged from its former isolation and gained growing prominence and had been granted imperial immediacy by Henry VII of Germany, in 1232), Schwyz, and Unterwalden formed an "Eternal Alliance." The signatories pledged "in good faith to assist each other with aid, with every counsel and every favor, with person and goods, within the valley and without" and not to recognize any "judge" who had not been elected and who was not their kinsman; furthermore, they reserved the right to settle disputes among themselves by means of long-established codes of conduct. In 1309, the Holy Roman Emperor Henry VII confirmed the exemption (first granted in 1240) of Uri and Schwyz from external jurisdiction. However, on November 15, 1315, the inhabitants of Schwyz were called upon to defend their freedom in the Battle of Morgarten on the shores of Lake Ägeri against a mounted army led by the Habsburg duke Leopold I of Austria; the cavalry found it difficult gaining a foothold on the rocky terrain, whereas the Confederates were equipped with crampons and, armed with halberds, set about the hapless riders "cleaving and hacking them to pieces as if with shears." This engagement stayed long in the collective memory and was recorded in the chronicle of the battle by Johannes of Winterthur, who as a boy had witnessed at first hand the retreat of the defeated Leopold: "This was no battle, but rather a slaughter of the foreign troops, as if they had been a herd of animals being led to the abattoir." The defense of freedom required weapons, and henceforth, the "Swiss" became some of the most feared mercenary soldiers in

Europe. The famous legends of William Tell and of the oath sworn on the Rütli meadow, which were immortalized by Friedrich Schiller's play *Wilhelm Tell* (1804), only began to circulate in the fifteenth century or even later. All nations, it seems, need their specific *loci* of commemoration.

The Papacy

In the late thirteenth century, the preeminence of the pope resided in a curious blend of secular and ecclesiastical authority. Popes claimed to represent a monarchical priesthood, hence their sporting of the three-tiered crown *(triregnum)*. As autonomous rulers, they reigned over the Papal States; while as supreme feudal lords, they effectively held sway over Sicily, Portugal, and England, and later over the kingdom of Sardinia, as well; on occasion, the same authority was also claimed, though never acknowledged, over Hungary and Aragón. On the basis of the translation doctrine, according to which the papacy had once transferred imperial power from the Greeks to the Franks in the person of Charlemagne, and from the Franks to the Germans in the person of Otto I, the popes demanded the right to approve the candidate for German king, since whoever was chosen would also in time become Holy Roman Emperor. General canon law was assigned to the sovereignty of the pope and the exegetical arts of the canonists. Finally, popes arrogated to themselves the supreme right to intervene in any kingdom's affairs "by virtue of sin" *(ratione peccati)*—in other words on moral or religious grounds: effectively a *carte blanche,* for who was without sin? In addition, the interests of the churches and especially the matter of electing bishops and abbots guaranteed extensive possibilities for the papacy to exert influence, at least indirectly, over national churches and by extension over the polities in which they were situated. Although such elections were officially in the gift of each cathedral chapter or convent, in practice these institutions were often divided among themselves, and in such cases of dispute the pope was empowered to name the new incumbent. Indeed, papal appointment of prelates became the norm over the course of the late thirteenth century; large sums of money were involved, providing a lucrative source of income for the Roman Church. And last but not least, the right of devolution, enacted by Boniface VIII and Clement V, gave popes the right to provide for a benefice in cases where the ordinary patron had failed to do so, with appropriate fees payable to Rome. It also became increasingly common for popes to grant special dispensation for the ordination of the illegitimate sons of priests.

All this gave ample cause for many complaints and over time for conflict with virtually every crowned head. Criticisms of the papacy were especially prevalent among the Franciscans; many a member of this order painted a gloomy picture of the situation. The Curia, they claimed, was corrupt, and the papal legates, whom one encountered everywhere, were open to bribes: "they thirst for gold, they drink gold while crushing the churches." Yet they did not dare to pass judgment on the pope himself, for "whosoever touches the mount shall be stoned like an animal" (cf. Exodus 19:12; Hebrews 12:20). Christ, they maintained, could not really be said to have been set free in a land where Christians were so beleaguered; and where the Hebrews had been robbed of their land and Egyptians had profited. Ways of life, scholarship, and Christian teaching had all gone to rack and ruin, and religious orders were in decline. Nor would the corruption of people's souls be reversed through the discoveries of philosophers or the edicts of secular princes. Yet the Mother Church, the Franciscans claimed, had made itself the handmaiden of the civil law, despite the fact that the writ of the Holy Roman Empire did not run either in France or in many other countries. There was a pressing need for change.[31] But even that correspondent of Gregory X from Germany, Bishop Bruno of Olomouc, was aware that the pope had convened a synod "because these are wicked times, in order to deliver the world from the evil to come" and "because a dangerous age has dawned." Bruno's comments set a thoroughly eschatological tone. And in the End Time, it was imperative that Christ should prevail against the Antichrist.

The political situation was in no less need of review. In 1261, with the help of the Genoese, the Byzantines had been able to recapture Constantinople. The new emperor, Michael VIII Palaiologos, seemed ready to heal the schism with Rome, but discussions to this end dragged on without resolution because of repeated changes of pope. Finally, in order to counter the Byzantines' "disobedience," Pope Gregory X convened the long-overdue Second Council of Lyons in 1274. When it met, the pope was at the height of his power, and the establishment of a Universal Episcopate seemed imminent. Even the Mongols were making efforts, albeit in vain, to forge an alliance with the "Latins" against the Mamelukes.[32] Plans for a new Crusade were afoot. Since the principal theme of the council was the planned reunification of Catholicism with Orthodox

Christianity, the key points of liturgical difference were high on the agenda, namely the Western doctrine of transubstantiation and the question of priestly celibacy, but also political matters such as Byzantine rule in Constantinople, the Orthodox mission to the Bulgars, and the Greeks' lack of allegiance to the *Vicarius Christi* in Rome. For a while, Palaiologus, who was keen to secure Western help and had traveled in person to Lyons, acceded to the pope's authority, but this union, which had been entered into solely for tactical reasons, only lasted a few years. By 1281, the Byzantine emperor found himself excommunicated, and his son and successor Andronicus repudiated the ecclesiastical union entirely. Constantinople remained firmly Orthodox; Venice continued to control the rump of the Latin Empire (or "Empire of Romania," *Imperium Romaniae*), where it found itself at war with Genoa, which now enjoyed the freedom of Constantinople and trading privileges with the city, which had once been the preserve of the Venetians.

Yet there were also some within the church who voiced their concern over the papacy's enthrallment with worldly affairs and who looked for a remedy. These concerns were once again mixed with millennial prophesies, such as those that were widespread among Franciscan mystics (though by no means exclusive to them). These prophesies were fueled by the teachings of Joachim of Fiore (ca. 1135–1202), who saw world history as falling into three phases guided by the Trinity: the first "under the Father," the second "under the Son," and the third "under the Holy Ghost." The mystics regarded themselves as the avant-garde of this third state and subscribed to Joachim's belief that it would begin in the year 1264, that unique and seminal date in European history which, as we have seen, witnessed Charles of Anjou's seizure of power in Sicily, the world's first "parliament," and the discovery of analytical "politics" (and which, as such, seemed to distill all the major historical trends of the preceding centuries). They looked forward to a cathartic initial purge, in which the millennial Antichrist would reveal himself and the worldly papacy would be divested of its power. Even the infallibility of the pope—insofar as such a concept existed then; that is, his hitherto unchallenged primacy in formulating doctrine—was called into question. Subsequently, in 1294, many people believed that the dawning of this new age had come in the form of an "angel-pontiff" when, after two years of inconclusive deliberations, the cardinals impulsively elected the hermit Pietro da Morrone (the site of his monastery) as Pope Celestine V. However, this holy anchorite, who dur-

ing his time as pope never set foot in the Papal States, let alone his episcopal city of Rome, proved unequal to the high office invested in him. His
main achievement was to confirm the peace between James II of Aragón
and Charles II of Naples. This peasant's son spent his time pacing up and
down his room, a hunk of bread clutched in one hand and a bottle of wine
in the other; the canon lawyer Giovanni d'Andrea lampooned him as a
"dull ox," and Dante (*Inferno* III, 59–60) accused him of being a cow-
ard.[33] After barely six months on the throne of Saint Peter, he abdicated
on the advice of Cardinal Benedetto Caetani, who then succeeded him (as
Boniface VIII).

In all aspects, Boniface represented the very antithesis of his predecessor; indeed, he overturned many of Celestine's decisions. He had statues
and images of himself put up all over Rome—on the city gates and in
churches, and immediately set about deploying the heaviest weapons in
his papal armory—excommunication and deposition—against the Colonna, a powerful Roman family that was in bitter rivalry with his own.
He even went so far as to invoke a Crusade against them. In the meantime, questions began to be raised about whether it was even possible for
a pontiff to abdicate. Given that Christ had not been able to renounce his
role, then surely the man who was Christ's representative on Earth could
not resign from his office? These questions sparked furious debates between various parties—theologians, canon lawyers, Franciscan mystics,
the Colonna—and even ultimately drew in the temporal powers as well.
This controversy placed great pressure on the pontificate of Boniface VIII,
whom some opponents accused of being a schismatic. These attacks only
increased when he issued the decretal *Clericos laicos* in 1296, in which he
inveighed against the taxes that the rulers of France and England had
imposed on their clergy in order to raise revenue to fund their wars. Boniface repeated the injunction of the Fourth Lateran Council, which had
threatened the sanction of excommunication against any temporal authority, even including kings, that attempted to tax church property without the express permission of the pope; Boniface's decretal occasioned the
first conflict between the papacy and Philip IV the Fair of France. In 1297,
the decretal was lifted in the case of France (and Aragón), before finally
being completely repealed by Benedict XI and Clement V. Thereafter,
nothing, not even the celebrated and challenging papal bull *Unam sanc-
tum* (1302) could conceal the failure of this pope. Its fierce injunction regarding the necessity of all, kings and commoners alike, to seek eternal

salvation could do nothing to mitigate people's tax liability in the temporal world.

In the interim, the balance of political power in Europe had shifted toward France, whose king had never at any time or in any worldly regard subjugated himself to the authority of the pope. Even for transgressions that would properly have been dealt with under canon law, the Most Christian King refused to countenance any interference by the Curia. The pope would sooner sin than the French king. And yet, in general terms, the major element that was missing now was the "emperor" as an opponent of the pope; as a result, all the tensions and conflicts that hitherto had been contested between the highest representatives of temporal and spiritual authority—and that were, so to speak, absorbed by the presence of the emperor—were displaced into each individual kingdom. All of these—eventually even the papal fiefdoms—freed themselves of every last vestige of the pope's *Potestas in temporalibus* (power over temporal affairs); nor were they at any time troubled by the question of whence their rulers derived their authority; and for their part, their kings governed as the representatives of God (that is, the divine right of kings). Bracton, for instance, naturally looked upon his king as the *Vicarius (Dei),* despite the fact that the English monarch was at that time a vassal of the pope. Similarly, Alfonso X of Castile regarded all kings without exception as the *Vicarios de Dios.* So it was that the actual power of the papacy foundered on the sheer multiplicity of kingdoms that came into being after the Holy Roman Emperor was removed from the picture as a major adversary and guarantor of protection. Thereafter the papacy shrank more and more until it was nothing more than a territorial power governing just one minor state. Boniface VIII was to feel the force of these momentous changes at first hand; he was deposed by the Colonna and imprisoned, and died soon after. But one upshot of these developments was the growing attention that popes were obliged to devote to their "Papal States."

Certain fundamental issues were at stake in this turn of events. Up until now, the world had been organized hierarchically, according to the sequence: kings, emperors, the pope, God. Dante's work was this emblematic of this way of thinking. Although his *Monarchy* criticized monistic papal authority, it still defended a bipolar hierarchy of pope and emperor. But henceforth, the trend toward dehierarchization grew ever stronger and succeeded in fashioning a polycentric world order. Furthermore, below the level of kings and princes, it also strove to legitimize and organize the participation of the masses in power. Now, an increasing flow of political treatises opposing any form of papal or imperial secular power began to appear—both at the universities and outside (though even then they were largely composed by graduates). One of the most famous of these was Marsilius of Padua's *Defensor pacis,* one of the most outspoken attacks on monism of all kinds (1324). Marsilius not only contested the supremacy of the pope, he also advocated, in a hitherto unheard-of manner, giving "the people" (by which he meant a select group of citizens) a stake in power by giving them legislative authority; so radical was this proposal that Marsilius was forced to leave Paris, where he had been teaching, and flee to the court of Louis the Bavarian in Munich, where his criticism of papal omnipotence was warmly received.

High Finance

This dissolution of hierarchical structures coincided with a secularization of thinking, a development that caused great alarm in some quarters. This, in turn, went hand in hand with the birth of new "saints" and a new "god," which so to speak gave rise to new cults. Their appearance was accompanied by a growth of interest in material matters, economic expansion, and a pleasure in audacious risk taking; these factors all helped increase production and created Europe-wide methods of marketing. The names of these new objects of veneration were "money, "gold," and "silver." As early as the twelfth century, the theologian Walter of Châtillon had paid mock-homage to the power of money in his satirical verse: *"Nummus vincit, nummus regnat, nummus cunctis imperat* ("Money is the victor, money is king, money reigns supreme over all"). Ironically, in adaptation of Byzantine practice, various coins of the medieval period and beyond displayed the proper wording of this Latin inscription (from the *Laudes,* with "Christ" in place of "Money") on the reverse: examples include Norman coinage from southern Italy, and especially (from the reign of Louis IX on) French *écus d'or* and later the *deniers d'or de la reine* of Philip IV. The application of Scriptural legends to money served, in some regard, to reinterpret the spirituality of Christ in material terms. To be sure, the monarchs by whose authority the money was minted and whose names and coats of arms appeared on the obverse of the coins intended, in their use of liturgical mottos, to convey the message that they held their kingdoms in fief from God. Many German princes on the Western borders of the

Holy Roman Empire, who had close political and economic ties with France, most notably the rulers from the House of Luxembourg, took to minting coins in imitation of French money, including the legend. However, Robert II of Artois followed the example of the satirist Walter instead and had stamped on his coins the words of Matthew 22:32: *Ego sum Deus*, "I am the God."[34] A presumptuous inscription indeed!

As ever, what the satirists revealed here was a radical societal change. Money was not just important in trade and commerce; its huge significance for popes and emperors, for the church and the realm, and for ordinary citizens and scholars was plain to see. An expanding currency market evolved, not least because every pope, king, prince, merchant, and student relied on credit. A form of protocapitalism took root, especially in the cities. On the one hand, certain individuals reaped large profits, but in their train came a new poverty, a clear impoverishment of large sections of the urban working class. Yet the rural knightly class also felt the impact of this great change, which often had consequences that it was unable to control.

Lombards and Caursines (professional moneylenders from Lombardy and the southern French city of Cahors—not Jews at all, but exclusively Christians) performed the role of early "bankers"; presently competitors from Tuscany, particularly Florence, established the first major banking houses handling "international" transactions. The activities of lending and the charging of interest revitalized and intensified the old accusation that was first leveled in the Bible, and repeated in early Christendom and during the Carolingian period: namely that lending money for profit was condemned as usury. Here, goods weren't being bartered, nor was money being exchanged for goods, but rather money was simply generating more money. Clearly, the devil had his finger in this pie. Any usurer who engaged in this activity with the clear intention of making a profit was in danger of being damned. Profiteering and the torments of Hell were two sides of the same coin.[35] And yet, while "usury," that is the charging of interest, was clearly beyond the pale in religious and moral terms and proscribed under canon law, it was in actual fact permitted under various exceptional rulings and special dispensations and even officially tolerated by the secular legal authorities, for the simple reason that it had become indispensable in economic terms. The practice helped free up capital that benefited the public good and paved the way for social advances. It was certainly true that interest rates could sometimes be astronomical; they fluctuated according to demand and, according to circumstances, typically ranged from a "modest" 10 percent, through 43.3 percent and upward to 100 percent or even higher.

Progress, therefore, did not come cheaply, and preachers such as Berthold of Regensburg found plenty of ammunition with which to rail against the deadly sins of usury, parsimony, and avarice and threaten their congregations with punishment in Hell. Fear became the hallmark of the age, and a truly effective way of exploiting people's concern for the fate of their souls. Preachers, fully devoted to the spiritual life themselves, fanned the flames of this anxiety; the examples they used to terrify and admonish their listeners and persuade them to change their ways, only served to emphasize once again that it was first and foremost Christians who were oppressing and exploiting their co-religionists. Yet was it possible to increase one's material wealth and improve one's chances of salvation at the same time, to defy the assertion of the tax-collector/apostle Saint Matthew: "You cannot serve God and Mammon" (Matthew 6:24). The first theories of money, capital, and the economy were developed at this time—remarkably, by Franciscans, who as the confessors of wealthy men sought ways to alleviate the fear they felt for their eternal souls. In truth, where the Bible and canon law were concerned, any "usurer" would have been duty bound to repay any profit made from charging interest, that is, the wages of his "usury," if he wished to save his soul; but under certain conditions, all profit could be turned to salvation. To bring peace to people's souls, it was necessary to develop an ethics of money that saw it as fulfilling some higher purpose rather than simply being an end in itself; for in the final analysis, the pull of money was stronger than any fear factor. So it was that the business of charitable endowments flourished, while the granting of indulgences raised hopes that were later, likewise, to sink without trace in a morass of money and profit. Morality and sound economic husbandry were constantly having to find new ways of reaching an accommodation.

IO

The Light of Reason

CAN WE SPEAK of reason in the Middle Ages? Or even Enlightenment? Who would have thought such a thing at all credible following the banning of the early obsessive adherents of rationalism? And yet there is no gainsaying the fact! The era of Charlemagne heralded the dawning of a new age of reason; indeed, the king and emperor himself advocated it. Numeracy was also at a premium at this time, as an essential skill for creating the calendar. Hardly any other period was as steeped in reason as the Middle Ages, especially its supposedly "enlightened" tenth century. Young people flocked to attend school, where they imbibed learning and practiced logic. At that time, the West and its scholars were just beginning to absorb the *Logica vetus,* the first part of Aristotle's *Organon,* in the original translation by Boethius. Students also pored over the *Isagoge* of Porphyry (the Introduction to Aristotle's *Categories*), the short manuscript of the *Categories* themselves, and his work on language and logic *Peri hermeneias (On Interpretation),* which by this stage were widely known. Even schoolmasters grappled with these ideas. The theory of categories was a way of classifying language; it taught people how to define different parts of speech, to systematically distinguish terms thus defined from others, and to understand the distinctions. Words used in conjunction with other words formed the subject of Aristotle's pronouncements on the composition of sentences; here, he discussed the role of the noun, verb, negation, affirmation, expression, and speech in general. People strove to grasp such concepts, since the ability to think logically and speak coherently was an indispensable stepping-stone to a successful career. Henceforth, everything was subjected to the yardstick of categorical thinking, given over to an application of reason that was governed by verifiable rules, and channeled into a mode of expression that was attuned to such a mind-set and into a logical form of verbal delivery, which for centuries thereafter was deployed by the best of the intellectual leadership and imitated by the less gifted and by everyone who attended Latin schools. Many things have changed on this particular path down to the present day, yet always with direct or indirect reference to the appropriation of the work of Aristotle from the "Dark" Ages onward; indeed, the interpretations of modern philosophers still use him as a touchstone, if only to then refute his approach. Throughout the High Middle Ages and the early years of the Late Middle Ages, Aristotle's entire oeuvre became known to the West through successive waves of reception. How, then, did this come about?

Certainly, the stage on which these developments unfolded only freed itself with some difficulty from the shackles of the magical and symbolical worldview that delimited the intellectual horizon of Early Medieval contemporaries. Reason has had an uphill struggle to assert itself in all historical periods. Yet the medieval period found it difficult to disengage action from thought. For example, the reader of Thietmar's *Chronicle,* which this bishop of Merseburg wrote shortly after the turn of the first millennium A.D., is confronted with a world of apparitions, symbols, and rituals. Thietmar, the son of a Saxon count, was not wholly unfamiliar with Aristotelian dialectics, but was nevertheless still wedded to "prelogical" modes of thought; before his consecration as a bishop he saw himself in a dream, poring over the Bible and holding a pendulum, which he was using to try and divine his future destiny. He did not harbor the slightest doubt about the truth of his reverie. At best, the full import of dreams would only be made known retrospectively to the human intellect, but even prior to this they would not remain entirely opaque to the person who had experienced them. Thietmar documented in minute detail the divine "signs" given in the natural world: two-headed animals, human freaks, demonic hoaxes, catastrophes, three wolves coming together to form a pack . . . the bishop interpreted these events as omens, construing them as a "language" through which the transcendental realm, namely God himself, communicated with his creations, and in common with his contemporaries saw these portents of doom as the consequences of people's sinfulness and as God's warning to sinners. Thus, not only fasting, praying, litanies, atonement, and weeping or ritual observance were called for in order to ward off the impending calamity; rather, it was necessary that a person's entire life should be geared toward this. Thietmar's work gave no hint of any dilution of this mode of thinking, no trace of any corrosive, enlightened skepticism toward the revelatory semiotic character of such occurrences.

However, over time, a growing acquaintance with Aristotle's dialectics changed the way in which people related one thought to another, the order in which they posed questions, and the manner in which they weighed up each answer. This had unforeseen effects on every form of planning, and every action or lack of action. A mode of thought began to spread that was no longer beholden to magic and God. Secularization became widespread, developing in leaps and bounds. The entire worldview—the way in which life was organized; the interaction between the sexes; the economic means of production within the manorial system, as well as at the princely courts and in the cities; and technology—and not just the world of earning in a narrower sense—became subject to the logical–dialectical process. Cosmology, the idea of man, ethics, and law came under corresponding pressure to redefine their terms of reference. Sooner or later, the whole of society, together with all its norms and values, was caught up in this rational, formal mode of thought and was transformed fundamentally.

Not least, rationalism presented a challenge not just to Christianity but to every other religion as well. However, it was in its clash with the Christian faith that it became most strident. Because of the unreasonable demand placed on the intellect by the Word of the Lord and its revelation to man, many a believer thirsted for it to have the same strict rules of rational thought applied to it that had been formulated by Aristotle. The dialectical methods that were practiced ever more effectively and enduringly by each successive generation of scholars equipped their adepts with skills that not only caused them to balk at the magical world view, but that also set them in opposition to all forms of miraculous faith, and called them to question many of the doctrines of the church and its popes. In effect, they dragged the doctrines of the church in front of the tribunal of reason. In return, the premises of faith demanded from it that it unquestioningly acknowledge the unfathomable mystery of belief and that it renounce all doubt and demands for proof. Furthermore, they also bade doubting voices be silent, under pain of damnation, incarceration, or—the ultimate sanction—being burned at the stake. And indeed, initially, school teaching took an utterly benign and unthreatening form.

In the Carolingian period, parish schools only furnished pupils with the most rudimentary of educations; they were taught to recite the Lord's Prayer and the formulaic confessional responses, and to renounce and erroneous beliefs or devil worship, but they were by no means versed in the "liberal arts," which only began appear in isolated places during the Late Middle Ages. There was a clear need for a more comprehensive form of education, and for schools that would be both more effective and, above all, long-lasting. Charlemagne, his aides, and his successors entrusted this task to the only institutions within society that could meet such expectations: namely, the monasteries. This was in no way a foregone conclusion; the Benedictine Rule had not envisaged such a role. Several monasteries hesitated to take on this task. However, either at royal behest or command, monks were presently compelled to give themselves over to the business of education and to put into practice the reconstruction of a new knowledge-based society. This task of rebuilding must have been made all the more difficult and laborious by the fact that the intellectual level of the Latin West had sunk to an absolute nadir as a result of the almost total decline of the ancient cultural and educational institutions. Even so, the first significant schools, where the entire canon of the seven liberal Arts and of Aristotelian dialectics was actually taught, were located in monasteries or other ecclesiastical foundations. The Carolingian royal court also played its own part in this process; it, along with other royal and princely courts that succeeded it, as well as the papal curia, proved itself to be a center of learning in addition to being a center for the organization and dissemination of knowledge. The royal chapel of both the Carolingians and the Ottonians repeatedly attracted gifted young scions of the aristocracy; this institution epitomized, so to speak, scholarship at the court. From the tenth century onward, the monastic schools found themselves increasingly supplanted by the cathedral schools, while from the thirteenth century, these were joined by the universities, which were founded and supported by kings, popes, municipalities, or local lords. The first Latin schools in cities also came into being at this time.

Women's life chances also improved. Their education did not remain unaffected by the general expansion of the school system that was taking place. Canonesses and nuns took a similar stance toward the revival of ancient learning as monks. For instance, it was in nunneries that the comedies of the Roman author Plautus were first transcribed. These learned women by no means confined themselves to the mystical speculation for which certain female authors of the twelfth and thirteenth centuries, such as Hildegard von Bingen and Mechthild von Magdeburg, became famous. The poet Roswitha von Gandersheim, who was active in the tenth century, was conversant with the most modern dialectics of the period; while the future bishop and chronicler Theitmar of Merseburh was schooled by his aunt, who was abbess of Quedlinburg Abbey in Saxony-Anhalt, a religious community where the daughters of the higher nobility were educated. Nor were middle-class girls expected to restrict their education to mere embroidery skills; the thirteenth century saw the establishment in several cities of public schools specifically dedicated to their education. And in Dante's *Convivio,* a work he wrote in the early fourteenth century to instruct lay readers about certain key question of philosophy, the author depicted a banquet at which women participated alongside princes and noblemen (I, 9, 5), for "all people naturally strive after knowledge" (I, 1, 1).

The examples of various remarkable teachers emphasize the major achievements of these monastery and cathedral schools. Even before the turn of the millennium, Notker of St. Gall had translated Aristotle's *Categories* into Old High German, in order to make this subject matter more accessible to his southern German pupils and so introduce it to a linguistic environment that had struggled to understand Boethius's Latin translation of this work. His contemporary Abbo of Fleury, meanwhile, acted as an advisor to the first kings from the House of Capet, and Wolfgang of Regensburg seems to have introduced new methods of teaching gifted students. Fulbert of Chartres won widespread acclaim for his scholarship; his reputation extended as far as Bavaria. It was said that anyone who listened him preach believed that they were hearing an angel singing. Mathematics first appeared on the educational landscape of the West in the final years of the tenth century thanks to the efforts of Gerbert of Aurillac (d. 1003); in any event, it was from that period onward that the abacus started to supplant the hitherto dominant method of counting on the fingers. The early eleventh century witnessed a fierce debate between masters from Liège and Cologne on the problem of squaring the circle. Hermann the Lame of Reichenau devised a complicated game based on Pythagorean number theory, which helped convey the principles of arithmetical ratios. Euclid's *Elements,* along with various other mathematical texts from the Arabic, first became known to the Latin academic world through translations in the late twelfth century.

Among the most skilled dialecticians of the period were Otloh of St. Emmeram and Manegold of Lautenbach, the latter of whom introduced the dialectical method to the circles advocating church reform. The outstanding figure of the mid-eleventh century was Lanfranc of Bec, a Lombard who established a widely renowned school in the Norman Benedictine abbey where he settled, which drew pupils from far and wide. Among them was the future Saint Anselm, who in time became Lanfranc's successor as head teacher and abbot of Bec, and thereafter was appointed archbishop of Canterbury.

The instruction offered by these outstanding scholars illustrated just how far dialectics had come within just a century; however, just like modern-day intellectuals, they were by no means in agreement with one another on all matters. Reason and learning generated a whole new set of disputes, which, as would soon become apparent, were inevitable. The first clash over the Lord's Supper erupted in the eleventh century, and was sparked by Aristotelian dialectics. It centered on the precise nature of the host—was it bread, or what? Nothing seemed to be self-evident any longer. Even the existence of God, it appeared, now required proofs, and although these were forthcoming at the time and were much admired, they were promptly refuted nevertheless. For advancing proofs only served to emphasize the primacy of reason over faith and every kind of authority. A certain Master Roscelin of Compiègne used remarks in Porphyry's *Isagoge* as a springboard from which to call the "reality" of universals into doubt; they were, he claimed, nothing more than "breath from the mouth." Unfortunately, we do not know any more about Roscelin's doctrines or the early phases of what later became known as the "universals dispute"; certainly, Anselm of Bec (Canterbury) took an opposing view to his.

Without more ado, this celebrated logician objected: "Reason must be the governor and judge of everything that resides within Man."[1] Yet how was this to be initiated? Anselm's answer was simple: faith should seek out reason. Indeed, Anselm's proof of the existence of God, which he evolved in the form of a prayer, was based on the premise of belief. As the most perfect and complete of beings, God necessarily had a real, and not just a notional, existence, precisely because nothing greater than Him can ever be conceived; hence, his existence was proved. This was an *a priori* ontological argument. Parodies of this position were not long in coming. The

Benedictine monk Gaunilo of Marmoutiers, of whom nothing else is known, accused the archbishop of false reasoning. The mere conception of the most complete being did not, he claimed, prove its real (and not just conceptual) existence.[2] The intellectual elites of Europe would henceforth prove their mettle, assert their legitimacy, and simply amuse themselves through the dialectical game of evidence and counter-evidence.

For this game required a skilled deployment of reason; time and again later logicians—such as Thomas Aquinas, Descartes, Kant, or Gottlob Frege—would come to address the fundamental question posed by Anselm. Their arguments became ever more sophisticated, as the triumphant march of rationality continued. Nothing remained untouched by it. Eagerly, thinkers seized upon every topic that seemed susceptible to the application of reason. And so, in the final years of the eleventh century, the discipline of astronomy/astrology, which had long been discriminated against, was finally taken up by Western intellectuals, in the context of a rational view of the world that was indebted to Arab science. This subject, which awakened people's hopes that they might gain sure insights into the future, found its way into the Western academic curriculum in concert with Greek–Arabic medicine. Astronomy taught people how to use the astrolabe and how to determine the position of the stars; the first evidence for the use of this instrument in the Latin West dates from 1092, when it was employed to determine the precise timing of a lunar eclipse. Subsequently, Walcher of Malvern produced a table of all lunar and solar eclipses from 1032 to 1112 inclusive.[3] Ptolemy's *Almagest,* the most extensive work of astronomy to have come down from antiquity, was available in Latin translation from around 1160. Horoscopes and prognostication went hand in hand with growing astronomical knowledge and with an increasing ability to make precise observations of the heavens; these became the most sought-after areas of activity for physicians and court astrologers.

This intensive engagement with Aristotle's theories of categories and predication had achieved the miraculous feat of prompting scholars to delve even deeper into dialectical reasoning, and to a growing, confident use of this facility—indeed, it brought about nothing short of the dawning of the Age of Reason. A new curiosity and understanding was awakened for all aspects of academic study and, moreover, for everything that could conceivably be viewed in an academic way. The upshot was a hitherto undreamt-of intensification of scholarly activity, in conjunction with a singular acceleration and concentration of its investigation; and in all this the application of reason taught people to see the world in a quite different light. Initially, faith was the beneficiary of this development; only later, in the twelfth and thirteenth centuries did the two realms diverge, when reason began to emancipate itself from belief and lay claim to an autonomous existence, and looked for "natural" explanations—that is, explanations that accorded with the dictates of "natural reason"—for the phenomena of nature. Thus, the rationalism practiced in schools by no means restricted itself to theoretical knowledge. Rather, as a consequence of this learning process, it began to govern the perception of all realms with which humans came into contact, became an integral part of political, social, and technological practice, and over time came to fundamentally alter every aspect of life.

In addition, from the early twelfth century onward, scholars began to study the second part of the *Organon,* namely the *Logica nova,* the collective name for the Latin version of the *Prior Analytics,* the *Topics* and *Sophistical Refutations,* which dealt respectively with causal (syllogistic) thinking; irrefutable arguments; and hypothetical arguments that avoid logical fallacies. Aristotle thereby bequeathed four logical axioms to the Middle Ages: the law of identity, the law of contradiction, the law of excluded middle, and the law of sufficient ground [*richtig, oder ist* "sufficient reason" *die herkömmliche Übersetzung?*]. The ramifications were immeasurable; it is only in contemporary logic that these principles begin to falter. But there were also some dangerous consequences for the Middle Ages: the position of Jesus Christ as God's only son; the virginity of the Blessed Virgin Mary; the doctrines of the Creation, the Trinity, Salvation, and Predestination; and the bishop of Rome's role as the Vicar of Christ—sooner or later, all these fundamental tenets of Christianity had to be defended against the onslaughts of reason. Doubt gripped faith communities. Henceforth, a growing culture of rationality nurtured the Late Middle Ages—analogous to the groundwater from which plants draw their sustenance. This change did not take place overnight, but rather unfolded over the course of several centuries. Its principal stages can be summarized here.

Despite the high achievements of certain monastic schools, in the long run the cathedral schools, which were intended for the education of the lay clergy, outstripped them. In particular, those in the Île de France, such as Chartres, Reims, Laon, and Paris came to prominence in the first half of the twelfth century. It was here that the discipline of dialectics was taught, and made receptive to further intellectual inquiry. Alongside the Seven Liberal Arts, a new "natural philosophy" began to evolve at these schools through the efforts of some outstanding teachers. Pliny the Elder's *Natural History* found an ever increasing readership, as did Plato's *Timaeus,* which had been partially translated and annotated by Calcidus (fourth–fifth century). His manuscripts were disseminated in ever greater numbers from the tenth century onward. The six days of Creation in the Bible were now interpreted with his assistance. Another key text was Macrobius's commentary on the *Somnium Scipionis* (Dream of Scipio) from Cicero's *De re publica,* a portrayal of a universe that likewise exhibited Platonic features (being modeled on The Myth of Er from Plato's *Republic*). Saint Augustine had already indicated that Plato and the *Timaeus* were in accord with the biblical account of the creation of the world; Boethius appeared to agree.[4] Yet people now began to read them again with renewed interest and with a method learned from Aristotle.

Natural philosophers of the twelfth century such as William of Conches attempted to explain creation logically according to "natural" principles. Accordingly, they tried to harmonize the *Timaeus* with the Book of Genesis. Nature was now regarded, pure and simple, as an tool used by God to bring his Creation into being and to maintain its existence. This position is very much akin to Immanuel Kant's later postulate of a single Highest Intelligence at the very inception of creation: "There is a God for just this reason, that nature, even in a chaotic state, can develop only in an orderly and rule-governed manner."[5] The cathedral at Chartres was built in the early to mid-thirteenth century in the spirit of this new learning, with theoretical knowledge being given tangible and visible form in the stone carvings decorating its doorways. Moreover, the Middle Ages also had a clear conception of the spherical form of the Earth; Macrobius, for example, had transmitted this fact. It did not take long thereafter for audacious scholars like Albertus Magnus to declare, in conscious opposition to Augustine, that the Southern Hemisphere was habitable;[6] though admittedly, it was for advancing precisely such a theory that the encyclopedist Cecco d'Ascoli was burned at the stake in Florence in 1327. It was only the superficial understanding of some in the Enlightenment period who mistakenly claimed that all preceding ages had conceived of the Earth as a flat disk. These Enlightenment figures only made this claim in order to legitimize themselves and their worldview; in actual fact, only a few ancient Romans had ever mentioned the possibility of a flat Earth.

All of this did not fundamentally distinguish the West from the schol-arship of the Christian East, where there were also high-achieving schools and teachers there. And yet, despite their outstanding intellectual achieve-ments and the enormous advantage they enjoyed in the availability of knowledge, neither Byzantium nor the Arab world succeeded in produc-ing the kind of scholasticism and the attendant culture of learning that characterized the evolution of the West. In the East, the legacy of antiq-uity was handled quite differently; over time, its intensity and even more importantly its variety faded over time. An impulse toward innovation was lacking, such as that experienced by the West with the rebirth of an-cient learning and its enhancement through transmission by Arab schol-arship. Nor was Islam even responsible for giving such an impetus to the Arab-speaking world, inasmuch as the first Muslim caliphs seamlessly adopted the scholarship of Late Antiquity as practiced by Greek and Syr-ian Christians. Yet a tradition of learning only goes hand in hand with a continuing active generation of learning.

In the West, over time the ever more diversified and ever more special-ized individual disciplines within the arts, along with the development of new branches of learning, called for a decisive concentration of resources on a few elite schools. These attracted thousands of students from across the whole of Europe. Paris was a particular focal point; the sheer numbers of scholars who flocked to the city were a major reason why the University of Paris was founded there in the vicinity of the royal residence. This insti-tution arose from the cathedral school, and soon found itself in competi-tion with the city's monastic and other religious institutional schools, as well as the school of Saint-Victor-hors-les-Murs and those established un-der the aegis of the abbey of Saint-Genevieve on the left bank of the Seine, the future Quartier Latin. The origin of the university was as a collective of masters who taught at the cathedral school with the permission of the canon chancellor. It was soon joined by other schools with particular academic specialties, such as Montpellier, popular for medicine and ju-risprudence, or Orléans (which tried with some success to rival Paris), or Toulouse, which came into being with the express aim of spreading or-thodox Catholic theology in an area formerly dominated by the Cathars.

These "High Schools," or universities, became the home of scholasti-cism, and of academic disciplines cultivated within the "school" *(schola)*. In scholasticism, Aristotelian dialectics was brought face to face with the doctrines of the church fathers. Immediately, contradictions were laid bare, which demanded a new methodology. In scholastic debates, even the doctrines of Saint Augustine of Hippo (who was not identified as such) were played off against those of the later Saint Augustine of Canterbury (again anonymous). Peter Abélard became a past master of such disputations. His "Sic-et-non" ("Yes-and-no") method taught scholars how to explain or harmonize such contradictions. Scholasticism's impact can scarcely be overstated. A reading of the Christian fathers prompted a clamor for the imposition of reason, which was at once made it necessary to arbitrate over the clear differences in their ideas. Abélard even sought to explain the Trinity in rational terms—an approach that stirred his traditionalist adversaries into action and led to his condemnation. Nevertheless, the onward march of reason could not be halted; the consequences were far-reaching. Now, in the twelfth and thirteenth centuries, theology came into its own as a discipline in its own right. Around the mid-twelfth century, Peter Lombard wrote the *Sentences*—a theological handbook that was adopted by scholasticism as its key text. Over the ensuing centuries, Lombard's work would be commentated upon time and again by every candidate seeking to earn his degree as a doctor of theology. Yet rationalism was not content to remain confined within the discipline of theology; instead, it concurrently created for itself a new and independent field of activity, in the form of the academic subject of philosophy.

Furthermore, Aristotle and Boethius were not the only ancient authors to stimulate the medieval mind. The discovery in the late eleventh century of one of the extremely rare manuscripts of Justinian's *Digests* was to prove just as momentous. The identity of the person who found this text is as uncertain as the location in which it had survived the half-millennium since the era of Justinian—it has been speculated that it was in Tuscany, Emilia-Romagna, or some other site within the domain of Matilda of Tuscany. Whatever the case may be, study of these texts gave rise to a new, highly specialized discipline that drew heavily on Aristotelian dialectics and soon established its main center in Bologna, so turning this city, too, into a magnet for students from throughout Europe. They flocked there and formed a cohesive group, despite the fact that, except for in Romagna and certain regions in southern France (referred to nowadays as the *pays du droit écrit,* "land of written law"), Roman Law was by no means universally in force. The university thus arose in Bologna, quite independently of Paris and was organized along very different lines as a cooperative of students. The legists of Bologna taught a method with which over time not only Roman Law and canon law fell into line with but which (with the sole exception of the common law system in England) came to characterize all academic dealings with the law. And so the rebirth of jurisprudence mirrored in an exemplary fashion the achievements of the new culture of learning that had evolved in the West. Nor, in its study and dissection of the ancient legal texts, did it simply take recourse to old authors such as Ulpian, Paulus, or Gaius; in any case, their original works had for the most part been lost and were only extant in fragmentary form in Justinian's *Digests*. Rather, the legal scholars of Bologna really did fashion something new, insofar as their technique of allegation, definition, glossing, and exegesis began to permeate the practice of all civil and criminal law and created a public form of law hitherto unknown.

This new academic discipline of law was not the invention of a single scholar. Instead it was evolved by generation after generation of legal teachers, *legum doctores,* beginning with the so-called Four Doctors who taught at Bologna in the early twelfth century, followed by Azo, Accursius, and Odofred during the course of the thirteenth, to name just a few of the great academic luminaries of the university. As Azo wrote in the introduction to his *Summa Codicis* (1208–1210; no self-respecting lawyer of the period would have dared to appear in court without having read this text): "As the invention of learning was later augmented by an abundance of divine grace, and since this endowed the human intellect with further blessings of nature, we should not be surprised that the human condition *(humana conditio)* seeks improvement through continuing exercise of the intellect. . . . Later commentators light upon specific details. . . . King Solomon, for example, teaches that everything is caught in a cycle of renewal and decline, and that human flesh and blood also is born and dies. Thus, there is a constant succession of new people, and scholarship flourishes because the early teachers of the arts and sciences at least made a start, for which reason they are certainly to be commended but by no means to be preferred over later scholars. For he who subtly improves upon a piece of work is worthy of greater praise than the person who devised it in the first place."[7] The young professor alluded to here as deserving praise over and above his predecessors is, of course, Azo himself. His claim prefigures a similar one made by Max Weber, namely that later scholarship is always superior to earlier.

The juristic method emerging from Bologna changed Europe. It prepared the ground for a comprehensive theory of society, which was initially adopted by the northern Italian municipalities and Holy Roman emperors in the thirteenth century before finding general acceptance in the knowledge-based society of Europe. Because it involved a theory of law, it was also able to embrace the whole structure of power, the church, and society. Feudal law, common law, and the new legal formulations of the municipalities, provinces, and kingdoms found themselves under the sway of this theory every bit as much as emperors, kings, and popes. Henceforth, theoretical learning and practice were inseparable. James I of Aragón summed it up succinctly and appositely when he stated that jurists were absolutely indispensable for his regime. And, indeed, it was at royal and papal courts that the new knowledge-based society first took root.

Innovations in the academic world did not begin and end with legal scholarship, either. In quick succession, they soon came to affect every corner of Europe. From the early 1170s on, Aristotle's *Physics* was introduced to the West via the courts of Frederick Barbarossa and William of Sicily. Once again, this process highlights the role of the princely courts as sites for the transmission and dissemination of knowledge. The new natural philosophy had as its subject phenomena that exist naturally—such as rocks, plants, and animals—and are not created by man, like tools or works of art; such a realm of investigation obeyed the principles of motion and repose. Studying nature thus meant comprehending the origins of movement, which were four in number in Aristotle's analysis of causation: the *causa materialis,* the *causa formalis,* the *causa efficiens,* and the *causa finalis*; in other words, material cause, formal cause, efficient cause, and final cause. All these could of necessity be traced back to a primary "unmoved mover," which had set everything else in motion; to Christian interpreters, this principle may well have been synonymous with God. Nonetheless, Aristotelian physics taught people to conceive of the world as a series of natural causes, as indeed the natural philosophers of the twelfth century were attempting to do, and in so doing prompted a radical shift in thinking, which over time entailed a move away from the notion of God creating the world in six days. In addition to establishing the theory of the four elements, and as a way of explaining the world of natural phenomena, the *Physics* also introduced the theory of the four sensible qualities—namely, hot, dry, cold, and wet, which appeared in four possible combinations when related to the elements: hot-dry; dry-cold, wet-hot, and cold-wet. This all provided plenty of material, when taken in conjunction with the long-familiar causality principle of the Greek philosopher, for a thoroughgoing reappraisal of the world. The introduction of the *Physics* in the universities, especially in Paris, was (as already noted) accompanied by a wave of scholarly heresy, as demonstrated by the trial of David of Dinant. His famous proclamation that "The World is God" could well have related directly to Aristotle's theory of causality.

Accordingly, faith and the natural sciences began to diverge from one another. As the German Dominican Albertus Magnus admonished his listeners: "In studying Nature, it is not our place to enquire how God the Maker according to His free will uses his creations to work miracles and thereby proclaim His omnipotence, but rather what Nature with its immanent causes may naturally bring to pass." On another occasion, he stated: "If anyone maintains that God's will could on one occasion disrupt the normal course procreation in a manner that has never happened before and then simply make it resume its normal course thereafter, then I would respond that God's miracles do not interest me when I am studying Nature."[8] This latter remark was highly controversial, given that it referred to the sexual act and because every one of his listeners would have known the article of faith concerning the Virgin Birth of Jesus to which it alluded. And so it became necessary for scholasticism to formulate the Catholic doctrine—still in force nowadays—that miracles are events that occur *contra naturam,* which lie outside the ambit of the laws of nature and happen in direct contravention of them.

As if to compensate for this welter of dangerous natural science, a desire grew for pastoral guidance—a factor that the Fourth Lateran Council had already provided for. The sermon was intended to admonish and correct the faithful, and through its terrifying message of the torments of Hell and the Day of Judgment strengthen people's faith. Religious seminaries in every diocese were established to teach the art of sermonizing. Confessions were to be heard at regular intervals. It was around this time that the doctrine of purgatory took root—a special place in the Beyond in which souls that were sorely in need of purification might be cleansed of the sins that prevented their immediate entry into Paradise. This idea brought together traditional notions, dating from pre-Christian and Early Christian times, of a weighing-up of souls, a cleansing fire, and the agonies of Hell. Such ideas raised and stoked up people's fears, but at the same time offered a ray of hope to sinners, especially if they were aided in their repentance in the Here and Now by the living by means of religious foundations, intercessions, and charitable works. Numerous sermons that preached fire and brimstone attested to the efficacy of such an approach. In this way, even deadly sins like usury could be lessened, yet without such a cleansing process people were threatened with damnation.

Piety in the Late Middle Ages, a highly inventive phenomenon, fed on this fear. This was not restricted to preachers, but also found expression through lurid depictions in all forms of visual media, be it murals, panel paintings, or images in prayer books, all designed to terrify the faithful. Here, condemned souls were shown suffering the worst torments imaginable, meted out by infernally grinning demons and devils. Fear was also whipped up among the intellectual elites, who found themselves as alarmed as other believers, despite the fact—or perhaps precisely because—they were occasionally assailed by doubt. When confronted with the mouth of Hell, the learned poet Dante Alighieri captured his sense of terror and despair in resonant verse: "Abandon all hope, ye who enter here" *(Lasciare ogni speranza, voi ch'entrate)*. These are the words that Dante imagined inscribed above the Gates of Hell.[9] He went on: "Here sighs and lamentations and loud wailings resounded through the starless air. . . . Many tongues, a terrible crying, words of sadness, bellowings of anger, voices shrill and hoarse" *(Quivi sospiri, pianti ed alti guai / Risonavan per l'aer senza stele. . . . Diverse lingue, orribili favelle, / Parole di dolore, accenti d'ira, / Voci alte e fioche)*. It was reason that, grappling with the traditional premises of faith, produced and fomented such fears.

The floodgates of knowledge were now open, never to be closed again. Around 1200 or soon after, the complete works of Aristotle were introduced to the West in a Latin version; ancient Greek was still largely unknown here at this stage. By now, Aristotle was regarded as "the philosopher" plain and simple. It was the task of High Scholasticism to study and interpret his theories. Alongside the *Organon* and the *Physics* were now added his writings on the natural sciences, psychology, and political theory. The new perspectives these offered had profound implications for the general worldview of the West, as well as its political order, and its attitude toward faith and learning. Moreover, they demanded a complete rethinking and overturning of all traditional values and ideas. No ban placed on the works of Aristotle could halt this inexorable process.

In particular, the work *De Anima* (On the Soul)—which was translated in around 1200—broke with convention by placing psychological questions in a wholly new light (up until then Augustine of Hippo's views had held sway), so triggering a debate that has lasted up to the present day.[10]

Yet from the late twelfth century onward, transmitted by scholars such as Dominicus Gundissalinus, Aristotelian psychology—with which Avicenna and Averroës had long since engaged—started to permeate through to the Latin West via Spain. Soon, the corresponding works by these Arab commentators also began to be studied at the universities. Aristotle had discussed the nature of the soul, arguing that it was immaterial and hence not a corporeal quality, yet was still definitely related to a person's body; his conclusion was that the soul had its own substance and, as the fundamental principle that gave form and life to the body, that it lay at the root of all human sensory perception, willed action, thought, and cognition. At the same time, *De Anima* touched upon the physiology of the senses, and the question of how the receptor organs for our five senses (this was the first time they were enumerated) serve a person's psyche; the faculty of reason was not assigned its own organ. Aristotle also ascribed a vegetative soul to plants and a sentient soul to animals; ultimately, the "ladder of nature" rose to the rational soul of human beings. Man's path to recognition of his own rational nature and learning passed through the stages of perception, recollection, imagination, and opinion. This was all eagerly seized upon by the teachers of scholasticism.

The other writings of Aristotle on the natural sciences, metaphysics, and ethics had a comparable effect on the Latin West. There is insufficient space here to go into each of these areas individually. One of the most famous texts, the *Nicomachean Ethics,* a psychologically based lesson in how to attain the greatest good and happiness, was translated and interpreted by Robert Grosseteste. This work placed at the very center of education the contemplative life, one guided by wisdom, devoted to learning and art, and characterized by its pursuit of the "golden mean," which charts a middle course between the extremes. Justice, too, was defined quite differently here than in Saint Augustine's work, namely as a virtue that creates a "mean" between two extremes of unfairness, in contrast to injustice, which drives people into those extremes. In general, the study of Aristotle can be said to have widened the gulf between the new learning and traditional, Augustine-led convictions and doctrines. These fundamental differences led to endless disputes both between theologians and natural philosophers, and even among themselves on occasion; despite the best efforts of scholars such as Thomas Aquinas to reconcile these positions, it ultimately proved impossible to reach any agreement. Intellectuals would henceforth argue endlessly about spirit and body, the suprapersonal and personal intellect and free will, and the immortality of the soul—to name just a few of the major controversies. And yet, in defiance of all previous proscriptions, the statutes of the Paris Faculty of Arts, drawn up in 1255, enjoined its students to interpret the writings of Aristotle. The thirteenth century was characterized by dissent and diversity. Only one factor would find itself indisputably strengthened by these wranglings—the appeal to reason.

However, according to Albertus Magnus, human reason was particularly prone to error and guaranteed no great certainty; it was only divine reason that was impervious to deception and that imparted its truths through inspiration.[11] Accordingly, Albertus advocated that people should observe Nature continuously, under the most diverse conditions, if they wanted to reach reliable conclusions. Emperor Frederick II, an exceptionally gifted ornithologist and student of animal behavior, followed this rule and contradicted Aristotle at several points in his *Art of Hunting with Birds (De arte venandi cum avibus)*. Yet Albertus contended that even this great authority on the natural world could sometimes be wrong—as indeed he could himself. The future lay wide open to this kind of "empiricism" (or "scientific method"), which took root especially in England. To be sure, Albertus's fellow Dominican Thomas Aquinas did attempt to reconcile and somehow harmonize theology and philosophy, faith and science, and Augustine and Aristotle. But even he was doomed to fail.

The last work of Aristotle to reach the lecterns of the academics was the *Politics*. By 1264, this text was available in the (admittedly somewhat clumsy) translation by William of Moerbecke and, with the ground prepared by both a pseudo-Aristotelian work known as the *Liber de causis* and by a new "Paris Mirror of Princes Compendium"[12] compiled especially for the French royal court, it was well received. Study of this work opened people's eyes to the way in which society, the ruling powers, and political activity were all interrelated, and taught them to see this order of things as a work of man, which was perfectly capable of coming into conflict with God's hierarchical world order. In addition, the *Politics* presented people with a completely unfamiliar image of humanity, which no longer placed the sinner, the person led astray, and the transgressor against divine commandments at the center of things, but chose instead to focus on man as a "communal animal" or a "political entity," the *animal sociale* or *ens politicum* (the two ways in which Aristotle's original term "zôon politikón" was rendered). Such a person "naturally" hankered after social and political order. Questions of "laws" and "statutes," in other words of justice, which had already been broached by the revival of jurisprudence, as well as the meaning of "equitable" distribution of goods, could now be reviewed in a far broader context, on an anthropological plane, so to speak. A whole new style of thinking began to evolve; in particular, a "political" mind-set became widespread, and a new group of specialists came into being: the *politici,* or "political scientists."

Once again, then, the ethics of rulership came under scrutiny. "Mirror of Princes" literature boomed, finding the kind of resonance that it had not enjoyed since the ninth century. In the ensuing years, works of this genre were written by Thomas Aquinas (or his pupil Tholomaeus of Lucca), Aegidius Romanus, Jean Quidort and others. However, these were not exclusively concerned with the question of morality. For "politics" at this period also embraced "economics," namely the doctrine of the house, household, and household finances. This did not confine itself to theory, but rather had far more practical matters in mind. In line with this, the "mirrors for princes" began to engage with practical aspects of ruling. Over time, extensive works on the economics of rulership started to appear, such as the *Oeconomica* (1353–1363) by Konrad of Megenburg, a cynic and an opponent of the philosophy of William of Ockham. Works such as this developed a feeling for the interconnections between academe, commerce, and politics. Why people necessarily have to live within societies, why it is better for them to be ruled by monarchs rather than democratically, and the insight that the prime social consideration is the maintenance of the common good—all these and related questions now became the focal points of the education of rulers and the related literature.[13] "For example . . . he [that is, the ruler] will have to determine which place is suitable for establishing cities, and which is best for villages and hamlets, where to locate the places of learning, the military training camps, and the markets for merchants." The ultimate aim of the community, too, was a life of virtue. Naturally, peace and justice were indispensable prerequisites of this.

In many cases, the new texts came from the Arab-speaking world. As a result, it is hardly surprising that, at the same time when the works of Aristotle reached the West, those of his Arab commentators should also have become known there. From the twelfth century, the philosophical, psychological, and scientific writings of Avicenna (Ibn Sina, d. 1037), a polymath from Bukhara, gradually spread throughout Western Europe via Spain; Michael Scotus, Thomas Aquinas, and John Duns Scotus all studied and commented on them. Even more significant were the works of Averroës (Ibn Rushd; d. 1198). The influence of this scholar can scarcely be overestimated; following the translation of his writings in around 1230, he quickly became known in the Latin West as "the commentator," or simply as "the philosopher." But the same strict application of logic that won him renown there also excited the animosity of several Muslim scholars; banished from his home town of Córdoba, he died in exile in Marrakech. He gained widespread notoriety for reputedly having said, "None of the religions are true, even if they are useful."[14] What is indisputable is that scholarship began to liberate itself from their shackles. The rift between reason and faith grew even deeper, and became irreparable.

Astrology finally established itself as an academic subject at this time, and also gained acceptance at the leading courts of Europe. It was based on the best and most reliable sources that both Greek and Arab scholarship had to offer. By the beginning of the thirteenth century, the astronomy of Ptolemy was well established in European seats of higher learning. This is abundantly clear from the treatise *De Spera*, an unassuming yet handy compendium that combined insights from Aristotle as well as from Arabic astronomy and remained in use up to the sixteenth century. It posited the generally held belief that the cosmos was spherical in shape and turned around a center formed by the Earth: the lowest sphere was the lunar, followed by those of Mercury and Venus, and then those of the Sun, and the outer planets of Mars, Jupiter, and Saturn, and above them the eighth stellar sphere containing the fixed stars (firmament), and higher still the "fiery heaven" or Empirium *(Caelum emphyreum)*, the seat of the angels and superhuman intelligences. Admittedly, certain authors envisaged the inner planets, namely Mercury and Venus, as orbiting around the Sun. Moreover, the dangers that astrology posed for faith became ever more clearly apparent. For it questioned not only the doctrine of creation but also that of predestination, and called man's free will into doubt. Was it the stars and planets rather than God that determined the course of the world? And did the stars hold sway over a person's will? Such a view could not be allowed to prevail; strict proscriptions were required to prevent it.

Even so, under the influence of astrology the first signs of materialism became apparent from the thirteenth century onward. However, in the midst of other academic disciplines, all geared toward theoretical knowledge, astrology remained firmly rooted in the practical sphere. Indeed, in the High and Late Middle Ages, there is scarcely another realm of learning that promoted the study of nature so assiduously as astronomy or astrology. It had long since allied itself with eschatology, which had consistently and for many decades called for the "signs" of nature and time to be studied; at the same time, this alliance lent eschatology a positively scientific precision. Their convergence was a significant contribution to the reliability of fundamental research. What astrology had to offer in terms of theoretical insights on cosmology, astral constellations, calculating the elevation of the pole, planetary orbits, mathematics, radiation theory, and subsequently also spherical trigonometry and the like, needed to be constantly measured against practice. Every false judgment—inaccurate horoscopes or prognostications about the weather or illness, or warnings of epidemics—only emphasized the need for methods to be improved. Reason could not stand still. The doubts that were being both raised and allayed by scholars everywhere—be it in schools or lecture theaters—embedded themselves ever deeper within society. The firmament above them acted as a permanent spur to further questioning.

The influence of the stars on the world and human existence, and the deciphering of what they revealed about the future of individuals, the Earth, and the cosmos, not only called for precise astronomical knowledge but also great mathematical aptitude, in order to work out the course of the sun and the planetary constellations. In addition, scholars in this field were increasingly required to have the capacity to discriminate between contingent earthly causes and cosmic causes of actual events. Without a doubt, Aristotelian natural philosophy was a helpful aid in this process; however, before long, it proved insufficient. Although it provided the indispensable theoretical foundation for the interpretation of phenomena and a basis for practice, at the same time it found itself subjected to growing criticism—criticism that increased as gradually, step by step, and almost imperceptibly, the astronomical mathematicians of the Late Middle Ages distanced themselves from ancient conceptions of the world.

Outstanding scholars of the age, such as Albertus Magnus, or Roger Bacon in the thirteenth century, or Regiomontanus (d. 1476) or Copernicus (d. 1543) in the fifteenth century, had no doubts about the effects of the planetary constellations on the sublunary world; at most, they saw them as limited. Albertus, for example, attributed to their influence every occurrence "which has taken place within mutable material, or is connected in some way to the material world," but demanded a quite independent status for chance, human free will, and planning *(consilium)*.[15] Prognosti-cation became widespread above all among physicians; Copernicus, for instance, was one such. But even before him, one Johannes Müller of Königsberg, who was commonly known as Regiomontanus, had set the study of the heavens on a new path. When he was still a boy, this genius had produced horoscopes, while a few years later he developed the disci-pline of trigonometry, improved the "Alfonsine tables," discovered the 10-degree magnetic declination of compass needles, translated and anno-tated Ptolemy's *Almagest* (in collaboration with the Greek papal legate Basilios Bessarion; it was published in 1496, thus creating an authoritative handbook that was still being consulted by Copernicus and Galileo), and finally reflected upon the heliocentric nature of the cosmos. This "impulse toward mathematicizing" fundamentally changed both eschatology and astronomy and at the same time generated new questions. How might the results of this development square with the view officially sanctioned by church authorities that the world would only exist for 6,000 years? An-swers to this were by no means clear at the outset. A new mode of calcula-tion and interpretation ensued, which sometimes concluded that the Apocalypse was alarmingly close at hand, while at other times suggesting that it was reassuringly far off. It also gave rise to a welter of questions, which called for an ever closer observation of the heavens and its physical aspects, as well as of earthly events, and in so doing subtly incorporated them into a mechanistic view of the world.

This all took place within an environment that was growing increas-ingly complex and thereby subject to ever more insistent demands for the application of rationality. Farming, trade, commerce, municipal adminis-trations, kings and the upper echelons of the clergy now found the new learning indispensable. "Economics," literally "household matters," was invented. "Such learning," Albertus Magnus once remarked with regard to plant cultivation and agriculture, "is not only pleasurable for he who studies Nature, but it is also no less useful for the life and survival of the cities."[16] In the long term, if those active in commercial life did not want to sacrifice their overview of the sector, they could not get by without lit-eracy at least, and often found they required rudimentary knowledge of Latin, too. The denser the population and the more labor-intensive com-merce became, so too the points of contention grew more frequent and more complicated. In accord with this, lawyers and notaries were increas-ingly in demand; jurisprudence and all other aspects of the law became more detailed and intricate, and their practitioners found their specialized knowledge at a premium for the organization of daily life, just as it had formerly been for the ruling elite.

In this development too, the Italian municipalities led the way, but Europe north of the Alps could not resist this trend either. The first public Latin schools were founded in the cities specifically at the urging of their citizens and merchants. The urban classes had a great need of mathematics. Zero as a "number," indeed the so-called Arabic numerals in general, including minus numbers, were introduced to Europe from India via the Arab world, and soon became widespread among merchants and town-dwellers. Leonardo Fibonacci of Pisa, the discoverer of the Fibonacci series, used Indian (Arabic) numbers and wrote what was in Western terms an innovative and influential primer at the behest of the mercantile community of Venice. There, because people lived through financial transactions and extending credit, it was imperative that they master the business of calculating interest. Maybe this was not a difficult exercise, but it was an unfamiliar one nevertheless. "A person takes out a mortgage of 100 pounds at an interest rate of 4 pence per pound and per month on a house that earns 30 pounds annually in rent. At the beginning of every year he is meant to use this 30 pounds to pay off the capital debt of 100 pounds inclusive of interest. How many years, months, days, and hours must he own the house before he can earn fourpence per pound per month?"[17] Gradually, double-entry bookkeeping gained a foothold in the trading houses, and a new form of arithmetic became widespread, even though the unfamiliar numerals and particularly calculations using zero did not become established either instantly or universally. Fibonacci himself, indeed, learned his mathematical skills among Muslims in the Maghreb and Egypt, where the new arithmetic had arrived from India much earlier.

Meanwhile, Maimonides (Moshe ben Maimon) astonished the Jewish world with the publication of his *Guide for the Perplexed* (or *the Confused*)—an introduction to the rational, practical interpretation of over six hundred precepts in the Jewish Bible. Here, too, the tradition of the Torah found itself confronted with Aristotelian dialectics and scientific learning, and here too reason ultimately prevailed, though Maimonides's thesis by no means met with unequivocal approval. This work by this remarkable scholar, who was born in Córdoba and died in Cairo in 1204, was originally written in Arabic, but was soon translated, first into Hebrew and then Latin *(Dux neutrorum)* and was much admired by Christian thinkers such as Thomas Aquinas. It appears to have first become known to the Christian West through the Sicilian court of Frederick II. However, a contrary trend that was also on the rise was Jewish mysticism; Kabbala spread far and wide at this time. Rabbi Moses ben Nahman of Girona (known as Nahmanides or Ramban; died ca. 1270) was its foremost exponent; despite the fact that he was no friend of Maimonides's theology, he defended him against his enemies.

The Mongol invasion of 1240–1242 prompted a singular shift in scholars' perceptions, forcing them to take issue with and correct ancient sources of knowledge on the nature of the Earth. Ptolemy's great *Cosmography,* which described (albeit only in a rudimentary fashion) the Silk Route, China, and the coast of Southeast Asia was as yet untranslated, and so remained unavailable to the Latin West before the early fifteenth century; as for Roman geographers, they had shown scarcely any interest in the Orient. Certainly, the work of the most reliable of them, Pomponius Mela (first century A.D.) had been transcribed several times (Petrarch, for example, owned a manuscript of this author). However, apart from mentioning a few names without providing any further context, Pomponius knew very little about the Far East. The work of the fourth-century geographer Gaius Julius Solinus was also widely known, though he was primarily concerned with supposed "wonders" rather than with an objective description of the Earth. His writings prompted Westerners to go off on wild goose chases for, say, cynocephalae (men with dogs' heads), sciapods (or monopods; men with a single, huge foot), troglodytes (a race of people who had taken refuge underground from the noise of the Sun), parossites (people who lived off the steam from cooked food), and other such beings, whose fictitious nature was not immediately seen through at the time. The Mappae Mundi of the early Middle Ages consigned such creatures to the fringes of the Christian world or sited them on remote islands; these maps generally only knew that Asia existed, but nothing else about it. The more accurate knowledge of well-traveled Arab geographers only gradually seeped through to the West. Certainly we know that Roger II of Sicily had a world map, which al-Idrisi had created on the basis of information from Ptolemy. But such documents were not commonplace. As the Mongols advanced into Europe, scholars were obliged, as it were, to rediscover the Earth, a task that they approached, rationally and systematically, with great curiosity, with the advantage of a thoroughgoing scholastic education, and with admirable tenacity.

In the process they tackled not just the question of the "Monstra," the fabulous creatures that peopled the pages of ancient literature. The reports that the first envoys to the Mongol Empire—Giovanni da Pian del Carpine and John of Rubruck—left behind testify to their extraordinary powers of observation and description, skills that a scholastic education had given them. These accounts are easily on a par with the ethnographic texts of antiquity; indeed, in many respects they actually surpassed these, as records of the way in which foreign societies viewed and interpreted the world. For example, they corrected Isidor of Seville's claim that the Caspian Sea was a gulf of the "world ocean." John of Rubruck produced what can only be described as a regular spy's dossier on the organization of the Mongol army, its weaponry, its fighting methods, and its military objectives. Further reports by missionaries were soon to follow. Yet these accounts also had a great impact on the sciences being taught at the universities.

Roger Bacon (ca. 1219–ca. 1292), an English-born Franciscan monk teaching in Paris, who was ultimately forbidden to teach and banished to a monastery, turned the prevailing fear of the Mongols to scientific and practical account. He regarded these all-conquering invaders from the East as great astrologers and mathematicians, who had a better understanding than Westerners of the motion of the stars and who knew how to use them to their advantage. Supposedly, if the planets joined together with human words and objectives, then they were capable of exerting enormous power (or "fascination"). The Mongols had mastered this technique, while the West was still to learn it. Stars, thoughts, and desires needed to converge if great things were to be achieved. Of course, all this was completely specious, but even so only someone who knew in advance what was going to happen would find this doctrine risible. For Bacon knew full well that only empirical experience, not argument, could provide incontrovertible proofs. Accordingly, he sought to corroborate theory through experience *(experientia)*. His scientific doctrine evolved its own theory of the "questioning way" *(via inquisitionis)*, which certainly owed much to the "reasoning way" *(via rationis)* but which drew on experience.

After studying in Oxford and Paris, Bacon became a university tutor. He won the backing of the future pope Clement IV, and dedicated his work to him. His wide-ranging oeuvre embraces every scientific discipline of the period, from mathematics through physics and optics to the study of foreign languages. He was the first person to correctly measure the angle between the arc of a rainbow and the sun's rays, and wrote the first

European grammars of Hebrew and Arabic. He also realized that the Caspian Sea was an inland lake and proposed the use of magnifying glasses as a military weapon. Yet he regarded all his scientific endeavors as subservient to the guiding discipline of theology.

It is evident that Bacon's works had far-reaching implications. For instance, his calculations on the circumference of the Earth and the distance between Spain and the Far Eastern Cathay—which would have been unthinkable without knowledge of the Great Khan of the Mongols— were the starting point for Christopher Columbus's plans when he set sail westward. His sketch of a network of coordinates between lines of longitude and latitude spans the entire globe, and as such went far beyond both the portolan charts of the period and the attendant narrow perspective of his European contemporaries that their own continent was at the center and everywhere else on the peripheries. But precisely the fact that many of his ideas were way beyond their time brought Roger Bacon into conflict with Bonaventure, the head of his order. He was arrested and ultimately debarred by the Curia from teaching and writing, and was compelled to spend the final years of his life in monastic isolation. Nevertheless, his ideas provide clear evidence of the wide perspectives that were opened up at that time by the interplay of Aristotelian dialectics, systematic questioning (Bacon's *via inquisitionis*), and empirical knowledge. This fundamental upgrading of eyewitness testimony and experiment, of empirical knowledge and theoretical and mathematical formulation, in short of the scientific method *(scientia experimentalis)* was to resonate right down to the modern period, to his namesake Francis Bacon and beyond.

"What is truth?" "What is reality?" "What is knowledge?" Experience, study, knowledge, and method all coalesced here. The sciences generated a never-ending series of new questions and in turn produced unpredictable answers, which had the capacity to shake the very foundations of the traditional worldview. The world became ever more subject to deep analysis, and God's creation was increasingly unlocked to logic and the natural sciences. For sure, every answer merely threw up new questions, with no end to this process in sight. And indeed, how could such a conclusion ever be envisaged, once the devil had tempted man to eat the apple from the Tree of Knowledge? So why not taste it? Why?—this is the fundamental question that even the smallest children ask. Curiosity was discouraged, at least for the follower of Saint Augustine, but even so it could not be quelled. Despite the fact that this church father had condemned the urge for knowledge for its own sake, the questions did not cease. Albertus Magnus recognized where all this would lead: "Curiosity provides the stimulus to research" *(experiendi incitamentum)*.[18] In time, William of Ockham would come to distinguish between demonstrating why something is the case *(demonstratio propter quid)* and demonstrating that something is so *(demonstratio quia)*; Ockham showed that no further question regarding the conclusion can remain after the first (the *propter quid* "why proof"), whereas a "that proof" *(quia)* necessarily calls for a further "why proof."[19] But scarcely has the "why" been revealed than it transforms itself into a "that," and the questioning continues to all eternity.

The universities saw to it that the new learning was publicized. From the thirteenth century on, an increasingly dense network of universities covered the south and west of the continent. They spread throughout Italy, France, Spain, Portugal, and England; indeed the only places where this trend was not replicated were the Holy Roman Empire and the Far East. Furthermore, not every one of these foundations in the West flourished either immediately or on a long-term basis. Yet no realm hesitated for as long as the Holy Roman Empire in embracing the university. It took extraordinary stimuli and hostile rivalry between the German royal families to bring the oldest universities in this region into being. It was only in the fourteenth century that this came about. Prague was the first to be established (1348–1360), followed within a few years by Vienna (1365), Heidelberg (1386), and Cologne (1388); in other words, the royal House of Luxembourg was the first to take the initiative, followed by the Habsburgs, the Wittelsbachs, and finally a town's citizenry. Krakow in Poland (1364) was an earlier foundation than all of these. The result was an ever tighter interweaving of academic communication networks and an acceleration of the transfer of knowledge throughout Europe.

Alongside the universities, religious seminaries of the various monastic orders also came into being. Dominicans in particular, but also Franciscans, were much sought-after teachers; at different times, the Dominican seminary in Cologne, for instance, boasted both Albertus Magnus and Thomas Aquinas as tutors. Admittedly, in Paris, rivalry between secular masters and teachers from the ranks of the mendicant orders led to worst conflict than the university on the Seine had to endure in the mid-thirteenth century. What was at stake here was not just the number of attendees at lectures, fame, and money, though all these factors of course did play a role. Rather, the main bone of contention was the way in which artists and theologians treated (or were expected to treat) the recently published writings of Aristotle and of his Arab commentator Averroës. There was no concurrence on this matter, even within the religious orders. For example, Albertus Magnus and Thomas Aquinas, despite both belonging to the Dominican order, took up diametrically opposed philosophical and theological positions. Nor by any means did the order later decisively come down in favor of Aquinas. The rivalry between the two great mendicant orders also increased the tension, and could sometimes even lead to one or the other side condemning certain teachings by its adversary as heretical.

The Dominican Albertus Magnus and the Franciscan Roger Bacon, on the other hand—and in spite of the growing differences between their orders—were in agreement on one particular question: observation and logically guided deduction should furnish the ultimate proof of what is true; error was possible, but correctable. Ockham and the younger nominalists were the first to register methodical reservations against this "naïve" empiricism. Small-scale experiments were already being conducted at this time to clarify commonplace observations, for instance the fact that down a well shaft, a candle would go out and people would faint, and to explain why this happened. While playing as a child, Roger Bacon had noticed the effect of saltpeter, and now as a man deduced that it could be used for military purposes; even so, he was not the inventor of gunpowder—the time was not yet ripe, though it soon would be. Also, experiments with mirrors gave him the idea that, if these had been deployed at the right time, England might have been saved from the Norman invasion. It was less the actual techniques that Bacon proposed and more the combination of observation, "experiment," and deduction applied to a specific purpose that pointed the way toward the future—in other words, the line of development that led directly from the lecture theaters of the theologians and philosophers and from the monks' cells into such practical realms as military research, the maintenance of sovereignty, the use of power, and other environments. What was still lacking as yet in these kinds of experiment was any continuity or systematic approach, with a focused scientific reductionism as the *modus operandi*.

All the same, some misgivings were voiced. Religion incontrovertibly had priority over all research, methodology, and logic. It was all the more urgent to call this fact to mind, since dangerous teaching had begun to spread despite all the bans imposed on the reading and teaching of Aristotle. Their principal exponent was Siger of Brabant, a secular preacher and philosopher from Brabant. Siger conducted intensive research into the works of Averroës and around 1265 formulated a series of logical inferences arising from the Arab philosopher's teachings, concerning the unity of the intellect, the permanence of the world, the denial of free will, the inability of the immaterial soul to suffer in the material infernal fire, and other topics that were at variance with church doctrine. Although Siger later recanted his earlier conclusions, they could not be unsaid once they had been disseminated around the academic world, and so continued to have an effect. In any event, at least some churchmen still considered Siger so dangerous that he was murdered in 1283, while on his way to a hearing at the papal court at Orvieto.

Could the writings of Aristotle ever be reconciled with Christian and ecclesiastical teachings? Many theologians doubted this, and even those who thought it possible were at pains not to question the premises of theology; at best, philosophy and indeed the Liberal Arts as a whole could only be a handmaiden to theology. If it ever usurped the role of mistress, like every rebel it was mercilessly persecuted, and if necessary condemned to death. Yet the formulaic metaphor of the handmaiden did not preclude independent thought, in some regards it even legitimized it, at least in the field of theology.

Singular thought games were indulged in at the universities. For example, one topic for disputation might run thus: "I propose that there is no God. Prove the contrary." This challenge was just another variant of endeavors to find a conclusive proof for the existence of God, which from the time of Saint Anselm on had actually only succeeded in evoking negations. Certainly, it was nobody's place to doubt, but when did this dialectical game become a serious metaphysical enquiry? And when was God's existence ever "proved" merely through some authoritative philosophical formulation? When did truth in a philosophical sense start competing against the truth of religious belief? When did such doubts become intolerable? A double truth, such as Thomas Aquinas feared might arise as a consequence of Averroism, could not be allowed to develop. Moreover, the barb of questioning and disputation kept awakening and heightening people's latent doubts, and now seemed lodged for all eternity in the flesh of Christianity. As a result, there arose in the course of the thirteenth century "the most comprehensive concept of rationality before Descartes,"[20] which even opposing theologians could not help but use the methods of

Aristotle to combat, and could only criticize by engaging with his ideas. In other words, even those who feared the inherent dangers of rationality could no longer challenge its substance.

This same situation was mirrored in the so-called Condemnation of 1277, in which the bishop of Paris, Étienne Tempier (on the occasion of a sermon for Laetare Sunday, the fourth Sunday in Lent) condemned 219 philosophical and theological theses as heretical. Taking them out of their context, Tempier lambasted them as "execrable errors, or rather vanities and false absurdities," and as "specious wisdom."[21] This condemnation had been preceded in 1270 by an initial denunciation (albeit with less discredited theses). Despite the fact that it also banned Andreas Capellanus's treatise *De amore,* as well as the practices of geomancy, necromancy, devil-worship, and astronomy, the document of 1277 is still evidence of the progressive enlightenment that was taking place in the Middle Ages, and the fruit of a continuing engagement with Aristotelianism and Averroism. The people at whom Tempier's sermon was aimed, as contemporaries knew only too well, were (first and foremost) the Parisian masters Siger of Brabant and Boethius of Dacia, the two leading Averroists of the period; however, it is by no means certain that these two individuals actually espoused the ideas decried in the Condemnation. Many ideas were only (even by them) expressed in the form of hypotheticals, and not put forward as their own doctrines. But at what point did a hypothesis become a binding personal conviction?

Statements or theses such as the following were the subject of condemnation: "God is not Three in One, because the Trinity is not compatible with the greatest simplicity. For where there is great diversity, there too addition and combination also necessarily occur. Take, for example, a pile of stones.—Nothing is eternal regarding its end, which would not also be eternal with regard to its beginnings" (a sentence which calls into question the eternal bliss or eternal damnation of created souls).—"When all celestial bodies are once again in the same alignment as they are present, a situation that will recur after 36,000 years, the same conditions as currently pertain will also arise then" (this statement contradicts the doctrine of the Creation of the World and the Day of Judgment and the ensuing Apocalypse).—"There was no original man, and there will be no final human being, but rather what there always was and always will be is the creation of a person from another person."—"There is more than one Prime Mover.—"'Humanity' is not a real entity but a rational construct" (a fundamental position of nominalism).—"In the exercise of will and intellect, these faculties are not self-motivated, but are driven by an eternal agent, namely the celestial bodies" (a renunciation of the doctrine of human Free Will). At the universities, for the purpose of training scholars' mental agility, people were free to think in highly radical terms, a situation that put faith on the defensive. The response of the religious powers that be, in alliance with the secular authorities, was to impose inquisitions, punishments, teaching bans, violence and terror.

The Condemnation of 1277 did not end the disputes that it had conjured up; on the contrary, they were exacerbated by it, insofar as it only succeeded in shifting them onto the plane of the rivalry between the two great mendicant orders and embroiling them in political conflicts. Even some theses of Thomas Aquinas fell victim and found themselves condemned as heretical utterances. But they, along with the list of ideas proscribed by the Paris Condemnation, continued to be added to both manuscripts and early printed editions of Peter Lombard's *Sentences,* making it the most important theological primer of the entire Late Middle Ages. But above and beyond this, Tempier's verdicts hint at further momentous differences between the tutors of Paris. For among the authors who were attacked there appear to have been adherents of a position that had already been the subject of much controversy around 1100. These scholars held that the *universalia* or general concepts were nothing more than mere terms, in other words only *nomina* and not *realia,* and that only individual things were real. It is unclear who may first have promulgated such an idea at that time. What was certain was that it was on the verge of a major resurgence, and that it would go on to triumph as never before.

It was only now that the heyday of nominalism dawned and produced its most astute thinker, William of Ockham. Although he had never been a pupil of his fellow Franciscan John Duns Scotus, this Oxford theologian and logician was his intellectual heir. Even when he was still a young theologian, Ockham was forced to defend himself against an accusation of heresy for his unorthodox questioning and responses; however, despite its long duration (1324–1328) and a series of incriminating statements, his trial in the presence of Pope John XXII in Avignon did not lead to a conviction. Based not least on Aristotle's *Logica Vetus* in Boethius's translation, Ockham's logic obeyed a strict terminological nominalism, which maintained that, apart from the thinking soul and apart from the idea-bound intellect, no "universals" existed. Instead, reality was ruled by contingency and individuality, chance and individual things. The ramifications of this position for scholarship were immense and are still felt today. Following Ockham's line of enquiry, it abandoned its treatment of things in favor of concepts and theses that represent those things. Accordingly, the findings of the sciences are of a logical and not an ontological nature. Superfluous stages of reasoning in reaching a conclusion were rejected; simple explanations took precedence over more complex ones. This requirement later came to be known as "Ockham's Razor."

Using these methodical insights, Ockham proceeded to investigate certain central tenets of the Christian faith, such as predestination, the Eucharist, the doctrine of grace, and so on—indeed, the whole question of the scientific basis of theology. In complete contrast to Thomas Aquinas, who had just been canonized by John XXII, he emphatically rejected such a premise; for however vital revealed truths might be for the business of gaining salvation, there was no empirical evidence to corroborate them. In the realm of theology, nothing could be proved. One could know nothing of God, only believe in Him. Scholarship, on the other hand, required clear premises. Doubts, however, unsettled even Christians, while no rational argument would ever win unbelievers or people of other faiths over to Christianity. In this way, Ockham drew a clear distinction between faith and knowledge. "It is childish to say: 'I know the conclusions of theology because God knows the principles I believe in, since it was he who revealed them in the first place.'"[22]

The trial against Ockham remained inconclusive. Instead, political controversies began to come to the fore, which forced the Oxford Franciscan to flee Avignon for Pisa and led to his excommunication. In 1327, the Franciscan minister-general Michael of Cesena's request that Ockham produce a report on the question of poverty saw the latter become embroiled in the so-called poverty dispute that had just erupted among theologians (the debate as to whether Christ and his disciples had ever owned anything). Ockham ended up defending his order's vow of poverty against the acquisitiveness of the Roman Church. He refuted the position that property and the regime of ownership was a product of natural law and God's Will, and instead concluded that they were the work of man. The implications of this position were radical, and Ockham did not shy away from stating them. The pope, who defended the wealth of Christ and the church, had fallen victim to a "heretical error," and through the decretals that he issued against poverty required that the faithful believe "everything that was heretical, erroneous, stupid, laughable, fantastic, insane and defamatory, and which likewise was at total variance and in conflict with the true faith, good manners, natural reason, reliable experience and brotherly love." In consequence, Ockham forswore any "obedience to this pseudo-pope."[23] Condemnation by John XXII was not long in coming, but the disputatious Ockham escaped imprisonment only in the nick of time by taking refuge at the court of the Holy Roman Emperor Louis IV (the Bavarian) in Munich, where he was to remain for the rest of his life. There, he met Marsilius of Padua, who following his own flight from Paris in 1324 had also found sanctuary at the emperor's court. The two most original thinkers of their age subsequently found themselves caught up in Louis's ongoing conflict with the popes. These circumstances played a leading role in Ockham's formulation of his ecclesiastical doctrine and in his political writings, as well as compelling Marsilius's political thought to engage with the politics of the day. Thereafter Munich would never again experience this intensity of intellectual dynamism.

The same period in Avignon that witnessed the excommunication of Ockham also saw the trial of the Dominican Meister Eckhart. He too—a man who at different times had been both Dominican Provincial for Saxony and professor of Theology in Paris—was obliged to defend himself against accusations of heresy leveled by Heinrich von Virneburg, archbishop of Cologne (and compiled by members of his own order). Eckhart is commonly regarded as a mystic, but was actually—under the influence of Dietrich von Freiburg—a trained logician, whose criticism of his fellow Dominican Thomas Aquinas earned him many enemies within his own order; by contrast, Dietrich's tuition had instilled in Eckhart a great admiration for the work of Albertus Magnus and Averroës. From the former, he had adopted the idea that God's Being was an active intellect and that this intellect was substance. However, such a conception of substance divested of its materiality contradicted Aristotle and could not be reconciled with the teachings of Thomas Aquinas either. Eckhart's aim, like that of Anselm of Canterbury, was nothing less than to delve into God's secrets, and even into the mystery of the Trinity, with the aid of "natural reason" (by which, admittedly, he meant in accordance with the method learnt from Aristotle and not starting from the premise of faith) and fathom their truth, and to use this insight to explain the visible world. Yet God exists because He is a cognitive entity. That had little to do with mysticism as it is commonly understood; instead, with this notion the theologian was harking back to the Neoplatonic tradition. Was there then, after all, a way out of the all-consuming rationalism and Aristotelianism?

Eckhart's trial appeared to dismiss any such notion. Twenty-eight theses from his complete works were condemned by John XXII as being either heretical or as being suspected of heresy, and he was struck from the list of approved Dominican writers. But what was actually written in these passages? For example, one of them stated that as soon as God came into being, He created the world; hence one could conclude that it had been there for all eternity. Another maintained that God's majesty was also manifest in evil deeds, and that anyone who blasphemed against God was praising him at the same time. Ideas of this kind were decried; and it is certainly true that, taken out of their context, they sounded strange and provocative, and truly "evil" *(male)*. The preacher Eckhart was accused of having overstepped the boundaries of faith and strayed into the realms of fable, and that he had sought to find out more than he was entitled to know. Furthermore, he had put forward many ideas that actually only obscured the true faith. Accordingly the theses in question and the books in which they appeared were condemned—in other words, the scholar's entire exegetical oeuvre.[24] And yet, when read in context, they made perfect sense, opening up the way to a new understanding and a new image of man; and it was precisely this that came under fire. Eckhart spoke in terms of the "New Man . . . who is within us," and of the "inner man" or the "heavenly man" and his divine core, the active intellect. This figure was placed in contrast to the "outer man," the "hostile . . . evil man," who had succumbed to the temptations of the Devil. However, within the intellect that was God time and space were suspended, along with the Past, Present, and Future, indeed the whole history of salvation. And it was through this realm that man, with his intellect, with his innermost soul, the uncreated "spark of soul" directly imparted by God, partook of the divine. As Eckhart put it, the "seed of God is within us" *(der sâme gotes ist in uns).*[25] This dictum above all was regarded as heretical; the church authorities were in no doubt that it and others like it were deeply dangerous. For if this theology of the intellect were to take root, then what need would there be henceforth for instruments of grace and above all for the teaching primacy of the church? Such a line of argument suggested an entirely new anthropology in which man, insofar as he even took cognizance of his divine origin, was ennobled in such a way as to throw all conceptions of ecclesiastical hierarchy overboard. Instead, in six stages described by Eckhart, man would be raised directly to the status of the Son of God. Immediately after the verdict was announced, Meister Eckhart died. Despite having been condemned, though, his work survived thanks to an apologia by Johannes Tauler and Nicholas of Cusa's reading of him; in particular, Eckhart's German sermons were frequently copied, and it may fairly be assumed that these became widespread among the Beguines and Beghards (lay preaching orders) within German-speaking areas of Europe, creating a ferment that transcended all theology and sermonizing. We know that Martin Luther was familiar both with them and with the writings of Eckhart's pupil Johannes Tauler.

The intellect thirsted for experience. The advent of rationalism brought with it a widespread urge toward mysticism. Johannes Tauler (d. 1361), whose sermons are the only writings to have survived, steeped himself in Eckhart's teachings, albeit colored with the Neoplatonic thoughts of Pseudo-Dionysius the Areopagite. Tauler preached about the "basis of the soul," the uncreated "soul-spark," which Meister Eckhart had also mentioned, and which originated from God and strove to become one with God. The path to this *unio mystica* appeared attainable and was described by Tauler as a psychogenic technique. Female mysticism in particular rose to new heights in the decades around 1300, although in this instance no scholarly background is discernible; it was especially prevalent among the Beguines. Ultimately, a direct line of descent becomes visible from mysticism—as, for instance, transmitted by Jan van Ruysbroek (1291–1381), admittedly not a follower of the "heretic" Eckhart—to the *Devotio moderna* and to the influential, established church-inspired religious revival movement of the fifteenth century.

Was it symptomatic of an era in which philosophers began to place the subject in the center of their thinking and when scholars found themselves troubled by growing concerns about the Apocalypse? Despite the triumphs of rationalism, a general anticipation of the End Time was on the rise, as though reason were once again looking to be counterbalanced by the irrational. The Day of Judgment, whose signs foretold the imminent second coming of Christ himself, came ever more ominously close for all those whose calculations were based on the world lasting for just 6,000 years (a figure derived from the Talmud and hence from the writings of the Christian fathers) and who closely observed the auguries. A list drawn up in the tenth century enumerated fifteen of these signs and omens: a solar eclipse, drought, scarcity of resources, hails of blood, and the like. People who could read and interpret such signs were much in demand. Astrology, with its prediction of the eternal recurrence of astral constellations on a 36,000-year cycle, was in a position to offer relief from this threat, but it was frowned upon for doctrinal reasons. Even so, it stimulated many scholars to speculate on this subject and heightened the atmosphere of eschatologically tinged anxiety. Time and again, people kept watch for signs, calculated time limits, and preached sermons on the need to prepare for the impending Day of Judgment.

In particular the early fourteenth century—the heyday of William of Ockham, one of the most effective rationalists and proponents of enlightenment—also saw the publication of a series of eschatological calculations and apocalyptic scenarios.[26] These went hand in hand with a growing fear and terror of magic and witchcraft. Rationality and irrationality were in close proximity to one another. Reason and speculative belief were not mutually exclusive; indeed, the connection between them contributed in large part to the rise of the natural sciences, which were just becoming established at this time. After all, it was essential that the signs be interpreted correctly, with different forms of darkness or of scarcity properly distinguished from one another, while at the same time saving the truth of God's revelation. In many cases, the inexplicable was treated as an expected, infallible sign. Thus it was that people began to calculate, investigate, ask questions, and seek criteria that would furnish them with certainty, in conjunction with a ceaseless interpretation of signs, texts, and speculations. The conflict over the role of astrology at the same time became a struggle for religious enlightenment, for an explanation of the world along natural scientific lines, and for a cathartic criticism of the church fathers.

Even though not every writer of the age treated such themes, it nevertheless constituted the great underlying tenor of the age. For example, in his autobiography Charles of Moravia, the future Holy Roman Emperor Charles IV, recalls being woken in great alarm by his manservant with the words: "My lord, wake up, the Day of Judgment is nigh! The world is teeming with locusts." The year was 1338. Artworks of the period were fond of invoking the Apocalypse; it was an ever-present feature of life. Even Luther's Reformation began under the auspices of the impending Last Trump. To stretch our field of reference even farther into the modern period, Isaac Newton was first and foremost a speculative apocalypticist and only coincidentally a brilliant physicist; nor was he the only thinker of his era of whom this was the case. The apocalyptic traditions of Christianity had never entirely disappeared. Sometimes proclaimed by only a few "prophets," and at other times believed by many, the imminent anticipation of the End Time and the Day of Judgment runs through the entire history of the West, coming through more or less strongly depending on the particular age.

Curiously, though, the *via moderna* may be said to have begun with Ockham—the "new way" as opposed to the old, the *via antiqua*; yet at the same time a strange inertia set in on an intellectual plane. Hereafter, only a few less well-known names are worthy of note, such as Jean Buridan (died shortly after 1358), who reflected on the mortality of the soul and the strictly temporal nature of human happiness. His name was immortalized in the image of "Buridan's Ass," which could not choose between two piles of hay placed at equal distances from it and so starved to death (a satire on his philosophy of moral determinism). Or the skeptic Nicolas d'Autrecourt, who questioned the traditional doctrine of causality, preferring instead to operate with hypotheses and probabilities, or Nicole Oresme, who imagined the sun as the center point of the cosmos, developed an original theory of money, and translated some of Aristotle's writings into French. All three of the aforementioned thinkers represented nominalist positions.

Yet dissenting voices made themselves heard, and all too soon a paralyzing conflict erupted over the correct path for philosophy and theology to take to the truth, namely the nominalist *via moderna* or the realist *via antiqua*. Presently, this "dispute about the ways" effectively blocked both paths, meaning that no progress was made on either. From the second half of the fourteenth century onward, philosophy slumped into the routine of a university discipline, devoid of any new impulses or fundamental new questions. It was left to a medieval collection of tales from the late fourteenth century, the period of the Black Death, to broach such vital questions: how is it that goodness may turn to evil, truth to falsehood, and justice to injustice? This work, the *Gesta Romanorum,* contained a tale in which four philosophers were required to answer the question. The reason given by the fourth was astonishing. For it simply stated: "God is dead," *Deus est mortuus.* People only did good out of their love for God, "but now we believe that he is dead." The Day of Judgment was forgotten.[27] Death held sway over the scene. Could life ever be regained? At least the Elector Palatine Rupert I managed at that time to persuade a proponent of the *via moderna,* the scholastic philosopher Marsilius of

Inghen, to move from Paris to Heidelberg, where he was instrumental in founding the university (1386).

However, the universities were not the prime movers behind the Renaissance. The debate over the works of Aristotle, the endless aphoristic commentaries, and the "dispute about the ways" had caused these institutions to lose sight of their nurture of the classical authors and of the elegance and beauty of language. It was precisely at the foremost university in the West, Paris, that a one-sided academic bias toward dialectics took root.[28] Accordingly, a fresh impulse was needed to ensure that the whole wide range of ancient thought and literature was rediscovered and that an entirely new direction was imparted to European culture. It began sometime before the middle of the fourteenth century in Italy and is associated with the names of Petrarch and the Roman revolutionary Cola di Rienzo. The movement grew stronger throughout the fifteenth century as its subject matter diversified; that period witnessed a revival of interest in Plato; now, for the first time in the West, study of the ancient philosopher could base itself on the original Greek texts. It also prompted some scholars to take serious issue with the biased and exclusive focus of the intellectual elite on Aristotle. The Renaissance could, as with Petrarch, take on a decidedly Christian character, but at the same time it was also capable, as in the fifteenth century under the influence of the Byzantine philosopher Georgius Gemistos Pletho, of succumbing to a curious form of new paganism. Likewise, it had the capacity to appear hostile toward all curiosity and investigation, or conversely to endeavor to delve ever deeper into the mysteries of the cosmos and life. Certainly, in the fifteenth century, the Renaissance distinguished itself more through its works of art than its philosophy.

Petrarch inveighed against Aristotelian scholasticism.[29] "What would it profit me to know the nature of animals, birds, fish, and snakes, and to ignore or despise the nature of men, the end for which we are born, whence we come, and where we go," he wrote. The writer in him took exception to the long-winded, unwieldy language of scholastic philosophers, while the Christian Petrarch bridled at their remoteness from everyday life and lack of religion and at the moral vacuity of their utterances. He railed particularly vehemently against contemporary philosophers who displayed insatiable curiosity; Petrarch's humanism warned against investigation that knew no boundaries: "Seek not what is above you and search not out things above your strength," he warned humanity, true to his great mentor and guide Saint Augustine. "The things that God has commanded to you, think thereupon always and be not inquisitive in His many works; for it is not necessary for you to behold what is hidden." "You, my God, are the Lord of Learning," he concluded, thereby implicitly denying Aristotle or any other mortal philosopher that distinction. "O saving Jesus, true God and true Giver of all learning and all intelligence, true King of Glory and Lord of all powers of virtue . . . I am born to love You dearly and adore You piously, not for learning."[30] In his principal historical text *De viris illustribus,* Petrarch elaborated on his image of Man; he chose not to make doctors, poets, or philosophers the subject of this work, as had been the practice since the days of Saint Jerome, but rather men "who have served the Republic with distinction through their martial skill or their great zeal." As a poet, he was blessed with an innate sense and apprehension of both linguistic beauty and human greatness, which—influenced by his reading of Cicero—far transcended the rhetorical and ethical teaching of his own day and which caused his chosen instrument of language to resonate like a hosanna and touch his readers' innermost beings. With him, poetry and literature attained new heights. One of his greatest achievements was to stress the practical relevance of learning for real life.

In the process, Petrarch and his fellow humanists talked more frequently and more extensively about themselves than all previous authors of the Middle Ages had done, including Peter Abélard. "It is possible that some word of me may have come to you . . . you may desire to know what manner of man I was, or what was the outcome of my labours." Thus Petrarch began his "Letter to Posterity."[31] The humanists were in pursuit of an entirely new objective. Their desire was to express something about themselves and their humanity. The letter was the ideal literary form for them; although some exemplary letters had been written in the past, it was they who truly rediscovered it as a significant literary form. Well over five hundred letters of Petrarch alone have been preserved. These authors wrote about themselves, yet at the same time they knew how to incorporate general human observations into their examination and stylization of their own lives in such a way that readers were gripped and involved, and felt themselves somehow on a par with the letter writer. "In my prime I was blessed with a quick and active body, although not exceptionally strong; and while I do not lay claim to remarkable personal beauty, I was comely enough in my best days. I was possessed of . . . lively eyes, and for long years a keen vision, which however deserted me, contrary to my hopes, after I reached my sixtieth birthday, and forced me, to my great annoyance, to resort to glasses. Although I had previously enjoyed perfect health, old age brought with it the usual array of discomforts."[32] Reflections like these had no place among the schoolmen at the universities. It was self-evident, however, that they were what motivated artists; it is no coincidence that, around this time, they began to apply their skills to lifelike portraiture. Petrarch himself, for instance, was portrayed as a portly figure with a full face, more fleshy than lean, and with a double chin.[33]

All the same, humanism was in no position to confine the scope of the sciences. Quite the contrary, fact: newly rediscovered texts such as Pythagoras's theory of the transmigration of souls (metempsychosis), Democritus's atomic theory, Epicurus's materialism, the theory of boundless worlds and the perpetuity of the world, and others such as the *Opus Hermeticum* only served to broaden the horizons of scholars and multiplied their questions. In addition, from the late fourteenth century onward, scholarship was increasingly opening up to vernacular languages; translations from Latin and Greek were initiated by royal and princely patrons. Not least Nicole Oresme, one of the most outstanding intellectuals of this period, wrote scientific texts about the cosmos and optics, plus a treatise against astrology, in French. Oresme was an advisor to King Charles V of France, and translated Aristotle's *Ethics* and *Politics* into the vernacular for him; he recorded expressly that he did this in order to allow Charles— who had had little schooling and was unfamiliar with Latin—to appreciate these difficult and useful texts and so further his education as a prince. Exquisitely illustrated manuscripts (produced sometime after 1372) were part and parcel of this enterprise.[34] Indeed, a new mania for collecting gripped kings and princes at this time and they began hoarding books (old manuscripts as well as recently published works) and compiling libraries systematically specializing in particular subjects of interest. Charlemagne and Otto II had, of course, done this in the past, but for a long time nobody had emulated them. This situation only began to change as the Late Middle Ages dawned. The learned emperor Frederick II of Sicily and his son Manfred amassed large numbers of priceless volumes, though the collection was broken up shortly after Manfred's death, so that it is now impossible to reconstruct it and know which works it contained. Alfonso X of Castile was renowned as wise thanks to his book collection; his library was also dispersed, however, as was that of the Holy Roman Emperor Charles IV. Presently, though, collections were made more enduring. Charles V of France laid the foundations of the modern *Bibliothèque Nationale*. The permanence of Paris as the nation's capital facilitated the development of a royal library there. The Renaissance also saw book collecting come into vogue among lay people. The *Biblioteca Laurenziana* in Florence still holds several complete collections that were originally assembled during this period.

After the high-water mark of philosophy during the thirteenth and early fourteenth century had passed, no more outstanding philosophers were to emerge (with the exception of Nicholas of Cusa, although he is primarily regarded as a theologian). Innovative thinking and study of the natural world migrated from university circles to the urban centers, as well as returning to the courts of kings and princes. The humanists of the Renaissance, which was spreading throughout Italy at that time, shunned philosophy as an academic discipline, studied Plato in Greek, and exulted in their own breadth of learning and the beauties of the soul and of humanity. Only theology was able to boast one or two remarkable scholars, yet even this discipline threatened to ossify into a late scholastic university-based enterprise. Yet at least it was the universities that were also at the forefront of calls for church reform.

Jean Gerson (d. 1429), the chancellor of the University of Paris, left behind an extensive body of theological writings. These were the fruit of an intensive study of the Bible, an enterprise in which he took a decidedly nominalist approach; even so, he described mysticism as the "experimental knowledge of God." Gerson was one of the leading theologians on the Council of Constance; he was concerned in particular with ecclesiological reflections and their impact on canon law. He justified the death sentence that the council passed on the Czech church reformer Jan Hus in 1415, while at the same time defending the whole idea of ecumenical councils, since he saw the church first and foremost as a community of the faithful and the pope merely as its representative, who could if necessary be deposed by that community. Conversely, the future cardinal Nicholas of Cusa (d. 1464) was an "anticonciliarist," although not to begin with. He was not unfamiliar with humanism, but in matters of philosophy he plowed his own furrow. His abiding motto was that the church was in constant need of reform *(Ecclesia semper reformanda)*. However, there was no consensus over how such reform might be achieved; furthermore, advocating "constant" reform was an implicit rejection of the view that there was a pressing need to enact it.

The ecumenical councils were convened at a time of intense political and social upheaval. While this unrest certainly gripped religion and scholarship, it also had a profound effect on realms outside the church and the universities. "Commerce" increasingly came to the fore at this time, as the towns of Constance and Basle profited from the church councils that were held there. Florence, the final place where a council was convened, was a major commercial center and its rulers, the Medici, who played an absolutely pivotal role in the Renaissance, had grown rich and powerful through the textile trade and financial transactions. Technical innovations such as spectacles (which spread from Florence in around 1300), bookkeeping, and cartography prospered in this urban society, quite apart from the numerous innovations and improvements in agriculture, crafts and trades, transport, and road and bridge construction. Academic life and business had long since formed a compact. Trade fairs served in many regards as showcases for innovation. For example, the first printed book, the forty-two-line Gutenberg Bible, was the star attraction at the Frankfurt fair in 1454; its significance was to spread far beyond the world of book collecting. It is possible that Gutenberg himself may have offered it for sale at this fair; if not, then it was certainly his business partner, the printer Johann Fust. Enea Silvio Piccolomini, who would presently ascend the papal throne as Pius II, examined a copy of the Gutenberg Bible and was fulsome in his praise, reporting that he could read it even without the aid of his spectacles, so clear and regular were the printed characters.

Johannes Gutenberg's invention heralded nothing less than a bloodless revolution. New dimensions of knowledge, its dissemination and networking were opened up by the media revolution that was set in motion by the cities of Mainz, where Gutenberg was active, and Frankfurt. These factors soon combined with the unresolved questions from the era of the councils to bring about fundamental changes in scholarship and religion, the church, and the world of trade. Over the following 50 years, more than 250 printing houses were established throughout Europe. This new technology was seized upon especially eagerly by French and Italian humanists; their earliest master printers established themselves at Subiaco near Rome (1465) or in Milan (1470), while the first two printing presses in Venice started operating in 1469 and 1471 respectively. The renowned humanist printer Aldus Manutius, whose press published the most important contemporary authors, set up shop there in 1489. But as a result of a book market becoming a regular fixture in Frankfurt in the wake of the trade fair held there, the first commission on book censorship, summoned by the city council at the behest of the archbishop of Mainz, also met in the city (probably in the town hall at the Römerberg) from 1485 onward. This was several decades before the Vatican's *Index librorum prohibitorum* (1559) took steps toward enforcing global control over the dissemination of knowledge.[35] Writing and reading, or even just printing books became a risky undertaking. Little wonder: humanists and witch finders, Lutherans, Calvinists, Reformists and Huguenots, scholars, prelates, and princes, as well as copper and wood engravers all went to the Buchgasse in Frankfurt to find new ideas, fresh impulses, and revolutionary literature. Martin Luther also visited the Frankfurt fair in search of the latest pamphlets and books.

The fall of Constantinople to the Ottomans in 1453, which coincided almost exactly with the date of the first printed book, brought a wave of emigrants to Italy and with them a definitive revival of Greek culture in the history of European ideas. The ground was already well prepared; for instance, Georgius Gemistos, commonly known as Pletho (d. 1452), had spent a brief spell in the West, in 1438–1439, as envoy of the Byzantine emperor John VIII Palaiologos to the Council of Ferrara/Florence. Pletho was a Platonist, and a very singular one at that. In his treatise on the differences between Plato and Aristotle, he chided the Latins for their preference for the latter and his commentator Averroës: Pletho's critique left a lasting impression on Western thought, not least in responses to the idea of establishing an "Academy" in Florence.

Pletho took a skeptical view toward the religions of his day—both Christianity, then in retreat from the advance of Islam, and Islam itself. He anticipated renewal coming through a Platonic-Pythagorean oriented "polity" that displayed neo-Platonic and polytheistic traits; Pletho took his cue from the ancient Greeks in calling the highest deity "Zeus." It was he who taught the humanists to revere Plato's *Republic*; their reading of this text lent new impetus to political thought in the Latin West. Various Utopian designs for the world and for society were soon to follow; Pletho's work *Nomoi* may well have had an influence on Thomas More's *Utopia*, the text that gave this whole genre of literature its name. His new paganism also impressed many writers of the Renaissance, who saw their astrological worldview conformed through his talk of Jupiter, Mars, or Venus. Christianity, Islam, and the Olympian pantheon appeared to undergo a form of symbiosis in the writings of this original thinker.

Pletho's pupil Basilios Bessarion (d. 1472), who also visited Florence in 1439, did not embrace his teacher's polytheism. Remaining in Italy, he became an advocate of ecumenical union between the Orthodox and Roman churches, and presently became a cardinal. Bessarion was instrumental in promoting Greek studies in the West (he had brought several ancient Greek manuscripts with him from Constantinople). Once established, this field of scholarship, which opened up a hitherto closed world and stimulated new ideas, saw many other emigrants from Byzantium welcomed with open arms. He eventually settled in Venice; his presence there became a focal point for humanists to meet and discuss ideas; his circle included Poggio Bracciolini, the former papal secretary and satirist, and Lorenzo Valla who revealed the Donation of Constantine to be a fake and who encouraged theologians and jurists alike to take a fresh approach to ancient texts.

The confusions that these upheavals provoked are perhaps reflected most clearly in the theological-philosophical work of Nicholas of Cusa. His notion of "learned ignorance" *(docta ignorantia)* was an imposition on both the church and the universities. Like his demand for constant ecclesiastical reform, it pointed to a new departure, in this case from the traditional methods of academic scholarship, and a renunciation of Aristotle and the endless scholastic commentaries.[36] Nicholas dreamed up and devised innovations that were hard to implement. To him, absolute extremes such as the largest, the smallest, complete stillness or the most violent movement were impossible to contemplate; there would always be something smaller, larger, calmer, or more agitated. In this way, stillness could actually became motion, and polarities merged into one. This, then, was his doctrine of the "coincidence of opposites" *(coincidentia oppositorum)*. Anyone thinking like this no longer saw a center at rest anymore, indeed could see no center at all, which was not at the same time infinity. The implications of this were truly shocking. The Earth could now no longer be conceived of as an immovable entity at the center of the cosmos. "The Earth, which cannot be the center, cannot lack all motion. In fact, it is even necessary that it be moved in such a way that it could be moved infinitely less. Just as the earth is not the center of the world, so the sphere of the fixed stars is not its circumference." Yet "we cannot discover motion unless it be by comparison with something fixed." But because bodies at rest and bodies in flux are one, so motion must always be relative to another body. Thus, "to those who are in the poles [unlike Saint Augustine, Nicholas acknowledged the existence of the Antipodes!], the Earth will appear to be in the zenith, and wherever the observer be he will believe himself to be in the center." Ultimately, then, God "is everything that there can be," and, as we comprehend or fail to comprehend him, the Something and the Nothing. Petrarch would have shaken his head in rejection at Nicholas of Cusa's relativistic theory and counted him among his enemies.

Even though his earlier works sounded less enigmatic and more engaging, Nicholas's entire way of thinking made him very much an outsider. He never underwent scholastic instruction; indeed, the universities rejected him. The new world, in any case, was now taking shape outside their precincts. Once more, it was the princely courts where such innovations as the Renaissance and humanism, the newly discovered discipline of hermeneutics, occultism, Pythagoreanism, the expansion of astrology, and full-blown New Paganism were unfolding. Here, then was where Nicholas of Cusa found an audience. The brilliant Count Giovanni Pico della Mirandola, for example, heeded his teachings, as did Lorenzo Valla and later Copernicus. The Italian city-states—Florence or Milan, ruled by princes who were close to the citizenry—were the first to embrace the new thinking, followed by royal courts such as that in Naples. Pico, the Lombard nobleman and cabbalist, belonged to these circles. In addition to Latin and Greek, this polymath also learned Hebrew and Arabic, and was an adherent of both Hermes Trismegistus and Savonarola. He was only thirty-one years of age when he died in Florence in 1494.

In his undelivered speech "Oration on the Dignity of Man," which he wrote when he was twenty-four as a kind of apologia against reproach by the church, he gave voice to the new picture of humanity that was being formulated by the Renaissance.[37] Man, he claimed, had been endowed with divine wisdom, love, and magnanimity. Yet the Creator had placed his creation in the center of the world, so that he might observe His work all around him, pass judgment on its disposition, admire its beauty, and marvel at its grandeur: "You, with no limit or no bound, may choose for yourself the limits and bounds of your nature. We have placed you at the world's center so that you may survey everything else in the world. We have made you neither of heavenly nor of earthly stuff, neither mortal nor immortal, so that with free choice and dignity, you may fashion yourself into whatever form you choose." This echoed the passage in the Bible that stated: "Ye are gods; and all of you are children of the most High" (Psalms 82:6). Precisely in his active existence, man was on a par with the highest of the angels, the Cherubim and Seraphim, while in the steadfastness of his judgment, the brilliance of his intellect, and the ardor of his love, he was akin to the Supreme Judge who rules over us all. Thus, to paraphrase John 17:21, man was in God and God in man. For all its Old and New Testament allusions, though, Pico della Mirandola's speech was more Neoplatonism and Hermeticism than Christianity. In any event, the image of man that this young writer painted has a persuasiveness that can still be felt today. It also underlined that humanism had come a long way since Petrarch.

In its latter phases, the new thinking crossed the Alps, induced its adherents to learn, say, Hebrew or Greek or to write treatises on education, and gave rise to collections like the Biblioteca Palatina and buildings such as the castle at Heidelberg (commissioned by the Elector Palatine Otto Henry d. 1559). Yet no more great writers were to emerge to rival Petrarch, Enea Silvio Piccolomini, Marsilio Ficino (d. 1499, the translator of the *Corpus Hermeticum*), or Pico della Mirandola. An elegance and beauty of language was lacking. It is thought-provoking to realize that the three-century long intellectual evolution that Europe underwent from the High Middle Ages onward ended up producing Machiavelli in Italy and the Reformation in Germany. The Florentine writer knew how to put the political experiences of his age into often shocking but ultimately apposite words. Luther on the other hand, unlike his later opponent the Dutch humanist Erasmus of Rotterdam (ca. 1466/67–1566), was a representative of Late Medieval university theological education, notwithstanding that he turned against it in order to emphasize the primacy of Faith alone and the Word of God as transmitted through the Holy Gospel. His schooling continued to resonate in his doctrine of authority, which drew heavily on Saint Paul: Everyone is subservient to his respective lord. He and Erasmus were at total variance over the question of Man's Free Will.

Without a doubt, the fall of Constantinople shook the West. Henceforth, deprived of its Byzantine defensive shield against the Ottoman Turks, it was left to its own devices. But even more unsettling was the discovery of the "New World." This prompted new scientific questions, not just regarding the geographical view of the world and cosmology, but more importantly the theological and presently also legal question of to what extent the "Indians" (so named because Columbus thought he had found the East Indies) could be considered humans. Now all the faculties that Europeans had developed in the preceding centuries were called into play: the capacity for reasoned, controlled thought; the readiness to integrate experiences, even cosmological insights, into a coherent view of the world; scholastic jurisprudence; the Aristotelian- and Platonic-influenced and "Utopian" attitude toward the common good; and not least Renaissance humanism's godlike view of Man, which endowed humans with dignity, status, and freedom. "Ye are gods; and all of you are children of the most High." All of you! What resulted was the notion of inalienable human rights, and although this principle was not (yet) enforceable, it was nevertheless still seen as a virtue worth protecting. The teachings of the Dominican theologian and advisor to Charles V, Francisco de Vitoria (d. 1546), which stood in the tradition of Late Scholasticism or of the Jesuit priest Francisco Suárez (d. 1617) might be cited here, though in a traditional division of historical eras, they already form part of the Early Modern period. In any event, though, de Vitoria's ideas, as expounded in his *De Indis et de iure belli,* a later (likely posthumous) spin-off of his *Relectiones theologicae,* were to have a significant influence on the development of international law and its originator Hugo Grotius. As in the realm of cosmology, these ideas brought a seamless transition of the insights and modes of thought of the Middle Ages into the Modern period.

II

The Monarchy

In summarizing subsequent intellectual developments and illustrating the trend followed by wider European history, the preceding chapter jumped far ahead in time. We should now return to the point where we left our general historical account, namely the thirteenth century. At that time, the decline of the Hohenstaufen dynasty and the ensuing "interregnum" in the empire that governed Central Europe left a power vacuum in whose wake the political balance of power shifted completely. It became the norm in the Holy Roman Empire for several kings to wear the crown simultaneously, some of whom had never even set foot in the empire; none of these monarchs wielded any real authority. Although Rudolf (r. 1273–1291), the first Habsburg monarch to ascend the throne, ultimately managed to put a stop to any further decline, the paralysis that the interregnum had brought to the empire's former power and authority could no longer be remedied. In any event, Rudolf abandoned Italy and Burgundy to their fate; he never entertained any idea of marching on Rome, at least; nor did he intervene in the endless round of conflicts between the Italian cities and municipalities or in the region of the empire west of the Alps that was steadily falling within France's sphere of influence.

Collapse of the Empire

This dwindling of imperial power also prompted the foremost poet of the Middle Ages, Dante Alighieri (ca. 1265–1321)—who was himself driven from his home town of Florence by the feuding between warring parties—to write a penetrating philosophical analysis of emperorship and the grounds upon which it asserted its legitimacy. In his *Three Books on Monarchy,* taking his cue from Aristotelian dialectics, ethics, and psychology, he proclaimed the divine right of the office of emperor, which was entitled to rule the world, where temporal matters were concerned, quite independently of the papacy.[1] Just as God directed the cosmos, so the emperor governed the world of men. The empire was founded, Dante maintained, on human rights *(ius humanum),* while its onward path was one of harmony, created by the unified will of all its subjects—a factor that was both brought about by the presence of the monarch and realized in his personage. Furthermore, the ultimate purpose of the empire was earthly happiness and universal peace bestowed upon a free race of men. Through God's providential design, this monarchy was invested in Rome and its contemporary emperors from Germany; and even Christ had subjugated himself to Roman rule. The canon-law experts were wrong to claim that the world was subservient to papal authority; Constantine, Dante asserted, had had no right to "donate" an empire, nor the church to receive it from him. The sole concern of the pope and the church should be to work for mankind's eternal salvation.

What Dante set down here in writing was a summation, as he envisaged it, of the century to come, which he was intent on portraying as fertile ground for the empire. This sensitive poet with a scholastic education had picked up on a political trend that had begun to have a general and largely positive impact upon the Western monarchies such as Spain, France, and England, and that was to grow even more intense from the start of the fourteenth century onward—one need only think here, for instance, of Marsilius of Padua. This trend saw a strengthening of the central monarchy, which in worldly affairs now disengaged itself entirely from the "sovereignty" of the papacy. Yet however rich in ideas and scholarly, and however widely disseminated Dante's *Monarchy* was, it only had the effect of spurring those whom it attacked to rebut its conclusions. Accordingly, soon after its publication, the work was denounced as heretical, and at the Council of Trent was among the first writings to appear on the Vatican's list of proscribed books (*Index Librorum Prohibitorum* 1564; the ban on it was only rescinded in 1881). So it was that Dante's principal philosophical work remained merely a utopian vision, a swansong, and not a realizable program. Nevertheless, inasmuch as it was characteristic

of a concerted effort during this period to provide a comprehensive theoretical underpinning to the notion of earthly authority independent of
papal control and approval, it pointed the way forward to the future.

Meanwhile, no learned discourse, no clarion call—however stirring—
and certainly no utopian musings could prevent or reverse the very real
decline in the empire's grip on power. It had been more than sixty years
since a Holy Roman Emperor had even shown his face in Italy, while the
German kings could not even hold undisputed sway north of the Alps.
The regional powers thus had to reorient and reorganize themselves. For
most of them, this signaled the start of a seemingly endless, exhausting,
and deeply confusing round of feuding over inheritances and heiresses,
small-scale increments of power, contested claims, and the pressing need
to assert their authority. The final decades of the thirteenth century and
the whole of the succeeding century were characterized by such skirmishes.
Rapidly shifting alliances tended to heighten uncertainties rather than
assuage them.

The counts of Luxembourg, to cite just one example of this trend, found
themselves embroiled time and again in disputes of this kind. Their most
famous scion, the king and emperor Charles IV, recalled such events in
his autobiography, remembering for example how he had been obliged to
assemble his forces in the Tyrol in support of his younger brother John
Henry, who was then just a child, and invade the Pustertal to attack the
count of Gorizia. John Henry hoped that his marriage to the Tyrolean
heiress—the later renowned and infamous Countess Margaret "Maultasch,"
then twelve years old to John Henry's eight—had already brought the region under his control. Charles remained there with his forces for three
weeks, noting that he "laid waste the country with his troops in the field,
since the count [of Gorizia] was a confederate of the dukes of Austria,"
and that they in turn were in alliance with a mortal enemy of the House
of Luxembourg, the emperor Louis of Bavaria. Charles duly advanced
from the Tyrol to attack the Bavarian Wittelsbach ruler, but when the
fighting there began to abate, returned to the Tyrol and thence, that very
same winter, set off on campaign with his father, King John of Bohemia,
against the heathen Lithuanians in Prussia—a favorite "winter sport" of the
Western nobility of the period.

Meanwhile, the Tyrol appeared to be secure. But then messengers arrived bearing news that John Henry's wife and Tyrolean aristocrats had
conspired against him, that the young countess was seeking a separation

and now wanted to marry his archrival, the son (also called John Henry) of the hated emperor Louis of Bavaria. Charles managed to put down the attempted coup. As he wrote in his autobiography: "We placed Tyrol Castle and Madame under guard." An equally plausible reading of the situation, though, is that the converse was true—namely that Margaret shut her young boy-husband out of the center of power and all other fortresses in her domain, and expelled him, his elder brother, and their Bohemian administrators from the country. The historical record does not permit a definitive answer in this matter. What is certain is that ultimately, whether locked in or out, Margaret disowned her husband on the grounds of failure to consummate their marriage (1341) and Tyrol was lost to the Luxembourg dynasty. Margrave Louis I of Brandenburg wed Margaret, and the scholars resident at the Munich court, above all Marsilius of Padua and William of Ockham, sharpened their quills to justify this marriage of convenience.

And so matters proceeded throughout the length and breadth of Europe—in France and Spain as well as in the Italian city-states: a life of constant low-level conflict, occasioned by dynastic circumstance, and steeped in betrayal, mistrust, broken oaths and scheming aides; in such conditions, one had to be permanently on one's guard. The long absence of any imperial authority in the empire north of the Alps as well as the steady shrinking of its former power hastened disintegration there, while south of the Alps, no authority could now prevail over the various cities, *condottieri,* and warlords, whose machinations to seize and maintain power were later analyzed so perceptively by Machiavelli. Admittedly, on occasion, though by no means regularly, the name of the Roman king or the Holy Roman Emperor was invoked by those seeking to legitimize their existing position of power. Dante, the poet who journeyed through Hell and Paradise and the theoretician of monarchy, expended many words lamenting this downfall. Nor did the rise of the "Papal States" bring any improvement. Not only did the "imperial lands" that Frederick Barbarossa had so painstakingly assembled in northern Italy disintegrate, becoming more or less totally lost to the Holy Roman Empire, but in addition, any sense of centrality in Germany or Italy had now been definitively squandered; precisely the opposite trend now set in throughout other Western realms, and proved all the more enduring; by contrast, it was 1871 before Germany finally acquired its own imperial capital.

Much the same fate as befell the counts of Luxembourg and the Tyrol also happened to other lords and rulers, including kings and emperors.

Moreover, in the event the humiliation in the Tyrol turned out to be less damaging to the House of Luxembourg than it did to the Wittelsbachs. Their ostensible success there plunged this dynasty headlong into catastrophe. All the advantages that the Bavarian emperor had previously won were nullified by the scandalous marriage of his son to the Tyrolean countess.[2] Charles took the divorce, as he himself hinted at the end of his autobiography, as an excuse to contest the Bavarian emperor's crown. By this stage, the Holy Roman Empire was bereft of any central authority with the power to enforce its decisions. Chaos ensued; in the following generation, the Tyrol duly fell like a ripe fruit into the lap of a third-party onlooker to the dispute, the House of Habsburg, where it remained until the post–World War I peace settlements of 1918–1919.

However, one aspect in particular characterized these activities: they literally drove their protagonists halfway across Europe, from Prussia and Lithuania via Krakow and Silesia to Tuscany and down to Rome, or over to Provence or Paris. These developments brought England, Spain, or Sicily into play as allies or foes; nor were the Nordic kingdoms excepted, either. For instance, Waldemar Atterdag, the famous Danish king and enemy of the Hanseatic League, had several meetings with the emperor Charles, including one in Prague. In this way, Europe began, as it were, to coalesce in people's minds into an entity that could quite literally be "experienced" and that was constituted by these direct encounters between princes. It was also regarded as a league of interrelated dynasties and of empires and principalities in a relationship of mutual dependence; a process thereby resumed that had first taken shape in the era of the papal schisms. This Europe started to emerge as a spiritual and spatial entity, hallmarked by the papacy, Christian monarchies, and a common intellectual, religious, and political culture distinguished by similar values, expectations, and chances—and an awareness of these commonalities. It was linked together by means of an ever denser network of diplomatic relations, and last but not least characterized by jealousies that never abated, rivalries that spilled over into open conflict, espionage, covert diplomacy, and wars.

The dynasts of the age were not alone in their propensity for travel. Concern for salvation, naked fear, and the many infirmities of life drove countless pilgrims and cripples onto the streets and impelled them to venture far and wide. Professional palmers undertook pilgrimages for others, who rewarded them financially for their pains. The graves of the apostles in Rome, the Way of Saint James to Santiago di Compostela, and Jerusalem were the favored destinations, holding out the promise of salvation and eternal redemption. Many other pilgrimage routes crisscrossed the whole of Europe: leading for example to Charlemagne's reliquary chapel at Aix-la-Chapelle, to the shrine of the Three Kings at Cologne, to Canterbury to visit the grave of the murdered archbishop Thomas à Becket, or to Assisi to see the tombs of Saint Francis and Saint Claire. From the late thirteenth century on, one could even journey to the grave of Werner of Oberwesel (allegedly murdered by Jews; see Chapter 9, under "Anti-Jewish Pogroms"), while the fifteenth century saw the creation of the shrine of the Fourteen Holy Helpers *(Vierzehnheiligen)* in northern Bavaria and those of Saint Gilles and Saintes-Maries-de-la-Mer in Provence, along with countless other sacred sites. Simple pilgrimage symbols announced which shrines the pilgrim had visited: a scallop shell for Santiago, the cross for Jerusalem, the keys of Saint Peter for Rome, and the Three Kings for Cologne.

Pope Boniface VIII—in all likelihood also for financial reasons—promoted the idea of attaining grace through pilgrimage. He proclaimed the year 1300 a Holy Year and a Jubilee, attracting tens of thousands to Rome to seek remission for their sins at the tombs of the apostles. This was the first time such an event had taken place since biblical times, when "jubilees" were celebrated every seven times seven years (the word is derived from the Hebrew *yo-bale*). As the Florentine chronicler Giovanni Villani ambiguously reported: "This endowed the church with a great treasure and enriched all Romans"; Villani went on pilgrimage to Rome himself at this time and was so enthralled by the festivities that he felt moved to start writing down his contemporary history, his chronicle. The *giubbileo* was such a resounding success that subsequent popes instituted these occasions ever more frequently; first at 100-year intervals, then 50, then 33, until finally, in 1470, Pope Paul II established the 25-year cycle of jubilees that is still observed today.

Another force for unification that transcended kings and kingdoms soon appeared on the scene: business and commerce. The economy experienced a boom at this period, as evidenced by the growing power and influence of cities throughout Europe. In a hitherto unimaginable way, commerce helped unify the continent. A growing population fueled demand. Provisions—herring and dried cod were the main commodities behind the huge expansion of the Hansa—and likewise luxury goods such as spices, silk, or furs also played their part in the overall increase in long-distance trade. Salt, the most important preservative of the Middle Ages, continued, as it always had done, to generate enormous wealth. The transport and communication that went hand in hand with the trade boom put regions that had formerly had no inkling of one another in contact and enabled them to forge ever closer ties, as well as fostering the dissemination of knowledge and stimulating its further growth. In this way, the new publishing industry boosted production, enabling many people, even those living in the remote countryside, to profit from the general increase in living standards. It now became possible to organize the production process much more efficiently than ever before through the division of labor. Rationalism also made its impact felt in this area, reflected for example in a much more precise differentiation of aspects of trade law than hitherto: this now encompassed contract law, cooperative legislation, insurance law, questions of liability, and trademark rights. No major trading or banking concern could now do without the services of notaries and lawyers.

In real terms, competition and rivalry were the order of the day, despite the fact that these were largely ignored in the market strategies and theories of the period. When the city of Siena wanted to promote its cloth-working industry, the city council summarily banned the import and even possession of (likely superior) textiles from Florence. Yet for a long while the stimulus provided by competition went unrecognized. The Italian municipalities continued to dominate the world of commerce; Milan, Florence, and Venice, not to mention smaller trade centers, supplied both their own manufactures and foreign goods to a supraregional market that extended as far as Africa and the Muslim Near East, as well as to Central Asia (Tartary). However, the domestic budgets of these municipalities sank ever deeper into debt; by 1340 Florence, for example, was encumbered with a mountain of debt amounting to 450,000 florins, an astronomical sum, while around the same time Siena made a failed attempt to institute a debt relief program.[3] Corresponding trends became evident in northern and western Europe as well. There, too, cities and their inhabitants had long since liberated themselves from the direct control of their erstwhile feudal rulers and were pursuing their own independent policies. Cities in Flanders and the Netherlands began to vie with the Italian municipalities. From the twelfth century on, from its origins in Lübeck, the Hanseatic League began to develop, and presently underwent a seamless transition, constituting itself first as the "Hanseatic League of Merchants," that is, a confederacy of traders, before morphing into the "Hanseatic League of Cities," a union of municipalities. By the fourteenth century, it had become the dominant economic and political force throughout the Baltic and North Sea region, with trading posts as far afield as Bruges, London, Lübeck, Bergen, and Novgorod.

Casting an Eye toward the Far East

Even the Mongol invasion of Europe now proved to be a stimulus for economic growth. The fear and terror that these steppe peoples had once inspired had long since given way to intensive trading relations. Though the Mongols had ventured halfway around the world, there was little rhyme or reason behind their migration. By contrast, the people who derived the real benefit from this global empire with its so-called Pax Mongolica were the Europeans, despite (or perhaps precisely because of) the narrow horizons of their world and the incessant internecine feuding that prevailed there. The Venetian adventurer Marco Polo, who dictated the famous account of his travels, the *Milione,* while languishing in a Genoese jail, was immodestly proud of his successful voyage to the Far East and the exotic experiences he documented. This pride emerges right from the opening paragraph of his *Milione*: "Ye emperors, kings, dukes, marquises, earls, and knights, and all other people desirous of knowing the diversities of the races of mankind, as well as the diversities of kingdoms, regions, provinces, and all parts of the East, read through this book, and ye will find in it the greatest and most marvelous characteristics especially of the people of Armenia, Persia, India, Tartary, and of many another country. . . . For let me tell you that from the creation of Adam to the present day, no man, whether Pagan, or Saracen, or Tartar or other of whatever progeny or generation he may have been, ever saw or inquired into so many and such great things as hath this Messer Marco Polo."

At first, the Venetians refused to believe the author of the *Milione,* taking Marco Polo for a braggart and a fantasist; indeed, arguments over the authenticity of the work continue to this day. Gradually, though, Europeans became aware of the limitations of their own world, and by contrast began to appreciate the immeasurable expanses and positively incredible diversity of peoples that existed in Asia, with its huge cities, its culture, and its teeming humanity. The situation changed rapidly. New handbooks on the "practice of long-distance trade" were published, especially in Italy; these texts reflect both a contemporary thirst for knowledge and the calculating mind-set of those who knew how to exploit the information they conveyed. Among them, the *Practica della mercatura* (ca. 1340) by the Florentine Francesco Pegolotti, is famous both for the richness of its content and the beauty of its design. In it, the author lists the trade routes to Cambaluc (Beijing) and Tabriz, and comments on such matters as travel conditions, commodities available, taxes payable on merchandise, various different systems of weights and measures, exchange rates, and a host of other important details. Pegolotti was a member of the *Compagnia dei Bardi,* a Florentine trading concern, which in its heyday was the largest banking house in Europe.

Later, Francesco Datini from the Tuscan city of Prato (1335–1410) came to prominence; he is now probably the most famous of all medieval merchants. Orphaned when still young, he began trading everything that could turn a profit: weapons and spices, cloth and silk, products both local and from far-flung sources. He soon amassed a huge fortune, spreading his various business interests, which he basically conducted in writing, between Florence, Pisa, and his home town. Acting as both a manufacturer and banker, he regularly had dealings with princes and kings. Some 125,000 business letters and 575 ledgers have survived in his commercial archive. These documents attest to his entrepreneurial acumen, as well as to his sheer energy and assertiveness. Datini founded the *Ceppo de' poveri,* or "poor people's stump," a charitable trust, and in his will bequeathed his entire estate to this institution. Through his generous endowment, the wealthy Datini hoped to avoid punishment in Hell for his usury and to purchase his own entry into the kingdom of Heaven. The institution still exists today, a miraculous survival. The medieval merchant class embodied a combination of curiosity, profit seeking, systematic thinking, communication, rationalism, financial skill and religion. As a later instruction on the education of apprentices issued in 1479 by the Ravensburg trading company puts it, the merchant was expected to have an "ingenious head on his shoulders" and to direct his intellect less toward complaint and more toward the cut and thrust of commerce.[4] Business, then, called for knowledge, creativity, and a rational outlook.

However, it was not merely economic imperatives that drove this new interest in the Far East. From the twelfth century, rumors had begun to circulate about a figure called Prester John, a Christian potentate who would, it was thought, come to the aid of Western Christianity in its desperate struggle against Islam. Popes and crusading kings placed their faith in him. The search for this mysterious ruler began at an early date. He was initially thought to reside among the Mongols, who had, after all, also attacked Islamic rulers during their incursion into the West. Apparently corroborating this idea was the intelligence that the Mongol realm harbored a Nestorian Christian community, namely the Uigur people. Yet when it became apparent that the Mongols were anything but Christians, this was simply viewed as a further challenge, with papal or royal envoys and above all missionaries joining the merchants' expeditions to the Far East. Odoric of Pordenone and John of Marignola became well-known missionaries, and their stories circulated in the West. In 1307, John of Montecorvino became the first archbishop of Cambaluc. Stories of Christian martyrs soon arose. One such martyr, a Franciscan, came from Siena, and his death in 1321 gave rise to the oldest drawn-from-life representation of Tatars known in the West, men with almond-shaped eyes, sparse beards, conical hats, and strange gestures, painted by the Sienese artist Ambrogio Lorenzetti.[5] The Christian mission demanded that the one true faith should be preached to the whole of humanity and that they should be brought under the wing of the Mother Church. And in truth, the whole of the known world, the globe, the cosmos, was embraced by this vocation. Religion, scholarship, and commerce combined to form an unstoppable campaign of conquest that took throughout the entire Earth; the secular powers swiftly followed in the wake of the missionaries, subjugating as many peoples and countries as they could.

The new learning manifested itself in the abstract entity of the map. The oldest portolan charts date from as far back as the late thirteenth century. These portrayed the coastline of the Mediterranean with astonishing accuracy and soon became so reliable that, right up to the present day, they have only had to be refined but not fundamentally redrawn. On this basis, the ancient *mappae mundi* were now improved, and from decade to decade began to show the continents and oceans, islands and the interiors of landmasses in greater detail and more accurately. Cartographic schools were established to nurture and further the mapmaker's knowledge. The Catalan Atlas that had been commissioned at the behest of King Peter V of Aragón and Mallorca and which was created by Jewish scholars as a gift for King Charles V of France is a key early example of the art of cartographic abstraction, depicting the whole of the Earth, and yet informed both by the fables of the ancient world and the latest discoveries of explorers.

Venice also came to the fore as a center of cartography. Opicinus de Canistris (d. sometime after 1352), a priest, astrologer, cosmographer, and papal notary in Avignon who originally hailed from Lomello near Pavia, created allegorizing and moralizing maps of the Mediterranean which relied heavily on the picture of the world presented in the charts made for the seagoing (and avowedly secular) municipality of La Serenissima. Opicinus's maps reflect the first stirrings of moral unease about the alarming consequences of the globalization that was unfolding all around and that was threatening to destroy all the accepted norms of behavior. Opicinus saw these revolutionary innovations and the collapse of all traditional values as giving an entirely new complexion to the world, one characterized by greed and the profit motive, shameless eroticism, and crude sexuality. And so, on one map by Opicinus, we see the continent of Europe, shown in the form of a monk, with the town of Lomello as a blood-engorged "thing" between his legs—and with Italy and the Greek peninsula representing his boots—bending lasciviously over the outstretched breast of Africa, in the guise of a nun. In this strange piece of pictorial cartography, Opicinus managed to combine both self-castigation and his vision of the future. Venetian cartography reached its high point with Fra Mauro's world map in the fifteenth century; created in around 1450, this masterpiece, which embraces all the latest findings of contemporary scholarship, presents an astonishing precise image of the Old World just prior to the discovery of the New.

The collapse of the Mongol Empire and the rise of the Ming Dynasty in China (1368), together with major shifts in the balance of power in southern Siberia prevented any further journeys to the Far East by travelers from the Latin West. This signaled the end of all missionary work that had occurred hitherto. The Mongol catastrophe also severely disrupted trade with East Asia. Nevertheless, Western knowledge of the wealth and the huge extent of Asia, and a desire to secure a share of its riches, remained as a constant spur to new exploration, a goal that Europe accepted as a mental and technological challenge. China, on the other hand, shunned any such challenge. For a brief period, the third Ming ruler, the Yongle emperor (r. 1402–1424) made preparations to dispatch an expedition fleet to the West (1405); under the command of Admiral Zheng He; its huge ocean-going junks, each crewed by over 1,000 men, sailed as far as Africa and possibly even ventured into the Atlantic. However, the undertaking was abruptly abandoned in 1433 on the grounds of "ill omens." China would not make another attempt at a global naval presence until the late twentieth and early twenty-first centuries.

The outlook in Europe could not have been more different. From the late thirteenth century onward, Europeans were planning to explore the entire world. The mercantile advantages were clear. The brothers Ugolino and Guido (or Vandino) Vivaldi, two reckless merchants from Genoa, set off in 1291 with two galleys, and two Franciscan monks on board, with the intention of sailing west or south to try and find a passage to India; they never returned. This was the first such endeavor that we know about; more were to follow. The rustle of silk and the scent of exotic spices were powerful stimulants to exploration. Though Dante regarded such acts of daring as "madness," and as a display of hubris beyond all human measure, warnings like his went unheeded. A few decades later, one "Sir John Mandeville" set sail on a circumnavigation of the globe—albeit only in fiction; 150 years before Magellan, this Jules Verne of the Middle Ages claimed to have successfully completed this epic voyage; Christopher Columbus even took Mandeville's account with him on his 1492 expedition. Step by step, stage by stage, Europeans' horizons were broadening. By the start of the fifteenth century, the most concerted attempts to pioneer a sea route to India around the southern tip of Africa were being made by the Portuguese, foremost among them Prince Henry the Navigator. In November 1497, Vasco da Gama rounded the Cape of Good Hope, as he called it, and on May 20, 1498, made land at Calicut in southern India. With this remarkable seafaring triumph, the onward march of globalization began in earnest.

The Age of Philip the Fair of France

Yet while the wide world beckoned to European adventurers, their home continent remained a claustrophobic hotbed of conflict. The corrosion of the Holy Roman Empire during the "Interregnum" in Germany had major implications for the future of Europe. It was at that time, namely the mid-thirteenth century, under the reign of Rudolf of Habsburg (who favored links to southeastern Europe) that an increasing orientation toward the west became apparent among those princes whose power bases were close to the western frontiers of the empire. They duly formed closer ties with France. When Rudolf's son King Albert I of Germany was murdered in a family feud in 1308, several of these princes—namely the duke of Brabant and the counts of Hennegau-Holland, Luxembourg, Namur, Juliers, and Loon—met at Nivelles near Brussels and formed an alliance against all comers, with the exception of "their lords" the kings of France and Germany. It may have been that they were already planning to elect one of their own number king; in any event, they turned their back on the murderous Habsburg family and let themselves be wooed by Philip IV of France, who at the time was trying to win over the three Rhenish archbishops to support the election of his brother Charles of Valois as the next Holy Roman Emperor. Soon, other princes such as the duke of Lorraine, the counts of Gelderland, Leiningen, Virneburg, Sponheim, and Katzenelnbogen found themselves drawn into these plans.

In the event, matters never came to a head. Nevertheless, both the princes' league and the French plan to secure the emperorship can be seen as the prelude to the advent of a new order in Europe, a redistribution of power and sovereign territories. While this process took many centuries to complete, its general line of development became ever more clear from this juncture on. Philip's intention was a symptom of this change. The "Holy Roman Empire" (which in the Late Middle Ages was only very seldom referred to as the "German kingdom") dwindled away ever more obviously to just the German-speaking regions, and even further. This centuries-long development culminated, as is well known, in the peace settlements of Münster and Osnabrück, which brought the Thirty Years' War to an end in 1648. At that time, several of these regions definitively seceded from the imperial federation, either by switching to French sovereignty or by becoming independent. Even Napoleon still stood in this tradition when he reorganized the political shape of Central Europe. Finally, after an eventful history, the Grand Duchy of Luxembourg, formerly the heartland of the Carolingians, brought this process to a conclusion when, in the London Treaty of 1867, it renounced its membership in the German Confederation, which it had been part of up to 1866, and declared itself "neutral in perpetuity," so turning its back on the "German Empire" that Bismarck was then busy fashioning.

Around 1300, when this trend first set in, the great winner and outstanding representative of his age was King Philip of France, who was known by the soubriquet of "the Fair." During his reign, the structural transformation of the public sphere that we have already discussed above recurred with renewed vigor. The expansion in the number of university-educated scholars and their induction into the council of princes saw the emergence both of new educated elites, and of a new public, which was now much more conversant with questions of rulership, society, and political theory and which gained increasing influence. When challenged, it articulated its position in memoranda, pamphlets, or treatises like Dante's *Monarchy*—variously directed at opponents, adherents, or strangers, or written in response to opposing treatises. By now, a rhetoric deriving from the realm of scholarship had entered into the political practice of kings, popes, and princes. And their style of rule now accommodated itself to the requirements of these new educated elites, just as conversely scholarship had long since addressed the political demands of the day. This tendency was also evident, especially so, in France.

Above all canonistics (the study of canon law) and academic theology were in great demand; particular priority was given to teaching these disciplines at the leading universities, especially Paris. Dante railed against this practice, but in vain. The mystical search for God was still represented a powerful strain in religious thought. When, in her *Mirouer des simples ames anienties et qui seulemant demouret en desir et vouloir d'amour* (The Mirror of Simple Souls)—written in the vernacular, Marguerite Porete described a seven-stage path of devotion by which the soul might attain mystical union with God, a process that culminated in absolute freedom, her refusal to recant her position—a synod was convened in Paris—the same Paris that was rife with fear of heretics and where the Templars' trial had taken place. This ecclesiastical body duly referred her case to the secular authorities, and she was burnt at the stake in 1310. Yet her book was widely read. However, the authorities could not, indeed dared not, tolerate the notion of freedom through the free spirit of love, or the concept of a soul that learned its lessons direct "from the school of godliness" and in doing so became "godlike."[6] If their souls were to be redeemed, all human beings were required to be subservient to the pope in Rome, as Boniface VIII had decreed precisely at that time in his infamous papal bull *Unam sanctam* (1302).

Indeed, any ruler had to have constantly at his disposal all the statute books of canon law, the *Decretum Gratiani,* and even more importantly all papal decretals—and, along with these, scholars who could interpret them. Jurisprudence had long since established its position as a vital discipline for the exercise of power; it set the tone for political manifestos, in which Aristotelian arguments—borrowed from the philosopher's *Politics*—began increasingly to appear. Such scholarship helped promote the escalating secularization of social and political thought, a factor which became ever more clearly evident in the fourteenth century, breaking down many existing barriers.

Thus, for instance, in the works of Marsilius of Padua one encounters the statement that the development of civil societies, including their government and other manifestations, must necessarily—both by means of natural processes and human artifice *(ars)* as well as their imitation—proceed from a state of lesser to greater perfection. During the reign of Philip the Fair, this renowned Italian scholar was teaching in Paris; in 1312–1313, he was rector at the university's arts faculty. However, he only published his epoch-making work *Defensor pacis* in 1324, and then anonymously, so dangerous did he consider it. After all, this treatise challenged papal omnipotence and even went so far as to claim that peace, that most precious earthly commodity, was jeopardized by it. And it truly was a revolutionary work. "People," Marsilius maintained, "only believe they truly know something when they have grasped its initial causes and first principles and understood its basic elements." The implications of this statement were unprecedented: according to this unequivocal commitment to enlightened thought, the restrictive norms imposed by the church hampered progress. In accordance with this, Marsilius concluded: "The Holy Bible itself requires that no one should be compelled by worldly punishment and coercion to obey the Ten Commandments." Ideas like these undermined not only episcopal power over the curriculum and the papal primacy in matters of teaching, but also the whole apparatus of spiritual jurisdiction that had been put in place to safeguard this primacy, and that had long since used the secular law to enforce its authority.

Yet the application of the scientific method now also took hold of politics, which from this period on gradually assumed its own identity as a distinct concept and began to be referred to by this term. The discourses of university scholars, pastors, and confessors, the ways in which traditional texts were read, interpretations of society and the exercise of power, and indeed the means by which the world was interpreted now changed fundamentally. A new "thought collective" now arose from the interplay between the monastic schools of the mendicant orders and the royal and papal courts, engendering in practice a whole new way of thinking. Marsilius seized upon certain older "conciliar" ideas, placing the general council of the church over the pope and bishops, and drawing conclusions from this for the secular realm as well. Harshly and provocatively, he criticized the hierocratic tendency of the age in the following terms: "For all their threats of inflicting torment or imposing worldly or spiritual punishments, the decretals and decrees of the Roman and other bishops have no authority over anyone without the express agreement of the secular ruler or of a general council." He continued: "Electoral principalities or other elected offices only obtain their authority through the ballot box"—in other words, he meant to imply, not through papal endorsement, for instance.[7] In its logical consistency and in the light of prevailing doctrines, such statements were tantamount to blasphemy and to insurrection against the primacy of spiritual affairs over human reason. Moreover, Marsilius's conclusions did not merely relate to the empire, but rather to each and every form of secular authority, from royal rule right down to municipal government. How different it had been just a few years previously when Dante in his *Monarchy* (the exact date is unknown) had exalted the traditional bipolar world order, according to which the pope and emperor co-operated but nevertheless each governed his own separate sphere of influence. In this arrangement, where spiritual matters were concerned, the world was subservient to the pope alone, although what constituted the spiritual realm was not specified. In fact, Marsilius was only expressing ideas that had long since been common currency among the intellectual elites of Europe. In spite of this, or rather precisely for that reason, he was persecuted for his views. After his identity was disclosed, he was forced to quit Paris and flee to the court of the excommunicated King Louis IV (the Bavarian) in Munich in 1326. Marsilius dedicated *Defensor pacis* to him.

Marsilius was never a habitué of the Parisian court; his ideas would not have found favor there. Even so, secular thought focused on the maintenance of power was a long-established fact there. Philip IV, whose confessor Guillaume Imbert was also inquisitor-general of Paris, surrounded himself with outstanding councillors who were thoroughly committed to a secular mode of thought: these men included Pierre Flote, Enguerrand de Marigny, Guillaume de Nogaret (who may have come from a Cathar family), Pierre Bellepeche, Pierre Dubois, and others. The king was well versed in putting both jurisprudence and theology—Aristotle's *Politics* and the cold reason of university disciplines as well as orthodox religious faith—at the service of his policies and deploying them all to legitimize his authority. How could it have been otherwise in a country renowned for its scholarship and universities, and with Paris at its capital, the undisputed world center of theology?

No less efficient was the practice of centralized financial administration and the introduction of the highest court of appeal, namely the *parlement* with its *conseillers* and its fixed sessions;[8] indeed, these institutions were of even greater significance for the genesis of the modern, rationally ordered nation-state. These were both already in place when Philip ascended the throne, yet in both cases, it was Philip who provided the decisive impetus for their transformation into efficient public bodies. And both epitomized the triumph of the new culture of rationality, which was steadily permeating all practical aspects of life. For example, the *parlement* was various chambers with distinct areas of responsibility (dealing, say, with appeal cases, petitions to the king, and criminal cases). This trend would be consolidated over the course of the Middle Ages. Two further factors finally also came into play around this time: painting (indispensable for the staging and publicizing of the *religion royale*) and historiography, which was put to service presenting selective accounts of events, separating the essential from the inessential, disseminating royal claims and preserving insights for future instruction.

The tax system, which was based on the leasing of land, provided the material basis for royal policies. The administration of these lands lay in the hands of *baillies* and *senechauds,* who in many cases had completed a course of legal study. This leasehold taxation arrangement proved to be of great benefit to the king, but the precise opposite where his subjects were concerned, since the leaseholders guaranteed the king's earnings and so tried to extract from their tenants more than they were due to pay. In any event, royal financial requirements regularly exceeded income. Philip was a genius at amassing debts, and revenue raising became a key issue. Jews and Christians alike suffered greatly as a result.

The French king set about expanding his realm in a way that may now seem wholly unscrupulous. Even the church, the still powerful Knights Templar, and the papacy were not spared. The illustrious Templar Order was liquidated with the help of the Inquisition, torture, and burnings at the stake. During this process, Philip the Fair even went so far as to claim that he was the "King and pope and Emperor," though Dante decried him as the "evil Frenchman" and (because of his arrest of the pope) a "new Pontius Pilate."[9] Philip stopped at nothing to assert the majesty of his authority, which he saw as grounded in the Christian Faith, employing extreme violence, as his persecution of real and alleged heretics or his root-and-branch expulsion of the Jews attests. Writing in the sixteenth century, the historian Yosef ha-Kohen recalled Philip's direction of the unforgettable catastrophe of 1306:[10] "Every Jew is required (under pain of death, as the order stipulates) to leave my realm without his possessions, or to choose another God to worship, then we shall finally become a single People." Finally, the canonization of Louis IX by his grandson Philip was intended to sanctify the French monarchy anew; this ritual orchestration of their sovereignty was without parallel in Europe. Henceforth, the French king alone was styled the *"Rex Christianissimus," "Le Roi Très Chrestien,"* His Most Christian Majesty.

The Capetian dynasty was thus able to achieve what the Hohenstaufens had never managed; namely, to force the papacy to be beholden to the French crown without any disadvantage to the monarchy. For a century, France's kings and church had provided staunch support for the papacy in its conflicts with the Holy Roman Emperors, but now the erstwhile protector revealed itself to be a thoroughly dangerous friend. Philip the Fair, so to speak, reaped the harvest that Frederick Barbarossa and his grandson Frederick II had sown. The clearly visible signposts on this path were: the accusation of heresy leveled at Pope Boniface VIII; his arrest in Anagni by Philip's envoy Nogaret and a handful of troops (1313); the smashing and eradication of the Knights Templar from 1307 onward; the preponderance of Frenchmen in the college of cardinals; the Council of Vienne under Pope Clement V (1311–1312), which was forced to give its blessing to French interests; and finally the exile of the Roman Church into its Babylonian Captivity in the form of the transfer of the papacy to Avignon. The symbolic import of the shift of the Roman Church from the Eternal City to a region that nominally still belonged to the Holy Roman Empire, but which was to all intents and purposes already a French "province," was unmistakable.

Philip the Fair only suffered one real setback, when Flanders eluded the direct grasp of the French crown. Just as his great ancestor Philip Augustus had once seized the royal fiefdoms of the English king John Lackland, so Philip hoped to dispossess the count of Flanders. But the populace of Flanders rose in revolt, and took the field against French knights at the Battle of Courtrai in 1302. After bringing down the charging horses, the Flemish infantry slaughtered the helpless knights in their heavy armor.

Although this so-called Battle of the Golden Spurs did not succeed in winning independence for Flanders, it did assure its citizens the right to co-determination in the government of the county, and the date of the battle (May 11) is still celebrated as a national holiday in Belgium. Despite this defeat, however, France now emerged as the model and yardstick for all the other crowned heads of Europe.

The thrones of kings and their realms now, so to speak, moved closer together. Henceforth, the fate of each crown was followed mistrustfully by all its neighbors and the great empires; there were potential rivals around every corner. The poet and philosopher Dante was wise to their machinations and duly consigned them all—including the Holy Roman Emperor Albert I, who neglected Italy but who saw fit to celebrate the marriage of Edward II of England in the company of Philip the Fair—to Hell.[11] Even the events that took place in far-off Poland and Lithuania concerned the monarchs of the western lands, whose noblemen set off every year without fail on their notorious "hunt" of Prussian heathens. No king could effect a reorganization of power any more without his fellow monarchs being involved in some measure. Any wrong note that was struck in their orchestra disturbed their ensemble playing. But, to continue the analogy, it was France who wielded the baton in this pan-European concert. Philip IV's relations with other crowned heads therefore come to the fore.

The marriage of Philip's daughter Isabella to the English heir to the throne Edward (later King Edward II), which at first was clouded by what was almost certainly a homoerotic affair between the king and his favorite Piers Gaveston, was to have catastrophic consequences. It guaranteed the bridegroom not just Gascony as a French fiefdom, but also—something Philip the Fair could admittedly not have anticipated—gave the Plantagenets the chance, by appealing to the right to succession after the main line of the Capetian dynasty had died out, to regain all the mainland possessions lost by John Lackland and even to lay claim to the French throne. It thus became the cause of the Hundred Years' War between France and England, or at least the pretext for hostilities. Yet in Britain, the old conflicts between the increasingly unpopular king and his barons continued unabated; a new factor that now came into play was the growing influence of the towns, especially London. Isabella ultimately made common cause with the opposition and led an invasion army commanded by her favorite Roger Mortimer and supported by the king's and her own son (the future

Edward III) against her husband; Edward II was taken prisoner, and under massive pressure from the municipality of London declared unfit to rule. In 1327, the queen herself finally issued the order for his execution, which was carried out in a bestial fashion and in such a way as to leave no external signs of violence (some historians claim it was by suffocation, while others maintain that a red-hot poker was inserted into Edward's anus). This was the first regicide in the House of Plantagenet, though others were to follow. The throne was now usurped by the murdered king's son Edward III, who soon had Mortimer hanged and his mother placed under arrest (1330). Prior to this, however, he had already staked his claim to the French throne, immediately after Charles IV's death in 1328. From 1337 onward, in alliance with Louis the Bavarian, he attempted to seize it by force of arms. So began the long-running war between England and France, which would drag out over more than a century and eventually involve the whole of Europe.

The French kings had long had dynastic connections with the Iberian peninsula. Philip the Fair, however, made no attempt to consolidate them. He himself was a grandson of James the Conqueror of Aragón; on ascending the throne, he immediately ended the crusade against his uncle, King Peter III. It was on that campaign, which had been called because the Aragonese monarch had intervened in Sicily, that Philip's father had met his death. But beyond this, it was only the smallest of the Spanish kingdoms, Navarre (the Basque country) that excited Philip's interest. The heiress to this realm, Joan, the daughter of Henry I ("the Fat") of Navarre, was Philip's queen consort. In 1305, she founded the Collège de Navarre in Paris, which was soon to become famous. Under her rule, albeit reluctantly, the kingdom attached itself to the French crown until 1328. Then, the kingdom regained a dynasty of its own when Philip III, the husband of a daughter of Louis X of France and a scion of the House of Évreux, ascended the throne. This dynasty remained in undisputed control of Navarre until the fifteenth century, when the kingdom found itself caught in the power struggle between France and the kingdom of Castile-Aragón and its last king, Henry, a Huguenot, who largely ruled Navarre in name only, ascended the French throne as King Henry IV (1589). Famously, to avoid bloody conflict, he was later to renounce Protestantism and embrace Catholicism, claiming "Paris is well worth a Mass."

Likewise, the future kings and emperors from the ducal house of Luxembourg got to learn about the kingship of France from their mother's knee, as it were. Indeed, the first-born of this dynasty were raised at the French court, a situation that was not without consequences. The first of these, the Holy Roman Emperor Henry VII, probably served as page to Queen Marie of Brabant, the stepmother of Philip IV; in any event, she acted as his patron, and after him Henry's son John too, the first king of Bohemia from the House of Luxembourg, whose sister Marie was briefly married to the French king Charles IV (she died in childbirth), and finally John's son Wenceslas who, though born in Prague, came to Paris at the age of seven and spent the next seven years there being schooled. It was in Paris, too, that Wenceslas was confirmed, taking the name of his sponsor, King Charles IV, and where he received the spiritual and religious instruction that would shape his character. The first members of the House of Luxembourg to be given a "home" education principally in Prague were Wenceslas's (that is, Holy Roman Emperor Charles IV's) own sons and Henry VII's great-grandsons Wenceslas and Sigismund. This amounted to an act of liberation from France's spiritual leadership and testified to a newly awakened sense of cultural self-awareness in the Bohemian Empire.

It appears that Henry VII of Luxembourg entered the stage of European politics as the compromise candidate for Holy Roman Emperor between Philip the Fair and the Rhineland electors. Philip had spared no expense in attempting to have his brother Charles installed as emperor, but the electors deliberately procrastinated, under the skillful leadership of Henry's younger brother archbishop-elector Baldwin of Trier (then just twenty years old). In all likelihood, the electors were also fearful of bending to the will of this worrisomely ambitious king, and accordingly opted for the count of Luxembourg, who had been bound to Philip since 1294 by the *ligesse,* an oath of fealty. Henry VII was a man without any great power base at home and whom, so the Electors' reasoning ran, no one needed to fear. Philip, too, appeared content with the choice, at least for the time being. And yet Henry turned out to be a man of action. By way of impressing upon the French who was an emperor and who was merely a king, he set about renewing imperial political involvement in Italy, something from which the first Habsburgs had shied away.

However, the act of anointment as ruler, the coronation ceremony, immediately made plain to the future emperor the constraints he was bound by. This investiture was arranged specially for Henry in Aix-la-Chapelle and provided a political spectacle in liturgical garb. There was no hint here of a *religion royale,* as in France. The holiness of the empire went no further than its name. Religion subjugated the dignity of the royal and imperial office to the authority of the pope and tied the monarchy to the electors, but in no way enhanced the sovereignty of the emperor. Certainly, the emperor was deemed to occupy his position through God's grace, but how this was to be realized in practice was left to the personal destiny of the person anointed as ruler. The cataclysmic upheavals that had occurred over the preceding century, and that had completely changed the face of Europe, were reflected in this ritual. Henry's investiture supplanted the older coronation ceremony that had been instituted under the Ottonians in the tenth century and remained in use in the same basic form for the next half-millennium until the demise of the Holy Roman Empire. As the senior clergyman responsible for Aix (Aachen), the archbishop of Cologne performed the anointment, while the crown was placed on the new king's head by the three Rhineland archbishops together, including Henry's brother Baldwin. The coronation oath, which the king was required to swear during the ceremony, contained the thoroughly new commitment to regain *(recuperare)* all the privileges that the kingdom and empire had lost, yet also the no less new pledge to treat the pope with the utmost reverence and show him all due "subservience and loyalty." Taken together, these two obligations amounted to squaring the circle. Nevertheless, the crowned monarch was "invested with the kingdom of God" and enjoined to act as the guardian of this realm *(defensor regnique a Deo tibi dati existas).*

The formal declaration that subjugated the king to the pope was the result of developments since the Hohenstaufen debacle; this took on major significance for the future of the monarchy. In general, no opportunity was neglected to model the coronation ceremony after the now authoritative conception of the monarchy, which stressed the prevalence of spiritual power. Following the accession to the throne in the framework of a liturgical observance, the archbishop of Cologne reminded the new king—once again departing from the corresponding older formulation—that he was not ascending this royal seat of power "by right of inheritance and in succession to his father" but rather that he "had been assigned it by virtue of the authority of the electors in the kingdom of Germany, and according to the will of God and through our present dispensation."[12] In other words, God, the electors, and the king unified the empire, and the pope watched over it.

The prevailing conditions in Europe and Germany left very little room to maneuver for the first member of the House of Luxembourg on the throne. In concert with his brother Baldwin, who supplied him with troops, money, and credit, Henry exploited this as best he could. The electors and their chosen ruler could scarcely have anticipated that an opportunity would soon present itself for Henry to consolidate his own power, in the shape of the marriage of his son John to Elysabeth, the last of the Premyslid dynasty, and the heiress to the kingdom of Bohemia. This union would lend Europe's destiny a new turn; the emperor may have lived just long enough to enjoy this decisive victory over his rivals for the Bohemian crown before his untimely death in 1313.

Probably in response to financial hardship, and most definitely in expectation of rich pickings (which did not remain entirely unfulfilled), Henry turned his attentions to Italy. With this move, he deliberately thwarted the interests of his friends the Capetian dynasty, whose cadet branch, the House of Anjou, ruled Naples and who viewed the whole of Italy as its sphere of influence. The Roman crown weighed heavily on those who wore it, imposing new obligations and unfamiliar actions on them. For the first time since the demise of Frederick II, a new ruler— welcomed by some yet feared by others—now appeared in Italy who intended to bring his authority to bear there and who aspired to become Holy Roman Emperor. The Ghibelline supporter Dante rejoiced. The pictorial chronicle *(Baldineum)* recording Henry's Roman campaign, which Baldwin retrospectively commissioned both as a tribute to the dead emperor and to enhance his own reputation, celebrated his brother's deeds. Was Henry perhaps planning a return to the Hohenstaufen tradition? There are serious reasons to doubt this. After all, the means at his disposal were strictly limited. Furthermore, we are lacking any programmatic statements or explanations by the emperor himself revealing the motivation of his actions or his aims. Dante hoped for great things from the emperor and, naming him *l'alto Arrigo,* duly accorded him a place in Paradise, despite the fact that he had failed.[13] The poet's theoretical treatise on monarchy could no longer hope to legitimize the immediate divinity of the empire in the case of any particular emperor, but did at least fundamentally dispel any papal claims against the empire, while also obligating it to cooperate with the papacy.

The Italy into which the future emperor rode in 1310 was not just a country of cities at war with one another, and even though it was riven by internal quarrels of ambitious *signori* and violent *condottieri,* at the same time it was also a country of scholarship and universities, art, music, and poetry—the land of Dante and the *dolce stil nuovo,* the land of the painters Cimabue and Giotto (d. 1337). There, buildings were still being constructed in the Gothic style, but new developments were appearing on the horizon. The universities of Bologna and Padua, and of Perugia and Siena, too, were attracting students from all over Europe. In particular, they came to study jurisprudence and to become notaries, with fewer taking courses in theology; others opted for astrology combined with medicine, a common joint course of study. Subsequently, they disseminated all the new trends originating in Italy across the continent.

Dante's picture of the world as articulated in the *Divine Comedy* may be regarded as characteristic of his time. The poet's journey through Hell, Mount Purgatory, and Paradise; the guidance provided by the heathen Roman poet Virgil, in whose care the Christian writer placed himself; encounters with a host of well-known heroes and contemporaries in the Hereafter; the reflection of the present; the sighs and laments, warnings and prophecies of the damned and the redeemed souls; the detailed portrayal of the Afterlife, with its forensic sense of locality; the depiction of the worst torments and the most liberating bliss; the fear, hope, and confidence that this all evoked in his readers and listeners had a lasting resonance. The literary figures of the High Renaissance were still celebrating the Florentine poet and their great artists such as Botticelli, whose captivating drawings illustrated the *Divina Commedia,* and even used Dante's work to chart their own religious worldview; indeed, it was Boccaccio who first added the adjective *"Divine"* to its title (its author simply called it the *Commedia*).

Italy, then, immediately sucked Henry into the intense feuding that was going on both between and within its cities. The nobility were ranged against the *popolari,* the Ghibellines against the Guelphs, the "whites" against the "blacks," or whatever the individual parties chose to call themselves. These were power struggles rather than class conflicts, and the bishops played only a subsidiary role in them. Genoa, Pisa, Florence, Milan, Mantua, Venice and the Papal States were all in dispute with one another. The old feudal system had long since collapsed with the rise of the municipalities. Nowhere were there any clear fronts visible; what was the emperor meant to achieve in such circumstances? The cities and their rulers were powerful because they were wealthy and had total command of the world of long-distance trade. Certainly, Henry did manage to collect lapsed land easements and taxes owing to the empire, dues that the cities and the *signori* grudgingly conceded. But to pacify the country, restore royal and imperial authority there, unify the *Regnum Italicum,* and bring about peace were all beyond his capacity. Here there was no idea of nationhood, like that embryonic unifying force that had motivated the French aristocracy; nor did the idea of the *Imperium* engender a feeling of community anymore, even if the odd person here or there, like Dante, still dreamed of such an ideal. Each city, each *signore,* each *condottiere* was striving after sovereign control, free of the "imperial reins" that the Golden Bulls issued by the emperors from the north constantly referred to over centuries. The only options were failure or withdrawal.

In Milan Henry VII (possibly prompted by plots against him) strengthened the position of the ruling Visconti family against their deadly enemies, the Torriani. This was a decision in favor of the Ghibelline party, and henceforth they became the emperor's allies. Genoa reserved judgment and awaited developments. Pisa pledged its support, which inevitably antagonized Florence. The city on the River Arno, which just a few decades earlier had been forced to submit to Pisa, was a stronghold of the Guelph party and paid no homage to the emperor. Its greatest son, namely the imperial loyalist Dante, died in exile and never returned to his home town, even to be buried—his grave can still be seen today in Ravenna. Rome, too, gave the future emperor a distinctly frosty reception. The House of Anjou prepared to fight him and cast about for allies. Henry himself entered into negotiations with the Aragonese, who since the Sicilian Vespers of 1282 had ruled over Sicily as the sworn enemies of Anjou. However, he fell victim to malaria and died in 1313 before these talks could reach a conclusion. At least, though, Henry had appealed to imperial authority, and in so doing had called into people's minds something that was thought lost forever. He was buried in the cathedral in Pisa—one of two medieval emperors' tombs south of the Alps, and the only one to have been preserved, at least partially (it was the work of the sculptor Timo da Camaino). The grave of his wife Margaret of Brabant, who died two years before Henry and who is buried in the church of San Francesco di Castelletto (near Genoa) was made by the famous sculptor Giovanni Pisano, and was a work of exquisite beauty.

Following Henry's death in Italy, the electors turned their back on his house and after lengthy deliberations ended up with a split decision; their main motive was to ward off any new Capetian candidate but being divided among themselves, some opted for Frederick the Handsome from the House of Habsburg, while others chose the Wittelsbach candidate Louis the Bavarian. So it was that for the second time in German history a grown-up royal (in this case, Henry's son John of Bohemia) did not succeed his father; and for the fifth time, two rival kings found themselves fighting one another in Germany—the other occasions had been the counter-kingships of Rudolf of Rheinfelden and Hermann von Salm against Henry IV (1076–1088), Heinrich Raspe and William of Holland against Frederick II and Conrad IV respectively (1246–1254), and finally Albrecht's revolt against Adolf of Nassau (1296–1298). The consequences of this unique situation in the history of Europe (not counting Byzantium) are self-evident, especially when Germany is compared to her neighbors. For during this same period, France had no such situation to contend with; as a result, its monarchy could constantly consolidate itself and ascend to heights from which not even the Hundred Years' War of the fourteenth century could dislodge it; though on occasion suffering terrible hardship, at no time did France have to face a remotely comparable situation to that confronting the German kings of the time. Fate also smiled upon the rulers of the Iberian Peninsula. Only in late medieval England did similar circumstances arise, with kings being murdered and their assassins coming to the throne. Shakespeare gleaned much of the subject matter for his historical plays from this turbulent period.

Yet the constant recurrence of this succession dispute in the middle of Europe left its indelible mark not only on German history but also on the history of Europe as a whole. From time to time, it plunged the monarchy in Germany into ever more serious catastrophes, hastened the selling-off of imperial privileges and royal property, eroded the prestige and the assertiveness of the crown, hamstrung the king's power, and exposed it and the empire it represented to external incursions. The upshot was immediate repercussions to the advantage of a variety of agencies: territorial princes, the universal papacy, the composition of the influential college of cardinals, and finally Germany's ambitious neighbors. And indeed, when we consider the inevitable long-term effects on people's mind-set, on national cultures and on culturally conditioned attitudes, these repercussions can still be felt in the present day.

The houses of Wittelsbach and Habsburg now vied for eight years for hegemony, before Louis the Bavarian finally managed to put his adversary out of the running with a decisive victory at the Battle of Mühldorf (1322). Immediately, like his predecessor, he turned his attention to Italy, earning in the process the implacable enmity of Pope John XXII; on the basis of the papal approbation theory, the pope had already denied the king (before he became emperor) the exercise of all ruler's rights prior to his, namely the pope's, approval. Throughout his period in office, the Bavarian ruler never succeeded in shaking off this burden, whatever methods he employed, be it force of arms, or legal, Aristotelian, or theological arguments (Marsilius of Padua and William of Ockham for instance wrote treatises in his defense). Louis's failure ensured that the House of Luxembourg once more got to ascend the Roman throne.

Nevertheless, Louis the Bavarian and his court deserve closer scrutiny. Theology, art, and scholarship in general were greatly prized there. A dispute about the historical role of poverty in salvation shook the Franciscan Order and with it a large part of Latin Christendom, to whom the Franciscans administered pastoral care and acted as confessors. The argument started as a disagreement with the "Spiritual" wing of the Franciscan order (the Fraticelli) over the controversial figure of Petrus Johannes Olivi, a theologian who took his inspiration from the prophetic writings of Joachim of Fiore in espousing an extreme interpretation of ecclesiastical poverty; John XXII persecuted Olivi's followers, ordering them to be burnt at the stake as heretics if they refused to recant their views. The dispute turned upon the fundamental matter of poverty, which stood in such glaring contrast to the wealth of the church and its lavish display of pomp. It had been sparked by the question of the poverty of Christ and his Apostles, and was fueled by the rivalry between the Franciscans and their fellow mendicant order the Dominicans. In 1323, the pope decided against the Franciscan position and in his decretal *Cum inter nonnullos* denied the poverty of Christ. The minister-general of the order, Michael of Cesena, was summoned to Avignon and, after Louis the Bavarian, who had already spoken out in favor of the Franciscans on the poverty issue, had himself crowned emperor in Rome by its citizens (1328), Michael was accused of heresy and threatened with excommunication. The Franciscan leader duly fled to the emperor's court and, having been immediately deposed by pope as minister-general, remained there until his death in 1342. William of Ockham, a Franciscan like Michael and Olivi, sided with Michael and accused the pope of heresy.

The pope thus found not only his teaching authority called into question—as Marsilius had done before. In his attack, Ockham did not follow the theoreticians who wrote on canon law in drawing a simple distinction between *Regnum* and *Sacerdotium*. Rather, he fundamentally questioned the legitimacy of the pope's claim to absolute power as well as his claim that he should be obeyed unquestioningly in secular matters. In this matter, the pope's authority was usurped and illegitimate, while the governance and control he postulated over the whole of mankind was tyrannical. This, Ockham claimed, made all Christians slaves of the pope and meant that all princes and kings could be arbitrarily stripped of their authority. Ockham expressly took issue with the common interpretation of the entrusting of the Keys to Saint Peter (Matthew 16:19), which he maintained related solely to spiritual concerns and not to worldly ones; in other words, to pastoral care and not secular rule. Therefore, Ockham concluded, a papacy that overstepped its boundaries was of necessity heretical.[14]

The real target of these remarks, John XXII, was known on a personal level for his frugality and his ascetic lifestyle, yet on the other hand he maintained a court that could rival the emperor's, indeed which even surpassed it in opulence. John was responsible for building the enormous Palais des Papes in Avignon and, once it was completed, for hosting elaborate functions there. We know that he paid for lavish court festivals there such as weddings, as well as bestowing appropriate gifts—mutton and a side of beef, mutton and venison, even a goat on one occasion—to certain ladies, namely his own relatives by marriage, as befitted a banquet for honored guests. The records also attest to the sumptuous quarters he laid on to accommodate several worldly "subsidiary courts" comprised of his knightly retinue outside the walls of the city, such as one in the wine-growing region of Châteauneuf-du-Pape.[15]

No ruler of this period was complete without his patronage of art and literature. Louis's Italian campaign exposed the royal and imperial court to new intellectual and artistic stimuli. Every self-respecting city south of the Alps sponsored—at its own cost but also to its greater glory— architectural works, paintings, and sculptures. Pisa and Milan were pioneers in this respect, patronizing the arts from the late eleventh century on, but other smaller municipalities had long since followed suit, quite apart from the major patronage provided by Venice.

The artists of Italy were no longer content to paint Byzantine icon-like symbolic representations with gold backgrounds and simple props. The saints, though still idealized and not true to life, became more human, and unlike in earlier works, now met the gaze of those contemplating their image at eye level, rather than looking down on them. So, Saint Francis for example was portrayed walking among ordinary people. At the same time, painters began to expand their visual horizons. The natural, living world and real landscapes were discovered as a painterly subject. The forerunners of this revolution were the Florentine artist Giotto and the Sienese Duccio (d. 1319), along with Simone Martini and the Lorenzetti brothers, but the entire guild of painters would soon follow. It was quite common for Giotto to forego a gold background and dare instead to paint a blue sky made from costly ground lapis lazuli (ultramarine), which had to be imported from abroad. And so the Saint Francis that he painted for the church where this saint was interred, in Assisi, performs his miracles against the backcloth of just such a blue blue sky; contemporaries even imagined that they could step into these frescoes, so lifelike was the scene before them. The most famous examples of art from the reign of Holy Roman Emperor Louis IV must be the frescos of "Good and Bad Government"—replete with contemporary allusions—painted by Ambrogio Lorenzetti for the Palazzo Pubblico in Siena in 1338–1339.

In these works, Ambrogio painted a wide panoramic landscape with a distant horizon line, while at the same time daring—the first painter to do so—to cast his eye over a cityscape; these two features were instantly copied by other artists.[16] Their setting in the building's Sala della Pace (Room of Peace; also completed 1338–1339) lent the allegories of good and bad government depicted in the frescoes an air of authenticity and persuasiveness that had never been achieved before. "Behold how sweet and tranquil life in the city is" runs the text beneath the painting of good government. According to contemporary conceptions, the *dolce vita* hinted at the joys awaiting a person in paradise; yet since Thomas Aquinas and Tholomaeus of Lucca respectively, the term "paradise" had come to be applied to earthly and political realms. Here, in Siena, Venus was believed to auspiciously guide the destiny of the city and so "the people rule and will rule in future and shall never decline," as one of the foremost astrologers of the period Cecco d'Ascoli wrote in specific reference to Siena. He went on: "The women are beautiful, because Venus has put her mark on them all." Trade flourished; Lorenzetti depicts wool and linen weavers, as well as cobblers and the city's university. An inscription expressly invited the viewer to tear his eyes away from the beauty of the round-dancing virgins and the commercial hubbub of the city and focus on the good governance, the *Comune,* under which justice, unity, and peace resided, while "security" presided over the region. Rich harvests were assured. Under tyrants *(Tyranni),* however, greed, pride, discord, envy, treachery, and violence held sway; fear *(timor)* hunted with a drawn sword through the land while "justice" lay in bondage on the ground. Here, Saturn directed the affairs of men, and destruction, firebrands, and hunger were the order of the day. Lorenzetti's fresco visualized the statutes and the political communiqués of the municipal government. It soon became renowned for its illustration of the political theories of the age.

Louis the Bavarian understood the message it conveyed. Henceforth, the imperial court in Munich began to display some distinctly Renaissance-like features. This is most clearly evident on the reverse side of the singular gold coins that he had minted, and which no other Holy Roman Emperor who followed him ever copied. There, plain for all to see, was the unmistakable image of the outstanding ancient and Christian monuments of the Eternal City, the widely renowned sights of the city of the emperors and the apostles and also the site of remembrance that every pilgrim to Rome carried in his heart. These coins were imperial pretension, but also something more. With them, Louis was staging the concept of *Aurea Roma,* the seat of the apostle princes, as proof of his piety—he, the ruler excommunicated by the pope and who in turn had denounced the pope as a heretic. Eminent émigrés gathered at his court, joining Marsilius of Padua (d. 1342) and his friend and fellow campaigner Johann of Jandun, as well as the remarkable logician William of Ockham. Michael of Cesena also arrived there, the excommunicated Franciscan minister-general, plus Bonagratia of Bergamo. At that time, then, imperial Munich was a gathering-place for an intellectual elite that elevated this city and its court into a unique cultural center of Europe for fully a generation. Last but not least, Louis knew how to deploy art for his own ends. Accordingly, his court became a hotbed of new ideas, which his court art lost no time in turning into a powerful propaganda tool.[17]

Yet the Bavarian emperor had coequal enemies. One of them, John of Bohemia—Henry VII's son, who had been passed over by the electors—was a prince who scorned danger, a king and hero universally revered by Europe's knightly caste. "The more enemies I have, the more booty I can seize," he reputedly once told Louis.[18] Like some knight of the Round Table, he rode out in search of "adventure." The Czechs felt no great love for him; yet while he never felt at home in Bohemia, he did manage to win over Silesia. His real love was for his homeland of Luxembourg in the west; his urge to get closer to home drove him to Italy, to Tuscany, where he waged war against the Habsburg allies, the dispersed followers of Frederick the Handsome. John was a consummate schemer, and campaigned in Italy with the full acquiescence of the pope and the Guelph party, which might well have been hoping that this conflict would split Italy away from the Holy Roman Empire. But John was also pursuing his own agenda, seeking to establish a power base there. Presently, in 1332, he journeyed to Paris in order to fetch his own fifteen-year-old son, the future Holy Roman Emperor Charles IV, and take him south to fight alongside him. There, the young man was required to prove himself as a military commander—in the midst of companies of mercenary, battle-hardened soldiers assembled from all four corners of Europe. Their officers were men like Castruccio Castracani, who had served under Charles's grandfather Henry VII in the 1310s, or the unscrupulous Werner of Urslingen, who was soon to conduct a reign of terror throughout Italy. Charles was knighted at this time. Incidentally, the *condottiere* Castruccio, an archetypal *Principe* figure, was to be immortalized two hundred years later by Niccolò Machiavelli in a biography that glorified him as a hero but which was historically extremely unreliable.

Before they left Paris, the father and son traveled to Fontainebleau to meet Philip VI, the first Valois on the French throne, and sign a treaty that committed the Luxembourg dukes to services of fealty in the Champagne and Vermandois regions, services that were indeed later called upon. Meanwhile, the objectives that John was pursuing south of the Alps burst like so many soap bubbles in the wind. Clear battle lines still persistently failed to emerge there; Charles got into serious difficulties, and although he gained the support of papal and French forces, he failed to take Florence, the most powerful city in Tuscany, despite the assistance of many Guelph commanders. He found himself forced to withdraw, only returning to Italy when he was king. Even so, Italy had made a lasting impression upon the young Charles and furnished him with experiences that would change his life, experiences that went far beyond war and the pursuit of power. He discovered a liking for the art, scholarship, and literature of Italy, for the beauty and power of the Italian language, for the country's light and its vibrant colors, and for the early Renaissance. He had also seen through the senselessness of war and learned to value the art of diplomacy.

Nevertheless, a martial existence lay in store for the young Charles, a common destiny for rulers of this period. For example, the future emperor found himself repeatedly having to go to war on behalf of his feudal lord, the French king. Thus, in 1339, the English king Edward III in his capacity as the imperial vicar of Louis the Bavarian in western Europe, attacked the town of Cambrai, together with a number of German princes, the Duke of Brabant, the margraves of Jülich and Berg and others. Cambrai still belonged nominally to the German Empire, but in actual fact was already under French control; the bishop of Cambrai was defending the city for the emperor, while the Luxembourger Charles, as the margrave of Moravia, was serving under the fleur-de-lys banner.[19] Where was the city to turn in this situation of confused loyalties? A short while later, in 1341, even Louis the Bavarian, the emperor, sought an alliance with Philip VI; scurrilous rumors soon spread that because Louis's coffers were empty, he had been bribed to do so by the wealthy French ruler. However, a crucial reconciliation with the pope foundered once more on the obstinacy first of Benedict XII and then of Clement VI. The latter pontiff, at the urging of his former student in Paris, Charles of Moravia, now prepared to engineer Charles's ascent to the Holy Roman throne. And so the conflict was not resolved, and the Hundred Years' War between England and France took its course.

Finally, along with his father and a contingent of Bohemian troops, Charles (who had just been elected as the (counter–)Holy Roman Emperor by the enemies of Louis but had not yet been crowned) joined the Battle of Crécy (1346) on behalf of the king of France, Philip VI. After Otto IV, who had fought alongside the hopelessly outnumbered John Lackland at the Battle of Bouvines in 1214, Charles thus became the second German king to become embroiled in person in the conflict between England and France while his crown was in jeopardy, and like Otto he also left the field of battle in defeat. Admittedly, unlike his predecessor, Charles fled the scene in good time and did not leave the imperial standard to be captured;[20] he thus avoided the fate of his father, who by this stage was blind yet still became involved in the thick of the action and died a hero's death.

Crécy was one of the last great set-piece knightly engagements of the Middle Ages; and just as Bouvines had been a springboard for France's rise to become the foremost power in Europe, so Crécy formed the first high-point of the Hundred Years' War between England and France, which had broken out over the old bone of contention concerning whether the closer female line or the more distant male line took precedence in matters of inheritance, but which in practice soon came to be simply about dominance over the continent. Now, as in 1214, questions of inheritance in Brittany provided the initial *casus belli*. Philip VI (d. 1350) fled the field of battle, his reputation severely damaged. The estates assemblies in Paris and Toulouse imposed adverse financial administration measures on the king. However, the victor of Crécy, Edward III, the son of a daughter of Philip IV of France, besieged and promptly captured Calais (1347). This incident gave rise to the legend of the Burghers of Calais, six prominent citizens who were ordered by Edward to surrender themselves up for execution and hand over the keys of the city, in return for which he would spare the rest of the populace; sixty years later, the chronicler Jean Froissart was the first to recount this story, and the subject has been treated several times since by writers and artists, most notably the magnificent if wholly fanciful 1889 sculpture by Auguste Rodin.[21] The costs of the war were gigantic; these were met through the extension of credit, which overstretched the royal budget and led to continual tax rises and concurrently to a strengthening of parliament. The war's catastrophic repercussions even reached Italy, plunging the Bardi banking house—at the time the largest in Europe, with at least twenty-five subsidiaries stretching from Seville to Constantinople and Jerusalem, and from Tunis to England—into bankruptcy.

Yet Charles was favored by fortune. He not only escaped disaster at Crécy, but fought his way back to Bohemia; the commendable fate of his father—*le plus noble roy,* as the contemporary and Anglophile Liègeois chronicler Jean le Bel dubbed him[22]—caused people to forget his own ignoble flight. Luckily, too, he had completed an account of his own deeds, his autobiography, just before the Crécy campaign, thus sparing himself from having to recount the bitter defeat. Charles also learnt lessons from this escapade. Henceforth, despite being offered the opportunity on three occasions, he avoided marriages with king's daughters, kept a judicious distance from France, and effected a rapprochement with the English king. He also kept himself out of their endless intrigues and conflicts. Even so, the French and English clashes failed to ignite a wider European conflagration, though Europe certainly got to feel the effects of their antagonism. In addition, Charles's great adversary, the Bavarian emperor Louis IV, met with a fatal accident while out hunting the following year (1347). The German princes and cities now broadly recognized the Luxembourger as Holy Roman Emperor; even the Czechs loved him, as he was a Premyslid on his mother's side.

A "European" Ruler: Emperor Charles IV

Although this young man, formerly known as Wenceslas but now going by the name of Charles, had only prevailed over the "Godless Bavarian Antichrist" in his attempt to gain the imperial crown with the active assistance of his old tutor in Paris, now Pope Clement VI (from 1342), he was not the "Cleric's King" *(rex clericorum)* that Ockham mocked him for being from the safety of his sanctuary at the royal court in Munich, however much Clement may have wished that he were.[23] Rather, Charles was the most "European" of all the medieval Holy Roman emperors; he surpassed even Charlemagne in this regard. He knew from first-hand personal experience about the problems of France and England, Italy and Spain, as well as the eastern lands of Silesia, Poland, and Hungary. This ruler was far from taking a narrowly "German" perspective; his reign can be taken as a guidepost through half a century of European history.

Charles's native language was Czech, French was spoken when he was growing up, he was educated in Latin, and he learned Italian as a youth while he was in Italy; it is not known how much, if any, German he knew. Like his father and grandfather before him, he spent seven key years in Paris, under the watchful eye of the French king, where he learned how to use power in a measured way and to govern flexibly, and also how to harness knowledge for the benefit of the realm. A pious ruler and an insatiable collector of religious relics, he got to know how to use the church to achieve his ends and to exploit it without sacrificing himself to it. Last but not least, he came to appreciate the power of money. The Florentine chronicler and banker Matteo Villani claimed resentfully that Charles had only come to Italy to fill his money bags and to carry off the imperial crown like some merchant.[24] The interest he took in financial matters was in accord with the radically changed times in which he found himself living, an age that had discovered and knew how to manage the concepts of capital, double-entry bookkeeping, and cashless monetary transactions across national frontiers. Many of the electors that brought him to power, such as the archbishop of Cologne, had demanded hard cash, and Charles could on occasion be exceedingly generous toward cardinals when it was a matter of facilitating the signature of treaties. Yet where his erstwhile mentor the pope was concerned, who had just reminded the newly elected emperor about the remit of papal jurisdiction also running in secular affairs and who now expected Charles to unequivocally assent to the papal right of approbation and swear an oath of obedience, the emperor, advised and supported by his great-uncle Baldwin, the archbishop of Trier, promised everything but in actual fact kept to none of his promises.[25]

The young Luxembourger assumed his new name of Charles and carried it like a victory banner through Italy. Close to the enemy city of Florence, the sixteen-year old hero established a castle at a strategically important location, which he named for himself: Montecarlo—nowadays a picturesque village in Tuscany.[26] The emperor's name was not chosen at random. Again, a French paradigm influenced his choice. For in France, in a thoroughly intentional expression of Carolingian tradition, there had already been a Charles IV (who had acted as this emperor's religious sponsor).[27] His very name proclaimed the doctrine of *Reditus,* which sought to establish a sense of implied suitability for imperial office and dynastic legitimacy through a "return" to the Carolingian dynasty.[28] In its earliest guise under Philip II and also later, this doctrine postulated the only very thinly disguised claim to the whole of Carolingian *Francia.* Regarding the polities of the thirteenth and fourteenth centuries, this meant a French claim to Lorraine, the lands right up the Rhine, indeed if the succession to Charlemagne was also taken into account, to the Holy Roman Empire as a whole. Furthermore, this doctrine blended with another theory that was formulated around 1200 by a combination of canon law and other legal experts and was intended to rebut imperial claims or juristic doctrines— namely the theory of the "king who is emperor in his own realm."[29]

In fact, Louis IX's brother Charles of Anjou, who deposed the Hohenstaufen dynasty from the throne of Sicily and had their last representative, the sixteen-year-old Conradin publicly hanged in the marketplace in Naples, had already ascended the Sicilian throne with designs on being appointed Holy Roman Emperor, while his uncle Philip the Fair, as we have already seen, was trying to gain the Roman royal crown, and hence the emperorship, for his brother Charles of Valois after the assassination of King Albert in 1308. Though Philip failed in this goal, the territorial claims attached to it endured for centuries. But when the Capetian monarch Charles IV gave the young Wenceslas his own name at the latter's confirmation in the French coronation church of St.-Denis in 1323, he no doubt did it in the assumption that the future king of Bohemia and elector—endowed with his symbolically resonant new name, and also related dynastically to the *lignée de Charlemaine le Grant* through his recently arranged forthcoming marriage to the king's cousin Blanche de Valois—would be instrumental in bringing about just such a *retournement.*

This change of name, though, also had the potential to be politically explosive.[30] It seems it was not taken as a provocation in Bohemia, despite the king having thereby renounced his connection to the national patron saint Saint Wenceslas. Yet presumably quite intentionally, the confirmation and name-change occurred at precisely the same time (1323) as the start of Pope John XXII's conflict with Louis the Bavarian. Emboldened by the support of the French king, the "man from Cahors," as the "man from Bavaria" disparagingly referred to Pope John XXII, the eloquent jurist and reorganizer of the papal finances, by now a stubborn and querulous old man of eighty, commenced hostilities against Louis IV from his seat at Avignon. The point at issue was Italy and Lombardy, which the pope wished to see detached from the German kingdom; the old confrontation between the Ghibellines and the Guelphs once again played into the politics of the empire, and the succession dispute between the houses of Wittelsbach and Habsburg resumed. The pope himself sought to enhance his own power, and new plans circulated for the Capetians to assume the imperial crown; John of Bohemia is reputed to have offered it to his stepson Charles of France. Meanwhile Louis's provocation, as the Roman Curia saw it, had now been answered with Wenceslas of Bohemia's change of name in the same symbolic language, with the evocation of the "stronger" and hallowed name of "Charles." The Luxembourger was expected subsequently to live up to his new name; as the second man to succeed John XXII on the Petrine Throne, Clement VI, admonished that Charles when approving his election as king, he should strive to be *katholicus . . . devotus et magnificus ecclesie,* a clear allusion to Charlemagne.[31]

Henceforth, the new king not only regarded Charlemagne as a saint and his heavenly patron, he also consciously placed himself within the imperial tradition of the Frankish king, summarily dismissing all foreign claims. Like no other ruler since Otto III—Barbarossa, who was responsible for canonizing Charlemagne, included—he revived the memory of the great ruler in Aix-la-Chapelle. There, on the feast of Saint James (July

25, 1349), almost three years to the day since his election as king of the Romans, he had himself anointed a second time, crowned the reliquary bust of Charlemagne (in all likelihood commissioned by him) with a precious crown, and consecrated an altar to Saint Wenceslas. It is also possible (though recent scholarship has cast doubt on this) that he was also responsible for extending the Palatine Chapel by commissioning the construction of the Gothic choir (built from 1355 on).[32] In Charlemagne's church and at his tomb, this unique memorial site, the Luxembourger was at pains to demonstrate that he was following in his footsteps.

Yet even that was not enough. Charles transferred Aix to the Czech metropolis of Prague, so to speak, by founding the Augustinian monastery of Karlov (Karlshof) in the new town there. Not only did he dedicate it to his titular saint, but also had the church there modeled after the royal church of Saint Mary in Aix (Aachen Cathedral), with an octagonal tower surmounted by a cupola. And when finally, after eight years of marriage to Anna von Schweidnitz, Wenceslas, the successor he so longed for, was born in 1361, in thanks he made an offering equivalent to his son's weight in gold to the cathedral at Aix, instead of making a pilgrimage there.[33] Elsewhere too, such as at Ingelheim, which at that time was believed to have been Charlemagne's birthplace, Charles founded chapels or altars dedicated to him. Admittedly, seen from the perspective of the empire as a whole, the earlier paradigm of "Charles" which the monarch christened Wenceslas may have brought with him from Paris had nothing more in common with the canonized "Charlemagne"; the Carolingian tradition remained firmly rooted in France. The next royal son to be born there was once again baptized in the name of Charles (Charles V, b. 1338) and likewise his son, and his grandson Charles VII (the king whose throne was saved by Joan of Arc), and so on down the lineage. The Holy Roman Emperor Charles IV, on the other hand, christened none of his sons in the Carolingian manner. The name had evidently served its sole purpose, as a counter to Louis the Bavarian.

Charles IV reigned, as far as he was able, in the French manner, as *ung tres grant sages homs* ("a great wise man"), who ruled his kingdom "more by wisdom . . . than by force" *(plus . . . par sens que par armes),* as one French chronicler noted approvingly.[34] The methods he employed had been tried and tested at the French court: diplomacy, a sophisticated "divide and rule" policy toward opponents, bringing pressure to bear either gently or firmly, making willing concessions when no great losses were at stake, and noncommittal silence occasionally dissembling approval in delicate matters. Moreover, he kept a close eye on financial policy, and shrewdly greased palms when necessary. An elaborate public-relations machine, in the form of Charles's royal patronage, served to legitimize and promote his policies and rulership. Finally, the king of Bohemia used historiography, that enduring repository of cultural memory, to dramatize his role as king and emperor. Before long, the Bohemian realm he had inherited was enjoying a new blossoming of culture.

The emperor himself was remarkably well educated. As a ruler, he surrounded himself to a far greater extent than his predecessor with scholars, and founded in Prague the first university to be situated within the domain of the Holy Roman Empire north of the Alps. These regions now found themselves, albeit after a delay of many centuries, being gradually introduced to the mainstream of European development and subjected to an urgently needed modernization program. Charles IV's royal rivals took their cue from him, first the Habsburgs with the University of Vienna, and then by the count of the Rhineland Palatinate, from the house of Wittelsbach, with the founding of the University of Heidelberg. These were followed by the municipal University of Cologne and the Studium Generale in Erfurt (within the archdiocese of Mainz). Above all, there was a pressing need for jurists and canonists to help the emperor steer his own rule and the empire as a whole safely through the perilous waters of ecclesiastical norms.

Charles IV did not fall in line with the general trend of the age, however. Although jurists played a major role in his council, permanent legal departments were not established in Prague, unlike in Paris and London; in this regard, then, the imperial court remained behind the times. Just under a half of Charles's advisors were clerics. In addition to notaries, the inner circle of the court was especially interested in doctors and astrologers; no physician in those days could hope to get far without the services of the latter. Innovations spread throughout Charles IV's realm via the royal chancellery. Charles's chancellor Johann von Neumarkt stylized the official correspondence of the Prague court in conscious imitation of the eloquent manifestoes of Frederick II; he corresponded with Petrarch, whose letters he likewise assimilated as models for the royal chancellery. In this way, the latest linguistic fashions and the literary Renaissance began to find their way, ever more rapidly, to the north. Yet all attempts to woo Petrarch to Charles's court were in vain. He was scared off by the "barbarian country" *(terra arbarica)* and its unappealing climate—this was, after all, the period of the "Little Ice Age"—although he did praise the serious-minded demeanor of its people *(virorum gravitas)* and was captivated by the beauty of Rhineland women: "Ye Gods! What a figure! What grace!" *(Dii boni! que forma! quis habitus!).*[35] The spoilt Italian turned down all royal and imperial blandishments and remained in the south; so it was that initial stirrings of a Renaissance were evident in Prague but never came to anything. Ultimately, Charles IV was not a Renaissance prince.

Charles had a tense relationship with Cola di Rienzo, the second representative of this proto-Renaissance. Rienzo was a popular notary who attempted to restore the "ancient jurisdiction of the city of Rome" *(antiqua iurisdictio Urbis).* This self-proclaimed "tribune of Rome" *(Tribunus Augustus)* had formerly, during the succession dispute, summoned Louis the Bavarian, Charles, and the electors to appear before him, and had called for the election of the emperor to be the preserve of "the Holy Roman people." Furthermore, he demanded that the *Imperium Romanum* should revert from the squabbling electors to Rome itself, and for all endowments to be restored to the Roman people, along with the return of all the authority, jurisdiction, and power that the Senate and People had ever possessed. Naturally, Charles had to condemn and punish such aspirations, yet could not help being impressed by the sheer force of the rhetoric of Rienzo, the son of a washerwoman.[36] Charles was no revolutionary or fantasist; he only planned what was practically achievable and indeed succeeded repeatedly in his aims. Nevertheless. he still had an appreciation of grandeur and of forward-looking innovations.

At least in the eyes of his contemporary, the chronicler Froissart, Charles was regarded as inquisitive and keen to explore the wonders of the world *(estoit bien enfourmés de toutes ces choses que li venoient à grant mervelles).*[37] Accordingly, a well-traveled man who was a lively conversationalist and experienced raconteur of wondrous stories, the Florentine Franciscan monk Giovanni de Marignolli, regularly enjoyed the hospitality of the emperor's table. After his coronation in Rome, Charles met Marignolli in Italy and invited the mendicant to accompany him back to Bohemia as his royal chaplain. The emperor commissioned him to compile a *Cronica Boemorum,* which he hoped would furnish edifying *Exempla* promoting peace and moral behavior, as well as imparting many useful facts. This didactic agenda was crucial to Charles; schooled in the works of Saint Augustine, he abhorred idle curiosity.

Giovanni de Marignolli duly got to work on his *magnum opus,* but disappointingly it turned out to be a rather insubstantial, unoriginal world history.[38] But the one notable thing it did contain, which must have roused the emperor's interest, was an account of the compiler's fourteen-year-long mission, at the behest of Pope Benedict XII, to the court of the Great Mongol Khan in Cambaluc (Beijing). Marignolli had spent a total of three or four years—his memoirs were not very precise on this point—living at the Mongol court. He wrote about the Gobi Desert and Cathay, about the island of Ceylon and the supposed earthly paradise on the mainland opposite, which Adam and Eve had been forced to leave, and went on to claim that he had personally heard the rushing waters of the rivers of Paradise. His report was alive with curiosity and all manner of miraculous sightings. In encouraging Marignolli to put his experiences down on paper, the Holy Roman emperor, lord of the world *(Orbis)* furnished himself with a picture of the world that blurred the boundaries between the accurate and the outlandish. The monk certainly demonstrated an extensive knowledge of the world such as only a few Venetian, Genoese, or Florentine merchants would have possessed at that time. But what both this well-traveled individual and his contemporaries lacked was an appropriate interpretive model by which to properly evaluate these new experiences and to extrapolate general insights out of the episodic narrative of his recollections. And so he couched these experiences in terms of a traditional interpretation of history and the world that leaned heavily on Saint Augustine and that failed to grasp the truly revolutionary implications of his findings for all previous learning.

Giovanni de Marignolli thus conceived of the world—and adduced his own experiences to corroborate this view—as a land mass floating on one vast ocean, which in turn was divided into four quarters in a cruciform arrangement; its two (probably northerly) segments, surrounding inhabited regions of the world, were navigable, whereas the two other, southerly, portions were impassable: "For God did not wish man to circumnavigate the earth on the oceans." On the one hand, Marignolli knew of the island of Sumatra ("the realm of the Queen of Sheba") and was aware that in that location, that is, south of the Equator, the sun was to the north and cast shadows to the south, and had it on good authority from a Genoese traveler and astrologer that one could not see the Pole Star from there, but that one could see the Southern Cross; he also decisively rejected the fanciful notion of "Antipodeans," namely people with feet at the opposite end of the body from Europeans, sprouting out of their heads. And yet on the other hand this papal legate was prone to seeing mystical signs of the Cross wherever he went in the world. In fact, it may have been this "discovery" that first attracted the emperor, a deeply devout Christian, to the stories of Marignolli. Charles, though, was also captivated by the miraculous; Marignolli recounts how the emperor took back to Prague with him a girl he had discovered in Florence whose face was completely covered in hair. Marignolli interpreted such miracles as entirely natural, as the malformed offspring of Adam or as the fabrications of poets. The monk's mind-set remained firmly rooted in a biblical view of the world and fixated on Europe, which he defined as extending from Hungary in the east via England and France to the ends of the Earth in the West; the chronicler maintained it was inhabited by people who, like himself, always hankered after new experiences, though they really ought not to.[39] Yet this intertwining of novelty with familiar concepts could, Marignolli claimed, produce some original constructs.

However, ultimately Charles IV was less concerned with global matters than with his own and others' perception of his rule. This perception was filtered through measures that had the same effect on common subjects and the country's nobility as they did on rivals and adversaries, and whose ultimate goal was legitimization of Charles's reign. Charles seized this opportunity, and the Bohemian aristocracy followed his lead. For example, all genres of visual art were harnessed to this end; Louis the Bavarian's example loomed large in this undertaking. Charles's long sojourns in France and Italy had opened his eyes to the beauty and power of new forms of representational art, namely High and Late Gothic architecture, sculpture, and painting, as well as literature and music. It is possible that he got to marvel at Andrea Buonaiuti's grand fresco depicting the "Triumph of the Church" in the Spanish Chapel of Santa Maria Novella in Florence, a work that was completed around the time (1365–1367) of his second journey to Rome. As always, such art facilitated official communication: art and propaganda, legitimization and aesthetic allure went hand in hand.

Europe's art scene was changing at this time. Musicians and painters were highly sought after. Political patronage boosted the demand for their works.[40] Even female artists were able to make their mark in this period: in his *Decamerone,* Giovanni Boccaccio celebrated a woman painter who— and this was an unheard-of novelty—displayed her works in public with a view to selling them. Meanwhile, at the French court, the poetess Christine de Pizan was hawking her verses, the first female writer to earn a living from her art. Nor were her poems confined to eulogies of the king. Other women were to follow in the wake of these two pioneers. The West began to experience widespread cultural exchanges. The greatness of the relatively small, polycentric continent of Europe started to manifest itself in the unique degree of integration of its available forms of culture—be it politics, religion, scholarship and art, or more abstract modes of thought, ways of living, or forms of social organization—an integration that was designed to safeguard its existence.

In the art of Charles's court, too, French and Italian influences were blended with native traditions. Artists, art works, and musical innovations reached Bohemia from Italy. Suddenly, a polyphony that had never been heard before resonated around Charles's court, while the ballata and rondeau forms were introduced to Prague. One of the first composers of the *Ars Nova,* Guillaume de Machault, had traveled through Bohemia in the retinue of Charles's father John the Blind, and he continued to reside in Prague during Charles IV's reign. The emperor arranged for major state occasions like the reception of foreign monarchs such as the king of Cyprus to be accompanied by this music.[41] Portraiture was also encouraged, and attained new heights of proficiency. Grandiose churches, public buildings decorated with painting and sculpture, beautiful Madonna statues in churches, illuminated manuscripts, publicly displayed priceless reliquary caskets, and crown jewels—all these art forms combined to create an instrument of legitimation that worked on several levels simultaneously, on both the senses and the soul, on the common people and the nobility, and among lay people and the clergy alike.

Even so, Charles took a very realistic view of the possibilities open to him. His customary approach was one of shrewd modesty; only rarely did he take an impulsive step. He assessed situations carefully and preferred peaceful, cost-saving solutions, agreements, and treaties rather than engage in costly wars. In fact, Charles was renowned for despising war. "Win victories by peaceful means," he is reputed to have advised his son; "desist from war if you can achieve your ends through diplomacy" *(Und sigest fridesam und was du mit gúte maht wol überkumen, do erlo dich krieges).*[42] In any case, the limited scope for action that was still open to the king and emperor obliged him to cooperate with his nobility, since direct rule or intervention in their territories was out of the question. Maintaining the peace called for consensus politics, and was no longer achievable, as it once had been, through coercion and monarchical *Terror*.

Charles identified a better chance of stabilizing his reign in the East than he did in the West. Here, he continued to pursue the policy of acquisition that both his father and he himself, in his capacity of duke of Moravia, had followed. He seized every opportunity to increase Luxembourg territory; patiently, he also added small and even tiny sovereign lands to his possessions. His clever marriage policies created favorable conditions for this. Beginning with Bohemia, he acquired first Silesia, which he completed through marriage to the heiress to the territories of Schweidnitz and Jauer; then came Egerland and Vogtland, the upper Palatinate and Franconia with the city of Nuremberg at its heart, and finally Upper and Lower Lusatia. In the final years of his life, he also, in return for massive payments, secured control of the margravate of Brandenburg; patrician Nuremberg bankers arranged the necessary finances for this transaction. From there, the mouth of the River Oder, the River Elbe, and the Baltic Sea were within his purview. The result of this eastward-directed activity was a stronger linking of northern and eastern Europe to the centers of culture in the west and south of the continent.

Charles, however, was not content with simply amassing new lands. It was his intention to reorganize the territories he had gained and to unify them under one jurisdiction. Accordingly, he set about developing them into a kind of royal demesne; here, too, we may surmise a French influence. He succeeded in doing what the Premyslids had attempted yet failed to achieve in the eleventh century, that is to raise the ecclesiastical status of Prague from a diocese to an archdiocese (1344) and so to release it from subservience to the archbishopric of Mainz. The concept of the "Bohemian Crown" as epitomizing all the lands, sovereign titles, and rights over which the king of Bohemia held sway was down to Charles IV. It also had the effect of integrating the Czech aristocracy. As far as he was able, the emperor incorporated his newly acquired territories under the Crown. This not only represented a decisive stage in the process of abstraction leading to the modern conception of statehood; in addition, this crown symbolized the crown of the Roman king and hence the emperor. In other words, the Holy Roman Empire was now to be governed from Prague and from nowhere else. The "Crown of Bohemia" also appeared as a very tangible symbol, inasmuch as Charles had a corresponding crown jewel commissioned to adorn the reliquary bust of Saint Wenceslas in Prague, which thereafter would be "lent out" by the country's patron saint for the coronation of the Bohemian king. The crown of Saint Wenceslas remains one of the most expensive royal treasures ever made, and copies of it and the great reliquary cross that Charles also commissioned are displayed in Prague.

France imposed itself as an exemplar upon the whole of Europe. This is especially evident in the city of Prague, which under Charles was turned into a much-admired royal residence on the French model. Charles, so to speak, imported Paris wholesale to his own capital, displacing it from the Seine to the Vltava. The records show that French courtiers were brought in to assist in this transformation, for example one Nicolas Sortes, who in 1347, shortly after Charles's coronation, came from Paris to the Bohemian court, and who only the year after had already filled the position of chief notary there, with responsibility for distributing the more important privileges on behalf of the Bohemian court. And just as the congruence of the royal and episcopal seat in Paris was symbolized in urban planning terms by the proximity of the royal palace and Notre Dame Cathedral on the Île de la Cité, so Charles also realized the architectural unity of the royal castle and Saint Vitus's Cathedral by siting them together on the Hradcany hill above the river. Charles was responsible for commissioning both buildings. A prestigious new bridge across the Vltava was also an essential feature of a royal capital, and Charles duly had it built, too. The programmatic sculptures decorating the tower of Charles Bridge left no doubt as to the identity of its creator; the bridge tower may well have been modeled on a famous similar structure that Frederick II designed for the city of Capua, the gateway to the kingdom of Sicily. The Charles Bridge linked the commercial center of the city to the seat of the king and archbishop, and rivaled the famous bridges over the Seine in its grandeur. Emulating Paris's long-standing institution, Prague likewise was now graced with a university and, with the Collegium Carolinum, a university college on the Parisian model.

Against the plans of Archbishop Ernst of Podiebrad, but fully in accord with the wishes of the king, the new cathedral in Prague was also built in the French royal Gothic style by a French architect, and endowed with special judicial and liturgical privileges. It combined in one building the episcopal church and the commemorative church for the two royal houses of Premyslid and Luxembourg. Its remarkably lifelike busts of rulers by the sculptor Peter Parler are reminiscent of the series of statues of deceased kings in the Grande Salle of the royal palace on the Île de la Cité and in the royal burial church of Saint-Denis.[43] Charles, who had been brought up in Paris, was responsible overall for a resacralization of the office of king and emperor, a phenomenon he had witnessed at first hand in the *religion royale* of the French. So it was that, directly after his election, and in a deliberate adaptation of an ancient practice (also by way of snubbing papal demands for the right of approbation and in assertion of his own jurisdiction by contrast) he introduced the regular reading by the Roman king and future emperor of a particular passage from the Gospel of Saint Luke (2:1): "And it came to pass in those days that there went out a decree from Caesar Augustus" *(Exiit edictum a Caesare Augusto)* into the Christmas matins service;[44] he also obtained from Pope Innocent VI the dispensation to hold a Festival of the Holy Lance and Nails of the Cross, which were publicly "displayed" annually on the appointed day (the eighth Friday after Easter) on Charles Square in Prague on a podium specially erected for the occasion—this devout act was recognized by the pope with a three-year indulgence for the remission of sins. Furthermore, anyone who celebrated Mass, no matter where, at the same time as the king and emperor did on this day, was granted remission of one hundred days.[45]

The religious cult instituted by the Bohemian king deliberately emulated the veneration of the Crown of Thorns and other saints' relics in the Sainte Chapelle of the royal palace in Paris. Similarly, Charles also ordered his own reliquary chapel of Karlstejn to be built some thirty kilometers southwest of the capital, together with its own seminary, the Collegium Caroli; from Paris, he even acquired a thorn supposedly from the original Crown of Thorns, and used it to establish a kind of imperial religious cult venerating the crown, the cross, the lance, the nails, and the vinegar-soaked sponge, namely the final instruments of Christ's suffering on Earth, and for all of this gained an indulgence of seven years.[46] There, to the castle that was named for him, and to the spiritual sanctuary of the seminary that likewise bore his name, Charles would, as it were, take refuge in himself and conduct his personal devotions. The salvation-bringing Imperial Regalia, the *sacre imperiales reliquie,* were also housed in Karlstejn for safekeeping. And so Europe arose as a cultural entity through rivalry, through imitation, and through a process of mutual learning and exchange. The Luxembourger on the Czech throne proved to be one of the great facilitators of this historical development.

All of this cost huge sums of money, of course. Money thus played a key role in the political machinations of the Bohemian king and Holy

Roman Emperor; this was something else that the young prince had learned in France. He was in the habit of "ending his wars through the power of gold and silver," according to the contemporary chronicler Jean de Noyal (d. 1396).[47] In addition, he had to hand the example of his great-uncle Archbishop-Elector Baldwin of Trier, who—advised by renowned Jewish bankers like Muskin, Baruch, or Jacob Daniels whom he employed as treasurers and chamberlains—was an outstanding financial policymaker. The rich silver mines at Kuttenberg (Czech: Kutná Hora) meant that the finances of the Bohemian kingdom were on a firm footing; but even these were insufficient to fund Charles's plans. The king and emperor showed himself open to considering economic matters on a Europe-wide scale. He listened to the advice of experts and collaborated closely with high financiers in his domains, to their mutual benefit.

In particular, the mercantile dynasties of Nuremberg, who were specialists in financial affairs and who had secured imperial privileges even during the reign of King John the Blind, enjoyed Charles's favor—foremost among them the Stromers. The emperor borrowed heavily from them, transactions that were financed by means of the common ploy of raising imperial liens, a peculiarly German form of security interest that had been in evidence since the succession dispute between the Hohenstaufens and the Guelphs. Even the home territory, the county or (after 1354) duchy of Luxembourg, did not escape this fate. Between them, John, Charles, and his son Wenceslas repeatedly mortgaged their homeland. The Bohemian and Roman crown only served to enhance the reputation of the mercantile dynasties, but did incalculable harm to the duchy of Luxembourg. Its territorial development proceeded in a discontinuous fashion, was constantly under threat, and eventually got caught up in the power politics of the dukes of Burgundy, and hence in the history of the Spanish Netherlands.

Even in this period, time was money. Financiers and merchants needed to keep a close eye on the most important currencies, whose exchange rates regularly fluctuated. Speculation made long-distance trade and the transfer of capital a difficult business; even at this stage, capital gains from exchange-rate fluctuations tempted people to speculate. Charles is said to have thought about introducing fixed exchange rates.[48] We are certainly justified in speaking of a targeted economic policy for the public good by Charles, and not solely for the benefit of his own realm either. The king appears to have conducted ambitious trade policies. Even leaving aside the important mining sector, he supported the fustian weaving industry, which used imported cotton, and particularly the trade in fustian finished goods in the imperial cities of Swabia. This called for an extremely diverse, supraregional interplay between regional government, long-distance merchants, providers of capital, entrepreneurs, and skilled labor. There are many examples of targeted commercial initiatives by the Luxembourg dynasty (not just Charles IV, but also, especially, by his son Sigismund). In an atmosphere of intensive Europe-wide rivalry, the competition to corner key markets began to shape the development of markets on the continent. The success of the great medieval trade fairs—in Amsterdam, Lyons, Geneva, or Frankfurt—was a yardstick of this growing economic activity. And Charles IV's realms were to gain their share of the profits.

The "chamber servants" of the empire, namely the Jews, found themselves constantly harassed by the king's demands for money. Worse still, in the royal household, they had always been regarded as assets that could be disposed of at the first opportunity. This was also the case now, even prior to the arrival of the Black Death in the Holy Roman Empire. When the plague did hit, the situation worsened, as familiar old prejudices were aired against the Jews—they were accused (a charge first attested in southern France) of having poisoned wells, of adulterating butter and wine, and generally of being responsible for the wave of deaths that overwhelmed Europe in 1348–1349. Subsequently, the sacrilege of host desecration was also laid at their door. Such charges were sometimes backed up with astrological deliberations, which claimed that the planetary alignment of Saturn with Jupiter had contributed to the outbreak. The mob was unleashed on the Jews, and like heretics they were condemned to be burnt at the stake. Even when the authorities were inclined to intervene, which was not very often, they were powerless. Despite the fact that the emperor was their greatest patron, time and again he withdrew his protection from the Jews; in other words he simply transferred his patronage, for which he had demanded high payments, to other groups that were willing to pay even more. Justifying his actions by claiming that "the Jews will soon be slaughtered anyway," he preemptively dispossessed them, legitimized pogroms, and turned "Jewish houses" and synagogues over either to looting, to financial exploitation by their parties, or to expropriation by municipalities and their citizens. In Nuremberg, which remarkably remained free of the Black Death until 1406, the Church of Our Lady was consecrated on the site of the former synagogue; for all the architectural splendor of the new building, this was a dark chapter in the history of the cult of the Virgin Mary.[49] The large and significant Jewish communities in such cities as Nuremberg, Frankfurt, and Mainz were wiped out at this time. Likewise in the major commercial centers of Regensburg, Augsburg, Basel, and Strasbourg. In addition to the monarch, the people to benefit from the slaughter of the Jews were the prominent urban trading dynasties like the Stromers in Nuremberg. Only in Prague, where the king himself was in debt to Jewish financiers, did he protect this community (some other local rulers also did so), his "court Jews." He also let it be known to the city authorities in Luxembourg that it was by no means proven that the Jews had poisoned the wells.[50]

The barbarity of these actions is in no way mitigated by pointing to the fact that similar things occurred in earlier times and in other countries, say England or France, where expulsions and pogroms had been carried out before and now erupted again, nor through the knowledge that such outrages were almost part of daily life in Western society of the time. For example, the Shepherds' Crusade and the Cowherds' Crusade of 1320 and 1321 respectively, which both started in southern France, and were aimed at helping the Christian reconquest of Aragón, also saw bloody atrocities committed against the Jews.[51] Time and again, promising new life through the Gospels but visiting death upon certain communities, Europe's Latin Christendom revealed itself to be a "persecuting society" (R. I. Moore). The Jews and heretics were its principal victims. Froissart commented on the plague year: "The Jews were seized and burned at the stake everywhere, throughout the entire world, and their property confiscated." The chronicler went on to claim, however, that the only place where things were different was under papal rule, while the kings of Navarre, Castile, and Aragón gave asylum to many Jews in their kingdoms. How far this was the case cannot be determined. Yet even in these places, the Jews were blamed for bringing down the plague on humanity "through their sinfulness." Again, they were attacked by the mob, and many cities in the kingdom of Aragón witnessed brutal massacres.[52] Toward the end of the century, in around 1391, Jewish communities south of the Pyrenees were once again subject to pogroms, with terrible loss of life.

Heretics were also mercilessly persecuted. Pope Clement VI gave the newly elected king Charles IV the following piece of advice in parting: "It is the duty of the Christian emperor to exterminate all heretics!"[53] And the emperor duly obliged, issuing countless edicts to this effect, especially in the Bohemian kingdom he inherited, but also in places where the Inquisition's remit ran, outlawing heretics, a group that now expressly also included the Beguines and the Beghards. Charles was suspicious of the tracts and sermons in the vernacular that circulated among the latter groups; albeit without mentioning him by name, the text of the relevant decree makes it clear that the works of the mystic Meister Eckhart were what was at issue here. His doctrine of the "basis of the soul" and the "soul's spark" took on a dangerous aspect; its adherents no longer sought communion in the Mass and also spurned Charles's cults of holy relics. Reason and religion had formed a close bond in Eckhart's doctrine. Yet unrepentant attachment to "heresy," as fundamentalists elsewhere also discovered, was punished by being burned at the stake. As the emperor proclaimed: "We shall wield the worldly sword against the enemies of the Faith until we have completely exterminated *(exterminium)* their heretical corruption." The pope, Gregory XI, had good cause to be pleased; he heaped praise on his "champion of the Faith" *(pugil fidei)*, expressing his gratitude to this "excellent and determined persecutor of heretics."[54] Charles's son Sigismund, too, would continue this holy war; notably, he promised the reformer Jan Hus safe conduct to Constance, but broke his pledge and had Hus burned to death in 1415.

Fear also drove people to do violence against their own persons; at that time, as the Black Death raged throughout the West, it gave rise to processions of flagellants. One rhyme sung by German-speaking practitioners ran: "Nun peitscht euch sehre / durch Christus Ehre, durch Gott, so laß die Hoffahrt fahren / so wird sich Gott unser erbarmen" ("Now whip yourselves raw / let us in the name of Christ and the Lord dispense with all pride / so that God may take pity upon us"). These desperate, half-naked penitents would roam in ceaseless processions from town to town, hoping to drive sin and death away both from themselves and from Christendom as a whole by thrashing their bodies with nail-studded scourges. Each group of flagellants would travel around for thirty-three and a half days at a time, corresponding to Christ's age in years when He was crucified. Originating in Germany, the penitential movement spread to the province of Hainaut (in modern Belgium). Froissart reports that several women, gripped by fear and mania, were given to collecting the blood spilt by the flagellants and, believing it to have miraculous properties, smeared it over their eyes. The penitents sang laments about the Passion of Our Saviour: "This they did in order to urge God to conquer Death," and in the process brought reconciliation and peace even to violent criminals and murderers, or at least so Froissart claimed. Fear, it seemed, could work wonders. Meanwhile, France was spared the penitential movement (though not the Plague itself): the pope in Avignon banned the gruesome practice of self-flagellation and threatened its exponents with excommunication. And yet even kings of France were known to use the scourge on themselves in their penitential devotions. The mid-fourteenth century was, it seemed, thoroughly steeped in violence.

Nevertheless, the Black Death seemed to make little impact on the crowned heads of this time; in scarcely any royal court do the records make any mention of it. Only Clement VI took an interest, commissioning his physicians to investigate the number of deaths it had caused. Otherwise, most contemporary accounts of the plague are those by the municipal chroniclers of Italy and elsewhere, and their reports tell us a great deal. From out of the blue, as God ordained it, the epidemic seems to have been visited upon mankind. Introduced, like Chinese silk, from the Mongol Empire by Genoese merchants sailing from the besieged port of Caffa in the Crimea, the first places it Europe that it affected were Italian sea ports. Before long, it reached both the larger and smaller trade routes that ran into the interior, before crossing the Alps and spreading to the rest of Europe—a "microbial unification of the world,"[55] a devastating and enduring globalizing effect of European expansion to the Far East.

The symptoms of the disease were described in such detail that the epidemic can nowadays be identified as a pulmonary and bubonic plague. However, at the time, no one knew the causes; the plague bacillus was only discovered and identified by Louis Pasteur in 1894. Doctors in the Middle Ages had no remedy; some advised sufferers to wear amulets. At least contemporaries found out that direct contact and exhalations when speaking appeared to spread the infection. Yet others speculated that it could be spread by the "evil eye," that is, a look that could convey death. In any event, the interpretive model of "contagion" was first devised at this time, with scholars somewhat helplessly referring to it as an *epydimie*.[56] Over time, physicians took to wearing beak-like masks to maintain some distance and protect themselves, covered their patients' eyes, or simply fled to safety. In addition, no one then had any inkling that the ever-present fleas were acting as vectors, transmitting the disease from rats to humans. The first wave of the Black Death swept over Europe from 1348 to 1352, and then abated, only to return at regular intervals of ten to fifteen years.

Eventually, the population in some places had been halved, while across Europe as a whole, it had been reduced by as much as one-third; for the time being, the survivors were immunized by exposure. One Italian commentator lamented that all the beautiful women and all honest men had been carried off by the plague, and that only rogues had survived, so that nobody could trust anyone else any more.[57]

All aspects of life seemed to have been affected by the plague, except one: the power struggle among princes and kings. They seemed to be immune to the general sense of unrest that gripped the populace. Even the "king of the Romans" was preoccupied with other matters. He was hankering after his coronation as Holy Roman Emperor in the Eternal City. Not everyone applauded this aim. The chivalrous-minded chronicler Jean le Bel, for example, thought that Charles's decision to venture across the Alps was unworthy of him and was the only major error of his reign.[58] And, certainly, Rome at that time, having been abandoned by the pope and the Curia, was in a state of chaos "full of immorality, wickedness, lawless and beyond all control."[59] The leading families of the city, the Colonna, the Orsini, the Caetani, and all the rest, were conducting vendettas against one another, seemingly unperturbed by the plague, which had arrived in Rome just in time to coincide with the Holy Year of 1350. The last thing anyone there wanted was the visit of a German emperor. There was scarcely any sign remaining of the blessings that the Roman Revolution under the tribune Cola di Rienzo had brought to the city, while the negative consequences of its failure were still in evidence; beyond the walls of Rome, the notorious German *condottiere* Werner von Urslingen and his Great Company of mercenaries were still rampaging, making Campania and Tuscany extremely unstable. Only a few lone voices, such as that of Petrarch, encouraged Charles to undertake his journey, in the hope that the king's arrival would help restore a sense of peace and harmony. Intoxicated by his celebration of antiquity, and by his hope for the dawning of a new era, which after a thousand years of darkness and ignorance would revive the pure glow of former times,[60] the poet Petrarch invoked the greatness of the Roman Emperors; Charles, he firmly believed, would follow in their footsteps.

Both Petrarch and Rienzo were in thrall to an imaginary Rome and an idealized Antiquity that they thought might set new standards for the contemporary world—and emphatically not to the enfeebled "Holy Roman Empire" that they encountered in the present. In addition, they each greatly admired one another. A new "Renaissance" was on the horizon, more a literary than a political phenomenon. When Rienzo, the son of an innkeeper and a washerwoman, rose to become the master of Rome, and called for a Roman revival without the emperor, indeed expressly set himself up against the pope and the emperor, Petrarch praised and celebrated the uprising: "O most illustrious citizens [of Rome], you have been living as slaves—you whom all nations were wont to serve . . . you have had as tyrants strangers and lords of foreign birth. . . . The valley of Spoleto claims this one; the Rhine, or the Rhone, or some obscure corner of the world has sent us the next. . . . They had themselves addressed as 'Lord,' something that even the Emperor Augustus, who truly was lord of all nations, would not tolerate. And now Rienzo has become the third Brutus, the third savior of Rome from servitude." "Hail, then, our Camillus, our Brutus, our Romulus, or whatever other name you prefer to be addressed by! Hail, you author of Roman liberty, Roman peace, and Roman tranquillity. The present age owes it to you that it may die in liberty; to you posterity will owe that it is conceived in liberty."[61] These kinds of sentiments were far removed from Dante, who had once, in his *Divine Comedy,* had consigned the second Brutus, the murderer of Julius Caesar—*e con paura il metto in metro* ("and it is with fear that I put it into words")—to the darkest depths of the Underworld, along with Judas Iscariot and the assassin Cassius, to suffer for all eternity in the maw of Lucifer, the prince of Hell (*Inferno* 34:10 and 65). Petrarch and Rienzo were representative of a new generation that, dazzled by the former glory of Rome, pursued more grandiose goals and harbored more audacious hopes than their predecessors, who lived far from Rome and its influence.

However, the Roman king chose to ignore Petrarch's urging; Charles was in no hurry to make his entrance into Rome. From his prison cell in Prague, the former "tribune of freedom, peace, and justice," the representative of Roman notaries and tradesmen, Cola di Rienzo,[62] wrote the following wistful reply to Petrarch, the preacher of revolution in Rome: "O [my friend], the ancient times that you call to mind were not beset by the adverse circumstances we are faced with today." By contrast, the lodestar of love *(caritas),* Charles's "greatest virtue," now sought to make adversity a thing of the past. An emperorship foisted upon Rome at the wrong time would only bring war. And so Charles put off the supplicant Petrarch, exhorting him to keep his peace "lest we let slip something that would be unworthy of the emperor."[63]

It was only four years later, after tough negotiations with the pope and with the cities of Lombardy and Tuscany and their *signori,* that Charles decided to visit the Eternal City, and even then only just long enough for his coronation and a brief pilgrimage tour of its main churches on Maundy Thursday and Good Friday. There was no question of his imposing a new order on the city or the surrounding countryside, or bringing it peace and freedom, or subjugating the pope-less city once more to imperial control, let alone leading the successor to Saint Peter back in triumph to the city of the apostles. Around this time, the Visconti were establishing their rule in Milan; yet by contrast, the king of Italy and the emperor of the Romans could not regard himself as a true *signore* who ruled unopposed and whom the people obeyed, in one single city in Italy. In words that Protestant historiography would later eagerly seize upon, Petrarch gave vent to his disappointment; "You are the bearer," he accused Charles, "of the empty name of emperor. People may call you emperor of the Romans, but in fact all you are is king of Bohemia."[64]

And yet Charles had a more modern outlook than the protagonists of the Renaissance; he paid homage to no political utopias. Before he could set off for Rome, it was essential that he agree upon the ways and means of his coronation with the pope. The old relationship of trust with Clement VI, having been placed under great strain by the obligations and traditions of the Roman monarchy, had long since given way to dissent and mistrust. Certainly, the pope's former student avoided any open conflict with the man to whom he owed his crown; rather, he assessed the situation coolly and objectively. The Luxembourger was far from launching a direct attack on the papal *plenitudo potestatis.* In fact, without actually supporting it, Charles had the utmost respect for this papal doctrine and the pope's claims to sovereignty in Italy, or at least chose to suppress any objection when it seem advantageous to do so. Rome, the city on the Tiber, the *caput mundi* that Petrarch still dreamt of, was long lost to the empire; no Rienzo, no Petrarch could ever conjure up imperial Rome again. Charles, the sober planner on the Holy Roman throne recognized what the Rome-intoxicated humanists failed to see, and so deployed smoke-and-mirror tactics. He became adept at preserving his royal-imperial sovereignty by a variety of means: ostensible compliance, dissimulation, and subtle deception of his adversaries until they came around to his way of thinking. It was as if the emperor had learned his craft at the knee of Machiavelli; however, alert thinkers like Froissart saw through the whole game.[65]

So, the journey to Rome had to wait until Charles could reach an accord with Clement's successor, Innocent VI. The long delay was caused by difficult negotiations, with deep mistrust on both sides prolonging matters. In return for agreeing to the imperial coronation, the Roman Curia hoped to receive financial support to help it regain control of Rome, in the form of massive credit—there was talk of 40,000 gold florins—advanced by the emperor. Charles balked at this, offering instead to lend troops to the pope's military commander in Italy, Cardinal Albornoz. In turn, the pope thought this too paltry an offer, and turned it down. It was only two decades subsequently that the emperor, under totally different circumstances, took a different attitude to the question of credit and threw his weight behind a return of the successor of Saint Peter to the City of the Apostles.[66]

Nevertheless, nine years after his election, it finally came to pass that the Luxembourger was crowned emperor. Peter, the cardinal-bishop of Ostia, officiated at the coronation in Saint Peter's on behalf of the pope (1355). Yet once crowned, Charles became, like his patron saint Charlemagne, a legislator. While it is true that he found it impossible either to enact his legal code, the *Majestas Carolina,* by means of which he had hoped to strengthen the rights of the Bohemian crown against the nobility and the royal family and to bind the country closer to the king, or to impose public peace on his realm; even so, there soon followed (1359) certain imperial laws concerning church freedom that were to have an enduring effect, inasmuch as they touched upon papal certificates of appointment for permanently delegated ecclesiastical judges (custodian mandates) and after the Council of Constance (1414–1418), supplemented with older and more recent privileges, were codified and brought together to form the Constitutio Carolina.[67]

The Golden Bull of 1356

Above all, however, the election of the king was newly regulated, and with the Golden Bull legislation was sealed that placed the future constitution of the Holy Roman Empire on a new footing. Charles exploited the opportunities that the conflict between the pope and the emperor had opened up. Excommunication and declarations of deposition, manifestos, legal rulings and their exegeses in canon law, and historical constructs such as the "translation doctrine" had indeed combined to make the office of emperor appear disposable. This latter doctrine had in the past implanted in the consciousness of the West the Curia's teaching that the papacy had transferred the emperorship from the Greeks to the Franks and Germans, that is, to the two great leaders Charlemagne and Otto; Dante had already written polemics against this notion. But the tradition of exegesis had blurred the clear separation of Regnum and Imperium. In fact, from John XXII on, the popes had already claimed the right of approbation for the Roman king to be raised to the status of Holy Roman Emperor; even in the Curia's own terminology, there was no longer any distinction made between the *Regnum Alemannie* and the *Imperium Romanum*. And it was in this that Charles identified the weak point of the whole construct. For the role of German king had never been at the disposal of the Apostolic See, no more so than the kingdom of Italy or the kingdom of Arles had ever been; in actuality the *Rex Romanorum* ruled both the *Regnum* and the *Imperium* in the same way. Charles drew exactly this conclusion from the Golden Bull; in consistently treating *imperium* and *regnum* as interchangeable terms, it not only blurred all distinctions, but also implicitly made the king who had been chosen by the electors (with a simple majority) the ruler of the *imperium*.

This bull, "our imperial statute book" (as Charles himself called it), was a basic law of the empire, which had been enacted at two imperial diets at Nuremberg and Metz through the formal assent of all the electors together with numerous other secular and ecclesiastical princes. Admittedly, it can in no way stand comparison with the great legislative achievements of the Italian municipalities or the simultaneous developments in constitutional law that occurred in the monarchies of Western Europe, about which the emperor had learned about in his youth. Even where Bohemia was concerned, Charles's plans took a much more modern approach. By contrast, this Golden Bull set in stone, so to speak, the backwardness of Germany and its monarchy, but still managed to remain in force for the next 500 years.

Moreover, the Diet of Metz took place at a moment of high tension throughout the whole of Western Europe—a factor that had an important bearing on the implementation of the Golden Bull. Twelve weeks before, on September 19, 1356, John II (the Good) of France had suffered a heavy and humiliating defeat at the hands of the English heir-apparent, Edward the Black Prince, at the Battle of Maupertuis (south of Poitiers). The king himself had been taken prisoner and was held captive for the next four years. Once more—as had happened ten years previously at the Battle of Crécy—the consequences were catastrophic. The French people were threatened with heavy ransom demands, and a situation of chaos ensued. Within barely eighteen months, the population of Paris (the *gens des communes*), led by the wealthy cloth merchant Étienne Marcel, rebelled; this was followed by a peasants' revolt (the *Jacquerie*) against the nobility. The "Kingdom's Day of Judgment"[68] that many commentators had feared seemed to be coming true. The dauphin had already fled Paris. Finally, Étienne Marcel was murdered, and Charles II of Navarre—who like the English king had been passed over as a candidate for the Holy Roman Emperorship in 1328; and who now became his ally and John the Good's mortal enemy—crushed the *Jacquerie* (1358) and successfully restored the aristocracy. Charles II made an unsuccessful bid for power; ultimately, John's son, the future King Charles V of France, was able to maintain the House of Valois's hold on power.

But before securing his throne, the dauphin had sought the support of the emperor and to this end had hurried to Metz to meet with him; the imperial diet that was convened in order to ratify the Golden Bull took place in his presence. The emperor could not have wished for a more favorable turn of events for his plans. In order to bring an end to the conflict that had attended his own succession ("durch dasz nit me krieg umb das rich wurde, als vor ime gewesen ist";[69] "so that there should no longer be the kind of warring that affected the empire before he [that is, Charles] came to power") Charles's bull definitively settled the matter of who was entitled to act as elector, and also regulated the distribution of traditional "arch-offices," and the electoral procedure not only for the position of Roman king, but much more importantly, whenever the "Imperium" fell vacant ("quando . . . sacrum vacare continget imperium" [4,2; 5,1]) for the post of future Holy Roman Emperor. The bull also established the prerogative of the seven imperial electors and their order of ranking and ruled all foreign claims inadmissible. This piece of legislation effectively stage-managed the "Holy Empire" by giving it a ritual underpinning. By establishing once and for all the sitting, voting, and processional hierarchy of the electors *(Sacra Imperii principes electores)*, it gave the empire (and not just the "Regnum") the appearance of gravitas and, as time would duly show, permanence.[70] Immediately after its demise, Goethe still found himself fascinated by the spectacle of the electors' assembly, an event he described admiringly in his memoirs. More than simply a piece of youthful nostalgia, Goethe's account is a eulogy to the glory of a past empire.

Yet Charles's "statute book" (unlike the Declaration of Rhens of 1338, where, almost certainly under the aegis of Charles great-uncle Baldwin of Trier, the electors formed a league that criticized the unyielding attitude of Benedict XII and firmly rejected any papal claim to approbation of the king whom they had chosen) studiously ignored any question of papal demands, regulating only in the vaguest terms the election of the "future emperor" and of the king "promoted to emperor," and leaving everything else to the destiny of the individual chosen. Furthermore, it was determined that this individual reigned even before being anointed as king, and hence, so the implicit suggestion ran, ruled legitimately even in the absence of the imperial title and of papal approbation over the *Sacrum Imperium*. Again, Charles's bull said nothing about the consequences that Louis the Bavarian, in reference to the Electoral Union of Rhens, loudly announced to the world in his notorious yet forward-looking law (formulated according to canon law principles) *Licet iuris:* namely that the person who was chosen as king by the king "is the true king and emperor of the Romans solely by virtue of the election" and that he enjoyed full sovereign power over the empire *(ex sola electione est verus rex at imperator Romanorum)*.[71] Charles IV thought the same and decreed accordingly; likewise, in the aftermath of his "statute book" all papal approbation claims came to nothing. But the difference was that he did it subtly, without any loud proclamation, and without any barbs aimed at the Holy See. Even when the emperor was engineering the election of his son Wenceslas as king of the Romans, and to this end entered into negotiations with Pope Urban V, he avoided any explicit regulation. And from the sixteenth century right to the end of the "Holy Roman Empire of the German Nation," this was how matters were left: the papal claim remained, but in practice was so empty as to have no force whatever.

Such flexibility ushered in precisely that change which both Frederick II and latterly Charles's great adversary Louis the Bavarian had tried in vain to bring about through rigidity and the use of force, and which ultimately really did liberate the empire from papal pressure. It played a decisive role in the ability of the Holy Roman Empire (of the German Nation), this shapeless entity, to survive for such a long time—right up until 1806. In an ironic twist of history, though, time and again Medieval and Early Modern historians asserted that Charles had achieved precisely the opposite: he had, so the *Historia Bohemica* by Enea Silvio Piccolomini (the future Pope Pius II; first published in 1475) claimed, "done more to win glory for Bohemia than for the Holy Roman Empire" and had "undermined its power" by offering inflated payments to the electors in order to get his son Wenceslas elected as king."[72] This judgment was echoed widely by subsequent historians, and it was only revised with the advent of critical historical scholarship. Charles had emphatically not failed; however, his sons Wenceslas and Sigismund found themselves faced with difficulties that they were unable to solve.

At the same time, the Golden Bull was a document of the House of Luxembourg; as such, it had European significance. By establishing the principle of the inheritability of the secular office of Holy Roman elector it accorded unique rights especially to the king of Bohemia—first and foremost the unrestricted active right to an electoral vote, a right that had long been denied to the Czech ruler as a non-German, and even recently had been called into question,[73] and also in particular the "iura non appellando" and "non evocando," which were accorded as matter of course to the other electors—together with precedence over the other secular electors. In addition, the electoral princes were now expected, from seven years of age onward, to learn Latin, Italian, and Czech *(Slavica lingua)* alongside their mother tongue of German, "so that they may both understand and be understood by more people." These languages were deemed to be the ones "best suited to the use and benefit of the Holy Roman Empire." This was, admittedly, a change envisaged for the future, for at that time, in 1356, Charles did not yet have a son and heir (only a brother who could inherit the throne); but later on, he did indeed arrange for the heir to the throne to be schooled in such a manner. Remarkably, this language decree left out French, despite the fact that large tracts of Francophone territories lay within his realm. Several factors may have some into play here: consideration for France, his pragmatism, and his far-sightedness. He may even have anticipated the eventual "falling away" of these areas from the empire.

Despite having the assent of so many princes, the bull issued by the emperor failed to secure just one thing, the most important all, namely to bring peace and security to the realm. This was hampered by the growing tendency in Germany toward fragmentation in small states. In vain, the Golden Bull forbade any sworn alliances between citizens or towns along with the phenomenon of "external citizenry," that is the granting by a town of citizenship rights to inhabitants of the countryside that lay outside its walls. The growing political significance of the cities with their rights of collective freedom could no longer be ignored by any emperor or lord. Protected by their walls, the town citizenry had the power to defy both princes and nobility. Finally, the knightly caste also came under increasing pressure—from two quarters simultaneously, the cities on the one hand and on the other dwindling revenue from peasantry that was bound to the land. The emperor could do little to help in this instance. Meanwhile the ramifications of the imperial edict for the rest of Europe were significant. Henceforth, not only the relationship between the Holy Roman Empire and the Curia was placed on a more even footing, but other far-reaching and long-lasting consequences also became apparent. For instance, the vote of the elector from the Rhineland Palatinate remained split, since the Wittelsbachs could not agree, meaning that it sometimes went to the Palatinate and sometimes to Bavaria. This was one of the causes of the Thirty Years' War, which was to turn into a European war on German soil.

The glory of the Golden Bull outshone a charter issued by another member of the House of Luxembourg just a few months earlier: the "Joyeuse entrée" granted to the duchy of Brabant. This decree was more forward looking and, because it more closely concerned the common people, also more modern than Charles's "statute book." Joanna, the duchess of Brabant and margravine of Luxembourg, issued this document in conjunction with her husband, Charles IV's brother Wenceslas, and with the cities and regions of her duchy. It became necessary because Brabant had been left to the duchess alone, and a clear legal stipulation was required establishing that only her natural heirs could succeed her as ruler, and not, say, the heirs of the duke's brother the emperor. Thirty-four long and detailed chapters, written in the vernacular, circumscribed sovereign rights by enabling the "country" as a whole to participate in them. The country's nobility and patrician class were the first to have a say, but soon wool weavers and cloth merchants were asserting their rights, too. The endless war between England and France did not leave either Flanders or Brabant unscathed, with the aristocracy leaning toward France and the weavers and cloth merchants toward England. "We promise you," the ducal pair now told their subjects, "that we shall form no future alliances with any party without the prior consent and agreement of our cities and the common people of our land, and that we shall seal no treaty with our

Great Seal that might reduce or infringe upon the borders of our Brabant in any way." In the "Joyous Entry" basic freedoms, the minting of coinage (in other words: currency stability), peace obligations, accountability of officials, property rights, along with traditional privileges and the like were all assigned to the joint control of rulers and their subjects.[74] It was the rich and powerful town citizenry that was in a position to wrest such treaties from their rulers and insist they be observed—charters like the "Joyous Entry" were milestones in the history of political rights. The effect of this charter was to be felt right up to the Netherlands' struggle for freedom from Spain in the Early Modern period and even beyond.

Formerly, in the Carolingian and Ottonian period, the emperor had been the very real guardian of the Roman Church; by the fourteenth century all that remained was the nominal obligation to offer protection. Yet Charles IV took this duty seriously. The growing influence of the king of France in the kingdom of Arles increasingly threatened the papacy's freedom of action there; it was not only the emperor who began to press for the head of the Roman Church to return from Avignon to Italy. The popes themselves also aspired to do so, but to realize this aim a Europe-wide consensus was called for. Charles's journey to the Curia in Avignon in 1365 clearly had this goal in mind. Moreover, new perspectives were opening up at this time. In the two kingdoms belonging to the House of Anjou, Naples and Hungary, acute problems over the successions were becoming apparent. Neither of their kings had so far produced male heirs. Their cousin on the French throne was already planning dynastic marriages. However, the succession question in Naples also affected the county of Provence, which nominally belonged to Arles, and this immediately brought the emperor into the arena. The Sicilian question, on the other hand, once the cause of serious conflict between the emperor and the pope, was of little concern to him.

Urban V did indeed return to Italy in 1367, first to Viterbo and then to Rome, where he took up residence in the Vatican (where all popes were to live henceforth) rather than occupy the old pontifical Lateran Palace, which had been used since the time of Constantine. Perhaps his intention had been to devote himself more effectively to the Neapolitan question from within Italy. At Urban's behest and in order to offer him his support, Charles IV duly embarked on his second journey to Rome (1368–1369), the military and diplomatic preparations for which took fully a year and a half,[75] and even this turned out to be insufficient. At their meeting in

Rome, the first summit of this kind to be held for almost 150 years,[76] since Frederick II had met with Gregory IX in 1230 to sign the fragile Treaty of Anagni, the emperor performed the traditional service of *strator* for the pope, leading the pontiff's horse by the reins and holding the stirrup, a gesture of subordination that offended many contemporary humanists, with their dreams of the majestic sovereignty of the emperors of antiquity.[77] In Siena—by now, he was already on the return journey—Charles was besieged by the people's militia and under severe duress was only able to secure the release of himself and his forces by granting privileges.[78] Meanwhile, back in Rome, in the absence of any outside help, the pope was unable to assert his authority. In 1370, he reluctantly returned to Avignon, where he died later that same year; he was succeeded by Gregory XI. Jointly, Charles IV, Charles V of France, Charles II of Navarre, and Louis of Anjou now informed Gregory that they were prepared to fund the return of the papacy to Rome with extensive credit totaling 230,000 florins (1372 and 1375).[79] When Gregory died after only a few years in office (1378), the cardinals elected Urban VI as his successor (1378–1379). However, French members of the college of cardinals objected to his election and, declaring him unfit for office, unseated him and elected in his place Clement VII. With Rome inaccessible to him, Clement returned to Avignon. The schism that this papal coup created would shake Latin Christendom for the next forty years.

Charles's journey into Provence culminated in his coronation in Arles in 1365. In this, the Luxembourg monarch was emulating Frederick Barbarossa,[80] who when he was likewise facing a difficult situation, had himself crowned there in 1178. Charles thus became the first emperor since Barbarossa to take control of the kingdom of Arles in this way. Yet the times had changed. There are so few historical records of this coronation and so few mentions of it by contemporaries, and it received so little attention even from the emperor himself that little significance has traditionally been accorded to it.[81] Against the contemporary historical background of the return of the Curia to Rome and the Neapolitan-Provencal succession, it must be regarded as a snap decision on Charles's part to assert a territorial claim. The coronation was a symbolic piece of political theater reminding all those present that Avignon was situated within the borders of the empire and that the county of Provence was a fiefdom of the emperor. Admittedly, in the kingdom of Arles, no real power devolved any longer upon the emperor, and Charles was almost certainly not planning to alter this situation. Only recently, he had detached the county of Savoy from Arles and integrated it into the empire.[82] The aspirations of Arles had long since turned westward, toward Paris, and even the most solemn of coronations could not hope to stem the tide in this direction. And indeed it is hard to imagine that this was ever Charles's intention.

A Paris Summit in 1378

Back in 1349, the last dauphin of the county of Vienne (or Dauphiné) in southeastern France, which was nominally a state of the Holy Roman Empire, ceded his province and title to then ten-year-old heir-apparent to the French throne, Charles, in return for a generous financial settlement. This Charles was the nephew of the Holy Roman Emperor Charles IV, and the son of his sister Jutta (also called Bonne)—who incidentally was the ancestress of all the kings of France and heirs-apparent to the French throne right up to the present day. Although, following his father's defeat at the Battle of Maupertuis (Poitiers) in 1356, Charles did swear an oath of fealty to the emperor, this was, as Charles likely realized himself at the time, a short-lived victory. Even by the following year, it was clear that the Western imperial fiefdoms could not be retained, as they were moving ever closer to France. Even the Diet of Metz in 1356 could not halt this westward drift. The emperor's nephew Charles V, having grown up and ascended the French throne, granted his son in turn sovereignty over the Dauphiné, and thereafter the title of dauphin transferred to all crown princes of France. The emperor not only accepted this, he even enfeoffed the French king's brother Louis with the duchy of Burgundy, which was then part of the kingdom of Arles, and appointed the dauphin, the future Charles VI of France, as permanent imperial vicar to the Arelat;[83] in doing so, he renounced (though not in name or in legal terms) any real sovereignty over the kingdom. This last act took place in Paris, where the ill and aged emperor had traveled; Charles of France proceeded to regale him at length about how the Hundred Years' War against England was proceeding, recounting the enemy's treaty violations and setting forth his *bonne querele et justice* ("well justified grievances"), which the emperor immediately conceded. At least, this is the picture painted by the *Grandes Chroniques,* and there are no other historical accounts by which to judge this account.[84] Dieter von Niem, a long-serving papal notary, and toward the end of his life a conciliarist, lamented the loss of imperial territory, claiming that the emperor had given away the kingdom of Arles for the price of a banquet.

Yet Dietrich was ill-informed; the emperor was not such a glutton that he would have done this. Charles only conceded positions that were indefensible anyway. Even his ceding of Arles was a calculated move. New opportunities were opening up in the east which seemed more worthy of his attention. And he surmised that his royal nephew could be of help in this. Charles V's own correspondence does indeed confirm that the emperor raised the question of Poland at their Paris summit. The letter mentioning this was addressed to Louis the Great, the last king from the House of Anjou to occupy the Hungarian throne, and also the king of Poland. Louis was advanced in years and had no male heirs, only three daughters, the oldest of whom, Catherine, was engaged to Charles of France's younger son Louis (who later became the duke of Orléans) and the second eldest of whom, Mary, was betrothed to the emperor's younger son Sigismund, who was then ten years old. Was it perhaps the case that the emperor, who is said to have cited family affairs as the reason for his visit to the French court,[85] hoped to persuade his nephew to share Louis the Great's expected legacy—in other words, the crown of Poland for Sigismund, who that same year was about to be enfeoffed with the margravate of Brandenburg, while the Hungarian throne would be occupied by the Valois?[86]

If that was indeed the case—and there is strong evidence to suggest so—then a preliminary decision was reached at the Paris summit that would have repercussions for the history of Europe until well into the twentieth century. For while Catherine died prematurely in 1378, meaning that a further connection between the Valois and the Angevin dynasties never came to pass, Sigismund married Mary as planned, accepted (albeit only after some initial difficulties) his father-in-law's inheritance (though Poland was subsequently, through his youngest daughter Hedwig, to fall to the Jagiellons, a dynasty of Lithuanian counts), became emperor in due course, as third in line of succession to his father, but died leaving only a single daughter, Elisabeth. She duly brought her husband, Albert of Austria, two royal crowns when they married; the electors ultimately chose him as Holy Roman Emperor (Albert II). Austria, Hungary, and Bohemia, in addition to the Roman crown—even though this triad of crowns was to fall apart once more, it was like a prefiguration of the later concept of *felix Austria*—namely the House of Habsburg's good fortune in amassing through dynastic marriage a vast empire, and whose luck was to hold out until 1918, when it was shattered by the First World War and its constituent peoples' urge for nation-statehood.

So it was that in Paris, the old emperor, accompanied by his son Wenceslas (who had already been crowned "king of the Romans," and his nephew, the young *roy lettré*, met one another in the heart of France. This was a meeting of two Carolingian traditions, the dynastic and the imperial, evoking folk memories of a glorious past. Moreover, this was the first time that a Holy Roman Emperor and a Roman king had met the king of France in his own country, going to visit him in the epicenter of his sovereignty, to take part in a unique summit where his power was at its most concentrated and striking, the heart of his realm where his inviolable sanctity was on display for all to see. This was the historical moment at which the phenomenon of the state visit was born. No Son of Heaven, no Great Khan, no Japanese Tenno, no Roman Emperor, no Persian Shah, and no Pharaoh had ever attended such an encounter. By this stage, the Holy Roman Empire had taken leave of all pretensions to world domination and had made a clean break with the doctrines of the global emperor that had circulated at the courts of the Hohenstaufens and latterly at that of Louis the Bavarian. Sober reality had taken the place of illusory dreams.

It was one of the earliest meetings of this kind, which it seems only began in the reign of Charles IV. Earlier meetings between royal rulers had been hallmarked either by mistrust or by the overwhelming superiority of one party. The only exceptions to this general rule were special cases like encounters between kings as one passed through the other's realm while on pilgrimage to Rome (such as happened between Canute II and Conrad II) or when a monarch traversed another's territory on Crusade, or meetings that took place in the context of a royal marriage or a court of arbitration (say Charles IV's meeting with Louis I of Hungary in the border town of Györ [Raab] in 1356).[87] Even John II of France's voluntary return to captivity in England in 1364 should be excepted here. Where deep mistrust was the order of the day, it was customary for two wholly independent rulers to meet exactly on the border between their two realms, with each of them punctiliously intent upon not exposing themselves to any danger to life or limb, and concerned not to cede even an inch to the other, lest this afford him an opportunity to ritually make some humiliating gesture of superiority and triumph.[88] In cases of dependency or subjugation, or even a relationship of patronage, this was ritually demonstrated by the subservient party visiting the victor. But on this occasion, the Luxembourg monarch broke with these meaningless traditions, journeying to France of his own volition and under no duress, just as he had traveled the year before, in 1364, to the court of the Polish king Casimir III at Krakow to meet with Louis of Hungary there in order to sign a peace treaty and discuss questions of the succession.

The ceremonial of the Paris summit reveal more than just doctrine.[89] It carefully preserved the rank of both princes. The "Roman" Charles was paid proper homage as emperor and accorded the honor due to a guest, but was not revered as a ruler of the world nor received as the sovereign of the host country. This was all made plain through an exchange of horses. The *imperator* and the *rex Romanorum* began their journey on gray steeds, the hallmark of the pope, emperor, and sovereign, but—dissimilar to the practice within their own realms[90]—the horses were adorned neither with caparisons nor with the emperor's personal or imperial coat of arms; then, just outside Paris, prior to the meeting with the king of France, Charles and Wenceslas mounted mares, which were bedecked with the caparisons of the French king and the dauphin—a gesture on the part of Charles V in honor of his exalted guest. While he was on French soil, the emperor was denied the use of any symbols or the practice of rituals that were specifically imperial—for example the reading of the Gospels on Christmas morning or having church bells rung to signal his entry into a city, nor was he allowed to display the imperial coat of arms openly.[91] He complied with these requirements, and refrained from any imperial gestures. The *Grandes Chroniques* recounted these conditions for the meeting of the rulers at length, noting that "in France, the King does not permit anything that is not a customary practice there." Following their initial greeting with a handshake, it was the French king, and not the emperor, who rode between the Holy Roman monarchs, with the emperor to his right and the young king to his left. Charles IV respected the *religion royale,* with whose rituals he had no doubt been well acquainted since his youth. The visit and its protocol appeared as a gesture of mutual friendship, not of claim and counterclaim, and as a ritual encapsulating equal sovereignty, not a relationship of superiority and subservience. The book illuminators, among them none other than the renowned Jean Fouquet (in Charles VII of France's copy of the *Grandes Chroniques*) illustrated the ceremonial aspects of this visit repeatedly in meticulous detail, to immortalize the occasion for all time and so that it might serve as a model for all future kings[92]—a magnificent incunabula of royal diplomacy (see the illustration of elderly emperor Charles IV visiting his nephew King Charles V of France in Paris).

The solution was as new as it was momentous. The rulers' summit in Paris was followed just a few decades later by a journey by the Roman king and future emperor Sigismund (the youngest son of Charles IV) to the English royal court. On this occasion, too, great care was taken to ensure that the ceremonial should not convey the slightest hint that the empire wielded sovereignty in a foreign country, yet at the same time without compromising the distinguished visitor's status. In turn, this journey was followed in due course by a seemingly endless stream of state visits, right up to modern times. There was only one apparent exception to the well-rehearsed formula of such events. This took place in 1416, during a visit to Paris by Sigismund (still not emperor by this stage) to the mentally ill ruler of France, Charles VI. During Sigismund's visit a carefully controlled infringement of protocol was staged with the intention of strengthening the sick king's hold on his disputed realm. The ritualized community of two *principes,* two sovereigns, such as that fashioned during 1377–1378, became an unmistakable symbol of the equality and equal ranking of European nations and of the unifying bond between them. Over the long process of globalization, Europe exported this model to the wider world. It bears the indelible stamp of Charles IV's whole political philosophy, which has survived the passage of time: namely, the propensity to settle matters through diplomacy ("with goodness," as Charles put it) rather than rush to take up arms.

The Consequences of the Papal Schism in Europe

The emperor, however, had not been able to prevent the Papal Schism from occurring in 1378. He died that same year. The whole of Europe was divided at this time, with all of the West from Scotland to Castile recognizing the "French" antipope Clement VII in Avignon, while Italy, eastern and northern Europe continued to pay homage to Urban VI in Rome. The Holy Roman Empire was also divided internally, with its princes and prelates as disunited as ever and switching sides as they saw fit. Finally, the territories of the House of Luxembourg were split: in Bohemia and the empire. King Wenceslas, Charles's eldest son and successor followed Rome, whereas the Luxembourg homeland in the west, under the control of

Charles's brother Duke Wenceslas, swore religious obedience to Avignon. This latter factor had a powerful effect, strengthening the westward drift of the German princes. Furthermore, the duke's failures drew the country into the conflict that broke out between Burgundy and Orléans (and Armagnac) in the 1390s. Luxembourg was first seized by the duchy of Burgundy, forming an intermediate realm between France and Germany, before Philip the Good finally conquered it for Germany in 1443. Following his demise, toward the end of the fifteenth century, it devolved to Charles the Bold and the Austrian House of Habsburg *(felix Austria)* through his heiress daughter Mary.

Only Aragón put off deciding in favor of one or other of the popes; the reasons for this lay in the special problems facing its king, Peter IV, "El Ceremoniós" ("the Ceremonious") as he would later be called, was seeking to impose a stricter order upon his realm and consolidate all the various ruling titles from the Aegean and Sicily to Aragón itself including the former fief kingdom of Majorca. The last heir to the Majorcan throne, James IV, Peter's distant nephew, was kept prisoner by Peter in an iron cage in Barcelona until his death. Peter's plan was to blend elements of Norman–Hohenstaufen administrative practice, Roman Law, and Alfonso the Wise's *Siete Partidas* with home-grown legal traditions. Peter's rule saw the final compilation of the *Llibre del consolat del mar,* a statute book of Catalan maritime law that represents one of the outstanding juristic achievements of the Catalan citizenry. The Aragonese king could count on the support of the towns and the mercantile class within his realm; the nobility, on the other hand, was opposed to their monarch's plans to develop sea power, but Peter was able to prevail over this alliance by means of military force.

A succession of wars had plunged Peter IV into financial difficulties. Now, though, in the Western Schism, he seized the opportunity to confiscate church property. This measure proved to be of little help, yet his mountain of debt required that he persist with this policy (albeit for quite different reasons, Henry VIII of England's later dissolution of the monasteries, may be ranked alongside Peter's actions). The struggle for supremacy between the two great kingdoms on the Iberian Peninsula—Portugal was independent by this time—led time and again to protracted wars. The cause of these, as so often, was dynastic entanglements. Peter's father Alphons IV had taken the Castilian *Infanta* Eleonora as his second wife, and she had borne him two sons. Peter refused them and also his elder brother Ferdinand the inheritance provided for them by their father and drove them into exile in Castile, which henceforth became a hotbed of intrigue against Aragón. The pay for the mercenary troops Peter employed to maintain order continued to be raised through credit. The situation was exacerbated toward the end of Peter's reign by a financial crisis, which caused a banking crash in Barcelona (1381–1383).

Peter's problems continued to mount. At the same time as he was fighting against the alliance of noblemen, the plague was raging in Catalonia, where it hit a population already weakened by starvation. Barcelona at that period had a system of social welfare, which with its hospitals and orphanages, care for the mentally ill, and provision for the education and marriages of orphans was far more advanced than elsewhere in Europe.[93] Shortly afterward, war with Castile broke out once more (1356); this kingdom was in the grip of succession disputes, which also spilled over into Aragón, with Peter's estranged brother Ferdinand entering the fray as a rival candidate to Henry of Trastámara. At the same time, Henry was the preferred candidate of the French king, although he was now caught up in renewed conflict with England. Trastámara was ultimately able to prevail with Aragonese and later French assistance, and ascended the Castilian throne in 1369 (the dynasty he founded was to retain this title until the end of the Middle Ages), but the costs of the war stretched the finances of the Aragonese crown to the breaking point and made it dependent upon the estates' approval of taxation. The Catalans even derived a part of their income from duties imposed on foreign trade; in their *Corts* (parliament) a fourth estate comprising an alliance of the lesser nobility and the urban patrician class now began to grow in strength, to the great disadvantage of the future king. This development severely curtailed the sovereignty of the monarch in the kingdom of Aragón, while considerably extending the rights of the estates to approve taxes. This system would take root elsewhere in the future.

Finally, what happened here in the kingdom of Aragón was accompanied by theoretical deliberations, formulated by one of the most important political writers of the Middle Ages Francesc Eiximenis (d. 1409)—and this fact gave events there a resonance that extended far beyond the kingdom and the historical moment. This Franciscan scholar, who had studied in Valencia, Cologne, Paris, and Oxford, and knew the papal court in Avignon, finally became a lecturer in theology at the University of Lerida and maintained a close connection to the Aragonese crown. In his principal work, *Lo Crestia,* Eiximenis placed the *cosa pública,* and the *comunitat* of the realm above the king, and claimed that the monarch should be bound by the law. It had long been the practice for the king of Aragón, either in person or through a representative, to swear an oath before the *justicia mayor,* a legal body which adjudicated in matters of dispute between the parliament and the king. Though no demonstrable connection exists, in many regards the pledges contained within this oath resembled the English Magna Carta: the monarch undertook to put no person to death, or dispossess, or exile them without a trial, and furthermore not to infringe against the laws of the land *(fueros)* or its freedoms.[94] Developments in Western Europe also militated, here and there, in favor of similar solutions. Eiximenis, who had found in the writings of Avicenna the notion that the *cosa pública* could be divided into three "parts": the "regents," the "servants," and the "jurists," drew conclusions from this for Catalonia. He declared the *Corts*—Catalonia had no *justicia mayor*—to be the appropriate court of law with jurisdiction over the ruler, and that it even had the power, should the monarch transgress against the country's laws—to dismiss the king from his post. The doctrine of the right of resistance, which John of Salisbury had first formulated in the twelfth century, now attracted ever more adherents: in many significant aspects, it approached the provisions of the modern constitutional state. But first and foremost Eiximenis accorded the estates' assembly control over all decisions that related in any way to its right to approve taxes, not least whether to wage war or sue for peace. In addition, Eiximenis is also nowadays regarded as an early theoretician of the bourgeoisie, since he was the first to identify a connection between *bon regiment*—that is, the common good—work, and merit and hence to broach ideas that were to resurface in the sixteenth century.

The Papal Schism only multiplied political complications throughout Europe. No single potentate was in a position to disentangle these problems. Too many multifaceted and conflicting interests were in play. Yet a common strategy by all parties concerned seemed an impossibly distant prospect. A dominant ruler to match Charles IV was nowhere in evidence; yet even he would have been able to make little headway. Peter IV of Aragón, who may well have been planning to establish a Mediterranean empire, left behind two sons, Juan and Martin, who ruled in succession; following their reign, their dynasty died out. In the few years of rule that each enjoyed, they were unable to make any great impact, not even when a Catalan, Benedict XIII, was chosen as the successor to the Avignon antipope Clement VII (1394). France refused to recognize his accession, and he was duly deposed by the Council of Pisa in 1409. Even so, he declined to step down, and lived out the rest of his days in the Catalan town of Peñiscola until his death in 1423. He is seen today as an Antipope. The crown of Aragón had this passed the zenith of its power, and Spain's future lay in unity, which became a reality in the late fifteenth century. However, the European system of power as a whole centered upon the autonomy and sovereignty of the prince and his "state," rather than on alliances of princes, community, and unity. The theory of the *status principis* ("the ruler as person") as widely expounded in the fifteenth and early sixteenth century, contained within it the germ of the modern state.

Europe existed in a state of permanent conflict, affecting the whole of the continent, with wars in Spain and France, wars between German regional rulers and between Italian municipalities, military action to protect the territorial interests of the Holy See, and unrest in the kingdom of Sicily. The Hundred Years' War, the Black Death, and increasing payments to the nobility took a heavy toll on both France and England. Peasants and the urban citizenry alike rose up against their masters and the king. In France "free companies," that is, tightly organized units of mercenaries usually drawn from several countries, who found themselves surplus to requirements between conflicts, roamed the countryside without any purpose or political aim, plundering villages, castles, and towns and spreading terror throughout the region between the Seine and the Loire. One of these companies, under the command of the notorious "Archpriest" Arnaud de Cervole even advanced as far as Avignon, threatening Pope Innocent VI, who only managed to rid himself of them by handing over large sums of money. The plague compounded people's misery, while the huge ransom demands made by the English for French knights taken prisoner at the Battle of Maupertuis in 1356 were a heavy burden on the peasantry. Social unrest became widespread. The first major uprising was the great peasant revolt of 1358 known as the *Jacquerie* led by Guillaume Cale (pseudonym, "Jacques Bonhomme"), which was directed at the nobility and its property and affected large tracts of the Île de France, Picardy, and Normandy—and this in a century that had begun so proudly for France. In addition, the citizens of Paris revolted against the national council that was governing the country while King John the Good was still languishing in English captivity. This badly organized uprising, though, quickly disintegrated after the murder of its leader Étienne Marcel and was brought to an end with a general amnesty. Even so, a state of fear remained.

A quarter of a century later, in 1381, England was also gripped by insurrection. The unrest had reached the island from Flanders. The reforming sermons of John Wyclif, an Oxford theologian and preacher, which castigated the wealthy church establishment, had been fanning the embers of discontent since the 1370s. Now the peasantry—"People created in the same image as their masters but treated like animals," according to the chronicler Froissart—also joined forces against the nobility. Their demands were more radical and systematic than those of the *Jacquerie,* and with a more coherent agenda. Under the leadership of John Ball, a priest, they called for root-and-branch changes in society and made freedom their rallying cry. Yet anyone who simply based their concept of freedom, as these rebels did, on the free will inherent in every individual implicitly called into question, or even totally discredited, any form of bondage. The social consequences of such a doctrine were only a matter of time. A favorite song of the rebels ran: "When Adam delved and Eve span, / who was then the gentleman?" Their cause was also aided by the economic crisis then affecting the country. Things were going badly in England was Ball's message, spread by Froissart, and would continue to do so "until private property is taken into public ownership and there are no more lords and servants." Social utopias abounded, raising such demands as "we want to be lords of the kingdom." This revolt would live long in the folk memory.

Wyclif's sermonizing did not just stimulate a movement against poverty, however; his translation of the Bible also began to circulate among Catholics. His pupils, the Lollards, rejected the church's doctrine of the Eucharist, stressing instead the message of the Holy Gospel, which, translated into the vernacular, they demanded should be accessible to all believers. Soon, their grievances widened into attacks on the primacy of the pope, religious orders, and the business of pilgrimages, and broached for the first time the notion of a "priesthood of all believers." From 1401 onward, they were declared heretics and threatened with being burned at the stake, This did little to deter them, however, and Lollardism remained a vibrant force. Fresh rebellions and unrest, allied with repeated succession disputes, kept England on a tense footing throughout the fifteenth century. The uprisings were emblematic of fundamental ecclesiastical and religious changes that were sweeping not just England but the continent, too. Not without reason, prelates and priests began to fear for their safety.

This widening social upheaval only served to heighten the general atmosphere of anxiety in the West that had been triggered by famine, epidemics, and the Black Death. As an anonymous chronicler from Pisa recorded in the late fourteenth century: "The plague spread so rapidly that almost everyone perished." He continued: "Fear was so widespread that people avoided one another, the father his son, the son his father, brother shunned brother, and wives their husbands."[95] The terrifying first-hand experience of death also held sway elsewhere: "Charity was a thing of the past, and all hope vanished," lamented the pope's personal physician, Guy de Chauliac.[96] Family ties and friendships were severed. Fear had the effect of isolating people, turning them in on themselves, and even the customary ritual observances paid to the dead were abandoned. The plague, which swept through Europe from the mid-fourteenth century on, had spared no one: patricians and day laborers, princes and paupers were carried off by in the same way; the Black Death was a great leveler. This devastating experience left a lasting impression upon society and its order and engendered a whole new conception of the world and of humanity. Significantly, the Dance of Death became a common motif in art at this time.

The light-hearted tales in Boccaccio's *Decameron* unfold against this dismal backcloth. The framework narrative constructed by the writer introduces us to a refined Florentine society comprising seven young women and three young men, who have withdrawn from the plague-ridden city to the countryside in order to spend their days in carefree pursuits and apparent safety and to ward off the threat of death by regaling one another with diverting, sometimes even erotic, tales and by giving themselves over to all the distractions life has to offer. In Boccaccio's work, with Death looming, a lust for life in the here and now comprehensively dispelled religion's shunning of all earthly things. A much more sober and somber atmosphere pervades a contemporaneous work, *Der Ackermann aus Böhmen* (The plowman from Bohemia), whose author Johannes von Tepl, speaking through his central character, rails against Death, "the slayer of all men." Death has carried off the plowman's beloved wife, an act he can never forgive or forget. But significantly in Johannes's dialog with the Grim Reaper, there is no longer any sense of Death being a force that liberates man from the Vale of Tears that every soul once believed that it was condemned to suffer here below. Nor was there any hint of the quiet death, which in the early Middle Ages was deemed to descend upon the dying man, or of the dutiful acceptance of death by the chivalrous knight on the battlefield. Even though the dispute between the Plowman and Death finally, and somewhat academically, concludes with the familiar *topos* of the transience of all earthly things—"all is vanity"—a traditional consolation for our mortal state, the new worldview presented by this text was unmistakable. Human feelings are embraced here for the first time—feelings such as despair and impotent rage—along with what provokes them, namely an emphatic affirmation of earthly existence in all its preciousness and beauty: "Death, be thou cursed!"

The plague hit Europe just as the continent was starting to feel the effects of a severe worsening of the climate. A series of appallingly rain-soaked years (1316–1318) formed the prelude to this; ears of corn failed to ripen in the field and rotted on the stalk; gangrene brought on by ergotism became rife and starvation became widespread. Storm surges like the notorious *Grote Mandränke* of 1364 inundated sections of the North Friesian coast in perpetuity. In this flood, the diocese of Schleswig lost two whole villages on the North Sea island of Sylt, which were completely washed away. Hand in hand with these disasters came a general decline in living conditions and a succession of epidemics. The cause of both may well lie in the perennial practice of cultivating rye; although this staple provided people with bread, its monoculture seems to have led to a general deficiency in diet (quite apart from the scourge of ergotism, caused by a fungus that grew on rye). The great agricultural advance of the late Middle Ages, the rise of cereal growing in the three-field system of crop rotation, thus proved to be a disadvantage, with debilitating effects on the population over time. But at the time, the causes remained unknown, so preventive measure were not taken. Moreover, the effects of the plague were worsened by a period of economic recession, which hit the peasantry and the knightly caste especially hard.

All these developments pointed to gradually evolving processes that the historian, with the benefit of hindsight and equipped with statistical data, can easily grasp but that anyone living at the time could scarcely have been expected to recognize. For people alive in the Middle Ages, the first great break with normality that changed everything was the Black Death. This change was evident everywhere. In an attempt to replenish their ravaged populations, the cities relaxed their former restrictions on incomers.

As a result, an extensive internal migration from the countryside to the towns ensued, which in turn caused economic shortages, for example from the shortage of agricultural laborers available at harvest time. The settlement of the East slowed to a trickle. Those members of the aristocracy who had survived suddenly found themselves inheriting rich legacies. As a chronicler from Florence noted, "Those who had nothing became wealthy overnight." Besides, when deaths from the plague ceased, people started paying attention to the way they dressed once more. Accordingly, "tailors began charging astronomically high prices; no sum was too extravagant for them. Man servants and maids shamelessly asked for higher wages, demands only curbed by punishing them severely. Peasants meanwhile called for a contract whereby virtually everything that they harvested should belong to them."[97] This was the situation in Florence, which had been shaken by serious economic crises in the past, but it was repeated all over Europe. Traditional social bonds were torn asunder, and the old world of Europe was cut loose from its moorings. The authorities intervened, sanctioning emergency restrictions and extending and centralizing their power. This helped lay the foundations for modern state authority.

Finally, the great fear abroad in Europe also came to afflict the ruling class, not so much fear of the plague as fear of the anger of their people and fear of one another. They barricaded themselves in their solidly built homes, strengthening the defensive walls and reinforcing the gates of their castles. Charles V of France not only had the Louvre extended but also fortified, and also built the Bastille, which would later became the symbol *par excellence* of the oppression of the French people. Major uprisings in Flanders and Languedoc (1379) lasted until Charles V's death the following year and even beyond. The general populace was seething with anger; already, the citizens of Ghent had expelled the count who controlled the city and his military contingent. "Rulers were gripped by terror, running head over heels to escape; the son did not wait for his father, nor the father for his son."[98] Kings and princes feared that they would be slaughtered, and their fears were well founded. In 1407, Louis I, duke of Orléans ended up murdered with his skull smashed in after being waylaid; it transpired that his assassination had been ordered by the duke of Burgundy. "Mourn, you men and women, old and young, poor and rich! For the sweet state of peace and tranquility has been snatched from you. War and destruction are on the horizon." So prophesied Louis's widow, Valentina Visconti. The French royal court began to dabble in magic and sorcery. This was a truly black period for the country. The arrival of these dark times was heralded by another assassination (1419); its victim was John the Fearless, duke of Burgundy, the man who had arranged the earlier killing. This time, the dauphin was suspected of having a hand in the murder. The ongoing dispute in Latin Christendom over the true pope continued to be a source of mounting insecurity and skepticism, hampering all attempts at reform. The advent of the Antichrist drew ever closer. Saint Catherine of Siena (d. 1380), according to her biographer, even picked up the stench of infernal vice at the Roman Curia. The pope to whom she confided this, Gregory XI, refused to believe her. Was this now an age where crime and fear reigned supreme?

Mosaic of Pope Innocent III, from the old Saint Peter's Basilica in Rome. When the old church was demolished, it was given by Pope Clement VIII to the Conti family, to whom he was related, and may now be seen in the Museum of Rome at the Palazzo Braschi. Scala / Art Resource, NY.

ILLE EGO PRECLARI TVLERAM QVI SCEPTRA SENATVS
REX SICVLIS CAROLVS IVRA DEDI POPVLIS
OBRVTVS HEV IACVI SAXIS FVMOQVE DEDERVNT
HVNC TVA CONSPICVVM TEMPORA SIXTE LOCVM

Charles of Anjou, the ruler who finally deposed the Hohenstaufen dynasty from the throne of Sicily. This statue, in a deliberately antique style and showing Charles clad in the toga of a Roman senator, is by Arnolfo di Cambrio (d. 1302/10) and is in the Capitoline Museum in Rome. Erich Lessing / Art Resource, NY.

The Chinese emperor Kublai Khan, the ruler whom Marco Polo visited on his travels. The Art Archive at Art Resource, NY.

The Holy Crown of Hungary. Tradition claims this as the crown of Saint Stephen (d. 1038), but analysis reveals that it comprises two different parts—the so-called Corona Latina and Corona Graeca—and was only assembled in the twelfth century. Since that time, all the kings of Hungary, even down to the last Habsburg monarchs, have been crowned with it. It is now kept in the Hungarian parliament building in Budapest. Foto Marburg / Art Resource, NY.

The "scissor arches" in Wells Cathedral in Somerset, England. This church, built between 1182 and 1260, represents the high point of the Early English style of Gothic architecture. The distinctive arches were added in 1338 to support a stone tower with a wooden spire, which was threatening to collapse. Gianni Dagli Orti / The Art Archive at Art Resource, NY.

This portolan chart from Pisa, dating from the late thirteenth century, is one of the earliest known examples of this kind of maritime chart. Scala / White Images / Art Resource, NY.

Notre Dame Cathedral in Paris is one of the most outstanding ecclesiastical buildings of the Middle Ages, and established many of the principles underlying the Gothic style of cathedral architecture. Its façade faced the original palace of the kings of France. Notre Dame, Paris, France / Peter Willi / The Bridgeman Art Library.

From the thirteenth century on, music came to play an increasingly important role not only in church but also in courtly life. This bas-relief by Luca della Robbia, from the Museo dell'Opera del Duomo in Florence, shows a group of singers and musicians from the so-called *Cantoria* (1341–1348). Alfredo Dagli Orti / The Art Archive at Art Resource, NY.

Bust of Holy Roman Emperor Charles IV of Luxembourg, who ruled as Holy Roman Emperor 1355–1378, by architect and sculptor Peter Parler. Saint Vitus Cathedral, Prague, Czech Republic / Art Resource, NY.

The only form of portraiture practiced in the Middle Ages comprised portraits of patrons, which might occasionally include family members. But from the late fifteenth century on, a new kind of secular family group portrait emerged: courtly representations of entire princely dynasties. This fresco by Andrea Mantegna (1465–1474) shows the family of Margrave Ludovico III Gonzaga of Mantua, Italy. The margrave is seated on the far left, looking up from a letter he has received from his son Francesco, who had just been made a cardinal, and turning his head to talk to his secretary. Scala/Art Resource, NY.

The so-called Echevins portrait of Joan of Arc, anonymous, sixteenth century.
Snark / Art Resource, NY.

In the central panel of the *Hay Wain* triptych by Hieronymus Bosch, sinful people from all ranks clamor to grab some hay, a proverbial symbol for worldly goods. The Art Archive at Art Resource, NY.

The nude arose as an artistic challenge to convention in
the Renaissance. The German painter Hans Baldung
Grien painted this subject matter on several occasions. One
example is his work *Woman with Cat: Allegory of Music.*
Alte Pinakothek, Bayerische Staatsgemäldesammlungen,
Munich, Germany / Art Resource, NY.

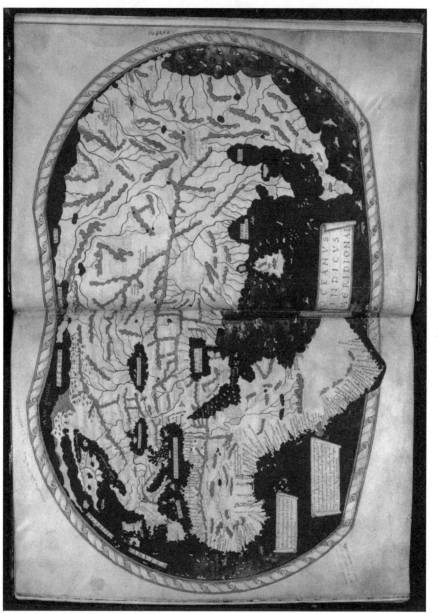

Henricus Martellus's world map of 1489 stands firmly in the tradition of Ptolemaic cartography, showing an image of the world following the first expeditions down the west coast of Africa by Portuguese explorers. However, it evidently predates Vasco da Gama's first rounding of the Cape of Good Hope in 1497. © British Library Board / Robana / Art Resource, NY.

This terracotta bust of Niccolò da Uzzano by Donatello is an outstanding example of the highly developed art of portraiture in the Early Renaissance, which placed a premium on close observation of real life. Erich Lessing / Art Resource, NY.

As a result of peace negotiations between the Republic of Venice and the Sublime Porte in Istanbul, the Venetian painter Gentile Bellini, brother of Giovanni, was given the opportunity in 1480 to paint the Ottoman ruler who had conquered Constantinople and was a great patron of the arts, Sultan Mehmet II. Gianni Dagli Orti / The Art Archive at Art Resource, NY.

This portrait of Charles the Bold, duke of Burgundy, is a copy of a painting attributed to Rogier van der Weyden. The only insignia of authority worn by the duke is the Order of the Golden Fleece on the chain around his neck. Erich Lessing / Art Resource, NY.

The cities of the Low Countries maintained a strong and independent stance toward their new ruler, the Holy Roman Emperor and German king Maximilian I, a position that the monarch was obliged to concede. The settlement that he reached with Bruges in 1488 was marked with a Mass and with a peace banquet, at which the king dined alone and was served by the burghers of the city. This sketch by the so-called Master of the Housebook shows Maximilian behind a curtain during the Mass. Kupferstichkabinett, Staatliche Museen, Berlin, Germany / Art Resource, NY.

Detail of a panel from the bronze "Bernward's Doors" (1015) at Saint Mary's Cathedral in Hildesheim, showing Jesus being brought before Pontius Pilate. The two wings of the doors, which were commissioned by Bishop Bernward, thirteenth bishop of the German city (d.1022) are both an artistic and a technological masterpiece. In antiquity, bronzes were cast in several pieces that were then soldered together. The first bronzes to be cast as a single piece were the doors to Aachen cathedral (from the Carolingian period), the Willigis doors at Mainz Cathedral, and Bernward's doors. Erich Lessing/Art Resource, NY.

Pisa Cathedral and the Leaning Tower. Construction took from the eleventh to the fourteenth century; the cathedral façade was designed by the architect Rainaldo in the twelfth century. The whole ensemble of ecclesiastical buildings at Pisa conveys the wealth and power of this medieval maritime city, which in its heyday rivaled the might of ancient Rome. Omniphoto / UIG / The Bridgeman Art Library.

12

Waiting for Judgment Day and the Renaissance

U P ON HIGH, enthroned in the firmament and seated upon a rainbow spanning Heaven and Earth, sits the Lord, who has come to judge the world at the End of Days. His fellow judges are the saints, while at his side Mary the Mother of God kneels in intercession; above them angels hover, some displaying the instruments of Christ's Passion while others blow the trumpets of Judgment Day. Down on Earth, mighty and all powerful, stands the Angel Saint Michael, the weigher of souls. Clad in shining gold armor, he performs his duty, separating those who are blessed from those who have been damned. Far into the distance, right to the horizon, the dead are seen rising from their graves; those few souls who have been saved turn toward Paradise, covering their nakedness. At the gates of Heaven, Saint Peter receives them with a handshake, and angels clothe them in the robes of the Blessed. Some of those who have awakened from the dead still hope for forgiveness and beg for mercy, but an angel use his cross staff to drive one such desperate sinner back into the clutches of a devil, whose terrible companions drag and push the great mass of the damned off to Hell. These unfortunates are all stark naked, stripped of all signs of worldly status, and their faces are etched with horror and fear. Crying, wailing, and contorted in agony, they are cast down into the fiery abyss of Hell, plunging head over heels into eternal damnation, and even as they fall they are tormented by demons.

The man who imagined and brought to life this awe-inspiring scene was the artist Hans Memling. Painted in Bruges in around 1470, it was commissioned by Angelo Tani, the Bruges representative of the Medici Bank. The painting was duly dispatched to its patron in Italy, but the ship carrying it was seized by vessels of the Hanseatic League, and the triptych confiscated and taken to Danzig (Gdansk), where it resides to the present day. Memling created for the Renaissance city of Florence a work that was fully in accordance with contemporary anticipation of a Day of Judgment that was thought to be drawing threateningly close. Devout believers at the time—at least wealthy citizens and princes—were greatly preoccupied with thoughts of the End of Days and the fear this engendered. Artists of the time in the Netherlands and Italy, in particular, painted this same motif time and again. They included Rogier van der Weyden, in whose workshop Memling had been apprenticed, Fra Angelico, Petrus Christus, and Luca Signorelli; later, Michelangelo would follow suit, while at the same time breaking new ground. And these were only the outstanding masters of their craft; countless lesser painters would also find themselves attracted to this same theme.

Granted, paintings of the Day of Judgment had always been part of the basic stock of imagery illustrating the Christian doctrine of redemption and the story of salvation; they were a familiar sight in every richly deco-rated place of worship: the tympana and spandrels above church doors in Paris, Bamberg, or Berne provide the ideal site for this theme, which was later also adopted by the illuminators of Books of Hours. But over time, the content of these depictions had changed fundamentally. Thus it was once the case, say in the famous mosaics decorating the sixth-century Basilica of Sant' Apollinare Nuovo in Ravenna, that the Lord was shown separating the sheep from the goats. Elsewhere, the Wise and Foolish Vir-gins appeared as metaphors for judgment. Then, in the tenth century, the damned were first shown in person in the works of the Reichenau school of illumination; before long, the gaping mouth of Hell was being por-trayed and devils had found their way into the pictures. Finally, it became commonplace to paint a beatific smile on the countenance of the Savior, while the faces of the damned were shown contorted in grimaces of terror.

Dante gave the fourteenth century powerful visions of Hell, the moun-tain of Purgatory, and Paradise, showing by turns scenes of despair and of blessed salvation. Illuminated manuscripts of the *Divina Commedia* conjured up images of terror and bliss. Sandro Botticelli, almost certainly with one of the Medici as his patron, was commissioned with just such a task, producing a unique cycle of drawings for Dante's work.[1] And it was precisely around the same time that he was active, namely the late fifteenth century, that images of the Day of Judgment began to take on a degree of vividness and unsettling drama never since surpassed, depicting almost unimaginable bliss on the one hand and agonizing "naturalistic" horror on the other. Memling's teacher Rogier van der Weyden had been renowned for his ability to imbue his pictures with emotion. Now, angels and devils could be seen engaged in a violent struggle for the soul of every dead person. Whether in a compact Book of Hours or a large-format triptych, the Day of Judgment revealed its terrifying face. Hope in trepidation and constant anxiety were the hallmarks of the century—for all the joyous affirmation of life, and despite the Renaissance and the agenda of humanism and their promise of a happy existence. Time and again, be it in Italy, Germany, or France, contemporaries clamored for news about what was to come. Astrology and prognostic literature were abiding features of the Renaissance period, and its most celebrated authors and artists treated such topics more intensely than most. Who could have known at the time that this was a blind alley? It appeared a perfectly rational approach, and all existing scholarship pointed to its being a worthwhile line of enquiry.

Concerns about the End Time were voiced even at royal courts, as well as in private. Aliénor of Poitiers, a lady-in-waiting at the court of the French queen, complained indignantly about the collapse of morality: "Nowadays, everyone does just as they please, and it is to be feared that this will all end badly" ("que tout ira mal"). Even though it was only small alterations in the court ceremonial or in good taste that awakened her anger—for instance, that women in Flanders were now in the habit of putting their bed in front of the hearth prior to giving birth—it still made her turn up her nose in disgust. How much store this age set by etiquette can be seen from Froissart's report on the visit of the French king Charles VI to Clement VII in Avignon (1389): "There sat the pope, all alone at a table, and held court. The king was seated lower down, also alone at a table, while the cardinals and dukes all filed in to take their places. And the banquet was long, drawn-out, impressive, and sumptuous."[2] The coronation feast of the German king retained this kind of ceremonial pomp right up to the end of the Holy Roman Empire. Yet even a glance out the windows of palaces, banqueting halls, and warm bedchambers would have served to show that all was not well. Two, sometimes even three popes were sitting on Saint Peter's throne at this time, or at least fancied that they were; kings were being deposed or murdered; the brave duke of Burgundy was unceremoniously done away with and buried without honor in his doublet, hose, and shoes rather than in his robe of state with all the pomp that befitted his status.[3] Meanwhile, "infidel" Turks were threatening Christendom, annihilating Crusader armies, and finally conquered the thousand-year-old Byzantium (1453). Popular uprisings were shaking Italy, France, and England, while religious wars were ravaging Germany. In France, a virgin girl saved the throne, as proud knights accustomed to victory went to the slaughter in their thousands. At the same time in France, Jean of Berry, a duke of royal blood, was having the most magnificent castles built and was commissioning the most opulent illustrated Books of Hours. Avarice and parsimony were the order of the day in the houses of the town citizenry, and even more so at the court of the pope and the king, as usury burdened poor and rich alike. Priests were not obeying their vows of celibacy, and courtesans plied their trade at the papal court. Bastards, sons of priests who had been born in sin, demanded and were granted ecclesiastical offices. Heretics and witches carried out their mischief in towns and in the countryside. Faith itself was in danger, and preachers of repentance called for people to renounce their sins, but few followed them. "We live in a time of fools, yet they alone wield power!" as one clear-sighted observer of the Roman Curia complained.[4] Everything, with no exception, was in a state of confusion; nothing and no one could be relied upon any more, downfall and chaos loomed, and everything was going awry. There was a desperate need for reform, but who could possibly set this in motion? And where to begin this process?

Are we, then, justified in seeing this period as the decline of the Middle Ages? Its autumn, so to speak, when all that it sowed would be reaped? The entrance of the Four Horsemen of the Apocalypse, perhaps? Or merely as a time of upheaval, hardship, and revolts? There was no denying that a new age was dawning here, which transcended all previous boundaries, which was more complex and hectic, and more multifaceted, fast-living, and turbulent also, as well as being more disruptive and more unsettling than any earlier age. In symbolic terms, we may see it as being prefigured by Petrarch's ascent of Mont Ventoux in 1336, though the storm on the mountain he described was most likely pure invention on the writer's part. This peak does indeed afford panoramic views all around, over the sea and the high mountains, even without a walker having to ascend all the way to the summit. So, even if Petrarch did fabricate his storm on the summit and write it with a classical model as his guide, he was still celebrating in the climb a sense of liberation, an expansion of his horizons, and the fact that his soul was opening up to the world. And yet, no sooner had he reached the summit than the words of Saint Augustine's *Confessions* came into his mind. "I wish now to review in memory my past wickedness and the carnal corruptions of my soul—not because I still love them, but that I may love thee, O my God," he imagined the saint calling out to him, he who just at that moment seemed to have the world at his feet: a warning to him not to lose himself. The poet himself then concluded that the only person who is truly happy is he who could be certain that all fear and all earthly desires lay beneath his feet.[5] The tempest on the mountain frightened the poet. Openness to the world demanded that he conquer his fear. Could he manage that, though? The terrifying images of humans plunging into the pit of Hell must have cast doubt into his mind.

In practical terms, the voyages of the Portuguese prince and administrator of the Military Order of Christ, Henry the Navigator, to try and find a sea passage to India burst open the confines of Europe. When, in 1418, Henry sent his ships out into the wide world to sail down the western coast of Africa and discover new routes into the unknown, this was targeted, deliberate exploration. Henry's expedition was an enterprise that Dante would still have considered an act of godless hubris, but which, after decades of missionary and trading journeys to the Mongol court at Cambaluc, had begun to seem entirely feasible. The first colonial empires began to take shape at this time. Portugal and Spain vied for the best jumping-off points from which to embark on their imperial adventures. The Canary Islands, the Azores, hitherto uninhabited, were occupied in the name of Portugal and promised to the country's king in perpetuity by the pope. Bases were established all along the west coast of Africa. The slave trade received a new boost from this, and experienced a revival not witnessed since ancient times.

Technical innovations both promoted and accompanied expansion. The magnetic compass is a prime example. Magnetism as a principle had been known about in some shape or form since Antiquity. Yet the first mention of the compass is by the English scholar Alexander Neckam in 1187. He cited a needle floating on water and aligning itself on a north–south axis and stated that "the sailor makes use of the twirling needle to show him the cardinal point to which the prow of his ship should be turned" *(De naturis rerum)*. The "dry" (and more accurate) compass was first described by Pierre Pélerin de Maricourt in 1269, and in around 1300 was made into a truly practical instrument by combining it with a compass-rose and mounting it (on gimbals) in a sturdy wooden box. Around 1400 compasses were installed on ships for the first time, giving them greater precision, an essential for navigation on the high seas. It was around this same time that the phenomenon of magnetic declination was first identified, namely the discrepancy between the direction indicated by the compass needle and True North; the first person to pinpoint this problem was the German astronomer Georg von Peuerbach (d. 1461), and sailors soon learned to compensate for it. The voyages of Christopher Columbus and other Atlantic seafarers would have been inconceivable without these developments. A series of seemingly inconspicuous inventions over several centuries thus enabled the process of globalization to take hold. Compasses showing True North were also used in mining in the thirteenth and fourteenth centuries. Presently, in a development of the astrolabes used in ancient and medieval times, the sextant made its first appearance. Weapons technology also came on in leaps and bounds. The Hundred Years' War was the first conflict in which gunpowder and cannon were used en masse, ultimately deciding the outcome of the war.

Peaceful advances also took place at this time. The invention of printing with movable type, the brilliant notion of Johannes Gutenberg (d. 1468), together with the development of paper as a writing and printing material, greatly speeded up the dissemination of knowledge. In 1454, the renowned forty-two-line Bible came off the presses. Books and the acquiring of learning became cheaper, while the networks of knowledge became more extensive, denser, and more readily accessible to larger sections of the populace. Swifter transmission of ideas promoted innovation in many fields, some quite unexpected such as mathematics, spherical trigonometry, mining, architecture, and art history. Other areas to quickly develop were propaganda, ecclesiastical reformation, and the reporting of "news." A new conception and consciousness of time arose. The mechanical clock incorporating a balance and pendulum, developed in the late Middle Ages, now became widespread; church towers were found to be ideal places to install them. Measured time, work calibrated by the hour, and the phenomenon of days subdivided mechanically into segments changed the life of the entire population, including children.

Knowledge of the world expanded as precise orientation in space and time became a possibility. These were all without a doubt massive strides forward, but at the same time they inevitably confused people, fostered insecurity, and stimulated a desire for some point of fixity in this situation of dynamic flux. Life was being increasingly overtaken by the passage of hours, standardization, and the monitoring of norms. The countryside, towns, and princely courts alike were pervaded by a sense of growing social control. In all these places, regulations had to be strictly observed, and courtly etiquette governed peoples' coexistence with ever greater regularity and efficiency. Reason, thrift, and rational organization also became an intrinsic part of the home, especially the bourgeois home. Diligence and luck—*virtù* and *fortuna,* were to become its guiding principles. For instance, the humanist, poet, art historian and architect Leon Battista Alberti (d. 1472) described this trend as it related to his own family, in which domestic order had been elevated to an art form: "The number of family members should multiply, and should never decrease; likewise, its wealth should not dwindle but increase; all manner of damage to the family reputation should be avoided, rather its good name should be loved and cherished; hatred, envy, and animosity should be shunned; instead acquaintance, fondness, and friendship should be secured, intensified, and maintained" (*Della famiglia* [On the family], 1437–1441).[6]

Such a reevaluation of the family unit was especially evident among the urban middle classes, but was by no means confined to them; not least, it manifested itself in the rise of the family portrait (a genre that had a loose precursor in the portraits of benefactors). Between 1465 and 1474, for example, Andrea Mantegna completed a fresco of the extended family, plus all the members of the court, of the ruthless *condottiere* Margrave Ludovico Gonzaga of Mantua. Portraits of the nuclear family comprising father, mother, and children, arranged according to age and height, soon became a familiar form. Humanism and the Reformation would in due course thrive on this genre: in such portraits, the new bourgeoisie, for all the feuding between guilds that sometimes afflicted it, was able to present itself as a countervailing force to ostentatious displays of wealth and pomp. Measured, modest forms of architecture, style, and dress were the order of the day: simple, black gondolas; small oriel windows; and no finery in the wardrobe. On the other hand, it cannot be denied that guild regulations held back competition and innovation in many trades. Taxes increased, at least for the lower echelons of society; the rules and regulations of social order and social discipline were everywhere in evidence. And yet, despite such restrictions, this new bourgeoisie was adept at self-presentation and promotion.

No less rigidly than in the bourgeois world, etiquette also played a key role in governing the world of the nobility, and of princely and royal courts at this time.[7] Elaborate feasts, lavish tournaments and jousts, public mourning, the use of state liveries, the arrangement of beds, indeed every last aspect of protocol demanded the minutest attention to detail. All this took place under the supervision of a whole army of court functionaries—heralds, chamberlains, and ladies-in-waiting. Anyone who transgressed against etiquette was regarded as an uncouth oaf or was deemed to have done so quite deliberately in order to provoke and offend. On one occasion, in 1463, when two kings met who, though not openly in conflict with one another, nevertheless didn't particularly like one another—namely, Louis XI of France and Henry II of Castile—both appeared in vestments that were inappropriate to the occasion. Without any words being exchanged, their apparel made it abundantly clear what they thought of one another. As the French diplomat Philippe de Commynes reported, "The king of Castile was ugly, and his clothes displeased the Frenchman . . . our king dressed himself in great haste, and as badly as he could." The smallest details were taken notice of. When the Elector Palatine Frederick I ("the Victorious") paid a state visit to Charles the Bold, duke of Burgundy in Brussels in 1467, lavish celebrations were laid on, but even so Commynes still reported overhearing the duke's men whispering that "the Germans were dirty, threw their muddy boots on the freshly made beds, and had no sense of propriety. And yet those same Germans still saw fit to carp enviously at the opulence of their surroundings. And indeed, the two princes fell out after this visit."[8] Clothes and manners were vital elements in political dealings.

And yet, in spite of this rigidly regulated life, insecurities still grew, uncertainty how to respond to all the novelties that were appearing; the world seemed to be governed by anxiety. Fears were stoked by violence and war, while various visions either heightened these fears or seemed to promise salvation; these visions were given form by religion and faith. Anticipation of the Day of Judgment intensified; the Antichrist, it was thought, was coming ever closer, devils were rampaging throughout the land; and spirits of the air, earth, and fire were just waiting to be summoned by sorcery. Reason thirsted after secrets, belief, and miracles; enlightenment, it seems, always comes up against frontiers that frustrate it. As early as the final years of the fourteenth century, new religious movements were coming into existence, founded by visionaries, reformers, and educated women. Even the young Charles IV was convinced that he possessed visionary powers. Brigitta of Sweden (d. 1373), who experienced a vision of the Virgin Mary, believed that she had a calling to bring about peace between England and France, and so moved to Rome; she lambasted her own king, Magnus Erikson, for having homosexual affairs and for his defiance of papal excommunication. Although she was a Dominican nun, the mystic Catherine of Siena (d. 1380), to whom Jesus, Peter, Paul, and the Beloved Disciple Saint John the Evangelist all appeared, experienced the stigmata, and—unusually for a woman—held public meetings; she was particularly well received in Italy.

Private devotion had long since found its way into both bourgeois and aristocratic households. The forms it took from the late twelfth century onward can be seen in the exquisite Books of Hours commissioned by patrons. These became luxurious prestige objects. Many patrons—notably the duc de Berry—collected them for their beauty, splendor, and sheer costliness. But for all their opulence, with their prayer texts and calendars, their cults of saints and instructions for doing penance, they are a reflection of the religious practices that gave rise to them in the first place. Moreover, with their images of devotion and meditation, they also mirror the devout belief in the Afterlife, the expectations of salvation, and the reasons behind the worldly fears and heavenly hopes harbored by those who used them daily.

The period from the late fourteenth century onward witnessed the spread of the religious movement known as *Devotio moderna,* which had its origins in Gerard Groote of Deventer in the Low Countries (d. 1384). Groote, the founder of the Brethren of the Common Life, was heavily influenced by mystics such as Meister Eckhart and Jan van Ruysbroek. The new mood of piety that Groote's movement fostered was consolidated and organized (along the lines of the Rule of Saint Augustine) by Gerhard Zerbolt of Zutphen and especially Groote's pupil Florence Radewyns of Utrecht, who recruited followers in Flanders, Brabant, Lorraine, Holland, and large parts of the German kingdom (the Congregation of Windesheim, for example, joined them) as far south as Basel (Saint Leonhard) and Interlaken. The Parisian theologian Jean Gerson is widely regarded as the driving intellectual force behind the *Devotio*. It never reached Italy or Spain. Despite being university trained, its founders turned their backs on scholasticism and sought a life of simple devotion to God. They attracted a large following particularly among lay people, and their influence can be seen not least in the writings of Luther and Calvin.

The most influential work of the *Devotio Moderna* was without a doubt the meditational text *De imitatione Christi (The Imitation of Christ)* commonly ascribed to one Thomas à Kempis' (d. 1471), though the actual authorship is unknown; it may even have been written by Groote himself. This was widely read, with some manuscripts of it even reaching Italy. For a long time, it was the second-most-popular Christian text, the number of copies printed only being surpassed by the Bible. The themes of its four books are: an admonition to lead a spiritual life and to renounce the vanities of the world; the inner life; inner consolation; and preparing oneself to receive the Holy Sacrament. In his introduction, the author exhorted his readers reader: "Let our chief effort, therefore, be to study the life of Jesus Christ. The teaching of Christ is more excellent than all the advice of the saints" (1:3–4). "What good does it do to speak learnedly about the Trinity if, lacking humility, you displease the Trinity? Indeed, it is not learning that makes a man holy and just, but a virtuous life makes him pleasing to God. I would rather feel contrition than know how to define it" (1:7–9).

A life of virtue rather than cold learning—such an agenda was bound to find favor among the humanists. All this comes across like an answer, driven by the mysteries of faith and the needs of the soul, to the rational, nominalistic waves of enlightenment in the thirteenth and fourteenth centuries, such as always appear in the wake of intensive trends toward rationalism. The *Devotio* was the religious correlate to the worldly affectations of the humanists. The dialectic of enlightenment called for inwardness, faith, and irrationality. Even the long-established orders were striving toward reform. The Benedictines experienced a new efflorescence through the Congregations of the abbeys of Melk, Kastl, and Bursfelde, while new religious forces were also stirring among the Augustinian Canons.

While no outstanding philosophers came to the fore at that time, in the fifteenth century, and while theology, by contrast, made its voice heard far more loudly through the works of Jean Gerson, say, or Nicholas of Cusa, this century is truly remarkable for its visual artists and its humanist-schooled writers. These stand in curious contrast to the religious needs of the era. When, somewhat earlier, Christine de Pizan raised eyebrows at the French court as the first woman poet to earn her living through her art, she heralded a sea change in intellectual affairs. Rhetoric, historiography, letter writing, schooling, and education henceforth occupied the center stage of both public and private spheres. The much-admired style of ancient pagan authors once again prompted writers to imitate and adapt their works. Intellectual elites found themselves gripped by a pervasive atmosphere of secularization. Even priests let themselves be seduced by the manifold delights of this world. Erotic stories like those recounted in Boccaccio's *Decameron* were highly popular. Likewise, the *Facetiae* by Poggio Bracciolini (d. 1459), a collection of humorous anecdotes and scurrilous tales of scandal such as those doing the rounds at the papal court in Rome ("and so the three of them repaired to bed together") mirrored the all-embracing "sensualization" of this society, which had the propensity to shock and make people aware of their sinfulness, but also to yearn for contrition, penitence, and expiation.

Preachers of repentance appealed to troubled souls. And Poggio was a serious humanist, who himself was highly critical of the vanities of the world. The gravity of the period was conducive to contemplation and reflection. For three years (1451–1454), the Minorite Giovanni Capestrano (d. 1456) traveled through the lands north of the Alps preaching against the Hussites and the Turks and drumming up support for the papacy; he was also active in Hungary. This mendicant friar invested great hope in the emperor and the diet. For three weeks, while the princes met at the Imperial Diet in Frankfurt in 1454, he preached daily—on work days in the Saint Bartholomew churchyard outside the cathedral, and on Sundays and holidays on the teeming Römerberg square in front of Frankfurt's town hall—castigating usury and adultery, as well as games of cards and dice, which he consigned to the flames of Hell. What a curious age this was, when all such things were seen as vices heralding the apocalypse! In vain, Capestrano called for a Crusade against the Turks, to try and contain the very real danger that was looming from the East.[9]

Hell was devious and scheming, though. Contemporaries were certain that it was intent on taking possession of people's bodies and souls, especially ordinary people's. As far as the rich and powerful were concerned, so long as they had not indulged in usury, they could easily escape censure by earthly judges. Yet on his journey through the Inferno, Dante had already met the likes of them in great numbers and seen them punished with the most ghastly forms of torture, and had not shied away from naming these damned souls. This served to turn up the heat on those in power: sin and the flames of Hell were ever present and were being stoked up incessantly. Contemporaries were shocked, terrified, and yet at the same time oddly captivated by the notion. The Devil devised ever more subtle methods of ensnaring them, using magic and sorcery to conjure up enticing pleasures. These forbidden arts "had taken root in the souls of so many men, be they of lowly or exalted status," including even the highest echelons of society. It was now of the utmost urgency to defend humanity against these works of the Devil. At the very beginning of the fifteenth century, this impelled the Heidelberg theologian Nikolaus Magni to compose a polemic, which, several decades later, in 1455, Johannes Hartlieb made more accessible and widely known when he incorporated it in his *Book of All Forbidden Arts,* dedicated to Margrave John of Brandenburg. Hartlieb gingered up this account with tales of his own encounters with the world of magic. He concluded that "many gullible people are led astray" by "Satan and his thousand tricks."[10]

In their condemnation of magic, these two scholars identified seven dark arts: necromancy, geomancy, hydromancy, aeromancy, pyromancy, chiromancy (palmistry), and scapulimancy—ranging, therefore, from black magic and the casting of evil spells to the reading of palms and augury using the shoulder blades (scapulae) of large animals or even of people. Hartlieb's book recounted how one high-ranking "captain of the Teutonic Knights" was a great devotee of this latter practice of divination, "which both princes and large sections of the common people swear by." Yet all this, the authors maintained, was just an illusion devised by the Devil to try and rob man of his free will. Listing several well-known books, which he claimed dabbled in these dark arts, Hartlieb sweepingly condemned the Jewish Kabbala and certain works of Arab astronomy. His polemic, then, was directed at the intellectual elites, despite the fact that he was himself a doctor and respected astrologer. The cleansing fires of purgatory were what awaited these practitioners of magic, whereas all ordinary sinners among the common people had to fear was being burned at the stake.

The Devil really did seem to be taking possession of more and more souls. Hitherto-unnoticed pitfalls suddenly came to light. These new dangers were formed of a blend of high scholarship and illiterate traditions and embraced a number of different elements: the superstitious beliefs of antiquity and the church fathers, scholastic theology and jurisprudence, trials of heretics and sorcerers, old superstitions and possibly also a very real obsessive behavior. Now these specters appeared in flesh and blood, and were given a terrifying new name: witches. No one knows where the belief in witchcraft originated, though the first reports of it come from the Valais canton in western Switzerland; not long after, it also cropped up in the Upper Rhine region. In 1446, it was reported that "a number of women were burned at the stake in Heidelberg for practicing witchcraft."[11] Belief in the existence of witches first became widespread in rural areas, less so in princely courts or among the nobility, while it seems that generally speaking it was very rare among town dwellers.

The Inquisition soon began to engage with the question of witchcraft. In 1484, Innocent VIII issued the papal bull *Summis desiderantes,* which triggered the persecution of witches on a grand scale. Soon after, the theoretical foundations of this practice were established with the publication of *Malleus maleficarum* ("Hammer of the witches") by Kramer (or Henricus Institor, as he liked to style himself, in the scholarly Latinized form; died ca. 1505). Kramer had formerly been the chief inquisitor of the province of Alemannia, and was also active in Innsbruck and Brixen. Jacob Sprenger was cited as his co-author, though it is doubtful whether this was in fact the case, since Sprenger later turned against the methods of persecution advocated in the book.[12] The *Malleus,* which in the late scholastic fashion was subdivided into various sections, had three main objectives. Its first aim was to provide evidence showing that there really were such things as (male and female) witches and why they existed. It then proceeded to demonstrate the effects of their evildoing and to suggest remedies against witchcraft. Finally, the book described in detail how to prosecute witches. The whole gamut of belief in demons and devils, the idea of incubi and succubi, of witches and warlocks, of fantastic practices of conjuration, of pacts with the devil and witches' sabbaths, of deviant sexual acts and evil spells was forged here into a hammer with which to beat witches, which was wielded to deadly effect over centuries and struck fear into people. First published in 1487, and sold at the Frankfurt Market, the book was reprinted many times over, right up to the seventeenth century. Its author boasted of having personally sent 200 witches to the stake. Although fear of witches had manifested itself earlier, and not just among peasant and village dwellers, it was really the *Malleus* that was responsible for generating mass hysteria about witchcraft. It was not long before artists like Albrecht Dürer and Hans Baldung Grien were producing drawings, or copperplate engravings for the general market, of these wicked creatures (male and female alike) showing them in all their nakedness and striking shameless poses: a titillating and repellent feast for the eyes that was designed to evoke a *frisson* of evil but have an alluring appeal at the same time.

In the midst of this widespread fear of devils and witches, artists and architects, painters and sculptors found themselves engaged in building churches, decorating them with frescoes and altarpieces, and creating beautiful illuminated prayer books and breviaries. Outstanding artists of the period were widely admired and learned how to market their great talents. It was around this time, in the mid-fifteenth century, that single-point perspective was discovered, the technique of making orthogonal lines in a painting converge on a distant vanishing point, and turning the planar surface of the picture into a cross-section of a "visual pyramid," namely a cone of rays with the apex at the viewer's eye. The theoretical foundations for this technique in mathematics and optics were laid in treatises by the architect Filippo Brunelleschi (d. 1446) and the polymath Leon Battista Alberti in 1410 and 1436 respectively. It was subsequently expounded (ca. 1470) in greater detail by the painter Piero della Francesca;[13] yet by that time, Brunelleschi's brilliant twenty-three-year old pupil Masaccio had put the theory into practice in the frescoes he painted for the Brancacci Chapel in the church of Santa Maria del Carmine and a daring portrayal of the Holy Trinity (1429) in Santa Maria Novella (both in Florence). This opened up a whole new view of the world; perspectivity became a key hermeneutic concept that was by no means confined to the realm of painting. Now the kind of golden icon background that even Giotto had once dispensed with disappeared entirely, to be replaced by ever more "realistic" scenes. A new building style became widespread; Alberti, in his role as architect, was the first theoretician of this development also (in his *De re aedificatoria* of 1452). The square, rectangle, and triangle and smooth surfaces now triumphed over the pointed arch and open-work tracery façades.

Contemporary sensibilities became receptive to the beauty of images from antiquity, which were discovered and excavated quite by chance—for instance the famous sculpture of Laocoön and His Sons, and the Apollo Belvedere—and now found their way into the first princely art collections that were then being assembled. Flavio Biondo (d. 1463), a humanist and secretary to four popes, played a prominent role in this, in his bold attempts at a first reconstruction of ancient Rome (*Roma restaurata*, 1444–1446). And reused materials from antiquity appear time and again in the walls and battlements depicted in Mantegna's paintings; his portrait of the martyr Saint Sebastian (now in Vienna) is seen standing amid ancient ruins, and has the self-conscious Greek inscription: TO EPΓON TOY ANΔPEOY (the work of Andrea). Painters and sculptors chose as their themes more earthly and secular subjects than those of the preceding centuries, and their scrutiny of these subjects became more intense. Observation of reality, the mass of details, the external appearance of objects, their materiality, and the way the light caught them all became more significant factors. The grace and beauty of the human body were accorded an attention never seen before; the body was idealized and its proportions studied, most famously in Leonardo's "Vitruvian Man." Adam and Eve were now portrayed as nude figures; soon, even the fig leaves were dispensed with (though subsequently their nakedness was often painted over). A realistic style of portraiture emerged, capturing every last wrinkle, facial expression, and wart, and every faint ghost of a smile. Much could be read from contemporary physiognomy; indeed, the portraits of courtiers and princely confidants from this period were often thought to reflect their masters' supposed secret insight into the innermost workings of their souls. Jan van Eyck's Madonna of the Annunciation now receives the salutation of the Angel Gabriel with her head raised and her eyes wide open; Italian painters who treated this same biblical passage depict their Madonnas as deep in prayer, hearkening as it were to an inner voice. Mantegna's self-portrait for his burial chapel unsparingly depicts the drooping corners of his mouth, his lined face, and his disillusioned look.

However, it was not only classical beauty that was celebrating a revival, but also ugliness, the backdrop against which the beautiful came into its own. Ugliness was born, so to speak, from the spirit of beauty. Repellent facial features, and crippled misshapen individuals were sometimes captured on canvas in order to evoke sympathy and compassion, but sometimes also simply for the sake of showing something unsightly or as a metaphor for evil. The devils in Renaissance art testify to the inexhaustible inventiveness of their creators in the wide range of terrifying, grimacing forms they take. The shocking scenes of Judgment Day, the vivid portrayals of the torments of Hell, and the eternal fury of the demons intensified to an intensely realistic evocation of unimaginable horror. Admittedly, some contemporaries were already all too painfully aware of the anguish of Hell in unvarnished reality, from the torture chambers of Christian rulers and the Inquisition.

The eruption of the supernatural into the real world was shown in ever more "objective" and "realistic" terms, incorporating a wealth of familiar details. Counterbalancing this realization of horror, though, were paintings of the heavenly "Afterlife," which in turn were also executed highly realistically, with angels and saints of captivating beauty and sensual magnificence, enchanting gardens of Paradise and delightful scenes of the Madonna and Child. In these works, the countenances of those who had been saved and redeemed were commonly suffused with overwhelming joy, rapturous ecstasy, and eternal beatitude. For instance, in this period, painters were wont to turn a private devotional picture of the Lamentation of Christ into a "true to life" drama, a picture staging that was tailor-made for the aristocratic art collections that were then coming into vogue.[14] In stark contrast, by the end of the century, deceit had become the abiding theme, exemplified by the works of Hieronymus Bosch—who still had no inkling of the impending Reformation—paintings like the mischievous *The Conjuror,* or his *Hay Wain* triptych. These were jaded observations of a hypocritical, dishonest world inhabited by deceitful humanity—urgent warning messages delivered from the prosperous Netherlands to that world and its people. Bosch's painting were thoroughly emblematic of the poor spiritual condition of Man in the prosperous regions of Europe at the end of the Middle Ages.

An alarming symbolism becomes apparent in them. The conjurer, who holds his stupefied contemporaries in thrall with his shabby tricks, while his assistant creeps up behind their backs and robs them, and the hay wain, careering headlong to Hell—these were vivid metaphors of everyday reality. Bosch painted no altarpieces, yet in this latter painting employed its classic form of the triptych. The three panels of the *Hay Wain* depict, on the left, Paradise, on the right Hell, and in the center the course of the world. For the reverse of the two folding outer panels, the painter chose the image of the "Wayfarer," a down-at-heel beggar and prodigal-son figure, condemned to wander the earth for all time. Bosch's message was clear: humanity's path led from where our forbears Adam and Eve had been cast out directly down to the realm of the Devil. Nowhere was any possibility of tuning back indicated, nor did any salvation beckon. An angel, who is seen accompanying the little group of people on top of the hay cart, vainly entreats the Great Judge seated on high above the scene in parted clouds; on the far side of the same group, a grotesque demonic figure is shown piping a merry tune. And so some people sit up high on the hay bales and let themselves, drawn on by angels and devils, be carried through a seemingly idyllic life devoted to courtly love and song, while others down below scurry around to gather up and purloin the few stalks of hay that fall off the moving cart, while still others fight among themselves over what they have stolen and stab one another to death; behind the cart, the pope and emperor parade in their finery and with their great retinue and, engaged as they are in a fierce dispute with one another, notice nothing. The world has been plunged into chaos, downfall, and Hell, while its spiritual and temporal leaders, who should really be leading the hay wain, are instead following it on its headlong course. The visible, longed-for presence of salvation, which was articulated in the late medieval cult of the host and religious processions, had the greatest urgency attached to it. Humans, ensnared in their belief in Heaven and Hell, desperately needed it for their consolation and in order to live.

Here, it was not just the faith of the simple, illiterate poor that was on display. Quite the contrary, in fact; the upper echelons and the elites also subscribed to this belief. After all, it was from such circles that Bosch's patrons came. According to his courtiers, Charles VI of France is supposed to have succumbed to madness through his devotion to magic and sorcery (1392). The aid of white magic was sought in an attempt to cure him; Marshal Louis de Sancerre and Philip the Bold, duke of Burgundy, financed this undertaking. When the king's condition failed to improve, at least five of these magicians were ultimately accused of fraud, condemned, and publicly burned at the stake.[15] Joan of Arc, the Maid of Orléans, was viewed by some of her compatriots—a least with hindsight—as a prophet, yet by others as a fearful witch. When the latter view prevailed, she was burned to death in Rouen in 1431. When the prophesies she had made came true, she was hailed by the populace and likely also by many a courtier, as a prophet sent to France by God. On the other hand, her great adversary the duke of Bedford, who acted as regent in France for the underaged king Henry VI of England and was an outstanding military strategist, reported to his king that the English defeat at the siege of Orléans had been brought about by "a follower and spy of the Devil, known as la Pucelle, who made use of evil spells and magic."[16] Wherever people looked, they saw supernatural forces at work.

A New "Joie de Vivre" and Spiritual Rebirth

It is open to speculation whether it was the Black Death that caused this disruption of normal life, or rather the repeated bouts of famine, or natural disasters, price rises, and incessant wars that destroyed the fixity of certain norms and ethics and confounded all plans laid by man. And what force was it that had conjured up new devils, but had also given life a new meaning in the Here and Now and engendered a new secularity? Whatever the answer, at no time is any comparable development documented from the early medieval period or from the height of the Middle Ages. People delighted in their bodies, in their sensory and spiritual impulses, in their humanity in its entirety. Erotic fantasies even dared to rear their head, as painters subtly introduced them into their works. "Women of uncommon beauty, who are seen stepping out of the bath and who with remarkable modesty conceal the more intimate parts of their bodies with gauzy linen; he has portrayed one of these women in such a way that she is revealing only her face and her breast, while the hind parts of her body are seen in a mirror painted on the opposite wall": a panopticon of male desire.[17] The painter being praised in this passage, Jan van Eyck, is widely regarded as the inventor of oil painting, which laid a seductive, glossy patina on the surface of pictures and made everything that was depicted shine with a beguiling light. Writers, too, treated sexual pleasures in a lighthearted manner, and revealed how quickly they could erupt into arguments: "Two Roman whores of my acquaintance, very different in both age and beauty, once went to visit the house of one of our Curia members, to cater to his needs and earn some money. While the man had his way twice with the prettier one, he only managed it once with the other, and even then only so that she wouldn't feel slighted, and to ensure that she'd come back again in future with her colleague." At the end, the two women argued about the fee, over whether the prettier was entitled to double what her friend was due.[18] However, it wasn't the lecherous curial member that attracted the interest of the papal secretary who recorded this anecdote, but rather the row between the two women—women "of my acquaintance." Clerics of the time, it seems, were all too familiar with such erotic exploits. When he was a young man, Enea Silvio Piccolomini, who later became Pope Pius II, delighted in the smoldering glances and dangerous sexual guiles of the women of Genoa.

In this atmosphere of sensual and intellectual *joie de vivre,* an admiration for pagan antiquity was rekindled. *"Ad fontes"* became the watchword of the age—in other words, back to the original sources in the original language. While attending the Council of Constance (1414–1418), Poggio Bracciolini discovered the old archive of early medieval manuscripts from the monastery of Saint Gallen and began to reveal the treasures they contained. Searching for old manuscripts became something of a general vogue. The shorter works of Tacitus, including the only surviving manuscript of *Germania,* were found in places like Fulda and Hersfeld. The monks at these monasteries had not realized how precious and uniquely valuable their holdings were, and it took the interest of Italian humanists to quite literally save these treasures written on parchment from being fed to the monastery pigs. By the mid-fifteenth century, cultural decline, lack of interest, and the desperate poverty of many of the old Benedictine abbeys in Germany, which had once been influential centers of learning and power, were plain for all to see—particularly so in the case of institutions that took no part in the great reform movements of this century.

Nevertheless, the early interest shown by Charlemagne and his contemporaries in the writers of antiquity now bore fruit a hundredfold once more. For it was Carolingian manuscripts, the oldest extant written records, that the humanists chanced upon. The Renaissance's whole conception of antiquity was built on early medieval foundations. Nor was it just Latin texts that benefited from their delving into the past; Greek and ancient Hebrew studies also blossomed as never before. The classical deities themselves—Jupiter, Venus, and Mars—seemed to return. Sandro Botticelli's painting *The Birth of Venus* (1486) is possibly the most famous manifestation of this classical revival. Ancient statues of gods and heroes were recognized once more as possessing an exemplary quality. Modern artists and writers stood before them as if transfixed by their compelling beauty.[19]

In place of Aristotle, whose tendency to "ruminate" even Petrarch had already found off-putting, and whose *Dialectics, Natural History,* and *Ethics* were monotonously dinned into university scholars, the "immortal God"[20] Cicero was now rediscovered, together with Quintilian—the two great rhetoricians of the ancient world. In addition, emigrants from Constantinople brought Plato to the attention of the West, along with the

Byzantine, Platonic theory of art. Yet Aristotle was by no means eclipsed in these new developments, but rather hallowed anew. Ancient Greek historians such as Thucydides also became known to the West for the first time; their works and those of Plato gave people an initial inkling of the Athenian state and the world of the Ancient Greeks, which many centuries later would come to exert a powerful emotional fascination upon Europeans. All this awakened a new sense of spirituality and opened up unknown, hidden insights and unfamiliar perspectives on the world. Roman architecture was now looked upon in a new way. As had already happened in Pisa, there was now a general celebration of the Roman origins of the modern polity. At times, contemporaries—as Petrarch had done before them—found themselves fascinated by the Roman Republic, while at others their attention focused on Caesar and Imperial Rome. Petrarch's successors distinguished themselves not only as writers and propagandists, but also as teachers, inspiring generations of students with an appreciation of antiquity. Coluccio Salutati, Leonardo Bruni, Poggio Bracciolini, Lorenzo Valla, and Marsilio Ficino were the heroes of this new cultural awakening, whose repercussions were felt far beyond Florence. Bruni had learned Greek and is thought to have owned the first manuscript ever available in the West of Ptolemy's *Cosmography* (sometime before 1405). Knowledge of this text now spread from Italy across the whole Latin world; a full Latin translation had already been completed by 1406. Henceforth, the knowledge of medieval cartographers would be supplemented by that of this distinguished ancient scholar, forming a link between Abraham Cresques's *Catalan Atlas* and ancient Greek cartography—a significant advance in learning. The result was the creation of new world maps like the one produced by Fra Mauro in Venice in 1459. The cities and *signorias* of Italy formed the hotbed of the Renaissance; the movement coalesced and intensified in cultural centers like Florence, where wealth, power, and education were concentrated, where astrology had long since found a home, and where memories of the ancient Roman past kept rising to the surface.

Private "academies" were founded there within the orbit of the Medici. The most renowned contemporary writers and the most outstanding artists of the age were active in Florence; its citizens watched in awe as the renovated cathedral, with its soaring new dome began to rise above the city: "Whoever would be arrogant or envious enough to deny praise to the architect Pippo [Brunelleschi] on seeing here such a gigantic structure, towering above the skies, and wide enough to cast its shadow over all the Tuscan people, and constructed without the aid of any beams or abundance of wooden supports?: . . . a work of art whose execution seemed incredible to contemporaries."[21] In 1470, Santa Maria Novella, which was formerly constructed in the Gothic style, was now given an imposing Renaissance façade, designed by no lesser a person than Alberti. And it was here in Florence that—to cite just a few of the outstanding artists and creations of the period—Fra Angelico worked, Botticelli's *Primavera* was painted (a work thoroughly steeped in the spirit of antiquity), Donatello's sculpture *David* saw the light of day (the first free-standing nude figure to be created since ancient times), and Leonardo da Vinci's talent was honed to mature perfection. This was all excellent publicity for the rulers of the city, men who—like Duke Lorenzo the Magnificent—were themselves given to composing poems imbued with the humanist spirit and the Neoplatonic tenor of the age.

These writers and artists and their patrons all gained their intellectual grounding in the *Studia humaniora,* and particularly in the study of history as a leading anthropological discipline, and in rhetoric, ancient languages, and the cultivation of letter writing. Coluccio Salutati (d. 1406), a friend of Petrarch and secretary of the Florentine Republic, not only distinguished himself as an author, he also collected manuscripts, promoted the study of Greek in the city, and—in imitation of the script style known as Carolingian minuscule—developed a calligraphic style that rejected Gothic black-letter in favor of clarity and easy legibility. The result was the elegant and aesthetically mature *littera antiqua* style of handwriting, which became a model for printing fonts, and remains so to the present day. Others soon followed his lead. Humanism (a term actually only coined in the nineteenth century) spread to become the dominant intellectual movement of the fifteenth century. It promulgated not just a new ideal mode of education, but also a whole new image of mankind, which posited the intellectually autonomous human being as the focus of its attention. Even more significantly, though, taking its cue from Pico della Mirandola and Hermes Trismegistos, it proclaimed man as the "great miracle" and "placed him in the very center of the world" *(in mundi positum meditullio),*[22] declaring him to be made in the image of his Creator, and the agent of His will. Furthermore, human beings were free to exercise their own will and creative spirit, and should never be subservient. A distinctive quality of man was his spiritual sensibility, while his ability to articulate emotions (far more nuanced than the rest of the animal kingdom) enabled him to express what he was feeling. Yet the study of Nature also benefited from this new attention to the world of the senses. Astrology and its sister discipline astronomy provided a long-established springboard from which to investigate new insights and explore new fields of study.

The triumphant march of the *studia humaniora* also continued elsewhere. Florence maintained a network of relationships, and was in regular contact with Milan, Mantua, Padua, Venice, Rome, and Naples. Yet while historical studies served the cause of general enlightenment, they could also prove dangerous to established forms of rule. For example, in 1440 the humanist Lorenzo Valla, who was active in Rome, Naples, and Venice, demonstrated that the Donation of Constantine, to which many scholars ascribed the papacy's secular authority, was a fake, a fact that Nicholas of Cusa, who had also been receptive to humanist ideology, had suspected some while previously. In Venice, the statesman Francesco Barbaro (d. 1454) was keen to foster intellectual exchanges and friendship with the Florentine ruler Lorenzo de'Medici, as well as Poggio Bracciolini, Flavio Biondo, and other humanists. Enea Silvio Piccolomini, an author, historian, and letter writer from a Sienese family, was first a conciliarist, then a papalist, before finally himself ascending the throne of Saint Peter. As Pope Pius II (r. 1458–1464) he commissioned many new buildings in Rome, and displayed a penchant for the classical style. Even so, rather than Rome, his first love was Corsignano, his birthplace, whose name he changed to Pienza, and which he intended to transform into a jewel of humanist–classical architecture through the construction of squares, palaces, and a new cathedral.

The roots of this humanism lay in the culture of the town-dwelling nobility, and from the educated elite of the urban laity rather than the corresponding clerical classes. Yet the movement spread among this latter group as well, and even found its way into certain monasteries.[23] Presently, it was taken up by the arts faculties at the universities, by princely and royal courts, and even Rome did not shun the new ideology. Indeed, quite the opposite: two avowed humanists, Nicholas V (r. 1447–1455) and Pius II, ascended the papal throne, while the *Studia humaniora* found many friends in the college of cardinals. The whole of Europe was gripped by humanism, with the exception of the Orthodox East.

Unlike all courses of study at the universities, however, a humanist education did not confine itself to men. On the contrary, in fact, the humanist program quite consciously and systematically included daughters, wives, and princesses, even if they were excluded from university entrance. Leonardo Bruni advised his correspondent Baptista Malatesta to begin her reading with the Christian fathers, primarily Saint Augustine. Yet the works of historians (Sallust, Tacitus, Curtius Rufus, and Caesar were mentioned by name) should also be studied, Bruni wrote, as well as orators and poets (Hesiod, Pindar, Euripides, Homer, and others were cited), quite apart from Plato, Socrates, and Pythagoras.[24] In England, meanwhile, Thomas More assiduously devoted himself to educating his own daughter.

In general terms, learning and a rounded education of young people were the primary focus of these studies, without which humanism could not have flourished. More's friend Erasmus of Rotterdam promoted this idea in his *Colloquies* (1518), a collection of dialogs on a wide range of subjects: "a woman who knows nothing yet thinks herself to be wise, is twice a fool." And indeed, many letters from women who are well versed in literature have come down to us from the early fifteenth century. These afford us a vivid insight into everyday life and common hardships, the misery of excommunication, and some of the indignities suffered by both the princely classes and the bourgeoisie in the Renaissance.[25] Moreover, with many of the early printing presses under their control, the humanists were guaranteed a wide dissemination of their ideas. Humanism provided a spiritual template for the future Protestant parsonage, as well as establishing the defining characteristics of the intellectual culture of the Early Modern Period in Europe.

Princes and Politics

Far-reaching changes were also taking place in politics. Wars continued to rage between princes, while conflict over territory and borders was the norm. Ambition and honor proved once again to be the driving forces *par excellence* of princely action; these qualities were celebrated and lauded by those humanists who—in their capacity as secretaries or advisors to the *signorie*, the *condottieri*, or princes, or alternatively as their ambassadors and diplomats—found themselves in the thick of the action on this stage. Indeed, it is their entrance and involvement that turns this political arena into a historical stage in the first place. Their much-vaunted ideals of *ratio* and *virtus*, namely informed reason and strenuous virtue, along with the blessings of "Fortuna"—the good luck that favored the decisive man of action—seemed to be realized in the successful upward climbers and violent individuals who came to the fore at this time; in any event, the men in question claimed these qualities for themselves. Their yardsticks were the despots of ancient times. Politics and culture became curiously intertwined at this stage, mutually interacting to the advantage of both.

In particular, with their incessant clashes and wars, the Italian cities and city-states offered extraordinary opportunities for advancement to the adventurer. Successful *condottieri* or bankers who had enriched themselves from conflict gained control over the municipalities, becoming tyrants of whom even the emperor went in fear. The Visconti and the Sforza in Milan, the Gonzaga in Mantua, the Este in Ferrara, and finally the Medici in Florence—these were all upwardly mobile families, who in some cases came from quite modest backgrounds. The ancestral forefather of the Sforza, for example, had been a small-town cobbler, sneered the haughty aristocrat Philippe de Commynes. This family's rise began with the "brigand captain" Muzzio Attendolo "Sforza," who served a string of masters; his son Francesco hired himself out to the last Visconti ruler of Milan and married his daughter and heiress apparent. Thereafter he secured his succession through the use of force. In turn, his grand-daughter Bianca Maria became the second wife of the emperor Maximilian, and through this—personally deeply unhappy—marriage ensured that her uncle was elevated to the status of duke.

Nor did the high clergy behave any differently. They, too, embraced and promoted humanism, while at the same time rushing headlong into conflict. They spared no expense in displaying their status, and acted just the same as the secular princes in paying hired assassins. They incurred debts and took out massive loans; usury thrived. However contradictory it might appear, all these men were hankering after was cultural legitimacy; and to this end, they needed the services of educated writers and artists. This legitimacy would serve to vouchsafe their public patronage, lavish self-promotion, and support for humanism, scholarship, and art, while beautiful artifacts, grandiose buildings, and enchanting rhetoric—in sum, the overwhelming power of representational art—would, they reasoned, both validate and act as an outward sign of the political power that they had attained or usurped, and accord it general acceptance. The need for this arose sooner in some places, and later in others. Schooled in ancient rhetoric, these men promised greatness, and in emulation of ancient historians formulated higher, worthwhile goals beyond the mere retention of power, laid down models of behavior, and provided an object lesson not only in how to succeed but also in how to combine spiritual matters, art, and politics. What did it matter that this was all built on the backs of an oppressed labor force? Posterity acclaims the movers and shakers, not the victims.

Florence under the Medici stood at the forefront of these developments. This family had acquired its vast wealth through the cloth trade and banking activities.[26] The crushing of the Ciompi Rebellion of 1378 by one of their number, Salvestro di Alamanno, first propelled them to prominence in the city's ruling elite. As bankers to the papacy—a risky but lucrative business—their wealth skyrocketed during the closing phase of the Hundred Years' War. Following a brief period in exile, Salvestro's grandson Cosimo il Vecchio (Cosimo the Elder) managed to attain leadership of the *signoria* and establish enduring control over the city. Then, in 1478–1479, Lorenzo the Magnificent (d. 1492) sealed the Medici grip on power after brutally suppressing the Pazzi Conspiracy, in which the archbishop of Florence and the Roman Curia were involved. Just as Cosimo had once done at the instigation and with the assistance of the Byzantine exile Georgios Gemisthos Plethon from Constantinople when, in imitation of ancient models, he promoted the program of the Florentine "Academy" from 1440 onward, so Lorenzo now also began to style himself as a generous patron, and a tyrant who was at the same time a friend of the sciences, scholarship, and the arts. Around this time, Leonardo da Vinci rushed to Florence to offer his services to "the Magnificent"; yet the all-powerful ruler of the city preferred instead to have Sandro Botticelli paint shaming portraits of the hanged or persecuted conspirators on the façade of the Palazzo del Podestà—the same Botticelli who had created images of Madonnas and saints. Was it the case, then, that high culture was inextricably bound up with tyranny and murder?

The social development of the Italian municipalities in the final years of the Middle Ages stood in strange contrast to the ideals of humanism that unfolded within their city walls. Despite attracting many disciples, this humanism reveals itself, at least in its embryonic stages, to be the culture of a small, competitive, violence-prone elite of social climbers in the service of noble lords. Beyond this elite, less exalted conditions held sway. Social unrest, such as that experienced in France or England, had long since taken hold in Italy, too. As early as 1345, before the arrival of the Black Death, Florence had witnessed an insurrection by the *popolo minuto* against the *popolo grosso,* that is, the poor against the rich. In the same year that Charles IV died (1378), the revolt of the Ciompi broke out, the first workers' revolution in the history of the West to enjoy at least temporary success. The Ciompi were workers in the wool industry who enjoyed no rights of citizenship, were not organized, and who were employed to carry out the most unpleasant part of the wool weaving process, namely carding, in return for a pittance. Their uprising swiftly collapsed, but it was so momentous that even Machiavelli recalled it over a century later. Moreover, it was far from being the last revolt to break out in the city on the River Arno.

The late fifteenth century saw the rise in Florence of the powerful public speaker and rabble rouser Girolamo Savonarola. This Dominican friar's attacks on privilege and appeals to the conscience of the rich fomented a new round of upheaval in the city. The ruling Medici regime regarded his radical penitential diatribes, which showed no respect for secular or ecclesiastical authority, as highly dangerous. Charles VIII of France's invasion of Italy in 1494 and the expulsion of the hated Medici ruler of Florence (Piero II) struck many people as clear evidence of God's impending Day of Judgment. This was an enormous success, but evaporated in no time at all. Meanwhile, Savonarola was hailed by the people of Florence as the "Prophet of God." Popular calls for revolution saw the Dominican preacher propelled to power and installed as dictator. Pope Alexander VI was forced to move against this upstart heretic and rebel. Savonarola was duly excommunicated, summoned to appear before a tribunal, condemned to be burned at the stake, and publicly executed on the Palazzo Vecchio in 1498. An unknown Florentine painter captured the event; the resulting painting is a curious work in which a serene architectural cityscape frames, in the foreground, a gruesome scene of violent revenge. At the time of Savonarola's execution, Niccolò Machiavelli was the secretary of the restored Florentine Republic.

At the beginning of that same century, both the political and ecclesiastical arenas had been beset by the gravest concerns. The whole of Europe was in an uproar. The pressure exerted by the advancing Ottoman Turks on Christendom was immense, and increasing all the time; at the same time as the Serbs were conducting a stout defense against Ottoman encroachment, they were also attempting to extend their empire westward, into Hungary. In the wake of the bloody Battle of Kosovo in 1389, the Turks had forced the expanding, flourishing Serbian empire, which had long since rid itself of Byzantine control, to recognize their suzerainty in the Balkans. The heroes of the Battle of Kosovo (Blackbird's Field)—Prince Lazar of Serbia, Miloš Obilić, and their brave compatriots, were feted in epic tales and their memory lives on undimmed in the national consciousness of Orthodox Serbs to the present day. The dangers threatening the southeastern corner of the Holy Roman Empire and the Mediterranean also cast their long shadow over the west and south. The anarchic conditions governing the kingdom of Naples, from where Elizabeth of Bosnia, the queen-dowager of Hungary, hoped to secure a son-in-law and heir to the realm where she was regent, enabled Sigismund, son of the Holy Roman Emperor Charles IV to ultimately prevail against Elizabeth by force of arms; in 1387, he asserted his claim to marry Mary, heiress to the Hungarian throne and receive the crown of Saint Stephen. Sigismund also made preparations to resist the Ottomans.

Sigismund tried to consolidate his weak position in his new realm and prove himself as king of Hungary by attacking Serbia, yet this only succeeded in increasing the danger from the Turks rather than dispelling it. He found himself unable to halt the onward march of the Ottomans. A Christian crusader army, led by himself and Duke John of Burgundy, who later earned himself the soubriquet "the Fearless," was defeated at the Battle of Nicopolis in 1396. John was taken captive and had to be ransomed. To restore his damaged prestige and promote solidarity among his nobility, in 1408 Sigismund instituted the Order of the Dragon; the intention was not just to bind the Hungarian aristocracy more firmly to the crown, but much more importantly to impose on them a bounden duty to fight the heathen. The new order did indeed foster solidarity among the nobility and bestow honor on its holders, but could still do nothing to alter the kingdom's military inferiority; the heyday of the knightly caste was by now long past. The next catastrophic defeat to the Ottomans, once more at Kosovo, followed in 1448, eleven years after Sigismund's death. As so often happens when a country attempts to assert moral superiority over a threatening adversary, horror stories were spread about the Ottoman attackers and their Janissary forces. Yet the Christian forces were no less brutal. The notoriously bloodthirsty cruelty of Vlad III Draculea, the ruler of Wallachia, who was known to the Turks as "the Impaler" has gone down in legend. Even Christian contemporaries described him as a "tartar who perpetrated many evil, murderous, and inhuman deeds."[27] Ultimately, as the "son of the dragon" (that is, Vlad II Dracul, who was a member of the Hungarian chivalric order), more recent times have turned him into a vampire and the horror figure of Count Dracula. None of his atrocities could halt the tide, however; in 1453, the death knell sounded for Christian Constantinople. With the fall of its mother city, Orthodox Christianity declined to a second-tier denomination, only observed by a small minority of the whole Christian community.

Sigismund's brother Wenceslas, the Roman king (r. 1378–1400) proved unequal to the task of handling the complexities of the political stage in Europe, which saw the center and east of the continent in particular engulfed in turmoil, but which also affected the situation in Italy. Neither of Charles IV's sons shared his talent or his good fortune.[28] Whatever their other achievements, they were never able to master the problems that assailed them; not the least of their shortcomings was their failure to produce any heirs. Wenceslas was commonly regarded as lazy (he was given the nickname "the Idle"), and while not devoid of talent was nevertheless politically maladroit and, as far as we know, an alcoholic, too. The simultaneity and intertwining of conflicting interests, the recurrent eruption of the Hundred Years' War (1337/8–1453), the Western Papal Schism (1378–1417), the challenges posed by regional rulers in Germany—around twenty secular and no fewer than ninety ecclesiastical princes vied for co-ownership of the "empire"—and the Bohemian nobility's urge to attain independence— all these factors outstripped Wenceslas's abilities and resources. As a result, he was incapable of securing peace within his realm.

The ongoing conflict between the houses of Habsburg and Wittelsbach was completely beyond the Luxembourger's influence. Moreover, the cities—even the smallest of which had more than 10,000 inhabitants, and most of them with defensive walls, towers, and fortified gates—united against the princes and the nobility and were able to prevail. The Rhineland city league was revived, and a similar confederation founded in Swabia. Companies of knights were established solely for the purposes of defending cities. Unrest spread among the peasantry and on manorial estates, which had repercussions for the whole of feudal society. This was a Europe-wide phenomenon that had already been developing for some time, and only now began to affect the Holy Roman Empire. To boost his finances, Wenceslas re-enacted the *Judenregal,* the crown's right to protect Jews and impose taxes on them, thus opening up Jewish property to a new round of despoliation. By order of the king, there then followed, in 1390–1391, an empire-wide *Judenentschuldung,* whereby all debts owing to Jews were amortized. Once again, the citizenry of Nuremberg was in the vanguard of this program of legalized looting (1384–1388). Though no bloody pogrom ensued on this occasion, there were persecutions, comprehensive dispossessions, and untold suffering.

Wenceslas was in even less of a position to exert any significant influence on the reorganization of the kingdoms in the East than in the empire. Events occurred without his input, and matters unfolded to his distinct disadvantage. The ascent of the Lithuanian Jagiellon dynasty to the Polish crown (1386) damaged the interests of the Teutonic Knights; Charles IV had largely neglected this military order, and Wenceslas now, belatedly and in vain, tried to strengthen them. After the Luxembourg possessions in the west fell vacant in 1383, the king could not even manage to save them for himself and his family. Here, he found himself outmaneuvered by the skillful dynastic marriage politics of the House of Burgundy, which took control of the duchy of Luxembourg for a century, and brought it great renown.

Similarly, the new Polish king, Władysław II Jagiello (r. 1386–1434) was also able to consolidate his rule. The center of coronation and the royal residence city was Krakow; back in 1364, Louis I of Hungary had founded the second-oldest university east of the Rhine and north of the Alps there. The first historical record of the *Sejm* dates from the fifteenth century; this body was originally the Great Council of the king, before becoming the representative assembly of the aristocracy, the churches, and the cities. Yet the kings of Poland more often convened the corresponding assemblies of the regions than they did the *Sejm*; there, too, the town citizenry had little influence over the cities in which they dwelt. In 1410, at the Battle of Tannenberg (Grunwald) a combined Polish and Lithuanian army comprehensively crushed the forces of the Teutonic Order under the command of the Grand Master Ulrich von Jungingen, a defeat that set in motion the protracted demise of the Monastic State of the Teutonic Order in Prussia. The final remnants of this state were finally absorbed, during the Reformation, by the electorate of Brandenburg in 1525.

As early as 1396, the drunkard on the German throne was placed under the legal guardianship of his younger brother Sigismund, and four years later was deposed, with the Palatine Elector Rupert being chosen as king in his place. Only the Bohemian throne now remained in Wenceslas's possession—much to the detriment of that country—right up to his death in 1419. Yet even in Bohemia, he was placed under the supervision of George of Poděbrady. If we were to judge Wenceslas by the things he held most dear—beautiful books—and which were his chief legacy to posterity, he might be regarded as one of the greatest rulers of his age. For he left behind a lavishly illustrated compendium of astronomy and astrology that incorporated all the latest scholarship, a prestigious display manuscript of the Golden Bull, and a Bible illuminated with the most exquisite miniatures, which abound with the sensuous joys of life. Yet however essential royal patronage of the arts may have been, it was not enough to constitute successful kingship.

The Palatine Elector Rupert, who built Heidelberg Castle and founded the university in the city, was equally unable to cope with the difficulties that troubled his new realm of Germany, but he died before his predecessor's fate could befall him. He likewise produced no successor in the direct line. At his death in 1410, the electors were divided, but ultimately found themselves reverting to the old royal family of Luxembourg, which offered two candidates bitterly opposed to one another: Jobst of Moravia, Charles IV's nephew, who ruled the Margravate of Brandenburg, given in pawn, and Sigismund of Hungary, the youngest son of Charles IV. Quite at variance with its original intention, the Golden Bull had failed to prevent this dual candidacy. Only Jobst's death in 1411 forestalled a renewed throne dispute, which would have posed serious problems for the House of Luxembourg. Sigismund was now free to assert himself as the sole king; he was the last of his line to "hold the reins of the world."

And yet, lacking the totality of power resources that were still available to his father, even Sigismund was unable to reassert royal authority to the full. The king and emperor seldom showed his face in his own realm, remaining principally in Transylvania and Hungary, where he had the castle at Buda rebuilt into a magnificent residence, complete with fabulous statuary, and made Bratislava the seat of his power. These opulent buildings served, as it were, to "make the king's presence real" even when he was physically absent. The unsettled situation on the eastern borders of his kingdom slowly sapped Sigismund's resources. Repeatedly, the uncertain circumstances within the empire compelled him to conclude shifting alliances with this or that elector and time and again required that he compromise. A root-and-branch reform of the empire in these conditions, no matter how urgent it may have been, was simply impossible. Neither the princes, whose main concern was generally to secure their limited spheres of influence, nor the electors, whose gaze was fixed on suprare-gional, Europe-wide concerns had the slightest interest in strengthening imperial power. Religious conflicts heightened tensions. The only lasting sign to remain of Sigismund's term of office, right up to the demise of the Holy Roman Empire in the nineteenth century, was the imperial coat of arms. For it was he who, following his coronation as emperor, introduced the heraldic device of the double-headed eagle, black on a golden background, which thereafter was reserved strictly for the emperor, whereas the king's emblem was the single-headed eagle facing right. Yet the heads of the imperial eagle were surrounded by halos, alluding to the transcendental aspirations that the emperor shared with many of his contemporaries.[29]

The Decades of the Ecumenical Councils

And indeed, the Great Western Schism, that cataclysmic division in the church, was highly conducive to stirring up once more that age-old theme of Christendom, namely the End of Days, which was thought to be drawing ever closer. The very real fear was that it might be imminent. Dire prophesies and the ongoing schism filled everyone with deep alarm—clergy and lay people, scholars and common people alike. Who was the legitimate successor of Saint Peter? For contemporaries and especially their rulers, caught up as they were in their divergent interests, this question was impossible to answer definitively. They decided in favor of one papal candidate or another, with no foreknowledge of whether their choice would eventually become God's Vicar on Earth. When other means of healing the rift between Avignon and Rome proved unworkable—for instance, the resignation of both popes, or having a commission appointed by both sides reach a binding decision—the decision was taken to convene a general papal council. Sigismund summoned this council to meet at Constance, and threw all his weight behind making it a success. His plans linked the question of the church schism with his own empire and the matter of imperial reform: as his letter of 1414 convening the Council of Constance stated, on the agenda were "not just matters pertaining to the church, but also those relating to the empire and matters of general concern," adding that "both are in grave need of advice and assistance."[30] It was also imperative to combat dangerous heresies, such as those that had recently arisen in England and Bohemia, and long known to be indications of the impending End Time. All in all, as Sigismund's missive went on to announce, the intention was to reform the church "from its head to its limbs." However, it soon became apparent, once the council

elders—by no means exclusively bishops; rather, the meeting had a preponderance of middle-ranking clergy and theology professors—had assembled, that the primary intention of this kind of reform was to bring
about a new redistribution of church resources and decision-making powers from the pope at the top, through the bishops in their dioceses, rather
than to devise a new ecclesiology, namely to change the fundamental nature of the church and its role in the world.[31] The delegates from Germany
and theologians from the University of Paris and other French institutions
found themselves at one on this question.

The ecumenical council to discuss the Western Schism took place in
several largely unsuccessful stages. An initial gathering at Pisa (1409)
ended in failure. Then came the emperor's call for it to meet in Constance
(1414–1418). After a brief intermezzo in Siena (1423–1424), it then reconvened, after a five-year pause and several years of planning, in Basel in
1431. A new split that occurred there (1437) then led to one element of the
council transferring to Ferrara (1438), Florence (1439), and finally Rome,
where there was an attempt to bring about a union with the Eastern
Church, a venture that ended in a total fiasco. The rump council that remained behind in Basel was finally expelled by emperor Frederick III and
moved to Lausanne before dissolving in 1448–1449. From time to time,
these meetings would proclaim their supreme authority over the pope, but
these blossomings of conciliarism were only brief and insubstantial. As
early as 1417, through the active intervention of the German king, a strong
and assertive pope was elected in the person of Martin V, who succeeded
in making Rome and the Papal States the center of his church once more.
However, this revival of the papacy in Rome would never regain the complete sovereignty it had enjoyed before the Schism. The great European
kingdoms, especially France, England, and now Aragón too all claimed
extensive authority over their own national churches (and, while this was
not true of the Holy Roman Empire as a whole, it was where its constituent princes within their individual territories was concerned). Martin V
and his successor Eugenius IV had to acknowledge and reluctantly accept
this state of affairs. At least the ecumenical councils, with delegates from
all the countries of Western Christendom, met on the soil of the Holy Roman Empire and not, as they had done previously, on French soil, or in
places where they were under the direct influence of the French crown.
Time and again, the Roman king, the "reeve of the church" acted as a

mediator between the pope and the Council; in this role in Constance, Sigismund expressly promoted the cause of reform.

Nevertheless, the ecumenical councils did not constitute a success for Sigismund's empire, and there are good reasons to doubt whether they had any beneficial effect on the church as a whole either. Reform of the church "from its head to its limbs," the primary objective of the council, was never achieved; moreover other matters like the union with Eastern Christians were endlessly deferred through specious solutions, which only further exacerbated the decline of Christian Constantinople. Not even the new start signaled by the return of the papacy to Rome, the tangible manifestation of the end of the Western Schism, set in train the far-reaching ecclesiastical reform that was so eagerly yearned for and anticipated, and indeed which was so urgently required. In full confidence that this would happen, in 1430–1432 Jan van Eyck painted his magnificent altarpiece for Saint Bavo's Cathedral in Ghent, depicting on its central panel "Paradise," the era that would ensue after the Day of Judgment (van Eyck took as his starting point the text of the Book of Revelation, 7:17: "For the Lamb which is in the midst of the throne shall feed them"), but this was to remain simply a utopian vision.

The one objective that was fulfilled was the fight against heresy. In the presence of Sigismund, enthroned in all his regalia, the doctrines of the Oxford theology professor John Wyclif, which criticized the Eucharist, the church, and the pope, were condemned. One of Wyclif's more inflammatory claims was that: "Excommunication by the pope or any other prelate should not be feared, since it is a punishment *(censurs)* of the Antichrist."[32] Furthermore Jan Hus, a priest and theologian at Prague University, a sworn opponent of the trade in indulgences and representative of the radical reformist clergy in the Bohemian capital, who was a champion of Wyclif's ecclesiology even though it rejected many of his own teachings, was damned as a heresiarch and burned at the stake in Constance in 1415. The king had promised the Czech reformer that he would be given safe conduct and return unharmed to Prague, but what price a monarch's historic pledge in the modern world of calculating power politics? Hus's opponents called for his arrest and Sigismund, finding it politic to heed their call, complied and arranged the burning, which Louis the Bavarian supervised.

Yet burning Hus at the stake did not, as hoped, destroy the "body of Sin" or expunge his teachings, despite the fact that a concerted campaign against the Hussites was organized, funded by new imperial taxes devised, and imposed by the experienced English financier and cardinal Henry of Beaufort. In the long term, the flames of his funeral pyre could not ward off the looming division of the church, either. The path that John Wyclif had prepared ran directly through Hus and the Hussites and the Moravian Brethren, to Martin Luther, who identified the Antichrist as sitting on Saint Peter's throne, and further on to Ulrich Zwingli and John Calvin, in whose circle the right to resist and murder tyrants was enshrined in law. This same path also led to the confessional division of Western Christendom into Protestantism and Catholicism, with all the attendant horrors that would later entail, and to a complete reorganization of society. As these developments unfolded, fundamental and hallowed tenets of faith that had been established over long centuries of spiritual struggle, such as the Power of the Keys, papal primacy, transubstantiation, and the efficacy of the confessional, were repudiated and condemned. But at the same time, worldly rule was transformed and consolidated in its unashamed secularity, a state of affairs that would be expressed in words by the likes of Niccolò Machiavelli and Cesare Borgia. The Florentine thinker Machiavelli was the first to formulate the fundamental insight—still largely valid to the present day—that ruthlessness is the single most important quality required to establish, extend, and retain political power.

If any socioreligious movement of the time warrants the term "revolutionary," then it was the Hussite Rebellion in Bohemia.[33] The Hussites not only called for but also put into practice the secularization of church property, the abandonment of all ecclesiastical estates and jurisdiction, and any remaining sovereign powers of the church. Their basic demand was that Christianity should exist "without masters and servants." They dispensed with any centralization of the church, and any form of hierarchy. Priests were required to be poor, namely to have no land holdings, but to act simply as proclaimers of the Word of the Lord. The radical wing of the Hussites, the Taborites, went even further, formulating principles of brotherhood and egalitarianism, and of common property, and harboring millenarian beliefs. Despite the fact that these groups were persecuted with crusades and burnings at the stake and ultimately failed to impose their ideals on Bohemia, their utopian thinking endured and went on to influence modern theories of society.

The death of the Czech reformer coincided with alarming reports of renewed fighting from the West. There, pressured by tensions with his barons, by revolts among the nobility, and the ongoing struggle against the Lollards, Henry V, king of England, had resumed the war against the French. His troops scored a string of stunning victories. The fleur-de-lys banner was trampled in the dirt, and the French monarchy was weakened by several factors. The throne was occupied by the mentally ill Charles VI, who was prone to hallucinations, while the regents of the kingdom were divided among themselves, with the duke of Burgundy on one side and the duke of Orléans and the count of Armagnac (from the House of Valois) on the other. French trade lay in ruins; merchants traveled to Burgundy and Geneva, bypassing France entirely. The catastrophic defeat suffered by French knights at the Battle of Agincourt (south of Calais) in October 1415, where English archers equipped with longbows slaughtered the charging French horsemen (by the end of the day some 5,000 knights, an archbishop, three dukes, and five counts lay dead on the battlefield), brought about the effective collapse of French military power. Even King Sigismund, who met with Ferdinand of Aragón in Narbonne to explore peace options and discuss ways of bringing the Western Schism to an end, then immediately traveled from there via the French court in Paris to London to try and mediate between France and England (1416) but ended up later that same year concluding an alliance with England against France. In the Treaty of Troyes (1420) Henry V married Catherine of Valois, and declared himself heir to the French throne. Philip of Burgundy recognized his claim, after his father Duke John the Fearless had been murdered in the presence of the dauphin and almost certainly with his complicity (1419). But Henry V died of dysentery just two years later, in the same year as the insane Charles VI (1422). Henry V's son, Henry VI, who would subsequently unite France and England, was only a baby when he came to the throne. The duke of Bedford, John Lancaster, acted as his regent in France during his infancy, continuing to pursue the war there. Charles VI's younger and only surviving son, Charles VII, who refused to recognize the Treaty of Troyes that had robbed him of his royal inheritance, was swiftly repelled: his opponents mocked him as the "king of Bourges," whence he had fled from Paris into internal exile, since it was the only region that remained loyal to him. English troops occupied the country right down as far as the Loire valley and now threatened even the duke of Berry. Orléans, which guarded the crossing over the River Loire, was surrounded and besieged in 1428. If the city fell, it would surely spell the end of the House of Valois.

Joan of Arc

It was then that a miracle occurred. Joan of Arc, la Pucelle, a maid in the guise of a warrior, appeared on the scene like some incarnation of the most fervent prayers of the French people, who even though living under English or (renegade) Burgundian rule still cleaved to the ancestral royal house of France. As the transcript of her heresy trial at Rouen in 1431 later reported, "She claimed that at the age of thirteen years she had experienced a revelation from Our Lord, in the form of a heavenly voice that told her to lead a good life. . . . Twice or three times, the voice told her to leave home and make all haste to France, where she would be granted the power to break the siege of Orléans."[34] She was, the voice assured her, destined to lead the dauphin to Reims to be anointed king there and that she would liberate France from the English. In her own words, she maintained that "Everything that I have done, I did at the bidding of Our Lord." Having heeded her inner voice and arrived in Chinon, Joan was led before the beleaguered and mistrustful dauphin. Later reports recalled her having told the king-elect that "she was sent by God to him to help him regain his kingdom." A peasant girl as an emissary from God? Only subsequently, after her victories, was her "mission" reinterpreted in this way as a prophecy. At first, she was sent to university theologians in Poitiers to verify her piety and to the women of the court to ascertain her virginity.

When both of these matters had been confirmed, the king equipped her with a sword and a suit of armor. She had "a banner, the field of which was sown with lilies. On it the world was represented and two angels at the sides. It was made of linen or white boucassin. There was written upon it, as it seems to me, these words: *Jesus Maria,* and it was fringed with silk." Joan then warned her enemy: "King of England . . . be assured that I am Chef de Guerre, and in whatever place I shall find your people in France, I will make them go whether they will or not; and if they will not obey, I will have them all killed." She was convinced, she said, that the English would be driven out of France. The English, on the other hand, were unnerved by her strange charisma, and feared this emissary of Heaven, calling her a "witch." A contemporary German commentator reported that they were "eager to challenge the Maid."[35] However, with Joan at their head and fired by her enthusiasm, the troops of the dauphin managed to break out of the encirclement of Orléans, which was completely enclosed except for a gap to the east, by storming the most important bastion of the English, La Tourelle to the south of the river. "She told her comrades that they shouldn't be afraid and that they would lift the siege. She also let them know that while storming the bastion, she had been wounded in the neck by a crossbow bolt, but that she drew great comfort from the example of Saint Catherine. . . . Despite being wounded, she stayed on horseback and continued to go about her business."[36] Was everything what it seemed at this engagement? The English were convinced that there was sorcery at work, while the French now believed fervently in the divine vocation of the Maid of Orléans.

Whatever the case, Orléans was now free once more. Thereafter, popular legend has it, Joan of Arc immediately led the dauphin on a triumphant campaign the like of which had never been seen before; relentlessly, the French advanced, first to Jargeau, where following a brief investment of the town, the English were brutally crushed, then to Troyes, which was stormed and duly surrendered, and then finally to Reims for the coronation (1429). The Maid stood with her banner raised next to the coronation altar as the king was crowned; this was the high point of her short life. "Noble King, now is accomplished the will of God, who desired that I should raise the siege of Orleans, and should bring you to this city of Reims so that you might receive your holy coronation."[37] This event marked a key turning-point in the Hundred Years' War and heralded the end of the conflict. Yet the newly crowned Charles VII abandoned "la Pucelle." He was now ready to negotiate with the enemy, whereas she wanted to pursue the war. Eventually, in Compiègne, she was taken prisoner by the Burgundians and sold to the English—barely two years after she first set off from her home village of Domrémy in Lorraine.

The French king allowed this all to happen without intervening. The inquisition, or rather sham trial, which began in Rouen in 1431 under the aegis of the ten-year old Henry VI, with the bishop of Beauvais (in whose diocese the town lay) presiding, and with the active and decisive collaboration of theologians from the University of Paris, recorded all of Joan's testimony in detail. The verdict was a foregone conclusion: "Because she wore men's apparel, Joan is clearly a heretic; she is also a recidivist (because she once again donned men's clothes in prison, in defiance of strict orders not to); she is evidently an obdurate heretic . . . we therefore declare you, Joan, commonly known as the Maid, an idolatress, an invoker of demons, an apostate from the faith . . . we further denounce you as a rotten member, which must, so that you shall not infect the other members of Christ, be cast out of the unity of the church, cut off from her body, and given over to the secular power." In contravention of due legal process, the sentence was immediately carried out, with Joan ("who claimed to be around nineteen years old") being burned alive at the stake, and her ashes cast into the Seine.[38]

Later, twenty years after Joan's execution, and six days after the death of his favorite mistress, the wise confidante Agnes Sorel, and when he had long since been hailed as the "Victorious" and had taken Rouen back into French control, King Charles VII once again fell to thinking about his erstwhile savior. He did not want to owe his kingdom to a convicted witch. And so he ordered the evidence and the conduct of the original trial to be reexamined. In 1456, following exhaustive questioning of eyewitnesses in Lorraine, Orléans, Paris, and Rouen, the original verdict—"tainted as it is by malice, false accusations, injustice, and lies"—was overturned, and Joan finally rehabilitated where the funeral pyre had once consumed her body in flames. "A solemn sermon was delivered and a commemorative cross erected to the eternal memory of the Maid."[39] The final engagements of the Hundred Years' War were decided by French cannon, which proved themselves far superior in both range and firepower to the English longbows; a new era of weapons technology and of competitive arms races had dawned. However, it was only a century later, in 1558, that the last English forces left Calais, their final stronghold in France. The goal of La Pucelle had finally been realized.

Interpretation of the phenomenon of the "Maid of Orléans" has always been a contentious issue, and remains so to this day. Modern commentators commonly light upon the psychology of the case, using psychoanalytical interpretive models, which posit that Joan's warlike activities were a sublimation of her unfulfilled sexuality. Groundless speculation over the years has made of her the illegitimate daughter of the king, or even the half-sister of Charles VII. The popular conception of her, though, was long that of a divine emissary. Even before the advent of "la Pucelle," female visionaries and prophets like Christine of Sweden or Catherine of Siena had created a stir for political ends. Certainly, they achieved nothing like the success enjoyed by the Maid from Domrémy. Even people at the time were struck by the uniqueness of *Jehanne la pucelle*. When Joan was still alive, Christine de Pizan composed a poem in her honor. The writer François Villon also recalled in rhyme "Jehanne la bonne Loraine . . . Vierge souveraine," and Pius II was filled with admiration for her. Shakespeare turned her into a witch, whereas Schiller made her the eponymous heroine of one of his tragedies. Later, writers and musicians as diverse as George Bernard Shaw, Jean Anouilh, Bertolt Brecht, Guiseppe Verdi, Pyotr Tchaikovsky, and Arthur Honegger made the Maid of Orléans the subject of dramas, operas, and an oratorio—not to mention the many films dedicated to her life. She was beatified in 1909; and in 1920, following the terrible ravages of the First World War that saw Lorraine and Domrémy revert to being French once more, she was finally canonized. Today, a monument in the marketplace in Rouen bears the words of the novelist André Malraux: "O Jeanne, without sepulcher, without portrait, you know that the tomb of heroes is the heart of the living."

The European Powers

Charles VII was a successful ruler, one of the greatest kings of France. At his court, which admittedly was no match for the artistically inclined Burgundian court, one of the outstanding painters of his age, Jean Fouquet, was active. The portrait that he painted of the king—one of the very first worthy of the name—shows a somewhat mistrustful-looking man with beady eyes, a large nose, and fleshy lips; a drawing of the beautiful Agnes Sorel, his mistress, survives, which may also be by Fouquet. The king was surrounded by highly capable courtiers, such as Jean Chartier (d. 1464), who became Charles's official historian, Jean Juvénal des Ursins (d. 1444), who ultimately was appointed bishop of Reims and who crowned the king, and his confessor Gérard Machet (d. 1448), who became the bishop of Castres. One last close advisor of the king was the merchant Jacques Coeur (d. 1456); appointed master of the mint at Bourges in 1436, Coeur was involved in financial misconduct, creating counterfeit currency by reducing the proportion of fine metal in coins to increase his profit, but still escaped with a fine, followed by a letter of remission. Coeur then showed his acumen as an international trader, recognizing early on the difference in value between East and West of precious metals like gold and silver. He advanced huge war loans to the crown, and finally was made banker to the king *(argentier du roi)*, amassing a vast personal fortune. His downfall came when he foolishly flaunted his wealth publicly in a lavish lifestyle, which raised the king's suspicions. Charles VII, who was massively in debt to Coeur, had him arrested, and condemned, but ultimately contrived a subterfuge to let him escape prison and flee the country while he,

Charles, seized Coeur's wealth for the Crown. The house that the financier had built for himself in Bourges remains as a magnificent example of Late Gothic bourgeois prestige architecture.

The Hundred Years' War did not completely destroy bureaucracy in France. It remained intact in the English and Burgundian-controlled regions, even while in exile, Charles apparently managed without any particular difficulty to establish a viable alternative administration. Especially personal contacts between the aristocracy, despite the front of mutual antipathy they kept up, continued unscathed. Having been crowned king, Charles set about reorganizing his country's bureaucracy. Above all, he succeeded in stabilizing its finances. He ensured that demobilized, dangerously marauding bands of mercenaries were either expelled from the country or—a momentous innovation—transformed into a standing army in his own service; this was a major step toward bringing peace to France. The duke of Burgundy, Philip the Good, presently found himself moved to conclude a peace settlement with Charles, which was finally signed, after protracted negotiations and mutual territorial concessions, at Arras in 1435. Though it was fraught with tensions and mistrust and compromised by irksome border disputes, this agreement nevertheless held firm. Burgundy was not won for France, for sure, but at least the agreement isolated England once and for all, especially after German princes whose lands bordered on Burgundy, declared in favor of the French side. In 1440, a revolt of the nobility known as the *Praguerie* (1440) broke out against the king's military reforms, and even involved the dauphin Louis, but Charles was able to suppress this without undue difficulty. Relations with his son remained strained and antagonistic; ultimately, Louis withdrew into "exile" at the Burgundian court. By contrast, the king was able to skillfully exploit the tensions between Eugenius IV and the Council of Basel, which the pope had never wanted convened. In the concluding phase of the period of ecumenical councils, the pope found himself forced to accept the Pragmatic Sanction of Bourges (1438), which accorded the French church freedom but in practical terms granted the king sovereignty over it. When Charles died (1461), he was regarded as the most powerful of Europe's monarchs. Once more, France seemed on the verge of a glorious rise to power, a process that was brought to fruition by Charles's wayward son, an equally mistrustful and superstitious man, but a highly adept diplomat.

The Hundred Years' War finally saw England thrown back entirely on its island kingdom; it was unable to prevent France's rebirth as a nation. Henry VI was unable to consolidate the successes of his father, and even in England found himself increasingly on the defensive; he was widely seen as mentally unstable. Insurrections and court intrigues subsequently combined to undermine royal authority. The country entered the era of the Wars of the Roses (1445–1485), the succession dispute between the houses of York (whose heraldic emblem was the white rose) and Lancaster (the red rose), which after decades of growing animosity between the sides now erupted into violence and murder. The two sides engaged in wide-ranging military campaigns and appallingly bloody battles, and deployed money and diplomacy to further their cause. The conflict only came to an end with the demise of the direct male line of succession in both houses and the marriage of Henry Tudor (1485–1509), a distant relative of the House of Lancaster through his mother, with Elizabeth of York in 1485. This union certainly helped reestablish the stability of the English monarchy, but beyond retaining its bridgehead at Calais, it never again returned to power on the continent. Alliances with Spain, Scotland, and the Holy Roman Empire secured the Tudor dynasty's external relations. Henry Tudor even concluded a peace treaty with France, and his adroit financial and taxation policies enabled him to consolidate his realm, still shaken by the ravages of civil war, internally as well. The infamous multiple marriages of his son contrived to jeopardize all the gains made by Henry VII, but even Henry VIII managed to survive—yet here is not the place to delve into this history any further. Shakespeare would later capture the memory of the Wars of the Roses in his history plays, though the characterization is more psychologically intriguing than historically accurate.

To the south, too, in the Mediterranean, affairs unfolded at a dizzying pace as the great powers armed themselves for the conflicts of the Early Modern era. Venice had long since come into conflict with the Ottoman Empire, its sultans and its fleets, and even concluded pacts with the Turks (1454) when necessary. Single-handedly, abandoned by the other Christian powers, it took a brave stand against the pressure from the East. Alfonso V of Aragón (1416–1458), "il Magnanimo" as he was rightly called, exploited the crisis of the papacy to extend his position of power. In the face of Martin V's opposition, and in his capacity as the adoptive son of the Neapolitan queen Joan II, who (so the rumors that circulated among papal secretaries claimed) was open to the odd amorous adventure, gained control of the kingdom of Naples.[40] Although he dramatically fell out of favor with Joan, he still managed to keep his hold on power and reunited her patrimony of Naples with the island of Sicily to form the Kingdom of the Two Sicilies (1432). Alfonso now held sway over Majorca, Sicily, Sardinia, and Corsica, which he had conquered in a war against the Genoese. Because he opposed the Angevin dynasty in Naples and brought their kingdom to an end, this earned him the enmity of the French crown. The social costs of this expansion were unrest on Majorca and in Catalonia, especially in Barcelona. After his death, however, Alfonso's Mediterranean realm dissipated. His brother John II, who succeeded him on the Aragonese throne and who survived serious rebellions against his reign, lost the Roussillon region to France, but successfully bequeathed Naples to his son Ferdinand II (1479–1516) "the Catholic," through whom it later devolved to a unified kingdom of Spain. Sardinia and Corsica presently broke away, but before this happened, the pope had had to forego the fiefdom payments for Sardinia, Corsica, and Sicily in favor of Alfonso V; the church livings on these islands could now only be occupied at the invitation of the king, while the church tithes were also at the king's disposal. Moreover, he now had the right to put forward the names of those whom he wished to be elevated to the college of cardinals.

The weakening of the papacy through schisms and the age of the ecumenical councils was clear to see. None of the following popes, be it Pius II (1458–1464) or any of the popes from the Medici or Rovere families, or the Borgias, could hide this basic fact. Little wonder, then, that radical voices were raised, calling for reform. It was in this context that, in 1439, an anonymous author on the fringes of the Council of Basel published the pamphlet *Reformatio Sigismundi*. This work, which surveyed the monarchy, the knightly caste, and the towns, as well as industry and trade, the legal system, vendettas, and peace, painted an extraordinarily unworldly picture of a king endowed with diaconal, even priestly, authority, and came up with ideas for truly revolutionary reforms like married priests, the secularization of church property in favor of the imperial cities and the lower aristocracy, and transferring responsibility for the maintenance of peace in the empire to the cities. The author claimed that it was the utopian conviction of his utopian Sigismund that the *klainen*, namely the poor, the weak and the oppressed would improve the world and castigate the proud and lordly. The old Christian and humanitarian dream of the poor and pure in heart, who would bring the world salvation, resurfaced here. The author went on to state that a *sacer pusillus* (or in the vernacular *cleiner geweichter*), that is, a lowly priest rather than any prominent prelate or pope, would accomplish the work of bringing about this new world order. Even though the time was not yet ripe for cataclysmic changes, this text was in wide circulation in both manuscript form and printed editions on the very eve of the Reformation, and acted as a spark that helped ignite both the Reformation and the ensuing Peasants' War.

Instead of engaging in discussion about much-needed reform, the debates of the council elders became bogged down in arcane wranglings over "curialistic" or "conciliar" theories. These debates dragged on indefinitely and sapped all the intellectual force of the Council. One key question was who held the reins of the church, the pope as the successor to Saint Peter, or the Council as the successor to the Apostles and the seventy-two disciples, which in addition was the "representative" of the entire church, which is the mystical Body of Christ. The members of the Council of Constance, the great majority of whom were delegates from the abbeys, monasteries, and universities, with scarcely any bishops or cardinals, had once issued the self-confident proclamation: "The General Council is the embodiment of the Church Militant; it derives its power directly from Christ; and each and every Christian, whatever his rank or social status—even if he should be the pope himself—is duty bound to obey it."[41] In the decree they issued called *Tres veritates* (Three truths, 1439), the delegates of the Council of Basel formulated in even more radical terms their belief in the superiority of the Council over the pope: "The truth of the authority of the General Council, which embodies the entire church, is the truth of the Catholic Church as a whole."[42] The Council followed up this decree by deposing Pope Eugenius IV. This revolutionary doctrine, which in many aspects recalled the ideas of Marsilius of Padua and particularly William of Ockham, threatened the whole constitution of the church, as it had evolved and established itself since the Gregorian reform, guided by the supreme authority of the decretals and shaped by the interpretative skills of the canonists (even though their teachings could also be used to justify the Conciliar theory, too).[43] Yet in the long run, all the maxims about cooperation and representation carried no weight; over time, the church, supported by kings and other figures in authority, reverted to the monarchical power of the *vicarius Dei*; indeed, this was the only viable solution if it was not to sink in the morass of interminable Council debates. The religious and spiritual concerns of the laity waited in vain for clarification. Subsequently, the vicar of Christ's authority as the head of the church proved only to be consolidated and strengthened by having weathered this crisis. The era of the Borgia popes, but also of Michelangelo, was on the horizon, in which the newly built Basilica of Saint Peter would come to symbolize the renewed power of the Petrine successor: as Christ stated in the Gospel According to Saint Matthew 16:18–19, "Tu es Petrus, et super hanc petram aedificabo ecclesiam meam" ("You are Peter, and on this rock I shall build my church").

As new dangers loomed, Sigismund died without leaving a son and heir. Although his daughter Elizabeth brought the Luxembourg inheritance to her marriage with Albert of Austria, he met an early death fighting the Ottoman Turks and did not have a chance to have any lasting impact on the destiny of the empire. The son born after his death, Ladislaus the Posthumous, was still a minor when he became king, and was placed under the guardianship of his uncle Frederick V. Now, finally, the provisions of the Golden Bull took effect, as the German electors chose Frederick as king, and forever thereafter the Roman crown, with just one exception, was to remain within the House of Habsburg.

Emperor Frederick III consciously attempted to model his rule on that of his namesake predecessor, the Hohenstaufen emperor Frederick II. Yet his subjects were deluded if they imagined he was about to do justice to this illustrious name. The German princes, first and foremost his brother Albert of Austria and the Bavarian Wittelsbach dynasty, set themselves up in opposition to him. He was keen not to relinquish either Hungary or Bohemia. The result was an endless succession of wars and conflicts, which only weakened the ability of the Christians to counter the Ottoman threat. The Turks had already invaded Transylvania, Serbia, and Hungary, and in no time had advanced to Carniola and Carinthia. Concerned that he might be usurped and deposed, Frederick tenaciously and jealously guarded the prerogatives of his royal status. These prerogatives were distinguished by notions of *superioritas* and of imperial *plenitudo potestatis* (jurisdictional power) deriving from Roman Law, and by a sweeping interpretation of what constituted crimes against the crown. Where he was able to, the emperor insisted upon absolute subjugation and obedience; faced with extreme danger, he passed an emergency act valid for five years imposing public peace and order (*Landfrieden*) on the empire; any transgression against it was liable to draconian punishment, and Frederick was rigorous in his enforcement of these sanctions. An yet, despite his lengthy reign (1440–1493), the longest of any German king or emperor, no particular successes are associated with his name. That astute observer of current affairs Philippe de Commynes declared Louis XI of France, the Hungarian king Matthias Corvinus, and the Ottoman sultan Mehmet the Conqueror as the outstanding rulers of his age, not the emperor. Rather, Commynes observed, Frederick was the "most avaricious ruler of our times."[44] His most significant achievement was simply to outlive his most dangerous adversaries both at home and abroad and to compensate so effectively for the many setbacks he suffered that at his death the Habsburg ancestral lands were once more successfully united and his grandson Philip was well placed to inherit one of the richest countries in Europe. Philip could scarcely have had any inkling of the turmoil and wars that would shortly be visited upon his realm and upon European history as a whole, and that would engulf the continent for many decades to come.

When he was still duke of Inner Austria, Frederick had devised for himself the strange motto *AEIOU*—unexplained in his lifetime but later (from the eighteenth century on) interpreted as meaning, either in Latin or German, "The whole world is subservient to Austria" (German: "Alles Erdreich ist Österreich untertan"; Latin: "Austriae est imperare orbi universo"). With this, the duke and later emperor was acting out a curious dynastic sense of destiny, which traced his family back, allegedly, to Julius Caesar (some other royal families also claimed similar genealogies, it is true). While he was open to the intellectual currents of his age, Frederick was no great trendsetter or patron. In the early years of his reign, the great Italian humanist Enea Silvio Piccolomini served as secretary to his chancellery; his inexorable rise to the papacy (as Pius II) began at Frederick's court. Later, renowned scholars like Johannes Reuchlin, Konrad Celtis, the mathematician and astronomer Regiomontanus, and others, including writers, met at Frederick's courts in Linz, Vienna New Town, and elsewhere. The emperor was also a great devotee of music. Even so, no new major contributions to the Renaissance or humanism were to emerge from this court.

In any event, after having recognized Eugenius IV as the pope in his schism with Felix V (a course of action he was advised to take by Nicholas of Cusa and Piccolomini), the king came to an accord with his successor Nicholas V. In 1448, he and the pope concluded the Vienna Concordat, *Pro natione Alamanica*. This pact established a set of basic guidelines for relations between the two sides, the German nobility and the empire on the one hand and the Roman Curia on the other. It remained in force right up to the end of the old empire in 1803. It also spelled the end for the Council; the king forcibly disbanded and dispersed the rump assembly of squabbling prelates. The Concordat put at the disposal of the Holy See all the vacant canonries and nonelective benefices in the empire during the six odd months of the year, declared that the election of bishops was to be free of all interference (while reserving for the pope the right of confirmation), as well as guaranteeing free elections to the imperial monasteries and abbeys. It also regulated the matter of payments of annates (the profits from benefices) to the Apostolic Camera, namely the papal treasury. Albeit through special agreements, over the following years the German nobility acknowledged the Concordat, thereby laying down an essential precondition for the creation of the future territorially established regional churches in Germany, and for the polycentric ecclesiastical constitution of Germany in the modern period. In all this, there was no longer a single mention of reform, however—a momentous omission that stored up trouble for the future. Yet the agreement with the Holy See did open up Frederick's path to Rome for his imperial coronation.

A few years later, he duly embarked on this journey, receiving first the Italian crown and then the imperial crown from the pope's hand. Unbeknownst to those involved, though, this also signaled an end-point: this was to be the last time that a German monarch was crowned as emperor in Saint Peter's. It was the dawn of a new age. After the coronations, Frederick hurried to Naples to visit the court of Alfonso V of Aragón, not only in order to seal his marriage, but primarily in order to forge an alliance against Milan under the Sforza. On his return to Germany, he was confronted with the catastrophic news of the fall of Constantinople (1453) to the forces of the Ottoman sultan Mehmet: "The loss of Constantinople was a great disgrace to all Christian rulers."[45] The Basilica of Hagia Sophia was turned into a mosque; the city's churches were closed and left to go to rack and ruin, while the magnificent Fatih Mosque and other places of worship were built, along with many madrasahs for the teaching of the Qur'an. The unique Topkapi Palace became the new residence of the victorious Mehmet within the city. The city on the Golden Horn, the city of the Christian Roman and Byzantine emperors, was now transformed into the capital of the Ottoman Empire. Propaganda ensured that these achievements became widely known in the West, where a sense of dread went hand in hand with awed admiration for the Grand Turk.

No sooner had the emperor returned from Italy than he found himself obliged to release the twelve-year-old Ladislaus the Posthumous from his wardship. The boy king was faced with insurmountable crises in both Hungary and Bohemia, and died only five years later, allegedly poisoned by a scorned lover[46] before he had any opportunity to achieve greatness. The Czechs elected George of Poděbrady as Ladislaus's successor, while the Hungarians chose Matthias Corvinus, the great bibliophile and patron of humanism. The emperor, whose own brother Albert contested his right to rule over the Austrian ancestral territories, had to acquiesce in these decisions. Reluctantly, he renounced both crowns (in 1459 and 1463) in order to save Austria at least, and even that he only managed with great difficulty.

However, the threat from the Ottomans as they pushed steadily westward should have required the consolidation of all available forces and the coordination of defensive measures rather than their fragmentation, not to mention wrangling over succession and dynastic rivalry. The Turkish troops—the feared Janissaries, an army comprised of slaves and sons of Christian peasants taken from the Balkans and trained as an elite bodyguard for the sultan—came inexorably closer. In 1448, a Crusader army under the command of John Hunyadi, was annihilated in a second battle at the Blackbird's Field in Kosovo. As soon as he heard news of the fall of Constantinople, the pope reiterated his call for a crusade against the Turks; but no one responded, except for Duke Philip of Burgundy. Intoxicated by tales of knightly adventures, Crusades, and the exploits of ancient heroes, Philip had long been spoiling for a fight against the Ottomans, and had found allies in the Mediterranean region, in the shape of Portugal and Aragón; together, they began to construct a battle fleet. Philip was intent on avenging his father's humiliation; even on his death bed, he was still talking about it. Just as happened years before with the founding of Sigismund's Order of the Dragon, the Order of the Golden Fleece instituted by Philip in 1430 was also designed to rally people to the defense of the faith and promote crusading zeal. The commercial interests of the Dutch also came into play. The Burgundian fleet duly saw action off Rhodes and in the Black Sea, but the attempt to assemble a new crusade collapsed before it gained any real momentum.[47]

While the Hungarian king Matthias Corvinus fought skillfully and inflicted a number of bitter defeats on the Ottomans, all his calls to the emperor for military assistance fell on deaf ears. Christendom and the Holy Roman Empire seemed incapable of taking any concerted action.

The Imperial Diet of Frankfurt in 1454 marked a sad low point of such inaction. Nicholas of Cusa issued dire warnings, but to no avail; likewise the papal legate in Frankfurt Enea Silvio Piccolomini directed all his oratorical skill toward persuading the delegates to support Hungary. Eventually, though, he was forced to conclude in resignation: "The Germans are faint-hearted; not one of them voted for a Crusade against the Turks." The emperor did not even bother to attend the Diet. Europe feared the Turks, yet put up no resistance to them. No matter how often Pius II continued to preach a crusade against them, or Philip kept pressing for action, even Louis XI, the latter's liege lord, denied him help for fear of provoking a new English invasion of his country, as well as for various other reasons. Might this total lack of unity within Christendom perhaps explain the fact that artists' depiction of the torments of Hell became ever more terrifying at this time? Whatever the case, danger increased throughout Europe, in the southeast and in the Mediterranean, and even in the Adriatic, the "Venetian lake."

For sixteen years, La Serenissima, left in the lurch by most of her fellow Christian powers, had been at war against the Turkish invader. Eventually, in 1477, Ottoman forces appeared quite unexpectedly outside the city gates of the lagoon republic. From the top of Saint Mark's Cathedral, the glow of fires across the devastated countryside beyond could be clearly seen. "The enemy is at our gates," Doge Andrea Vendramin was warned, "The ax is at the root. Unless divine help comes, the doom of the Christian name is sealed." The city of Venice, which had never been conquered before, was obliged to sue for an inglorious peace, which entailed the loss of its most important possessions in the Aegean and Morea (the Peloponnese) and the surrender of huge compensation payments. On the credit side, the same settlement of 1479 did guarantee Venice exclusive trading rights with the Ottoman empire. Proud Venice had been humiliated; contemporary Venetians wistfully recalled their own conquest of the city of Constantinople almost three centuries earlier (during the Fourth Crusade of 1204); these nostalgic visions of past triumphs stiffened their resolve, but even so it would be almost another century before Venice regained her Mediterranean dominance at the naval Battle of Lepanto (1571).

Mehmet II the Conqueror (r. 1444/51–1481), an extremely well educated man who spoke several languages, was himself keen to emulate the exploits of the heroes of the past, and was not intimidated by the threat of a new crusade.[48] Commynes reported that he possessed "more intelligence and guile than boldness and daring" and that he was "a gourmet without measure."[49] After the peace treaty of 1479, at the invitation of the Grand Turk, the doge sent one of the foremost painters of Venice, Gentile Bellini, to the Sublime Porte. Bellini was permitted to paint the sultan's portrait—the first authentic image of a Muslim ruler. The Venetian master depicted him in quarter-profile, in a red cloak with a heavy fur collar, wearing a red and white turban on his head, and with a dark beard, narrow lips, a hooked nose, and his gaze fixed either somewhere in middle distance or directed inward. This was a portrayal of a determined conqueror to truly strike fear into European hearts. Three years before Bellini's visit, some 200 Janissaries, who after fierce siege warfare had been forced to cede the important border fortress of Shabatz (Sabac) to the Hungarians, and who after fleeing the town had managed to battle their way back to the safety of the Sultan's main army. The sultan had them summarily drowned in the Danube, with millstones round their necks. Mehmet had been beside himself with fury at their "cowardice"; it was their duty, he raged, to defend their position to the very last man. The Ottoman armies advanced deep into Hungary. The defenders were just about holding the line against them, but the country's strength was dwindling daily.

The rise of Burgundy made warding off the Ottoman threat even more difficult. This duchy generated mistrust and animosity among all its immediate neighbors. The ascent of Burgundy had begun under Philip the Bold, a son of the House of Valois, when he became duke in 1363, and was successfully sustained by John the Fearless, and was finally echoed in Philip the Good's audacious plans for a Crusade. The duchy's prominence was far more than a mere flash in the pan. Between England, France, and the Holy Roman Empire, a new major power now came into being, extending from the Netherlands down to the borders of the Swiss Confederacy; its rise had a major impact on the European balance of power, shifting it fundamentally. As duke, the younger Philip presided over a strict, almost harshly Spartan, regime, which weighed heavily upon its tax-paying subjects. Uprisings of the town citizenry against the authorities increased, especially in the duchy's largest city of Ghent. "I love you, but I will show you no mercy," Charles the Bold is reputed to have reproached the inhabitants of Ghent after suppressing their revolt of 1467;[50] his father Philip the Good thought no differently and acted accordingly. Nonetheless, the Burgundian court developed into a magnificent spectacle without equal in the whole of Europe. The pomp and pageantry presented by the duke

497

was second to none; the wealth of the Netherlands provided the where-withal for a display of luxurious extravagance. Trade and commerce thrived here, and art too. The most important painters of the age such as the Limburg brothers, Jan van Eyck, Robert Campin, Rogier van der Weyden, Petrus Christus, and Hans Memling (who moved to Bruges from Hesse) were all active here. In 1425–1426 the duke and the city estab-lished the University of Louvain, which soon became one of the foremost European seats of learning, a magnet for outstanding scholars of the age. However, Burgundy's splendor ultimately turned out to be bedazzling: Charles the Bold, the fourth of the great dukes of Burgundy, continued the policies of his father but at the same time pushed them too far. His motto was *Je l'ay emprins* (I have dared to do it), but his audacity did not serve him or his realm well. After his death in battle in 1477, Burgundy abruptly ceased to expand; its legacy was to weigh heavily on the other European powers until far into the modern period.

The most famous portrait of the warlike Charles the Bold, possibly painted by Rogier van der Weyden or his workshop, shows a young man seemingly lost in thought, with an almost dreamy look about him and soft facial features. He is wearing no prince's hat or crown; the only deco-ration in evidence is the chain of the Order of the Golden Fleece round his neck. His hand appears to be resting on the hilt of his dagger. And yet this was the man whom his own country and his neighbors feared as a tyrant. Luxembourg was already incorporated into his realm, Savoy had been brought to heel, and Lorraine was just about to fall into his grasp. Charles then set his sights on the Lower Rhine and Alsace; even the Swiss Confederacy, with which Charles's father Philip had concluded a friend-ship treaty in 1467, felt threatened. In alliance with Edward II of England, Charles was able to field an impressive fighting force. He planned to seize control of the whole of the Rhine valley down to the county of Pfirt in southern Upper Alsace, which he already held in fee from Austria. "The duke had so many and such great things in mind that they quite over-whelmed him."[51] Yet it wasn't just naked power that Charles hankered after, rather he was seeking legitimacy and tangible recognition of what he had achieved—in sum, a revival of an independent kingdom of Bur-gundy and Lorraine (Lotharingia). The duke was after nothing less than the crown of the Holy Roman Emperor on his head. The marriage of his daughter Mary to the Emperor's son Maximilian would, he calculated, smooth the path to his coronation; a letter of recommendation and a diamond-studded ring were dispatched to underline the seriousness of the duke's intention.[52]

Frederick III did indeed enter into negotiations with Charles the Bold concerning this marriage, but at the same time covered his back by also entering into secret negotiations with the Swiss and Louis XI of France, the sworn enemy of all Burgundian expansion. Frederick and Charles met in Trier in 1473. Although the emperor declared that he was prepared to bestow the status of kingdom on a duchy that was a fiefdom of the empire, in other words to confer the title of king on Charles the Bold, he still enfeoffed him with money in his capacity as duke of Brabant; the only matter that was still unclear, it seemed, was what the new kingdom would be called. But Charles held out for more, demanding that he be put forward for election as the Roman–German king, and hence as successor to the office of Holy Roman Emperor, and this led to a split. Frederick left the duke without any formal farewell; his pride deeply wounded by this deliberate snub, Charles duly threatened the emperor with war.

For their part, the Swiss were allied with Louis XI, and with his support the eight Old Cantons had finally succeeded, after decades of struggle against the Habsburgs, in concluding a peace agreement (the so-called *Ewige Richtung* [Eternal direction]) with Duke Sigismund of Austria in Constance in 1474. This treaty really did bring about a fundamental change, although the French king did not by any means adopt all of its provisions for his ancestral lands. Most importantly, the treaty left the Swiss, who were also in alliance with René of Lorraine, free to combat the threat posed by Burgundy; presently, war was declared. Charles lost three battles, at Grandson and Murten in the canton of Vaud (1476) and finally in the following year outside the town of Nancy, which he had hoped to capture from the duke of Lorraine. In this final battle, bold to the last, Charles was in the thick of the fighting and lost his life, his face disfigured so badly by the blows of a Swiss halberdier that he was barely recognizable when his body was found. The booty carried off by the victors was immense, including jewelry, ceremonial robes, insignia of high office, and even Charles's artillery. A similar haul of treasure and weaponry had already been taken after the Battle of Grandson, which was distributed among the cantons involved in the conflict. The Burgundian Wars and Burgundian treasure are still a source of great pride for the Swiss, constituting an historical episode that helped forge a sense of national identity.[53]

New conflicts and upheaval continued to arise in Europe. Straight after the death in battle of Charles the Bold, Louis XI sent his troops into the various provinces of the duchy to take control of Burgundy. Mary, Charles's twenty-year-old daughter and heir, was chosen to marry the dauphin, a boy just ten years of age. But under the leadership of the estates-general of the Netherlands, Burgundy resisted the French invasion; the Dutch compelled the duchess Mary to reform the existing regime and accord them more autonomy, but still remained loyal to her. Mary, "the Rich" went on to marry the eighteen-year-old emperor's son Maximilian in 1477 to whom she had recently been betrothed. The bridegroom came to Ghent with a retinue of 700 or 800 horsemen. The following year, Mary bore a son, Philip the Handsome. Through him, the greater portion of the Burgundian inheritance, which the dukes had built up over decades of fighting, namely Flanders, Brabant, Luxembourg, and the Netherlands, including all the royal residences and centers of industry and commerce and the great cities such as Brussels, Bruges, Ghent, Antwerp, and Amsterdam, was passed down to his son, Charles the Bold's grandson Charles, the fifth Holy Roman Emperor of that name, on whose empire the sun would never set. Only Burgundy itself, with Nancy and Dijon, fell to France. This situation soon generated further conflict in Europe.

The great triumph of the Swiss Confederacy thus altered the face of the continent. Venice's peace settlement with the Ottomans, however fragile it may have been, may also be seen as a key turning point. The Hungarian king Matthias Corvinus now turned his attention to fighting the emperor. Frederick found himself caught up in a new cycle of conflict. Corvinus's objective was to seize the crown of Bohemia and so secure himself a role as an imperial elector. To this end, he allied himself with the Swiss and the Wittelsbachs, and succeeded in overrunning most of the Habsburgs' Austrian ancestral territories. At this stage, the old emperor, who up until then had steadfastly opposed any election to the kingship, allowed the imperial nobility to elect Maximilian as king of the Romans/Germans in 1486. Maximilian was only able to regain the ancestral lands after the death of Corvinus (1490). At the same time, the cities of Flanders rose up against their government; Mary had been killed in an accident while out pursuing her beloved sport of hunting with falcons in 1482; but her "subjects accorded her greater honor and respect than they did her husband. Yet she loved her husband dearly and had a good reputation." It was true, the Burgundians had little love for their new duke Maximilian. "He had," complained Commynes, "no idea about anything; that came from his youth and from the fact that he found himself in a foreign land and had been brought up very badly; in any event, he had not the slightest notion how to conduct the great affairs of state."[54] The Habsburgs clearly had a lot still to learn.

The uprising forced the emperor to launch a military campaign against the Netherlands. The region was plagued by unrest right up to his death. Plagued by painful arterial sclerosis in his legs—shortly before his death, his surgeons amputated one of his feet—the seventy-eight-year-old Frederick died in 1493 without having managed to banish the Turkish threat and before he had a chance to learn about the discovery of America the previous year. A war with France and new revolts in the Netherlands were just about to break out. His son, the "last knight," was not taking on an easy inheritance.

The young man had received a humanist education and was a quick study.[55] He had brokered an alliance between Castile and the Habsburgs, a union that would presently cause the kings of France a great deal of trouble. And at the Diet of Worms in 1495, he put the constitution of the Holy Roman Empire on a firm footing that was to last for centuries; in the face of fierce opposition, he also secured for his family the right of succession to both the Hungarian and Bohemian crowns (1515), as well as being a keen patron of the arts and sciences throughout his realm. Maximilian's only major flaw was that, throughout his life, he was bad at managing money, taking massive loans from Jakob Fugger of Augsburg; the privileges he granted in return made the banker an extremely wealthy man. Yet despite these huge injections of cash, he still found himself obliged, after Mary's death, to enter into a new marriage arrangement—as it turned out, a total mismatch—with the beautiful Bianca Maria Sforza of Milan, in order to use the immense dowry of 400,000 guilders in cash, plus a further 40,000 in jewels, that she brought with her to pay off at least some of his mountain of debt. Scarcely had he remarried, though, than the king of the Romans began to complain about his wife's stupidity, and neglected her thereafter. Even so, Bianca Sforza's uncle Ludovico il Moro, who had arranged the whole marriage, was rewarded by being enfeoffed with the duchy of Milan—a realm that he had already seized by force from Bianca's brother Gian Galeazzo Sforza, whom he promptly had imprisoned and—according to Commynes—murdered. Machiavelli drew his lessons from this skulduggery; however, Leonardo da Vinci, whose patron Ludovico was, lent legitimacy to the perpetrator through his writings, his extraordinary works of arts and scientific inventions, and through organizing festivities for the Milanese court. It was at the behest of this suspected murderer that the artist created his unique *Last Supper* for Santa Maria delle Grazie, the church of the Milan *signoria,* in 1497. As so often, even nowadays, the violent abuse of power and art made close bedfellows.

The tensions between Milan and Florence shook Italy, drawing in both the emperor and the pope, and ultimately prompting Charles VIII of France to launch an invasion of the country. The immediate cause of the invasion was the friendly policy adopted toward Naples by Piero II de'Medici, who had succeeded his father Lorenzo as ruler of Florence; alarmed by this alliance, Ludovico Sforza turned to the French king for help. Piero's too hasty surrender of Tuscan fortresses to Charles, in a deal signed with the French invader in 1494, led to a revolt in Florence and the expulsion of the ruling Medici family that same year. Yet another branch of this family, headed by Giovanni "il Popolano," a nephew of Lorenzo the Magnificent, was sympathetic to the populist cause espoused by Girolamo Savonarola. His circle included Sandro Botticelli, formerly renowned for his paintings of heavenly round-dances and graceful allegories. In accord with the violent upheaval in the city, Botticelli's art now underwent a fundamental change, as the artist began to incorporate themes of political and social revolution into his works. For example, in the *Calumny of Apelles* (ca. 1494) three allegorical figures representing "Calumny," "Subterfuge," and "Deceitfulness" (clad in the sort of rich robes once worn by the sublime figure of Beauty in his works, but which now epitomized the tyranny that just had been overthrown) drag their naked victim, Apelles, by the hair before the throne of the king. Powerless to intervene, the naked figure of Truth implores Heaven for help, while envious Hatred, clothed in a tattered monk's habit, stands in front of the king-judge and harangues him and black-robed Regret casts a furtive glance at Truth. Elsewhere in Botticelli's late work, the mythological ancient Roman heroines who embodied freedom and hatred of tyranny—Virginia and Lucretia—make an appearance. Violent scenes unfold in these paintings; in a radical break with tradition, the unrefined, almost coarse faces of the protagonists mirror the real, down-to-earth milieu of the rebellious populace. Government is shown in a state of impotence, while brutal violence is visited particularly upon women, as the quintessential symbol of all those who are perennially embattled and oppressed. We search in vain here for the slightest hint of the exaggerated, unreal, ethereal beauty evident in the painter's earlier works like *Primavera* or *The Birth of Venus*. In his *Lives of the Painters* (1568), Giorgio Vasari claimed that the older Botticelli burned all his earlier works depicting naked figures from Antiquity. Here, then, was yet another sign of the dawning of a new age, which saw humanism adopt a political and social revolutionary face. In later life, the painter may have been influenced by the fire-and-brimstone sermons delivered by Savonarola; his eventual burning at the stake must have hit the painter hard. And yet it would still be almost another twenty years before the Medici regained power in Florence. In the meantime—and despite the continuing presence of Michelangelo, a lover of freedom and a lifelong opponent rather than friend of the ruling classes—the former revolutionary cultural vibrancy of the city had long since dissipated; Botticelli died in 1510.

North of the Alps, society, the church, and the ruling classes were also in a state of turmoil, though here, too, both humanism (as represented by Jakob Wipfeling) and Greek studies (through the influence, say, of Johannes Reuchlin) likewise made their mark. In around 1500, the so-called Revolutionary of the Upper Rhine took an even more radical and inflammatory stance than, some generations previously, the author of the *Reformatio Sigismundi* had done. The anonymous author of this tract, who was clearly connected in some way with the imperial court—all we can surmise is that he was a jurist with astrological knowledge—it has proved impossible to identify him more closely—clearly yearned for the day when divine justice would be visited upon the world. This utopian goal, a mixture of eschatological and astrological insights, would be realized through radical reforms in the church and in society. The general decline in moral values that had taken place would inevitably call down the Day of Judgment on Earth. The author vented the full force of his righteous anger on the children of priests, social climbers who became bishops and prelates. They were, he claimed, the offspring of the Antichrist. Furthermore, the practice of serfdom was born of naked avarice, the unjust use of coercion, and oppression, and as such must be abolished forthwith. The only figure who was entitled to wield earthly power was the Emperor from the Black Forest, a mythical apocalyptic German messiah-king. He would castigate the clergy, dissolve the monasteries, seize the property of the aristocracy and territorial rulers, dispossess the rich merchant class, and protect the poor. All vital state expenditure would be met by moderate levels of taxation. An equitable justice system would be guaranteed by pastors and judges and regular confession. The language of the church would henceforth be German, not Latin. Even though millenarian texts like these were not widely distributed or read, they do still reflect the revolutionary mood of the expectations of contemporaries on the eve of the Reformation in Germany. Anger at wealth and the tyranny of money was hardly surprising; yet neither this revolutionary, nor any since, has been able to alter this state of affairs.

The economics and politics of the Late Middle Ages, and the exercise of both imperial and papal power in that period, were ruled by money and credit, and their influence remained just as strong thereafter. The struggles and wars in Hungary, Italy, and Spain and the rebellions that broke out here and there continued unabated. Charles VIII of France invaded Italy in 1494, though he and his army were forced to withdraw by the ravages of the "malady of Venus" (syphilis), and the Ottoman sultan dispatched his Janissary armies ever further west. Presently the settlements of Pest and Buda were under threat; Matthias Corvinus had developed the latter town into a magnificent royal residence in the Renaissance style. The ambition of princes knew no bounds. And so it was that the Middle Ages—with its wars, uprisings, financial crises, legal statutes, and hopes of reform, with its religious and humanistic values and doctrines, with its political insights, its superstitious belief in witches and the devil, its predictability, its urge to explore the world, its scholarship, and with its burgeoning commitment to rationality—and which the last remaining vestiges of "political immaturity" and irrationality, however tenacious, could not stop—crossed seamlessly over into a similarly constituted Early Modern period. No contemporary observer had any sense of standing on some "threshold between eras"; indeed, it was only later commentators and historians who, without possessing the requisite knowledge anyhow, cobbled together such a construct in the first place.

The Dark Middle Ages?

Tᴏ ᴀ ᴛʜᴇ ᴠɪᴇᴡ ᴛʜᴀᴛ the Middle Ages was an era hopelessly ensnared in a kind of self-inflicted intellectual immaturity seems very wide of the mark. The "Soldier King" Frederick William I of Prussia, the father of Frederick the Great, demanded that his son be given a thorough historical education, but strictly forbade him to study either the ancient world or the Middle Ages.[1] On reflection, Frederick William concluded that antiquity might just about be acceptable, but this staunchly Protestant monarch regarded the Middle Ages as spent, effete, and simply too Catholic. Others, like Immanuel Kant, the great thinker and author of famous *Critiques* (though, it must be said, a man with little experience of the world) shared these misgivings, but voiced even more damning criticisms, which condemned the Middle Ages out of hand. At the end of his 1764 work *Observations on the Feeling of the Beautiful and Sublime,* eight editions of which were published in his lifetime, the renowned Königsberg philosopher turns his attention to both the ancient world and the medieval period, first conceding that: "The ancient times of the Greeks and the Romans exhibited unequivocal signs of a genuine feeling for the Beautiful as well as the Sublime in poetry, sculpture, architecture, legislation, and even in morals." He then goes on to remark, however, that "the government of the Roman Emperors" changed all that and concludes that "in sympathy with the general decline of the state, even this bastard relic of the purer taste was extinguished." In this assessment, Kant was merely giving voice to what many of his fellow intellectuals at the time believed.

Yet almost every word of Kant's argument carried devastating weight, simply because it was Kant expressing it. The *Observations* drew together and neatly summed up the whole spectrum of negative preconceptions about the Middle Ages that were then current. This frequently reprinted text served to disseminate this view widely, and set the seal on popular repudiation of an entire millennium of history. For, moving on to consider the Germanic peoples, Kant wrote the following: "The Barbarians, after having established their power on the remains of the Roman Empire, introduced a peculiar form of corrupt taste which is called the Gothic, and which amounted to a passion for the childish and grotesque. This passion manifested itself not merely in architecture, but in the sciences and in all other matters and usages. Once having been expressed through false art, this debased sentiment proceeded to adopt every other unnatural form that it possibly could rather than the old form of simple nature, and the results were either exaggerated or foolish. The highest point to which the human genius was allowed to soar in its attempt to master the Sublime was the Barbaresque. Romances, both temporal and spiritual, were then exhibited on the stage of nations, and oftentimes a disgusting and monstrous abortion of both in combination—monks, with the missal in one hand and the battle flag in the other, followed by whole armies of deluded victims destined to lay their bones in other climates and in a holier soil; consecrated warriors, solemnly dedicated by vow to outrage and the perpetration of crimes; and in their train a kind of a strange breed of heroic visionaries, who styled themselves knights and rode off in search of adventures, tournaments, duels, and other romantic exploits. During this period, religion together with the sciences was disfigured by miserable follies, and we have occasion to observe that taste does not easily degenerate on one side without giving clear indications of corruption in everything else that has to do with finer feelings. . . . Finally, after the genius of man has fortunately, through a kind of palingenesis, managed to raise itself up once more to its former heights, we see in our own age the proper taste for the Beautiful and the Noble blossoming anew both in the arts and sciences, as well as in moral sentiment."[2] To this compendium of accusations leveled by Kant, the unchurched proponent of the Enlightenment, we might also add the words of the poet and historian Friedrich Schiller, who wrote that the Middle Ages were pervaded by "the depressed spirit of Nordic Barbarians."[3]

Enough of all this, however. These three testimonies—the judgment of a Prussian king, the verdict of a Königsberg philosopher, and the malicious defamation offered by a poet—are representative of many such views. In the Enlightenment, everyone was in agreement that the Middle Ages was a backward era that exhibited no yearning for enlightenment, no sense of dynamism, and definitely no spirit of rebellion.[4] This attitude is a curious phenomenon; no other advanced civilization on Earth has ever dismissed and denigrated a period of its own past so comprehensively, or even wished to airbrush it out of existence entirely through neglect, in the way that Europeans have done with the medieval era. The "Middle Ages" is a typical European, or to be more precise, Western European, phenomenon. In the search for the origins of their own culture, neither the advanced civilizations of India or the Far East, nor of Christian Byzantium or the Islamic countries have any comparable conception of an *aetas media* that is clearly defined, yet dismissed as being inferior, and even sometimes wished away lock, stock, and barrel. The conception of the Middle Ages does not include either Byzantium or Arab-Muslim culture, yet horizons do widen to the extent that even in the medieval period Europeans—thanks both to diplomatic contacts and the missionary calling enacted by Latin Christendom—begin to adopt a global perspective.

Granted, there is another quite different image of the Middle Ages, which became especially prevalent in Germany—namely a fanatically romanticizing one that saw in that era nothing other than a unified Christianity devoted solely to observing the Faith, a harmonious Christian community not yet debilitated and undermined by overintellectualization, and a sure and certain trust in salvation that exulted in armed pilgrimage to the Holy Sepulcher. Consequently, such a viewpoint made of the Middle Ages some utopian dream age. Every bit as much a caricature as the other false perspective—albeit in the opposite direction—this image likewise failed to do proper justice to the medieval millennium. It failed to take into account the eruption and triumphal procession of precisely that normalized rationality into all aspects of culture, the secularization of thought that permeated the whole of society, and the way in which all modes of existence, even religious ones, were becoming increasingly secularized and concerned with the Here and Now, rather than with transcendence. Those responsible for creating this romantic image misjudged the power of systematic doubt, which Peter Abélard instilled into Western scholarship, failed to identify the return of skepticism and the rise of the academic discipline of philosophy, which steadily eclipsed faith, and ignored the triumph of a sheer joy in experimentation and empirically based learning that became evident from the Late Middle Ages on, together with the beginnings of a rational, analytical form of natural science that was organized primarily according to the laws of logic rather than religious premises. These same romantics also completely left out of their idealized picture of the medieval world such factors as the mounting unrest among the peasantry, the collective emancipation of the middle classes, and the growing division of labor that accompanied social processes of differentiation, increasing professionalization, and the emergence of new elites. Finally, they overlooked the sheer radicalism of apostate critics of the church and the unstoppable forward march—in defiance of all the burnings at the stake and crusades against heretics that were instigated—of the so-called heresies of mystics and reformers such as Meister Eckhart, John Wyclif, or John Hus, along with the very first stirrings of materialism. In short, they chose to ignore the thesis "God is Dead."

Significantly, none of the authors of the "Renaissance," who were the first to develop the idea of the Middle Ages, rushed to pronounce such a damning verdict. Philology, language, and eloquence, and the whole picture of man were the focus of their urge for renewal; and although, from Alberti on, their buildings were influenced by the writings of the Roman architect Vitruvius, this did not lead them to condemn all previous architecture. Above all, they did not sweepingly repudiate an entire era, but at most confined themselves to criticizing and renouncing individual building idioms or transgressions against the classical rules, or the sterility of rigid, university-based Late Scholasticism. Not even Giorgio Vasari (1511–1574), who coined the negatively loaded concept of the "Gothic" style in painting and architecture, intended it to condemn an entire epoch; rather it was meant as a targeted critique of a particular style of building and order of column design; "May God protect every country from such ideas and style of building. They are such deformities in comparison with our buildings that they are not even worthy of further discussion."[5] Like Vasari, these authors of the Renaissance greatly revered Dante, say, or Cimabue, whose image of the Madonna against a golden background "garnered much fame and admiration" and yet who still "provided the first impetus to the revival of painting," or Giotto, or Nicola, or Giovanni Pisano—all of them poets, painters and sculptors of the thirteenth and early fourteenth centuries—as "modern" artists, or at least as having blazed a trail for modernity. For example, Vasari states that Simone Martini (d. 1344) "was an excellent painter, remarkable in his own times and much esteemed at the court of the pope"; thus, while Vasari deemed him to be not so adept at drawing, he stopped short of condemning this medieval painter out of hand.[6] Admittedly, the historical Goths, whose sacking of Rome in A.D. 410 gave this supposedly worthless style its bad name, devised no "Gothic" style themselves, nor did they even destroy Rome. Ironically, they were in fact the first people to embark upon a revival, a "Renaissance" of the moribund Roman Empire.

And so, this "peculiar form of corrupt taste which is called the Gothic" was nothing more than a fabricated historical composite; even so, this mélange, in the writings of Kant and his ilk, had been used to ostracize a whole era, its religion, its art, its chivalric order, its scholarship, and all its "other usages." This method of passing judgment on the part of the Enlightenment is reminiscent of the trial of Galileo Galilei. For here, too, judges passed sentence on a phenomenon without actually realizing what they were condemning—effectively cutting away the ground on which they stood, their own roots. For in the absence of such roots, who could possibly appreciate who they were, what criteria they were basing their judgment on, and why their thought patterns, interests and outlook had developed in the way that they had? Who could have known at that time what this provenance and its condemnation, what the implications of this process of blackening and suppression on his own life and future might be, indeed what this might mean for the future of a whole society and culture? Awareness of the potential impact of the unconscious and the suppressed only began with Sigmund Freud.

The concept of "rebirth" has as its premise that of "demise." Yet who could say when that latter process was deemed to have started, when the *aetas media* began, and when the descent into darkness set in? Flavio Biondo had only treated the so-called *inclinatio imperii,* the downfall of the Roman Empire, claiming that this started with the Sack of Rome in 410; he had nothing to say about the demise of thought and civilization, or about the "almost complete destruction" of the genius of man. This latter hypothesis was only brought into play in the work of Kant, in fact. But the question still remained as to when the wellsprings of ancient high culture were supposed to have run dry? Or when European civilization had begun to embrace the "childish and the grotesque" and, divested of all its previous rationality, hide itself away in a state of "self-inflicted immaturity." Perhaps this occurred when Roman antiquity or Late Antiquity forgot the last vestiges of Greek? Or maybe when it no longer understood Aristotle? Then again, it may have come with the spread of the monotheistic, Judeo-Christian faith, which not only shunned polytheism but also in the Middle Ages, posed the greatest challenge to any attempt to renew Aristotelianism? Or could it have been with the final renunciation of animal hunts and gladiatorial contests? With Constantine the Great, maybe, that son of an Illyrian—a barbarian no less—and a barmaid, a man who ordered the execution of his own wife? Or did decline first set in when Theodosius the Great, the hitherto warlike emperor, knelt down in penitence at the feet of Saint Ambrose, the highly educated archbishop of the royal residential city of Milan? Or with the abolition of the ancient practices of augury and bloody animal sacrifices? Or the closure of heathen temples, and the cessation of the cults of Jupiter, Dionysus, Mithras, or Cybele (the Great Mother, or Magna Mater)? Or the transformation of the cults of Venus and *Dea Roma* into that of the Blessed Virgin Mary? Or finally with the much-maligned Goths, who took the first steps to renewing Rome and imparted the key foundations of dialectical reasoning to the Middle Ages? And how long did these supposed Dark Ages last?

In fact, nowhere did any such beginning or end worthy of the name, signifying clearly identifiable breaks or dramatic sea changes (proclaiming, say, that "from, or up to, this and this point, the Middle Ages began or darkness reigned") ever become apparent, nor were such junctures ever analyzed by proponents of the Enlightenment. Were Theodoric the Great and Chlodwig, who were traditionally regarded as "Germanic" warriors, and were contemporaries of Justinian, that peasant's son and barbarian from Illyria, to be seen already as "medieval" or rather still as "ancient" rulers? And consequently should the great compendia of Roman Law, first collected by that same Justinian, and which came to form the basis of the jurisprudence arising during the "Middle Ages," be seen as "medieval" achievements? And did the "Middle Ages" begin at a later date in Constantinople than they did in Italy or Gaul? Again, Enlightenment thinkers did not posit any cultural theory of the simultaneity of the dissimilar. The authors of the Renaissance unconsciously employed that three-phase model of time that is so familiar to modern ethnologists: the distant, golden Age of Heroes; the period within human recollection; and the "We" time of their own present. Nor was Kant beyond such schematic conceptions when he spoke of a "taste for the Beautiful and the Noble . . . in our age." He, too, came up with no clear, comprehensive answer on this score, nor did he propose any typology or sociology of total decline into darkness and the grotesque and test it against history. In fact, all Kant did was rely upon collective prejudices and on a fallacious cultural memory. He only had a vague conception floating before his mind's eye of the sixteenth and seventeenth centuries as the point when things changed for the better. However, unfounded theories are not merely groundless, they are above all uncritical. Indeed, they are akin to a state of irrational immaturity.

Definitive answers are a moot point here, anyhow. Every great civilization declines in a gradual way; and even while in decline it sets in motion transformations and transmissions of cultural knowledge; in other words it stimulates innovation in knowledge. Ancient Egypt and Babylon did not collapse in a day, nor did Rome, and no culture that learned from the Egyptians, such as the ancient Greeks for instance, ever built pyramids again. Rather; world history can be said to resemble the *Silva,* that primeval forest, which ancient and scholastic natural philosophers claimed had been the source of all the world's building material, or a well-tended vineyard in which the world-gardener uses a sharp blade to clear away old vines ready for burning. Dead wood and new shoots are in evidence at the same time. If one really wanted to try and posit a beginning and an end, one might rather point to the gradual worsening of the climate, to catastrophes that affected the whole of Europe and brought about drastic declines in population, notably the great waves of epidemic that broke over the continent in the sixth and the fourteenth centuries, when the deaths of hundreds of thousands of people awakened a desire for rebirth and a fresh start. Yet militating against such a "nature-based" periodization, and in favor rather of a consideration of the Renaissance era of beauty, poetry, and art that is supposed to have supplanted that medieval era, is the self-evident fact that the whole notion of the *aetes media* is founded in intellectual history. At best, this rebirth brought about the final fulfillment of a previous endeavor, which had going on for centuries, to appropriate the works of the Christian fathers, and the pagan poets, historians, and philosophers and to thereby effect a revival of ancient Rome. But how could this conscious, targeted, and systematically enacted desire for rebirth, this careful groundwork and all its early successes, be counted as the Middle Ages, and yet its later ramifications be counted as the modern age?

So it was that, just before the plague wave of the sixth century, Boethius, the proud history-conscious Roman whom the Gothic king Theodoric put to death, preserved for later "medieval" generations—who for various reasons had become alienated from ancient scholarship—the foundations that enabled such scholarship to be reborn. And so, whatever may have led up to it, the Renaissance—which actually began at the time of the Black Death, the reign of Charles IV, and the construction of Milan Cathedral—undoubtedly belongs to that same Middle Ages, while the modern age began—if indeed it did begin then, which is highly questionable, and is not merely a retrospective interpolation—sometime later. But every delimitation of "ages" is quite arbitrary; such ideological constructs only reveal the stance of the ideologue who devised them, and do not represent any objective structures of world history.

And yet we should not be berating the Enlightenment philosopher Kant as a person, but rather reserve our harshest criticism for him as a representative of an age eager for enlightenment, which in defiance of its own agenda propagated misjudgments that its proponents, appealing to the ideal of "Enlightenment," then proceeded to implant in the collective consciousness of subsequent centuries. In doing so, they completed a gradual process of defamation that had been going on for some three hundred years, which began in the realms of language and academic life, then drew in art and architecture, and finally ended up embracing the cultural totality of a long era. However exalted Kant's contribution to critical philosophy may have been, in matters of anthropology, art appreciation, and historical understanding, the bewigged Königsberg scholar was, like his Enlightenment comrades-in-arms, simply a child of his age, and these men not only knew nothing about the Middle Ages but also did not want to learn anything about it. Yet prejudices only obfuscate and blind people to truth.

The application of reason does not owe its existence to that Enlightenment of the seventeenth and eighteenth centuries; its "rebirth," namely the focus on a logic and dialectic that was strictly bounded by rules and hence susceptible to criticism, and the gradual evolution of the operations of formal logic, as described by developmental psychology, began many centuries earlier, almost a millennium before Kant, at the court of Charlemagne, and then intensifying in the tenth century. Constantly evolving through a process of ongoing cultural regeneration, it ultimately enabled Kant to stand on the shoulders of giants he knew nothing of, and gaze down condescendingly and develop his thoughts. Long before the "modern age," Europe had sallied forth to discover the world through an interplay of experience and critical thought.

This widening of horizons took place both close to home and farther afield, sometimes occurring in small steps and sometimes in giant leaps. At the start of the Middle Ages, to take an example from close to home, the area that would later become Germany (apart from the far west) had a small population and was backward, but abounded in marshland and dense primeval forests. Like islands in a sea, settlements were surrounded by vast swathes of barren land. The language spoken by its inhabitants, an early variant of the language of Kant, was wholly unsuited to any form of scholarship. This would only change over the coming centuries, as a result of historical developments. By the end of the medieval millennium, when the future Pope Pius II (r. 1458–1464) journeyed through these lands, the region had been transformed into a blossoming cultural landscape. The great forested regions of earlier times had been felled and settled, and the swamps had been largely drained. Lübeck, Hamburg, Magdeburg, and Leipzig were major urban centers whose influence spread beyond their localities, not to mention Frankfurt, Cologne, or the economically powerful cities of the Low Countries like Ghent or Bruges or others. Yet Königsberg in Prussia, the place that Immanuel Kant never left his whole life, owed its very existence to the crusading and chivalric posturings of the Bohemian king Ottokar, for whom this city's most famous son had nothing but vitriolic scorn. Its population grew, while efficient industry, a dense network of roads, and ever more ambitious feats of maritime exploration furnished it with extensive trading contacts. The country and people played an active part in the innovative, dynamic forces that shaped the age. Finally, Renaissance and humanism, and the rediscovery of ancient pagan poets and rhetoricians whose work was already widely known in the tenth and twelfth centuries, also reached the Germans.

Soon, this new learning went to the Germans' heads; disregarding their fundamentally Christian attitude, they found themselves in thrall to a fiction. Just then, around the middle of the fifteenth century, Italian humanists had found at Hersfeld Abbey a manuscript of the *Germania* by the ancient Roman historian Tacitus and taken it back to Italy to rescue it "from the prison of barbarism." When the Germans, first and foremost humanists like Jakob Wimpfeling, Beatus Rhenanus, Konrad Celtis, and Aventis, came to read this text, they suddenly discovered their "Germanic" roots, imagining themselves to be an ancient people—even more ancient, some gloated, than the much-vaunted French, Italians, Romans, and Greeks, older even than the peoples of the Bible, with a glorious early history that supposedly began with Noah's "son" Tuyscon. This divine ancestor figure taught them writing, songs, and laws. This, so these authors claimed, represented the beginnings of all civilization. German nationalism was to feed off this myth until well into the twentieth century. What did it matter that this history was all pure fabrication? The overabundance of German self-confidence that this tale engendered proved durable, surviving debunkings of the myth and over time revealing its darker sides. This catastrophic delusion of a glorious Germanic past, which no Enlightenment could stop or even efface, had its origins, then, precisely in this humanism. The beautiful and the terrible often share the same root.

The successive stages in the opening up of geographic and cultural horizons following the collapse of the Western Roman Empire speak for themselves; they also facilitated the expansion of trade throughout the whole of Europe. All manner of things that the fathers of the church, in their hostility to learning, might once have banned now found themselves challenged by diverse influences from far and wide: Byzantium (through the coronations of Charlemagne and Otto the Great); Asia Minor and the Middle East (through the Crusades, chiefly organized by the French); and Islam and Arabian science (through the Spanish *Reconquista*). In addition, in all Western centers of education, through the presence of Jewish scholars with their wide experience of the world, people and ideas that were once rejected or persecuted now sparked curiosity and scholarly enquiry. Indeed, it was precisely the knowledge that was brought by Jews, through their religious observance and deep understanding of the Bible, and the lasting cross-cultural transfer of learning that they set in train, which proved to be a thorn in the side of the church's deep antipathy to much scholarly research and enquiry. Without them, the whole academic culture of the West would not have developed in the way it did.

The Mongol invasions of the thirteenth century opened the eyes of the "Latins" to the Far East, to places like Karakorum and Cambaluc (Beijing), to the Indian subcontinent and Burma, Malaysia, and Indochina, and to Indonesia. As far as we know, the ancient Romans only penetrated as far as southeast Asia, though they did somehow seem to be aware of the existence of China. The advance of Mongol mounted warriors into the West proved to be an historic turning point, a decisive step in the process of globalization: for Europe reacted to the threat by undertaking a "learning offensive," countering the danger by dispatching expedition after expedition to the Far East, and sending papal legates and royal envoys, merchants, missionaries, and adventurers; the outcome was a positive welter of field reports on these unknown lands. Europe learned to explore the world, and the more it discovered, the more comprehensive and precise the intelligence it demanded. For the first time, there arose a form of global knowledge based on first-hand experience, an awareness of the sheer size of the Earth and the diversity of its peoples, and the desire to use the knowledge thus gained.

Thereafter, layer by layer, the clouds obscuring the West's centers of learning began to lift; new experiences opened up a panoramic view of unimagined expanses, raising new questions and constantly demanding new answers. From this point on, missionaries, merchants, and explorers from the beleaguered West prepared to go out into the world, taking the trade route along the Silk Road, venturing to the Middle East and China, sailing round the southern tip of Africa, and working toward the religious and commercial appropriation of the entire globe. This knowledge of the world soon brought with it—for good or for ill—a far-sightedness in strategic concerns. For example, it was this new sense of geostrategic awareness which, in around 1330, prompted the well-traveled and urbane diplomat, missionary, and Dominican monk Guillaume Adam (Guilielmus Adae) to prepare a sober, businesslike report born of his own experience (*De modo Sarracenos extirpandi*; "On the method of wiping out the Saracens"), which advocated a blockade of the Red Sea at the Straits of Aden by four war galleys with a complement of 1,200 men in order to choke off supplies to Egypt and so gain a decisive advantage in the crusading struggle for control of the Holy Land. Henceforth, for all the ostensibly diverse ends they were pursuing, all these missionaries, merchants, and military adventurers would set forth to explore the world quite literally hand in hand.

Yet silk or baptism, or winning gold or souls, were by no means their primary concerns. Rather, their ventures were driven by an unbounded thirst for knowledge. It was in this spirit that the Franciscan friar and adventurer Giovanni de Marignolli addressed Emperor Charles IV when he returned from exploring the Far East for fifteen years: "I, the most inquisitive explorer of all Indian lands, I who possess a more enquiring than virtuous cast of mind, desired insofar as I was able to know everything, and so exerted myself to a greater extent than any other that I have ever read about or known, to seek out the Wonders of the World."[7] The Chinese were amazed by such inquisitiveness. Odoric of Pordenone, another Minorite friar from Italy who traveled to China, had a troop of monkeys brought and displayed to him, precisely in order that he might see something amazing *(mirabile)*, "and, when he returned home, might report what novelties *(quid novum)* he had discovered."[8] The East soon came to realize that Westerners were in the grip of a mysterious, insatiable curiosity. An intercultural exchange of knowledge ensued, whose consequences can scarcely be exaggerated. When Rabban Sauma, a Uighur born in Cambaluc and a Nestorian Christian, was sent to the West in 1287 as an envoy of the Mongol Ilkhan Argun, then resident in Baghdad, and visited several seats of royal power, he remarked with astonishment in Naples on the restrained fighting taking place there at the time, which spared the civilian population. In Paris, he was less impressed by the Sainte-Chapelle than by the presence of "thirty thousand students" studying all kinds of different disciplines and who "busied themselves unceasingly with writing, and each and every one of them sustained by a grant from the king."[9] And indeed, universities and public, urban schools revolutionized the educational potential of the West from the twelfth and thirteenth centuries on. This observer from the Far East was astonished by this new departure; in fact, he saw it more clearly than the Europeans themselves, who were busy bringing it to fruition.

Ever since the "barbarians" had irrupted into the advanced civilization of the Mediterranean world, since the age of Alaric and Athaulf, a willingness to learn had become apparent that showed no signs of abating. Not least, this thirst for knowledge manifested itself in the form of a wave of renewal. Consequently, many far-reaching innovations and momentous advances can be observed throughout the centuries of the Middle Ages, in many different areas, repeatedly undermining the traditional body of knowledge and view of the world. These brought a new dynamic approach to thinking, faith, and experimentation. That "debased sentiment" that Kant decried discovered new logical modes of thought, which the logician in Könisgberg, due to his lack of knowledge of medieval manuscripts, had no inkling of. In his condemnation of Meister Eckhart, John XXII summarized this state of affairs in words that he adapted from the Epistle of St Paul to the Romans (12:3), accusing him of "desiring to know more than he ought to."[10] The effects and ramifications of these medieval waves of learning and research, observation, reflection, and experimentation are still very tangibly present nowadays. The general principle of scholarship, the Western culture of rationality, the Enlightenment, and globalization can all trace their origins back to this period.

The expanded educational sector by no means simply benefited the sciences. The secularization of thought, and its reorientation toward temporal affairs, was every bit as evident in daily life as in matters of faith, and among merchants just as much as in the upper echelons of the clergy. Anyway, for the most part clerics were those who constituted the intellectual elites, and it was from their ranks that the innovators and revolutionaries came. Countless organizational, institutional, and technical innovations became possible, and gained economic, political, or general cultural significance. As a characteristic example, we may cite early medieval efforts to impose a rational system of time, an innovation decreed by Charlemagne. These endeavors resulted in a calculation of time according to the now familiar system of B.C. and A.D. Despite the fact that this system is thought to have been devised by Eusebius, the Arian (and hence heretical) bishop of Caesarea in Palestine and the chronicler and biographer of Constantine, this mode of reckoning originally remained restricted to the Latin-Western world, before spreading right across the globe, irrespective of religions of cultural boundaries. Byzantine-Orthodox Christendom used the age of the Earth, the *Annus Mundi,* as its basis for calculating time—just as Judaism still does (albeit somewhat differently); while from early on, Islam measured the passage of time from the *Hijra* (622), the date on which the Prophet Muhammad migrated from Mecca to Medina; other civilizations used different methods again. Even the former West Gothic kingdom of Spain employed a curious "era" system that was peculiar to this realm. Ever since the reign of Charlemagne, it was only the Catholic Western world that consistently organized time according to the "Year of Our Lord"; and nowadays, under the rubric "common era; C.E." the entire world has fallen in line with this schema.

The medieval age was imbued with an uncommonly advanced sense of the practical, which manifested itself in several ways. For example, by then people were fully conversant with the workings of the crankshaft and the cogwheel, which enabled them not only to utilize water power in new ways but also to develop and apply new technologies—say, grain mills, fulling mills, hammer mills, pumping stations, and deep mining— all of which were later to ensure that the great philosopher, sitting at home in frosty Königsberg, did not have to fear hunger or the cold. In fact, the whole mining industry underwent a revolution at this time. Ore smelting witnessed great advances, which improved the quality of the castings and streamlined working practices.[11] In making their monumental bronze figures, the ancient Greeks and Romans could not make large castings; instead, they welded together smaller sections. But Charlemagne's bronze gates, the cast bronze doors known as Bernward's Doors that can now be seen at Saint Mary's Cathedral in Hildesheim, the cathedral doors in Gniezno (Gnesen), the Brunswick Lion, and the Capitoline She-Wolf *(Lupa Capitolina)* in Rome are all works of the Early and High Middle Ages that were cast in a single piece. We will never know the names of the technicians, engineers, and inventors who developed such technologies, but their skill and know-how have stood the test of time. From the fourteenth century on, a combination of these new highly developed metallurgical casting techniques with the introduction of gunpowder in the West revolutionized warfare (gunpowder had been invented in China some time before, but weapons technology had not kept pace there). Henceforth, firearms and cannon would decide the outcome of wars and power struggles. War in the Middle Ages, then, was also a child of rationality.

Similarly, medieval master builders could bring to bear outstanding technical expertise in their construction of truly free standing domes and cupolas—an engineering feat that the much-praised Greeks and Romans had never managed. And precise observation and rational mathematical extrapolation enabled the visual artists of the Late Middle Ages to apply single-point perspective to their paintings; this was an illusionistic technique that was never mastered by the advanced civilizations of antiquity, including ancient Greece and Rome. Unlike the Italian creators of the Renaissance, who single out the master builders of Pisa for praise, Immanuel Kant knew the architectural marvels of, say, Chartres Cathedral, the ensemble of ecclesiastical buildings in Pisa (the cathedral, baptistry, the Camposanto, and the Leaning Tower) only at second hand, from travelers' accounts or inadequate engravings, and not from his own experience. Likewise, he remained ignorant of courtly love poetry (Minnesang) and the epic poems of Middle High German, indeed of poetry and music in general, for his entire life. Kant's renowned "categorical imperative" comes across as a bloodless and contrived construct in comparison to the very true-to-life struggles that are played out in the Minnesang to keep passions in check, express higher ideals of "courtliness," "chivalry," "urbanity," and reconcile the desires of the flesh with eternal redemption. This tension informs the whole civilizing process of the Middle Ages and pervades our system of ethics to the present day.

Another achievement of this much-misunderstood era was to create, out of nothing, a rationally based monetary economy. The banking system was developed and the concept of "capital" devised, along with cashless money transfers. An elegant solution was also found to the problem of usury, resulting in the extension of credit becoming a respectable and legitimate business. This all manifested itself in the advent of an early form of European high finance, which in turn saw the increasing participation of wealthy individuals in political power. Here, then, were the origins of the triumphal onward march of entrepreneurship, money, and capital, which all financed Kant's university teaching program and nowadays provides the driving force behind the globalization of the world. Furthermore, the need to distribute financial risks saw the beginnings of maritime insurance. Publishing also blossomed, facilitating an economic expansion that had not been seen since antiquity. Techniques of trading were perfected; new forms of mercantile societies like the Great Ravensburg Trading Company (1380–1530) came into being and benefited from improved methods of production. Water and land transport became more efficient, with shipbuilding experiencing an upturn the like of which had never been seen before. Not only merchant vessels like the Hanseatic cog and the caravel became more sophisticated as a result; fighting galleons also became larger and developed more rakish lines that made them faster and more dangerous. Even as far back as the Carolingian period, the harnessing of horses was made more efficient by the invention of the horse collar, a device that enabled teams to pull heavy carts. The construction of roads that were suitable for commercial transport and not, as in Roman times, simply for military purposes, saw the growth of a dense communications infrastructure.

World maps and the study of nature underwent profound change during this period. The improved state of knowledge in the medieval period clearly rendered obsolete the view of the world reflected in the map produced by the ancient geographer and astronomer Ptolemy. Mathematical knowledge and skills played their part in this momentous change. One thing led to another: from astrology and astronomy, mathematics and expanding geographical knowledge developed. Emperors, kings, and popes, in fact all kinds of rulers, took a keen interest; after all, they reasoned, such knowledge would accrue to their benefit. For instance, the mathematician, astronomer, and astrologer Regiomontanus was active at the court of Frederick III. And with his so-called earth apple (1493–1494), which incorporated information gleaned from Portuguese scholars connected to that country's royal court and which is reckoned to be history's first "globe," the Nuremberg geographer Martin Behaim provided a summation of all the terrestrial and cosmological knowledge of the Middle Ages.

Although the Earth had long since been regarded as a sphere (a radical departure from some ancient authors' conception of it as a disk), for many centuries it has also been seen, in line with the worldview of Ptolemy, which was approved by the fathers of the church, as resting immobile in the center of the Cosmos. Albertus Magnus and Nicholas of Cusa succeeded in shifting the Earth away from its central position, and even in establishing the idea of it as a body in motion. And now Behaim had managed to depict in three dimensions all the known continents of Europe, Asia, and Africa (not yet America), the Azores, India, Indonesia and all the world's great oceans and trade routes on his globe—a masterpiece of scholarship, abstraction, and technical expertise. Somewhat earlier, Paolo Toscanelli began to calculate distances from Europe to China and India. The German Georg von Peuerbach (d. 1461), a friend and teacher of Regiomontanus, attempted to work out the distance from Earth of Halley's Comet, which appeared in 1456. Peuerbach's ambition was to work out the total dimensions of the Cosmos. Vasco da Gama and Columbus both took copies of his *Ephemerides* on their voyages of exploration to uncharted shores.

And now, it seemed, this "earth apple" was beginning to turn on its own axis and to rotate around the Sun. As early as 1509, in his *Comentariolus*, Nikolaus Copernicus, who had studied law in Krakow, Bologna, and Padua, and who had earned a doctorate as a physician, first broached and advanced proofs for his doctrine that the sun stood at the center of the Cosmos and that the Earth moved around it, along with the other planets. His next publication on the subject, his most important work *De revolutionibus orbium caelestium,* only followed several decades later, in 1543. As is so often the fate of innovative theories, it by no means met with universal acclaim straightaway, Even so, it was a scientific revolution, a paradigm shift, although the groundwork for this breakthrough had occurred some decades previously, in the work of Nicholas of Cusa and Regiomontanus. This momentous finding lay, so to speak, on the outstretched palm of the Middle Ages as it quit the stage, ready for the modern era to pick it up and run with it. And yet, the notion of the Earth no longer being at the center of creation, and of Man no longer being God's crowning achievement, was deeply alarming to contemporaries. Unrest and fear gripped humanity at this "'narcissistic wound' inflicted on the humanist ego by the Copernican revolution."[12] For sure, though this kind of knowledge had virtually no effect on the peasantry, its impact was all the greater on the university-trained theologians, astrologers, and other scholars. Creation was clearly in need of a new interpretation—but where to begin? With questions such as this, the Middle Ages laid down an unprecedented challenge to the modern era, which even now has not found any conclusive answer.

The measuring of the entire Earth from West to East and (an even more revolutionary step) from North to South—that is moving from the temperate zone to what, according to ancient theories was the zone closest to the Sun, where everything was overheated, burning up and boiling, and where consequently, no man dared set foot—this steady advance across the world quite literally set in motion the process of globalization that is now, remorselessly, coming back to haunt the "Old World." This encroachment took place on various levels: those of scholarship, thought, the realm of personal imagination and interests, and communication, as well through trade, war, and commercial activity. When Columbus, equipped with a magnetic compass, set sail westward in 1492 to try and find a passage to the East, he was only logically continuing a process that had already begun long before. This Genoese seafarer, who was sailing in the name of His Most Catholic Majesty of Spain, carried in his baggage the *Milione* of the Venetian explorer Marco Polo and the (wholly fictitious) travel report of the English adventurer "John Mandeville." Once Europeans set foot in the Americas, medieval inventions such as improved swords, firearms, and cuirasses, plus the warhorses of the conquistadors, brought about the demise of the indigenous civilizations of the Incas and the Aztecs, whose most deadly weapons were nothing but sharp blades made out of obsidian, a volcanic rock. The fact that even Columbus hunted down native people in the Americas, refusing to have his captives baptized so that he could sell them on the European market reveals something about the tension that subsequently occasionally arose between missionary and mercantile interests, but in essence underscores the tried and tested cooperation that had been going on between them for centuries.

Before long, the most violent excesses were being perpetrated, as entire alien cultures were wiped out; it was a long time before these Indian "savages" were accorded any human dignity.

The Middle Ages created the bases of modern nations and "invented" the burgher—a member of an urban community who was furnished with collective privileges and protected by an autonomous jurisdiction, and who proceeded to completely unhinge the aristocratic-agrarian world of Late Antiquity and the Early Middle Ages; his later descendants continued to dominate European politics and culture right up to the eighteenth and nineteenth centuries. Not least, then, freedom—political and social freedom, and freedom of thought—may be counted as a signal achievement of those much-maligned centuries of the Middle Ages, for they laid the theoretical foundation of such a concept through their recourse to the notion of "free will," in just the same way as proponents of the Enlightenment. But they formulated the idea through the clash between the pope and the emperor, between temporal and spiritual authority, between the city ruler and the citizenry, between the manorial seigneur and the village community. In particular, it was those burghers who had attained wealth and power who out of their very real, daily needs formulated and laid claim to the large majority of those rights to freedom, which centuries later would come to be enacted as universal human rights.[13] This notion of free will even put faith and the church under pressure, as evidenced by the newly revived history of heresy and then the Inquisition from the eleventh century onward. Kant had not the slightest conception of all this when he sweepingly decried the ways of life, learning, art, ad manners of the centuries before Michelangelo and Milton as being disfigured by the "childish and grotesque." But, as we have seen, his judgment carried much weight, and still counts for much even now.

Not just faith, church, and heresies succumbed to this great change, but entire kingdoms, principalities, and collectives. They became, as it were, the first "victims," or beneficiaries, of the medieval culture of learning and the secularization processes to which this gave rise. Ever since the ninth century, the various descendants of Charlemagne, from the twelfth century the kings of Europe, and subsequently the nation-states of the continent had regarded one another with deep suspicion. The result was an endless succession of political, economic, intellectual, religious, or confessional conflicts. The development of a self-balancing European system of power, bringing together antagonistic secular and religious authorities, facilitating political freedom, and generating diplomacy, expressed itself in a smooth process of abstraction of all public authority, relentlessly spurred on by contemporaries, which impelled such authority toward the formation of states. Finally, in his infamous work *Il Principe (The Prince)*, Niccolò Machiavelli (1469–1529) displayed an aptitude for analysis of social questions that can definitely be interpreted as a summation of all the experiences of the final decades of the Middle Ages, which its author— who in his capacity as former secretary to the Florentine Republic had served it by acting as an envoy to the king, emperor, and pope, and who had experienced the torture perpetrated by princely rule at first hand— was intent upon passing down to succeeding generations. Only "armed prophets have conquered, while all unarmed ones have been destroyed," as one of the passage in *Il Principe* (Chapter 6) informs us. The "Holy Roman Empire and the German Nation" played no part in the insights offered by Machiavelli. This medieval *imperium* mutated into an entity that the historian Samuel Pufendorf would later call a "misshapen monstrosity."[14] Rome, the locus of memory that for so long had fueled its once universally valid doctrines, had now fallen into desolation and neglect. Its Roman name may have remained to the last, but this empire gradually lost more and more of its Roman-ness and instead became with each new generation increasingly "German" and provincial.[15] The Western monarchies were to reap the benefit of its decline.

Machiavelli's insights, his pessimistic view of humanity, and his didactic *Discorsi* all fed off examples from the ancient world. Livy was his Bible. As he stated in Book 1 Chapter 10 of *The Discourses*: "From the study of Roman history we may also learn how a good government is to be established." And the *Principe*, his introduction to how such a successful regime might be created, straightaway recommended in its dedication to Lorenzo de'Medici, the nephew of Pope Leo X, the *"continua lezione delle (cose) antique"* ("a constant reading of all things ancient"), yet it did not shun more recent, that is medieval, examples either. It was the political experience of the final decades of the medieval period and at the same time the turning away from that era that was being articulated here and that availed itself of an idiosyncratic interpretation of Roman antiquity that was wholly focused on contemporary circumstances. Thus, Machiavelli claimed, it is generally true to say of men that they are "ungrateful, fickle, false, cowardly, and covetous" (Chapter 17). The Prince, the Florentine author maintained, should therefore rely solely upon himself and, as

Machiavelli concluded in what was soon to become a notorious phrase summarizing his thesis, should understand how to avail himself "one of both the beast and the man" ("*a uno principe è necessario sapere bene usare la bestia e l'uomo*"; Chapter 18). This Prince or king figure rose above the condition of mere humanity. His status, the "status principis" was in fact the starting point for all early modern, and hence modern conceptions of the "state." Such a "state" was not a collective or confederation; rather, the state was the Prince. He became a fictitious personage, released from all the countless individuals guided by various interests, a single personage that guaranteed unity of action, and who dispensed both Good and Ill, and from whom his subjects might expect both oppression and help, and who possessed both an attractive and a forbidding face. Indeed, this emerging state now had a face, which could take on the countenance of a man or of a beast.

The Enlightenment thinker Kant and his contemporaries were heirs to the age they denigrated, not its conquerors. They stood on the shoulders of others, yet were unaware of doing so. They despised what was in fact supporting them. Of course, these Enlightenment figures were passing judgment before the discovery of historicism, prior to the experience of the change not only of reality but also of modes of perception and experience of reality itself and the associated relativism of values, even prior to an awareness of the phenomenon of cultural evolution.[16] Trammeled by the traditions of their youth, they paid homage to an idealized image of antiquity which was not affirmed by critical academic history, and which itself had been formed and shaped by the final decades of the Middle Ages. Moreover, they speculated, and put their thoughts down on paper, before their own movement, namely the Enlightenment, had developed any sense of how devastating the methodical insufficiencies of an anachronistic approach were, which led all scientific research astray, and before the corresponding conclusions had been drawn for the study of all past ages. They still had no inkling of the immediacy of every era to God, whose existence admittedly many of them doubted anyway.

Nevertheless, their judgment, their misjudgment, embedded itself in the cultural memory of Europe, and still resonates to this day. Yet things suppressed have also left their mark there. "We are still in the midst of the Late Middle Ages," wrote one journalist recently when criticizing the loutish victory celebrations of the German national football team.[17] Everything that is reprehensible, repellent, and brutal, like torture, religious fanaticism, fundamentalism, or obscenity is popularly regarded as a "relapse back to medieval times," even into the "Dark Middle Ages," instead of being viewed as the outbreak of a newly minted kind of immaturity that has everything to do with current social failings and nothing to do with the Middle Ages. In this way, such behavior is conveniently pigeonholed into some fictitious, alien, and shunned age, and in the process shunted off and covertly excused: it's not our fault, runs the reasoning, but that of our dark past. Once again, at least in Germany, it appears as though this sort of prejudice is being officially endorsed, in the same way as the Soldier King once struck the Middle Ages from the curriculum. These are in fact the "childish and grotesque" manifestations of the present, just as those who condemned the medieval period in the eighteenth century were the ones at fault. In truth, the Middle Ages were more mature and wise, more inquisitive, inventive and with a finer feel for art, more revolutionary in their deployment of reason and their thinking than the Enlightenment gave them credit for, and than most people living now, at the start of the twenty-first century, also commonly imagine. At the same time, this medieval age was more humble and modest in its own assessment of itself. Even its most outstanding, groundbreaking thinkers considered themselves mere dwarfs standing on the shoulders of giants, on the shoulders, that is, of the collective experience of past ages; as a result, they saw much farther than the tallest of the giants supporting them. And this enabled them to point the way forward to a reason-based future.

The groundwork for the intellectual and cultural unity of Europe, the unity of the many kingdoms and nations, was laid in the Middle Ages.[18] In its questing, surging, expanding ferment, it was one of the most unsettled, innovative periods of European history. It rescued for posterity the better part of the scholarship of antiquity. Without the monks of the ninth and tenth centuries, without the scholars of the eleventh, twelfth, and thirteenth centuries, all that would have survived of this great body of knowledge would have been the stock of manuscripts held in the archives of Byzantium and by the Arabs, along with the ruins and treasure hoards buried in the ground. But who else, after the fall of Constantinople and the religion-induced ossification of Arab scholarship from the thirteenth century onward, would have shown the slightest interest in the treasures of the ancient world? It was the Latin Middle Ages, which, since Charlemagne, had repeatedly revisited and appealed to Antiquity and schooled its cultural elites in the language, art, and thought of the ancients, and which then used this learning to hone its view of the world, and to strive to perfect its expertise so that it might prove itself in that world. This same tendency also led that era to adopt a receptive approach to each and every encounter with things passed down and alien, even things hostile, and to inculcate in it a robust attitude that did not shun foreign religions. Time and again, the people of the Middle Ages proved themselves adept at appropriating the knowledge that was handed down to them and developing it further, originating and shaping new concepts, and revolutionizing science and their own worldview. This Middle Ages was eminently creative. It discovered and trod the path into the wider world, and in so doing became the springboard from which the world advanced to the modern era.

ABBREVIATIONS

NOTES

SELECTED BIBLIOGRAPHY

INDEX

Abbreviations

Cod. Car	Codex Carolinus
DA	Deutsches Archiv für Erforschung des Mittelalters
HZ	Historische Zeitschrift
LexMA	Lexikon des Mittelalters
MGH	Monumenta Germaniae Historica

Editions are abbreviated as follows:

Capit.	Capitularia regum Francorum
Conc.	Concilia
Const.	Constitutiones et acta publica imperatorum et regum
Epp.	Epistolae
Epp. Sel.	Epistolae selectae
LdL	Libelli de lite imperatorum et pontificum
SS	Scriptores
SS rer. Germ.	Scriptores rerum Germanicarum in usum scholarum separatim editi
SS rer. Germ.	Scriptores rerum Germanicarum, Nova series
Migne PL	(Migne) Patrologia Latina
QFIAB	Quellen und Forschungen aus italienischen Archiven und Bibliotheken
Reg. Imp.	Regesta Imperii (sources and research findings from Italian archives and libraries)
VSWG Beihefte	Vierteljahrschrift für Sozial- und Wirtschaftsgeschichte Beihefte
ZRG	Zeitschrift der Savigny-Stiftung für Rechtsgeschichte
Germ.	Germanistische Abteilung
Kan.	Kanonistische Abteilung

Notes

1. Boethius and the Rise of Europe

1. Quoted from Brian E. Daley, "Boethius' Theological Tracts and Early Byzantine Scholasticism," *Mediaeval Studies* 46 (1984): 158–191, quotation at 160.

2. Theologia "Scholarium" I,25 and II,9 ed. C. J. Mews (Corpus Christianorum Cont. Med. 13), 329 and 410–411.

3. Ulrich Schindel, "Zu spätantiken Wissenschaftsgeschichte: Eine anonyme Schrift über die Philosophie und ihre Teile" (Paris: BN 7530). Nachrichten der Akademie der Wissenschaften zu Göttingen I. Phil-Hist Klasse 2006, I (Göttingen, 2006).

4. Though criticized by some scholars, for its unparalleled analysis of the research findings of the Soviet neuropsychologist Alexander Luria, see Walter J. Ong, *Orality and Literacy: The Technologizing of the Word* (London, 2002). This approach was successfully adapted for historical analysis by Hanna Vollrath, "Das Mittelalter in der Typik oraler Kulturen," *Historische Zeitschrift* 233 (1981): 571–594; cf. Johannes Fried, *Der Schleier der Erinnerung: Gründzüge einer historischen Memorik* (Munich, 2004), 80–152.

5. Orosius, *Historiarum adversum paganos,* libri VII, VII,43,5–6, ed. Carl Zangemeister. *Corpus Scriptorum Ecclesiasticorum Latinorum* 5 (Vienna, 1882), 560.

6. Ulfilas, as reported almost a century later by the church historian Philostorgios the Arian, Ecclesiastical History II,5; quoted in Herwig Wolfram, *Die Goten von den Anfängen bis zur Mitte des sechsten Jahrhunderts* (Munich, 1990), 84.

7. This example is from Elfriede Stutz, *Gotische Literaturdenkmäler* (Stuttgart, 1966), 60.

8. Cf. for example Variae IV,32: Magni Aurelii Cassiodori Senatoris, *Opera* I, ed. A. J. Fridh. Corpus Christianorum Ser. Lat. 96. Turnhout: 1973.

9. Aarne Stüven, *Rechtliche Ausprägungen der civilitas im Ostgotenreich: Mit vergleichender Berücksichtigung des westgotischen und burgundischen Rechts*. Europäische Hochschulschriften, Reihe 2: Rechtswissenschaft 1742. (Frankfurt a.M. and elsewhere: 1995).

10. *Edictum Theoderici regis*, ed. Friedrich Blume, MGH Leges 5 (1868).

11. Detlef Liebs, *Römische Jurisprudenz in Gallien (2. bis 8. Jahrhundert)*, Freiburger Rechtsgeschichtliche Abhandlungen NF 38 (Berlin, 2002), 157–163 and 166–176.

12. *Anastasis Childerici I. Francorum regis sive Thesaurus sepulcraris . . . auctore Ioanne Iacobo Chifletio* (Antwerp, 1655). The many illustrations in this volume are uniformly devoid of any color; all colored editions are the result of reconstruction suggestions made by the Central Museum of Roman and Germanic History in Mainz; cf. Michael Müller-Wille, *Zwei religiöse Welten: Bestattungen der fränkischen Könige Childerich und Chlodwig*. Abhandlungen der Geistes- und Sozialwiss. Klasse der Akademie der Wissenschaften und der Literatur Main, 1998 I. (Stuttgart, 1998).

13. It should be noted that certain of the prestigious grave goods placed in Childeric's grave, such as the golden bull's head decoration of the horse harness and the more than 300 golden bees, do not point to hybrid culture, being of apparently eastern provenance. Cf. Fried, *Der Schleier der Erinnerung*, 272 and 337–338.

14. Cf. Liebs, *Jurisprudenz in Gallien*.

15. *Kommentar zu den Liedern der Edda*, ed. Klaus von See et al. (vols. 1–5 published so far), (Heidelberg, 1997–2006).

2. Gregory the Great and the New Power of the Franks

1. Hermann Nehlsen, "Die Entstehung des öffentlichen Strafrechts bei den germanischen Stämmen," *Gerichtslauben-Vorträge. Freiburger Festkolloquium zum 75. Geburtstag von Hans Thieme*, ed. Karl Kroeschell (Sigmaringen, 1983), 3–16; Nehlsen, "Reaktionsformen der Gesellschaft auf Verletzung und Gefährdung von Gemeinschaftsinteressen in Spätantike und frühem Mittelalter bei den germanischen Stämmen" (Vortag gehalten auf dem 33. Deutschen Rechthistorikertag, Jena, September 12, 2000).

2. Decree of Childebert II from the year 596: MGH Capit. I Nr. 7 cc. 2 and 5, pp. 15–16.

3. Cf. for example Lex Baiuvariorum I, 14; however, the threat of punishment goes back to the sixth century. On the dating of the law, cf. Peter Landau, *Die Lex Baiuvariorum. Entstehungszeit, Enstehungsort und Charakter von Bayerns ältester Rechts- und Geschichtsquelle*. SB München 2004,3 (Munich, 2004).

4. Contin. Fredegar. c. 13 cf. Also ibid. c. 17 and 20, in *Quellen zur Gechichte des 7. und 8. Jahrhunderts*, Unter der Leitung von Herwig Wolfram, 284–291. Ausgewählte Quellen zur Deutschen Geschichte des Mittelalters: Freiherr vom Stein-Gedächtnisausgabe IVa (Darmstadt, 1982).

5. Cf. Bonifatius ep. 80, MGH Epp. 3, pp. 356–361.

6. MGH Conc. 2, pp. 1–4.

7. First substantiated in Cod. Carol. 6 of 755, MGH Epp. 3, p. 488,36.

8. On the anointing of 754: "Vita Stephani II," ed. Louis Duchesne, *Le Liber Pontificalis* I (Paris, 1886), 448; on the identification with Saint Peter: Codex Carolinus 10, MGH Epp. 3, pp. 501–505; the missive from Pope Zacharias on the royal anointing of 751, which we might expect to encounter, does not exist; presumably the two editors of the so-called Fredegar and independent chroniclers Childbrand and Nibelung (c. 33 and c. 36), father and son, who alternate in 751/753, mistakenly date the papal assent that was only given at the anointing of 754 (which they make no mention of) back to 751: Contin. Fredegari (see note 4 in this chapter), 298–303.

9. For Saint Peter as a helper in battle, see Contin. Fredegari c. 37 (see note 4 in this chapter), 302–305.

10. Cod. Car. 10, MGH Epp. 3, pp. 501–505.

11. "Vita Stephani II," ed. Louis Duchesne, *Le Liber Pontificalis* I Paris 1886, pp. 454–455.

12. Cod. Car. 11 (March/April 757), MGH Epp. 3, pp. 504–507. In actual fact, a series of towns in the Romagna, the exarchate, and the Pentapolis that should be restored to the pontificate were mentioned here by name. This process of restoration seems to have taken place step by step.

13. See section entitled "The Crisis of the Carolingian Empire under Louis the Pious" in Chapter 3.

14. Cod. Car. 45, MGH Epp. 3, pp. 560–563. Here p. 561, 13–14.

3. Charlemagne and the First Renewal of the Roman Empire

1. Here, from a theological standpoint, see Karl Kardinal Lehmann, "Augustinus als Lehrer der "Gnade"—Ein Blick auf Wirkung und Rezeption in der Gegenwart," in *Gnade—Freiheit—Rechtfertigung: Augustinische Topoi und ihre Wirkungsgeschichte*, ed. Cornelius Mayer, Andfreas E. J. Grote, Christof Müller, pp. 73–94. Akademie der Wissenschaften und der Literatur zu Mainz, Abh. der Geistes- und Sozialwiss, Klasse 2007, 3 (Stuttgart, 2007); the quotation from Saint Augustine appears there on p. 74.

2. On calculation at the court and in the environs of Charlemagne, see Arno Borst, *Die karolingische Kalenderreform*. MGH Schriften 46 (Hanover, 1998); also Borst, ed., *Schriften zur Komputistik im Frankenreich von 721 bis 818*. MGH Quellen zur Geistesgeschichte des Mittelalters 21 in three parts (Hanover, 2006): here Part 1 Introduction, pp. 1–204, Part 2 p. 867 for the following quotation.

3. "Vita Karoli," c. 16, ed. O. Holder-Egger. MGH SS rer. Germ 25 (Hanover and Lepizig, 1911), 20.

4. On the so-called Cologne Memorandum, cf. Johannes Fried, "Papst Leo III besucht Karl den Großen in Paderborn oder Einhards Schweigen," *Historische Zeitschrift* 272 (2001): 281–326.

5. The so-called Symmachian Falsifications from the period around 500: Constitutum Silvestri: *Nemo iudicabit primam sedem,* which in an altered form was included in the *"Decretum gartiani; C.* 9 q. 3 c.13. Cf. Leo II's purification oath of 799, MGH Epp. 5 p. 63: *a nemine iudicatus.*

6. "Charlemagne (the most pious) and exalted, crowned by God, the greatest and most peace-bringing emperor (of the Romans), to you be given life and victory!"— the two principal sources are: *Annales regni Francorum,* ed. Friedrich Kurze. MGH SS rer. Germ [6] (Hanover, 1895), on 801 see p. 112 (remarkably, the editing changed the wording of the proclamation, by having the coronation, the acclamation, and the *Laudes* occur at the same time, ibid p. 113); *Liber Pontificalis,* ed. L Duchesne, vol. 2 (Paris, 1892) p. 7. On the interpretation of this acclamation, cf. Ernst H. Kantorowicz, *Univeristy of California Publications in History,* vol. 33, *Laudes regiae: A Study in Liturgical Acclamations and Mediaeval Rulership* (Berkeley/Los Angeles: University of California Press, 1946), 83–84. Einhard mentions Charlemagne's anger, Vita Karoli c.28, ed O. Holder-Egger (MGH SS rer. Germ. [25]), Hanover 1911, p. 32.

7. MGH Capit. I, No. 46 c.13 p. 132.

8. On this point, cf. Wolfram Brandes, *"Tempora periculosa sunt:* Eschatologisches im Vorfeld der Kaiserkrönung Karls des Großen," *Das Frankfurter Konzil von 794: Kristallisationspunkt karolingischer Kultur,* ed. Rainer Berndt SJ, vol. 1, pp. 49–79. Quellen und Abhandlungen zur mittelrheinischen Kirchengeschichte 80, 2 vols. (Mainz, 1997).

9. On the following, see MGH Capit. I pp. 91–102 No. 33 as well as pp. 120–126 No. 43–44 (805 December/806 January).

10. *"Insipientia, quae tegeabatur pallio caliginis."* Paschasius Radbertus, Vita s. Adalhardi c.50 Migne PL 120 Sp. 1534C.

11. *"Quis senatum populi ad tantam ineptiam deduxisset?"* On this and the following, see Johannes Fried, *Donation of Constantine and Constitutum Constantini: The Misinterpretation of a Fiction and Its Original Meaning,* Millennium-Studien 3 (Berlin and New York, 2007), 88–109.

12. Gelasius ep. 12, Andreas Thiel, Epistolae Romanorum Pontificum genuinae I, Braunsberg 1867, pp. 349–358, here pp. 350–351.

13. Johannes Fried, "Der karolingische Herrschaftsverband im 9.Jh zwischen 'Kirche' und 'Königshaus,'" *Historische Zeitschrift* 235 (1982): 1–43; also Fried, *"Gens* und *regnum,* Wahrnehmungs- und Deutungskategorien politischen Wandels im frühen Mittelalter. Bemerkungen zur doppelten Theoriebindung des Historikers," in *Sozialer Wandel im Mittelalter: Wahrnehmungsformen, Erklärungsmuster, Regelungsmechanismen,* ed. Jürgen Miethke and Klaus Schreiner, 73–104 (Sigmaringen, 1994).

14. Johannes Fried, "Ludwig der Fromme, das Papsttum und die fränkische Kirche," in *Charlemagne's Heir: New Perspectives on the Reign of Louis the Pious (810–840),* ed. Peter Godman and Roger Collins, 231–273 (Oxford: Clarendon Press, 1990).

15. Adelheid Hahn, "Das Hludowicianum: Die Urkunde Ludwigs d. Fr. für die römische Kirche von 817," *Archiv für Diplomatik* 21 (1975; published 1977): 15–135.

4. Consolidation of the Kingdoms

1. Nicholas I, ep. 71 = Decretum Gratiani D. 19 c. 1.

2. First quotation: *Annals of St Bertin to 864,* ed. Reinhold Rau. Quellen zur karolingischen Reichsgeschichte 2 (Freiherr von Stein-Gedächtnisausgabe 6), 130; second quotation: Anastasius's dedication to Pope Nicolas I: MGH Epp 7, p. 397, 15–6: *vicem namque in terris possides Dei.*

3. Cf. Heiko Steuer, "Das Leben in Sachsen zur Zeit der Ottonen," in *Otto der Große, Madgeburg und Europa,* ed. Matthias Puhle, 2 vols. (Mainz, 2001), here the essay volume, 89–107.

4. Joachim Wollasch, *Cluny, Licht der Welt: Aufstieg und Niedergang der klösterlichen Gemeinschaft* (Zurich, 1996), here, p. 167 for the quoatation by Urban II, and pp. 238–245 on the depredation of the monasteries.

5. The End of Days Draws Menacingly Close

1. Cf. Johannes Fried, "Die Endzeit fest im Griff des Positivismus?" *Historische Zeitschrift* 275 (2002): 281–321, here p. 289.

2. Elisabeth Magnou-Nortier, "La place du concile du Puy (v. 994) dans l'évolution de l'idée du paix," in *Mélanges offertes à Jean Dauvillier,* ed. Elisabeth Magnou-Nortier, 489–506, here p. 499 (Toulouse, 1979).

3. *Ælfric's Colloquy,* ed. G. N. Garmonsway, pp. 33–34 (Exeter, UK: Exeter Medieval English Texts, 1978).

4. On this process, cf. "Introduction," *Dialektik und Rhetorik im früheren und hohen Mittelalter.* Schriften des Historischen Kollegs 27, ed. Johannes Fried, vii–xviii, here xii–xiv (Munich, 1997).

5. Quoted in Fried, "Introduction," xvii.

6. See section entitled "The Consequences of the Papal Schism in Europe" in Chapter 11.

7. Nithard, *Historiarum* III: 5, "Strasbourg" (MGH SS rer. Germ. 44), ed. Ernst Müller, 35–37 Hanover 1907. On the matter of allegiance, compare the oath sworn by Charlemagne in 802: MGH Capit. I S, 102 Nr. 34. On "Fulbert," see *The Letters and Poems of Fulbert of Chartres,* ed. Frederick Behrends. Oxford Medieval Texts 39 (Oxford, 1976), 90–92; in the "Decretum" C 22 q. 5 c. 18 and in the Libri Feodorum 2F6.

8. Fulbert, *Tractatum contra Judeos* (Migne, OL 141, 307–308).

9. Chronicon S. Benigni Divionensis, MGH SS 7, p. 236.

10. Anselm, *Gesta episcopum Leodeciensium* c.58 and c.66, MGH SS 7, p. 230.

11. "Roman superstition should be put on trial, Roman adultery is destroying the Empire. In contravention of ecclesiastical law, one Pope is sitting over another. Such evil was devised in order to acquire gold and silver." Hermann Grauert, ed., "Rom und—Gunther der Eremit?" *Historisches Jahrbuch* 19 (1898): 240–287, here 254–255.

12. "De sancta Romana Ecclesia," *Kaiser, Könige und Papst,* vol. 4,1, ed. Percy Ernst Schramm, 143–170 (Stuttgart, 1970).

13. Ludwig Schmugge, *Kirche, Kinder, Karrieren: Päpstliche Dispense von der unehelichen Geburt im Spätmittelalter* (Zurich, 1995).

14. MGH Const. I pp. 539–541, Nr. 382. The quotations are taken from Horst Fuhrmann, "Die Wahl des Papstes—In historischer Überblick," in *Geschicht in Wissenschaft und Unterricht* 9 (1958): 762–780, here p. 769 ff. (abridged and updated) in Fuhrmann, *Einladung ins Mittelalter* [beck'sche Reihe] Munich 2000, pp. 135–150.

6. "The True Emperor Is the Pope"

1. Hubert Mordek, "Proprie auctoritates apostolice sedis: Ein zweiter Dictatus papae Gregors VII.?" in DA 28 (1972), 105–132; here 129 c.15; cf. Myron Wojtowytsch in ibid. 40 (1984), 612–621.

2. Matthew 24:12, quoted in Gregory VII. Reg. I,18; I,29; II, 40; VIIII, 2; ed. Erich Caspar (MGH Epp. Sel. 2) vag.51 ed. *The Epistolae Vagantes of Pope Gregory VII,* ed. and trans. by H. E. J. Cowdrey. Oxford Medieval Texts. (Oxford, 1972).

3. Gregory VII. Reg. II, 45 (ed. Caspar).

4. The extensive body of literature on the papal legates cannot be enumerated here; the older institution of the legates is treated in Stefan Weiis, *Die Urkunden der päpstlichen Legaten von Leo IX bis Coelestin III (1049–1198).* Beihefte zu J. F. Böhmer, Regesta Imperii 13 (Cologne, Weimar, Vienna, 1995); as an example of the jurisdiction of the delegations, see Harald Müller, *Päpstliche Delegationsgerichtsbarkeit in der Normandie (12. und frühes 13. Jahrhundert)* Studien und Dokumente zur Gallia Pontificia 4, 1/2, 2 vols. (Bonn, 1997).

5. From collections of letters from the reign of Henry IV, MGH Briefe der deutschen Kaiserzeit 5 (Weimar, 1950), 33–35, no. 15.

6. Reg. IX, 3 mentions donations of Constantine and Charlemagne, and undoubtedly alludes in the case of the latter to the "Pacta" of the Carolingian and Ottonian kings for the Roman Church; likewise, the reference to Constantine may primarily refer to the patrimonies of the Roman Church, which according to the "Liber Pontificalis" the first Christian emperor generously donated to the Roman Church, and not to the "Constitutum Constantini."

7. Luis Weckman, *Las Bulas Alejandrinas de 1493 y la Teoria Política del Papado Medieval. Estudio de la Supremacia Papal sobre Islas 1091–1493,* introducción por

Ernst H. Kantorowicz. Universidad Nacional Autónoma de Mexico. Pubblicaciones del Instituto de Historia 11 (Mexico City, 1949).

8. On the following subject, cf. Johannes Fried, "Der Pakt von Canossa: Individuelles und kollektives Gedächtnis, Schritte zur Wirklichkeit durch Erinnerungsanalyse," in *Die Faszination der Papstgeschichte: Neue Zugänge zum frühen und hohen Mittelalter,* ed. Wilfrid Hartmann and Klaus Herbers. Beihefte der Regesta Imperii 28 (Cologne, Weimar, Vienna, 2008), 133–197.

9. Ep. vag 18, ed. Cowdrey.

10. *Liber de unitate ecclesiae conservanda* c.38, MGH LdL p. 266.

11. On this question (in opposition to Alfons M. Stickler), see Hartmut Hoffmann, *Die beiden Schwerter im hohen Mittelalter,* I: DA 20 (1964), 78–114.

12. Manegold of Lautenbach, *Liber ad Gebehardum* c.30, MGH LdL 1, p. 365f.

13. For a general view, cf. Arno Borst, *Die Katharer.* Schriften der MGH 12 (Stuttgart: 1953); for a Marxist interpretation, see Ernst Werner, *Pauperes Christi: Studien zur sozial-religiösen Bewegungen im Zeitalter des Reformpapsttums* (Leipzig, 1956).

14. Richard William Southern, *Saint Anselm: A Portrait in a Landscape* (Cambridge, 1991); *Gangolf Schrimpf, Anselm von Canterbury Proslogion II–IV: Gottesbeweis oder Widerlegung des Toren?* Unter Beifügung der Texte mit neuer Übersetzung. Fuldaer Hochschulschriften 20 (Frankfurt a.M.: 1994); idem, *Die Frage nach der Wirklichkeit des Göttlichen: Eine wirkungsgeschichtliche Hinführung zu klassischen philosophischen Texten.* Fuldaer Hochschulschriften 35 (Frankfurt a.M.: 2000); Joachim Ringleben, Erfahrung Gottes im Denken: Zu einer neuen Lesart des Anselmschen Argumentes (Proslogion 2–4). Nachrichten der Akademie der Wissenschaften in Göttingen I. Phil.-Hist. Klasse 2000, 1 (Göttingen, 2000).

15. Liber contra Wolfelmum c.20, ed. Wilfried Hartmann, MGH Quellen zur Geistesgeschichte 8 (Weimar, 1972), 88–89; *finis seculorum* (p. 88,4); *ad demeciciendas plagas celi et planetarum concursus . . . discernendos* (p. 89, 3–5).

16. Robertus Monarchus, *Historia Iherosolimitana* I, 1, from Urban II's sermon in Clermont-Ferrand, *Recueil des Historiens des Croisades, Hist. Occidentaux* 3, pp. 728–729.

17. Balderich von Dol, *Histroia Jerosolimitana,* c.5, Rec. des Historiens des Croisades, Hist. Occidentaux 4. pp. 15–16.

18. *Analecta Hymnica Medii Aevi* 14b, ed. Guido Maria Dreves (Lepizig, 1894), No. 95, pp. 76–79.

7. The Long Century of Papal Schisms

1. Philippe Wolf, "Quidam homo nomine Roberto negociatore," *Le Moyen Âge* 69 (1963): 129–139.

2. Roberto S. Lopez, *The Commercial Revolution of the Middle Ages* (Princeton, NJ: Princeton 1971).

3. Ulrich Meier, *Menschen und Bürger: Die Stadt im Denken spätmittelalterlicher Theologen, Philosophen und Juristen* (Munich, 1994), here p. 75, including footnote 23; *De bono comuni*, ed. Maria Consiglia De Matteis, La 'teologa politica comunale' di Remigio de'Girolami (Bologna, 1977), 18.

4. Robert von Keller, *Freiheitsgarantien für Person und Eigentum im Mittelalter: Eine Studie zur Vorgeschichte moderner Verfassungsgrundrechte*. Deutschrechtliche Beiträge, Forschungen und Quellen zur Geschichte des deutschen Rechts 14, 1 (Heidelberg, 1933).

5. Barbara Frenz, *Gleichheitsdenken in deutschen Städten des 12. bis 15. Jahrhunderts*. Städteforschung A/52 (Cologne, Weimar, Vienna, 2000).

6. *The Chronicle of John of Worcester 1118–1140*. ed. J. R. Weaver, 32–35. Anecdota Oxoniensisa 4,13 (Oxford, 1908).

7. On the following, cf. the popular history by Derek W. Lomax, *The Reconquest of Spain* (London, 1978).

8. Alexander Fidora, *Die Wissenschaftstheorie des Dominicus Gundissalinus. Voraussetzungen und Konsequenzen des zweiten Anfangs der aristotelischen Philosophie im 12. Jahrhundert*. Wissenskultur und gesellschaftlicher Wandel 6 (Berlin, 2003).

9. Johannes Fried, *Der päpstliche Schutz für Laienfürsten: Die politische Geschichte des päpstlichen Schutzprivilegs für Laien (11.–13. Jahrhundert)*, Abhandlungen der Heidelberger Akademie der Wissenschaften, Phil.-Hist. Klasse 1980, 1 (Heidelberg, 1980), 214 including note 144.

10. William of Malmesbury, *Gesta regum Anglorum*, ed. William Stubbs (London: 1889), 2:467.

11. This rendition of the sermons of Saint Bernard draws on the translation by Hans Eberhard Mayer, *Geschichte der Kreuzzüge* (Stuttgart, 2005), 124–126 ff.

12. *Die ältere Wormser Briefsammlung*, bearb. von Walther Bulst. MGH Die Briefe der deutschen Kaiserzeit 3 (Weimar, 1949), No. 25, pp. 46–47.

13. *Sic et non*, "Prologue," ed. Blanche B. Boyer and Richard McKeon (Chicago and London, 1976), 103, 34–39.

14. See Chapter 10.

15. Peter Abélard, *Theologia summi boni*. Latin–German, trans. with introduction and notes, ed. Ursula Niggli (Hamburg, 1997), 66. On Abélard, see Michael T. Clanchy, *Abaelard: Ein mittelalterliches Leben* (Darmstadt, 2000).

16. Epistola 337, S. *Bernardi opera*, vol. 8, *Epistolae* ed. J. Leclercq O.S.B., H. Rochais (Rome, 1977), 276, with the cross-reference to Migne PL, Sp. 540–2.

17. Johannes Fried, "Über den Universalismus der Freiheit im Mittelalter," *HZ* 240 (1985): 313–361, here pp. 347–355.

18. Gavin I. Langmuir, "Thomas Monmouth: Detector of Ritual Murder," *Speculum* 59 (1984): 822–846; and again in Langmuir, *Toward a Definition of Antisemitism* (Los Angeles, 1990), 209–236.

19. Peter Dronke, *Die Lyrik des Mittelalters: Eine Einführung* (Munich, 1973), 88. "My Lord Ibrahim, o you sweet man, come to me tonight."

20. Johannes Heil, *Kompilation oder Konstruktion? Die Juden in den Pauluskommentaren des 9. Jahrhunderts.* Forschungen zur Geschichte der Juden Abt. A Vol. 6. (Hanover, 1998).

21. "That Peter, who offered the Holy Church his treasure."

22. Bernard of Clairvaux, *Epistola* 191 (see note 16 in this chapter), 41–43.

23. Peter Herde und Hermann Jakobs, eds., *Papsturkunde und europäisches Urkundenwesen. Studien zu ihrer formalen und rechtlichen Kohärenz vom 11. bis 15. Jahrhundert.* Archiv für Diplomatik, Beiheft 7 (Weimar, Vienna, 1999).

24. The image appears in the so-called "Institutio Traiani" of the Pseudo-Plutarch; to date, it has not been explained whether it is based on models from Late Antiquity or is a pure invention of John of Salisbury, *Policraticus V and VI*, ed. C. C. I. Webb, 2 vols. (London, 1909), here vol. 1; the passages in question are interspersed throughout the works of John of Salisbury, cf. on this topic the two following literary references. On the theory of the antique models: Max Kerner, *Die Institutio Traiani—spätantike Lehrschrift oder hochmittelalterliche Fiktion?* in *Fälschungen im Mittelalter* I. Schriften der MGH 33, 1 (Hanover, 1988), 715–738; on the question of its being an invention, see Peter von Moos, "*Fictio auctoris:* Eine theoriegeschichtliche Miniatur am Rande der Institutio Traiani, in ibid., 739–780. Whatever the truth of the matter, John of Salisbury, who moreover refers to C. 9.8.5., treated the image appropriately and used it to make clear the advances in abstraction in conceptual thought, whereas in the ninth century, one Claudius of Turin did not really know how to handle an analogous image borrowed from Saint Ambrose; cf. Johannes Fried, "Der karolingische Herrschaftsverband zwischen 'Kirche' und 'Königshaus,'" in *HZ* 235 (1982): 1–43, here 18–20.

25. MGH Diplomata 10,2 pp. 27–9 No.237.

26. Diego Quaglioni, "Il diritto comune pubblico e le leggi di Roncaglia: Nuove testimonianze sulla l. 'Omnis iurisdictio,'" in *Gli inizi del diritto pubblico: L'età di Federico Barbarossa: legislazione e scienza del diritto: Die Anfänge des öffentlichen Rechts. Gesetzgebung im Zeitalter Friedrich Barbarossas und das gelehrte Recht,* ed. Gerhard Dilcher, Diego Quaglioni (Annali dell'Istituto storico italo-germanico in Trento), *Jahrbuch des italienisch-deutschen historischen Instituts in Trient.* Contributi/Beiträge 19. (Bologna and Berlin, 2007), 47–65.

27. John of Salisbury, Letter 124 to Ralph of Sarre. *The Letters of John of Salisbury,* vol. 1, ed. W. J. Miller, S. J. and H. E. Butler, rev. C. N. L. Brooke (London, 1955), 204–215, here 206.

28. MGH *Die Urkunden Friedrichs,* part 3, ed. Heinrich Appelt, No. 687.

29. Johannes Fried, "Friedrich Barbarossas Krönung in Arles (1178)," *Historisches Jahrbuch* 103 (1983): 347–371.

30. Klaus Schreiner, "Die Staufer in Sage, Legende und Prophetie," in *Die Zeit der Staufer. Geschichte–Kunst–Kultur.* Catalogue of the exhibition held in the Württembergisches Landesmuseum (Stuttgart, 1977), 3:249–262.

31. Matthias Thumser, "Letzter Wille? Das höchste Angebot Kaiser Heinrichs VI. an die römische Kirche," *Deutsches Archiv* 62 (2006): 85–133.

32. Abaelard, *Die Leidensgeschichte und der Briefwechsel mit Heloisa,* trans and ed. Eberhard Brost, with an afterword by Walter Berschin (Heidelberg, 1979), 81 and 108.

33. On this subject, see Erich Maschke, "Die Wirtschaftspolitik Kaiser Friedrich II. im Königreich Sizilien," *Vierteljahrsschrift für Sozial- und Wirtschaftsgeschichte* 53 (1966): 289–328.

8. The Vicar of God

1. "Die Register Innocenz" III, 1, 401, ed. Othmar Hagenauer and Anton Haidacher. Publikationen der Abteilung für Historische Studien des Österreichischen Kulturinstituts in Rom II/I, I. (Graz and Cologne, 1964), 599–601 (the translation is abbreviated); cf. X, I,1, 33, 6, Vo *inter solem et lunam.* On this passage, see Othmar Hagenauer, "Das Sonne-Mond-Gleichnis bei Innocenz III: Versuch einer teilweisen Neuinterpretation," *Mitteilungen des Instituts für Geschichtsforschung* 55 (1957): 340–368, here pp. 340–341.—Boniface: on the confirmation of King Albrecht (1303), see MGH Const. 4,I p. 139. Cf. in general: Wolfgang Weber, "Das Sonne-Mond-Gleichnis in der mittelalterlichen Auseinandersetzung zwischen Sacerdotium und Regnum," in *Rechtsgeschichte als Kulturgeschichte: Fschr. f. Adalbert Erler,* ed. Hans-Jürgen Becker et al., 147–175 (Aalen, 1976).

2. Cf. X 2,2,10 and its gloss Vo *vacante imperio.*

3. A good introduction to this topic can be found in Harald Müller, "Streitwert und Kosten in Prozessen vor dem päpstlichen Gericht—eine Skizze," *ZRG Kan.* 118 (2001): 128–164; cf. also idem, "Päpste und Prozeßkosten in späten Mittelalter," in *Stagnation oder Fortbildung? Aspekte des allgemeinen Kirchenrechts in 14. und 15 Jahrhundert,* ed. Martin Bertram, 249–270 (Tübingen, 2005).

4. The pamphlet *Eger cui lenia* presents itself as a tract written by Innocent IV, but it could equally be the work of an author in his close circle: cf. Johannes Fried, *Donation of Constantine and Constitutum Constantini: The Misinterpretation of a Fiction and Its Original Meaning,* Millennium-Studien 3 (Berlin and New York, 2007), 26, footnote 77.

5. In X 3,34,8 and X 1,2,1.

6. Extrav. Comm 1,8,1.

7. Arnoldi Chronica Slavorum e recensione I. M. Lappenberg ed. Georgius Heinricus Pertz, MGH SS rer. Germ [14] (Hanover, 1868), 240. Cf. Johannes Fried, "Schuld und Mythos: Die Eroberung Constantinopels (1204) im kulturellen

Gedächtnis Venedigs," in *Festschrift für Elmar Wadle,* ed. Tiziana J. Chiusi and Heike Jung (Berlin, 2008), 239–281.

8. Papal bull *Etsi karissimus* of 24.8.1215: *Selected Letters of Pope Innocent III concerning England (1198–1216),* ed. C. R. Cheney, W. H. Semple (London and elsewhere, 1953), No. 82, 212–216.

9. X, 2, 1, 13.

10. X, 4, 17, 13.

11. Alexander Patschovsky, Kurt-Viktor Selge, eds., *Quellen zur Geschichte der Waldenser.* Texte zur Kirchen- und Theologiegeschichte 18) (Gütersloh, 1973), 16–17 and 70.

12. From the letter: Gervasii monachi Cantuariensis, *Opera historica,* ed. William Stubbs. Rerum Britannicarum medii aevi scriptores, Rolls Series 73, 1 (London, 1879), 269–271.

13. Kurt-Viktor Selge, in *Probleme um Friedrich II.* Vorträge und Forschungen 16 (Sigmaringen, 1974), 309–343, here p. 328.

14. Llibre dels fets c.9.

15. Caesarius von Heisterbach, *Dialogus miraculorum,* dist.5 c. 21 ed. Joseph Strange (Cologne, 1851), 301–302.

16. Malcolm Lambert, *Häresie im Mittelalter: Von den Catharen bis zu den Hussiten* (Darmstadt, 2001), 122.

17. *The Formation of a Persecuting Society: Power and Deviance in Western Europe, 950–1250* (Oxford, 1987).

18. *Monumenta diplomatica S. Dominici* nr.4. Monumenta Ordinis Fratrum Paedicatorum Historica 25 (Rome, 1966), 11–13.

19. *Chronica fratris Jordani,* ed. Heinrich Boehmer. Coll. d'Études et de Documents 6 (Paris, 1908).

20. On the following topic, see Wilhelm Preger, *Geschichte der deutschen Mystik im Mittelalter: Nach den Quellen untersucht und dargestellt,* part 1 (1874), 60–64. Further reading listed in Peter Dinzelbacher LexMA 3 Sp. 1918 and 6 Sp. 242.

21. *Summa theologica* I qu. 92 art. 1 ad sec. and ibid., Qu. 93 art. 4 ad prim.

9. The Triumph of Jurisprudence

1. Othmar Hageneder, "Das päpstliche Recht auf Fürstenabsetzung: Seine kanonische Grundlegung," *Archivum Historiae Pontificiae* I (1963): 53–95; Peters, *Shadow King*; Helmut G. Walther, "Das Problem des untauglichen Herrschers in der Theorie und Praxis des europäischen Spätmittelalters," *Zeitschrift für Historisch Forschung* 23 (1996): 1–28.

2. First formulated by the canonist Alanus Anglicanus, in his gloss to D. 96 c.6 V⁰ *cursu: Unusquisque* (sc. *Rex vel princpes*) *enim tantam habet iurisdictionem in regno*

suo quantam habet imperator in imperio, ed. Alfons M. Stickler, "Alanus Anglicanus als Verteidiger des monarchischen Papsttum," *Salesianum* 21 (1959): 345–405, here 363–364. On the further development of this theory, cf. Francesco Calasso, *I glossatori e la teoria della sovranità,* (Milan, 1951); for an opposing view, see Sergio Mochi Onory, *Fonto canonistiche dell'idea moderna dello Stato.* Pubbl. dell'Università catt. del sacro cuoro, nuova serie 389 (Milan, 1951); also E. M. Meijers, *Tijdschrift voor Rechtsgeschiedenis* 20 (1952): 113–125; Robert Feenstra, "Jean de Blanot et la formule Rex Franciae in regno suo princeps est," in Feenstra, *Fata iuris Romani: Études d'histoire du droit,* (Leiden, 1974) pp. 139–149 (first published in *Festschrift for G. Le Bras,* vol. 2, [Paris, 1965]); Bruno Paradisi, "Il pensiero politico dei giuristi medievali," in *Storie delle idee politche, economiche e sociali,* diretta da Luigi Firpo, 5–160 (Turin, 1973).—The following quotation is from the *Siete Partidas* II,I,5: "God's representatives on Earth are the kings, each sovereign within his own kingdom; they are—like the emperor in his empire, and as far as the temporal realm is concerned—set above the common people, to hold them to the path of justice and truth."

3. J. L. A. Huillard-Bréholles, *Historia diplomatica Friderici Secundi,* vol. 6 (Paris, 1861), 685ff.

4. In his lifetime, Pufendorf's work appeared under the following pseudonym: Severini de Monzambano Veronensis, *De statu imperii Germanici ad Laelium fratrem* (Geneva, 1667), and thereafter in German as Samuel Pufendorf, *Die Verfassung des deutschen Reichs,* trans, notes, and afterword by Horst Denzer (Stuttgart, 1976), here 106 (Chapter 6, § 9). Pufendorf may well have known of Bartolus's treatise *De regimine civitatum,* which cites as the seventh form of constitution the Holy Roman Empire, describing it as a *monstruosa.*

5. Cf. on this latter question Elmar Wadle, "Gerichtsweg und Fehdegang in Mainzer Reichsfrieden von 1235," in *Festschrift für Heike Jung,* ed. Von Heinz Müller-Dietz, et al., 1021–1031 (Baden-Baden, 2007). This contains the most important secondary literature.

6. *Die Konstitutionen Friedrichs II für das Königreich Sizilien,* ed. Wolfgang Stürner. MGH Const. 2, Suppl.; cf. Wolfgang Stürner, "Rerum necessitas und divina provisio: Zur Interpretation des Prooemiums der Konstitutionen von Melfi (1231)," *Deutsches Archiv* 39 (1983): 467–554.

7. Johannes Fried, "In den Netzen des Wissensgesellschaft: Das Beispiel des mittelalterlichen Königs- und Fürstenhofes," in *Wissenskulturen: Beiträge zu einem forschungsstrategischen Konzept,* ed. Johannes Fried und Thomas Kailer, 141–193. Wissenskultur und gesellschaftlicher Wandel I (Berlin, 2003).

8. Gregor IX und Friedrich II, in *Kaiser Friedrich II in Briefen und Berichten seiner Zeit,* ed. und trans. Klaus J. Heinisch, 423 and 424 (Darmstadt, 1968). On Salimbene: *Cronica.* Scrittori d'Italia 232/3, ed. G. Scalia, 2:507 (Bari, 1966).—For the following anonymous quotation in the text, see *Das Brief- und Formelbuch des*

Albert Behaim, ed. Thomas Frenz und Peter Herde, MGH Briefe des späten Mittelalters I, pp. 192–193.

9. Ernst H. Kantorowicz, "Zu den Rechtsgrundlagen der Kaisersage," in *Selected Studies* (Locust Valley, NY, 1965), 284–307 (first published in *Deutsches Archiv* 13 [1957]: 115–150).

10. *Chartularium Universitatis Parisensis* I, ed. Heinrich Denifle, (Paris, 1889), pp. 209–211 Nr. 178.

11. Cf. X 5.6.16 *blasphemus Christi,* the gloss elucidates further: *id est blasphemans Christum.*

12. On this general topic, see Wilhelm Berges, *Die Fürstenspiegel des hohen und späten Mittelalters.* Schriften der MGH 2 (Stuttgart, 1938), 185–195 and 303–313. On the individual texts: Vincent of Beauvais, *De eruditione filiorum nobilium.* The Academy of America, Publ. Nr.32, ed. Arpad Steiner (Cambridge, MA, 1938); Vincentii Belvacensis, *De morali principis insitutione.* Corpus Christianorum Cont. Med. 137, ed. Robert J. Schneider (Turnhout, 1995).

13. Matthew Paris, *Chronica majora.* Rolls Series 57, 3, ed. Henry Richards Luard (London, 1876), 75–76.

14. This Latin quotation is taken from the petition of the barons, while the French comes from the Provisions: *Select Charters and Other Illustrations of English Constitutional History*, arranged and ed. William Stubbs (Oxford, 1913), 375 (c. 15) and 379.

15. II c.24 and III,I c.9 in Stubbs, *Selected Charters,* 413.

16. See, for example, the *Llibre del Fets* c.370. Jaume I—Bernat Desclot—Ramon Muntaner—Pere III, Les quatre gens cròniques. Revisió del text, pròlegs i notes by Ferran Soldevilla (Barcelona: 1971); English: *The Book of Deeds of James I of Aragon: A Translation of the Medieval Catalan Llibre del Fets.* Crusade Texts in Translation, ed. Damian Smith and Helena Buffery (Aldershot/Burlington, 2003).

17. This negative critique of Alfonso X began in the fourteenth century and largely went unchallenged by historical scholarship right up to the twentieth century; Barbara Schlieben's unpublished dissertation *Verspielte Macht: Politik und Wissen am Hof Alfons' X* (Frankfurt a.M: 2007) offered a fundamental reassessment of this monarch. The two quotations here are taken from this study; their respective sources are Juan de Mariana, *Historia de rebus Hispaniae*, libri XX (Toledo, 1592), 649; and the Portuguese *Crónica Geral de Espanya de 1344*, IV,791, ed. Luis Filipe Lindley Cintra, vol.4 (Lisbon, 1990), 384.

18. Johannes Fried, *Der päpstliche Schutz für Laienfürsten: Die politische Geschichte des päpstlichen Schutzprivilegs für Laien (11.–13. Jahrhundert),* Abhandlungen der Heidelberger Akademie der Wissenschaften, Phil.-Hist. Klasse 1980, 1 (Heidelberg, 1980), 213–219 and 239–241.

19. From Ibn al-Hatib, Kitab A'mal al-a'lâm, quoted in Wilhelm Hoenerbach, *Islamische Geschichte Spaniens* (Zürich/Stuttgart, 1970), 483–484.

20. *Llibre del Fets* (see note 16), c. 396.

21. These quotations are taken from Louis IX's *Enseignments au Prince Philippe* (c. 25 and c. 8). The original text of the *Enseignments* is virtually impossible to reconstruct.

22. *Les Grandes Chroniques de la France*, publ. by Jules Viard, 10 vols. (Paris, 1920–1953), here vol. 7, p. 7. On the topic of the Capetian monarchy, see Karl Ferdinand Werner, "Die Legitimität der Kapetinger und dir Entstehung des 'Reditus regni Francorum ad stirpem Karoli,'" *Die Welt als Geschichte* 12 (1952): 203–225; Gabrielle M. Spiegel, "The *Reditus regni ad Stirpem Karoli Magni:* A New Look," *French Historical Studies* 7 (1971): 145–171. Spiegel rightly points to the fact that, prior to its use in promoting dynastic legitimacy, the *Reditus* doctrine was employed in a territorial sense in the realm of power politics, that is, signifying the dispossession of the Plantagenets and the "return" of their lands to the French king.

23. Cf. Anne D. Hedeman, *The Royal Image: Illustrations of the Grandes Chroniques de France, 1274–1422* (Berkeley, 1991); see in particular chapter 1, pp. 9–29, and especially pp. 24–28.

24. On this subject, see Willibald Sauerländer, "Die Sainte-Chapelle du Palais Ludwig des Heiligen," in *Jahrbuch der Bayerischen Akademie der Wissenschaften* (1977): 92–115.

25. For near-contemporary accounts of the collecting of holy relics, see Natalis de Wailly, *Récit du treizième siècle sur les translations faites en 1239 et en 1241 des saintes reliques de la Passion*. Bibl. de l'École des Chartres 39 (1878): 401–415.

26. On Louis IX's crusades, see the following summary: Hans Eberhard Mayer, *Geschichte der Kreuzzüge* (Stuttgart, 2005), 302–214.

27. On the subject of the secret report written by the bishop of Olomouc (Olmütz) in 1273, see Constantin Höfler, "Analekten zur Geschichte Deutschlands und Italiens: Bericht des Bischofs Bruno von Olmütz an Papst Gregor X. über die kirchlichen und politischen Zustände Deutschlands bei der Thronbesteigung Rudolphs von Habsburg," in *Abhandlung der Hist. Classe der Königl. Bayerischen Akad. d. Wissenschaften* IV,3,B (Munich, 1844), 1–28.

28. Winfried Trusen, *Spätmittelalterliche Jurisprudenz und Wirtschaftsethik dargestellt an Wiener Gutachten des 14. Jahrhunderts*. VSWG Beihefte 43 (Wiesbaden, 1961), 91–95.

29. Cf. for instance the Glossa ordinaria for X. 5.19.18.

30. We can only make passing reference here to the debate between Armin Wolf and Franz-Reiner Erkens about the genesis of the Electors' College; cf. Franz-Reiner Erkens, in *ZRG Germ.* 122 (2005): 327–351, which has a concise summary of both scholars' differing positions.

31. Cf. The "Collectio de scandalis ecclesiae," ed. P. Autbertus Stroick O.F.M., in *Archivum Franciscanum Historicum* 24 (1931): 33–62.

32. Burkhard Roberg, "Die Tartaren auf dem 2. Konzil von Lyon 1274," *Annuarium Historiae Conciliorum* 5 (1973): 241–302.

33. Peter Herde, *Cölestin V. (1294) (Peter von Morrone): Der Engelpapst.* Päpste und Papsttum 16 (Stuttgart, 1981), 97, 127, and 120.

34. Ernst H. Kantorowicz, *Laudes Regiae: A Study in Liturgical Acclamations and Mediaeval Ruler Worship* (Berkeley/Los Angeles, 1958), 1–12 and Appendix II, 222–230. Furthermore, as early as the late tenth century, Abbo of Fleury had attributed nobility, wisdom, and power to money *(nummus),* cf. ibid., 6, note 17.

35. See Jacques Le Goff, *Wucherzins und Höllenqualen. Ökonomie und Religion im Mittelalter* (Stuttgart, 2008).

10. The Light of Reason

1. "Epistola de incarnatione verbi" c. 1, *Opera omnia,* ed. Franciscus Salesius Scmitt, 10 (Stuttgart-Bad Canstatt, 1968); cf. Kurt Flasch, ed., *Aufklärung im Mittelalter? Die Verurteilung von 1277: Das Dokument des Bischofs übersetzt und erklärt.* Excerpta classica 6 (Mainz, 1989), 15 and footnote 2.

2. This discussion can be found in Anselm of Canterbury, *Proslogion Anrede* (Latin/German), trans., notes, and afterword by Robert Theis (Stuttgart, 2005).

3. Olaf Pedersen, "Astronomy," in *Science in the Middle Ages,* ed. David C. Lindberg, 303–337, here 312 (Chicago/London, 1978).

4. Saint Augustine of Hippo, *The City of God* XI,21; Boethius, *The Consolation of Philosophy,* III, 9.

5. Immanuel Kant, *Universal Natural Theory and Theory of the Heavens.*

6. *De natura loci* I,12, ed. Auguste ct Emile Bognet, vol.9 553–555; cf. Albertus Magnus, *Ausgewählte Texte* (Latin/German), ed. and trans. Albert Fries (Darmstadt, 1987), 94, No.144.

7. Azonis *Summa super codicem*: Instituta extraordinaria. Corpus Glossatorum Iuris Civilis II (Turin, 1966), 1 (after the Pavia printed edition of 1506).

8. First quotation: *De caelo et mundo,* ed. Paul Hossfeld (Edition Coloniensis vol.5), 103; second quotation: *De generatione et corruptione* I tr. c.22, ed Borgnet vol.4, 363b. For both citations, cf. *Ausgewählte Texte* (see note 6 in this chapter), 6 No. 17 and No. 18.

9. *Divine Comedy,* "Inferno" 3:9 and 22–27.

10. This first treatise to make use of Aristotle's work and Gundissalinus's translation of Avicenna's work on the same theme was by the English scholastic philosopher John Blund: *Tractatus de anima* (ca. 1200).

11. *Super Dionysium de divinis numinibus,* ed. Paul Simon (Ed. Colon. vol.37), 6; cf. *Ausgewählte Texte* (see note 6 in this chapter), 242 No.262.

12. See section entitled "Thinking in Terms of 'Politics'" in Chapter 9.

13. As for example in the "mirror of princes" by Thomas Aquinas, *De regimine principium* (On the rule of princes). This work is fragmentary, and only the parts definitely written by Thomas are quoted here.

14. Cited in Aegidius Romanus, Giles of Rome, *Errores philosophorum* c. 5,1 ed. Joseph Koch (Milwaukee, 1944), 24. cf. Kurt Flasch, ed., *Aufklärung im Mittelalter? Die Verurteilung von 1277: Das Dokument des Bischofs übersetzt und erklärt.* Excerpta classica 6 (Mainz, 1989), 17 and footnote 4.

15. Compare, for instance, De IV coaequavevis q. 18 a. I, ed. Borgnet vol.34, 450; cf. *Ausgewählte Texte* (see note 6 in this chapter), p.96 No.146a; this also contains further passages on the independence of the free will from the influence of the planets and stars.

16. *De vegetabilibus et plantis* 7 tr. I c. I, ed. Ernst Meyer and Carl Jessen (Berlin, 1867), 590; cf. *Ausgewählte Texte* (see note 6 in this chapter), 8 No.21.

17. Federigo Melis, *Documenti per la storia economica di secoli XIII–XVI con una nota di Paleografia commerciale a cura di Elena Cecchi.* Ist. Int. di stor. Econ. F. Datini Prato, Pubbl. Ser. I. Documenti I (Florence, 1972), 556 No.199—The solution to this problem is: 6 years, 8 days, and five and thirteen twenty-ninths hours, at a moderate 20 percent interest.

18. On Daniel 14:15, ed. Borgnet vol.18, p.636b, cf. *Ausgewählte Texte* (see note 6 in this chapter), 6 No.19.

19. *Summa logicae* III 2, 17–19, ed. by Philotheus Boehner, Gedeon Gál, Stepeh F. Brown. Opera Philosophica I (New York, 1974), 532–537.

20. Flasch, *Aufklärung im Mittlealter?* (see note 14 in this chapter), 73.

21. Edited and interpreted most recently by Flasch, *Aufklärung im Mittlealter?* (see note 14 in this chapter). The quotations are taken from the bishop's edict on publication.

22. In *Librum primum sententiarum,* ed. Gedeon Gál. Opera theologica I, Franciscan Institute, St. Bonaventure. (New York, 1967), 199.

23. From Ockham's *Epistola ad fratres minores.*

24. The papal bull *In agro dominico* was edited by Heinrich Denifle, "Meister Eckeharts lateinische Schriften und die Grundanschauuungen seiner Lehre: Acten zum Prozesse Meister Eckeharts," *Archiv für Literatur- und Kulturgeschichte des Mittelalters* 2 (1886): 417–687, here pp. 636–640.

25. "Vom edlen Menschen," in *Meister Eckhart, das Buch der Tröstungen,* trans. Kurt Flasch (Munich, 2007), 94–115, here 94–99; in *Meister Eckhart, die deutschen und lateinischen Werke* (critical-text ed.). *Deutsche Werke* vol.5, ed. Josef Quint (Stuttgart, 1963), 106–136, here 106–111.

26. On the following, see Johannes Fried, *Aufstieg aus dem Untergang: Apokalyptisches Denken und die Entstehung der modernen Naturwissenschaft im Mittelalter* (Munich, 2001), 113–153.

27. Olaf Pluta, " 'Deus est mortuus': Nietzsches Parole 'Gott ist tot!' in einer Geschichte der *Gesta Romanorum* vom Ende des 14. Jahrhunderts," in *Atheismus im Mittelalter und in der Renaissance,* ed. Friedrich Niewöhner and Olf Pluta, 239–270 (including the text of the story). Wolffenbüttler Mittlealter-Studien 12 (Wiesbaden,

1999); cf. Pluta, "Materialismus im Mittelalter," in *Das Licht der Vernunft: Die Anfänge der Aufklärung im Mittelalter,* ed. Kurt Flasch and Udo Reinhold Jeck, 134–145 (Munich, 1997).

28. Cf. Martin Grabmann, *Geschichte der scholastischen Methode* II, 63.

29. Karlheinz Stierle, *Francesco Petrarca* (Munich, 2003).

30. The following Petrarch quotations (from "On His Own Ignorance") are taken from *The Renaissance Philosophy of Man,* ed. Ernst Cassirer et al. (Chicago: University of Chicago Press, 1948).

31. From Petrarch, *Letters,* trans. James Harvey Robinson and Henry Winchester Rolf (New York: G.P. Putnam's Sons, 1909).

32. "Letter to Posterity," see note 32 in this chapter.

33. See, for example, the portrait reproduced in Florian Neumann, *Francesco Petrarca* (Reinbek bei Hamburg: 2005), 117 and 120.

34. Claire Richter Sherman, *Imaging Aristotle: Verbal and Visual Representation in Fourteenth-Century France* (Berkeley/Los Angeles/London, 1995).

35. Johannes Fried, ed., *Die Frankfurter Messe, Besucher und Bewunderer: Literarische Zeugnisse aus ihren ersten acht Jahrhunderten* (Frankfurt a.M.: 1990), 26–27.

36. On the following, see Kurt Flasch, *Nikolaus von Kues in seiner Zeit: Ein Essay* (Stuttgart, 2004).

37. See Pico della Mirandola, *Oration on the Dignity of Man: A New Translation and Commentary,* ed. Francesco Borghesi, Michael Papio, and Massimo Riva (Cambridge, 2012).

11. The Monarchy

1. A useful English edition is Dante Alighieri, *Monarchy and Three Political Letters,* with an introduction by Donald Nicholl (London, 1954).

2. Paul-Joachim Heinig, "Gescheiterte Inbesitznahme? Ludwig der Brandenburger und die Mark," in *Vielfalt und Aktualität des Mittelalters: Festschrift für Wolfgang Petke zum 65. Geburtstag,* ed. Sabine Arend et al., 1–26 (Bielefeld, 2006).

3. William M. Bowsky, *Le Finanze del Comune di Siena 1287–1355* (Florence: 1976), 405 on Florence; English edition (Oxford, 1970).

4. Cf. Johannes Fried, "Kunst und Kommerz: Über das Zusammenwirken von Wissenschaft und Wirtschaft im Mittelalter vornehmlich am Beispiel der Kaufleute und Handelsmessen," *Historische Zeitschrift* 255 (1992): 281–316, here p. 293.

5. *Pietro e Ambrogio Lorenzetti a cura di Chiara Frugoni* (Florence, 2002), 186–191 (S. Francesco, Siena).

6. Margareta Porète, *Der Spiegel der einfachen Seelen* trans. from Old French with an afterword and notes by Luise Gnädinger (Zurich, 1987).

7. *"Defensor Pacis"* I,3,2; III,2,7 and III,2,9.

8. Joseph R. Strayer, *Die mittelalterlichen Grundlagen des modernen Staates*. Böhlau Studien-Bücher (Cologne, 1975).

9. Johannes Fried, Wille, "Freiwilligkeit und Geständnis um 1300: Zur Beurteilung des letzten Tempelgroßmeisters Jacques de Molay," *Historisches Jahrbuch* 105 (1985): 388–425, here p. 417, for the quotation by Philip. A new discovery of sources on the trial of Molay in 2001 saw the publication of a comprehensive facsimile edition: *Processus contra Templarios* (Venig, 2007); see also Barbara Frale, *L'ultima battaglia dei Templari* (Rome, 2001). Also Dante, *Divina Commedia,* Paradiso 7:109 and 20:91; the poet accuses the king of counterfeiting in Paradiso 19:118–119.

10. Quoted in William Chester Jordan, *The French Monarchy and the Jews from Philip Augustus to the Last Capetians* (Philadelphia, 1989), 214; on the threat of the death penalty, see ibid., 215.

11. Dante, *Divina Commedia,* Paradiso 19: 100–148.

12. The wording of the Coronation Ceremony is reprinted in Eduard Eichmann, *Staat und Kirche*, part 2: *Von 1122 bis zur Mitte des 14. Jahrhunderts.* Quellensammlung zur kirchlichen Rechtsgeschichte und zum Kirchenrecht I (Paderborn, 1925), 56–69; the quotations here are from pp. 59, 65, and 66 respectively.

13. Dante, *Divina Commedia,* Paradiso, 17:82 and 30:137.

14. Cf. Ockham's *Breviloquium de principatu tyrannico,* ed. Richard Scholz, *Wilhelm von Ockham als politischer Denker und sein Breviloquium de principatu tyrannico.* Schriften der MGH 8 (Lepizig, 1944), 38–218; extracts from this in Wilhelm von Ockham, *Texte zur Theologie und Ethik* (see Chapter 10, note 23), 288–313.

15. Stefan Weiss, "Die Rolle der Damen am päpstlichen Hof von Avignon unter Papst Johannes XXII. (1316–1334)," in *Das Frauenzimmer: Die Frau bei Hofe in Spätmittelalter und früher Neuzeit,* ed. Jan Hirschbiegel und Werner Paravicini, 401–409. Residenzforschung II (Stuttgart, 2000).

16. On the following, see Max Seidel, *Dolce Vita: Ambrogio Lorenzettis Porträt des Sieneser Staates.* Vorträge der Aeneas-Silvius-Stiftung an der Universität Basel 33 (Basel, 1999).

17. Robert Suckale, *Die Hofkunst Ludwigs von Bayern* (Munich, 1993).

18. Charles IV, *Vita,* ed. by Karl Pfisterer and Walther Bulst (Heidelberg, 1950), c.18.

19. Charles IV, *Vita,* c.14, 47–48.

20. The imperial standard is mentioned in Froissart, cf. Heinrich Neureither, *Das Bild Kaiser Karls IV. in der Zeitgenössischen Französischen Geschichtsschreibung* (Diss. Heidelberg, 1964), 166.

21. On the heroic mythologizing of the "Burghers of Calais" up to the twentieth century, cf. Jean-Marie Moeglin, *Les bourgeois de Calais: Essay d'un mythe historique* (Paris, 2002).

22. Quoted from Neureither, *Das Bild Kaiser Karls IV,* 94.

23. *Impius Antichristus Bavarus:* MGH Const. 8 Nr. 100 p. 160,32.—On Ockham, see Richard Scholz, *Unbekannte kirchenpolitische Streitschriften aus der Zeit Ludwigs des Bayern (1327–1354).* Bibliothek des Kgl. Preußischen Historischen Instituts in Rom 9–10, 2 vols. (Rome, 1911–1914), here 2:358.—Pope Clement VI's papal bull approving Charles's election as king reveals similar expectations: MGH Const. 8 Nr. 100, pp. 142–163.

24. Giovanni, Matteo, e Filippo Villani, *Croniche,* edited and published by A. Racheli, vol. 2 (Trieste, 1858), 139.

25. A fundamental text on this topic is Edmund E. Stengel, *Avignon und Rhens: Forschungen zur Geschichte des Kampfes um das Recht am Reich in der ersten Hälfte des 14. Jahrhunderts.* Quellen und Studien zur Verfassungsgeschichte des Deutschen Reiches in Mittelalter und Neuzeit VI, I (Weimar, 1930), 204–225; for a general overview, see Ludwig Schmugge, "Kurie und Kitche in der Politik Karls IV.," in *Kaiser Karl IV: Staatsmann und Mäzen,* 73–87.—for a memoir of this event, see *quare papa et pontifices etiam de temporalibus habent iudicare:* MGH Const. 8, Nr. 100, p. 158,31.

26. Ellen Widder, "Mons imperialis, Baldenau, Karlstein: Bemerkungen zur Namengebung luxembergischer Gründungen," in *Studia Luxembergensia: Festschrift Heinz Stoob zum 70. Geburtstag,* ed. Friedrich Bernhard Fahlbusch and Peter Johanek, 233–284 (Warendorf, 1989).

27. The numbering of the kings is unclear. For after Charlemagne, Charles II, Charles III, and Charles the Simple, the final Capetian should have been Charles V (rather than Charles VI, which was the actual case). Clearly, Charles III was passed over, while Charles the Simple appeared in the *Grandes Chroniques* as a weak ruler, whom the first Capetian to ascend the throne, Odo, had temporarily ousted from the throne. According to this, the *Reditus* doctrine and the principle of *princeps in regno suo* did not incorporate the French monarchy without more ado into the imperial tradition and succession.

28. See section entitled "France" in Chapter 9.

29. See section entitled "The King Is Emperor within His Realm" in Chapter 9.

30. Reinhard Schneider, "Karolus, qui et Wenzeslaus," in *Festschrift für Helmut Beumann,* ed. Kurt-Ulrich Jäschke and Richard Wenskus, 365–387 (Sigmaringen, 1977).

31. MGH Const. 8 p. 146, 16–24.

32. For a summary, see Sascha Schlede, "Ausdruck einer tiefen Verbundenheit? Karl IV und Aachen," in *Der Aachener Dom als Ort geschichtlicher Erinnerung.* Werkbuch der Studierenden des Historischen Instituts der RWTH Aachen, ed. and with an introduction by Max Kerner, 493–508 (Cologne, 2004); also Karsten C. Ronneberg, "Das Aachener Glashaus—zur Entstehung und Deutung der Chorhalle der Aachener Marienkirche," in ibid., 509–526.

33. *Die Chronik Heinrichs Taube von Selbach,* ed. Harry Bresslau. MGH SS rer. Germ. NS I (Berlin, 1922), 117, 22–24.

34. This was the verdict of the *Chroniques des quatre premiers Valois*, as quoted in Neureither, *Das Bild Kaiser Karls IV*, 92.

35. Paul Piur and Konrad Burdach, *Petrarcas Briefwechsel mit deutschen Zeitgenossen. Vom Mittelalter zur Reformation* 5 (Berlin, 1933), 1.

36. On the summoning of the emperor and the Bohemian king to Rome: Cola di Rienzo ep. 27 ed. Konrad Burdach, and Paul Piur, in *Briefwechsel des Cola di Rienzo*, third part, *Vom Mittelalter zur Reformation* 2,3. (Berlin, 1912), 100–106, here 104–105. On the election of the emperor: ibid., 37–41.—On the revocation of the "rights of the Holy Roman people" see, for example, ep. 41 (Z.23–51, 153–54); cf. Gustav Seibt, Anonimo Romano, *Geschichtsschreibung in Rom an der Schwelle zur Renaissance. Sprache und Geschichte* 17 (Stuttgart, 1992), 108–110.

37. Neureither, *Das Bild Kaiser Karls IV*, 160.

38. Anna Dorothee v. den Brincken, "Die universalhistorischen Vorstellungen des Johan von Marignola OFM: Der einzige mittelalterliche Weltchronist mit Fernostkenntnis," *Archiv für Kulturgeschichte* 49 (1987): 287–339. Yet precisely the conception of the Earth as a flat disk, which van den Brincken claims Marignolli subscribed to, does not square with his knowledge of the Equator, his division of the world's oceans into four, and his rejection of the notion of "Antipodeans."

39. *Sinica Franciscana* I, p. 548 (Sumatra, das Reich der Königin von Saba), 549 (Antipodeans), 545–546 (the Florentine girl), p. 546 (on curiosity).

40. Johannes Fried, "Mäzenatentum und Kultur im Mittelalter," in *Die Kunst der Mächtigen und die Macht der Kunst: Untersuchungen zu Mäzenatentum und Kulturpatronage*, ed. Ulrich Oevermann, Johannes Süssmann, and Christine Tauber, 47–72 (Berlin, 2007); Barbara Schlieben, "Herrscherliche Wißbegier und politisches Unvermögen: Historische und allegorische Lesarten der Herrschaft Alfons' X," ibid., 89–104.

41. For an introduction to this topic, see Miroslav Basta, "Die Musik am Prager Hof," in *Die Parler und der schöne Stil 1350–1400: Europäische Kunst unter den Luxemburgern*, ed. Anton Legner, vol. 3, 133–134 (Cologne, 1978).

42. Jakob Twinger von Königshofen, *Deutsche Chronik*, ed. Carl Hegel. Die Chroniken der deutschen Städte 8 (Leipzig, 1870), 493.

43. The "Grande Salle" and its busts of kings were destroyed by fire in 1618, but Jean de Jandun left behind a brief sketch from the time of Charles IV: "you might almost believe they were alive"; cf. Hedeman, *Image* (see Chapter 9, note 23), 35 with footnotes 13 and 14.

44. See Hermann Heimpel, "Königlicher Weihnachtsdienst im späteren Mittelalter," *Deutsches Archiv* 39 (1983): 131–206.

45. Gustav Pirchan, *Karlstein*, in *Prager Festgabe für Theodor Mayer*, ed. Rudolf Schreiber, 56–90, here p. 68. Forschungen zur Geschichte und Landeskunde der Sudetenländer I. (Freilassing/Salzburg, 1953).—On its effect cf. Heinrich Taube, ed. *Bresslau* (see note 33 in this chapter), p. 82. This report suggests that the cult of the Crown of Thorns was imitated in France.

46. Cf. Pirchan, *Karstein* (see note 45 in this chapter), passim.

47. Quoted in Neureither, *Das Bild Kaiser Karls IV,* 91.

48. Cf. Erling Petersen, "Studien zur Goldenen Bulle von 1356," *DA* 22 (1966): 227–253, here 230–231.

49. For a summary and further treatment of this topic, see Klaus Schreiner, "Antijudaismus in Marienbildern des späten Mittelalters," in *Das Medium Bild in historischen Ausstellungen,* contributions by Klaus Schreiner et al., 9–34. Materialien zur Bayerischen Geschichte und Kultur 5/98 (Augsburg, 1998).

50. For a summary, see Willehad Paul Eckert, "Die Juden im Zeitalter Karls IV." in *Kaiser Karl IV: Staatsmann und Mäzen,* 123–130; cf. Also Wolfgang von Stromer, "Der kaiserliche Kaufmann—Wirtschaftspolitik unter Karl IV.," in ibid., 63–73, here 64; on Luxembourg, see Thomas, *Deutsche Geschichte,* 224.

51. See David Nirenberg, *Communities of Violence: Persecution of Minorities in the Middle Ages* (Princeton, NJ: 1996).

52. Nirenberg, *Communities of Violence,* 234–245.

53. MGH Const. 8 Nr.100, 159–160.

54. Cf. Michael Tönsing, "Contra hereticorum pravitatem: Zu den Luccheser Ketzererlassen Karls IV. (1369)," in *Festschrift Heinz Stroob* (see note 26 in this chapter), 285–311, here 304 for the quotation by Charles IV (in the edict of July 9, 1369) and 285 for the quotation from the papal bull of 1371.—The quotation from Saint Paul's Epistle to the Romans (12:3) comes from the bull of John XXII *in agro domenico* against Meister Eckhart—something that does not appear to have been remarked upon before now, though the wording makes it clear.

55. Emmanuel Le Roy Ladurie, "Un Concept: L'Unification microbienne du monde (XIV–XVII siècles)," *Schweizerische Zeitschrift für Geschichte* 23 (1973): 627–696; also Neithard Bulst, "Der Schwarze Tod: Demographie, wirtschafts- und kulturgeschichtliche Aspekte der Pestkatastrophe von 1347–1352: Bilanz der neueren Forschung, *Saeculum* 30 (1979): 45–67.

56. Cf. Bulst, "Der Schwarze Tod," 59.

57. Ibid., 66.

58. Cf. Neureither, *Das Bild Kaiser Karls IV,* 90–91.

59. The Anonimo Romano, quoted in Seibt, *Anonimo* (see note 36 in this chapter), 83.

60. Petrarch formulated this idea in his epic poem *"Africa."*

61. Petrarch to Rienzo and the Romans: Konrad Burdach, Vom Mitelalter zur Reformation. *Forschungen zur Geschichte der deutschen Bildung,* vol.2: *Briefwechsel des Cola di Rienzo,* ed. Konrad Burdach and Paul Piur, 4 parts (Berlin, 1912–1928, here II,3, 63–81 Nr. 23 (June 1347), here 68, 99ff.; quoted in the abridged version of Karl Brandi, *Vier Gestalten aus der italienischen Renaissance: Dante, Cola Rienzo, Machiavelli, Michelangelo* (Munich, 1943), 52–53.

62. Anonimo Romano, quoted in Seibt, *Anonimo* (see note 36 in this chapter), 12.

63. Konrad Biurdach and Paul Piur, *Petrarchs Briefwechsel mit deutschen Zeitgenossen. Vom Mittelalter zur Reformation*, Bd.7 (Berlin, 1933), Nr.71,406–10; the first quotation is from p. 407, 13–14, while the second is from p. 410, 52–33 in Burdach's paraphrase (on line 52f).

64. Biurdach and Piur, *Petrarchs Briefwechsel*, Bd.7, 51–54 (1355).

65. Cf. Neureither, *Das Bild Kaiser Karls IV*, 160–161.

66. Stefan Weiss, "Kredite europäischer Fürsten fur Gregor XI: Zur Finanzierung der Rückkehr des Papsttums von Avignon nach Rom," *QFIAB* 77 (1979): 176–205.

67. Peter Johanek, "Die 'Karolina de ecclesiastica libertate': Zur Wirkungsgeschichte eines spätmittelalterlichen Gesetzes," *Blätter für deutsche Landesgeschichte* 114 (1978): 797–831.

68. Armin Wolf, "Das 'Kaiserliche Rechtbuch' Karls IV. (sogenannte Goldene Bulle)," *Ius Commune* 2 (1969): 1–32; on the genesis of the Golden Bull, cf. Petersen, "Studien"; on the conditions of the age, cf. Neureither, *Das Bild Kaiser Karls IV*, 103–104.

69. From the report on the agenda of the Diet of Nuremberg, quoted in Karl Zeumer, *Die Goldene Bulle Kaiser Karls IV. Quellen und Studien zur Verfassungsgeschichte des Deutschen Reiches*, 2 vols. (Weimar, 1908), here 2:70–71.

70. Bernd Schneidmüller, "Die Aufführung des Reichs: Zeremoniell, Ritual und Performance in der Goldenen Bulle von 1356," in *Die Kaisermacher: Frankfurt am Main und die Goldene Bulle, 1356–1806. Aufsätze,* ed. Evelyn Brockhoff and Michael Matthäus, 72–92 (Frankfurt a.M.: 2006).

71. The *Licet iuris*, reprinted many times, is conveniently found in full in Karl Zeumer, *Quellensammlung zur Geschichte der Deutschen Reichsverfassung im Mittelalter und Neuzeit,* vol. 1 (Tübingen, 1913), Nr.142, 184.

72. See Beat Frey, "Karl IV. in der älteren Historiographie," in *Kaiser Karl IV: Staatsmann und Mäzen,* 399–404, here 399 for the Piccolomini quotation.

73. On doubts regarding the Bohemian right to an electoral position: cf. Wolf, "Rechtbuch" (as per note 68 in this chapter), 9, note 37.

74. Cf. Reg. Imp. 8 Nr. 4483 (1367 January 21).

75. Not counting Louis the Bavarian's imperial coronation by an Antipope, Nicholas V.

76. For instance, Coluccio Salutati, cf. Reg. Imp. 8 Nr. 4696f.

77. Cf. Reg. Imp. 8 Nr. 4708A and 4709.

78. Stefan Weiss, "Kredite" (as per note 66 in this chapter).

79. Johannes Fried, "Friedrich Barbarossas Krönung in Arles," *Historisches Jahrbuch* 103 (1983): 347–371.

80. Cf. Reg. Imp. 8 Nr. 4l71a.

81. Reg. Imp. 3695 and 3698 (1361 May 17 and 29).

82. Reg. Imp. 5861–5863.

83. Quoted in Neureither, *Das Bild Kaiser Karls IV*, 138–139.

84. According to the *Grandes Chroniques,* cf. Neureither, *Das Bild Kaiser Karls IV,* 119.

85. Anders Thomas, *Deutsche Geschichte,* 297–298.

86. Cf. Reg. Imp. 8 Nr. 2433. See Bernd-Ulrich Hergemöller, "Der Abschluß der 'Goldenen Bulle': zu Metz 1356/57," in *Festschrift Heinz Stoob* (as per note 26 in this chapter), 123–232, here 130–131 and 218–219.

87. Things were different when the subordination or superiority of one king to another was a point at issue, or where family celebrations were concerned.

88. See Martin Kintzinger, "Der weiße Reiter, Formen internationaler Politik im Spätmittelalter," *Frühmittelalterliche Studien* 37 (2004): 315–353 (with plates IX–XII).

89. On this topic, see for instance the illustrations by Jean Fouquet of the Second Crusade, which Conrad II (who is depicted here as emperor) and Louis VII of France jointly embarked upon. Here, Conrad is shown riding a white horse in his own realm, and clearly emblazoned with his own imperial crest, while Louis is seen mounting a chestnut horse, caparisoned with his royal coat of arms. Moreover, Conrad was on Louis's right side.

90. Moreover, on his entry into Cambrai, which in strictly legal terms still formed part of his realm, Charles IV rode a white horse without insignia; the miniature thus gives not the slightest visual indication that this town belonged to the empire. The "lack" of any coat of arms points, then, to the dashing of any French hopes of gaining control of this episcopal city.

91. Heimpel, "Königlicher Weihnachtsdienst" (as per note 44 in this chapter), 162–169 and illustrations; here, 163, and 165 for the quotation from the *"Grades Chroniques"* of Charles V of France.

92. Uta Lindgren, *Bedürftigkeit, Armut, Not: Studien zur spätmittelalterlichen Sozailgeschicht Barcelonas* (Münster, 1980).

93. Cf. Victor Fairen Guillen, "Die aragonesischen Verfassungsprozesse," *Zeitschrift der Savigny-Stiftung für Rechtsgeschichte Germ. Abt.* 91 (1974): 117–174, here 124–125 with the full text of the oath of 1348 (after Peter IV's victory over the aristocratic alliance!).—On Eiximenis, see Uta Lindgren, "Avicenna und die Grundprinzipien des Gemeinwesens in Francesc Eiximenis' Regiment de la cosa publica (Valencia, 1383)," *Miscellanea Mediaevalia* 12 (1980): 449–459; cf. ibid., *Bedürftigkeit* (as per note 92 in this chapter).

94. Quoted in *Die Pest 1348 in Italien: Fünfzig zeitgenössische Quellen.,* ed. and trans. Klaus Bergdolt with an afterword by Gundolf Keil (Heidelberg, 1989), 74.

95. Guy de Chauliac, *La grande chirurgie, composée en 1363,* ed. Edouard Nicaise (Paris, 1890), 170; cf. Bulst, "Der Schwarze Tod" (as per note 55 in this chapter), 57.

96. Cf. *Die Pest 1348 in Italian* (note 94 in this chapter), 72–73.

97. This account is from Froissart, quoted in *Burgund und seine Herzöge in Augenzeugenberichten,* ed. and with an introduction by Christa Dericum (Munich, 1977), 48.

98. Enguerrand de Monstrelet, *Chroniques,* ed. Louis Douët-de'Arcq, 6 vols (Paris, 1857–1863), here 1:44; quoted in *Burgund und seine Herzöge* (as per note 97 in this chapter), 90.

12. Waiting for Judgment Day and the Renaissance

1. Hein.-Th. Schulze Altcappenberg, *Sandro Botticelli: The Drawings for Dante's Divine Comedy,* with essays by Horst Bredekamp, et al. (London, 2000).

2. Quoted in *Burgund und seine Herzöge in Augenzeugenberichten,* ed. and with an introduction by Christa Dericum (Munich, 1977), 54.

3. Jan Huizinga, *Herbst des Mittelalters: Studien über Lebens- und Geistesformen des 14. und 15. Jahrhunderts in Frankreich und den Niederlanden,* ed. Kurt Köster (Stuttgart, 1965), 327 *(tout ira mal)*; 68 (burial of John the Fearless, 1419).

4. Quotation from the *Facetiae* of Poggio Bracciolini.

5. Francesco Petrarca, *Le Familiari* IV, I, ed. critica percura di Vittorio Rossi, vol. 1, 157, 150–153, and 159–160 (Florence, 1933). Petrarch's "Ascent of Mont Ventoux" appears in English in *The Renaissance Philosophy of Man,* eds. Ernst Cassirer et al. (Chicago, 1948); an online version is also available at the Internet Medieval Source Book website http://www.fordham.edu/halsall/source/petrarch-ventoux.asp (Fordham University)—On the strong influence on Petrarchs work of the *Itinerarium mentis in Deum,* an account written by Bonaventura of his ascent of the Mons Alvernae (near Arezzo, Tuscany) in 1259, see Dieter Mertens, "Mont Ventoux, Mons Alvernae, Kapitol und Parnass: Zur Interpretation von Petrarcas Brief Fam. IV, I 'De curis propriis,'" in *Nova de veteribus. Mittel- und neulateinische Studien für Paul Gerhard Schmidt,* ed. Andreas Bihrer and Elisabeth Stein, 713–734 (Munich/Leipzig, 2004).

6. Leon Battista Alberti, *Books on the Family* (I libri della famiglia); for an English translation, see *The Family in Renaissance Florence: I Libri della Famiglia,* ed. and trans. Renee Neu Watkins (Columbia: University of South Carolina Press, 1969).

7. Huizinga, *Herbst,* 67ff.

8. Philippe de Commynes, The Memoirs of Philippe de Commynes, ed. Samuel Kinser, trans. Isabelle Cazeaux (Columbia: University of South Carolina Press, 1969).

9. Heribert Müller, *Kreuzzugspläne und Kreuzzugspolitik des Herzogs Philipp des Guten von Burgund.* Schriftenreihe der Historischen Kommission bei der Bayerischen Akademie der Wissenschaften 51 (Göttingen, 1993).

10. *Das Buch aller verbotenen Künste von Johannes Hartlieb,* ed. and trans. into modern German Frank Fürbeth (Frankfurt a.M.: 1989); quotations from 19–20 and 127–128 of this edition.

11. "Ettlich Frauen zu Haidelberg verprannt umb zaubreye": quoted from *Hexen und Hexenprozesse,* ed. Wolfgang Behringer, 82 (Munich, 1988), from Hartlieb's *Buch der verbotenen Künste.*

12. *Malleus maleficarum,* ed. and trans. Christopher S. Mackay (Cambridge, 2006).

13. *De prospectiva pingendi,* ed. Giusta Nicco Fasola (Florence, 1984): on Piero, see *Bernhard Roeck, Mörder, Maler und Mäzene: Piero della Francescas "Geißelung,"* Eine kunsthistorische Kriminalgeschichte (Munich, 2006).

14. Cf. Hans Belting, *Giovanni Bellini Pietà: Ikone und Bilderzählung in der venezianischen Malerei* (Frankfurt a.M.: 1985).

15. Peter Gorzolla, *Magie und Aberglauben im Frankreich Karls VI. Studien zu ihrer Kritik bei Jacques Legrand, Jean Gerson und Heinrich von Gorkum.* Diss. phil. Masch. (Frankfurt a.M.: 2006).

16. Quoted in Herbert Nette, *Jeanne d'Arc* (Reinbek bei Hamburg: 2002), 49.

17. Bartolomeo Facio, *De viris illustribus* (1456) See also *Die Kunstliteratur der italienischen Renaissance: Eine Geschichte in Quellen,* ed. Ulrich Pfisterer (Stuttgart, 2002).

18. From Poggio Bracciolini's *Facetiae.*

19. See the 1370 report by Giovanni Dondi dell'Orologio of Padua, quoted in Pfisterer, *Kunstliteratur* (see note 17 in this chapter), 221–222.

20. See the account of Leonardo Bruni in his missive "De studiis et litteris liber" to Baptista Malatesta, in Hans Baron, ed., Leonardo Bruni Aretino, *Humanistisch-philosophische Schriften* (Leipzig, 1928), 5–19, here 8.

21. Leon Battista Alberti in the dedication of his work "Della pittura" (1436), quoted in Pfisterer, *Kunstliteratur* (see note 17), 224–225.

22. Pico della Mirandola, *Oration on the Dignity of Man: A New Translation and Commentary,* ed. Francesco Borghesi, Michael Papio, and Massimo Riva (Cambridge, 2012), 4–8.

23. On so-called monastic humanism, see Harald Müller, *Habit und Habitus: Mönche und Humanisten im Dialog.* Spätmittelalter und Reformation 32 (Tübingen, 2006).

24. Bruni's letter to Baptista Malatesta is cited in this chapter in note 20.

25. A source still worth consulting is Lothar Schmidt, *Frauenbriefe der Renaissance.* Die Kultur 9 (Berlin o.J.: 1900).

26. Volker Reinhardt, *Die Medici* (Munich, 2004).

27. *"Wüttrich vil boshaftiger, mortlicher und onmenschlicher sachen."* This was the verdict of Gebhard Dacher (1472) in *Die Chroniken der Stadt Konstanz,* ed. Philipp Ruppert (Constance, 1891), 233.

28. For an overview of Sigismund's reign, see *Sigismundus Rex et Imperator: Kunst und Kultur zur Zeit Sigismunds von Luxemburg 1387–1437,* ed. Imre Tekács. Exhibition catalogue (Mainz, 2006).

29. See Bettina Pferschy-Maleczek, *Der Nimbus des Doppeladlers: Mystik und Allegorie im Siegelbild Kaiser Sigmunds, Zschr. f. hist. Forschung* 23 (1996): 433–437, especially 451ff.

30. *"Nit allein der kirchen sunder ouch des richs und gemeines nuczes sachen. . . . den beiden rates und hilf sere not ist,"* Reichstagsakten Ältere Reine 7 (Gotha, 1878), Nr. 176, 269–270.

31. Alexander Patschovsky, "Der Reformbegriff zur Zeit der Konzile von Konstanz und Basel," in *Reform von Kirche und Reich zur Zeit der Konzilien von Konstanz (1414–1428) und Basel (1431–1449),* ed. Ivan Hlavácek and Alexander Patschovsky, 7–28 (Constance, 1996).

32. This was one of the sentences of Wyclif (30) expressly condemned in Pope Martin V's Bull *Inter cunctas* of 1418.

33. Frantisek Smahel, *Die Hussitische Revolution.* Schriften der MGH 43/I–III (Hanover, 2002).

34. See note 40 in this chapter.

35. *"Begerten die Jungfrowen zu bestritten"*; Markus Twellenkamp, "Jeanne d'Arc und ihr Echo im zeitgenössischen Deutschland," *Jb. f. westdeutsche Landesgeschichte* 14 (1988): 43–62, here 46; the following quotation is by this same anonymous eyewitness.

36. These quotations from Joan of Arc come from a collection of excerpts from her trial: *Der Prozeß der Jeanne d'Arc,* introduced by Georges und Andrée Duby (Berlin, 1985).

37. *Journal du siège d'Orléans et du voyage de Reims (c. 1460),* quoted in Nette, *Jeanne d'Arc* (see note 16 in this chapter), 59–60.

38. *Jeanne d'Arc: Dokumente ihrer Verurteilung und Rechtfertigung 1431–1456,* trans. with an introduction by Ruth Schirmer-Imhof (Cologne, 1956), 123, 125–126. The estimate of her age comes from Duby, *Der Prozeß der Jeanne d'Arc* (see note 36 in this chapter), 21.

39. Schirmer-Imhof, *Jeanne d'Arc* (see note 38 in this chapter), pp. 267–269; cf. Duby, *Der Prozeß der Jeanne d'Arc* (see note 36 in this chapter), 181–182.

40. This characterization of Joan II appears in Poggio Bracciolini *Facetiae.*

41. Sessio V, 6 April 1415, Mansi 27, 590 = Codex Oecumenicorum Decreta. Ed. Istituto per le Scienze Religiose, Bologna 1973, p. 409.

42. Last printed in *Quellen zur Kirchenreform im Zeitalter der Großen Konzilien des 15. Jahrhunderts 2,* selected and trans. Jürgen Miethke and Lorenz Weinrich. Freiherr von Stein-Gedächtnisausgabe 38b. (Darmstadt, 2002), 396–397, Nr. XXIII (16 June 1439).

43. Brian Tierney, *The Foundations of the Conciliar Theory: Contributions of the Medieval Canonists from Gratian to the Great Schism.* Studies in the History of Christian Thought (Cambridge, 1998).

44. See Commynes, *Memoirs* VI, 12; on the varice of the emperor, VI,2.

45. See Commynes, *Memoirs* VI, 12.

46. Ibid.

47. On Philip and his plans for 1454, cf. Herbert Müller, *Kreuzzugspläne und Kreuzzugspolitik* (as per note 9 in this chapter).

48. Franz Babinger, *Mehmed der Eroberer: Weltenstürmer einer Zeitenwende.* Serie Piper 621 (Munich and Zurich, 1987; first published 1953).

49. See Commynes, *Memoirs* VI, 12.

50. Quoted in Walter Prevenier and Wim Blockmans, *Die burgundischen Niederlande* (Weinheim: 1986), 216 (after the *"Excellente cronike van Vlanderen"*).

51. See Commynes, *Memoirs* IV, 1.

52. See Commynes, *Memoirs* VI, 2.

53. An overview of this period is given in the catalog: *Bernisches historisches Museum: Die Burgunderbeute und werke burgundischer Hofkunst* (Berne, 1969). See also *Karl der Kühne–Charles le Téméraire–Charles the Bold (1433–1477): Catalogue of the Exhibition at the Berne Historical Museum* 25.4.–24.8 (2008).

54. See Commynes, *Memoirs* VI, 2.

55. The most recent biography is Manfred Hollegger, *Maximilian I. (1459–1519): Herrscher und Mensch einer Zeitenwende* (Stuttgart, 2005).

Epilogue

1. Arnold Berney, *Friedrich der Große*: Entwicklungsgeschichte eines Staatsmannes (Tübingen, 1934), 9.

2. Quoted from Immanuel Kant, *Werke,* 10 vols., ed. Wilhelm Weischedel, Sonderausgabe vol. 2 *Vorkritische Schriften bis 1768* (Darmstadt, 1983), 883–884.

3. Friedrich Schiller, "Was heißt und zu welchem Ende studiert man Universalgeschichte?" in *Schillers Werke,* Nationalausgabe vol. 17, ed. Karl-Heinz Hahn (Weimar, 1970), 359–376, here p. 370. Cf. Arno Borst, "Was uns das Mittelalter zu sagen hätte: Über Wissenschaft und Spiel," *Historische Zeitschrift* 244 (1987): 537–555, here 537.

4. This theory of dynamic and moribund ages is put forward in Heinrich Mann, "Ein Jahrhundert wird besichtigt," *Gesammelte Werke,* vol. 24 (Berlin and Weimar, 1973), 5; here, as is so often the case, the Renaissance and Reformation are assigned to the first type.

5. Giorgio Vasari, *Vasari on Technique, Being the Introduction to the Three Arts of Design, Architecture, Sculpture and Painting, Prefixed to the Lives of the Most Excellent Painters, Sculptors, and Architects* (New York, 2000).

6. Ibid., 100, 109.

7. *Sinica Franciscana* 1, ed. P. Anastasius van den Wyngaert O.F.M. (Quaracchi-Florence, 1929), 546.

8. *Sinica Franciscana* 1, p. 466.

9. J.-B. Chabot, "Histoire du Patriarche Mar Jabalaha III et du moine Rabban Çauma," *Revue de l'Orient Latin* 2 (1894; French translation of the original Syrian text) here 87–122.

10. Cf. Chapter 10, "The Light of Reason," note 24.

11. Dieter Hägermann, "Das Reich als Innovationslandschaft," in *Heiliges Römisches Reich Deutscher Nation 962 bis 1806: Von Otto dem Großen bis zum Ausgang des Mittelalters, Essays,* ed. Matthias Puhle and Claus-Peter Hasse, 439–451 (Dresden, 2006).

12. Umberto Eco, *On Beauty: A History of a Western Idea* (London, 2004).

13. Robert von Keller, *Freiheitsgarantien für Person und Eigentum im Mittelalter. Eine Studie zur Vorgeschichte moderner Verfassungsgrundrechte,* with a preface by Konrad Beyerle. Deutschrechtliche Beiträge 14,1 (Heidelberg, 1933).

14. Samuel Pufendorf, *De statu imperii Germanici,* VI,9, first pub. (under a pseudonym) Geneva 1667, then Berlin 1706. However, in his treatise *De regimine civitatum,* c. 7, the legist Bartolus of Sassoferato had already called the constitutional form of the Holy Roman Empire *monstruosa.*

15. Cf. Peter Moraw, *Von offener Verfassung zu gestalteter Verdichtung: Das Reich im späten Mittelalter 1250 bis 1490.* Propyläen Geschichte Deutschlands 3. (Berlin, 1985), 17.

16. On the problem of relativism, cf. Karl Mannheim, "Historismus," *Archiv für Sozialwissenschaft und Sozialpolitik* 52 (1924): 1–60.

17. This example appears in Christian Thomas: "Die nächste Pose ist nicht mehr die schwerste," *Frankfurter Rundschau,* June 15, 2006.

18. Michael Mitterauer, *Warum Europa? Mittelalterliche Grundlagen eines Sonderwegs* (Munich, 2003).

Selected Bibliography

The following bibliography is not intended as an exhaustive list of all the primary sources and secondary literature consulted in the writing of this book, but rather to provide suggestions for further reading.

Algazi, Gadi. *Herrengewalt und Gewalt der Herren im späten Mittelalter.* Frankfurt a.M., 1996.

Ambos, Claus, et al. *Die Welt der Rituale: Von der Antike bis heute.* Darmstadt, 2005.

Angenendt, Arnold. *Heilige und Reliquien: Die Geschichte ihres Kultes vom frühen Christentum bis zur Gegenwart.* Munich, 1994.

———. *Geschichte der Religiosität im Mittelalter.* Darmstadt, 1997.

———. *Das Frühmittelalter: Die abendländische Christenheit von 400–900.* Stuttgart, 2001.

———. *Liturgik und Historik: Gab es eine organische Liturgie-Entwicklung?* Quaestiones Disputatae 189. Freiburg, 2001.

Ariès, Philippe. *Centuries of Childhood: A Social History of Family Life.* Translated by Robert Baldick. New York, 1962.

———. *The Hour of Our Death.* Translated by Helen Weaver. New York, 1981.

Assmann, Jan. *Das kulturelle Gedächtnis: Schrift, Erinnerung und politische Identität in frühen Hochkulturen.* Munich, 1997.

Belting, Hans. *Das Bild und sein Publikum im Mittelalter: Form und Funktion früher Bildtafeln der Passion.* Berlin, 1981.

———. *Bild und Kult: Eine Geschichte des Bildes vor dem Zeitalter der Kunst.* Munich, 1990.

———. *Florence and Baghdad: Renaissance Art and Arab Science.* Translated by Deborah Lucas Schneider. Cambridge, MA, 2011.

Benson, Robert. *The Bishop Elect: A Study in Medieval Ecclesiastical Office*. Princeton, NJ, 1968.

Berg, Dieter. *Die Anjou-Plantagenets: Die englischen Könige im Europa des Mittelalters*. Stuttgart, 2003.

Berman, Harold J. *Law and Revolution: The Formation of the Western Legal Tradition*. Cambridge, MA, 1983.

Beumann, Helmut. *Die Ottonen*. Stuttgart, 1993.

Blickle, Peter. *Das alte Europa: Vom Hochmittelalter bis zur Moderne*. Munich, 2008.

Bloch, Marc. *The Royal Touch: Monarchy and Miracles in France and England*. Translated by J. E. Anderson. New York, 1989.

Borgolte, Michael. *Europa entdeckt seine Vielfalt 1050–1250*. Handbuch der Geschichte Europas 3. Stuttgart, 2002.

———. *Christen, Juden, Muselmanen: Die Erben der Antike und der Aufstieg des Abendlandes 300 bis 1400 n. Chr.* Siedler Geschichte Europas. Munich, 2006.

Borgolte, Michael, Cosimo Damiano Fonseca, and Hubert Houben, eds. *Memoria. Erinnern und Vergessen in der Kultur des Mittelalters*. Bologna, 2005.

Borst, Arno. *Die Katharer*. MGH Schriften 12. Hannover: 1953. With an afterword by Alexander Patschowsky, Freiburg, 1992.

———. *Der Turmbau von Babel. Geschichte der Meinungen über Ursprung und Vielfalt der Sprachen und Völker*. 6 vols. Stuttgart, 1957–1963. Paperback ed., Munich, 1995.

———. Introduction to *Schriften zur Komputistik im Frankenreich von 721–818*. MGH Quellen zur Geistesgeschichte des Mittelalters 21. Hanover, 2006, 1–326.

Borst, Arno et al., eds. *Tod im Mittelalter*. Konstanzer Bibliothek 20. Constance, 1993.

Boshof, Egon. *Die Salier*. Stuttgart, 2000.

———. *Europa im 12. Jahrhundert: Auf dem Weg in die Moderne*. Stuttgart, 2007.

Boswell, John. *Christianity, Social Tolerance and Homosexuality: Gay People in Western Europe from the Beginning of the Christian Era to the 14th Century*. Chicago, 1980.

———. *The Kindness of Strangers: The Abandonment of Children in Western Europe from Late Antiquity to the Renaissance*. Chicago, 1998.

Braudel, Fernand. *The Mediterranean and the Mediterranean World in the Age of Philip II*. 3 vols. Berkeley, 1996.

Brown, R. Allen. *The Normans and the Norman Conquest*. Woodbridge, 2000.

Bruchhäuser, Hanns-Peter. *Kaufmannsbildung im Mittelalter: Determinanten des Curriculums deutscher Kaufleute im Spiegel der Formalisierung von Qualifizierungsprozessen*. Dissertationen zur Pädagogik 3. Cologne and Vienna, 1989.

Brundage, James A. *Law, Sex and Christian Society in Medieval Europe*. Chicago, 1987.

Buc, Philippe. *The Dangers of Ritual: Between Early Medieval Texts and Social Scientific Theory.* Princeton, NJ, 2001.

Bumke, Joachim. *Courtly Culture: Literature and Society in the High Middle Ages.* Translated by Thomas Dunlap. Berkeley and Los Angeles, 1991.

Burckhardt, Jacob. *Die Kultur der Renaissance in Italien: Ein Versuch. Gesammelte Werke.* Vol. 3. Darmstadt, 1962. First published 1869.

Bynum, Caroline Walker, and Paul Freedman, eds. *Last Things: Death and the Apocalypse in the Middle Ages.* The Middle Ages Series. Philadelphia, 1999.

Carruthers, Mary. *The Book of Memory: A Study of Memory in Medieval Culture.* Cambridge, 1990.

Christe, Yves. *Les Jugements Derniers.* Paris, 1997.

Christiansen, Eric. *The Norsemen in the Viking Age.* Oxford, 2002.

Clanchy, M. T. *From Memory to Written Record: England 1066–1307.* Oxford, 1993.

Cohen, Mark R. *Under Crescent and Cross: The Jews in the Middle Ages.* Princeton, NJ, 1994.

Cohn, Norman. *The Pursuit of the Millennium: Revolutionary Millenarians and Mystical Anarchists of the Middle Ages.* London, 1957.

Colish, Marcia L. *Medieval Foundations of the Western Intellectual Tradition 400–1400.* New Haven, CT, and London, 1997.

Cordes, Albrecht. *Spätmittelalterlicher Gesellschaftshandel im Hanseraum.* Quellen und Darstellungen zur Hansegeschichte NF 45. Cologne, 1998.

Delumeau, Jean. *Sin and Fear: The Emergence of the Western Guilt Culture, 13th–18th Centuries.* Translated by Eric Nicholson. New York, 1990.

Dollinger, Philippe. *The German Hansa.* Translated and edited by D. S. Ault and S. H. Steinberg. Redwood City, CA, 1970.

Drabek, Anna Maria. *Die Verträge der fränkischen und deutschen Herrscher mit dem Papsttum.* Veröffentlichungen des Instituts für österreich. Geschichtsforschung 22. Vienna, 1976.

Duerr, Hans Peter. *Nacktheit und Scham: Der Mythos vom Zivilisationsprozeß 1.* Frankfurt a.M., 1988.

Eco, Umberto, ed. *The History of Beauty.* New York, 2010.

———, ed. *On Ugliness.* New York, 2011.

Ehlers, Joachim. *Das westliche Europa Die Deutschen und das europäische Mittelalter.* Munich, 2004.

Ehlers, Joachim, Heribert Müller, and Bernd Schneidmüller, eds. *Die französischen Könige des Mittelalters: Von Odo bis Karl VIII.* Munich, 1996.

Elias, Norbert. *The Civilizing Process: Sociogenetic and Psychogenetic Investigations.* Oxford, 2000.

Emmerich, Bettina. *Geiz und Gerechtigkeit: Ökonomisches Denken im frühen Mittelalter.* Vierteljahrschrift für Sozial- und Wirtschaftsgeschichte, Beiheft 168. Wiesbaden, 2004.

Erdmann, Carl. *The Origin of the Idea of Crusade.* Translated by Marshall W. Baldwin and Walter Goffart. Princeton, NJ, 1978.

Erkens, Franz-Reiner. *Herrschersakralität im Mittelalter: Von den Anfängen bis zum Investiturstreit.* Stuttgart, 2006.

Favier, Jean. *Gold and Spices: The Rise of Commerce in the Middle Ages.* Translated by Caroline Higgitt. New York, 1998.

Flasch, Kurt. *Das philosophische Denken im Mittelalter: Von Augustinus bis Machiavelli.* Stuttgart, 2001.

————. *Nikolaus von Kues in seiner Zeit: Ein Essay.* Stuttgart, 2004.

————. *Meister Eckhart: Die Geburt der "deutschen Mystik" aus dem Geist arabischer Philosophie.* Munich, 2006.

Flasch, Kurt, and Udo Reinhold Jeck, eds. *Das Licht der Vernunft: Die Anfänge der Aufklärung im Mittelalter.* Munich, 1997.

Fleckenstein, Josef. *Rittertum und ritterliche Welt.* Berlin, 2002.

Flint, Valerie. *The Rise of Magic in the Early Medieval Europe.* Oxford, 1991.

Freedberg, David. *The Power of Images: Studies in the History and Theory of Response.* 1989.

Frenz, Barbara. *Gleichheitsdenken in deutschen Städten des 12. bis 15. Jahrhunderts: Geistesgeschichte, Quellensprache, Gesellschaftsfunktion.* Städteforschung A/52. Cologne, 2000.

Fried, Johannes. *Der päpstliche Schutz für Laienfürsten: Die politische Geschichte des päpstlichen Schutzprivilegs für Laien (11.–13. Jahrhundert).* Abhandlungen der Heidelberger Akademie der Wissenschaften, Phil.-Hist. Klasse 1980, 1. Heidelberg, 1980.

————. *Der Weg in die Geschichte: Die Ursprünge Deutschlands bis 1024.* Propyläen Geschichte Deutschlands. Vol. 1. Berlin, 1994.

————. *Aufstieg aus dem Untergang: Apokalyptisches Denken und die Entstehung der modernen Naturwissenschaft im Mittelalter.* Munich, 2001.

————. *Der Schleier der Erinnerung: Gründzüge einer historischen Memorik.* Munich, 2004.

————. *Donation of Constantine and Constitutum Constantini: The Misinterpretation of a Fiction and Its Original Meaning.* With a Contribution by Wolfram Brandes: "The Satraps of Constantine." Millennium-Studien 3. Berlin and New York, 2007.

Fuhrmann, Horst. *Überall ist Mittelalter: Von der Gegenwart einer vergangenen Zeit.* Munich, 1996.

————. *Einladung ins Mittelalter.* Munich, 2000.

————. *Die Päpste: Von Petrus zu Benedikt XVI.* Munich, 2005.

Geary, Patrick. *Phantoms of Remembrance: Memory and Oblivion at the End of the First Millennium.* Princeton, NJ, 1994.

————. *The Myth of Nations: The Medieval Origins of Europe.* Princeton, NJ, 2002.

Geuenich, Dieter, and Otto Gerhard Oexle, eds. *Memoria in der Gesellschaft des Mittelalters*. Veröffentlichungen des Max-Planck-Instituts für Geschichte III. Göttingen, 1994.

Goetz, Hans-Werner. *Europa im frühen Mittelalter 500–1050*. Handbuch der Geschichte Europas 2. Stuttgart, 2003.

Goez, Werner. *Kirchenreform und Investiturstreit 910–1122*. Stuttgart, 2000.

Goitein, Shlomo Dov. *A Mediterranean Society: The Jewish Communities of the Arab World as Portrayed in the Documents of the Cairo Geniza*. 6 vols. Berkeley, CA, 1967–1993.

Görich, Knut. *Die Staufer: Herrscher und Reich*. Munich, 2006.

Grafton, Antony. *Leon Battista Alberti: Master Builder of the Italian Renaissance*, Cambridge, MA, 2002.

Gurjewitsch, Aaron J. *Das Individuum im europäischen Mittelalter*. Munich, 1994.

Haas, Wolfdieter. *Welt im Wandel: Das Hochmittelalter*, Stuttgart, 2002.

Hammel-Kiesow, Rolf. *Die Hanse*. Munich, 2004.

Hardt, Matthias. *Gold und Herrschaft: Die Schätze europäischer Könige und Fürsten im ersten Jahrtausend*. Europa im Mittelalter 6. Berlin, 2004.

Haverkamp, Alfred, ed. *Geschichte der Juden im Mittelalter von der Nordsee bis zu den Südalpen. Kommentiertes Kartenwerk*. Vol. 1, Forschungen zur Geschichte der Juden, Reihe A / 14. Hanover, 2002, S. 267–274.

Hawel, Peter. *Das Mönchtum im Abendland: Geschichte, Kultur, Lebensform*. Freiburg i. Br., 1993.

Hechberger, Werner. *Adel im fränkischen Mittelalter: Anatomie eines Forschungsproblems*. Ostfildern, 2005.

Henning, Joachim, ed. *Post-Roman Towns, Trade and Settlement in Europe and Byzantium*. Millennium-Studien 5,1–2. 2 vols. Berlin. New York, 2007.

Herbers, Klaus. *Jakobsweg: Geschichte und Kultur einer Pilgerfahrt*. Munich, 2006.

Herzig, Arno. *Jüdische Geschichte in Deutschland: Von den Anfängen bis zur Gegenwart*. Munich, 2002.

Hinrichs, Ernst, ed. *Geschichte Frankreichs*. Stuttgart, 2002.

Hoensch, Jörg K. *Die Luxemburger: Eine spätmittelalterliche Dynastie gesamteuropäischer Bedeutung 1308–1437*. Stuttgart, 2000.

Huizinga, Johan. *The Autumn of the Middle Ages*. Translated by Rodney J. Payton and Ulrich Mammitzsch. Chicago, 1996.

Hülsen-Esch, Andrea v. *Gelehrte im Bild: Repräsentation, Darstellung und Wahrnehmung einer sozialen Gruppe im Mittelalter*. Veröffentlichungen des MaxPlanck-Instituts für Geschichte 201. Göttingen, 2006.

Jäschke, Kurt-Ulrich. *Europa und das römisch-deutsche Reich um 1300*. Stuttgart, 1999.

Joas, Hans, und Klaus Wiegandt, eds. *Die kulturellen Werte Europas*. Frankfurt a.M., 2005.

Jussen, Bernhard. *Der Name der Witwe: Erkundungen zur Semantik der mittelalterlichen Bußkultur.* Veröffentlichungen des Max-Plack-Instituts für Geschichte 158. Göttingen, 2000.

―――, ed. *Die Macht des Königs: Herrschaft in Europa vom Frühmittelalter bis in die Neuzeit.* Munich, 2005.

Jussen, Bernhard, and Craig Koslofsky, eds. *Kulturelle Reformation. Sinnformationen im Umbruch 1400–1600.* Veröffentlichungen des Max-Planck-Instituts für Geschichte 145. Göttingen, 1999.

Kantorowicz, Ernst H. *Laudes Regiae: A Study in Liturgical Acclamations and Mediaeval Ruler Worship.* University of California Publ. in History 33. Berkeley and Los Angeles, 1946.

―――. *The King's Two Bodies: A Study in Mediaeval Political Theology.* Princeton, NJ, 1957.

―――. "Gods in Uniform." *Proceedings of the American Philosophical Society* 105, no. 4 (1961): 368–393.

―――. *Selected Studies.* Locust Valley, NY, 1965.

Keller, Hagen. *Zwischen regionaler Begrenzung und universalem Horizont: 1024–1250.* Propyläen Geschichte Deutschlands. Vol. 2. Berlin, 1986.

―――. *Die Ottonen.* Munich, 2001.

Kerner, Max. *Karl der Große: Entschleierung eines Mythos.* Cologne, 2001.

Klapisch-Zuber, Christine. *Women, Family, and Ritual in Renaissance Italy.* Chicago, 1985.

Kleinau, Elke, and Claudia Opitz, eds. *Geschichte der Mädchen- und Frauenbildung.* Vol. 1, *Vom Mittelalter bis zur Aufklärung.* Frankfurt a.M., 1996.

Koziol, Geoffrey. *Begging Pardon and Favor: Ritual and Political Order in Early Medieval France.* Ithaca, NY, 1992.

Kretzmann, Norman, Anthony Kenny, and Jan Pinnborg, eds. *The Cambridge History of Later Medieval Philosophy from the Rediscovery of Aristotle to the Disintegration of Scholasticism.* Cambridge, 1982.

Krieger, Karl-Friedrich. *Geschichte Englands von den Anfängen bis zum 15. Jahrhundert.* Munich, 1996.

―――. *Die Habsburger im Mittelalter: Von Rudolf I. bis Friedrich III.* Stuttgart, 2004.

Kuchenbuch, Ludolf. *Bäuerliche Gesellschaft und Klosterherrschaft im 9. Jahrhundert.* Studien zur Sozialstruktur der Familia der Abtei Prüm. Wiesbaden, 1978.

―――. *Die Grundherrschaft im früheren Mittelalter.* Historisches Seminar. Neue Folge 1. Idstein, 1991.

Lange, Hermann. *Römisches Recht im Mittelalter.* Vol. 1, *Die Glossatoren.* Munich, 1997.

Langholm, Odd. *Economics in the Medieval Schools: Wealth, Exchange, Value, Money and Usury According to the Paris Theological Tradition, 1200–1350.* Leiden et al., 1992.

LeGoff, Jacques. *Your Money or Your Life: Economy and Religion in the Middle Ages* Translated by Patricia Ranum. New York, 1988.

———. *The Birth of Purgatory.* Translated by Arthur Goldhammer. Aldershot, 1990.

———. *Intellectuals in the Middle Ages.* Translated by Teresa Lavender Fagan. Oxford, 1993.

———. *The Birth of Europe* .Translated by Janet Lloyd. Oxford, 2005.

Liebs, Detlef. *Römische Jurisprudenz in Gallien (2. bis 8. Jahrhundert).* Freiburger Rechtsgeschichtliche Abhandlungen NF 38. Berlin, 2002.

Lindberg, David C. *Theories of Vision from al-Kindi to Kepler.* Chicago, 1976.

———. *The Beginnings of Western Science: The European Scientific Tradition in Philosophical, Religious, and Institutional Context, Prehistory to* A.D. *1450.* Chicago, 1992.

Lindgren, Uta, ed. *Europäische Technik im Mittelalter: Tradition und Innovation.* Berlin, 1996.

Linehan, Peter, and Janet L. Nelson, eds. *The Medieval World.* London and New York, 2001.

Little, Lester K. *Religious Poverty and the Profit Economy in Medieval Europe.* Ithaca, NY, 1978.

Löwith, Karl. *Meaning in History: The Theological Implications of the Philosophy of History.* Chicago, 1957.

Lutterbach, Hubertus. *Sexualität im Mittelalter: Eine Kulturstudie anhand von Bußbüchern des 6. bis 12. Jahrhunderts.* Cologne, Weimar, and Vienna, 1999.

Lutz-Bachmann, Matthias, und Alexander Fidora, eds. *Juden, Christen und Muslime: Religionsdialoge im Mittelalter.* Darmstadt, 2004.

Mayer, Hans Eberhard. *The Crusades.* Translated by John Gillingham. Oxford, 1988.

Meinhardt, Matthias, Andreas Ranft, and Stephan Selzer, eds. *Mittelalter.* Oldenbourg Geschichte Lehrbuch. Munich, 2007.

Miethke, Jürgen. *De potestate papae: Die päpstliche Amtskompetenz im Widerstreit der politischen Theorie von Thomas von Aquin bis Wilhelm von Ockham.* Spätmittelalter und Reformation 16. Tübingen, 2000.

Mitterauer, Michael. *Why Europe? The Medieval Origins of Its Special Path.* Translated by Gerald Chapple. Chicago, 2010.

Mitterauer, Michael, and John Morrissey. *Pisa: Seemacht und Kulturmetropole.* Essen, 2007.

Moore, Robert I. *The First European Revolution: c. 970–1215.* Oxford, 2000.

———. *The Formation of a Persecuting Society: Power and Deviance in Western Europe, 950–1250.* Oxford, 2007.

Moraw, Peter. *Von offener Verfassung zu gestalteter Verdichtung: Das Reich im späten Mittelalter 1250–1490.* Propyläen Geschichte Deutschlands. Vol. 3. Berlin, 1985.

Morris, Colin. *The Sepulchre of Christ and the Medieval West From the Beginning to 1600.* Oxford, 2005.

Muhlack, Ulrich. *Geschichtswissenschaft im Humanismus und in der Aufklärung: Die Vorgeschichte des Historismus.* Munich, 1991.

———. *Staatensystem und Geschichtsschreibung. Ausgewählte Aufsätze zu Humanismus und Historismus, Absolutismus und Aufklärung.* Edited by Notker Hammerstein und Gerrit Walther. Historische Forschungen 83. Berlin, 2006.

Münkler, Marina. *Erfahrung des Fremden: Die Beschreibung Ostasiens in den Augenzeugenberichten des 13. und 14. Jahrhunderts.* Berlin, 2000.

Murray, Alexander. *Reason and Society in the Middle Ages.* Oxford, 1985.

Neureither, Heinrich. *Das Bild Kaiser Karls IV. in der Zeitgenössischen Französischen Geschichtsschreibung.* Diss. Heidelberg, 1964.

Nirenberg, David. *Communities of Violence: Persecution of Minorities in the Middle Ages.* Princeton, NJ, 1996.

Nitschke, August. *Bewegungen im Mittelalter: Kämpfe, Spiele, Tänze, Zeremoniell und Umgangsformen.* Historisches Seminar 2. Düsseldorf, 1987.

Noonan, John Thomas. *Contraception: A History of Its Treatment by the Catholic Theologians and Canonists.* Cambridge, MA, 1965.

Oexle, Otto Gerhard, ed. *Memoria als Kultur.* Veröffentlichungen des MaxPlanck-Instituts für Geschichte 121. Göttingen, 1995.

Oexle, Otto Gerhard, and Michail A. Bojcov, eds. *Bilder der Macht in Mittelalter und Neuzeit: Byzanz—Okzident—Rußland.* Veröffentlichungen des MaxPlanck-Instituts für Geschichte 226. Göttingen, 2007.

Paul, Eugen. *Geschichte der christlichen Erziehung.* Vol. 1, *Antike und Mittelalter.* Freiburg i. Br., 1993.

Pečar, Andreas, and Kai Trampedach, eds. *Die Bibel als politisches Argument.* Historische Zeitschrift Beiheft 43. Munich, 2007.

Peters, Edward. *The Shadow King: Rex inutilis in Medieval Law and Literature, 751–1327.* New Haven, CT, 1970.

Phillips, J. R. S. *The Medieval Expansion of Europe.* Oxford and New York, 1988.

Postel, Verena *Die Ursprünge Europas. Migration und Integration im frühen Mittelalter.* Stuttgart, 2004.

Reichert, Folker. *Begegnungen mit China: Die Entdeckung Ostasiens im Mittelalter.* Beiträge zur Geschichte und Quellenkunde des Mittelalters 15. Sigmaringen, 1992.

Reinhard, Wolfgang. *A Short History of Colonialism.* Translated by Kate Sturge. Manchester and New York, 2011.

Rexroth, Frank. *Das Milieu der Nacht: Obrigkeit und Randgruppen im spätmittelalterlichen London.* Göttingen, 1999.

Reynolds, Susan. *Fiefs and Vassals: The Medieval Evidence Reinterpreted.* Oxford, 1994.

Rösener, Werner. *Peasants in the Middle Ages.* Translated by Alexander Stützer. Urbana, IL, 1992.

———. *Einführung in die Agrargeschichte.* Darmstadt, 1997.

Rubin, Miri. *Corpus Christi: The Eucharist in Late Medieval Culture.* Cambridge, 1991.

Rüegg, Walter, ed. *Geschichte der Universität in Europa.* Vol. 1, *Mittelalter.* Munich, 1993.

Ruh, Kurt. *Geschichte der abendländischen Mystik.* 5 vols. Munich, 1990–1999.

Saliba, George. *Science and the Making of the European Renaissance.* Cambridge, MA, 2007.

Schieffer, Rudolf. *Die Karolinger.* Stuttgart, 2006.

Schimmelpfennig, Bernhard. *The Papacy.* Translated by James Sievert. New York, 1992.

Schmeiser, Leonhard. *Die Erfindung der Zentralperspektive und die Entstehung der neuzeitlichen Wissenschaft.* Munich, 2002.

Schmieder, Felicitas. *Europa und die Fremden: Die Mongolen im Urteil des Abendlandes vom 13. bis in das 15. Jahrhundert.* Beiträge zur Geschichte und Quellenkunde des Mittelalters 16. Sigmaringen, 1994.

Schmitt, Jean-Claude. *La raison de gestes dans l'Occident médiéval.* Paris, 1990.

Schmugge, Ludwig. *Kirche, Kinder, Karrieren: Päpstliche Dispense von der unehelichen Geburt im Spätmittelalter.* Zürich, 1995.

Schneidmüller, Bernd. *Die Welfen: Herrschaft und Erinnerung.* Stuttgart, 2000.

———. *Die Kaiser des Mittelalters: Von Karl dem Großen bis Maximilian I.* Munich, 2006.

Schneidmüller, Bernd, and Stefan Weinfurter, eds. *Die deutschen Herrscher des Mittelalters: Historische Portraits von Heinrich I. bis Maximilian I.* Munich, 2003.

———. *Salisches Kaisertum und neues Europa: Die Zeit Heinrichs IV. und Heinrichs V.* Darmstadt, 2007.

Schreiner, Klaus. *Maria: Jungfrau, Mutter, Herrscherin.* Munich and Vienna, 1994.

Schuster, Peter. *Der gelobte Frieden: Täter, Opfer und Herrschaft im spätmittelalterlichen Konstanz.* Constance, 1995.

Seibt, Ferdinand, ed. *Kaiser Karl IV: Staatsmann und Mäzen.* Munich, 1978.

Shahar, Shulamith. *Childhood in the Middle Ages.* London, 1990.

Siems, Harald. *Handel und Wucher im Spiegel frühmittelalterlicher Rechtsquellen.* MGH Schriften 35. Hanover, 1992.

Steinen, Wolfram von den. *Homo caelestis: Das Wort der Kunst im Mittelalter.* 2 vols. Bern, 1965.

Stengel, Edmund E. "Die Entwicklung des Kaiserprivilegs für die römische Kirche 817–962: Ein Beitrag zur ältesten Geschichte des Kirchenstaats." In idem. *Abhandlungen und Untersuchungen zur mittelalterlichen Geschichte.* Cologne and Graz, 1960, 218–248.

Stock, Brian. *The Implications of Literacy: Written Language and Models of Interpretation in the Eleventh and Twelfth Centuries.* Princeton, NJ, 1983.

Stromer, Wolfgang von. *Oberdeutsche Hochfinanz 1350–1450.* Vierteljahrsschrift für Sozial- und Wirtschaftsgeschichte Beiheft 55–57. Wiesbaden, 1970.

———. *Bernardus Teotonicus e i rapporti commerciali tra la Germania Meridionale e Venezia prima della istituzione del Fondaco dei Tedeschi.* Centro Tedesco di Studi Veneziani. Quaderni 8. Stuttgart, 1998.

Sturlese, Loris. *Die deutsche Philosophie im Mittelalter: Von Bonifatius bis zu Albert dem Großen 748–1280.* Munich, 1993.

Stürner, Wolfgang. *Friedrich II.* 2 vols. Darmstadt, 1992–2000.

Suckale, Robert. *Kunst in Deutschland von Karl dem Großen bis Heute.* Cologne, 1998.

Van Engen, John. *Devotio Moderna: Basic Writings.* New York and Mahwah, 1988.

Vones, Ludwig. *Geschichte der Iberischen Halbinsel im Mittelalter 711–1480: Reiche—Kronen—Regionen.* Sigmaringen, 1993.

Wasserstein, David. *The Rise and Fall of the Party-Kings: Politics and Society in Islamic Spain, 1002–1086.* Princeton, NJ, 1985.

Wenzel, Horst. *Hören und Sehen—Schrift und Bild: Kultur und Gedächtnis im Mittelalter.* Munich, 1995.

Wollasch, Joachim. *Cluny, Licht der Welt: Aufstieg und Niedergang der klösterlichen Gemeinschaft.* Zürich, 1996.

Yerushalmi, Yosef Hayim. *Zakhor: Jewish History and Jewish Memory.* Seattle, 1982.

Zimmermann, Albert, and Ingrid Craemer-Ruegenberg, eds. *Orientalische Kultur und europäisches Mittelalter.* Miscellanea Mediaevalia 17. Berlin and New York, 1985.

Zinner, Ernst, ed. *Entstehung und Ausbreitung der copernicanischen Lehre.* With additional material by Heribert M. Nobis und Felix Schmeidler. Munich, 1988.

Index

Index

Index

Index

Index